THE BUILDINGS OF WALES
ADVISORY EDITOR: NIKOLAUS PEVSNER

POWYS
(MONTGOMERYSHIRE, RADNORSHIRE, BRECONSHIRE)

RICHARD HASLAM

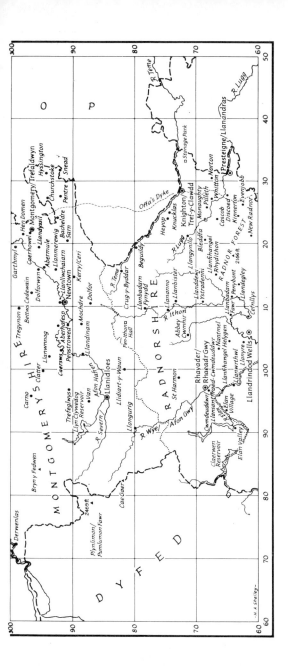

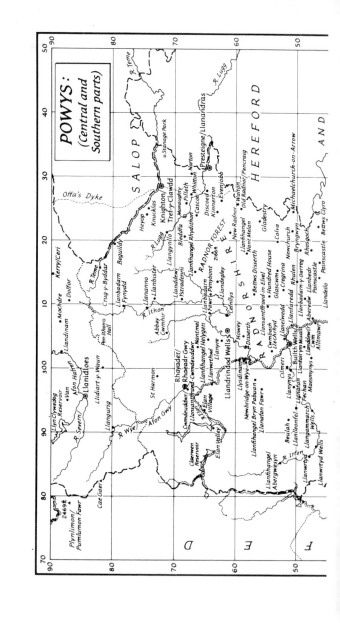

POWYS:
(Central and
Southern parts)

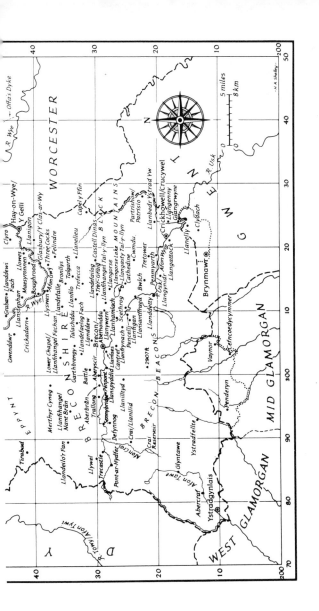

The preparation of this book has been greatly helped by grants from
THE TRUSTEES OF THE DAVIES CHARITY
and from
THE BOARD OF CELTIC STUDIES OF
THE UNIVERSITY OF WALES

THE BUILDINGS OF WALES

Powys

(MONTGOMERYSHIRE, RADNORSHIRE, BRECONSHIRE)

BY

RICHARD HASLAM

★

PENGUIN BOOKS

UNIVERSITY OF WALES PRESS

Penguin Books Ltd, Harmondsworth, Middlesex, England
Penguin Books, 625 Madison Avenue, New York, New York 10022, U.S.A.
Penguin Books Australia Ltd, Ringwood, Victoria, Australia
Penguin Books Canada Ltd, 2801 John Street, Markham, Ontario, Canada L3R 1B4
Penguin Books (N.Z.) Ltd, 182–190 Wairau Road, Auckland 10, New Zealand
University of Wales Press, 6 Gwennyth Street, Cathays, Cardiff, CF2 4YD

First published 1979

—

ISBN 0 14 0710.51 5

—

Copyright © Richard Haslam, 1979

—

Made and Printed in Great Britain
by Butler and Tanner Ltd, Frome and London
Set in Monotype Plantin

To Frances and Diccon

CONTENTS

Map References

★

The numbers printed in italic type in the margin
against the place names in the gazetteer of the book
indicate the position of the place in question on the
index map (pages 2–3), which is divided into sections
by the 10-kilometre reference lines of the National
Grid. The reference given here omits the two initial
letters (formerly numbers) which in a full grid
reference refer to the 100-kilometre squares into
which the country is divided. The first two numbers
indicate the *western* boundary, and the last two the
southern boundary, of the 10-kilometre square in
which the place in question is situated. For example,
Merthyr Cynog (reference 9030) will be found in the
10-kilometre square bounded by grid lines 90 and
00 on the *west* and 30 and 40 on the *south*; Castle
Caereinion (reference 1000) in the square bounded
by grid lines 10 and 20 on the *west* and 00 and 10
on the *south*.

The map contains all those places, whether towns,
villages, or isolated buildings, which are the subject
of separate entries in the text.

FOREWORD

Since this is the first volume of The Buildings of Wales, *a few prefatory remarks on the contents and arrangement may be helpful.*

Wales generally is rich in minor buildings and poor in major ones, and this is particularly true of Powys. Readers of The Buildings of England *will therefore notice some widening of the range of what is described. The country churches and chapels are often moving; the farmhouses have their poetry. Their vernacular qualities are not easily conveyed in photographs or academic prose, but they justify their inclusion. Most of Wales is deep country still, and its unpretending buildings form the most tangible documents of the past and present.*

Then, on boundaries, I decided to follow the historic counties within the new county framework – not from perversity or old fogeydom, but because large and diverse areas are involved, and to mix all the towns, parishes, and hamlets into one gazetteer would be to lose the benefits of easy concordance with previous literature. For those not familiar with Welsh place-names it could produce confusion in the many beginning with Llan-. The maps, introduction, photographs, and index on the other hand are in one, and will I hope lead the user to the gazetteer entries without difficulty. In the case of Powys, several parishes formerly in Breconshire have been transferred to Mid Glamorgan and Gwent; they are to be printed both in their old and their new location.

The protracted tasks of researching and of visiting were made fruitful, and indeed possible, through the work and kindness of many people. My first and best thanks go to Sir Nikolaus Pevsner, who from the start has had faith in The Buildings of Wales. *What is owed to his example is evident; without his acute and tactful surveillance, his friendly helpfulness, and his examination of the book before printing, all would have been far less worthwhile. Mr Peter Howell has befriended the enterprise all along, joined in visits, and read drafts untiringly; quantities of Victorian information and insight have come from him, and above all enthusiasm to revive my flagging spirits. In preparation, I was greatly helped by Miss Clare Ross, who undertook Breconshire. She made an excellent job of extracting from and ordering the published material – how competent I knew by comparing my results for Montgomery and Radnor. When it came to driving, Miss Rosemary Trant was ready to finish Radnorshire and go bravely on* with Breconshire during the very wet summer of 1974; she contributed not only efficiency but also a knowledge of farming. Mr Adam Naylor began the driving in Montgomeryshire, the first carefree days of the process, in autumn 1973. Accommodation in the area, all-important for understanding as well as convenience, was offered to me first at Gregynog, a residential centre of the University of Wales; to the University, to Dr and Mrs G. T. Hughes and to their staff, my gratitude is due not only for a Montgomeryshire base and use of the library, but for their kind welcome, which was renewed when I was writing up. In Radnorshire, Mr and Mrs Paul Carlisle and their family gave me great hospitality and an invaluable background in their home. In Breconshire I was fortunate in staying with Mr and Mrs R. H. C. Lyons, who thus put a central point in the county at my disposal. To their names I should add that of Mr Timothy Bacon, not in Wales but in London, when access to libraries etc. was made easy from the comfort of a room in his house.

For their successful efforts in translating my untidy pages into type-script I am particularly grateful to Mrs Fiona Dobson, and also to Miss K. Flanagan and Miss L. McCurry. At the University of Wales Press, Dr R. Brinley Jones, the recent Director, gave me help-ful advice. More recently at Penguins' I would like to thank Mr Peter Wright, Mrs Judy Nairn for her sure-handed editing and proof-read-ing, and Mrs I. Lorquet; they have given much pains to getting the final stages right. Nearly fifty photographs were taken specially for this volume by Mr Martin Harrison, a task which despite difficulties of lighting and others has allowed a variety of little known subjects to be illustrated, to the great benefit of the book. The archaeological entries were contributed by Miss Frances Lynch, and because of the moorland setting of many they are given OS grid references. Mr H. A. Shelley drew the maps and Mr Ian Stewart prepared the plans of Brecon Cathedral and Powis Castle. Mr Colin McWilliam gave me the benefit of his Buildings of Scotland glossary, and Miss Charlotte Dorrien Smith typed it. Mr F. W. How most kindly read the book in page proof.

The list of those whose knowledge I have drawn on is headed by two bodies directly concerned in Wales: the Cambrian Archaeological Association and the Royal Commission on Ancient and Historical Monuments in Wales. The Cambrians meet for a week each summer and attendance at their meetings has been an education. Of the many people from whom I have learned, Dr C. A. Ralegh Radford in par-ticular has been a deeply interesting guide to the main medieval monu-ments. The staff of the Royal Commission (abbreviated RCAM) includes the Secretary, Mr Peter Smith, to whom I am admiringly

*indebted for a disciplined approach to vernacular structures and for
being saved from errors; Mr C. J. Spurgeon, who has answered problems on castles; and Mr H. Brooksby and Mr Gwyn Thomas, who
have helped on houses and on churches. Mr Brooksby, Mr Smith, and
Mr Thomas kindly checked parts of the text. I am also indebted to
Mr J. T. Smith's accounts of Breconshire houses. I am truly grateful to
them. Other friends have been a tremendous support in other ways;
I should like to mention Mr Edward Hubbard, my companion
in travail, a source of good humour as well as of facts; Mr Vernon
Hughes, who allowed me to use his extensive indexes of Welsh buildings and has been ready with help including reading part of the proofs;
Miss Frances Lynch; and Mr Peter Reid on Georgian houses. Dr
Prys Morgan went to the trouble of reading the entire typescript,
meticulously checking my accounts and making suggestions. Mr
F. G. Dimes of the Geological Museum in London told me about the
geology of Powys, and my brother Dr H. W. Haslam helped me to
elucidate it. Mr D. Evinson gave me lists of Roman Catholic
churches; Mr Martin Harrison identified some Victorian stained
glass; Mr P. Joyce gave me information on G. E. Street as did Mr
Jeremy Knight on Montgomery Castle and Mr Anthony Quiney on
J. L. Pearson. Mr Christopher Wakeling let me make use of his
researches on chapels, which provided details very difficult to come
by otherwise. Mr Merlin Waterson and the National Trust were
generous with their time and in drawing plans of Powis Castle.
Professor G. Zarnecki gave me the benefit of his knowledge in the
examination of Romanesque sculpture, for which I am especially
thankful. Mr J. Lawson told me about the Shrewsbury artists;
Miss E. P. Roberts gave me information, more than I could use,
on the poets of the gentry.*

*Much material was gathered in the Library of the Society of Anti-
quaries in London and in the National Library of Wales, and I am
very grateful for the assistance offered in both. The National Monuments Record (NMR) in London have custody of the late H. S. Goodhart-Rendel's index of Victorian churches (GR), and at the time of
writing they still have 120 boxes of Welsh photographs. The other
photographic collection is run by the Royal Commision in Aberystwyth, so remote that it is a pity the two are to be united. I am grateful
to them both. The statutory lists of buildings of special architectural
interest compiled by the Department of the Environment (DOE) have
been very generously made available by the Welsh Office. All these
sources have proved invaluable in locating buildings.*

*Coming to individual counties, Montgomeryshire received the care-
ful encouragement of Dr J. D. K. Lloyd and Mr C. E. V. Owen;*

where I, on my first county, should have been without them does not bear thinking of. Dr Lloyd offered his long experience of the Montgomery area, Mr Owen his of the Llanidloes area. No general topographer can know a single region so thoroughly, but Dr Lloyd in his notes helped spread a spirit of inquiry, as did Mr Owen in the field. I owe them my warmest thanks. Among those who also helped were Mr W. N. Clare of Powys County Architect's Department, Major and Mrs H. P. M. Lewis (Newtown), Mr Malcolm Pinhorn, and Mr J. L. Russell and Mr Garbett Edwards of Newtown Development Corporation. It was Mrs Elisabeth Walters who first introduced me to Radnorshire. My subsequent informants there include Mr J. S. Bishop of the Welsh National Water Development Authority. For Breconshire, those who answered questions include Mr A. D. R. Caröe, who kindly looked out details of the work of W. D. Caröe, Miss Josephine Cormier of Gwent County Planning Office, and Canon Josiah Jones-Davies, who very kindly checked the proofs. I wish to express my sincere thanks to them. To these names I should add the very large number of people who showed me the buildings in their charge, for giving up their time and for their indispensable local knowledge, all too much of which cannot be included for reasons of space. To them all I owe the firm statement that mention of a building in the gazetteer does not mean that it is open to inspection by the public.

The principles on which this gazetteer is founded follow those of The Buildings of England, more or less. All medieval and Georgian churches are included, and most Victorian and C20 ones. Their principal non-movable furnishings – screens, stained glass, etc. – are described, and some altar tables, bells, chests, hatchments, etc., together with their Early Christian and sculptured monuments; but plate is excluded. Restorations both by local and national architects are set out. All chapels before 1800 are mentioned, and a selection of those of the C19 and C20, particularly in towns. Public buildings such as town halls, hospitals, schools, and bridges are described. Perambulations are suggested for towns. Castles, both stone and earth; country houses and their adjacent stables etc. and estate buildings; and larger farmhouses are given in some detail. The numbers of late medieval cruck buildings, of rural industrial buildings such as barns and mills and of other types, exceed the scope of the gazetteer, though many are included. Selections are also made in the fields of modern architecture and industrial buildings. The criteria throughout rest on assessing a structure's significance in the light of architectural history; a few important demolished or badly ruined buildings are therefore treated fully. Where I have not seen a building but describe it from *another source, that source is given and the entry placed in brackets. In principle buildings are grouped beneath the heading of the ancient church, which is usually the name of the civil parish and village also; geographical directions are usually in relation to the church or else a hamlet. This may not be ideally clear, but it seemed the readiest means of arranging buildings widely scattered over a hilly and intricate landscape.*

Despite the vigilance of many well-wishers, I fear that all too many errors remain; they are mine only. Would users of this book be good enough to bring them and any omissions to my notice?

PREHISTORIC AND ROMAN
REMAINS

BY FRANCES LYNCH

THE prehistory of Powys is difficult to categorize; like the countryside itself the material remains are subtle and elusive, and the picture is neither clear nor complete. Mid Wales is a landlocked area cut off from both the Bristol Channel and the Irish Sea by high mountain ranges and thus removed from the direct cultural influences brought to the seaboard of Wales from the W and the S. However Powys is penetrated by three major and several minor river valleys, and it is these natural routes and their complementary ridgeways which are the significant factors in the spread of men and ideas in the early as well as the later history of the region. Unfortunately the prehistory of the west Midlands is itself far from clear; the heavy clay soil made it an area of sparse population, and recent development has obliterated much of the evidence. It is not surprising, therefore, that the prehistory of Powys, which partakes both of filtered western and poorly defined eastern trends, should lack unity and – since the area has been little studied up to the present – clarity.

Breconshire S of the Usk shares many of the characteristics of the north Glamorgan moorlands, and the passes through the Beacons provide a means of contact with the prosperous lowland of the Vale and the Bristol Channel. The Usk and Wye valleys give other points of access for south-eastern colonizers, notably those who built the remarkable series of tombs near Talgarth. The N half of the region is dominated by the broad and fertile valley of the Severn and the smooth moorland ridges such as the Kerry Hills which gave easy movement and good grazing to the pastoralists of the Bronze Age. The projection of English influences into the heart of Wales via this route is most clearly demonstrated in the distribution of Late Bronze Age metalwork, but the pattern is repeated in the spread of Anglo-Norman motte-and-bailey castles.

The earliest evidence of man's activity in Mid Wales is a few scatters of small flint tools, the composite tips of arrows and the waste of their manufacture. The bulk of Welsh MESOLITHIC material has been found on coastal sites, and until recently it was thought that these small hunting bands never penetrated the mountainous inland areas. However, within the last few years

several discoveries of Mesolithic flint implements have been made
on the Breconshire moorlands and more may be expected.

It was not until the arrival of the first farmers that any appreciable settlement took place in Mid Wales. These farmers needed
to clear the primeval woodland to plant their crops and graze their
sheep and cattle; we can recognize their advent by their impact
on the forest cover, evidenced for us by the record of the pollen
fall trapped and preserved in bogs. More tangible evidence for
certain groups of these settlers can be seen in their great stone
tombs which survive to this day as striking features of our landscape.

In the Talgarth (B) area between the Usk and Wye valleys is a
surprising concentration of these MEGALITHIC TOMBS; sixteen
within an area of a few square miles. The long cairns cover stone
burial chambers of curiously complicated designs which were the

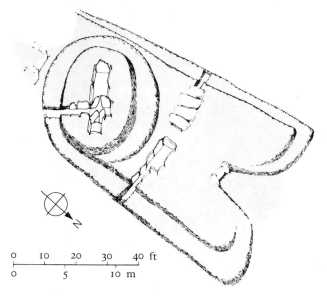

Castell Dinas (B), Ty Isaf long cairn: isometric view. Roofing slabs have
been restored over the western chamber. These would have been covered
by additional cairn material which might, in fact, have concealed the dry-
stone walling. Opinion is divided about the final external form of the cairn
and the stepped profile shown here is conjectural. Note that the entrances
to the passages are blocked (after W. F. Grimes)

communal vaults of the local farming communities over many centuries and must also have been the focus for their religious activity. These monumental tombs reflect a tradition which is very widespread in western Europe at this time, although the architectural details of the tombs vary from place to place. The Breconshire tombs are similar to those in the Cotswolds and the Vale of Glamorgan, where transepted and lateral chambers may be found. In Breconshire these two elements are usually found beneath the one mound, suggesting that their builders were a secondary group of colonizers coming from the S E and conflating two styles current in their homeland. For instance the well-known tomb at Ty Isaf is a long, wedge-shaped cairn with two rectangular chambers reached by short passages on either side and a more complex, T-shaped structure at the end. In the front is a forecourt centring on a 'dummy portal' or blind entrance. The chambers contained the unburnt bones of several individuals and a quantity of broken pottery. A similarly complex design was revealed by excavations at Pipton, but in both cases the chambers are now filled in and inaccessible. At Little Lodge, however, a badly ruined transepted chamber can be recognized at the southern end of the cairn. Another characteristic of this 'Severn Cotswold' style is the neat dry-stone walling which marks the edge of the cairns, though this, too, is seldom visible today. Consequently these tombs may seem architecturally disappointing to the modern visitor; the elaborate ground plans can seldom be made out and the scale of the chamber is small compared with the exciting structures which were being built elsewhere in Wales at this time (mid third millennium B.C.).

Apart from this concentration of tombs in Breconshire the evidence for NEOLITHIC settlement in Mid Wales is small; stone and flint axes are relatively common finds, and there are scattered instances of Neolithic occupation at Llanelwedd (R), Ffridd Faldwyn (M), and the Breiddin (M), but it is not yet possible to combine these facts into a coherent picture of settlement, beyond saying that there must have been farming groups further N who did not, for one reason or another, follow a tradition of monumental burial. Their preference for decorated pottery suggests that they did not settle this area until relatively late in the Neolithic.

Towards the end of the Neolithic period (c. 2000 B.C.) a new group of settlers, the BEAKER PEOPLE, came to these islands, bringing with them a distinctive style of pottery and, more importantly, the germ of a new social system leading to greater individualism, wealth, and social stratification and a knowledge of metallurgy which gradually replaced the old stone tools by weapons and implements of copper and bronze. It is conceivable that these new people also brought with them the Celtic languages which still survive in the west. The Beaker People came to Britain mainly from the mouth of the Rhine, and their chief areas of settlement were on the east coast and in southern England; they appear in Wales chiefly as a result of secondary movement from these new centres. Their small individual graves, which contrast so strongly with the earlier communal tombs, are rare in Mid Wales. There are examples of these stone cists or boxes beneath round cairns in south Breconshire which relate to a larger group in Glamorgan, and in the Severn valley, the result of penetration by settlers from the N W perhaps attracted by the picrite rock at Hyssington (M) so suitable for their heavy axe-hammers. The graves normally contain a crouched skeleton accompanied by weapons, bow or knife, and a Beaker.

Houses have nearly always been made of wood, especially in Mid Wales; so we know little of the homes of the living, and archaeology has been forced to rely on graves and the personal belongings left with the dead for information about their way of life. For no period is this more true than for the BRONZE AGE, which is characterized for us by the ubiquitous ROUND BARROW standing out against the skyline on high moorland ridges.

These mounds of earth or stone constitute probably the commonest field monuments in Powys, but few have been excavated. The investigation of one on Caebetin Hill, Kerry (M), revealed that the mound had covered a series of stake circles which had originally surrounded the burial; work on others such as the small cairn at Ynys Hir, Mynydd Epynt (B), showed that the capping was only the final act in what had been a long and complex history. The bodies covered by these barrows were normally cremated, and the bones gathered up into a large storage jar or urn and sometimes accompanied by a few personal possessions, a knife, a few beads, or a specialist tool. Sometimes there is only a single burial in the centre; sometimes the one mound may cover several cremations and urns either all buried in one ceremony or added on different occasions over the years. Consequently it is difficult to generalize about the details of construction or ritual in these numerous barrows, but it is safe to say that the vast majority were built in the Early Bronze Age (mid second millennium B.C.), a period of great wealth and prestige for the descendants and successors of the Beaker People, the cattle-owning chieftains who were buried under them.

Their interest in cattle and grazing lands is reflected in the distribution of the barrows on the open ridges such as the Kerry Hills where there is a very striking concentration, and in what are now bleaker areas such as the moors above the Elan valley and Llanbrynmair. However, their mounds may also be found in the valley bottoms close to rivers, and a fine series is to be seen in the Teme valley above Knighton. The Bronze Age interest in mountain areas may also have been connected with hunting, for there are notable concentrations of arrowheads at Llyn Bugeilyn (M) and Pant Sychbant, Fforest Fawr (B). The upland distribution is repeated by the more enigmatic Bronze Age monuments, the stone circles and alignments or stone rows which may be found in similar districts such as Rhos y Beddau in the Tanat valley, at Kerry (M), and further s on Fforest Fawr (B). These circles of small upright stones are assumed to mark religious or ritual sites connected perhaps with the worship of sky gods. The details of religious practice within them are the subject of much controversy and will never be known with certainty, since excavation has provided disappointingly little information about their use. A similar uncertainty attaches to the large standing stones set up in this period, though in south Breconshire there is an interesting association with mountain passes.

The more mundane activity of Bronze Age men is chronicled not by their houses and farms, which have not been found in Wales, but by the chance finds of their tools and weapons of bronze. From these we may postulate the distribution of population, the growth in prosperity, and the fluctuating fortunes of various centres of manufacture. In spite of the number of Early Bronze Age barrows in the region, the number of bronze implements of that date is insignificant. Large-scale manufacture begins only in the Middle Bronze Age, reflected in this area by the hoard of thirty-eight palstaves (axeheads), almost certainly a trader's hoard, found on a well known E–W route at Cemmaes (M). It is at the end of this period, in the Penard Phase (1050–950 B.C.), that the area becomes significant for wider developments, especially in weapon types. Continental knives and spears were being imported (Ffynhonnau hoard (B) in Brecon Museum) which were to influence British smiths in their designs and techniques for many years to come. Later – in the C8 B.C. – the northern part of the region was to see the main impact of new fashions and techniques with the remarkable series of finds in the Severn valley (Guilsfield, Buttington, and Churchstoke) of metalwork emanating from English centres of manufacture collectively known as the 'Wilburton Complex' after a very characteristic founder's hoard from Wilburton, Suffolk. These new styles made little impact on the rest of Wales, which remained faithful to older types. Later still Breconshire was a flourishing market for the socketed axes produced by the 'South Welsh' group of smiths centred on the Bristol Channel area. Radnorshire has not featured much in this survey, but there are two remarkable finds of Middle/Late Bronze Age goldwork from the county: the valuable hoards of torcs (twisted neck rings) from Heyop and Llanwrthwl. These ornaments are in an Irish style, but it is possible that they were actually made in Wales, since there is a good source of gold, rapidly exploited by the Romans when they arrived, not far away at Dolaucothi, Carmarthenshire.

The record of Bronze Age settlement is extremely meagre, but there is one instance of both metalwork and pottery of Middle Bronze Age date from a cave, Ogof yr Esgyrn, near Craig y Nos (B), a shelter used again in the Romano-British period. Another rare instance of a specialized form of late prehistoric dwelling is the 'crannog' or artificial island found when the level of Llangorse Lake (B) was lowered in the last century. Some comparable sites in Ireland are as old as the Bronze Age, but it must be admitted that there is no evidence for the true date of Llangorse. Recent work on hilltop settlements may eventually go further towards filling this vacuum, for radiocarbon dating is showing that man was beginning to occupy strategic high ground long before the Iron Age, the traditional period of the 'hillfort' whose ramparts crown so many hills in Wales and the border country.

These defended hill-tops are usually seen in military terms, and classical writers record that the native chieftains on the eve of the Roman invasion could withstand fierce attacks from their neighbours behind their carefully designed circuits of ramparts and ditches. However, it is possible to look at these sites in more peaceful terms as social and economic centres each controlling a surrounding territory of farmland and grazing. Excavation has tended to concentrate on the ramparts and the entrances in order to elucidate the history of the defences, which were often refurbished, remodelled, or enlarged through several centuries of occupation, but to understand the life of the community it is necessary to study the remains of houses and other buildings in the interior. Such large-scale excavation has not been carried out in any Mid Wales hillfort except the Breiddin, where rectangular and, later, round wooden houses have been found in large numbers. Indeed there has been little excavation even of the rampart sequences, so that any comment or classification must rely on surface study of the siting, number of ramparts, and design of entrances.

Powys has examples of most varieties of hillforts, from very large multivallate enclosures such as Pen y Crug NW of Brecon and Cefn Carnedd near Caersws (M), through smaller bivallate or univallate forts such as Caer Fawr and Caer Fach on either side of the Honddu valley (B), to hill-slope enclosures like Panty Hill, Felindre (R), whose military strength was minimal and which may have been harmless farms or cattle pounds. Equally a variety of building techniques may be seen in the surrounding ramparts – a simple, wide stone wall at Castle Bank near Llansantffraed-in-Elvel (R), or high earth banks with sloping fronts such as those at Ffridd Faldwyn near Montgomery. Excavation may show these earth banks to have been elaborately laced with timber to provide a firm vertical face, or sometimes built with an intentionally loose sloping front.

Whatever the date of the earliest palisades around hill-top settlements, it will no doubt remain true that the bulk of the hill-forts in Mid Wales were built in the pre-Roman IRON AGE. Few other remains of this period have been found in the region, though the recent discovery of a carved stone head in the river at Bontdolgadfan near Llanbrynmair (M) hints at the existence of some native shrine, and the discovery of finely decorated metalwork in other parts of Wales suggests that the standard of living of some of the local chieftains could have been high.

The pre-Roman strongholds are concentrated in the Severn and Banwy valleys in the N and overlooking the Usk and Wye rivers in the S, and it was by these traditional routes that the ROMAN armies entered Powys in the middle of the CI A.D. The conquest of the western parts of Britain – and Wales must be seen as such rather than as a separate entity – occupied a high proportion of the period 48–78. Mid Wales was a border area between the territories of the Ordovices, based mainly in the N, and the Silures of South Wales, just as it was to be divided between the commands of Chester and Caerleon under the Romans. These two tribes are recorded as being very hostile to the Romans, and it was in mid Wales that the Cativellaunian chief, Caratacus, who had taken refuge among the Silures, was finally defeated by Ostorius Scapula in A.D. 51. The various campaigns of subsequent governors were based on a three-pronged advance from Usk/Caerleon, Wroxeter/Leintwardine, and Chester. The period of active campaigning, up to the final conquest under Vespasian, produced a number of auxiliary camps, such as Clyro (R) on the Wye, and marching camps such as those on Trecastell Mountain (B), which were of only temporary importance. The stabilization of the occupation after A.D. 80 resulted in the foundation of major forts for auxiliary troops at Forden Gaer and Caersws on the Severn, 7 at Castell Collen near Llandrindod Wells, and at Brecon Gaer on the Usk, with lesser forts at Discoed (R), Beulah (B), and Pen y Gaer (B) which were closed down during the Antonine re-organization of the mid C2. However, this redeployment did not represent a serious reduction of the Roman presence, for the surviving forts were consolidated at this time, their defences and internal buildings strengthened and rebuilt in stone (although this improvement was carried out piecemeal, and in some cases, such as Castell Collen (R), a reduction in size was also involved).

From the end of the C2 A.D. the Roman military presence was being quite markedly reduced in both North and South Wales, but it is interesting that the main forts of mid Wales, Forden Gaer, Castell Collen, and Leintwardine, and probably Caersws and Brecon Gaer as well, continued to be occupied right into the C4 and the end of Roman rule. Presumably the native tribes in this region were resistant to Romanization to the end and could never be trusted completely. However, the final abandonment of even these outposts was effected eventually, perhaps when Magnus Maximus (Macsen Wledig) took Britain's troops with him to support his claim to the Imperial throne in A.D. 383, though the details are far from clear even in the archaeological record. The reoccupation of hillforts such as the Breiddin perhaps hints at a return to older ways of life amongst the native population, but many of the legacies of Rome survived – notably the network of well-designed and well-engineered roads which must have been still in use in the C6–7, when Christian memorials such as Maen Madoc near Ystradfellte (B) were set up beside them.

INTRODUCTION

POWYS is a region of the happy mean – not so rich as Clwyd to the N or so wild as Gwynedd to the NW, so remote as Dyfed to the SW or so industrialized as the Glamorgans to the S or as Gwent to the SE. As an entity this is Mid Wales, its LANDSCAPE characterized by green grassland, oaks and ashes, and beautiful east-flowing rivers. More than anything else one sees hills, of any shape and sort, and lots of them. The distinction between the English lowlands and the Welsh hills is that Wales is appreciably windier, wetter and cooler. Throughout Powys there are areas above 2,000 ft, affecting one's present-day journeys just as, for other reasons, they did prehistoric routes. Much of the land surface lies over the 1,000 ft contour, and so do many of the dwellings. This factor has determined a history of military campaigns and mines, of early Christianity and romantic tourism, traces of which crop up everywhere. Isolation has engendered an independent religious outlook, and also, till very recently, some poverty. The landscape dominates to the extent that one could almost speak of it as though it were uninhabited; but, as in Tuscany, it is precisely the presence of the farmsteads on the hills which delights one.

Powys is the name of the jumbo administrative area – it covers a quarter of Wales – created by the local government changes in 1974. Its constituents are Montgomeryshire, Radnorshire, and Breconshire, counties established by the Act of Union in 1536 from former medieval princedoms and Marcher lordships. Montgomeryshire marches with North Wales, sharing the Berwyn moors with Merioneth and Denbigh, and it has the unique distinction of both an English border (with Shropshire) and a west coast (on the Dovey estuary). Its historic loyalties were to the Princes of Powys Wenwynwyn. Breconshire is just as clearly a South Wales area, its tallest hills, the Brecon Beacons, being the mass in the S of which the coal- and iron-rich valleys are hollowed. The old county boundary (under the new one, followed here, three parishes were ceded to Gwent and three to Mid Glamorgan) lay S of the Heads of the Valleys road which now joins the towns at the tops of the industrial valleys. Radnorshire, George Borrow was told, is neither Wales nor England, but simply Radnorshire.

The total land area was 2,001 square miles, of which Montgomery-shire has roughly 510,000 acres, Radnorshire 301,000, and Brecon-shire now only 453,000; the total population in 1971 was 114,475, Breconshire with only 37,675 (it had 55,000) now coming between Radnorshire with 18,280 and Montgomeryshire with 43,120. Powys thus ranks second by area and eighth by popula-tion in the Principality. Within this general region, each county has its own topographical character.

MONTGOMERYSHIRE is visually pastoral, its neat counter-panes of grassy fields reaching right over the tops of the ridges. Of the border counties it has more observable English features than the other two. The Shropshire plain extends as a fertile promontory up the Severn valley among the outlying hills on the E. Abundant oak woods grew there and peopled this valley, and those of its tributaries the Banwy and the Vyrnwy, with black-and-white timber buildings. This heartland of the medieval princedom was called 'Powys paradwys Cymru' (the paradise of Wales) by the C6 poet Llywarch Hen. Except in the wilder N and W, there are endless varieties of this open country in which man-kind and nature look established in a civilized balance. It is most splendid along the Severn between Llanidloes, the great arena of Caersws, and Welshpool.

The upper Severn and the upper Wye enclose RADNORSHIRE, more or less. Both rise in Plynlimon (2,468 ft), the N part of the unpopulated uplands that divide Powys from the western sea-board. The Wye gives Radnorshire its grandest scenery, but generally this gentle and intimate county does not impose itself, its farms occupying an elevated plateau of lesser streams and recent hedged enclosures, of plantations and ancient commons. Away from the lush Herefordshire border, these lie dispersed amongst abrupt, bracken-covered hills. Such countryside tends naturally to the picturesque. In spite of its remoteness, Radnor-shire has nearly as high a proportion per head of buildings of some interest as any rural area in Britain.

BRECONSHIRE is the dramatic one. The Usk between Brecon and Crickhowell passes through a valley on a really majestic scale. The Beacons' rugged, glaciated outline to the S reaches almost 3,000 ft; Mynydd Eppynt to the N, on the other hand, is smooth, barren and remote. This drama contrasts with the good agricul-tural tract in the gap between the Usk and the Wye; a gap where old routes converge near Talgarth. Llangorse Lake, the largest natural water in South Wales, is part of this red-earth, formerly cider-producing district. The Black Mountains on its E, dividing

Wales and Breconshire from Herefordshire, have a different magic quality. Deep cwms run into the massif from the s, whilst on the w and n the cwms are steep and short. These hills are formed of the Old Red Sandstone (it outcrops in horizontal beds) which supplies the purple-grey material for local buildings. Bare uplands cover surprisingly much of the county, both s of the Beacons round the reservoirs, and w of the Wye. In this it differs from the other two.

Glaciation is the factor which has most affected scenery – and the three great glacier systems moving E and s from Plynlimon and n from the Beacons have left the courses of the rivers Severn, Wye, and Usk. In the s the ice did not overtop the Black Mountains (2,660 ft) or the Beacons (2,907 ft), and an aberrant flow diverted the Usk from its confluence with the Wye to seek a way s to the Severn estuary. The landscape of Montgomeryshire, and of Radnorshire down to the Forest (2,166 ft), results from erosion of a peneplain.

In these million hilly acres the principal occupation is, as ever, sheep- and cattle-farming. Rural depopulation – or at least stability through emigration – has limited manpower on the farms, and with new technology many of their traditional buildings will inevitably disappear. At the same time towns are still very few (there are only fifteen or so) and very small. Brecon is the most historic; Welshpool has a busy market; Newtown, as the Mid Wales development town, will soon be Powys's largest. The C19 industrial townships in the s valleys do not fit this view, for various enterprises have brought their people together in the rows and terraces of another tradition – and often on high and exposed sites. The Montgomeryshire weaving towns grew up from Edwardian boroughs. A nearly universal particularity of Welsh society is revealed by the rarity of nucleated villages (including modern council housing), the pattern of settlement being a remarkably even scatter of churches, castles, houses. The effect of that is to make it seem that buildings of architectural interest are much scarcer than is in fact the case. It contributes to the first obstacle for the architectural traveller in Wales: the difficulty of finding his goal.

The GEOLOGY of the three Powys counties is extremely complicated in detail, but calls for a summary of those aspects which have influenced the scenery and the choice of building materials. Apart from small occurrences of hard pre-Cambrian rocks at Hanter Hill and the Stanner rocks near Old Radnor (R), and of Ordovician dolerite and other rocks which form the sudden peaks of the Breiddens (M; 1,202 ft) and Corndon Hill (M; 1,684 ft) and which also outcrop near Llanwrtyd (B), the rocks are sedimentary.

Muds laid down in Ordovician times and subsequently compressed under the weight of overlying strata compose the hardish grey shales in the N part of the area, e.g. near Machynlleth and near Welshpool (both M). Further fine-grained shales and flags were deposited in Silurian times in the deep water which covered much of central Wales. During the Caledonian earth-movements these strata were uplifted and fairly strongly folded. Material eroded from the Ordovician and Silurian rocks of this raised mass – known as St George's Land – was laid down in a basin to the S during and after the mountain-building. A total thickness of 6,000 ft of sandstones, marls, breccias, and conglomerates was deposited, and this constitutes the Old Red Sandstone formations which now underlie most of Breconshire, the S of Radnorshire, and the W of Herefordshire. The sediments were laid down in deltaic, lacustrine, and shallow marine conditions; they are mostly stained red with ferric oxide but are interbedded with some green and grey sandstones. The Old Red Sandstone gives rise to richer soils than the rocks to the N. A hard quartzitic layer is responsible for the table-top appearance of the Brecon Beacons. At the S margin, continued sedimentation and changes of level produced the Carboniferous Limestone, the Millstone Grit, and finally the Coal Measures (particularly deep near Ystradgynlais, B).

Clearly, not much good BUILDING MATERIAL can be won from such sources. Because the stones of the N half of Powys are so fissile, everything except churches and castles has tended to be built of the oaks that the climate and elevation encouraged. Dearth of wood led to the local use of brick from c. 1700, and its widespread use from c. 1825. In this the Ordovician and Silurian areas contrast with the Old Red Sandstone of the S, for there the slightly more workable stone continued without substitution until the mid C19, and could be split for roofing tiles as well. Breconshire's architectural character is thus closer to Monmouthshire's; and its stone has encouraged conservatism.

For buildings of the highest status, needing stone capable of being ashlared, it was usually necessary to import. In the finest part of Brecon Cathedral the wall-shafts are of a fine pink stone. A Triassic sandstone from Grinshill in Shropshire (known as White Grinshill) was used even for the Cwmhir Abbey (R). At Powis (M) the castle outcrop itself yielded red sandstone. Red stones actually were much employed both for Early Christian carving and – particularly – for Norman work. They vary from pinkish to vermillion (Red Grinshill?).

The inadequacy of Montgomeryshire stone even for walling probably led to the adoption of timber bell-stages designed to prevent vibration from cracking the towers. Absence of a suitable freestone clearly limited the potential for Gothic tracery designs everywhere. Some rudimentary windows were done in the local old red sandstones, but better ones seem to have been done in yellow-green-grey sandstones (perhaps the Soudley or Downton Castle sandstones from Herefordshire?). More research could be done on locating quarries and their use; there were for instance two on the Usk, at Bwlch and Crickhowell. One stone, Criggion Green, an olivine dolerite quarried near Welshpool, enjoyed popularity in the C19 (e.g. for *Street*'s Llandysilio church) as did Sweeney Mountain stone, a sandstone from Shropshire. Montgomeryshire's roofing resources, between thatch – which has totally disappeared – and the late C19 slates from the North, included Rhiwarth slate from Llangynog and tile-stone from Corndon Hill (in the C15).

Not till the industrial age, however, was there extensive use of – perhaps even a new demand for – stones for elaborate cutting. Then Cefn stone from the Millstone Grit of Flintshire was brought by canal, and Somerset oolite and other distant materials like Derbyshire oolite began to be chosen for large houses. Breconshire nonetheless clung to its almost uniform grey-pink rubble; at Hay-on-Wye it was ashlared successfully. Modern extraction is confined to the getting of roadstone (near Builth, B, Rhayader, R, Old Radnor, R, and Criggion, M) and the use of clay at Buttington (M) for the brickworks.

OFFA'S DYKE, the extraordinarily long earthwork that defined the frontier between Mercia and Wales in the late C8, bears the name of the king of Mercia from 757 to 795. Now thought of as a real military barrier, it runs from near Prestatyn on the North Wales coast to the Beachley peninsula on the Severn estuary, and appropriately as much through present English counties as Welsh. Though not everywhere of the same design, it lies, formidable still – ditched mostly on the Welsh side and up to 16 ft high – on hill and plain alike. How effective was it, one wonders, as a deterrent against raiding parties reaching agriculturalists on the E, and how soon were matters settled legally instead? In some border areas, especially near Presteigne and Welshpool, Welsh and Saxon settlements seem to have co-existed.

Of the EARLY CHRISTIAN ORIGINS, the most widespread

and familiar signs are the names of the Celtic saints to whom most of the churches on the most ancient sites are dedicated. Preceded by 'Llan-' ('the enclosure of...'), these founder-evangelists (or St Mary or St Michael) lend their names to about eighty places in Powys. Some farms also have this prefix, possibly indicating an earlier religious building, more often a corruption. The Welsh dedications outnumber the Norman by more than two to one. However it seems very unlikely that any fragment of any church built between the C6 and the late C11 survives. The one exception is the SAXON work at Presteigne (R), where part of the N wall and part of the semicircular chancel arch of a simple two-rectangle church of the C10 or C11 are exposed.

What have come down are some twenty EARLY CHRISTIAN CARVINGS, either fonts or else stone pillars not necessarily associated with their present homes. Of the former, Old Radnor's (R) is perhaps the oldest (C8), a cyclopean boulder. Then Newchurch (R), C10 or C11; and then two C11 carved fonts with leaf-forms of Winchester manuscripts, Defynnog (B) and Partrishow (B). Defynnog's has leaf and other ornament, and inscriptions in Runic and Lombardic letters on the rim; Partrishow's a leaf design on the rim together with an interpretable inscription in Latin. The oldest of the incised memorial pillars, particularly plentiful in Breconshire, are much older than these fonts. A number date from the C5 or C6 (e.g. the Cunocenni stone, Trallong (B), the stone of Turpillius (Brecknock Museum), Maen Madoc, Ystradfellte (B), and the Rustece stone, Llanerfyl (M)); the typical ornament on the later ones is the Celto-Irish ring-cross symbol (a Greek or Latin cross within a circle). Some stones were carved with knots and elaborate interlacing, starting in the C9. The most important, the C8 or later Llywel Stone (B), is in the British Museum; its designs are pictographs, and pre-representational. Three C10 Breconshire stones, at Llandefaelog Fach, Llanfrynach, and Llanhamlach, do have reliefs of crude Crucifixion scenes combined with knotwork; but the standards of representation, and of conception of the decoration as related to the cross-form, are not high. At Meifod (M), a slab on that Dark Ages Christian site has similar motifs, but no figures except Viking animals. At Llowes (R) the C11 cross clearly belongs to a purer sculptural tradition. All the same, the slender C10 pillar cross from Neuadd Siarman (B) stands out for its integration of the wheel-shaped head with the interestingly moulded shaft. Breconshire is particularly rich in monuments with burial inscriptions in Latin and in Ogams.

If nothing helpful can be said even of plan-types, the SITES of the churches at least may be of great age. Many are approximately circular. Some are also raised. They are commonly either quite high up in the hills, or on the bank of a river. For secular dwellings of the period there are PLATFORM SITES, terraces of soil thrown outwards from the slope, with a 'hood' or bank to divert seepage from the top end. Whether actually used before the Norman Conquest or not, there are examples at Beili Bedw and Ddyrysgol, Rhayader (R), and Castell-y-Blaidd, Llanbadarn Fynydd (R). The houses on them had rectangular stone foundations.

By the C10 or earlier the Welsh form of monastery or Mother Church had become a CLAS, to which the churches each had founded contributed dues. Composed of an abbot, a priest, and hereditary canons, *clasau* were centres of scholarship. The institution lasted until absorbed into the Roman Church by *c.* 1200. In Powys there were seven such churches: Llandinam (M), Llangurig (M), Meifod (M); Glasbury (R), Glascwm (R), St Harmon (R); Llanddew (B). The last of these retains in its C13 form the cruciform plan associated with *clas* status. Two churches, Partrishow (B) and Pennant Melangell (M), possess graves of saints for which special plans were later made; at the former the Cell-y-Bedd is W of the nave, at the latter it is in an elongated chancel.

The MEDIEVAL PARISH CHURCHES are in many cases of extremely mixed architecture. Aesthetically it is the vernacular qualities of the fabrics which are usually the most enjoyable. At their extremes, e.g. at Rhulen (R), a small rectangular building, undoubtedly of great age, possesses practically no features which are datable in terms of style. In general, whether because of conservativeness and even backwardness in the adoption of new ideas, or because of inaccessibility or lack of the means to pay, the result is that two factors haunt the mind of the investigator. Any particular style or technique, once adopted and proved, tends to be retained, and so late datings (by comparison with some English counties) should not be regarded as exceptional or surprising. At some periods the work is fully comparable with events elsewhere; at others the time-lag is fifty years or more – for example, in timber construction, the square-framed houses of Montgomeryshire and the cruck barns of Radnorshire, with dates well into the C18. Secondly, what we see is often genuine work of its period, not replaced, and on occasion its survival is a matter for excitement.

The dominant PLAN-TYPE in Montgomeryshire is the

undivided nave and chancel, though that seems mostly to be the result of rebuilding in the C15. Radnorshire and Breconshire use a chancel arch and (usually) a narrower chancel. Cruciform plans are few and restricted to the C13 or C14, apart from Meifod (M) in the mid C12, and Llanddew (B) perhaps by c. 1180. Montgomery (M) became cruciform c. 1280; Machynlleth (M) was of this type and so was Talgarth (B), where the N transept remains. Crickhowell (B) was built complete with transepts c. 1310. Breconshire has a small group of two-naved churches W of the Black Mountains, similar to North Wales churches where the plan is more common. The old churches at Llanfair Caereinion and Newtown (both M) had double naves.

That leaves the MONASTIC FOUNDATIONS. A Benedictine priory of the Norman Battle Abbey was established at Brecon after 1100. Cistercian abbeys were founded by Welsh princes, on the other hand, at Strata Marcella (M) in 1170 and at Cwmhir (R) in 1176 (but perhaps initially in 1143); and a Cistercian nunnery, small and wholly gone, at Llanllugan (M) by 1236. The Cistercians were the great propagators of Gothic in Wales and also of the farming of marginal land. The Dominican friary outside Brecon was in existence by c. 1240, and there was a cell at Rhayader (R). The friary simply had a choir and nave with a N aisle added in the C14. The Knights Hospitaller were settled at Carno and Llanwddyn (both M), etc. Cwmhir and Strata Marcella, tragic victims both of the Glyndŵr iconoclasm and of the Dissolution, were very large and splendid churches, the former perhaps c. 300 ft long, with crossing towers, transepts, and aisled naves. Their loss is the greatest that Powys has suffered. Brecon, though smaller (205 ft), is cruciform too, with a central tower. The chapels E of the transepts are rectangular and staggered, the system adopted for priories along the S of the British Isles (cf. St Canice's Cathedral, Kilkenny, Ireland). Its C14 nave is aisled and has a clerestory.

AISLED NAVES are a feature of important churches only. Three Montgomeryshire churches had them in the C12 – Meifod (1155), Kerry (1176), and perhaps Llandrinio – as did the town church in Brecon, St Mary. Of c. 1300, a fine pair of arcades remains at Presteigne (R), and of the later C14 a pair at Guilsfield (M). For the C15 there is Old Radnor (R), and of course the single arcades of the Breconshire two-naved churches (see below). For the C16, there is Welshpool (M). Fewer still are the clerestories; Presteigne's are of c. 1310, Brecon Cathedral's of c. 1350, Guilsfield's not till c. 1500, and Welshpool's (destroyed) of c. 1550.

Finally in this outline of plan-types, the EARLY TOWERS should be listed. The earliest is probably the massive one at Kerry (M), C12–14. Michaelchurch (R), Llanddew and Merthyr Cynog (both B), as well as Brecon Cathedral, belong to the late C13 or *c.* 1300. Of the latter date or after also Guilsfield and Llandinam (both M), Disserth and Gladestry (both R), and Builth and Crickhowell (both B). Towers that are in part of the C14 include perhaps Knighton and Pilleth (both R) and Llanfrynach (B). They are all totally plain. Llywel (B) and Llanidloes (M) have late C14 towers with W doorways; at Llanidloes the belfry stands on a stone vault. Perpendicular towers are described below.

The ROMANESQUE style arrived in Powys *c.* 1100 and was employed for the largest building then attempted, the vanished first priory at Brecon. Of this first phase of Norman, Presteigne (R) retains what may be a tower arch and two blocked round-headed windows. By the mid C12 a plain form of the style was fairly widely used, though nothing very elaborate was done either architecturally or in sculpture. What survives is very fragmentary, but deserves attention either for its intrinsic interest or as positive proof of the oldest elements in the churches. Thick cylindrical piers bearing semicircular arches, the essence of the system, can be seen at Meifod and Kerry, and immured at Llandrinio (all M); 14 and at Presteigne. Capitals are circular and decorated with a chamfer; also with beading below, and once with a toothed motif. Two scalloped capitals survive, at Old Radnor (R) and St Mary, Brecon. Churches with small Norman windows include the square-ended Llanfechain (M). Other churches with partly Norman unaisled plans include Pennant Melangell (M), which had a long round-apsed feretory; a semicircular apse was also found in foundations of the small timber chapel excavated at Hen Domen (M).

As for Romanesque SCULPTURE, there are a few pieces well worth mentioning. One is exceptional – probably unique in the entire country: the reconstructed shrine of St Monacella at Pennant Melangell (M) of *c.* 1160. This is a delicate design of a sarco- 15 phagus with a saddleback roof, supported on six colonnettes with scroll and leaf motifs on their cushion capitals. There is more leaf-carving on the spandrels between the arches, and on the gable ends, which are crocketed. The only comparisons to be made are with fragments of another C12 shrine near by at Llanrhaeadr-ym-Mochnant, Clwyd. The altar shrine is of a different type from e.g. Edward the Confessor's of 1241; perhaps it is of Carolingian origin. The revival of ancient motifs in the carving is curious

but could be explained by the context. The best tympanum (of
the only two) in Wales is in the s doorway of Llanbadarn Fawr
13 (R), *c.* 1100–50, a Tree of Life with fabulous animals and thus to
be considered an outlier of the Herefordshire school of carvings.
Other bits of architectural sculpture are diaper-carved lintels at
Llanddew and Llanfilo (both B), a doorway at Llanddewi
Ystradenni (R), and a head corbel from Cwmhir (R). At Presteigne
12 there is a relief of St Andrew. One font, Brecon Priory's (*c.*
1130–50), has its side richly carved with masks, interlace, birds,
etc., in roundels in the manner of the South-West (cf. St Woollos,
Newport, e.g.). Llandrinio's (M) has intersected blank arcading on
the sides. Others are plain or cable-moulded, e.g. Llangenny
(B). There is a group of a more primitive type, on which four
human or bestial heads project from the bowl; they are at Rhayader
and St Harmon (both R), Llanwrthwl (B) – all circular and of the
CII or CI2 – and at Guilsfield (M), which is octagonal and so of
the CI3. In the Romanesque in Wales there is a marked recourse
to Anglo-Saxon forms among others.

The EARLY ENGLISH style of Gothic architecture arrived,
fully-fledged, with the Benedictines and Cistercians, and is repre-
20 sented in work of the finest quality. The chancel of Brecon Cathedral shows the accomplishment of its master mason; serenity and
nobility are present already *c.* 1200 in the articulation of walls and
windows, which repay analysis of their intelligent flexibility. The
style makes an interesting contrast with the Transitional doorway
now at Old Gwernyfed (Felindre, B), which, despite a date perhaps
thirty years later, still uses heavy mouldings and scalloped
capitals. The classic phase of E.E. escaped, *mirabile dictu*, to
18 Llanidloes (M) in the shape of the Abbey Cwmhir (R) arcades. The
piers have eight clusters of triple shafts attached, i.e. visually
speaking three sets a side, on the pattern widespread in the western
counties. The lavishness of this profile, continued in the arches,
19 is equalled by the abundance of the foliage in the capitals. The
beauty of the stiff-leaf types as they progress from formality to
free and open forms belongs to *c.* 1200–1230. It is heart-rending
to reflect that Strata Marcella (M), building in these same years,
is still more utterly levelled than Cwmhir. Aesthetically Powys was
not to regain such a level of excellence until the remodelling of
Powis Castle after the Restoration. In its later stages the local E.E.
appears less expressive. The chapels and transepts at Brecon and
21 the chapel of Christ College, Brecon, perpetuate the lancet window; shafts re-attach themselves to the wall surfaces except for
piscinae and sedilia. No other churches afforded indulgence on

this scale. Llanfair Caereinion (M), Montgomery (M), and Llandefalle (B) have ornate shafted doorways. Buttington (M) has a big
stiff-leaf capital, perhaps from Strata Marcella, as its font. The
period spans the origin of several more churches. Llanfigan (B)
with its crude arcade is of *c.* 1272; Llanigon and Llanddew (both
B), Gladestry, Cascob, Bryngwyn, and Bleddfa (all R), and Montgomery (M) have some lancets. The lancet unit may come in
groups of three of unequal height, or in small pairs. At Welshpool
(M) bar-tracery appears, with circles introduced as tracery
between the lights. By the early C14, multiplication of lights was
coming, either by mullions dividing a window up to its arch, e.g.
Brecon Cathedral; or by enclosing three or more lancets in one
frame, e.g. the E and Awbrey Chapel windows at Christ College;
or else by the more widespread Y-tracery which in a three-light
window becomes intersecting tracery, e.g. St Mary, Brecon.

At this point the more elaborate geometrical profiles of the
DECORATED style start appearing, though there are few significant examples to cite. It is in odd windows that it occurs most
often. Decoration of window heads by cusping the points of a trefoil is an early manifestation. Tracery lights tend towards cusped
quatrefoils and then less symmetrical shapes. There are Dec windows at Buttington and Llandrinio (M), Llanbadarn Fynydd (R),
Brecon Cathedral nave, etc. Llandegley (R) has a doorway with
a septifoil head, as has a tomb recess in Brecon Cathedral. This
recess, of *c.* 1340, also illustrates two other characteristics: the
ogee curve which first seems to occur *c.* 1310 in the clerestory at
Presteigne; and ballflower, also used on a doorway at Brecon and
on the early C14 arcade at Kerry (M). This brings us to C14 arcades.
Presteigne's is composed of octagonal piers and pointed arches,
Kerry's of octagonal piers and semicircular arches. The grandest
example is the nave of Brecon Cathedral. There the chamfers are
hollow; later in the C14 the wavy pattern develops, as on the N
doorway at Christ College, and the tower of Strata Marcella. At
Guilsfield (M) the columns are clusters of alternate wave-moulded
and rectangular members. The fluent repetition of the ogee in
reticulated windows exists at Meifod and Welshpool (M), Pilleth
(R), and elsewhere.

CHURCH FURNISHINGS of the C14 scarcely survive. In Breconshire wooden screens with buttressed pointed central openings
exist at Llanfigan and Merthyr Cynog, and a remarkable veranda
screen complete with painted tympanum divides the nave and
chancel at Llanelieu. A number of recumbent stone EFFIGIES
have escaped mutilation; they include one of St Monacella

33 (*c.* 1315) at Pennant Melangell, and Dafydd ap Gruffydd Fychan
(in armour; *c.* 1400) at Llanfair Caereinion (both M); Sir Grimbald and Lady Sybil Pauncefoot (*c.* 1325) at Crickhowell (B); and
27 the earliest and crudest in Brecon Cathedral, to Walter and Christina Awbrey (dated 1312), a single slab with both figures in relief,
and the rood and angels carved in the canopy at their heads.

Returning to secular buildings, NORMAN DOMESTIC ARCHI-
TECTURE can be described from one example: the shell keep of
16 Tretower Castle (B). Hall and solar, of reasonable size, were on
the first floor, above the kitchen and what was possibly a cellar.
The archways of the former are ornamented with chevrons, of
the latter with spiral shafts and capitals, the typically elaborate
motifs of the later C12. This shows how securely the Normans
had settled in the Usk valley.

At least twenty-three STONE CASTLES were erected in Powys
as the involved processes of border struggles intensified after the
mid C12. Previously, innumerable motte and bailey castles of earth
had been thrown up all over the country by Norman and by Welsh
potentates. The new builders were again the Marcher families and
23 the Welsh rulers, and the English king joined them in 1223 at
25 Montgomery. The C12 type was the rectangular tower, as at Powis
17 (M; for Gwenwynwyn?), Hay (B), and Castell Dinas (B), etc.
There were also shell keeps on the mottes at Brecon, Crickhowell
(B), and Tretower (B). About 1220 the Marcher families de Clifford
24 and Picard introduced at Bronllys (B) and Tretower the tall
cylindrical keep on a battering base, perhaps modelled on
Pembroke's and French in type. Llewelyn ap Gruffydd used it at
Blaencamlais (B). At most of these Mid Wales castles, e.g. Colwyn
or Knucklas (both R), there is little to see now. Following excavation, however, Montgomery Castle (begun in 1223 for Henry III)
is revealed as exceptionally important, since its twin-towered
gatehouse is the first in the series of famous castles constructed
in North and South Wales up to the end of the century. The prototype was Richard I's Château Gaillard. Further castles which were
17 strengthened for Henry III were Painscastle (R; 1231) and Hay
(B; 1233).

Little distinguishes the later C13 plans – basically rectangular
curtains with angle towers – built by Welsh and English partisans
at Dolforwyn (Llewelyn ap Gruffydd's desperate act of rivalry with
Montgomery) or Gwyddgrug (both M); Aberedw, Cefnllys, Dinboeth, New Radnor (all R); Blaenllynfi, Brecon, Pencelli (all B).
But Castell Coch, Ystradfellte (B), seems to have the Welsh D-
shaped tower. Powis (M), refortified for Gruffydd ap Gwenwynwyn,

the last Prince of Powys, *c.* 1280 or later, has kept its twin-towered gatehouse intact. It is unique in that it is still lived in, and therefore the layout of the wards, curtains, and gates is substantially unchanged. Edward I's only castle in the area, Builth (B; begun 1277), still awaits excavation to establish the earliest concentric scheme of his master engineer *James of St George,* and any trace of timber buildings by *John Fitz Adam* of Radnor. Following the death in 1282 of Llywelyn the last native Prince of Wales, in Breconshire, the Statute of Rhuddlan (1286), and the final English victory at Maesmoydog in Montgomeryshire in 1295, new castle building in Powys dwindled; the Marcher strongholds at Crickhowell (Pauncefoot) and Brecon (de Breos) (both B) are two exceptions.

The companion of enforced peace was what would now be called the infrastructure of civil prosperity, i.e. the GRID-PLANNED TOWNS of the C13 and their accompanying market charters. Montgomery was early established (*c.* 1223) under royal protection (cf. Caernarvon, etc.) and early too in being walled. No walls or gates remain at Brecon, Crickhowell, or Hay (all B), and their plans are confused. But regular layouts are obvious at Knighton, at New Radnor (with its earth banks), Presteigne, and Rhayader (all R); and in the more stable Montgomeryshire, the streets and indeed blocks of late C13 Newtown, Llanidloes, and Machynlleth remain easily identifiable. The ₃ rationality of this urban development bears comparison with the chequerboard plans of Edward I's Winchelsea in Sussex (1283) and with the Bastides of the English in Central France. In the countryside a bit of the Cistercians' system of granges or farms managed by lay brothers is visible at Clyro Court Farm and Monaughty (both R). That much cannot be said of the monasteries of either Cistercian abbey; though there are portions of the conventual buildings of the priory and the friary at Brecon. With this we leave the C13, which was for Powys a time of achievement in church and military architecture as well as in town planning.

From the later C14 individual HALL-HOUSES survive. The fundamental division between the stone- and timber-building areas should be stated here: this is that Breconshire uses stone walls almost exclusively, Montgomeryshire makes nearly everything except churches out of oak, and Radnorshire does half-and-half. The tendency towards timber in the fertile east and towards stone in the wet west is also marked. More will be said of this later. So it is Breconshire that can claim the first three in the list (though they are not houses): the C13 Large Hall at Christ Col-

lege, Brecon, quite long and with a semi-octagonal end; the quite ruined early C14 hall of the Palace of the Bishops of St David's
34 at Llanddew; and the lofty late C14 Small Hall at Christ College again. Here the original roof is of three collar trusses braced with big trefoil arches. An aisled timber hall of the period has recently been found at Upper House, Painscastle (R). Two aisled halls in
See Montgomeryshire came next. Ty Mawr, Castle Caereinion (*c.*
p.
90 1400?), is of composite type, combining a spere truss alongside the entry passage with base-cruck construction for the one and a half bays of the hall. Cwrt-Plas-y-Dre, Newtown (early C15; moved from Dolgellau, Merioneth), also has the aisled passage truss of the north-western counties, with two arch-braced collar-trusses over the hall. In the latter respect it resembles the later C15 stone-walled Parliament House at Machynlleth (M). Stone halls also in-
38 clude the two complete ranges at Tretower (B) of *c.* 1460 and *c.*
39 1470; the former is on the first floor, like the C12 castle's, and actually has one timber-framed wall. This, the largest medieval house in Powys, was the property of Sir William ap Thomas and his family as was Raglan Castle in Gwent. Others in the s are Great Porthaml, Talgarth (B; *c.* 1460), and the Old Vicarage, Glasbury (R; *c.* 1400). On a similar smallish scale are the timber halls, for instance Ciliau, Llandeilo Graban (R; late C15); a fragmentary town house, now Messrs Bennett's, Presteigne (R; early C15?) and two roofs in Knighton (R); and the vanished hall at Cefnllys Castle (R; *c.* 1440) which earns its mention because we know the name of its 'architect' (pensaer, literally 'master carpenter') – he was *Rosier ab Ywain*, Roger son of Owain. Where now lived in, these halls are filled with rooms.

In stone-building Breconshire, two three-storey early C14 TOWER HOUSES should be noted, at Talgarth and at Scethrog. These small defensible houses are to be found infrequently in Glamorgan and Pembroke, much more generally in the Scottish Borders and in Ireland.

ROOF STRUCTURES in the C15 are roughly parallel in stone-walled halls and in churches. The commonest type is a double-framed roof, which has arch-braced principal trusses, and
38 a secondary mesh of purlins and wind-braces. The great hall at Tretower is a good example. These techniques are particularly widespread in the western English counties. In some roofs a scissor truss is inserted as an ornamental variant, in churches as at Bettws Clyro (R; *c.* 1400?), Aberhafesp (M) and Disserth (R), and in houses as at Great Porthaml (B), and the Old Vicarage, Glasbury, and Maes Treylow, Discoed (both R). The Old

Vicarage has figure carvings at the spring of the roof. At Llanywern (B) and Llanbadarn-y-Garreg (R) these are single-framed scissor-truss roofs.

The most frequent early house, in the western Midlands as a whole – and Powys is central to that area – and in Wales at large except for the south-west and the western seaboard, is the CRUCK HALL. A pair of crucks are two symmetrical timbers, each forming the vertical wall as well as the sloping roof of a barn-like space. The term first appears in a building account for Harlech Castle of 1305; one might suppose that so elemental an invention could have originated much earlier. It occurs mostly in NW Britain (and NW France), but, ephemeral by nature, its physical survival from early times is rare or non-existent. In Powys the design of the basic house indicates the fruition of an evolutionary process. The crude examples are barns in the C17 and C18 decline. The period for houses is perhaps roughly from the early C15 to c. 1600. In all there are about 100 such structures in Montgomery, over 50 in Radnorshire, over 25 in Breconshire. Five couples used together provide the frame for a compact rectangular dwelling. The set of components is found often on flat earth platforms at r. angles to the downhill slope (for drainage). Their virtue was to provide a hall, of two bays spanned by a central couple, sometimes arch-braced and frequently with ornament in the apex timbers, with a storeyed room or rooms at either end. The whole box (the wall cladding was chiefly of square-framed timbers) was as skilfully used as a modern flat. Height to the apex roughly equalled width. The largest, Great House, Newchurch (R), spans 28 ft; Bryndraenog (Beguildy, R) with base crucks, spans 19 ft. * See p. 219
These halls are most easily appreciable where they have become barns (Middle Maestorglwydd, Llanigon, B; Old Rhydycarw, Trefeglwys, M). Inside many an upper floor and chimney have been built, hiding the roof, with the glorious exception of Bryndraenog (R), where a Jacobean gallery solved the problem of access between the upper floors of the wings. The grandeur of this Gothic design derives from repetition of the pointed arch forms, for the arched braces, in the crucks themselves, and for the arcades between collar and tie. The like would be worthy of church architecture, but of cruck-built churches there are none.

As the cruck tradition weakened, hall-houses came to be built with the BOX-FRAMES of the south-eastern English vernacular. At

* These figures compare with modern use of the technique; e.g. Rhayader (R) Community Centre, with laminated crucks, spans 40 ft; see also Welshpool R.C. church (M).

Bryndraenog the secondary hall in the cross-wing has an ornamental box-frame; in Montgomeryshire there are four, e.g.
Gwernfyda, Llanllugan. The halls were the dwellings of the leading families, of officials, and even of yeoman farmers. Their size
was modest, however; only Ciliau, Llandeilo Graban (R), and
Bryndraenog have even the cross-wings of the familiar H-plan.

Tudor GATEHOUSES stand in front of the Herbert family's
former house (Porthmawr; early C16), of Great Porthaml, Talgarth (c. 1525), and of Tretower (c. 1480). Tretower is quite
exceptional in that the gatehouse completes the medieval courtyard house. Considered as a group, Tretower, Porthaml, the
partly ruined Aberbrân, the lost Porthmawr, and Llywelyn ap
Ieuan's Bryndraenog have in common a plan with adjacent halls
for the use of the old established families who lived there and of
their feudal households. It is an interesting picture.

An arrangement of obvious antiquity for the shelter of humans
and animals in one farm building is the LONG-HOUSE, once
characteristic of all Wales. The ground floor of the end of the
house below the hall was fitted as a byre, and this could be reached
from the cross-passage, as could the hall. Great House, Llanfihangel Nant Melan (R) retains the connecting doorway; Cileos,
Penybontfawr (M) is a ruined C16 cruck house of this type; Hepste
Fawr, Ystradfellte (B) is one of the last instances where internal
communication between men and cattle is still possible.

Before finishing with the Middle Ages, the PERPENDICULAR
style in church building, the last to make much impact in Powys
till the C19, may be outlined. Perpendicular denotes prosperity
in C15 England, and it is not surprising to find that little was
rebuilt in C15 Powys. Old Radnor and Presteigne (both R), on the
border, possess good work, as does Llandefalle (B). Gracefully
slender piers in the arcades, ample proportions everywhere, and
the admission of more light with the multiplication of mullions
and panel traceries in the larger windows are, as everywhere, the
characteristics. The absence of a suitable freestone as much as
the absence of lucrative trade inhibits any tendency to verticality
or to great display. The broad aisled nave at Welshpool (M) has
perhaps the loftiest piers, and with its Tudor arches belongs to
the C16. There are Perp arcades in the two-naved churches of
Llanbedr Ystrad Yw, Llangattock, and Llangenny (all B). By and
large Perp means alterations to windows, doorways, etc., and
appears perhaps later in Breconshire than further N. Only Montgomery (M) boasts an E window of any complexity. Coming to
towers, Breconshire leads, not only with the noble steeple of St

Mary, Brecon, almost Tudor and the work of a Somerset mason 45 c. 1510, but also with many plain, unbuttressed towers in the early C16 (Defynnog, Llangattock, Talgarth, and others). Radnorshire has Old Radnor and Presteigne, with diagonal buttresses; Montgomeryshire has only Llangurig with diagonal buttresses, and Bettws Cedewain (c. 1520?) with angle buttresses. One might add the E tower of Powis Castle on account of its lierne stone vault.

The Perp style chiefly flourished in TIMBER – in BELL-STAGES of towers and BELL-TURRETS, in ROOFS and SCREENS, in fact in those elements which, because they are of the locally plentiful oak, carvers could enrich. This was impossible in the case of stonework. It is strange that in Montgomeryshire there is only one timber-framed church, Trelystan, seeing how the county parallels Shropshire in other respects; Llanbrynmair has an arcade of wood, as formerly did Llandinam, Meifod, and New-town. Perhaps there were more once. Timber bell-stages on towers and timber bell-turrets perched on nave roofs are typical sights in the county, though fewer than a century ago. The object was to keep the bell-frame from shaking the poor masonry of the towers to pieces; they may be a C17 feature. They cap the towers at Bettws Cedewain, Kerry, and Llanidloes and are restored at 30 Llandinam, Newtown, etc. Cascob (R) has a timber bell-stage. They appear in Gwent too, but not in Breconshire. In towerless churches, e.g. Buttington, Llanbrynmair, Tregynon, bell-turrets were raised through the roofs on colossal baulks of wood. In Radnorshire the square bell-turret is not uncommon.

The ROOFS of the churches are often their unifying part. Although apparently mostly of the period 1430–1530 (very few are accurately datable), they fall into three main groups according to region. Square-panelled barrel ceilings, of moulded wooden ribs with foliage bosses and plaster infill, are almost universal in Breconshire (Llandefalle etc). Their distribution extends through Radnorshire a little and even as far as Montgomery (M). They may be segmental, of full tunnel section, or more rarely Tudor-arched (Llangattock, B). Some (e.g. Llywel, B) have no plaster in-fill. Radnorshire roofs have one common component, the tie-beam, which is often employed alternately with arch-braced collar trusses (e.g. Glascwm). N Breconshire follows suit. Poor walling stone is part of the answer. The wholly arch-braced pattern of Montgomeryshire is common to very many churches in Hereford-shire and Shropshire, besides some cases in the S of Powys (Gladestry, R; Merthyr Cynog, B). The earliest may be at Kerry

(M; nave, C14). The structure is susceptible of decoration in two places: the apex struts can be cusped in various ways, e.g. Cemmaes, Llanfechain (both M), etc.; more obviously, wind-braces can be ranged between the purlins and the principals – at first merely cusped, they later take the form of quatrefoils, as in the two rows at Bryngwyn (R) or in the four at Montgomery (the W half of the nave). The latter roof is of hammerbeam construction, and in Montgomeryshire there are two other church roofs of this type: Llanidloes and Mochdre. Llanidloes', dated 1542, is certainly the finest roof in Powys. The spandrel pieces have figure-carved bases and each hammerbeam has its winged angel. Mochdre too has angels on the hammerbeams.* Decorative ceilings of a quite different, Tudor, kind are at Old Radnor (R), and at Guilsfield and Welshpool (both M).

Double-framed roofs are thus the overwhelmingly dominant type, and single-framed techniques, native to the SE of England, were used only in the nave at Presteigne (R), where the fine span has a collar purlin, supported by angled braces; at Bettws Clyro and at Llanbadarn-y-Garreg (also R); and at Llandeilo'r Fan (B).

The analysis of SCREENS was meticulously pursued by the late F. H. Crossley and Canon M. Ridgway and only some of the main groups need be enumerated here. Welsh screens of c. 1500 differ from English in being less Perp in style: instead of the verticals of the posts running uninterrupted down to the floor, they have the rail and dado interposing a horizontal stress: instead of vaulting below the loft, with ribs gathering to a shaft, they have a flat coving of square panels. The oak is in general dark and of heavy scantling. Traceries are not necessarily consistent in one screen. There is a tendency not to have a unified architectural design, even in the lofts. The very ornate and fretted parapets are composed of bands of interlace carving, one above the other, these being visually more important, and only decipherable from close to. The most inventive craftsmen, the 'Newtown school', produced work of extraordinary sensitivity and interest, to judge from Llananno (R) and the fragments of Newtown (M) screen. Their arabesques of open knotwork and twining stalks seem like a revival of the Celtic and Nordic designs of the Dark Ages. Other idiosyncrasies of the Powys scheme include the doorhead traceries and their shallow triangular profile and the pairs of posts supporting the loft both E and W of the doorway (formerly at Llanwnnog). Of

* The only other instances of hammerbeams are the unproven truss at Glasbury old vicarage; and possibly the vanished new roof to the hall of Brecon Castle, c. 1550 (cf. Raglan Castle).

nearly twenty screens still fairly intact, only four preserve their lofts. These are at Llanwnnog (M; restored in 1873); Llananno (R; restored in 1880 with twenty-five figures by *Boulton*); and Llanfilo and Partrishow (B; both restored under *W. D. Caröe, c.* 1926 and *c.* 1909). They combine foliage trails with a few dragons, wyverns, etc. English work is represented by the much-pinnacled E screen and the loft at Montgomery; and by the fluent vaulted screen at Old Radnor and a lesser example at Michaelchurch-on-Arrow (both R). Bronllys (B) is of Tudor date with carved spandrels. At Llywel (B) Renaissance features first appear.

The very few Perp CHURCH FURNISHINGS that call for a special mention are widely dispersed. Kerry (M) has a font carved with the Instruments of the Passion. Christ College, Brecon, and Montgomery have misericords. Remnants of an early C15 ciborium exist at Michaelchurch-on-Arrow (R). At Llanerfyl (M) a little reliquary like a chapel, and a two-niche shrine for statues, both of wood, were found immured. More remarkably, two C15 rood figures, a Christ and a St Mary, were found at the restoration of Mochdre (M) church. They are now in the National Museum of Wales, Cardiff. Of Tudor date and possibly connected with Crown patronage, the lovely organ case at Old Radnor (R) combines panels of linenfold with extraordinary Early Renaissance carving.

Still less is there of MEDIEVAL STAINED GLASS. A late C15 St Catherine at Old Radnor is the most intelligible piece. Fragments can be seen at Buttington, Llanllugan, Llanwnnog, and tracery lights at Llanwrin (all M); at Presteigne (R) and at Llandefalle (B); and some early C16 foreign glass at Bettws Cedewain (M). In the latter church is Powys' one pre-Reformation BRASS, with the figure of the Rev. John ap Meredyth, dated 1531.

With the figure sculpture of ELIZABETHAN MONUMENTS, and with their architectural settings where they survive, we come to full Renaissance art, even if the figures are mostly still not free of the stiffness of medieval conventions. That trait is still uppermost in the wooden figure from the Games monument (*c.* 1555; Brecon Cathedral). Fragmentary tombs exist at Builth (B; John Lloyd † 1585), at Welshpool (M; Sir Edward Herbert, † 1594), and at Berriew (M; Arthur Price † 1597 and two wives). The monument to Richard Herbert (attributed* to *Walter Hancock*; 1600) at Montgomery would hold its own in any company. The Elizabethan love of luxuriant colours is happily indulged in it, and the pictorial, and ceremonial, qualities of what is almost a free-

41

47

42

See p. 81

52

* By Dr J. D. K. Lloyd.

54 standing chapel are well explored. Sir David Williams † 1613 and
wife, in Brecon Cathedral, are good examples of the Jacobean
fashion for the rendering of lavish costume in alabaster.

ELIZABETHAN DOMESTIC ARCHITECTURE is represented at
its best by one work, as enjoyable as it is typical: Sir Edward Herbert's long gallery at Powis Castle (M). It is supported on a purely
49 Italian, stone arcade. The delightful gallery itself dates from 1592
and 1593. Because of its irregularity and intimacy, it is not a grand
room. Its leafy plasterwork shares this informality. Of stone-built
51 houses Monaughty (R; c. 1575), Old Gwernyfed for Sir David
53 Williams (Felindre, B; c. 1600), and Dderw (Llyswen, B; after
1590) are H-planned. Monaughty still has its hall screens with
two ornate doorways, and a decorated ceiling in the chamber
above. Old Gwernyfed's screen is confected out of C17 woodwork;
the lower room has ceiling decoration, the room above the hall
a bit of wall painting. The innovation in domestic plans of the
late C16 on is the double pile, deriving from villa designs in North
50 Italy. In Powys it is present already in Newton (Llanfaes, B; 1582)
for the distinguished Games family, and at Pencelli Castle (B;
1583) for the Herberts. Newton shows the trend for South Wales
houses of c. 1600 to go very tall; in this case there is a partial
explanation in the two-storey great hall and screen in continuation
of the Tudor tradition. The centrally-planned and pyramid-
roofed Cemmaes Bychan (Cemmaes, M; 1632) follows Sir Richard
Clough's Bachegraig, Flintshire, of 1576. The stone or brick
houses curiously have finer woodwork than those in timber areas.
56 In support of this statement one could cite the figures on the overmantel at Far Hall (Llanfihangel Rhydithon, R; c. 1600), wainscot
at Llanddewi Hall (Llanddewi Ystradenni, R), and the Jacobean
staircases formerly at Hay Castle (B) and at Montgomery Castle
(M; 1622). In addition there is the Dutch Mannerist heraldic
58 carved room for the Blayneys at Gregynog (Tregynon, M; 1636).
Clearly, for more than a century after Henry Tudor became King
of England and Wales, some Welshmen achieved the rank and
wealth to foster fine works of art.

Large HALF-TIMBERED houses may not have been as frequent
as stone, and all have been pulled down, anyway: for instance,
Montgomeryshire has lost Aberbechan, Llanllwchaiarn (C16 and
C17); Garthmyl (C17?); Lymore, Montgomery (c. 1675 and
earlier); and Pontysgawrhyd, near Meifod (early C16, 1593, and
C17). Lymore had an arcaded loggia which recalls Condover,
Salop (1608).

The HOUSE-TYPES OF THE C17, from which period large

The typical seventeenth-century Breconshire farmhouse (type B), of stone, with the chimney backing on to the cross-passage, based on Trewalter, Llangorse (Royal Commission on Ancient and Historical Monuments in Wales)

numbers of farmhouses survive, developed from the medieval and Elizabethan plans. There are three main ones, classified according to the positioning of the chimneys as they were introduced, both as improvement to hall-houses and *de novo* in storeyed houses, from the second half of the C16 onward.* TYPE A, characterized by chimneys on the outside walls, is most common in North Wales. The chimneys may be in the gable walls: or, in their earliest datable positions, lateral to open halls as well as early storeyed houses, on the side walls. Of the first group Breconshire has 14 (e.g. Pantllefrith, Llanfigan); Radnorshire has 3 (e.g. Llan-

* The categories are those of Peter Smith, *Houses of the Welsh Countryside*, 1975.

bach Howey, Llanbedr Painscastle); Montgomeryshire has none.
Of the second group Breconshire has 22 (e.g. Llwyncyntefin, Sennybridge); Radnorshire has 15 (e.g. Fforest Colwyn); and Montgomeryshire has 5 (e.g. Grofft, Llanwrin). TYPE B comprises
houses where the chimney heating the main room is built internally, with its back to the cross-passage running between the two
outside doors in opposite walls. This is the dominant Breconshire
(and South Wales) plan; there are about 100 (e.g. Tynllyne,
Llanigon). About 110 Breconshire houses also have the stair
beside the fireplace. Radnorshire has about 25 type B houses (e.g.
Ffaldau, Llandegley), Montgomeryshire has 15 (e.g. Esgairgeiliog, Mochdre). The TYPE C house derives from the introduction
of chimneys – often two, back to back, to heat two rooms – in the
middle of the cross-passage, thus creating an entry lobby. Its distribution is in the NE Welsh counties. In its most integrated and
satisfactory form this is easily the most recognizable Montgomeryshire house – especially when it is half-timbered and has a
porch. Montgomeryshire has some 260 examples, concentrated
particularly in the Severn valley. Radnorshire has some 60 – the
county actually shows no marked division between types, but does

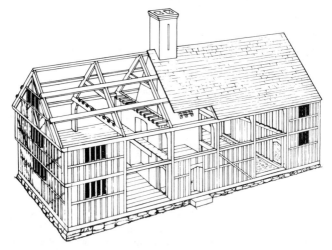

The typical seventeenth-century Montgomeryshire farmhouse (type C),
of timber, with a central chimney and lobby-entry, based on Talgarth,
Trefeglwys (Royal Commission on Ancient and Historical Monuments
in Wales)

shew a bias towards timber in the NE (e.g. Lawn Farm, Beguildy).
Breconshire has 3.

Geographical factors seem to determine whether houses of
these types or other buildings are made of stone, of timber, or
at the very end of the C17 of brick. In Breconshire stone is the
norm, and there are merely 20 or so timber-framed houses; but
the C17 town of Brecon must, like Herefordshire, have had many
more such buildings, e.g. *John Abel's* ornate Town Hall of 1624.
Radnorshire still has about 100; Montgomeryshire has some 500,
almost to the exclusion of stone. Stone may replace rotting timber
walls (e.g. Ciliau, Llanstephan, R; Cemmaes Bychan, Cemmaes,
M). W of the Montgomeryshire hills, stone is more common than
timber (e.g. the C15 'Parliament House', Machynlleth; Abergwydol, Abercegir – a type C house). Llynlloed, Machynlleth, had
a stepped gable in the North Wales fashion. In this county the
same preference for stone is true, later, in relation to brick (cf.
Montgomery with Machynlleth). Timber remained the material
for the few public buildings, e.g. Llanidloes Market Hall (M; 55
c. 1600), till the C18 (Rhayader Market Hall, R; 1762;
demolished).

The BLACK AND WHITE HOUSES of the Severn Valley (M)
and nearby possess strong regional characteristics. Plasau Duon,
Clatter perhaps comes closest to exemplifying them all. But before 59
the details of craftsmanship, a word on the general appearance
of the timbers. In all essential respects Montgomeryshire follows
Shropshire techniques. The two basic frames for load-bearing
walls are first, of large square panels of beams morticed together;
and second, of narrowly spaced uprights tenoned into a sill and
a horizontal beam above. Diagonal braces are introduced to keep
the corners at right angles. Upper floors are jettied, at first just
at the parlour end and under the gable above, then on three sides.
The bressumer beams are supported by diagonally set dragon
beams in the ground-floor ceilings; the bressumers are enriched
with roll-mouldings or strapwork (Broniarth Hall, Guilsfield),
and their external brackets are carved with scrolls or acanthus
(Trewern Hall, 1610). Accompanying motifs include vertical ropes
(Llyswen, Guilsfield, etc). Decorative arrangement of those struts
which are secondary to the framework may take the shape of
lozenges or herringbone or criss-cross; in gables particularly
small knotty circles like quatrefoils were popular. Of H fronts
there are Penarth (Newtown), Trewern Hall, and Trederwen
House (Arddleen; 1616). The type C plan often goes with a two-
storey porch. The open sides of the lower storey frequently have

shaped or turned balusters; a small room occupies the first floor. Examples of this handsome type are Berriew Vicarage (1616), Bacheldre House, Glanhafren (Llanmerewig), Lower Cil (Berriew), Middle Sylfaen (Castle Caereinion), Rhydycarw (Trefeglwys). With these the date is already the mid C17; substantial houses were still built in this way in the early C18, e.g. Maesmawr (Caersws). The technique or style is even strong enough to withstand a change of plan, e.g. the close-studded Plas Newydd (Carno; 1704) which is double-pile with a central stair. The porches are additions of astonishingly late dates: Buttington church is of 1686, Aston Hall (Pentre) 1691, Hurdley Hall (Hyssington) and Upper Treffin (Sarn) both 1718.

Some features of VERNACULAR CRAFTSMANSHIP in Montgomeryshire, apart from the mouldings and stops on the beams of important rooms, merit a short description. Montgomeryshire was so given to the use of wood that in thirty-two houses there are still timber-framed fireplaces. Chimneys in many cases are star-sectioned, both in stone and (in the later C17) in brick. A few C17 doorways have depressed ogee heads, the counter-curves in fact going lower than the sides of the doorhead. In the Trefeglwys area at least six houses have or had attractive floors of smooth pebbles pitched in geometrical patterns, a former craft of the whole Severn valley area.

The early C17 timber houses of Radnorshire, on the Hereford border, are a definable group. Close-studded construction was usual (Radnorshire Arms, Presteigne, 1616). Houses of sufficient standing to have an ornate solar upstairs, or solar upstairs and parlour downstairs, are none the less small; cf. Burfa, Walton; Upper Dolly, Norton; Wegnall, Presteigne, all of c. 1600. At Old Impton (Norton, c. 1625) the carved porch is consistent more with Herefordshire dating than with Montgomeryshire.

The INTERNAL DECORATION of the larger yeoman or gentry houses of the Jacobean period was not elaborate in Powys. More than a hundred have stud-and-panel partitions, mostly facing the fireplace; one, Pen-y-bryn (Llangynidr, B), still has attached to it the bench for the master of the house. The big late Elizabethan houses (Monaughty, R; Newton (Llanfaes) and Old Gwernyfed (Felindre), both B, and of course Powis Castle, M) had geometrical ribbed plaster ceilings in the main rooms. Intricate wooden ceilings were fashionable after c. 1600 in the N; for instance Aberffrydlan (Llanwrin), Abergwydol (Abercegir), Penarth (Llanmerewig), Plas Rhiwsaeson (Llanbrynmair), and Plasau Duon (Clatter) (all M) have moulded joists arranged in squares and turned so that those in one panel are at right angles to those in the next. Ornament was chiefly reserved for the staircase, and there are fine dog-leg ones at Trebarried (Llandefalle, B), at several smaller Radnorshire houses (Boughrood Court; Great House, Rhosgoch), and more heroically at Devannor (Abbey Cwmhir, c. 1670). Montgomeryshire has open stair-wells, as at the Cain Valley Hotel, Llanfyllin and at Messrs Anderson's, Welshpool. Whatever the scale, till the late C17 the preferred shape for newels and balusters was the geometrical, elaborately moulded inverted taper, with flat cut-out balusters (occasionally pierced) for the less important flights.

The C17 layout known as the UNIT SYSTEM occurs in three places in Breconshire, as well as sparsely elsewhere in Wales and England. Whether simply by way of enlargement, or as a result of a condition of the inheritance of property (such as division between heirs by gavelkind), quite separate dwelling-houses were built at Llandefailog tre'r-Graig, at the present Tretower Court Inn, and at Llanddegman nearby. These added units just touched the other houses at the corner, but now are usually made to interconnect. Whether other more complex houses are in fact composed of two or more household units it is always difficult to say. All these late C16 and C17 houses, made from the substances of the countryside and – taken with its medieval churches – making an entity to be treasured, are rather off the beaten track. From the late C17 Powys again followed more promptly the innovations and styles of the rest of the country.

The introduction of RED BRICK as a building material came to a considerable extent with the introduction of the more comfortable WILLIAM AND MARY HOUSE. This coincidence does not hold good for Breconshire, where stone was used for Llwyncyntefin, Sennybridge (porch dated 1634) and Pool Hall, Crickadarn (1670), of the early C17 plan, just as for Trefecca Fawr and Penpont, two large houses of the 1660s, and also as for the more Dutch-looking houses with hipped roofs and sometimes a central staircase, e.g. Cribarth (Llanafan Fawr), Abercynrig (Llanfrynach), Llangattock Cwrt, and Scethrog, all of c. 1690. These handsome late C17 houses are for some reason quite plentiful in Breconshire. Their counterparts in brick (e.g. Abercneiddon, Maesmynys; c. 1690) are as rare as stone is in Montgomeryshire. It was in the latter county that brick was widely used in the C17, often made with the clay on the site. The earliest dated example is of 1622 (the vanished New Building in Montgomery Castle). Brick remains the visually dominant material, except for C19 churches, to the present day – with particular benefit to the towns, especially Llanfyllin, Montgomery, Welshpool, and Newtown.

Montgomeryshire's C17 BRICK ARCHITECTURE began with the domestic buildings of the older families, e.g. the Blayneys' Gregynog (Tregynon, 1636?; demolished) with a long front recessed between wings, and Vaynor Park (Berriew) of c. 1640 for George Devereux. Then came Llandrinio Hall (c. 1670), Criggion Hall (c. 1670), and the new gateway at Powis Castle (1668). In the William and Mary fashion there were the large Aberhafesp Hall (c. 1675) for the Morgans, Bodynfoel (Llanfechain, c. 1690), 63 Maesmawr Hall (Meifod; begun 1689) for the Lloyds, and Nantcribba (Forden, 1697) by *Henry Pagett*. At Maesmawr Hall, as at Llangattock Cwrt (B), the construction of the tall hipped roofs was achieved with the use of upper crucks – an earlier technique. There are also anachronistic farmhouses, e.g. Abernaint (Llanfyllin) and Haughton Grange (Llandrinio), of c. 1700. Limited ecclesiastical use soon followed, with Dolobran Quaker Chapel, Pontrobert (1700) and Llanfyllin church (1706–10?).

Of interiors generally, STAIRCASES were still the focus of elaboration and have survived much more frequently than decorated rooms. Jacobean designs lasted late, only yielding to turned balusters near the end of the C17 (e.g. Bodynfoel, Llanfechain, 60 M); Aberhafesp Hall (M) has a splendid strapwork balustrade. Caroline grand stairways of c. 1670 with carved balusters exist at Powis and at Vaynor Park (M). The turned baluster appears at Penpont (B; for the Williams family) c. 1660; this is a well stair, which is less common, but see Llandrinio Hall and Maesmawr Hall (M). The Powis stair has two flights in the dog-leg arrangement – the popular sort in Breconshire especially (Trefecca Fawr and Dderw (Llyswen), c. 1680; then Abercynrig (Llanfrynach) and Scethrog, c. 1690, with two each). Trephillip (Bronllys, c. 1700) has twisted balusters. Each of the late C17 patterns continued into the C18.

Dutch and Italian styles in ROOM DESIGN reached their apogee at Powis Castle (M). Aristocratic patronage, first by the Herbert Earls of Powis and later by the Earl of Rochford, a kinsman of William III, led to the design of grandiose classical doorcases with double-curved open pediments and a scheme of Baroque decora- 61 tion on the Grand Staircase; and to the still more opulent (though 62 less aesthetically satisfactory) State Bedchamber and Blue Drawing Room. The architect responsible was probably *William Winde*, c. 1668; the painters on the staircase were *Verrio* and *Lan-*

scroon (*c.* 1705). In houses on a small scale, there is bolection panelling at Vaynor Park (M), Maesmawr Hall (M), and Abercynrig (B); Abercynrig also has 'furniture pictures'. Contemporary plaster ceilings exist at Trefecca Fawr (B), with a profuse incrusta- 64 tion of fruits, and at Penpont (B). An appendage to C17 houses of manorial status, the gatehouse, was built at Vaynor Park, at Llwydiarth (M; demolished); the sole timber-framed example is at Glyn Clywedog (Llanidloes, M).

At the HANGING GARDENS at Powis Castle, formed between the Restoration and the accession of George II, a breathtaking work of art grew out of the labours of engineers, architects, smiths (gates by *John Warren*, *c.* 1710), sculptors, and generations of 68 gardeners. Poised between the dull red walls of the castle and the bluish views down the Severn valley to the Breiddins, they are in a class of their own.

The EIGHTEENTH CENTURY gave Powys far fewer buildings than the seventeenth. No large country houses were created though several small ones were; nothing distinctive in vernacular architecture; and, except in Brecon, Presteigne, Montgomery, and Llanfyllin, and in early C19 Hay, few examples of town architecture. First, the PUBLIC BUILDINGS. Montgomery (M) retains 70 its Town Hall, by *William Baker* (1748); Llanfyllin's (M; by *John Yenn*, 1789) has gone. Since this was an age of improvements in communications, BRIDGES became important. The Usk in Breconshire is still crossed by five admirable stone rubble bridges of the C16 and C17, at Crickhowell, Llangynidr, and Brecon, and then by the private bridges of Penpont and Abercamlais. Their prominent cutwaters and narrow arches were still a tradition for the more graceful Pont Llwyncyntefin in 1750, and are even perceptible features of Usk bridges at Glangrwyne (by *Andrew Maund*, 1773), at Aberbrân (by *James Parry*, 1791), and at Cefn Brynich, Llanhamlach (a late C18 road bridge). Two well known Wye bridges, at Builth (by *James Parry*, 1779) and at Glasbury (by *William Edwards*, 1777), no longer stand unaltered. Montgomeryshire on the other hand has some fine classical bridges of ashlar stone over the Severn and the Vyrnwy. Pentreheylin near Llandysilio dates from before 1773; Llandrinio bridge (1775), the 74 best architecturally, is in the style of John Gwynn; Carreghofa aqueduct is of 1796. More competent neo-classical bridges followed at Llanymynech and Newtown (both by *Thomas Penson*, 1826) and at Boughrood in Radnorshire (*c.* 1830).

In the context of travelling, the establishment *c.* 1749 of a HOTEL, Llandrindod Hall, at the Radnorshire spa is an example of the random occurrence in Wales of items of considerable significance in view of their early date or their rarity. Moreover the mobility of the Shrewsbury architects – *Pritchard*, *Bromfield*, the *Haycocks*, and so on – no doubt affected the minor gentry house-builders from the mid c18 on.

EARLY GEORGIAN HOUSES, some in towns, are of the usual types. They include the Manor House, Llanfyllin (M; 1737) and Calcott Hall, Llandrinio (M; c. 1725); Maesllwch House (R; 1729; demolished for Lugar's castle); Abercamlais, Penpont (B; c. 1710), the Youth Hostel, Crickhowell (B; 1719), Trevithel, Three Cocks (B; c. 1710?) with its attempt at a façade, and the more familiar types of No. 4 Lion Street, Brecon (c. 1740) and Peterstone Court, Llanhamlach (B; 1741) for the Powells. Their architectural vocabulary does not differ essentially from that of houses anywhere in England. Of LATER GEORGIAN HOUSES, Montgomeryshire has the Trewythen Arms, Llanidloes (c. 1770), Trawscoed Hen, Guilsfield (1771, in the style of Henry Holland; the wings only remain), Trawscoed Hall of 1777, and Bryngwyn, Bwlch-y-Cibau (c. 1774 by *Robert Mylne*; partly rebuilt); all are of brick. Radnorshire had the Lewis's Harpton Court, and still has Cefndyrys, Llanelwedd (1787–90), an eyecatcher for the Thomas family, the plainer Boultibrook near Presteigne (c. 1810), and Boughrood Castle (begun 1817) for the Fowkes family. Brecon-
[72] shire's houses, of stone like Radnorshire's, included Moor Park, Llanbedr (c. 1760, on an eccentric centralized, quatrefoil plan), Thomas Harris's Tregunter (c. 1775; demolished) near Talgarth, and Gwern-vale, Crickhowell (c. 1795, by *John Newby*). *Nash*, documented at Harpton Court (R) in 1805–12 and at Glanwysc (Llangattock, B; altered) in 1795, is not really represented, except possibly by the ascription of Porthmawr House, Crickhowell (B).

Their DECORATION is similarly too scarce to warrant much examination. Plaster ceiling decorations were made at Maesmawr Hall (M) in the early c18; at Llwyn, Llanfyllin (M) in 1759 (demolished); and at Glandulais, Penstrowed (M) and Downton House, New Radnor (R) in the later c18. Fine staircases belong to Abercamlais (Penpont) and Trevithel (Three Cocks) (both B); to Gladestry Court, and a 'Chinese' design to Kinnerton Court (both R); and one in the Gibbs style to Trefnant Hall, Castle Caereinion (M). Berthddu, Llandinam (M; c. 1820) has the only double-return staircase, now that Garth (Guilsfield) is pulled down. Peterstone Court, Llanhamlach (B) has a room with a little Rococo carving. *Baker* has left no interiors at Powis Castle (M), and *Pritchard* only the very plain ballroom.

LANDSCAPE GARDENING can show only fragments of schemes by *William Emes* at Gregynog, Tregynon (M; 1774) and at Powis (M), and an interpretation of *Humphry Repton*'s proposals for Stanage Park (R) for the Rogers family (after 1803). Of course, nature's gifts to Powys really need such attentions no more than local squires had the means to pay for them.

Nor was this a significant period for CHURCH BUILDING. But six new churches were built in Montgomeryshire – Llanfyllin c. 1710, Criggion in 1774, Berriew in 1803–4, and Llanllwchaiarn in 1815, all in brick with towers; and Churchstoke in 1815 (by *Joseph Bromfield*) and Machynlleth in 1827 (by *Edward Haycock*, in stone). In Radnorshire only St Harmon (1821 by *W. Evans*), and in Breconshire only Hay (1834 by *Haycock*), Tirabad, and Capel y Ffin (1762?) were rebuilt. The last-named, however, is interesting as a point of comparison with chapel buildings, though this is to anticipate. Some Radnorshire parish churches have remained practically arrested in time since this period; examples include Disserth, and the gallery and schoolroom at Llanbister (1716).

FUNERARY MONUMENTS, on the other hand, became more numerous and exhibit a higher quality. Few enough have figures in the round, a sense of the Baroque: a bust of Bishop William Lucy † 1677, and the tomb of the Rev. R. Lucy with a conversation piece of three statues by *William Stanton* (1697), both at Christ College, Brecon; and children beside the bust of Richard Jones, † 1788, at Kerry (M). *John Nelson* of Shrewsbury carved attractive wall-monuments in a restrained Rococo style, of which examples dating from between c. 1772 and c. 1800 can be seen in Guilsfield, Llangynyw, and Llansantffraid-ym-Mechain churches (all M).

NEO-CLASSICISM makes itself felt in sculpture more than in architecture at the end of the C18. Plain materials replace richness and the forms are simplified to become more linear and less plastic, in emulation of the purity of Greek art. *John Bacon* the Elder carved reliefs for Sir John Meredith † 1780 (Brecon Cathedral), and for Arthur Blayney † 1795 (Tregynon, M) – a fastidious memorial. *Flaxman* signed tablets at Old Radnor († 1797) and in Brecon Cathedral († 1812).

The work of the Brecon sculptor *John Evan Thomas* (1810–73) can be introduced here. A pupil of Chantrey, he passed from early neo-classical works to an easy Victorian naturalism at the end of his working life. There are signed monuments dated between 1840 and 1858 in Brecon Cathedral and Dr Coke's Chapel, Brecon, and at Glasbury, Llanfrynach, Llanspyddid, and Penmyarth (all B).

There is also the bronze figure of Wellington (1852) in Brecon and the bronze group of The Death of Tewdric Mawr (1856) in the museum at Welshpool (M).

Another local scion, *David Evans* (1793–1861), born at Llanllwchaiarn (M), established the well-known stained glass works at Shrewsbury. His firm produced perhaps six windows for Montgomeryshire churches between 1837 and 1858; they are at Castle 88 Caereinion, Llansantffraid-ym-Mechain, Llanwnnog, Meifod, Trelystan, and Welshpool. His windows are easily recognizable by their large, usually frontally placed, single figures and their large areas of strong, even colour.

A third aspect of craftsmanship, the delightful tablets made by the *Brute* family of Llanbedr (B) and others, is to be found only in churches surrounding the Black Mountains, in Breconshire (at 73 Garthbrengy, Llanbedr, Llandefalle, Llanfilo, Llangattock, Partrishow), in Gwent, and in Herefordshire. Dating between about 1720 and 1840, these slate and stone tablets cheerfully combine a variety of incised letter-forms with extraordinary frames in low relief. Some are architectural; others – the most original – introduce chubby-cheeked cherubs, not very dire angels, heraldry, and so on, encircled in wreaths of leaves, branches, and sprays of flowers, all gaily picked out in gold, red, blue, and green. Broadly Rococo in spirit, they are executed with unabashed primitivism. The best are signed by *Thomas Brute* (fl. 1721–82), by *Aaron Brute* (fl. 1754–83), and by *J. Brute* (fl. 1773–1840).

The history of NONCONFORMIST CHAPELS begins, as mentioned above, with the rudimentary rectangular plans of churches of Puritan times and after, such as Capel y Ffin (B). This post-Reformation type in turn probably derives from the basic Counter-Reformation hall-nave, developed for preaching in the later C16. Powys possesses early examples of the two perennial variants: that with the pulpit on the long wall, with two doors 65 opposite, as at Maesyronnen (Independent; R), after 1696; and that with the pulpit on the short wall, as at Caebach (Independent; Llandrindod, R) *c.* 1715. Of early Quaker meeting houses there are Dolobran (Pontrobert, M; 1700) and The Pales (Llandegley, R; 1716).

The most characteristic of all Welsh building types, visually the focal point of so many rural communities and of so many landscapes and townscapes, the Welsh chapel is essentially an expansion of these humble buildings. Vastly numerous, almost all of the C19, and uncompromisingly four-square, chapels brood over clusters of cottages, greet one on entering a square, or stand in incongruous isolation in the countryside. The building type is certainly idiosyncratic; is full of variety within the stereotype; is frankly disappointing in detail. As architecture the chapels are naive, in that their architects had little knowledge of the classical rules; yet within this hermetic style they are designed with confidence. Besides the pulpit and *set-fawr*, the main internal feature is the gallery. As designs for letting many hear one voice, or for choral singing, they were effective and also cheap. As recognizable missions, their exteriors frequently announce their (Old Testament) name, sect, and dates of foundation and of rebuilding, in a plaque on the façade.

Yet chapels elude a strict analysis. From a matrix of classicism, each branch of Nonconformity chose a different pattern. This following brief attempt at drawing the picture will no doubt change as this series progresses. Independents kept to the plain classical scheme, e.g. at Ty'n-y-Coed, Abercraf (B; 1829). Baptists started in a similar manner, e.g. Bethabara, Crickhowell (B; 1840), with a two-storey façade, then leaned towards more grandiose architecture, e.g. the temple-fronted Treble Hill, Glasbury (B; 1866), and the opulent Zion at Newtown (M; 1881) by *G. Morgan*. Congregationalists also preferred the classical on the whole, as in Tabernacle, Rhayader (R; 1836) by *T. Hope* or the distinguished Sion, Llanidloes (M; 1878) by *John Humphreys*; but they built in Gothic as well, e.g. Horeb, Builth (B; 1869). Calvinistic Methodists entertained the greatest profusion of styles, from the conventionally sub-Regency, wholly typical Gerizim, Adfa (M; first half of the C19), through the Italianate chapel at Cemmaes (M) to the determined Second Pointed of the Howell Harris Memorial Chapel, Trefecca (B; 1872) by *R. G. Thomas*, and on to the quiet Art Nouveau of the Ann Griffiths Memorial Chapel, Dolanog (M; 1903) by *C. Dickens-Lewis*. Presbyterians paid most heed to Anglican Gothic, and their churches are mostly in a Dec style, e.g. those at Brecon (by *W. F. Poulton*, 1872), at Llandinam (M; an enterprising plan by *Szlumper & Aldwinkle*, 1872), and at Machynlleth (M; 1867). Other denominations are less definable. Exteriors generally do not need specific description, and interiors generally are without much stained glass, or memorials.

Chapels have led on prematurely to the NINETEENTH CENTURY, an epoch in which, as in the C17, Wales was transformed in terms of buildings. Terraces of compact post-Georgian houses and chapels compose hamlets and towns wherever extractive or other industry could give an alternative to the land and its ephemeral buildings. From the standpoint of architectural history, there is much more than this: significant buildings on the national and local levels – and in a wide range of styles.

NEO-CLASSICISM in its strict sense receives lucid expression
77 at *Joseph Bromfield*'s perfectionist Glansevern Hall (Berriew, M; *c.* 1801–7) for Sir Arthur Owen; there is also the unattributed and slightly incoherent re-fronting of Penpont (B; *c.* 1810) and Gunley Hall, Forden (M; by *J. H. Haycock*, 1810). Then there are Regency and George IV houses – Penylan (Meifod, M; 1812), Ffrwdgrech (Llanfaes, B; 1828), etc. The more irregular and picturesque white-painted small mansion was popular (e.g. Dol-llys, Llanidloes, M). The Greek Revival made itself felt in PUBLIC BUILDINGS as much as anywhere. The importance of the Shire
83 Halls called for new works; Brecon got *Wyatt & Brandon* in 1839 for what is now the Brecknock Museum; Presteigne (R) had a new Shire Hall in 1829; Montgomery's was partly rebuilt in 1828 by *Thomas Penson*. Crickhowell (B) built a Market Hall in 1833 (by *T. H. Wyatt*), and Brecon in 1857 (also by *T. H. Wyatt*); Newtown and Llanidloes (M) built them *c.* 1830. There were new open markets at Hay (B) for butter (1833) and cheese (1835). Another building type, the workhouse, took shape; the colossal Bryn Hyfryd (Forden, M; 1794–5) is by *Joseph Bromfield*. Next came Machynlleth (M; 1834); then on more spreading, radial plans came Hay (B; 1837) and The Meadows, Llanfyllin (M; by *Penson*, 1838). Caersws (M) followed in 1840. The similarly planned Gaol at Montgomery (1830–2) is also by *Penson*.

By way of contrast, COUNTRY SEATS of the early C19 inclined strongly towards Gothic and Tudor romanticism. The roots of this fashion, which the gentry of 1800 to 1830 made into a passion, lie in the elegant Gothic of the mid C18, of which Powys can show
71 a very curious example, Howell Harris's College at Trefecca (B). Nothing is known of why Harris chose Gothick in 1752, but his religious community, mid-way between monasticism and modern craft-based societies, caught the revival in full flight. Lady Huntingdon brought a more accomplished manner for her College at Trefecca (1768). Ty Mawr (Llanfrynach, B; *c.* 1820) is a C19 house in the style.

The borderland between Powys, Herefordshire, and Shropshire was one of the cradles of the PICTURESQUE, where a taste for the irregular in landscape was developed, and then a desire for irregular buildings in keeping.

For a statement of aesthetic theory, *Humphry Repton*'s words
78 to Charles Rogers on Stanage Park (R; begun 1807) are the best
80 guide. Llanerchydol (M; 1820) for David Pugh can be seen as

another realization of such ideas. The attitude which took pleasure in the things of the past did not shrink from travesties in the present: the young *John C. Loudon*'s Garth (Guilsfield, M; 1809) 79 for a chaplain of the Raj, the Rev. Richard Mytton, now sadly demolished, was a wild example of a Regency villa in Islam-influenced Perpendicular. A tendency to extremes of size and monumentality developed in the 1820s. *Robert Lugar*'s Glanusk (Penmyarth, B; begun 1825), in Elizabethan, for Sir Joseph Bailey the ironmaster, and his Maesllwch Castle (R; begun 1829), in castellated Tudor, for Walter de Winton have both been largely pulled down, but the Elizabethan Doldowlod (R; *c.* 1827 and 1878) for the Watt family still stands. *Sir Robert Smirke* is represented by the rebuilding of Boultibrook for Sir Harford Jones Brydges (Presteigne, R; 1812–15), and by works to intensify the antique appearance of Powis Castle (M; 1815–18). Clyro Court (R) was built in a florid Dutch style *c.* 1840. This wave of revivals is succeeded in the 1840s by a return to a Roman classicism, as at Penoyre (Battle, B; 1846–8) for Lloyd Vaughan Watkins by *Anthony Salvin*, 84 and as in *Edward Haycock*'s staircase at Stanage Park (R; 1845).

Among PROVINCIAL ARCHITECTS, *Thomas Penson* (1790–1859) of Oswestry, a pupil of Thomas Harrison of Chester, was outstanding. He was County Surveyor of Montgomeryshire from 1826 and also of Denbighshire, and his career spanned thirty years of rapid change. His work in Montgomeryshire includes five bridges, two churches, and three public buildings. The stone bridges came first, in 1826, at Llanymynech (with advice from *Telford*, County Surveyor of Shropshire) and Newtown. The first iron bridge in the county was at Llandinam (1846); then came 82 Brynderwen (Abermule; 1852) and Caerhowel (1858). The stone ones are neo-classical, the iron ones slightly Gothic. Classicism Penson used for his public buildings – the remodelling of Montgomery Town Hall (1828), the new Gaol at Montgomery (1830), 70 and for Llanfyllin's grandiose Poor Law Union (1837), mentioned above. His Christ Church, Welshpool (1839–44) is in neo-Norman 81 and notable for its bold use of terracotta (cf. his no less extreme St Agatha, Llanymynech, Shropshire, of 1845); at St David, Newtown (1843) he achieved a surprisingly powerful C13 building. It is typical of his age that between these two he skilfully remodelled Vaynor Park, Berriew in Jacobean (in 1841). His elder son, *Richard Kyrke Penson* (1816–86), succeeded him as County Surveyor, till 1864 (see his Cilcewydd Bridge, 1861). More of an anti-quarian by bent, he designed simple churches at Pontrobert (1853) and Penybontfawr (1855), and carried out church restorations at Llanfechain (1859) and Llanwnnog. Sarn church was designed by the younger brother *T. M. Penson* in 1859.

   T. H. Wyatt played a rather similar role in Breconshire. We have already seen his neo-classicism in Crickhowell Market
83 (1833), and the Shire Hall (1839–43) and Market (1857) at Brecon. His extensive practice was chiefly in country houses and churches. The former include the neo-Tudor Llangattock Park House (*c.* 1838) for the Duke of Beaufort – whose agent in Monmouthshire his father was – and Craig-y-Nos (Glyntawe; 1841–3) for Rhys Powell. He restored St Mary, Brecon in 1856, and built new, tasteless churches at Llandyssil (M; 1863–6) and Evenjobb (R; 1866). A contemporary figure of interest was the Rev. Thomas Price (1787–1848; his bardic name was Carnhuanawc). During his curacy the little Radnorshire church of Llanfihangel Helygen was repaired. He became rector of Cwmdu (B), and that church was carefully remodelled in 1831–3, at a time when other parish priests did not share his interest in archaeology. He also contributed to Cwmdu rectory and to Ty Mawr, Llanfrynach (B).

   The GOTHIC REVIVAL provided Wales with substantial new churches and with rescues of the old ones (usually admirable, but at times certainly not). Neglect, abetted by the climate and indifference, had reduced many valuable buildings to the point of collapse. Today's debt to the great efforts, for small rewards, of C19 architects and parishioners deserves to be set out in some detail. As a yardstick to indicate what might have been, one could point to the brief ANGLO-NORMAN phase, outrageous at *Penson*'s Christ Church, Welshpool (M; 1839–44), unappealing in *Vulliamy*'s Glasbury (B; 1837) and *Thomas Nicholson*'s Llanfihangel Nant Melan (R; 1846), and in remodellings like Llanfyllin (M; *c.* 1863) by *Walter Scott*, or Nantmel (R). Or one could cite *Edward Haycock Senior*'s minimally E.E. church at Hay (B; 1834), or else New Radnor church (R; 1843).

   Listing some of the best churches according to whether in Early English or Decorated etc. gives a picture of the spread of quality through a doubtless still inaccessible region. After *T. Penson*'s E.E. at Newtown (M; 1843) came *Sidney Smirke*'s Penrhos (M; 1845) in terracotta, *J. L. Pearson*'s pure and early Llangasty Tal-y-llyn (B; 1849–56), *R. K. Penson*'s Pontrobert (M; 1853), and *Benjamin Ferrey*'s Pont Llogel (M; 1854); then *Sir George Gilbert Scott*'s attractive Bwlch-y-Cibau (M; 1862–4), *John Norton*'s Beulah (B; 1867), *C. Buckeridge*'s unfinished Monastery, Capel y Ffin (B; begun 1870); then *Pearson*'s Tretower (B; 1876), *S. W. Williams*'s Llansantffraed (B; 1884), and *John Fowler*'s elaborate

Cwmbach Llechrhyd (R; 1886). In the Dec style the earliest is
W. H. Gee's showy church at Leighton (M; 1851–3); there are
further *T. H. Wyatt*'s Llandyssil (M; 1863–6) and Evenjobb (R;
1866–70), *J. W. Poundley*'s interesting Abbey Cwmhir (R; 1866); 91
then *G. E. Street*'s Llandysilio (M; 1867–8) and *T. Nicholson*'s
Forden (M) of the same year, *Scott*'s Norton (R; 1868), *Norton*'s
Builth (B; 1875), and finally *Williams*'s Newbridge on Wye (R;
1883). The revival of Perpendicular begins with Bettws Cedewain
(M; 1868) by *W. E. Nesfield* and with *Pearson*'s Heyop (R; 1880).

Scott's report on Brecon Cathedral (*c.* 1860) set a high standard
for painstaking RESTORATION, as did *J. P. Seddon*'s work at
Christ College chapel, Brecon (1859–72). Besides putting the
stone vault on the cathedral chancel, *Scott* rebuilt Penpont church 20
(B; 1864) and restored Llywel (B; 1869). Radnorshire's churches
were put into repair by *John Norton*, *E. V. Collier*, *F. R. Kempson*,
and others; *Thomas Nicholson* restored six in Radnorshire and
Breconshire and *Nicholson & Sons* another six, and *J. B. Fowler*
of Brecon also worked in six places. In Montgomeryshire, *Benjamin Ferrey* restored Llanwrin (1864) and Meifod (1871). *Edward
Haycock Junior* worked at Llanfair Caereinion (1868) and Berriew
(1876). *J. Oldrid Scott* worked at Llansantffraid-ym-Mechain
(1891–3), and *John Douglas* of Chester at Llanfechain (1883) and
Manafon (1898).

Five architects can be singled out as particularly active in their
own areas. *J. W. Poundley* (1807–72), a ward of William Pugh
of Kerry (M) and an apprentice of *Thomas Penson*, became County
Surveyor of Montgomeryshire in 1861. His *œuvre* consists of the
iron Broniarth Bridge, Meifod (1862); the Baroque gateway to
Montgomery Gaol (1866); Kerry School (1868); and designs for
farm buildings and cottages. In partnership with *David Walker*
of Liverpool, he worked extensively on churches in Denbighshire
as well as Montgomeryshire. In the latter county he partially
rebuilt Machynlleth church (1864) and Trefeglwys (1864–5), and
erected new churches at Carno (1863), Darowen (1864), and Llanbrynmair (1868; ruined). Castell Forwyn, Dolforwyn (1867),
a yellow brick house, is one of his domestic buildings. In Radnorshire two more able buildings, Abbey Cwmhir church (1866) and 91
Abbey Cwmhir Hall (1867), illustrate his unusual ecclesiastical
designs and his liking for polychromy.

G. E. Street's amazing output included one new church and
six restorations in Montgomeryshire. The new one, Llandysilio
(1867–8), shows his originality in grouping, and his restraint in 92
detail. The restorations luckily happened to the finer of the

county's churches – Llandinam (1864–5), Welshpool (1870–1), Montgomery (report, 1875), Guilsfield (for Christ Church, Oxford, 1877–9), Llanidloes (1880–2), Kerry (1881–3) – and wholly for their good. His reinstatement of appropriate arcades at Llandinam, Welshpool, and Montgomery, and his new roofs and windows (e.g. at Welshpool and Llanidloes), are a tribute to his thoughtfulness. This approach went by the board, however, when he came to refurnish Guilsfield as extravagantly as he did.

A pupil of Scott and an admirer of Street, *Charles Buckeridge* of Oxford (1832–73), incidentally, toiled at the restoration of twelve Breconshire churches between 1860 and his early death. These were: Aberyscir and Merthyr Cynog in 1860, Trallong in 1861, Llanwrtyd in 1862, Llangenny, Llyswen, and Nantddu (Cefncoedycymmer) in 1863, Llanafan Fechan in 1866, Cantref in 1867, Llanfihangel Bryn Pabuan in 1868, and Llanspyddid and the garth of the Monastery (Capel y Ffin) in 1870; the latter's church was begun in 1872. He did so at the instigation to the Rev. Gilbert Harries of Aberyscir. He was conscientious but unimaginative, with the result that where – as often – more than repairs had to be done, too much was thrown away or plastered over.

J. L. Pearson took over from Buckeridge at Father Ignatius's replica of Llanthony; he was then mid-way in a long career which included a number of Welsh buildings. The earliest was Treberfydd for the Raikes family, begun in 1848, together with Llangasty Tal-y-Llyn (B) church, also begun in 1848. The house, in a wholly-understood Tudor, reaches a level of sobriety that is inherent in the best of the Victorian age; in this it is at one with the church, for all that the house is much the more decorative. After work at Crickhowell church (B; early 1860s) and a new church and hall at Tretower (B; 1876–7) came a series of church restorations: Heyop (R; 1880–2), Llanfihangel Nant Brân (B; 1882), Presteigne (R; 1889–91), Knighton (R; 1896–7), and, perhaps the most sympathetic, Llanbedr Ystrad Yw (B; 1897).

Fifthly, a prolific architect–antiquary of Rhayader, *Stephen W. Williams* (1837–99). He worked with Benjamin Piercy on the Cambrian Railway; later, as County Surveyor of Radnorshire, he designed the Gaol at Presteigne and a small iron bridge at Hundred House. In addition to eleven somewhat middling restorations in Radnorshire and Breconshire (respectively Aberedw, perhaps Kinnerton, Llanbadarn Fynydd, Llandegley, Llanddewi Ystradenni, Llanfihangel Rhydithon; and Cathedine, Glyntawe, Llanafan Fawr, Llanfigan, Llanhamlach) between 1876 and 1894, there were six new churches. Llanbadarn Fawr (R; 1878) is slightly Romanesque; Newbridge-on-Wye (R; 1883) is Dec; Llansantffraed (B; 1884), Llanyre (R; 1885), Rhayader (R; 1887–97), and Nantgwyllt (Elan Valley, R; not built till 1903) are all E.E. and rather severe. He rebuilt Llysdinam (B), altered Llwyn-barried (Nantmel, R), added to Doldowlod (R; 1878), and built the Market Hall, Baths, and Pump Room for the Rock House, Llandrindod (R). In Breconshire he replaced Buckland (now Crosfield House, Bwlch) for the Gwynne-Holford family in Elizabethan in 1895. It was Williams who excavated Strata Marcella Abbey (M).

VICTORIAN CHURCH FURNISHINGS in Powys are mostly not of the highest quality, but do satisfactorily complement the architecture at e.g. Beulah (*Norton*), Christ College, Brecon (*Seddon*), and Llangasty Tal-y-Llyn (*Pearson*) in Breconshire. In Montgomeryshire, Leighton has *Gee*'s, Guilsfield has *Street*'s, and Manafon has *Douglas*'s fitments. Four reredoses with figures by *Thomas Earp* exist in the same county, at Llandysilio (*c.* 1868), Welshpool (*c.* 1870), Montgomery (*c.* 1878), and Berriew (1896). At Welshpool too the medievalizing tomb designed by *Scott* for the second Earl of Powis († 1848) should be noted.

VICTORIAN STAINED GLASS is quite plentiful, on the other hand, and there are worthwhile examples by many well-known makers. Aberhafesp (M) contains some by *Baillie*, Berriew (M), and Llanfrynach (B) some by *Hardman*; Christ College, Brecon has a moving window designed by *Seddon*; Forden and Llanllwchaiarn (both M) have windows by *Morris & Co.*; Llandysilio, Llanidloes, and Tregynon (all M), Vaynor (B), and perhaps Penmyarth (B) have windows by *Clayton & Bell*; at Abbey Cwmhir (R) there are good windows by *Heaton, Butler & Bayne*, and at 93 Kerry (M) there is glass by *Kempe*.

SECULAR ARCHITECTURE of the Gothic Revival was adopted for several prominent buildings in the years after *Pearson*'s earnest Treberfydd (B) of 1848–52. *W. H. Gee*'s enormous Leighton Hall (M), begun *c.* 1850 for the banker John Naylor, is in no way comparable with Treberfydd in external refinements; but internally both contained work designed by *Pugin* and executed by *Crace*, 86 in the impetus created by the Great Exhibition. The gardens around, by *Edward Kemp*, epitomize the formality of the period with their copious statuary and regular walks. In institutional building, *John Prichard* developed at Christ College, Brecon 89 (about 1861), a flexible polychrome Gothic that could accommodate itself to a variety of building types. Still on this plateau of High Victorianism belongs the many-tiered Lewis Memorial 90 at New Radnor (R; 1864) by *John Gibbs* with figures by *W. For-syth*; and possibly even the less sane Clock Tower at Machynlleth (M), by *Henry Kennedy*, 1873.

For LATER VICTORIAN HOUSES, as in those earlier in the century, it is the nationally established architects who bring in the most influential innovations. *J. K. Colling*'s Garthmyl Hall (M; 1859) for Major Gould represents the urbane Italianate side of the possible styles, as does Gliffaes (Penmyarth, B; 1881) by an unknown architect. At the other end of the spectrum there is the wishful-thinkingly half-timbered Gregynog (Tregynon, M; *c.* 1865?), also by an unknown architect, for Lord Sudeley; then two
95 houses by *W. E. Nesfield*, the lively Plas Dinam (Llandinam, M; 1873–4) for Captain Crewe-Read, and Gwernyfed Park (Three Cocks, B; 1877), where his enthusiasm for C17 vernacular looks a bit exhausted; and then *Douglas*'s Henllys Hall (Manafon, M; 1898). The Nesfield houses reflect the revival of interest in the domestic as opposed to the ecclesiastical architecture of the Middle Ages. *G. F. Bodley*'s embellishment of Powis Castle (M; up to 1904), with its lavish plaster-, wood-, and ironwork, can be seen as the culmination of a by then conservative taste. On
94 the other hand his Cefn Bryntalch (Abermule, M; 1869), so fresh and clean-lined, seems to bridge the gap between the preceding historicist fashions and the Georgian revival of the 70s and 80s, and even the style of 1900; but this may be due to *Philip Webb*.

In the field of CIVIC BUILDING, Welshpool (M) acquired a new Town Hall (by *B. Lay*, 1873–4) in a weak François Ier style. New Market Halls were erected at Builth (B) on an Italian medieval pattern by *Haddon Brothers* (1875), and at Presteigne (R) by *Thomas Nicholson* (1869). *David Walker* erected a small Museum for the Powysland Club at Welshpool (1874). Most unexpectedly, Dame Adelina Patti settled at Craig-y-Nos (Glyntawe) in the Upper Swansea Valley (B) and commissioned her own theatre (1890 by *Bucknall & Jennings*, with decorations by *Jackson & Sons*). It is a unique survival, both as a type and with its décor. Schools, until the early C19 usually held in the churches (where evidence of the schoolroom often survives), began to have their own buildings; there are National Schools of 1821 and 1845 at Welshpool, Llanidloes (both M), etc., and then the innumerable rural schools of the 1850s and 1860s.

Hills and rivers present challenges to communications, and Powys has several impressive works of ENGINEERING. Canals were built only in the Usk and Severn valleys. The Monmouthshire and Brecon Canal was carried over the Usk by the Cefn

Brynich aqueduct (Llanhamlach, B) by *Thomas Dadford, c.* 1800, and the Montgomeryshire (or Shropshire Union) Canal over the Vyrnwy by the Carreghofa aqueduct (Pentreheylin, M), by *John Dadford, c.* 1796. Both are of stone. The railway age engendered two viaducts on the Brecon and Merthyr line, the magnificent one at Cefncoedycymmer (1865–6) and another at Pontsarn (1866); their engineers were *Alexander Sutherland* and *Henry Conybeare,* and the contractors were *Savin & Ward.* The Cambrian railway built two good stations, in 1864 at Llanidloes and *c.* 1866 at Welshpool (both M), by *Benjamin Piercy* and perhaps *S. W. Williams.* The hills also gave opportunities for huge reservoirs to the nearer industrial centres of England. The sinister coniferous landscape round Lake Vyrnwy (M) was made for Liverpool Corporation; the 84 ft high masonry dam, then the tallest in Britain, was built between 1881 and 1888 by *Thomas Hawksley* and *George Frederick Deacon.* Birmingham Corporation followed suit with a series of dams in the Elan Valley (R), including the Caban Coch (122 ft high), completed by 1904. The Claerwen Dam, still in stone, is by *Sir William Halcrow &* 100 *Partners.* The new colossal concrete Clywedog dam (M; begun in 1964), by the same engineers, is 237 ft high.

Powys was not without its own INDUSTRIES; weaving, the largest, can readily be studied in Montgomeryshire, thanks, in part, to the Textile Museum at Newtown. This occupies a typical row of houses with upper weaving floors in Penygloddfa, a whole quarter of red-brick early C19 terraces and mills which is well worth conserving. Two other types of housing, now very rare, are the 'double-decker' terraces in Canal Road, Llanllwchaiarn (M), and the 'back-to-back' brick terraces in Victoria Road, Llanidloes (M), both perhaps as late as *c.* 1840.

The three counties border on two of the earliest IRON-MAKING AREAS of Britain; not far to the E is Coalbrookdale, not far to the S are Clydach and Llanelly (both formerly in Breconshire), and also Blaenavon, Nantyglo, and Ebbw Vale. Within their boundaries, however, such early activity was restricted, e.g. to the Lloyds' forge at Dolobran (Pontrobert, M), and to Walter Watkins's forge at Glangrwyne (B), though there are considerable remains of large mid C19 furnaces and later buildings of the Ynys-Cedwyn company at Ystradgynlais (B). The use of IRON in architecture, however, developed neither particularly quickly nor particularly originally. Staircases in a few C18 and C19 houses, and verandas, especially round the stables at Garth (Guilsfield, M), employed it decoratively. A substantial number of cast-iron window frames were in use. At Ystradgynlais church (B; 1861) iron is used structurally, for the arcades, as a substitute for stone; Churchstoke (M; 1870?) is another case. Far more commonly, plain thin columns with cast foliate capitals were inserted to support the galleries of chapels, from the mid C19 on. Bridges, the most significant, prefabricated, designs in the metal, have already been discussed; to recapitulate, there are three by *Penson* in Montgomeryshire – Llandinam (1846, made at Hawarden), and Brynderwen (Abermule; 1852) and Caerhowel (1858), both made at Brymbo; also *W. N. Swettenham*'s Gothic span at Buttington (1872). Less noteworthy are bridges at Broniarth, Meifod (M; 1862) by *Poundley*, and at Glangrwyne (B; 1856?).

More surprising is the innovatory use of CONCRETE by the fourth Lord Sudeley on his Gregynog estate (Tregynon, M) in the 1870s. A school and schoolmaster's house, a pair of cottages, several farmhouses, and in 1880 a bridge were built entirely of the material, either poured *in situ* or set in moulds, though without reinforcement. The venture did not catch on. There is a gap till the reinforced concrete bridge at Newbridge-on-Wye (B and R; 1910).

In so large and so rural an area, it is pleasant to be able to point to a number of works of the TWENTIETH CENTURY, particularly since the small population has probably been declining since 1900. In Breconshire there is Llangoed (Llyswen; 1913–19) by *Sir Clough Williams-Ellis*, a house in which a reconciliation between a traditional and an individual modern outlook was pursued in several different manners. Of single buildings, *Frank Hearn Shayler*'s Free Library at Newtown (M; 1902) is an excellent interpretation of Norman Shaw's ideas; the Town Hall at Llanidloes (M; by *Shayler & Ridge*, 1908) lacks vigour, by comparison, though it is more than competent. The ideals of the ARTS AND CRAFTS movement were perhaps more fruitful in villages, parish halls, and in unpretentious small housing schemes that have not been improved on till now. Examples are the Wesleyan Church at Llanrhaeadr (M; by *Shayler & Ridge*, 1904); Elan Village (B) of 1906–9; *T. Alwyn Lloyd*'s roughcast 'garden suburbs' at Llanidloes and Machynlleth (both M and 1913); and Llanfair Caereinion Village Hall (M; 1922). Of sculpture there is *Alfred Gilbert*'s statue of David Davies at Llandinam (M; *c.* 1890) and *Alfred Toft*'s Art Nouveau ironwork for Robert Owen's grave in Newtown (M; 1902). Capel y Ffin (B) epitomizes the ideals of the period, with the craftsmanship of *Eric Gill* and others pursued in a rural – and monastic – setting. Of stained glass, there are

Expressionist windows by *Leonard Walker* at Tregynon (M; *c.* 1921) and at Llanwrthwl (B; 1936); and one perhaps by *Sir N. Comper* at Glasbury (B; *c.* 1933).

Breconshire was fortunate indeed in finding so sensitive a restorer for its most interesting medieval churches as *W. D. Caröe.* We appreciate the self-effacement which has given so much back to Partrishow (1908–) and to Llanfilo (1913–). In Radnorshire Caröe restored Llanbister (1908); and after the War came St Mary, Brecon (1928), a reredos at Crickhowell, and of course work at Brecon Cathedral, where the little St Laurence's Chapel was recreated (1930), the high altar reredos installed (in Perp, 1937), and the monastic buildings modernized from 1925. Caröe's one church begun from scratch is Llangammarch (B; 1913–16) in a gentle Perp-influenced manner. After World War II, *G. G. Pace* made plans for eleven churches in Breconshire, and at Bleddfa (R) he redesigned the old church layout more flexibly.

In recent years it is no use pretending that all has gone for the best, from the standpoint of visual man. A great talent for vernacular design has been replaced by imported brick boxes, sometimes thoughtlessly sited. New farm buildings are often too bright for their size, as are some new industrial buildings. As for road design, Powys has fared less badly than, say, Gwynedd – so far. Major valley routes and N to S links have been carried on. There is a striking concrete road viaduct at Cefncoedycymmer (B; 1964, by *Rendel, Palmer & Tritton*). Colossal dams in the later C20 impound lakes to regulate river flows; Clywedog (M) has been built, Craig Goch (R) is still under discussion.

Montgomeryshire has most that is positive in POST-WAR ARCHITECTURE. *Herbert Carr*, County Architect from the early 1930s till his death in 1965, initiated a programme of primary and secondary school building, as did C. H. Aslin in Hertfordshire. There are area schools at e.g. Abermule (1951), Dolfor (1953), and Trewern (1954); and high schools at Llanfyllin (1955), Llanidloes (a big campus finished in 1955), and Welshpool, etc. They combine sensitive, ample plans with elevations partly of glass and partly of brick. By Carr also are some public buildings: the County Offices at Welshpool (1941–64); and at Newtown e.g. the County Library (1963), with its concrete-ribbed barrel roof.

The abandonment of traditional stylistic elements has only recently been tried. Newtown (M) possesses a new Town Hall (1965) by *Colwyn Foulkes & Partners*, which is still conceived as a capitol; *S. Colwyn Foulkes & Co.* are responsible for the Mynydd Illtyd Mountain Centre (Llanilltyd, B; 1965). Brecon, on a tighter

medieval plan than Newtown's, is less happily served by the
wholly modern County Library (1969, by *J. A. McRobbie*).

Newtown is the scene of the most exciting work now in progress
in Powys, the planning and realization – on the principles of a
New Town and with the co-operation of Cwmbran Development
Corporation (Chief Architect *J. L. Russell*) – of a Development
Town in Mid Wales. Up to 7,500 will be added to its population.
To date there are articulate housing schemes of great interest, in
101 the locally appropriate red brick at Trehafren (1970–5, by *Gordon
Redfern* and by *J. L. Russell*), and in the current North Wales
fashion at Treowen (begun 1974), by *Brian Lingard & Partners*.

As for matters of conservation, Powys has of course to contend
with the results of scattered settlement – there are few village
centres to preserve, while outlying farmhouses get abandoned (in
Radnorshire particularly). Of towns, Brecon should be valued for
its extensive medieval plan; Llanfyllin (M) has fared the worst,
and recently, too. The list of country houses lost is really small, in
this century only Glanusk (Penmyarth, B) and Maesllwch (R) by
Lugar, Garth (Guilsfield, M) by *Loudon*, and Lymore (Montgomery, M). The hand of the Historic Buildings Council can be
detected in an encouraging number of places, such as Llanidloes
Market Hall (M) and Treberfydd (B). The many dispersed parish
churches may yet prove the greatest anxiety, but so far these
treasures are being maintained (except a very few) in admirable
condition.

So this survey of the long, varied, and substantial history of
the buildings of Powys (always remembering that, aesthetically
speaking, there are far more foothills than peaks) can justly end
on an optimistic note.

FURTHER READING

THE most comprehensive source for monuments of all kinds in Wales is *Archaeologia Cambrensis*, published from 1846 by the Cambrian Archaeological Association; there are indexes for 1846–1900 and 1901–1960. Samuel Lewis's *A Topographical Dictionary of Wales* (in two volumes, 1845) is endlessly useful. Coming to the present, the indispensable work of reference on vernacular buildings is *Houses of the Welsh Countryside* by P. Smith (1975), which gives an abundance of detailed drawings, photographs, and map references. In *The Historic Architecture of Wales* by John B. Hilling (1976) there is at last a general study, with many plans. For the historical background, Sir John Edward Lloyd's *A History of Wales* (2 vols., 1912) is a standard work, and *The Dictionary of Welsh Biography down to 1940* (1959), published under the auspices of the Honourable Society of Cymmrodorion, should be consulted. William Rees's *An Historical Atlas of Wales* (new ed., 1972) is also helpful.

Coming to each county specifically, Montgomeryshire has been well served by its own periodical, *The Montgomeryshire Collections*, published by the Powysland Club, since 1868. Some of the churches fall within Archdeacon D. R. Thomas's *The History of the Diocese of St Asaph* (2nd ed., 3 vols., 1908–13). For the other two there are both old county histories and newer periodicals. Jonathan Williams's *A General History of the County of Radnor* (compiled by Edwin Davies, 1905) and W. H. Howse's *Radnorshire* (1949) have been supplemented by the *Transactions of the Radnorshire Society* from 1931 on; in the latter the recent articles on houses by H. Brooksby are useful. Theophilus Jones's *A History of the County of Brecknock* (enlarged and edited by Sir Joseph Bailey, first Baron Glanusk, 3 vols., 1909–30), is particularly thorough, and since 1955 *Brycheiniog* has been published, with, from 1963 to 1970, full studies of houses by S. R. Jones and J. T. Smith. There are early *Inventories* by the Royal Commission on Ancient and Historical Monuments in Wales and Monmouthshire, on the *County of Montgomery* (1911) and on the *County of Radnor* (1913), which should be read in conjunction with the other literature.

Where previously there had been a dearth of good guidebooks there are now plenty; Elisabeth Beazley and Peter Howell's *Companion Guides* to *North Wales* (1975) and *South Wales* (1977) are informative on a range of topics complementary to a study of buildings, yet excellent on buildings as well; they say everything I should have liked to, only more wittily. Montgomery and Radnor are in the first, Brecon in the second. David Verey's *Shell Guide to Mid-Wales* (1960) covers the same area as this book, perceptively and succinctly, and is illustrated with praiseworthy photographs. In Welsh there is the *Crwydro* series, especially *Crwydro Sir Faesyfed* by Ffransis G. Payne (2 vols., 1966). Of older tours there are Thomas Dineley, *An Account of the Progress of the Duke of Beaufort through Wales* (1684); Thomas Pennant, *A Tour in Wales* (1784); and the Rev. E. Nicholson, *A Cambrian Travellers' Guide* (3rd ed., 1830). *Country Life* has published on some of the houses. There are guides to Powis Castle and Brecon Cathedral; DOE guides to Tretower Court and Castle and to Montgomery Castle; and many churches have guide pamphlets. On towns, Dr J. D. K. Lloyd for Montgomery, W. H. Howse for Presteigne, and at greater length G. L. Fairs for Hay-on-Wye (1972). The *Shell Book of Offa's Dyke* is by Frank Noble.

On more specialized topics, there are authoritative works by Colin A. Gresham on *Medieval Stonecarving in North Wales* (1968), by Dr Mostyn Lewis on *Stained Glass in North Wales up to 1850* (1970), by V. E. Nash-Williams on *The Early Christian Monuments of Wales* (1950), etc. Beyond these is the standard bibliography for *The Buildings of England*, beginning with H. M. Colvin, *A Biographical Dictionary of British Architects, 1600–1840* (2nd ed., 1978), Rupert Gunnis, *A Dictionary of British Sculptors, 1660–1851* (1953), and so on; a full bibliography would take more than the space available.

As for archaeology, the list for further reading is similar. Both *Archaeologia Cambrensis* and *The Montgomeryshire Collections* contain articles relevant to Powys, and the *Transactions of the Radnorshire Society* and *Brycheiniog* have also contained important archaeological work. The RCAM *Inventories* for Montgomeryshire and Radnorshire need to be supplemented by later works; that for Breconshire is in course of preparation. The Roman period has been conveniently reviewed in V. E. Nash-Williams's *The Roman Frontier in Wales* (2nd ed., 1969, edited by M. G. Jarrett), but there has been no similarly comprehensive volume on prehistory. However *Prehistoric and Early Wales* (edited by I. H. Foster and G. E. Daniel, 1960) provides a general introduction, and useful articles may be found in *Culture and Environment* (edited by I. H. Foster and L. Alcock, 1963) and *Prehistoric Man in Wales and the West* (edited by F. M. Lynch and C. B. Burgess, 1972).

MONTGOMERYSHIRE
SIR DREFALDWYN

★

ABERCEGIR

w of Penegoes

There are two former flannel factories on this tributary of the River Dovey. FACTORY ISAF has a water-wheel *c.* 20 ft in diameter, made by Samuel Owens, Newtown Foundry, 1859. The other, though ruined, still has a (smaller) wheel.

ABERGWYDOL, 1 m. NW. A regional type-C house of stone, unusually deep, with a square central chimney dated 1693. Handsome stone porch with segmental doorhead and room over. In the hall a nine-compartment beamed ceiling and a post-and-panel partition. Stone and half-timbered addition of the later C19 to the S.

ABERFFRYDLAN *see* LLANWRIN

ABERHAFESP

ST GWYNNOG. In a round raised churchyard, extended to the S. Nave, chancel, S porch, and embattled W tower. Rebuilt very extensively *c.* 1857 by the rector, *Richard J. Davies*. It appears to be a single-chamber church cased in new stone with new windows and recast with a chancel arch and short chancel, taller tower, porch, etc. The nave roof is a fine early C15 one with six arch-braced and three scissor trusses, and a tier of trefoiled wind-braces below a tier of quatrefoiled ones. There are eight bays in all, quite shallow and low. The sequence is a scissor truss after one, two, two collar trusses. The scissor trusses have cusping in the apex and are themselves slightly arched. The massiveness of the frames suggests an early date. Another incumbent had the C18 furniture removed in 1866. The fitments are mostly post-1886; only the W panelling is of interest – New Testament scenes done in pokerwork in an attractive Arts and Crafts fashion by Mr *E. B. Proctor*, of the Hall, in 1893. – STAINED GLASS. E, a Raphaelesque composition in three lights, of Christ taking leave of his Mother, in a C16 Italian landscape. 'Painted glass', with hardly any leading to disturb the picture. By *Baillie* of London, 1857. – Nave N, an angel leading a lady to heaven, in the Early Victorian chocolate-box style, also by *Baillie*, 1856. – MONUMENTS. Meredith Morgan † 1701, called a 'marble manuscript', though the visual fiction is to treat the stone as a piece of fabric. – Matthew Morgan † 1705 and Frances Morgan † 1710. A fine pair of Early Georgian wall-monuments dated 1712, his with plain columns and urns with cherubs below, hers with twisted columns and flaming vases with cherubs' heads below. – Abigail Waring † 1753. A nicely cut Rococo cartouche. – George Green † 1843. Neo-classical sarcophagus with a draped urn. – Louisa Proctor † 1857. Large neo-classical tablet. – Others of the mid C19.

ABERHAFESP HALL, ¼ m. w. Large two-storey brick house of *c*. 1675, six bays by five, with a tall hipped roof and originally with dormers. Casement windows with a continuous stringcourse one brick thick rising above them as dripmoulds; the first-floor windows at the rear still have their moulded brick mullions and hoods. The s fenestration and much else altered in the C19. Inside, a stairwell in the Jacobean position beyond

60 the former hall. The distinguished staircase rises through two floors by three flights and a landing each. It has handsome open strapwork balustrades, newel posts, and wooden cornices of the period. Formerly the home of the Morgan family.

THE OLD RECTORY. Hipped-roofed Regency stucco, with a bow.

PLAS-YN-PENTRE, ½ m. NW. A little four-bay medieval cruck hall, with two later central fireplaces built independently. Walls clearly raised and floors inserted. Square-framed porch added in 1706.

ABERMULE

BRYNDERWEN BRIDGE, ¼ m. N. A single 109-ft span across the Severn (and a smaller span across the canal) on five iron girders. The openwork lettering on the outer ones reads 'This second iron bridge constructed in the county of Montgomery was erected in the year 1852'; '*Thomas Penson*, County Surveyor'; 'Brymbo Company, Ironfounders'.

BRYN DERWEN, ¼ m. N. An early castle on the Severn. The motte has gone and the bailey area is occupied by a farm.

ABERMULE PRIMARY SCHOOL AND COMMUNITY CENTRE.

By *Herbert Carr*, County Architect, 1951. Red brick, single-storey ranges beside the hipped-roofed hall. The classrooms with large window-areas in small panes, and brick pillars between.

CEFN BRYNTALCH, 1¼ m. NE. By *G. F. Bodley*, 1869, and 94 regarded as the start of the Georgian Revival of the 1870s. It is highly relevant that when Bodley fell ill, he asked *Philip Webb* to take charge.* The interior is indeed whole-heartedly neo-Georgian, though the plan is arranged with the main sides at r. angles. The staircase has the best of the detail – a broad flight towards a Venetian window and then two flights doubling back to a gallery. The exterior is of cleanly detailed red brick. SE front with three big gables and a careful balance of irregular chimneys and windows, and many C18 features - a hipped roof, two bays, sash-windows, and the C18 centrepiece – as well (cf. Joldwynds, Surrey). On the entrance front the balance is rather towards the local Jacobean vernacular – a tall thin porch with timbered upper storey, and lattice windows; but still the porch has rusticated pilasters and a pediment, and a mannered window surround above. The ancestor of so many garden city houses. Sensitive outbuildings etc.

Protection from the prevailing rain-storms is provided partly by the MOTTE AND BAILEY CASTLE to the SW. The motte is at the NE end of a scarped natural ridge, and a cross-ditch divides it from the bailey.

A half-timbered COTTAGE *c.* 300 yds SW was the LODGE built by *Bodley* for Cefn Bryntalch.

DOLFORWYN. *See* p. 101.

ADFA   *oooo*

¾ m. SSE of Llanllugan

GERIZIM CHAPEL. Built in 1790, enlarged *c.* 1820. The side to the road has two short, two tall windows. A timber-framed hipped-roofed SCHOOLROOM was added to the E also *c.* 1820. The school was founded in 1789. – MONUMENT outside to Lewis Evan † 1792, a pioneer of Calvinistic Methodism in North Wales, and the founder of the chapel here.

NEUADD GOCH, ¾ m. NE. A good example of a little type C Severn valley house of *c.* 1600, with one overhang and the stair beside the chimney in the middle.

LLANLLUGAN. *See* p. 146.

* Information on Cefn Bryntalch was kindly given me by Mr Peter Howell.

ARDDLEEN

TREDERWEN HOUSE. Two black-and-white wings (one actually
replaced in brick) and a central section. In the r. angle an overhung porch dated 1616. The r. wing has two overhangs with
quadrant timbering and the upper bressumer carved with
strapwork. Its side is close-studded, and the upper bressumer
is held on corbels which have ropes carved below them. This
carving, and the long upstairs corridor, are features the house
has in common with Broniarth Hall, Guilsfield.

MAERDY, ¾ m. N. Three-bay, three-storey mid C18 brick farm.
Two string-courses on the front, which has early C19 tripartite
windows. (C18 stairs.)

BACHELDRE

2 m. WSW of Churchstoke

BACHELDRE HOUSE. A well preserved small type C Severn valley house of the early C17. Close-studding with the l. end overhanging. Oversailing porch with a double-ogee bressumer and
carved corbels below the jetty of the gable. The central chimney
has been replaced by a stone one to the r., and its space used
for an C18 stair with turned balusters (cf. Berriew Vicarage).
Original front door. C18 fittings.

BACHELDRE HALL. Timber-framed house with the date 1613
on the overhang, embedded in a stone enlargement with a
three-bay, three-storey Regency front.

BACHELDRE MILL. With a water-wheel made by J. Morris,
Welshpool; in working order.

PENTRENANT FARMHOUSE, ¾ m. S. Mid C17. Renewed in stone,
except for the timber oversailing porch with open sides, and
a contemporary stair.

PENTRENANT HALL, ¾ m. S. Mid C19, gabled, with a battlemented porch. The staircase has a ribbed plaster vault above.

PIED HOPTON, 1 m. SW. A small early C17 Severn valley house,
box-framed, the r. overhang supported on corbels and
colonnettes.

CHURCHSTOKE. *See* p. 93.

BERRIEW

ST BEUNO. Beuno's early home is supposed to have been at Berriew: the name Maen Beuno given to a Bronze Age standing
stone 1 m. ENE is a reminder of his teaching here. He settled

at Clynnog Fawr near Caernarfon, where he founded a *clas* and where he was buried in 642. He has been called the patron saint of North Wales.

The church, in a circular churchyard, consists of nave, N and S aisles, chancel, N porch, and W tower. The medieval building (which once belonged to the Knights of St John and later to Strata Marcella), single-chamber, with a wooden W bellcote and a N chancel aisle (perhaps once the Price Chapel), was replaced in 1803–4 with a handsome larger church by an unknown architect – from Shrewsbury? Typical of its time, it was of brick with stone dressings, and had the entry under a pinnacled W tower to a galleried nave with four round-headed windows a side. What we see now is a Victorian correction of this structure carried out by *E. Haycock Junior* in 1876. The W tower has the doorway blocked, stone facing for brick, and Gothic windows except for the circular ones on its second stage. But the slight set-off is there, and ashlar quoins all the way up to the steeper-than-traditional pyramid of the remodelling. Ashlar quoins too at the NW, SW, and SE angles of the nave, which is of C18 proportions. Rooms either side of the tower and an E arch also survive from 1804. Victorianization therefore consisted of inserting the arcades of alternate circular and octagonal piers, the aisle windows and open roofs, and of adding a chancel. – REREDOS. 1896. Apostles and saints below ogee canopies, designed by *F. R. Kempson* with figures by *T. Earp*. – LECTERN. Eagle type, by *Rattee & Kett*. – ORGAN CASE with trumpeting angels, 1923. – STAINED GLASS. E by *Hardman*, c. 1859, an excellent window with strong colouring. The E window of the 1804 church, which it fitted, must have been a Venetian one. – S aisle E window by *Heaton, Butler & Bayne*, 1907. – W by *Powell*, 1907.

MONUMENTS. In the N aisle, three recumbent marble effigies from a raised tomb in the old church, of Arthur Price of Vaynor Park † 1597 and his two wives. The man is in Elizabethan armour with helmet and gauntlets; the ladies have ruffs and headcloths. Four figures of children are in the Powysland Museum, Welshpool. S chancel wall. – William Owen of Glansevern † 1837. Tablet on a corbel, and a relief portrait on a base supporting a shrouded urn, signed *R. Baily*, 1838. Under the tower. – A sarcophagus-shaped memorial to members of the Owen family, early C19. – Rev. E. Jones † 1806. Grecian with an urn and a snake. – In the churchyard a WAR MEMORIAL by *Comper*.

The village is justly reputed for its many black-and-white houses picturesquely grouped either side of the River Rhiw. In fact the timber-framed houses were largely restored by the Vaynor Estate c. 1880 and given large moulded brick chimneys. This imaginative operation saved an interesting layout of the C17 or earlier; preserved pre-industrial villages are not common in Wales. Other houses are C18/19 brick and painted, which is another strong local custom. RHIW HOUSE (the old malt house) is mostly restored and has a cluster of four chimneys. BRODAWEL had four separate stacks. Next of interest round the churchyard the OLD SCHOOL HOUSE, founded in the C17 and rebuilt c. 1819, and the little SMITHY, rebuilt in 1774 and again with four hefty chimneys. THE FARMHOUSE is C17; so is RECTORY FARMHOUSE. THE VICARAGE is by far the best example here of a C17 timber-framed house. It is dated 1616 with the initials of the rector, Thomas Kyffin. Vertical studding with diagonal braces, the upper floor jettied on a moulded bressumer, on a stone base. Remarkably preserved porch with railed sides and oversailing room above with quadrant decoration. The plan is unusual: two rooms, with a staircase now replacing the central chimney, and one floor of service rooms at the rear. Addition to the l. of c. 1700.

At the other end of the village GRO COTTAGE and YR EFAIL are two more successful renovations of the 1880s, gabled and chimneyed as *cottages ornés*.

LUGGY MOAT, 1 m. NW. A thirty-foot-high motte, with a top diameter of c. sixty feet, and in front an earthwork bailey roughly fifty yards square. The Luggy Brook has eroded the N side and revealed that the mound is composed of layers of rubble consolidated with bands of clay.

BRITHDIR HALL, 1¼ m. NW. Traditionally the site of a grange of Strata Marcella abbey. A timber-framed house of c. 1610 faced in stucco c. 1814, including the oversailing porch. The Regency restyling gave it deep eaves and some plasterwork; a stable and bakehouse were added in brick to the l. and the r. rather as pavilions.

(Nearby was BODHEILIN, a late C18 fantastic villa long since burned down. Engravings show an odd façade of five Gothic towers fronted with a neo-classical portico.)

BELAN CHAPEL, 2 m. NE. Small and late C19. – Inside the chapel is preserved the late Norman FONT from Llandysilio church.

LLWYNDERW HALL, 2 m. NE. Early C19; with blank segment-headed windows in the middle of its E side and verandas tucked into angles on the N and S.

LOWER CIL, ½ m. NW. A well-preserved farmhouse. Its l. side is early C16, possibly a hall-house enlarged to the standard Severn valley C17 pattern. So it has the central chimney with triple-moulded brick stacks, behind an open turned-rail porch with its original door and hinges and a room over. The r. side is close-studded and slightly jettied out.

RHIWPORT, ¾ m. WNW. Of c. 1815. Very plain stucco façade, five bays and three storeys, the central bay with a pair of giant pilasters up to the architrave and a blank attic above. Two bays with ground-floor bows, and a veranda curving round them.

(Y BRYN, 1½ m. NW. A barn (formerly a house) constructed with three cruck couples.)

VAYNOR PARK, ¾ m. SW.* The substantial medieval house built for Edward ap Hywel ab Ieuan Llwyd is described by Guto'r Glyn in the C15. About 1650 this seems to have given place to the present brick structure, perhaps built for George Devereux, High Sheriff in 1658. Vaynor is one of only four big brick houses of its date in the county. Flemish bond. John Ingleby's drawings show the back of the house with two storeys of eight bays beneath four equal gables. The W front had a five-bay centre flanked by half-hipped wings two bays wide by one deep. External chimneys on the side walls (cf. Llandrinio Hall). The home of the Moxon, Lyon, and Corbet Winder family from 1748, its two fronts were remodelled by *Thomas Penson* the County Surveyor in 1840–53 for John Winder Lyon Winder, the E one being brought forward several feet. The style chosen was Jacobean, a reflection of taste changing from the austere medieval of earlier in the century towards more opulent decoration. So on the W the mullioned windows were enlarged and given pediments, big shaped gables were substituted, and a carved porch with pilasters and a strapwork crest was added, to give an E plan. Inside, the plan was reordered by Penson, but most of the fittings are those of c. 1670, which is a tribute to him. In the hall a C17 carved overmantel from Crutched Friars. The library, whose l. part held the staircase, has a plaster ceiling and woodwork to Penson's designs, excepting a mid-C17 overmantel. In the drawing and dining rooms, ceilings by Penson, and in the latter a fireplace carved by *Henry Street*. The fine staircase, dog-leg, with its fluted pear-shaped balusters

* Colonel J. L. Corbet-Winder kindly gave me access to much new information about Vaynor.

and bold bolection panelling, was reassembled – which might account for some crude details in the open triangular pediments over the doorcases.

The house stands at the E of a courtyard which had two-storey pavilions halfway down the side walls. The long C17 gatehouse and stables had curly gables which were lowered by Penson, who added three gables facing the house. The florid Elizabethan frontispiece on the outer side came last, by *S. Pountney Smith* of Shrewsbury, 1853. By *Penson* also the terraces and LODGE.

AQUEDUCT, $\frac{1}{4}$ m. SE. Built *c*. 1796 to carry the Montgomeryshire Canal across the Rhiw. Four brick arches, repaired in 1889; two are land arches. The engineers were *John* and *Thomas Dadford*.

77 GLANSEVERN, $\frac{1}{2}$ m. SE. An austere Greek Revival house of Cefn stone, built for Sir Arthur Davies Owen by *Joseph Bromfield*, *c*. 1801–7. Very coolly and crisply detailed S façade of five bays with four giant Ionic pilasters – none at the angles – supporting an architrave. Porch of the same order, with half-columns *in antis*, a pair of doubled columns breaking forward between square piers to carry a plain entablature, and at the sides applied columns. The stone is different and it looks an afterthought. Modillion cornice and parapet below the roof. The S side has a central curving bow but is astylar. Originally all the windows were sashes. In the library are parts of the C15 screen of Llangurig church – the central opening, a four-centred arch with triangular tracery, and some side lights with various tracery heads. Also a C17 overmantel and Elizabethan panels from Montgomery church. Standard early C19 fittings otherwise, from Shrewsbury and London makers.*

Early C19 brick STABLES AND BREWHOUSE behind.

THE LODGE, designed *c*. 1808, is in the severest Greek Doric, with the doorway behind two columns *in antis*. At the ends a pair of columns, supporting a reticent pediment, break forward round the window.‡

BETTWS CEDEWAIN

ST BEUNO. In a circular churchyard. Single-chamber with a W tower, one of the very few Perp towers in the county, albeit a modest example, with its angle buttresses and moulded W

---

* I wish to thank Mr and Mrs Massy for their help on Glansevern.
‡ Demolished for road widening in 1978.

Bettws Cedewain, brass to John ap Meredyth, 1531

doorway below a Late Perp three-light window with a drip-mould, stops, and relieving arch. The partly renewed upper part has a wooden bell-stage and a pyramidal roof in two stages. The nave was rebuilt in 1868 by *W. E. Nesfield*, a near replica of the old. Perp fenestration; totally renewed arch-braced roof and wind-braces. – FONT. Heptagonal, with cusped circles on the sides; cut on the design of the old one. – REREDOS. White figures against coloured marble; 1871. – STAINED GLASS. E by *Wailes*, after 1868. – S. In a jumble of decorative bits, a small early C16 Nativity and Crucifixion, and later figures, all continental. – BRASS to the Rev. John ap Meredyth, dated 1531, showing the tonsured figure in mass vestments holding a chalice and wafer. He helped build the tower. This is the only pre-Reformation brass in the county. – The church once belonged to the Llanllugan nunnery.

Bettws is an attractive village grouping, the church on the hillock and the houses circled below. Little to note individually: a brick CALVINISTIC METHODIST CHAPEL, 1839, with a pedimented tabernacle behind the minister's seat; cottages whose timber-framing is being replaced by black-and-white-painted plaster; a Regency VICARAGE outside to the E.

CAER SIAC, ½ m. NE. Mutilated motte, on a ridge and protected by ditches either side.

GLAN BECHAN, 1 m. S. Square-framed Severn valley house with an E wing; dated 1651 on a jettied gable.

PONTYPERCHYLL, 1½ m. S. Timber-framing of two builds, a square-framed wing and, at r. angles, close heavy studding on an overhung gable.

HIGHGATE, 1½ m. SE. Large timber-framed farmhouse of two wings joined together to form an E-plan. The s wing seems from the internal details (brackets, partitioning) to be *c.* 1670. Heavy close-studded walls with bracketed jettying on three sides, and with a moulded bressumer above on carved corbels supporting quadrant timbering in the gable. Jetties round all the rest are bricked up. Later C17 staircase.

BRYNYCIL, 1 m. ENE. One of the all-concrete farms built on the Gregynog estate *c.* 1870 (*see* Tregynon).

PENTRE LLIVIOR CHAPEL, 2 m. NE. Small, red brick, with 'Regency Gothic' round-headed windows – i.e. *c.* 1850, though a plaque outside reads 'Wesley's Methodist Chapel 1798'.

BODFACH *see* LLANFYLLIN

BODYNFOEL see LLANFECHAIN

THE BREIDDIN see CRIGGION

BRONIARTH HALL see GUILSFIELD

BRYNGWYN see BWLCH-Y-CIBAU

BRYN Y FEDWEN
2 m. NW of Dylife

8090

There are two CAIRNS on Bryn y Fedwen (SN 841 953 and 844 954) which may be reached easily from the road. The peaks of Plynlimon are crowned by several impressive summit cairns (all damaged), and the discovery of dozens of flint arrowheads in the vicinity of Llyn Bugeilyn indicates a considerable Bronze Age presence in these bleak uplands. Game may have been more plentiful in the milder climate of that time.

BUTTINGTON

2000

ALL SAINTS. Single-chamber, roughcast and whitewashed, with a weatherboarded W bell-turret and a S porch; in a small raised churchyard. Only window details are visible outside: two Dec ones in the sanctuary, two-light with quatrefoils; a taller W window with the quatrefoil circled; and the E window, Perp, with panel tracery. Timber porch, dated 1686, with open sides with pierced balusters. Over the nave and chancel a good C15 roof of arch-braced principals with cusped braces in the apex, and three tiers of foiled wind-braces. They stop over the altar. Below the third truss from the E a rood beam, cusped on the E side, spans the church. Two foiled struts remain between it and the principals, but no other remains of a screen. Small restorations in 1876 – nave windows to the pattern of the sanctuary ones, new pews, etc. – FONT. A fine E.E. capital of c. 1220, with three tiers of tightly curling foliage, said (on good stylistic evidence) to have been brought from Strata Marcella Abbey. It belonged to a free-standing pier, possibly one supporting the groined vault of the aisled chapter house. – STAINED GLASS. W, pieces of a C15 Crucifixion (reconstructible?), two saints jumbled in modern borders, and a complete C16 shield.

Immediately by the church a hipped-roofed RECTORY of 1836;

and a single-span iron BRIDGE over the Severn (1872) with a pretty trefoiled cast-iron parapet, inscribed *W. N. Swetten-ham*, County Surveyor. BUTTINGTON BRICKWORKS, about a mile NE, has since *c.* 1870 been making a very hard, very red brick.

TREWERN. *See* p. 205.

TREWERN. *See* p. 205.

BWLCH-Y-CIBAU

CHRIST CHURCH. An interesting little church by *Sir George Gilbert Scott*, 1862–4. The exterior is plain E.E. with bellcote, s porch, and buttresses. Inside, the eye at once goes to the E end, a short choir with a semicircular apse. Its roof is of close-set rafters forming a semi-dome. Wagon roof over choir and nave in a similar technique. Chamfered chancel arch supported on corbels with capitals naturalistically carved with roses and leaves. The apse is lit by five lancets and the w end by a rose window and triple lancet. Nicely carved pulpit. – STAINED GLASS. E by *Wailes*, 1873. – w by *Powell*'s, 1877, designed by *J. W. Brown*.

BRYNGWYN, ½ m. N. Built *c.* 1774–6 by *Robert Mylne* for Mr Mostyn-Owen, for whom he also built Woodhouse, Oswestry. Partially burned in 1802 and rebuilt. Brick. The garden façade remains – two windows either side of a three-sided bay rising two full storeys and hipped like the main roof. No quoins. A stone string is used as a sill for the windows on the bay but broken for the others. The main additions were made after 1813 for Martin Williams, including the six-bay w front with a simple break forward (Mylne's was similar but had a pediment) and larger windows, and a Doric screen on the stairs. Chimney-pieces from Dublin. The gardens and the lake were also created at this time. The porch is by *A. McGarel Hogg*, 1914. Bryngwyn was formerly the seat of the Kynaston family.*

BRYN DERWEN, ½ m. NW, is a gabled High Victorian house of little interest. On the edge of the park a C17 farmhouse with a tall stone chimney abutted.

COED-OER-LE, ¾ m. WNW. A square-framed cottage internally constructed with four cruck couples. Later chimney of the C17, giving a lobby entry. Another four pairs of crucks in the adjacent BARN, sited cross-contour, and yet more in another BARN nearby, also called COED-OER-LE.

*I am grateful for the help of Mrs G. Mackeson-Sandbach.

YSGUBOR COED-OER-LE, ½ m. W. The tithe barn for the
  Bwlch-y-cibau district, cruciform in plan and built (on the old
  site?) soon after 1800.

CEFN LLYFNOG, ¾ m. ENE. A timber-framed farmhouse of considerable interest. Cruck-framed centre, perhaps C15, with
  three trusses. The oak post-and-panel wall opposite the fireplace in the former hall shows the space beyond the beam in
  which the original seat and hood were recessed. Large, later
  chimney supporting a double stack of brick with the usual star-
  pattern section of c. 1650. Close-studded parlour wing added
  at the lower end, along the contour. In its S gable a projecting
  bressumer and three bands of quadrant decoration. Two
  Madonnas and two devils in plaster in an upper room.

CAE GAER

8080

5 m. WNW of Llangurig

A very small ROMAN FORT (SN 824 818) built on an awkward
plateau strangely remote from the contemporary road system.
Excavation at the beginning of the century did not produce any
Roman finds, but the damp site had preserved the wooden palisade which topped the low turf rampart; the timbers were 4
in. thick and stood 2 ft apart.

CAERHOWEL

2090

CAERHOWEL HALL. Mid C18 brick hipped-roofed block.
  Façade of five bays and three storeys, with semicircular-headed
  windows in the projecting centre, the upper one breaking into
  the pediment. Additions include an early C20 single pilastered
  storey along the front.

CAERHOWEL BRIDGE, ½ m. W. The third iron bridge in the
  county, built in 1858, and wider than those at Llandinam and
  Abermule. By *Thomas Penson*, County Surveyor, as a replacement for a suspension bridge of 1852 which he had advised
  against – and which did indeed collapse with loss of life, under
  the weight of three wagons of lime from Garthmyl Wharf.

MONTGOMERY. *See* p. 163.

CAERSWS

0090

Caersws occupies part of the site of an important Roman fort
and road-junction. Since it lies at the confluence of the Trannon

and Carno with the Severn, it also became a junction for roads and railways following the river valleys. Its magnificent setting in a bowl between the hills is best seen from the slopes above Llanwnnog and Aberhafesp. It would have been more or less the focus of the Mid Wales Growth Town (proposed in 1966 and rejected), consisting of industries and a population of 50,000 disposed in villages beside lakes, developed up the valley between Newtown and Llanidloes.

ST MARY. C19 single-chamber; of no interest.

PRESBYTERIAN CHURCH. By *E. Jones* of Newtown. Chapel with spire in the Dec of *c.* 1900. The roofs of the nave and the transeptal wings curve out at the bottom.

BRIDGE. Three long elliptical arches with cutwaters; *c.* 1821.

LLYS MALDWYN HOSPITAL, ½ m. NE. Formerly the Poor Law Union for Newtown and Llanidloes. 1840. Cruciform. Four-storey brick central block with lower radiating wings. Grim N front of stone, eleven bays on a basement with a double staircase.

MAESMAWR HALL HOTEL, ½ m. E. Well-preserved T-plan regional-cum-Renaissance house, sympathetically enlarged behind by *W. E. Nesfield* in 1874. Burned and rebuilt *c.* 1712. Close-studded on the lower storey; the upper storey, jettied on three sides, has a layer of baluster timberwork (formerly a common local motif), and then square frames with quadrants. Central stone chimneys, set diagonally. The parlour on the r. has a later C17 wainscot, the hall on the l. a typical ceiling with beams stopped at the intersections and early C18 plaster in the nine compartments. An elaborate stair was built behind the chimneys; the lower flight has been replaced, but the second flights branch from the landing. They have bulky turned balusters, again confirming an C18 date.

RHOS DDIARBED, I m SE. A splendidly clear Norman motte-and-bailey layout near Moat Farm. The tall ramparts of the bailey, 200 ft by 150 ft, have a central entrance. The 40 ft high mound is independently ditched. A larger area, 605 by 350 ft, immediately below, also banked, is known as Camp Field. The castle was probably built by Roger de Montgomery before 1086 to guard Arwysth.

BRON FELEN, I m. SE. A small motte-and-bailey castle. The motte is 33 ft high.

CAERSWS ROMAN FORT was sited at the crossing of five Roman roads. The modern roads have tended to cover the Roman ones, but the latter can be well seen in places such as SO 052 922 and SO 046 956. The first Roman fort in the area was NE of the village at SO 042 925, but at an early stage in the Roman occupation a replacement was built at the confluence of the rivers, although the new site under the village was liable to flooding. The unimpressive remains of the turf rampart, to which a stone facing was added in the C2, can be seen where it is crossed by the A489. The fort and the civil settlement outside it had a long history, continuing in occupation until after A.D. 400, no doubt because of its strategic position at the junction of so many lines of communication.

CEFN CARNEDD (SO 017 900), set at the confluence of the Cerist and the Severn above Caersws, is an elongated hillfort to rival Ffridd Faldwyn and Gaer Fawr in the splendour of its setting and the probable complexity of its history. The earliest fort on the hill was at the W end. Its presence is revealed only by the illogical kink in the N scarp or rampart and a cross bank which shows well on air photographs but can scarcely be seen on the ground since it was slighted when the fort was enlarged to enclose the full 8 acres of the top of the ridge. At this second stage the fort was defended by three banks and ditches (the banks have been reduced by ploughing to scarps) curving in to inturned entrances at either end. At the E end there is a small annexe outside the entrance. At the W end, inside the fort, a straight line of bank without an entrance from the E seems to belong to a final phase of use when the fort was reduced to only 1¾ acres. This final phase may be Romano-British or Dark Age in date, but there has been no excavation to confirm this speculation.

CLATTER. *See* p. 94.
LLANWNNOG. *See* p. 151.

CALCOTT HALL *see* LLANDRINIO

CARNO

ST JOHN THE BAPTIST. A medieval church on the site belonged to the Knights of St John. The present building is by *J. W. Poundley* (County Surveyor), 1863, single-chamber, with a prettily detailed tower abutted W of the S porch. It needs repair at the time of writing. Geometrically cut stone decoration; conical slated spire above a wooden bell-stage. The windows have plate tracery (wheel motifs above lancets) – the E window is especially bold – and red and yellow stone dressings. The chancel is marked by quatrefoil ironwork on the roof ridge and inside by a wooden arch corbelled on stone colonnettes – an unusually restrained accent for the local C19 church builders. – MONUMENT. An Early Christian stone of the C7/8 incised with two superimposed circled crosses.

In CAE NODDFA, the field N of the church, excavation has revealed foundations of a medieval building in a big banked enclosure, possibly the HOSPITIUM of the Knights Hospitaller. N again is the factory of LAURA ASHLEY, with its offices' front wall of random coursed stone and full-height slit windows (1973) and vast, sprawling warehouses etc.

PLAS NEWYDD, $\frac{1}{2}$ m. E. A large timber house surviving in mutilated form, and demonstrating the endurance of the timber tradition even for a proper C18 plan. The date is 1704. Close-studded, and originally three storeys to the N and four storeys to the S (because of the sloping site). Renaissance plan of four main rooms at the corners, lit by large eight- and ten-light wood-framed windows (now partly blocked). Central entrance through the broad original door; then at the far end of the hall a fine dog-leg staircase with thick balusters with slanted mouldings on the first flight up, and fret-cut balusters for the second flight and the flight down to kitchen level. At the top of the latter is a dog-gate with turned uprights. The panelling was moved to Wynnstay, Denbighshire, and burned there in 1858. In 1811 the roofs were reconstructed a bit lower. W wall rebuilt in stone. Two BARNS form a courtyard in front of the house.

TRANNON. Where the cross-ridge tracks cross this moor there is an interesting group of Bronze Age monuments, sited around the head of a small stream and placed so as to be visible to travellers coming along the ridge routes from the S. The largest monument is TWR GWYN MAWR, a very badly ruined cairn (SN 918 959) which produced at least two burials when it was 'excavated' in the last century. Arrowheads and a piece of bronze were also found. A shepherd's house has been built beside it, contributing to its further ruin. A little to the SE are two small cairns with very large and conspicuous kerb stones; a smaller version of this design in which the kerb is the dominant feature may be found on a lower shelf of the moor some 2–300 yds ENE of Twr Gwyn Mawr. Further SW of the large cairn is a fallen alignment of seven stones, the S one extremely large. E of them, lower down the slope, is a ring cairn, very low and not always easy to see. TWR GWYN BACH is another simple cairn about $\frac{1}{2}$ m. S of Twr Gwyn Mawr.

CASTLE CAEREINION   *1000*

ST GARMON. Nave, chancel, w tower in a large banked churchyard. Rebuilt from scratch in uninspired E.E., by *T. H. Wyatt*,
   1866, for the nave and chancel, and by *Thomas Batt*, 1874, for
   the tower with the porch beneath. At least its broach-spire
   looks exciting at a distance. Its C15 predecessor was a typical
   Montgomeryshire unitary church with a w timber bell-stage.
   – STAINED GLASS. Nave s, interlaces with a roundel of the
   Ascension, probably by *David Evans*, *c.* 1840.

TWMPATH GARMON. The mound in the N corner of the
   churchyard has been suggested as the site of the motte of the
   castle, and the churchyard as the area of its bailey. It was built
   in 1156 by Madoc ap Mareddudd (his nephew Owain
   Cyfeiliog was driven from it eleven years later by the North
   Wales princes).

In this small farming village the black and white ORCHARD
   HOUSE, the C18 IVY HOUSE, and a little SCHOOL of 1852
   stand by the church.

PEN Y LLWYN, ¼ m. SW. Formerly a grange of Strata Marcella
   Abbey. Timber-framed in two sections: a C16 (?) square-
   framed part, and a C17 square-framed wing with an end
   jetty complete with the customary bressumer, brackets,
   simple quadrant woodwork, and strapwork-carved upper bressumer.

TY MAWR, ½ m. SE. The unusual aisled hall, perhaps of *c.* 1400,
   and long used as a barn, is in D O E guardianship. It is the only
   one of its kind found in Montgomeryshire. Ty Mawr is a good
   building for seeing the timber structure of a medieval open hall
   and, incidentally, how it was converted into a storeyed house
   in the C17, because there are no solid walls or floor. The hall
   was *c.* 25 ft by 30 ft, on a platform running out from the hill.
   Its two internal trusses are a single pair of chamfered wooden
   speres or posts set in the floor and forming a box-frame which
   carries the roof, and a pair of arch-braced base-crucks with two
   tiers of cusped struts above the principal, which spanned the
   whole width. The analogies are with the partly aisled halls of
   important houses in NE Wales and NW England. Gable and
   partition trusses also aisled. The roof was half-hipped. Wind-
   braces were employed both below the wall-plate and along the
   purlins. C17 additions include the timber-framed double fireplace with its tapering wattle-sided chimney, and stairs beside;
   and the beams for the upper floor resting on this, and on two

Castle Caereinion, Ty Mawr (Royal Commission on Ancient and Historical Monuments in Wales)

corbel-posts set near the speres. At the time of writing it awaits major repair.

TREFNANT HALL, 1½ m. SE. Probably the Trefnant acquired from Owain Cyfeiliog by Strata Marcella Abbey at the time of its foundation in 1170. In the C18 a home of the Lloyds of Dolobran. Approached by an avenue of walnuts, at 700 ft. Of the S front only the central triangular-pedimented doorway with a pulvinated frieze and four bays to the l. remain. Above the door a Venetian window, its centre with Gibbs surround, and fluted pilasters. The staircase, centrally placed for the complete house, and with another Venetian window behind, is a fine example of *c.* 1740. Lobby with fluted pilasters and triglyph frieze. Three turned balusters a tread, the treads inlaid with holly and with foliate sides. Gallery returning round three sides. Downstairs a room with wooden Georgian pilasters and a dentilled cornice.

MIDDLE SYLFAEN, 1 m. NE. A good specimen of the central-chimneyed regional Renaissance-house of *c.* 1650. The entire front is jettied on moulded bressumers, supported on scroll corbels, though now as so often underpinned with brick. Projecting timber porch with turned rails in the sides; the over-sailing room, again on scroll corbels, is decorated with fleur-de-lys timberwork.

About 1 m. N of Middle Sylfaen, behind Y Golfa hill, is MAES MOYDOG, the flat ground which has been identified* as the site of the battle in 1295 at which the English completed the conquest of Wales.

PEN Y FOEL (SJ 178 059) is crowned by a trapeze-shaped HILLFORT which relies mainly on the steep natural slopes for its defence. There is scarcely any evidence for a built rampart except on the SE, but the slopes have been artificially scarped all the way round. The main defences enclose an area of 3½ acres, and an impressive annexe to the SW adds a further 1½ acres to the fort. The entrance has been damaged by the farmhouse and garden, but both the main scarp and ditch and the annexe scarp have a recognizably original gap on this SW side.

On either side of the Luggy Brook are two small ENCLOSED SETTLEMENTS (SJ 170 035 and 172 041) which in spite of erosion by ploughing and flooding illustrate well the siting of many non-defensive enclosures which may be tentatively assigned to the peaceful period of Roman rule in E Wales. Neither of these sites is well preserved; the triple banks of the SW one have been reduced by ploughing to scarps and berms, and the E one has been confused by the digging of a drainage ditch. Analysis of the two banks and ditches suggests that the E one is of two periods.

* By Sir Goronwy Edwards.

CEFN BRYNTALCH *see* ABERMULE

CEFN CARNEDD *see* CAERSWS

CEGIDFA *see* GUILSFIELD

8000   CEMMAES

A village of stone houses of 1800 and after in a beautiful stretch of the Dovey valley.

ST TYDECHO. A single-chamber church with a W bellcote in a large circular churchyard; perhaps of the C14 or C15. Some old stonework is visible in the N, E, and S walls, but the last was raised in the C19, when the W gallery was removed and the E and other windows were changed (from Perp) to the customary C13/14 style. S porch faced with dressed stone and dated 1742 on the timberwork. The bare interior was much restored c. 1902. The best feature is the roof with its C15 arch-braced trusses, three at the E boldly cusped in the apex. A fragment of the vine-leaf cornice of the C15 SCREEN is fixed behind the altar. – STAINED GLASS. E, garish Crucifixion, Resurrection, Ascension, dated 1864. – S lancet of St Melangell, monogrammed ML, 1905. Art Nouveau brass tablet below. – W by *Ward & Hughes*, 1889. – MONUMENTS. Roger and Elizabeth Mostyn, erected 1744. Strong relief with two flowing oil-cruses and an asymmetrical shield above the entablature. – Anne Morris † 1729. Stone tablet with raised lettering.

CALVINISTIC METHODIST CHAPEL. A gay Italianate façade painted grey with white quoins. The central feature, three tall windows grouped under a steep gable, projects slightly from the narrow side-bays. Balustrades and vases above.

CAPEL SAMMAH, CWM LLINAU, 1 m. NE. Solid 'side-on' type, with severe classical detail; porches later. Typical of mid C19 country chapels.

GORPHWYSFA, next to the church, is a good specimen of the common type of c. 1800 – three bays, sash-windows, chimneys at the ends. The pattern was employed for rebuilding many of the local farms. Here the front is constructed of large coursed stones.

CEMMAES BYCHAN, ¼ m. SW. Approached by an avenue of ash-trees, with a small water-wheel on the r. and a lime-tree of huge girth on the l. The house was built in 1632 by Lewis Anwyl, formerly High Sheriff of Merioneth. Square on plan, with steep roofs hipped to a central cluster of four stone stacks. Originally timber-framed with two tiers of dormers, it was faced in stone *c.* 1850. Its appearance must have been influenced by Sir Richard Clough's Bachegraig (1567), Denbighshire. Besides the main timbers which tie the roof to the chimney, several rooms preserve their C17 wainscots.

GROFFT, 2 m. SW. A stone barn with two cruck trusses inside was perhaps a C15 house, aligned cross-contour. The farmhouse is early C17 and timber-framed, with a tall stepped lateral chimney to the N. Added to the S is a tiny parlour with C18 panelling and pilasters.

CERI *see* KERRY

CHURCHSTOKE

2090

ST NICHOLAS. In a circular raised churchyard. W tower, nave, N and S aisles, short transepts, chancel, S porch. Rebuilt by *Joseph Bromfield* in 1815 for £2,500, and remodelled to High Victorian taste *c.* 1870. Massive tower, C13 at the base, with small openings higher up. By Bromfield the wooden bell-stage with round-headed windows and the stumpy conical shingled spire with ball-finial. His nave and the aisles, under one roof and with stone covings, have been completely rearranged inside. By whom? The iron columns with bases at box-pew height, presumably once supporting galleries, now carry wooden arcades and tie-beam roofs with cusped trusses. Aisles with big traceried windows and buttressed walls. Chancel added: octagonal piers, leaf capitals, intersecting E window, panelled roof. – SCREEN. Of *c.* 1870, with Welsh motifs, carved on one side only. – PULPIT. Perhaps of 1815. – MONUMENTS. Thomas Browne † 1811, signed *H. Wood*, Bristol. Mourning figure garlanding an urn. – Thomas Browne † 1874. Brass in a carved alabaster frame.

A scattered village. Near the church are the gabled stone REC-TORY by *E. Haycock*, 1846, built beside a late C18 stone house facing the other way; and the SCHOOL and SCHOOLHOUSE, four bays with a pedimental gable over the door and a domed lantern, converted from an early C19 factory. Then CHURCH-STOKE HALL, whose early C17 N block has stone chimneys with triple shaped brick stacks abutted either end. The timberwork is much renewed in stone. Extension to the s of *c.* 1650 with moulded bressumers and a handsome door and frame with carved brackets. Good staircase inside. The rest of the house is modern. On the r. opposite is FIR COURT, with two diagonal-timbered gables on a three-bay square-framed front, and with the inscription 'What is here by man erected, let it be by God protected. Richard Middleton, gent, 1685, aetatis suae 27...'. In succession along the Bishop's Castle road are TODLETH HALL, an attempt to dignify the usual house of *c.* 1840 with a façade; SIMON's CASTLE, the foundations of a small Norman stone castle on a motte of natural rock covered with soil; BROADWAY HOUSE, a four-bay grouping of Regency roofs with early C19 additions; and IVY HOUSE, late C18, with a tall hipped roof, Tuscan porch, and some window improvements. Across the bridge in the village is a small two-storeyed stone house with arched windows dated 1778.

MELLINGTON HALL, 1½ m. SW. By *Evan Powell* and dated 1876. In rather hideous Victorian industrialists' medieval (C14), and ugly inside too. The hall, faced with small rough stones and ashlar dressings, has transomed, trefoiled windows and sharp semi-dormers. Tower with a Gothic parapet. Additions of *c.* 1900.

The LODGE, in the form of a gatehouse, is by contrast likeable enough.

In the previous house *S. W. Williams*, the Radnorshire architect, was born in 1837.

BACHELDRE. *See* p. 76.

CLATTER

1½ m. NW of Llanwnnog

59 PLASAU DUON. A former home of the Glyns and the Myttons, dating from just before the Civil War, and surviving in exceptional condition. Plasau Duon is a Severn valley regional house (type C) – with a central chimney between the two main living rooms – but it is a Renaissance type in its orientation and cruciform arrangement, i.e. the main block is placed along the contour instead of across it, and the service rooms are behind it instead of alongside. They seem to be an earlier (C16?) fabric, to which the porched house was added. Ground floor of close stud with wind-braces, first floor framed in squares and jettied

out on three sides in the usual way. The porch is a particularly good specimen: it has a (very much) depressed ogee doorhead, thin turned balusters in the sides, and the original door. The upper part has bold diamond framing. It is well off-centre because the hall is twice as wide as the parlour. Plain stone chimney of untypical form. The parlour has a later wainscot and overmantel. Cellar beneath. Hall ceiling divided into nine compartments by beams, the joists in them arranged in counterchanging directions. Its notable C17 floor (beneath modern boards) is of small smooth stones set in earth in geometrical patterns, a technique then widespread in the Trefeglwys area. Behind the chimney the stair climbs round a little well. Most of the doorways still have depressed-ogee heads and their original doors. In all an outstanding example of vernacular craftsmanship in oak.

CAERSWS. *See* p. 85.

LLANWNNOG. *See* p. 151.

CLYWEDOG *see* LLANIDLOES

CRAIG RHIWARTH *see* LLANGYNOG

CRIGGION   2010

The village lies on the Severn valley bottom directly and dramatically beneath the Breiddin Hills. 1,000 ft above is ADMIRAL RODNEY'S PILLAR, erected in 1781 to commemorate his defeat of a French fleet at Dominica in the West Indies in ships built of Powysland oaks. The order is Doric; of rubble stone except for the dressed capital and cornice of the plinth. On the NW side of the hills a roadstone quarry is eating high into the cliffs. At their base the huge pylons of the POST OFFICE INTERNATIONAL MARITIME RADIO STATION. Ancient settlements have been found on the hills and Anglo-Saxon settlements begin at the foot of the slopes. The farms were below on the marshes, which were drained by the monks of Alberbury, Shropshire.

ST MICHAEL AND ALL ANGELS. A little brick church of 1774 in a raised churchyard. Stone quoins and dressings. Entry under the W tower, which retains round-headed and circular windows and till recently had battlements and pinnacles. The nave windows are now lancets. The interior is a weird mixture of ecclesiological fashions. It is still fitted with the neat box pews, a bit of the altar rails, and the C18 pulpit and sounding-board of a hall-church on the N wall. But the hood of a restorer's window cuts the latter, the roof is rebuilt with lofty trusses, and, most discordantly of all, a dominating chancel arch (of red and white stone and resting on bold foliated capitals and ringed shafts) opens into a raised chancel, whose reredos consists of intersecting Romanesque chevron arcading. Is it all by *Thomas Nicholson*? The choir is of stone with lancet windows. Brick vestry with Norman décor added on the N. Quite a succession in less than a century.

CRIGGION HALL. Three brick gabled sections arranged side by side, with external chimneys, three at the ends and one on the side. The details of raised gable ends, mullioned and transomed windows, and some tumbled brick heads are all consistent with a date about 1670. What the exterior doesn't show is that the NE gables case an intact type C house whose front doorway has been moved to the parlour. Stair and chimney are in the centre, as is usual in the early C17. In the third wing a stair with turned balusters.

BRIMFORD HOUSE, ½ m E. Double-fronted three-bay three-storey house with the two chimneys still – c. 1740 – placed externally on each side. Porch with fluted columns and fanlight.

THE BREIDDIN (SJ 292 144), the largest of the defensive enclosures on the dramatic, volcanic hill of Criggion, has been badly damaged by forestry and quarrying and is now difficult to visit. However the destruction of parts of the site has given opportunity for excavation both before the last war and within recent years, and consequently the Breiddin will, when fully published, be a key site in understanding the history of the later prehistoric period in the Severn valley. The remains consist at present of a triple rampart on the SE side of the hill. The inner walls are of stone and the outer one is an earthen bank, though, where it turns up the hill, it too is of stone. The main entrance, in the centre of this SE side, is inturned. Excavation, however, has shown that this stone rampart replaced earlier palisades and timber-laced banks which are almost certainly associated with Late Bronze Age occupation of the hill. Behind the stone ramparts of Iron Age date the inhabitants lived in round wooden huts scattered over the rocky hill-top wherever a level platform could be found or contrived. These huts were built of stakes and wattle but were surprisingly robust; copies have been built at the Avoncroft Museum of Building in Bromsgrove, where their spaciousness and convenience can be well appreciated.

The arrival of the Romans seems to have led to an abandonment of the hillfort, but it was occupied again when they left, and the Breiddin is one of the few sites which has provided good evidence for Dark Age settlement, though the dilapidated defences do not seem to have been refurbished at that time. The latest excavations have also revealed evidence for occupation of the hill in Neolithic and Early Bronze Age times, but there is nothing to suggest that these early settlements were large or defended in any way – such formalization and enclosure of the settlement began only in the Late Bronze Age (a statement which would have been considered controversial only a few years ago).

CEFN Y CASTELL (SJ 306 134) is a small contour fort crowning one of the S spurs of the Criggion massif on which the Breiddin is the main fortification. Strong earth and stone rampart with inturned entrances at either end; annexe outside the SW one.

CASTLE CAMP (SJ 322 145) is a small multivallate fort on a spur from Kempster's Hill. The number of ramparts varies from two to four according to the natural steepness of the land, and though there has been some damage from ploughing, they remain impressive in places. The entrance is at the SW end.

CWRT PLAS-Y-DRE see NEWTOWN

CYFRONYDD

2½ m. ENE of Llanfair Caereinion

1000

CYFRONYDD SCHOOL. Formerly the home of the Pryce family. Large square brick house of c. 1865 with vaguely French detail, particularly on the three-storey entrance tower with its château roof.

CEFN DU UCHAF, 1 m. NE. The W part, which may be of c. 1600, square-framed, with diamonds on the gable, has two rooms with deeply chamfered beams and a central chimney. Beyond is an extension with late C17 woodwork and stairs, and another addition in brick with C18 details and stairs.

CEFN DU CAMP (SJ 150 094) is heavily wooded, but the double ramparts and ditch can still be made out. At the entrance on the NE end, an extra length of bank and ditch. There are a number of small fortified hills at the junction of the Banwy and the Vyrnwy, an area whose strategic importance is reflected later in the situation of the important Dark Age site of Mathrafal.

DAROWEN

The village enjoys wide views of the surrounding hills. Pwll-Iwrch, Cefn Coch Uchaf and the rest are survivors of isolated C15 hill settlements far from modern valley routes.

ST TUDYR. Nave and chancel with a bellcote over the chancel arch: entirely rebuilt by *J. W. Poundley* and *D. Walker* in 1864, in E.E. style, with plain trefoiled lancets. The w window is of four quatrefoils in plate tracery. Well proportioned nave with a scissor truss roof. Exemplarily light sanctuary. – MONU-MENT. Tooled brass plate from the old church, 1627, headed 'Iesus, Be My Iesus: The Epitaphe of Theodor Morgan which he made for himself a little before his Death', followed by nine heroic couplets.

(PEN-Y-BANC, $\frac{1}{2}$ m. ESE, was cruck-framed, but rebuilt in stone in the C17.)

PWLL-IWRCH, $\frac{1}{2}$ m. SE. The lower half of a cruck hall-house of *c.* 1480 within C17 and C19 additions, now restored. The (former) central truss has chamfered braces forming a pointed arch below the collar-beam, with a king-post above. The next (above the screen) has just a king-post and collar; the end one is box-framed. The timber partitions here are an exceptional survival; part of the post-and-panel screen and a blocked doorway are C15, and gave in to the lower (storeyed) room whose end wall had in-and-out boarding. A C17 central chimney replaces the open hearth, and there is also C17 wood-work.

CEFN COCH UCHAF, I m. NNE. Three pairs of crucks. The w couple are arch-braced and have two cusped struts in the apex – so they would have spanned the hall.

DERWENLAS

2 m. s of Machynlleth

Formerly a small river port on the Dovey estuary, with C19 ter-races.

GLANMERYN is an altered lobby-entry house. Over the fireplace in the former parlour the Griffith arms and supporters in plaster, much obscured. 1644.

RHIWLAS HALL. A small C18 double-pile house, much altered.

DEYTHEUR

2 m. SE of Llansantffraid-ym-Mechain

GWERN-Y-PANT PRESBYTERIAN CHAPEL. 1816. Whitened brick; two round-headed windows a side.

HEN DOMEN, ½ m. E. Motte only; the ditch is filled.

PLAS YN DINAS, ¾ m. W. A large moraine in a loop of the Vyrnwy, scarped in the C12 to make a castle on top with an area of 330 by 240 ft. This naturally defended position was still the llys of a manor in the C14.

TRE-WYLAN ISAF, 1 m. W. A timber-framed house with some early C18 brick, and two external chimneys on the lane. Brick BARN dated 1710, with a string-course. Stone quoins on the doorway and angles. CIL BRIDGE has been washed away.

COLLFRYN FARM, 1¼ m. SW. Two three-storey gabled sections, C18 and C19, one built against the other.

BANK, ¼ m. SE. Three bays and two-and-a-half storeys, with a thin, slightly projecting pedimented bay in the centre and chimneys at the ends. The typical Montgomeryshire farmhouse as rebuilt from c. 1800 on.

DOLANOG

ST JOHN. Nave and chancel, by *R. K. Penson*, 1853. E.E., with a similar roof to Pontrobert church, but more austere.

ANN GRIFFITHS MEMORIAL CHAPEL. 1903 by *C. Dickens-Lewis* of Shrewsbury. Buttressed front with pleasant Dec detail on porch, bellcote, and turrets. The furnishings are all gently Art Nouveau. Corbel heads of Ann Griffiths, David Davies, D. Roberts, and John Hughes. A chapel so sensitive to the Arts and Crafts movement is a rarity.

Dolanog lies in an exceedingly pretty stretch of the Vyrnwy valley. A bridge spans the river below the church beside a pool overhung with oaks, and a ford at the lower end of the village is crossed by stepping-stones near the attractive former corn- and fulling-mill. A scattered village; in the centre a well-designed new public lavatory in stone.

PLAS DOLANOG, ½ m. NW. A home of the Williams-Wynn family. Partly timber-framing dated 1664 and partly stone. Dressed stone chimneys set diagonally. A small stone dwelling on the r.

DOLWAR FACH, 1 m. N, was the home of the remarkable hymnologist Ann Griffiths (1776–1805). The house has been rebuilt since her lifetime.

DOLWAR HALL, 1¼ m. NNE. A long, low, cruck-framed house, externally of stone, except for a thin band of black-and-white. A central chimney with a stair beside it has been introduced between two of the couples.

LLYS Y CAWR – the Giant's Court – is the name of the defended top of Allt Dolanog (SJ 064 133), where the two ramparts, almost 10 ft high, may be well seen from the N.

DOLFOR

ST PAUL. A little buff brick single-chamber church with a three-sided apse, by *T. G. Newenham*, 1851. He made much use of terracotta, especially for the flamboyant tracery of the W window and S doorhead, and for various foliage hoodmould-stops and corbels, for example on the (now reduced) W belfry. Tall arch to the rib-vaulted sanctuary – chancels were not built for local churches of the 1840s and 50s. Delightful roof of scissor trusses above hammerbeams, supporting a secondary trellis of diagonal ribs springing from corbels and linked by collars between the trusses. The only horizontal lines are the boards beneath the slates.

SCHOOL. A pleasant-looking new school was built by *Herbert Carr*, County Architect, in 1953. It faces the red-brick school of 1866 by *W. White*.

GLOG. A steep, dramatic ridge SW of the village with nine earthen barrows on its high peaks. At the E end are two barrows, one obscured by a plantation; in the centre two very fine clay-capped mounds, one carefully sited on the topmost point and now crowned by a triangulation pillar. To the W the sharp ridges each appear to have an artificial mound built on them (some might be disputed – it is not always easy to distinguish between natural and artificial mounds). The westernmost barrow is the most dramatic and satisfying of the group, well shaped and dizzily sited above the precipitous drop at the end of the ridge. The E end of the ridge is cut off by a well preserved section of CROSS DYKE – a ditch between two banks, the larger bank on the E side. In the centre a number of early tracks run through the dyke, and this 'entrance' would appear to be original. The dyke ends at the N on the steep forested slope, and on the S it runs into a marshy area; both might be considered natural barriers, although it must be admitted that the purpose of these short dykes, whether defensive or simply demarcatory, is not fully understood. Nor is their date known with certainty; they are assumed to belong to the later centuries B.C. or the first millennium A.D., but there is no necessary connection with the larger and much more consistent Offa's Dyke.

TWO TUMPS (SO 117 850), two conspicuous Bronze Age barrows, were both excavated at the beginning of this century and provided evidence of burnt and unburnt burials; the cremation in the E barrow was contained in a large Food Vessel urn. A length of CROSS DYKE can be seen just to the W of them. Excavation of the barrow to the NE, on CAEBETIN HILL (SO 126 865), revealed evidence for a series of concentric stake circles beneath the mound. Such special arrangements predating the construction of the final stage of the monument may have been quite common.

DOLFORWYN   *1090*

½ m. NW of Abermule

DOLFORWYN CASTLE was the last of the native Welsh castles to be built. It stands on a ridge 400 ft above the Severn at Abermule. Llywelyn ap Gryffydd, Prince of Gwynedd, built the stone castle in 1273, probably to control the Prince of Powys, then his vassal. It was captured by the English (from Montgomery Castle) in 1277, and seized from Roger Mortimer III for the King in 1321. At this time the inventory included a round tower, square tower, chapel, hall, lady's chamber, pantry, buttery, kitchen, cellar, brewery, and bakehouse. It was a ruin by 1398. What remains now is scanty – a rectangular walled enclosure, 240 ft by 90 ft, with a projecting round tower at the NW. It has not been excavated. Deep rock-cut ditches protect either end. Platforms and banks along the ridge to the W are probably the site of the market town established there by Llywelyn ap Gryffydd.

DOLFORWYN HALL. The front is a nice piece of romantic Gothic of *c.* 1830, three bays, stucco, the door and windows with four-centred Gothic traceried heads under hoodmoulds. Quatrefoil section columns to the porch. The central bay has a flat embattled parapet. This part was built by John Pryce, vicar of Bettws Cedewain. Behind is the C17 timber-framed house, and behind this again an C18 wing with good woodwork details.

CASTELL FORWYN. By *Poundley & Walker*, and dated 1867. Of yellow brick.

ABERMULE. *See* p. 74.

DOLOBRAN *see* PONTROBERT

FFRIDD FALDWYN *see* MONTGOMERY

FOEL

(Garthbeibio parish)
1½ m. WNW of Llangadfan

ST TYDECHO. Above the village part of the medieval church remains inside a circular churchyard wall. Before restoration in 1862 it was longer to the E; the W and S walls of the unitary nave and chancel are still old. The reset E window is vestigially Perp: three lights below a transom. S sanctuary window also Perp, two-light and trefoiled. – FONT. Crude, octagonal; C15?

FORDEN

ST MICHAEL. Nave, N and S aisles, chancel, and SW tower by *Thomas Nicholson* of Hereford, 1867. Medium-sized, in yellow-grey Minera stone bonded with Red Grinshill sandstone, built to replace a small medieval single-chamber church on another site. Porch under the big-buttressed tower, where Coombe Down stone was used for carved work, as also for the E.E. capitals in the nave. Arcades of red and white stone. The chancel arch rests on green marble shafts placed on head-corbels. – REREDOS. Bath stone, designed by *Nicholson*, 1879; Trecento. – Fine brass LECTERN. – FONT. An oval marble bowl on an octagonal stem; dated 1794. – STAINED GLASS. E, three lights and tracery with an excellent St Michael and good colour, by *William Morris & Co.*, 1873. The middle scene is of the Adoration, the l. of Raphael. Three musician angels in the roundels. Three predella scenes also. It was made from cartoons by *Burne-Jones*.

LOWER MIN-Y-LLYN, I m. W. A motte 30 ft high and with an oval top 50 by 60 ft. Farm buildings occupy the supposed site of a bailey. Probably built by Roger Corbet of Caus and the Gorddwr districts at the time of the Domesday survey.

BRYN HYFRYD HOSPITAL, I m. SW. Built in 1794–5 by *Joseph Bromfield* as the House of Industry for the Montgomery and Welshpool districts. Brick, fifteen bays, with wings returning nine bays behind. It cost £12,000 and was to house up to one thousand persons. Males were to farm, females to knit, etc. In the Rev. E. Nicholson's words, 'a splendid receptacle of misery'. It was given up for a time *c.* 1840, and the folk, mostly children and the elderly, returned to their cottages and had their rents paid instead.

NANTCRIBBA GAER has been identified by C. J. Spurgeon as Gwyddgrwg Castle, thought to have been built in the border district of Gorddwr by Thomas Corbet of Caus, Salop, *c.* 1260, and destroyed by Gruffydd ap Gwenwynwyn in 1263. On a tall natural outcrop is a C13 ditched rectangular masonry enclosure, *c.* 130 ft by 110 ft. Remains of towers are visible on the W and S sides. In 1784 Pennant noted on this summit the ruins of a square structure 'with a round tower probably at each corner'. He also saw 'small square rooms with doorcases of good free stone'. The FARM beyond was built as part of the Leighton Hall estate.

HEN NANTCRIBBA seems to represent a C17 timber house with the W wing and S side rebuilt in stone in the C19, and with a tall shaped brick chimney abutted to the N.

NANTCRIBBA HALL. The hill-top site of the house of the Viscounts Hereford. Nothing of that remains from a fire *c.* 1900. John Ingleby's drawing (1796) shows a brick façade of three storeys and seven bays with a one-bay central break with a Venetian window. The house behind that was a William and Mary one, two storeys, cross windows, with a hipped roof and dormers. It was being built in brick 'according to a draught or plott drawing' by *Henry Pagett* of Bridgnorth in 1697, for Arthur Devereux. The present house comprises outbuildings that were not burned.

GUNLEY HALL, 2 m. E. Five-bay, two-storey stucco front of 1810 by *John Hiram Haycock*, with pediments over the windows and an Ionic porch, for Richard Pryce. This was the front of a Jacobean house removed in 1966. In the three bays added to the E in the same style in 1882 late C19 Arts and Crafts decoration. A reprehensible planning decision *c.* 1960 permitted the building of a bungalow directly to the l. of the façade. Behind this a panelled C18 WINEHOUSE, and a fine brick DOVECOT. STABLES behind to the r.

FORDEN GAER (SO 208 989). A large Roman cavalry fort built on low ground by the Severn which may be identified as the Lavobrinta of the Ravenna Cosmography. The fort was defended by a large clay and turf rampart which can still be clearly seen from the road. The defences never seem to have been revetted in stone although the fort appears to have had a long history and the discovery of some dressed sandstone in the interior suggests that the headquarters and even the barracks may have been of stone. The layout is unusual in that it has only two entrances, N and S.

FOURCROSSES

GOLDEN LION INN. Mid C18. Rendered brick front with big stone quoins, three bays and three storeys, with Venetian windows on the lower two.

GREENFIELDS. A brick house of c. 1860, four bays by three, with a Tuscan stone porch. Beside it a big brick WAREHOUSE of c. 1810 with cambered small-paned windows.

Beyond the site of Rhysnant Hall ($\frac{3}{4}$ m. SW) is the remains of a motte, RHYSNANT DOMEN.

FRON

2 m. SSW of Berriew

PROVIDENCE WESLEYAN CHAPEL. A small, plain red brick chapel of 1839, with two round-headed windows and a brick dentil course.

TAN-Y-FRON and the POST OFFICE possess one of Montgomeryshire's curiosities: Regency metal-framed casements. They are quite large, each with two mullions, a transom, many small panes, and intersecting Gothic pointed panes under the flat top.

THE RED HOUSE, $\frac{1}{2}$ m. SW, an L-plan close-studded farmhouse built round a central chimney, is early C17, though the date on the SE gable is indecipherable.

PENNANT, $\frac{3}{4}$ m. S.W. A red brick house of 1755. Five bays, with brick quoins on the ground-floor angles and on the wide middle bay. On the first floor pilaster strips are carried instead through the brick cornice up to the attic. Straight window heads. Staircase with one fluted and one twisted baluster to each tread. Other C18 details. Brick DOVECOTE and outbuildings behind.

GAER FAWR see GUILSFIELD

GARTH see GUILSFIELD

GARTHBEIBIO see FOEL

GARTHMYL

NAGS HEAD INN. A typical early C19 brick house, but with one-bay wings either side. It has the C19 metal Gothic-paned windows special to the locality.

GARTHMYL HALL. Two storeys and five bays; six bays deep. Dated on the shield in the pediment 1762. To an earlier brick front Major Gould (High Sheriff in 1864) added, to plans by *James K. Colling*, 1859, the stone quoins, windows, pediment and arms, and four-column Tuscan porch. The interior is entirely Victorian, with lavish Italianate plasterwork, a characteristic Ionic screen between the hall and stairs, and extensions behind. The large and ornate black-and-white house of the Johnes family still existed *c.* 1800.*

GLANSEVERN *see* BERRIEW

GLYN CLYWEDOG *see* LLANIDLOES

GREGYNOG *see* TREGYNON

GUILSFIELD/CEGIDFA

ST AELHAIARN. Nave, W tower, two-storey S porch, N and S 32 aisles, but no distinct chancel. Architecturally one of the richest medieval church interiors in the county, lavishly restored in 1877–9 by *G. E. Street*. The patron of the living then was Christ Church, Oxford, with Capt. D. H. Mytton contributing. The sturdy W tower of *c.* 1300 (see two windows) indicates the axis and width of the vanished C12/13 church to which it was abutted. The doorway to the nave has two hollow chamfers. Early Perp windows (of the early 1400s) in the bell-stage. Around 1400 the porch and S aisle were built on to this single-chamber church, with piers in line with its S wall. Some years after came the N arcade, well outside the former nave and with its arches out of alignment. The church was then extended by one chancel bay beyond the earlier choir to give four arcades of similar Dec piers. They are basically square-sectioned with bold wavy mouldings. The resulting chancel is off-centre. There are shafted corbel-heads on two nave piers, and the third pair from the W include short sections of wall, with a stair on the N for the rood loft. No chancel arch. The outer door jambs of the porch have quadrant mouldings like those of the

---

* I am grateful to Mrs Bromley-Way for her help on Garthmyl Hall.

aisles. The stoup is probably early C16. Inner doorway with two chamfers and no capitals; its inner frame is Perp. The door too is C15, with its original ironwork.

The clerestory, of Late Perp triplets, came in the early C16, when the roofs were raised from their early C15 level. These are excellent indeed. Three tiers of quatrefoiled wind-braces in the nave, with rather elegant cusped struts above the collars. A very fine Late Perp ceiling, ribbed and with bosses at the intersections painted red and white, covers the area E of the screen and one bay of the nave too. The aisles have lean-to roofs, still with much original timberwork and bracing from corbels on the columns. In the S aisle some carved bosses, e.g. a man with his tongue out. Also Perp are many of the windows – the S aisle E window with blank tracery between two lights (like the restored porch upper window), a S chancel window in Early Perp (like the tower's), a S aisle window with a four-centred head, a N aisle triplet with tracery. The tower was probably cased in masonry at this time. It was given a battered base and diagonal buttresses, raised a stage, and battlemented. Modern pinnacles and a short shingled spire. The model of the fabric before Street's restoration (at the back of the church) shows the exterior with seven dormers to light the S aisle gallery, and the higgledy-piggledy plan of the C18 pews. The elliptical W doorway to the N aisle has a studded door with the date 1737. A lean-to hearse house by the porch is dated 1739 and the room over the porch 1750.

Practically all the fittings and part of the roofs were renewed in Street's restoration and are successfully homogeneous. His designs include the E window (Dec for Perp) tracery; the REREDOS with statues of four Prophets on the l. and four Church Fathers on the r. and linenfold panelling; the carved ALTAR with frontal reliefs including a pelican and a phoenix, on steps of *Minton* tiles; the PARCLOSE SCREENS (in fact the nave screens of c. 1500 remodelled, but including some fine old heads with various wheel motifs in the traceries); and the tremendous Geometrical CHANCEL SCREEN with unrestrained wheel and ogee tracery, a reversal of Street's attitude to the style in late career. The S aisle screen again incorporates old work. – PULPIT with oak figures of the four Evangelists, also designed by Street. – Throughout, nice traceried Streetian PEW ENDS. – FONT. Octagonal, with two human and two beasts' heads alternating with blank sides. Symbolic motifs (a cross, an anchor) underneath the bowl beneath the blank sides.

C13? – STAINED GLASS. W by *Heaton, Butler & Bayne*, 1890.

MONUMENTS. In the chancel: William Edwards † 1780, by *Carline & Linell*. – In the S aisle: the Rev. Richard Mytton † 1828, chaplain of Barrackpore, Bengal, and to the Governor-General of India. White marble relief of a lady kneeling, book in hand, beside an urn inscribed VIVIT, and a melodramatic weeping willow. By *C. Smith*, London. – At the W end: John Owen and Thomas Lloyd † 1772, festoons on a shaped pink marble tablet, by *John Nelson* of Shrewsbury. – Rev. James and Rev. Juckes Egerton † 1772, also by *John Nelson*, but bigger and more rococo. Pink marble pyramid (made with matching veneers) on a shaped base, surmounted by a putto blowing a trumpet. Superimposed on this is a yellow marble plaque supporting a sarcophagus and mourning putto. – Brochwel Griffiths † 1742, again by *John Nelson* (but not so early?). Memorial as a piece of fabric tied at the corners. – Richard Mytton † 1801, by *G. Lewis*, Cheltenham. Female figure with a cross. – Devereux Mytton † 1841, by *G. Lewis*, to match, female figure with column and wreaths. – John Jones † 1854, by *J. H. Foley*, London, 1857. Group of three mourning ladies, still neo-classical, beside a casket with his profile in bas-relief. – In the N aisle: a beautifully lettered brass to Elizabeth Whittingham † 1678. – Rev. Charles Luxmoore † 1863, in a double canopy of E.E. shafts with crocketed arches. – Three late C18 BELLS by *Thomas Rudhall* of Gloucester.*

The little village is the most varied in the county, its compact centre now surrounded by many new small houses. There are also a number of buildings of interest within not much more than a mile. The W branch of the Montgomeryshire Canal was built a couple of miles up the valley, then abandoned. The old houses roughly follow round the circular churchyard wall. THE OAK, a farmhouse of *c*. 1630, has exposed timberwork typical of the period. The RED HOUSE is five-bay two-storey brick of *c*. 1770, a good English Georgian village type. Then PORCH COTTAGE, a row of mid C19 cottages with double lancet casements. TRAWSCOED HOUSE, facing the church, is a double-pile Late Georgian brick house with the central bay slightly projecting and four Venetian windows. It was built as a dower house. Down a lane to the r. is the RECTORY of *c*. 1823, beyond an avenue of limes, two storeys with a three-sided bay to the

* I am grateful to the Rev. J. L. Todd for his help on the church.

front. ONENWEN, a small cruck-built cottage, and CLEMATIS COTTAGE, with a semi-octagonal end and triple lancet casements of the early C19, are two of the prettiest. BOD ISSA beyond has been much interfered with. It is a C17 box-framed house with brick battlements and an early C18 brick wing with step-gables. TRAWSCOED LODGE, a charming cottage orné of c. 1810, stands at the end of the long drive to Trawscoed Hen. A modillioned cornice runs beneath the eaves of its hipped roof. Trellised veranda with roofs of the same pitch surrounding the ground floor.

TRAWSCOED HEN, 1 m. NW, was the home of the Lloyd family, one of whom built a substantial brick house on this isolated hill in 1771. It burned in 1858 and has recently been demolished, except for two small wings and the stable dated 1767. On the evidence of C19 watercolours the house was an attractive composition, the main part joined by triple blank arches to two-storey single-bay wings that formed a courtyard behind. These all remain, with stone string-courses at sill level and between the floors. Their smooth blocks in the style of Henry Holland are of some architectural quality, but the designer is not known. The central block stood in front on a basement with two curved flights of steps leading to the door. The façade was in three parts, the outer ones of three storeys and two bays with hipped roofs, the middle one projecting as a three-sided bay of two storeys with a balustrade on top. The STABLES are also brick with stone bands; the centre projects slightly and has a pediment and volutes beside. Why were they built before the house?

TRAWSCOED HALL, ½ m. WNW. Red brick Georgian on a hilltop, on the site of a house of 1583 built by the Hayward family. Small, unarticulated five-bay front with three bays breaking forward slightly beneath a pediment. The date here – 1777 – is the date of the house, not the 1771 on the rainwater heads, which come from Trawscoed Hen. Stone door frame with tapering pilasters and restrained Adamesque capitals, brackets, and frieze. A small room is panelled with late C16 wainscoting and some work of 1650 removed from Trawscoed Hen. Addition on the l. The DOVECOTE behind, with hipped roof and lantern, is of c. 1774.

BRONIARTH HALL, 1½ m. NW. A timber-framed early C17 house with a rebuilt brick front. At the r. end a strapwork-carved bressumer supported on corbels, beams carved with a rope motif, and herringbone timberwork in the gable. Moulded brick central chimney. Addition of *c.* 1700 to the l. An unusual interior feature is the upstairs passage straight through the middle of the house (cf. Trederwen House, Arddleen). Broniarth was the birthplace, about 1600, of George Griffiths, later Bishop of St Asaph, who was responsible for the Service of Baptism for those of Riper Years in the 1662 Prayer Book, and helped to prepare the Act of Uniformity.

LLYSWEN, 1½ m. NNE. Square-framed with a herringbone l. gable, extended in close-studding to the r. The good overhung porch is an addition of *c.* 1650. Its open sides have shaped balusters. Contemporary door. Corbels support a room above with moulded bressumer, quatrefoil timbering, angle-posts carved with ropes, and an oriel window. The bressumer of the gable is jettied out again, carved with spearheads, and is again on brackets. Original wood-mullioned window.

BRIDGE FARM, 1½ m. NE. Three cruck trusses (one pair is jointed). Square-framed walls, nogged with red brick.

FOLLY, 1 m. E. C17 type C timber house.

TRELYDAN HALL, ¾ m. SE. Large and much altered. A low timber wing to the w looks the earliest part; two overhangs in heavy C16 square framing. In the C17 it was made roughly E-plan close-studded, with some diagonals and chevrons on the two-storey porch projection. Its s wing has elaborate patterns of quadrants, ovals, and so on. On the E side again a variety of C17 timber patterns – lozenges, circles – and a three-sided timber projection at the end of the staircase wing. To the N a late C18 brick addition with ogee doorhead, to the s a further wing of Buttington brick, *c.* 1900, both painted black-and-white. Much C18 woodwork inside, including a good staircase.

The DOWER HOUSE stands at r. angles to the NW. It was built of brick *c.* 1700 and still has mullioned and transomed windows to the N; brick gable copings. The s front was rebuilt *c.* 1765 with five bays of sash-windows, a little projection, and a cupola (on the roof a clock whose weights hang in the hollow so formed).

GARTH, ½ m. SW. Demolished in 1946 – the saddest of Powys' recent losses.* House and stables were begun in 1809 by *John C. Loudon* for the Rev. Richard Mytton, on his return from Calcutta (see his memorial in Guilsfield church). This imaginative nabob's house was a square two-storeyed pavilion in a Perp-cum-Indian style, all slender diagonal buttresses and graceful crocketed spires. The smooth, rather bare walls were

* The National Monuments Record, London, has photographs.

faced with yellow-grey Darley Dale sandstone. Windows with flat ogee profiles. Merlons of Dutch-gable shape, with ball-finials. From the centre of the s the saloon projected – turreted, and with a vast traceried window above which the crenellation rose and fell. A veranda along this front was wrapped round the octagonal bows at either end. Though the detail is more bizarre, the inventive milieu seems close to S. P. Cockerell's Sezincote, Glos. In fact the executed house, costing nearly £100,000, was more imaginative than the one Loudon published in 1811 as a 'Mansion, Farmery and Stables calculated to form One Pile of Architecture'. But surely it is by Loudon, since it is so reminiscent of his (Turkish) Hope End, Herefordshire. The still flamboyant but prettier internal plasterwork ribbed vaulting (the *pièce de résistance* being the Islam-influenced octagonal canopy above the stairwell) seems to have been by another hand. Porden even? Loudon's stables were derived from Porden's Riding House at the Royal Pavilion, Brighton (1804–8) – they were circular, 84 ft in diameter, with triangular merlons, ogee windows again, and with an external covered passage (with cast-iron finials) all round, where horses – even carriages – could be exercised out of the rain. The loose-boxes etc. were arranged radially, like engine-berths in a round-house. This was built according to the published design. In John Ingleby's drawing (1796) the preceding house looks *c.* 1700, but had a tall three-window wing of *c.* 1780. Only the later c19 brick FARM survives. The arrangement is a huge three-sided courtyard, entered between barns at the top; at the ends of the arms are two cottages.

LOWER GARTH, 1 m s. Basically an early c17 house on a documented medieval site. Close-studded front of one build with an added two-storey timber porch, but always with the two little wings. c18 brick additions at the N and E. In one room a Jacobean wooden overmantel of diamond-faceted patterns, with tapering balusters, on pilasters, and early c18 panelling.

BROOK HOUSE, 1¼ m. s. A gabled wing jettied on moulded bressumers and with chevrons in the gable, with a large stone chimneystack behind, and a lower close-studded range; all c17.

BROOKLAND HALL SCHOOL, 1 m. ssw. Large, irregular mid-Victorian building of yellow brick. The detail is a mixture of Gothic (porch decoration) and French c16 (steep roofs and lots of tall chimneys). The plan however is quite symmetrical around a hall and a stairwell with a Tuscan screen. Later additions. By *W. H. Hill* of Shrewsbury, *c.* 1860.

GAER FAWR (SJ 224 130). A fine and potentially very interesting multivallate hillfort, unfortunately obscured by trees. It is a long, ridge-top contour fort reminiscent of Ffridd Faldwyn and probably with a similar history of changes and enlargement. The earliest fort enclosed 3 acres on the very top of the ridge, defined by scarped slopes rather than ramparts. The enlargement, more than doubling the size, was on the NW and must be later, for the new bank rampart can be seen to ride up over the earlier scarped slope. The enlarged area was defended by a double rampart and ditch which was further duplicated at either end where the entrances were placed.

CROWTHER'S CAMP (SJ 248 113) is now mutilated and overgrown, but it merits a mention because the famous GUILSFIELD HOARD was found only some 100 yds away, along the ridge to the S. This deposit of bronze weapons and tools, many showing influence from England (Wilburton Complex), dates from the Late Bronze Age and raises questions about the date of the earliest fortifications on hilltops such as these, which have been traditionally assigned to a later period (Iron Age). Recent excavations at the Breiddin have shown that some of the Montgomeryshire hillforts may be expected to go back into the Bronze Age.

GUNLEY HALL see FORDEN

HAUGHTON GRANGE see LLANDRINIO

HEN DOMEN   2090

The original Montgomery and the earliest recorded castle in the county, built by the Conqueror's kinsman Roger of Ste Foy de Montgomery (Calvados), Earl of Shrewsbury, between 1070 and 1074, to dominate the road into Mid Wales. On the death of Roger's son in 1131, Henry I granted the castle to Baldwin de Boulers. After c. 1216 it played little part in border struggles, but it continued in occupation at least to the late C13 as an outpost of the new castle. It consists of a motte and ditched bailey within an oval bank c. 380 by 280 ft. Excavations have disclosed that c. 1200 an apsidal timber chapel stood in the bailey, and there was a stout palisade on the banks. New layout of slighter buildings of c. 1223.

MONTGOMERY. See p. 163.

HENLLYS HALL see MANAFON

HIRNANT

ST ILLOG. Single-chamber with a W bellcote, prettily sited in its near-circular walled enclosure. The Roman Sarn Helen between Llanfyllin and Llangynog passes it on the W. The N wall with one- and two-light windows is late medieval; the remainder was rebuilt with rock-faced stone and odd W turrets by *Laurence Booth* of Manchester, 1886–92. He had some of the woodwork of the old church at Llanwddyn brought over (before it was submerged under Lake Vyrnwy), including some roof-trusses and the pulpit and altar rails, but not St Illog's C18 pews, now wainscoting in the sanctuary. – FONT. Circular. C13. – Six-branch C18 brass CANDELABRUM. – Small BRASSES to Lewis Jones † 1754, in a classical wooden frame; and to the Rev. John Humphreys † 1796.

The former VICARAGE was rebuilt in 1749, re-using C16 beams. Its appearance, apart from a hipped roof and quoins of 1819, is characterized by a giant Gothicizing arrow slit and reinstated matching Gothick windows.*

FOELORTHO, ¾ m. ESE. Cruck-framed house (one pair complete) on a stone platform at the head of the Brithyll valley, which is a typical medieval – and cruck house – site.

HYSSINGTON

ST ETHELDREDA. Rebuilt in 1875. Single-chamber with a W bellcote. – PULPIT. Early C17.

CASTLE HILL. Motte and bailey on a plateau on a small hill. Remains of a C13 tower 30 ft square. Indications of a hall have been found in the bailey.

HURDLEY HALL, 1 m. W. A box-framed Severn valley house of *c.* 1630 with its original chimney. The porch, which is dated as late as 1718, has close-set uprights and diagonals and is decorated with ropework, carved corbels, and a curious fertility(?) figure by the door.

GREAT BRITHDIR, ¾ m. NW. Dated 1695. Stone on a stone platform, with the original chimney and curly doorheads.

KERRY/CERI

ST MICHAEL. In a round churchyard. W tower, nave and chancel, N aisle and its own chancel, S porch. The stalwart

* I am grateful for information from Mr Donald Buttress.

tower, whose walls are of rough masonry 6 ft thick with no out- 30
side door, perhaps replaces a C12 predecessor. On the N a
primitive square stair-turret. The tower is much buttressed. It
has C14 ogee windows to the S and shouldered embrasures, and
a top stage added slightly wider than the rest, capped with a
two-tier wooden Montgomeryshire bell-stage. Then the development of the church from the inside. There are three 14
Romanesque round piers to the N of the nave with cushion capitals, and a respond several feet from the W wall; on the exterior
of the S wall, bases of three corresponding piers. Do these
represent the enlarging of a single nave to a basilica, and was
this the church whose rededication for St David's diocese is
described by Giraldus Cambrensis, Archdeacon of Brecon, in
1176?* The Norman work is of red sandstone. The N W respond
has a toothed band. The N E respond is half-octagonal in section,
with four two-step round arches, the inner chamfered with
mitre stops; but the last is askew, and the third pier from the
W has only half a capital, so it must be the E nave respond made
into a pier in the early C14. The chancel arcade of this date
follows the narrower line of the C12 chancel. Octagonal piers,
four double-chamfered round arches with two patterns of
moulded capitals and two rows of the English ballflower on the
middle one. The N aisle of the nave may have been re-formed
in the C15. The S aisle disappeared in the C17. The reset S doorway with quarter-round mouldings and the priest's doorway
with a half-round filleted moulding and a hood with headstops
are early C13. In the N chancel a Dec window in the N wall,
a restored intersecting E window, and a C14 PISCINA. The
main E window is Early Perp. Fine roofs of the C14 and later:
four arch-braced principals and one hammerbeam, with three
tiers of quatrefoils and arcaded wall-plate, over the nave; a
wagon roof over the chancel; and an open rib-and-boss canopy
over the sanctuary. In the N aisle, arch-braced principals with
foiled apex struts and two tiers of trefoiled wind-braces. Similar
roof over the N chancel, but at a lower pitch and without wind-
braces. The renovation of 1881–3, particularly thorough for
walls and windows, was begun by *G. E. Street* and carried on
after his death by *A. E. Street* and *A. W. Blomfield.* The walls
were wholly replaced in Llanymynech stone.

* Actually an amazingly unseemly to-do, since the Bishop of St Asaph was
only dissuaded from claiming the church for his own diocese by violence.
Giraldus pronounced his excommunication while his followers jangled the
bells.

FONT. Tall, Late Perp, and octagonal, with the Instruments of Christ's Passion carved on three facets. – SCREENS. Five lights and canopy, made at the restoration but made well. – A contemporary N parclose screen divides the choir from the organ and vestry. – PULPIT. Victorian, with fragments from the C15 screen. – LECTERN also of c. 1883, with a Welsh Bible of 1690 chained to it. – STAINED GLASS. E by *Kempe*, 1871. – MONUMENTS. Margaretta Herbert † 1838. Female figure with a book; a dove and light descending. – Harriet Lang † 1847. Two Gothic arches and canopy. – John Herbert † 1807, by *C. Lewis*. Mourning woman leaning on a broken pillar, the capital lying upturned beside. – Rev. John Catlyn † 1717. Slab with an angel crudely incised. – John Owen Herbert † 1821, by *Boobyer*, Bath. Draped urn above an oval tablet in a rectangle. – Richard Jones † 1788, a Royal Navy Purser who founded the Black Hall Institution. An elaborate memorial: two free-standing children, one reading and one writing, beside a yellow marble sarcophagus, with a bust of Jones on top – it cost £525. Superfluous details of the trustees' stewardship are inscribed below. – Two HATCHMENTS with the Herbert arms (N aisle).

KERRY MOAT, ¼ m. s. Motte and bailey castle of the second quarter of the C12. A small mound deeply ditched. Possibly built by Madoc ap Idnerth († 1140) as the caput of the Commote of Ceri. Until the C12 Kerry was part of Maelienydd (subsequently in Radnorshire).

TOMEN MADOC, ½ m. N. A large motte at 925 ft overlooking Kerry and the Severn valley.

DOLFORGAN HALL, ¼ m. NW. A former home of the Herbert family, built c. 1800. Possibly by *John Johnson*? Regency stuccoed house of two five-bay, three-storey façades. The E (entrance) front has a pair of exiguous full-height pilasters supporting urns above a parapet, a four-column Ionic porch, and a fan-lunette over the middle window. On the s side the ground storey projects slightly and the central three bays are screened by four Ionic columns *in antis*. Near the church are a pair of Regency Gothic LODGES to the former drive, built in 1818.

A stranger use of Gothic is the SAWMILL W of the church. At the E of the village a yellow brick SCHOOL by *J. W. Poundley*, 1868.

Just outside the village on flat fields beside the river (SO 150 902) are two enormous rounded mounds, said to be called BRYNAR and RIDDLE, which are most probably Bronze Age barrows, though some have doubted their artificial origin – perhaps because of their exceptional size. Nothing is known of anything found in them, though there are rumours that they have been 'opened'.

BRYNLLYWARCH SCHOOL, ½ m. SSE. The home of William Pugh (1783–1842), who financed the extension of the canal to Newtown, introduced power looms, and backed the Flannel Exchange and the graded, curling road to Llandrindod. Of his house on the S of the present fabric a stair with a little six-column screen on the landing, of 1829, survives. The enlargement of 1887 includes a grand staircase with perforated panels as balusters and a gallery on two storeys. Outside a Beaux-Arts ironwork veranda and second-floor loggia.

THE MOAT, ¼ m. S. Built in 1810–11 for the Rev. John Jenkins (Ifor Ceri) as the vicarage, for £890, at the time when Nash was Diocesan architect. The site was moved from a little lower to this position, consciously picturesque beneath the castle earthworks. Four bays and two storeys with small one-bay wings. Gothic windows throughout. Almost of the same date are the bow added to the r. wing and the arcaded veranda along the front. John Jenkins was a pioneer of the Eisteddfod.

MIDDLE CWMYDALFA, 1 m. SW. A Severn valley house of c. 1650 with a stone chimney added to the E. The cross-wing, whose rooms were wainscoted, has a stone reading G.E.H. 1736.

BLACK HALL, 1 m. SE. A five-bay mid C19 red brick rebuilding with two C19 iron bridges in the garden. Formerly the home of John Wilkes Poundley the architect.

GLANMULE, ¾ m. ENE, is a cruciform, gabled, and prettily bargeboarded cottage by *J. W. Poundley*.

KERRY POLE GROUP. Three of the four ridge-summit barrows in this group are rather badly obscured by forestry, but the small ditched barrow called Shenton's Tump (SO 158 862) and the stone circle (SO 157 860) can still be found easily from Kerry Pole. The ditch around SHENTON'S TUMP can be clearly seen. Although such ditches from which the mound material was obtained are common in England, they are rare in Wales, where burial mounds are normally built either from gathered stone or from turves stripped from a large surrounding area.

The STONE CIRCLE is set on sloping ground with wide views to the S, but the siting is unusual for monuments of this class.

The stones of the circle are all low but vary in bulk; one is duplicated. In the centre is a single large stone lying on its side, another unusual feature of this monument, although some other examples could be cited.

The four large barrows on Beacon Hill can be clearly seen on the s horizon.

KINGSWOOD
¾ m. NNE of Forden

2000

EDDERTON HALL. A villa of *c.* 1840 in its own park. Porch of two Tuscan columns *in antis* supporting an attic, between two two-storey curved bows. In the hall a screen of Doric columns with an arch, in front of the staircase in its curved rear projection.

At CILCEWYDD, 1 m. to the N, a mid C19 five-storey brick MILL with stone dressings, and a BRIDGE built by *R. K. Penson*, County Surveyor, *c.* 1861.

LAKE VYRNWY

9020

The reservoir supplies water to Liverpool down 70 miles of conduit, and also statutory compensation to the River Vyrnwy. Its DAM was the first large masonry dam to be built in Britain; the engineers were *Thomas Hawksley* and *George Frederick Deacon*. More facts: the works were begun in 1881 and the lake was filled from 1888; the dam is 84 ft high and holds back 13 million gallons of water which takes 48 hours to reach Liverpool, going via Oswestry and Tarporley, a drop of 550 ft; the total cost was more than £2 million. The dam is at its most dramatic when surplus water is running white down its sloping face. Small arches carrying a roadway along the top make a consciously arcadian view from the lake. The STRAINING TOWER, 1 m. to the N, a plum for students of C19 waterworks, is strikingly disguised as a stone fortress protected by a bridge. It is by *Deacon*, who also built the water tower on the aqueduct at Norton, Cheshire. Circular and machicolated, it has a stair-turret and a skyline of two copper spires with weathervanes, which all goes to intensify the Germanic feel of the conifer-grown lakeside. The LAKE VYRNWY HOTEL however is of no architectural merit.

LLANWDDYN. *See* p. 151.

LEIGHTON

HOLY TRINITY. By *W. H. Gee* of Liverpool, 1851–3. Nave, N and S aisles, SE octagonal chapel, colossal NW tower and stone broach-spire. 'A perfectly preserved and unaltered specimen of nouveau-riche-dom in the 1850s', Goodhart-Rendel remarked. There's a bit of everything outside – flying buttresses, flowing traceries, gargoyles on the tower, crockets on the spire. Actually the last is a splendid landmark in the Severn valley, which does something to redeem the brassiness of the Cefn stone exterior seen close to. The interior is unexpectedly small and rather splendid. *The Ecclesiologist* criticized it in 1855 because the pews which occupy the entire centre make the church awkward to use and spoil it aesthetically; and because where space for the sacraments and the choir is needed there is just a tiny presbytery. Now for the architecture. Two arcades of enriched quatrefoil pillars, tall pointed arches, clerestory, and very steep hammerbeam roof – with Dec tracery in the spandrels. Exceptionally tall moulded arch to the chancel, which has spiky wall arcading, a handsome E window, and a Perp but gabled rib and boss ceiling. – *Minton* TILES throughout. – STAINED GLASS. E and W in deep colours, by *Forrest & Bromley*. – MONUMENTS. The mausoleum to the SE, beyond the Naylor family pew in the S aisle, contains tablets to members of the Naylor family, and in the middle a not very accomplished statue of an angel by *Georgina Naylor*. Here is patronage by an enterprising family expressed as though they lived in the Middle Ages or the C18; the Victorian idiom available to them doesn't do so well. But taken together, Leighton church and Leighton Hall are a comprehensive document of a High Victorian's idealism, historicism, and belief in scientific progress.

LEIGHTON HALL. Built for John Naylor, High Sheriff in *c.* 1850–6. His wealth derived from the Leyland and Bullen Bank, Liverpool, and it was the otherwise little-known Liverpool architect, *W. H. Gee*, whom he commissioned to build the house and church. Naylor bought the Leighton estate in 1849 and set about developing it with the most advanced technology and at great cost. The large brick HOME FARM, halfway along a vista from the gardens to the church, was part of the most ambitious scheme. Small streams were channelled to drive a turbine there; and later a by-pass channel was cut for the Severn to drive a water-ram which pumped water to a huge tank (which still exists) on Moel-y-Mab, a spur of the Long Mountain. Raw materials were brought up by funicular railway to make liquid manure in the tank. This was then distributed round the farms in copper pipes. Naylor's own gasworks sent gas through pitched fibre pipes to the Hall, the home farm, and the church. Other estate buildings, including a poultry house, were also of brick. In addition to land improvement – drainage, sawmill, dairy – he planted evergreen woodlands, including California Redwoods, which are now managed by the Royal Forestry Society. The Leyland cypress was first grown here. The whole estate was broken up before the First World War.

THE HALL matches the scale of this landscape. Sited in front of an oak of good age and facing across to Powis Castle, it is in hard yellowish Cefn stone, Gothic, and arranged to give a continually shifting skyline when seen from the gardens. The house consists of a main block of 1851 facing W and N but also S and W to the gardens; a partly demolished courtyard of 1852; and beyond an amazingly tall eight-stage octagonal tower with projecting circular stairwell, of 1854–5. The entrance is by the W porch, which has a clockwork carillon by *J. Wagner* in the tower – a glorified musical box with interchangeable drums, to deafen visitors with a folk air or their national anthem. The interior of this porch is lavishly decorated with linenfold wood-work, a carved ceiling, and *Minton* tiles on the floor; to designs by *A. W. N. Pugin* and not unlike his interiors for the Houses of Parliament. The great hall following is gigantic, built for paintings, now dispersed, and for marble sculptures (by *Siddon* and *McBride*) now in the Walker Art Gallery, Liverpool. It dwarfs Pugin's fireplace and galleries, the frieze of Welsh family shields beneath its hammerbeam roof, and the iron chandeliers. The original L-shaped library on the r. has a quatrefoiled stone fireplace, also probably by Pugin. To the l. three rooms again by the Houses of Parliament team: the decoration is by *J. G. Crace* to Pugin's designs (in the Victoria and Albert Museum). The first two have carved alabaster fire-places and overmantels (inlaid with lapis lazuli), richly com-partmented ceilings with polychrome stencil painting, and gilt linenfold doors in battlemented frames. In the third the ceiling painting is simpler and in deeper colours, and there is a cornice of intricate open woodwork like the vernacular C15 screenwork. For some reason the house was never finished or fitted up. The cost of it all was £275,000, of which a good part must have gone to the GARDENS. These were laid out *c.* 1860 by *Edward*

86

Kemp, a pupil of Paxton. They are of many kinds, from woodland to formal, arranged as a number of set-pieces with pools
and stone sculptures linked by broad paths. A dry bridge leads
from the library garden and the tower across a hollow to the
main walk and over another bridge (carvings of creatures including an elephant). Below is a delightful figure of Icarus
falling headlong through the surface of a pond. At the end is
the view to the spire of the church, and another bridge leads
back to the house. The High Bridge (1858) is a lofty viaduct,
with a series of stone cascades made below it in 1874. At the
bottom of the funicular a summer-house was built. To a county
of the small in scale the superhuman size of everything here
is quite foreign. No other tycoon did the same.*

(LEIGHTON BRIDGE. Of iron, 1871.)

LLAN *see* LLANBRYNMAIR

LLANBRYNMAIR   *8000*

In the old village, now called 'Llan', 2 m. SW of the new.

ST MARY. A church of strongly rural character which has never
been tidied up by learned architects; moving to visit and beautifully positioned in a raised circular churchyard on top of a little
hill. Fabric and upland parish seem as one, and long may that
last. The church is a single chamber of C14/15 type, but with
a transept added to the N and a C16 S porch. Pyramidal W bell-
turret supported on oaken uprights built inside the church, as
at Tregynon; C17 perhaps. The nave has two C16 windows in
the S wall and the sanctuary two plain PISCINAS, the N with
a pointed head, the S with a rounded head. The nave is roofed
at the W with arched braces and at the E with king-posts on
collars. The N addition is post-Reformation and was once
boarded off as the school. Its two-bay arcade to the nave is
wooden and has a twelve-sided oak support for the beam; its
roofs are of queen-posts with massive tie-beams; its N window
is Late Perp, three-light, reset in 1688. Repair is the apt term
here, not restoration: roofs and gables 1748, the W gallery
removed and some windows replaced 1860 under the Rev. I. G.
Kirkham, and so on. Solid oak pews. – FONT. C13 circular bowl
on an octagonal stem. – STAINED GLASS. N, with coloured
interlaces, by *D. Evans & Sons*, 1860. – S, patterned glass of the

* Notes for the entry on Leighton Hall were kindly supplied by Dr J. D.
K. Lloyd, and I must thank Mr and Mrs Lee for their help.

same date. – MONUMENT. Anne Browne Russell † 1831.
Crocketed and canopied, with blank tracery; by *R. Brown*,
London.

PLAS ESGAIR, ½ m. N. Late C18 of three bays.

ST JOHN. 1868 by *Poundley & Walker* for the new village. Now
ruined.

HEN GAPEL, 1 m. SE. Side-door type, with a gallery on the usual
three sides. Much rebuilt – last in 1904. – STAINED GLASS.
Two windows by *A. L. Moore*, 1906. – The chapel was founded
in 1739 (a photograph inside shows a lean-to at Ty Mawr where
Nonconformist worship took place for about sixty-four years
before this date). Abraham Rees, the C18 encyclopedist, was
one son of the chapel house; another, Samuel Roberts,
was minister in 1834–57 at the peak of his career as a Radical.

TAFOLWERN, ½ m. W. The motte and bailey castle of Owain
Cyfeiliog, in a strong (and picturesque) place on a neck of land
at the confluence of Afon Twymyn and Afon Rhiw Saeson.
Owain was granted the Commote of Cyfeiliog in 1149, but the
first reference to this castle is to its capture in 1162. Owain's
son Gwenwynwyn was still occupying it after Henry II's invasion, and it is last mentioned in 1244.

PLAS RHIW SAESON, 1½ m. N, was the home of the Owen family
from the C11. The present fabric is L-shaped. The wing
parallel to the road is Georgian in character externally, but a
bedroom ceiling within has joists of *c.* 1600 counterchanged in
the ceiling compartments, as at Aberffrydlan, Llanwrin. The
wing towards the road is C17 but cased in boulder stone – work
of 1710 for Athelstan Owen, according to the arch-headed
plaque on the NE. At the join of the two wings is a post-and-
panel partition with shallow incised mouldings. It rises through
both storeys and has an original doorway in the centre of the
ground floor.

0080

LLANDINAM

ST LLONIO. The monastic church of a *clas* which had an abbot
till the late C13, and the mother church of Llanidloes and
Llanwnnog. As so often, the broad W tower is the earliest bit
of the present fabric surviving. It has a stair-turret projecting
like a clasping buttress on the NW angle, and a tiny C13 window.
Entry under it via the S porch. A tall arch with a roll-moulding
on engaged shafts, now on the inner side of the Perp S doorway,
was perhaps the C13 opening to the nave. The present larger

triple-chamfered tower arch is of the late C14. The nave, with a modern chancel arch, retains its medieval walling at the NE only: re-used dressed red sandstones from the Roman fort at Caersws. On the N sanctuary wall two sepulchral recesses, one with a hoodmould with label-stops, and on the S wall the PISCINA, are perhaps of the earlier C14. S nave on the earlier foundations, and formerly divided by a wooden arcade. In the late C18 the naves and aisle were roofed in one pitch (see the model in the church) and a gallery put in. In 1864–5 the fabric underwent a major remodelling by *George Edmund Street*; he replaced the arcade in stone and saved a few things from the dilapidations. The E and S walls and windows were remade in a C14 style together with the S arcade of one circular and two quatrefoil piers, and a new chancel arch. He also renewed the timber bell-stage with its uncharacteristically steep pyramid roof – for the region, that is, not for Street. – PEWS. The pew ends are of medieval oak cut to a curly silhouette; deeper seats have been made from the little ledges. – CHOIR STALLS with some C17 panels. – SCULPTURE. In the vestry, assembled as a reredos, five wooden panels – a Temptation relief (perhaps C16) and the symbols of the Evangelists (C17). On a sill beside them, a C16(?) grotesque ceiling boss of three faces sharing four eyes. It comes from Trefeglwys church. – FONTS. The Perp octagonal bowl, much mutilated, now with a modern cover by *Jonah Jones*, was set up by *Street* beside his Victorian one. – STAINED GLASS. E by *Clayton & Bell*, 1857, and good. – Vestry S, centre light with St Paul explaining the Gospel to Caratacus (*see* Cefn Carnedd, Caersws, by tradition his hillfort). – BELL of c. 1450.

PRESBYTERIAN CHURCH. 1872–3 by *Szlumper & Aldwinkle*, 96 an ornate chapel in an idiosyncratic C14 style. Large banded slate roof above gable dormers. The fine interior has two (later) E transepts and a wooden barrel-vault from which hang a pair of good ironwork chandeliers.

DAVID DAVIES' STATUE. By *Alfred Gilbert*, in bronze; a replica of the statue at Barry Docks. A sturdy figure of the Llandinam-born industrialist and contractor (1818–90) who substantially developed the railway system in South Wales, the coal-mines in the Upper Rhondda Valley, etc. It stands by the abutments he built for the new bridge over the Severn.

BRIDGE. The first iron bridge in the county: 1846 – a pretty, 82 single-carriageway, 90 ft span across the Severn. Designed by *Thomas Penson* the County Surveyor, and marked by the

makers, Hawarden Iron Works. The parapet railing more
Georgian than Gothic.

95 PLAS DINAM, ½ m. N. The home of David Davies' descendants,
but actually built for Capt. J. O. Crewe-Read, by *W. E.
Nesfield*, in 1873–4. The plan clearly divides into three portions, as though based on a medieval fabric: the tall gabled
porch wing with the stairs behind, the service wing l. of this,
and a deeper block of living rooms and bedrooms on the r.
One sees some stylistic correspondence with Leyswood in
Sussex on the irregular and exciting entrance front. Nesfield
and Norman Shaw were partners in 1866–9; work on Leyswood (the relevant part of which is demolished but is well
known from the 1868 perspective) began in 1866 and ended in
1871.* Plas Dinam is therefore a significant example of the
revival of the domestic building style of the Middle Ages. The
central feature is the oversailing timber storeys above the stone
porch, in which the door is deeply placed behind relieving
arches; they have pargetting and wood-framed leaded windows. The longitudinal spine of the house is lower to the l. than
to the r., and from it gabled wings and dormers project. It is
of stone with stone-framed windows on the ground floor, then
slate-hung with wooden windows. This treatment all round.
The hall on the r. has a characteristic large transomed oriel
with a lead parapet ornamented with 'pies'. Tall roofs of
pleasing small pale slates, amongst which finials of open ironwork and iron sunflowers appear. Dramatically tall chimney-
stacks of sharply ribbed red brick – yet another material; but
most were rebuilt by *E. S. Hall*, who used harder orange
pressed bricks instead of handmade ones. Hall extended the
house at r. angles to the N in 1926. His wing, of coursed stone
with the roof behind parapets, has a little tower at the join.
All the detail is less delicate than Nesfield's. The main hall has
a ribbed plaster ceiling – it curves forward directly from the
chimneybreast – with the Crewe-Read monogram, ships, sunflowers, etc. in the panels. In the dining room an overmantel
from Pertheirin, Llanwnnog.‡

BEECHCROFT and ASHDENE on the road below were built
c. 1900 as offices for Plas Dinam. Unobtrusively Arts-and-
Crafts.

LLANDINAM HALL, 1 m. N. Later C17 close stud with diamond framing on the first floor. Porch and a room over added

* See Andrew Saint, *Norman Shaw*, pp. 44–53.
‡ I must thank Lord and Lady Davies for their help on Plas Dinam.

in 1700. Made into a larger black-and-white group in the C19.

THE LITTLE HOUSE, 1 m. NW. A very small example of the regional timber house type, dated 1692.

BRONEIRION, ½ m. W. Built for David Davies in 1864. Five-bay faintly Italianate E front with the first storey of coursed stucco. An unimaginative building. By *David Walker*.

BERDDU BARN, 2 m. SW. Square-framed with four pairs of crucks, on a stone base. A good example.

BERTHDDU, 1½ m. S. Ashlar, of c. 1820, with Regency details. The W front is of three bays with two short wings, but the N side is asymmetrical (a shallow two-window bow), and so is the E side with the porch placed in the angle of a wing. Large but plain double returning staircase inside. (In the valley above Berthddu one finds a whole group of structures employing crucks. These are: GLYNFACH, 2½ m. SSW; GWERNGIG-FRAN, 2¾ m. SSW; BRYN COCH, 3 m. SSW, with five pairs of crucks; and GLYN-FEINIAN, 2 m. SSW, with two.)

LLANDRINIO   2010

This border parish lies either side of Offa's Dyke. Thomas Dinely noted in 1684 that 'the plain countrey towards Salop [is] inhabited by Saxons and Normans'.

ST TRUNIO (or ST PETER). Single-chamber with W tower steeple and S porch, in a three-acre churchyard. The first build is Norman, see the arch and two round piers immured in the outside of the N wall at the W end. As elsewhere, the material employed is red sandstone. The E end probably represents the C12 chancel, see the little N lancet. The slight discrepancy of its axis, visible outside both the N and S walls and inside on the N (where there is a fragment of carved stone), suggests that its walls were retained when the N aisle and the apse disappeared in a medieval rubble stone rebuilding. The S doorway is Norman too; no sign of a S aisle. Three-light E window with reticulated tracery. The S chancel window – Perp, of three lights – served as model for new nave windows in 1859. The roof is still ceiled. The W gallery, enlarged in 1829, remains; of the 1829 restoration also the W wall of coursed stones and the pyramid-roofed bell-turret. – FONT. Deep circular stone carved with blank arches and columns linked again at the bottom. The arches have linked hoods and the columns ring/annular capitals. Late Norman. – PULPIT. Good, Jacobean. – READING

DESK. Jacobean in style, the railing dated 1689. – COMMUNION RAILS. Turned balusters alternating with pegs; C17. – Oak REREDOS made in 1891, with some C17 carvings in the middle. – EARLY CHRISTIAN CROSS, in the porch – a fragment with two bands of interlace. C10? – MONUMENT. Archdeacon Thomas † 1916; the historian of the Diocese of St Asaph.

YR HENBLAS, formerly the rectory, s of the churchyard. A long C17 timber-framed house, cased in brick in the C18 and much altered. Five bays and three storeys. A library was added by *Thomas Penson* in 1848. Guto'r Glyn, in a mid C15 *cywydd* to the rectory of the priest, Sion Mechain, describes a stone-built hall, roofed with tiles, 'with nine rooms', surrounded by a moat with a bridge and gateway.

NEW HALL, opposite the church on the N, is a four-bay red brick farmhouse. The stairs and parlour dragon-beams suggest a late C17 date, with an attic floor raised in the C18.

74 LLANDRINIO BRIDGE, over the Severn, 1775. Is it by *John Gwynn* of Shrewsbury? A humped narrow roadway, 132 ft across, yet a most graceful line when seen from the bank. Ashlar. Three semicircular arches of pink sandstone, pointed, and rusticated voussoirs, with triangular cutwaters with ball-finials placed against pilaster strips, which join with the parapet. Rather Baroque compared with the near-level roadways achieved by Rennie only a few years later.

DOMEN CASTELL. A motte and bailey almost totally obliterated in the building of a flood embankment on the N bank of the Severn, near the bridge.

HAUGHTON GRANGE, I m. NE. Something of a rarity – brick used in the late C17 for a house otherwise in the vernacular timber tradition. The brick was made locally of course and used for the prestige part of the house, the porch. Here in fact there are two porches, and they are most odd – very low, with the usual rooms above, and then shaped brick gables. The l. one also has two urns of sorts. Brick dentil course all along the front.

CALCOTT HALL, 1¼ m. NNW. Built *c.* 1725. An early Georgian house – a type that is rare in Montgomeryshire. It is three bays square, of two storeys, with a tall hipped roof. Above the attics an octagonal look-out tower – which might be an addition of *c.* 1800, like the strange, large stone-coped ogee pediment and the very big tripartite windows. The detail of the original house is more conventional – just stone quoins and a brick string.

Interior with fanlight doorheads. Fine contemporary newel stair at the back with bulgy turned balusters.

DOMGAY, $1\frac{1}{2}$ m. NNW. Two restored C17 cottages remain; the timber-framed Hall has been demolished.

POST OFFICE, $\frac{3}{4}$ m. WNW. C18 red brick; it has a little pedimented door grouped with two sash-windows under one beam.

LLANDRINIO HALL, $\frac{1}{2}$ m. WNW. A sizeable house of c. 1670, of Caroline type, in deep red brick,* at the end of an avenue of poplars and beeches. It is H-plan with two tall chimneys either side external to the walls. Originally with two, three, two windows in front: the present fenestration (apart from one mullioned and transomed window at the back) is of c. 1790, five tripartite windows with flat brick arches above plaster fan heads. The door surround is thin fluted Doric half-columns and a quatrefoiled entablature. Thermal lunettes in the attics and the deep-eaves roof complete the remodelling of the C17 hipped roof. Inside are two original late C17 staircases: in the l. wing a large stairwell with strongly moulded rails and solid reel-turned balusters; in the r. wing a smaller stair also with turned balusters. In the farm to the W a brick MALTHOUSE with a date 1798 (on a stopped beam).

LLANDYSILIO

$\frac{1}{2}$ m. N of Fourcrosses

ST TYSILIO. In the old circular churchyard an entirely new church‡ of 1867–8 by *G. E. Street* for the Rev. Waldegrave Brewster. Nave with N aisle, chancel, S timber porch, and a round NW tower with a conical cap to the belfry. It cost only £2,400. The exterior is conscientiously 'Middle Pointed', or E.E. to Early Dec, in greenish Welshpool stone with Cefn stone dressings. The interior is ornate and equally successful. N arcade of four tall pointed arches on round piers, and a cusped arch in the N chancel wall to the organ chamber. Nave roof of traditional C15 type. Some excellent furnishings. – REREDOS in Caen stone, by *T. Earp.* – Circular stone PULPIT. – Stone CANCELLI, wrought-iron LECTERN, ALTAR TABLE and RAILS, CANDELABRA, STALLS, etc., are all to *Street*'s designs. – STAINED GLASS. E, three-light in white borders, with the date 1868, made by *Clayton & Bell* and designed by *Street*. – Nave S, a three-light window of Christ walking on the sea

---

* Since this was written the house has been rendered.

‡ The previous church had chancel and nave with a tall timber belfry.

(a memorial to young sailors lost in the China Sea), 1879 by *Powell's*. – w paired lancets, small panels of prophets and saints by *Clayton & Bell*, 1868. – N by *Curtis Ward & Hughes*, 1898. – BRASS (w wall). Mary Eyton † 1674, plate engraved with heroic couplets, and with classical decoration by *Sylvanus Crue* of Wrexham. – Tablet to the Lloyd family, dated 1779. – By the door an C18 pillar SUNDIAL.

On the s edge of the churchyard is the former NATIONAL SCHOOL, with a Dec quatrefoiled window-head and a three-light C17 window from the old church set in the walls.

LLANDYSSIL

ST TYSSIL. By *T. H. Wyatt*, 1863–6, on a new site, at a cost of £3,000. Nave, N aisle, chancel, sw tower and spire. Plate tracery. Big pretentious interior with polished red granite columns and red and white stone arches, Caen stone REREDOS, and bright *Maw* chancel TILES. *Archaeologia Cambrensis* called it 'larger and more medievally correct, but of a style which has no prototype amongst, nor any connection with, the ancient ecclesiastical buildings of the district'. That is quite correct. £400 would have restored the medieval church.

OLD ST TYSSIL, higher on the hillside, now consists only of a stone porch with an C18 doorway standing in the churchyard. The single-chamber medieval parish church had the normal series of vernacular builds. It had also the most elaborate of the Montgomeryshire timber w bell-turrets, with an open gallery corbelled out from the supporting framework built inside the nave.

SCHOOL, opposite the new church. Perhaps by *T. H. Wyatt*. Panelled with woodwork from the old church's box pews.

Nearby a small green with early C19 houses.

RECTORY. Built *c.* 1800–10. Front of four bays, the centre two recessed; one bay added to the l. As in other Regency rectories, the hipped roof is low-pitched and has deep eaves. Later C19 dripmoulds above the windows, and a railway-age iron veranda with circles in the spandrels of the arcade.

PHIPPS'S TENEMENT, ¼ m. E. Two tiny box-framed former almshouses dated 1630, with their own barn at r. angles to the r.

LOWER BRYNTALCH, 1 m. WNW. Early C19 brick farmhouse with a pedimental projection.

LLANERCHYDOL *see* WELSHPOOL

LLANERFYL   0000

St Erfyl. In a raised circular churchyard reached through a lychgate of 1843. Rebuilt in 1870 by *Edward Haycock Junior* in rough blue stone with red Shelvocke sandstone dressings. The principal remnants of the old church are the six arch-braced trusses of the roof with their cusped apex struts and cusped wind-braces; they look early – *c.* 1400 perhaps. Modern chancel roof. – FONT. Late Perp, octagonal, the under-facets of the bowl carved with Tudor leaves. – SHRINE or wooden niche for two statues. Late C15. It is of two narrow bays with septifoil heads, traceried spandrels, and a cresting of battlements and pinnacles. – RELIQUARY. Shaped like a little chapel, with one- and two-light trefoiled windows and roughly made with cut-out gables. Also mid or late C15. It would have held a casket for processions. These two unusual objects survived plastered into the vestry wall. – Some interesting doctrinal PANELS dated 1727 from the gallery front also survive. They are painted in oil with texts and rather weak illustrations of Christ's Baptism and Crucifixion, Moses, St Paul, and the War in Heaven. – STAINED GLASS. W by *Done & Davies* of Shrewsbury. – An EARLY CHRISTIAN GRAVESTONE was found beneath the large yew. The Latin inscription reads: HIC (IN) TUM-(U)LO IA/CIT R(U)STE/ECE FILIA PA/TERNINI AN(N)I(S) XIII IN PA(CE). It is dated to the late C5 or early C6.

Llyssun, ¼ m. NE. Rebuilt after a fire in 1961. In the C17 a home of Lord Herbert of Chirbury; in the C16 the squire was another poet, Bedo Gwyn. Just below on the flats by the Banwy is a small C12 MOTTE AND BAILEY castle.

LLANFAIR CAEREINION   1000

St Mary. In a large churchyard overhanging the River Banwy, in whose SE corner is the stone-spired Presbyterian church. St Mary was granted by the Bishop of St Asaph in 1239 to the Cistercian nunnery at Llanllugan. The only evidence of the church existing at this time may be the fine S doorway, if it belongs to this building. It has two orders of triple shafts, the outer with a filleted middle shaft and rings above the bases, which are of cushion type. Capitals carved with rings and inverted fleurs-de-lys with bands passing from shaft to shaft

under billets. Above square thin abaci the order is continued as roll-mouldings to a pointed arch. The capitals are transitional from Norman to E.E. and comparable with those on the slype archway at Valle Crucis Abbey, which was founded in 1201. Otherwise the church is an uninteresting rebuild by *Edward Haycock Junior* of 1868. It consists of a nave – with four C15 arch-braced trusses and their foiled apex braces and wind-braces from the old one – and chancel in one, with a lean-to N aisle with round piers to the nave. The old church had a N aisle of equal length – or a double nave. Its separate wooden W tower has been replaced by a sturdy stone one at the SW angle of the nave, by *A. E. Lloyd Oswell*, 1884. – FONT. Monolithic, octagonal, *c.* 1300. – STAINED GLASS. E by *Ward & Hughes*; S by *Clayton & Bell*; cathedral glass by *Done & Davies*. –
33 MONUMENTS. In the sanctuary the recumbent effigy of Dafydd ap Gruffydd Fychan, a knight in armour, *c.* 1400. The detail of the armour is well preserved and has been described by Mr Colin Gresham. – David Davis † 1790, by *John Nelson*, ingenuously inscribed, 'He directed that Six-pence should be given to every Poor Person attending his Funeral, at which one thousand and thirty were present, and received Sixpence each.'
The town was a place of craftsmen – particularly in the cottage weaving industry in the C18 – but it is known better to the holiday public for its LIGHT RAILWAY. This line ran to Welshpool from 1903 to 1956, and in 1963 was reopened for tourists as far as Sylfaen. Of the old agricultural centre there is little now to be seen but the street plan; still, the situation of its small C19 houses perched above the river is a lovely one. In MARKET SQUARE there was a customary market. From the C18 the BLACK LION INN partially remains, but the central stone TOWN HALL, a nice late C18 building with an open ground floor two arches by four, and then a schoolroom and cupola above, was demolished *c.* 1890. Going up past the church, the houses are timber-framed but refronted, the WYNNSTAY HOTEL contains a late C17 stair, and the C18 brick SPINNING WHEEL also still has cobbles outside. The L turn from the square leads to the three-storey, three-bay front of the VICARAGE. The blank arch and pedimental gable are characteristic of the date: 1801. MOUNT HALL, further up the hill, is a neat Liverpool villa of 1873 with paired and triplet window frames in red and yellow banded stone and good E.E.-style carving on capitals. Asymmetrical planning, but bows, gables, chimneys end in counterpoise. Returning towards the

river, passing C19 weavers' housing with minute back court-yards, one finds on the l. the LLANFAIR INSTITUTE, built in 1922 by Lord Davies. The architect was, possibly, *F. H. Shayler*. It is an Arts and Crafts building and rather eclectic – stone tower with hooded casements, a black and white block with gables and dormers partly pargetted with vines. The BRIDGE was rebuilt in 1971, in stone but with ugly railings. Cottages and old chapel and millhouse make another pleasing if frail group around it.

EITHINOG HALL, 1¼ m. NE. Front section brick, of five by three bays and two storeys, with a hipped roof; *c.* 1870.

NEUADD LLWYD, ¾ m. N. A C17 timber-framed house, close studding below, then a course of diagonals, and box-framing on top. On a stone base. In good condition. Post-and-panel partitions inside.

GARTHLLWYD, 1 m. NNW. Three-bay front with cambered windows and a third floor added in the C19. C18 staircase with turned balusters.

BRYN GLAS, 2 m. NW. A Regency front range above the average. In the projecting wings are large tripartite windows with pointed Gothic traceried heads; in the centre a porch with an ogival window over. Central hall with an elegant stair with qua-trefoils on the risers. Panelling in the room to the l.

GIBBET HILL ROMAN FORTLET (SJ 106 044) is very well preserved, with a sharply defined turf rampart and a clear entrance on the E side. Excavation revealed that it had never been completed and had been left with neither palisade nor gate.

CYFRONYDD. *See* p. 97.

LLANFECHAIN

1020

The village spreads loosely round the large raised churchyard, and has evidently been a place of settlement from early times. It has acquired a pleasing variety of houses. The church is dedicated to St Garmon, as are some half-dozen others in North Wales. Garmon is now thought to have been a missionary from the Isle of Man and not the C5 Bishop of Auxerre, sent to confute the heresy of Pelagius. Llanfechain was the birthplace (in 1761) of the poet and antiquary Gwallter Mechain.

ST GARMON. Single-chamber, with a shingled W flèche and a S porch. In some respects the most complete Norman church remaining to Montgomeryshire, and at the same time a good example of *John Douglas*'s ecclesiastical work. The overall effect of his slender wooden spire and red-tiled roof on the low stone walls is strikingly Germanic. The late C12 church is a simple rectangle with three deeply splayed E windows – one square – above two round-headed ones. It had two S doors: the priest's (blocked), chamfered and with a semicircular hood, and the present S doorway with rounded jambs and a roll-moulding on the arch. Capitals but no bases. Chamfered dripmould on stops. In 1883 *Douglas & Fordham* stripped the masonry of plaster inside. The two-light windows are replacements of 1859 by the earlier restorer, *R. K. Penson*, who also rebuilt the W wall and gave it a wheel-window. It seems there was a W bell-turret which Penson rebuilt, and that Douglas altered this. The nave has a fine C15 roof of arch-braced principals with foiled struts in the apex and bicusped wind-braces. Over the choir Douglas erected a wagon ceiling with six bays of blank tracery. The timber porch is C17. – FURNISHINGS. STOUP by the priest's door. – FONT. Of *c.* 1500. Octagonal, the stem tapering and trefoiled, the bowl also with sloping sides: each has a rose in a quatrefoiled circle. – PULPIT. Pentagonal and carved with classical ornament. Dated 1636. Lit by a dormer. – Much of the WOODWORK is *Douglas*'s, 1883, and Perp to Tudor in style. Admirably simple STALLS. The SCREEN is of residual local type, with a wide ogee doorway and two sorts of heads in the compartments. Calvary crosses and Tudor cresting. The REREDOS of 1890 was designed by Douglas and carved by *Griffiths* of Chester. – MONUMENT. T. Evans † 1826, by *J. Carline*, Shrewsbury.

DOMEN CASTELL. Motte and bailey behind The Mount.

At the C17 and Regency farm also called Domen Castell is a good brick CORN BARN of the first half of the C18. On this far side of the road too is TY COCH, a restored C15 house with three cruck trusses, and the usual C17 conversion of central chimney with stair beside and post-and-panel partition opposite. In the crescent round the churchyard wall and beyond are a number of black-and-white houses, the best preserved PLAS-YN-DINAS INN, which might be of *c.* 1600, with later stairs. Later buildings beyond the Cain, and to the l. the RECTORY, superficially the work of the Rev. Madocks Williams, who also gave £416 for R. K. Penson's work on the church. For him *Edward Hodkinson* added the W rooms and faced the house in Ruabon brick; but the core of the house and the staircase are 1736, and older.

PENTRE. A cruck-built house of the late C16 preserving, after its conversion to type C, a number of old fittings, and Jacobean stairs. The best external feature is the elaborate and tall stone chimneystack with its zigzag-section ornament all round. Stone also replacing timber in the walls.

BODYNFOEL HALL, ¾ m. W, is a neo-Jacobean gabled stone house of 1846.

BODYNFOEL FARMHOUSE, ¾ m. NW, the former home of the Trevor family, is a rare example of the English pattern of a manor house of the late C17. The front has two projecting wings and is seven bays in all and two storeys high. Brick with flush stone quoins, and a stone string-course. All roofs are hipped. Broad central chimney. Cambered windows and still some cross frames; five dormers. Quite handsome. The interior is much changed, but there is an C18 fireplace with quatrefoil frieze, and the original staircase. Its upper two flights have turned balusters, while the lower, to the cellar and well, has fret-cut ones.

LLANFIHANGEL-YNG-NGWYNFA   0010

ST MICHAEL (in the Winds). A near-round churchyard at almost 1,000 ft. The old church was demolished c. 1862 (at a cost of £9 10s 6d) and replaced with the present one by *Benjamin Lay* of Welshpool. Nave and chancel with paired lancets, narrow chancel arch, and scissors truss roof. C19 panelling at the W, with C16 painted shields of arms formerly on the Llwydiarth pew. Only three stones carved with CROSSES, in the vestry, survive from earlier: a four circle cross of the early C14; a cross raguly of c. 1340, inscribed in Lombardic capitals X HIC IACET MAD(OC) AP KELYNNINE (Madog ap Celynin, ancestor to the Vaughans of Llwydiarth); and a fragment of another cross raguly.

OLD RECTORY. C17, modernized (with a long iron veranda) c. 1840.

LLWYNDERW, 1½ m. NE. Timber-framed, and dated 1583 on the dentilled bressumer. Much altered.

LLANFYLLIN   1010

One of the six market towns of Montgomeryshire, Llanfyllin received its charter from Llewelyn ap Gruffydd in 1294. It has the character of places either side of the border, and the branch railway line down the Cain valley to Oswestry emphasized its position as a regional centre. Maltings and tanneries thrived. What is noteworthy architecturally about the town is the quality and quantity of buildings in brick (bricks were made here) – the earliest which can be approximately dated is the church of *c.* 1710. The loss of Llwyn and the brick Town Hall recently, and of the Old Rectory, together with the ill-advised painting of frontages, are changing the rich red look of an area that would be one of the most suitable for constructive conservation. This is all the more lamentable since Powys possesses so few C18 buildings, so few good built-up spaces.

69 ST MYLLIN. A big embattled church without a separate chancel, of Llanfyllin-made red brick with stone dressings, replaced the old nave and chancel sometimes after 1706. The weathered triangular-pedimented doorway between the two easternmost of the five s windows and the diminutive crocketed pinnacles on the corners are of this date. Round-headed window frames, all renewed, the s ones in Norman. Brick w tower, totally plain, but for diagonal buttresses and small-paned windows. Six bells made by *Abraham Rudhall* were set up in it in 1714. Attached to the N of the nave the girls' schoolroom of 1826; it has six pretty Regency windows still. Boys were taught in the Town Hall. The churchyard was partly cleared of memorials in 1972; a pity, but it has gained in amenity. An C18 baluster sundial stands by the s door.

The entry under the deep C18 gallery is to a plain hall-church with a coved ceiling. On the gallery front are parish benefaction boards of the early C18 giving details of amounts raised to build the new church (£1,030) and of local education in 1720. The improvement or restoration here is in a sort of Norman, *c.* 1863 – a late date – and the architect was *Walter Scott* of Birkenhead. A sanctuary was formed by inserting three arches with dogtooth ornament, the centre much broader than the sides. The short N aisle (occupying part of the schoolroom) is divided by a similar two-arch arcade. Two E windows with attached shafts. Normanizing furnishings in keeping: two-decker PULPIT and reading desk with blank arcading, ALTAR RAILS with varied capitals. – COMMUNION TABLE. 1744. – Wainscoting of the early C18 from the rectory has been re-erected in the sanctuary. – STAINED GLASS. E, three roundels by *Clutterbuck*, 1857. – Chancel, N by *Heaton, Butler & Bayne*, 1903; s by *Smith & Taylor*, 1859. – Nave s by *Alexander Gibbs*, 1839.

PENDREF CONGREGATIONAL CHAPEL is said to be the oldest Welsh independent church in the county; Vavasour Powell was its first minister, in 1640. Built in 1708 and destroyed by Jacobites in 1715, it was re-erected at government expense. The present building, of 1829, has a classical side elevation to the road, four windows and cornice; the pressed-brick door frames are a C20 addition. C19 interior of little interest.

WESLEYAN CHURCH. By *Shayler & Ridge*, 1904, in a Wrenaissance style.

The TOWN HALL of 1789 by *John Yenn* was demolished *c.* 1960. It replaced a timber hall (burned 1775) on the square where the war memorial now is, and was a delightful building with arches below for the market and a room 45 ft by 20 ft for the petty sessions etc. over. It had a hipped roof.

The streets of this compact small town have sustained qualities of townscape. HIGH STREET is graced with plenty of undisturbed C18 and C19 detail, to be seen at its modest prettiest by the church in bows, window frames, and doorways, particularly at No. 24. The COUNCIL HOUSE has a pleasant C18 pedimented doorway, and a C19 shop-front attached: C18 stairs within lead the visitor to an upper room decorated with thirteen mural paintings – strange neo-classical mountainscapes in blue and ochre, peopled with figures, bridges, and ruins. They are by Captain *Augerau*, a French officer held prisoner here in the Napoleonic Wars, who later married the Rector's daughter; only such a story could explain this urban theatricality in gentle green Wales in 1812/13. The POST OFFICE, tall late C18 red brick with iron-railed steps and a modillioned shop-window, is alive with late C18 near-Gothic windows including two versions of the Venetian form. The little SQUARE has more C19 plaster fronts.

NARROW STREET – the former main street – leads to the r. into VINE SQUARE. Here stands the best house in Llanfyllin, the MANOR HOUSE, with a very English five-bay, two-storey Early Georgian front of local brick dated 1737: segmental windows and stone keys and quoins. Staircase, doors, and panelling in a bedroom are contemporary. Early C17 features behind and two rows of old dormers in the roof. Above is the HALL, with an elaborate porch and Tudor windows with lozenge panes. This is work of 1830–2; all that remains of the historic C16 Hall is the central chimney and stacks, and the beam dated 1599 set over the door. The third side of the square was the site before its demolition in 1957 of the RECTORY, a hipped-roofed Queen

Anne house with mullioned and transomed windows and a step-gabled Jacobean wing of 1851 along the road. At the top of MARKET STREET is BROOKSIDE, C19, with plaster fan-fluting in the cambered window heads, and opposite the Gothic stone-fronted CALVINISTIC METHODIST CHAPEL of 1857 by *Thomas G. Williams*. The broad section of the HIGH STREET s of the Square, once used for cock fights, has considerable amenity value as a meeting place and so on. Its changes of level and its trees keep the informality of a village. The CAIN VALLEY HOTEL on the l. has a handsome brick front of *c.* 1800, now painted, of seven bays and three storeys, with a Tuscan porch. Inside, a late C17 staircase with roughly carved newel posts and fret-cut balusters. The Regency façade facing it, also garishly painted at the time of writing, has fan-plasterwork in the window heads, too. The porched EAGLE CAFÉ and the irregular group of ABEL HOUSE are both painted black and white. Gabled houses follow with dormers – a feature of Llanfyllin's skyline. Where the raised terrace of houses, one dated 1820, begins, there is a taller counterpart in the Regency BACHIE PLACE. At the s of the town is the gabled OLD PEOPLE'S HOME of 1972 and a SCHOOL of 1853 forbiddingly inscribed, ' "Take fast hold of instruction, she is thy life" – Solomon'; below them the bargeboarded former railway station.

LLANFYLLIN HIGH SCHOOL has occupied the site since 1946. Further buildings were added by *Herbert Carr* (County Architect) in 1955, but they are not among his best or most sympathetically arranged.

LLWYN, the nearer of the two large houses of Llanfyllin, was begun *c.* 1710. The plain brick front is seven bays wide and three storeys high. The drawing room was made in 1759, and its plaster ceiling is the best of the period in the county – a circular floral garland and four Rococo cartouches with trophies of musical instruments and a few bars from Handel's 'Messiah' in the corners. The overmantel is similarly enriched. By *T. F. Pritchard*? A fine Georgian stair with turned balusters rises through all three storeys.*

BODFACH, the home of the Kyffin family, in its own park beyond a C19 cruciform lodge, was rebuilt in 1661. Bell Lloyd was the owner in the C18 and rebuilt in 1767. During Thomas Pennant's visit in 1781, Moses Griffith drew a hipped-roof block and barn. The Gothic COACH HOUSE is probably the second of these,

---

* Demolished in 1975. The plasterwork is a real loss.

quoined and hipped-roofed, and with an ogee cupola and ogee windows in the pedimented blocked arch beneath. Bell Lloyd's small house itself survives in details, particularly the Georgian staircase, within a larger house of c. 1870. The park he created also remains. (His son, who became Lord Mostyn, is said to have planted 171,000 trees on the estate.) The exterior now is largely Victorian Italianate, five bays by five, with a Tuscan porch and triglyph-and-metope frieze. The contemporary interior decoration consists of a two-column screen in the hall, a weird later fireplace, and some plasterwork in the drawing room and elsewhere.

THE MEADOWS (formerly POOR LAW UNION), ½ m. SE. The union of twenty parishes was formed in 1837, and this workhouse (1838), for 250 persons, was built by *Thomas Penson*, the County Surveyor. The plan is as usual basically cruciform; but three of the wings radiating from the octagonal centre branch again to form four courts, those to the SE being three-sided only. The main elevation, to the NW, has a certain grandeur as a composition. Blank arcading is a motif all along the middle block and the two wings either side; in addition the middle block has seven bays of round-headed windows on the upper floor and Venetian windows in projections on the lower. Beyond this the three-storey centre can be seen, with its cupola above. In this it seems to belong more to the C18 tradition of public works.

Up the valley of the Fyllon to the NW are a number of vernacular buildings.

(GLANFEIGLO, 1½ m. WNW, has five pairs of crucks intact enclosing small rooms at either end of a hall. Central truss with cusped struts. Half-hipped gables.)

ABERNAINT, 1¾ m. NW. A brick house dated 1700, very early for the locality and apparently on the tried timber model with overhanging porch and gables, and so without concessions to the new material employed. Or is it just a casing of a C17 house?

(BODYDDAN-ISAF, 1¾ m. NW. Three cruck trusses.)

CORNORION FAWR, 2¼ m. NW. An Early Georgian brick block, dated 1729, added to a timber-framed house. It has stringcourses, cambered windows, and a stair with sturdy balusters.

RHOSFAWR, 2¾ m. WNW. A three-unit rectangular hall-house perhaps of the C15, complete and unchanged since it became a barn in the C17. The gable trusses are crucks, as is the arch-braced central one in the hall. Those of the dais partition, and of the open partition dividing off the large lower room (possibly byre?), are box frames. Walls of square framing including the internal partitions. Entry and dais doorways with slightly cambered lintels. Like the barn alongside, it is downhill-sited (cf. Old Rhydycarw, Trefeglwys).

LLANGADFAN

9010

ST CADFAN.* An early C19 LYCHGATE with a stone arch stands like the trees on the margin of a circular raised enclosure, now enlarged. The church walls have been roughcast and the roof is still ceiled, so all that can be told of the fabric is that it is probably basically C15 (if not earlier), with a Perp E window of three lights with seven tracery lights and with its original roof. Stoup by the S door. Restorers in 1867 replaced the other windows, added a square W bell-turret, and divided the unitary nave and chancel with a meagre arch. – STAINED GLASS by *Wailes*.

CANN OFFICE HOTEL of the early C19 was a stage for the mails. Behind are remains of a MOTTE AND BAILEY castle, on a bend of the river Banwy.

ABERNODWYDD has been re-erected at the Welsh Folk Museum, St Fagans. A small square-framed hall (now thatched again), apparently converted to a storeyed house in the C17, it demonstrates the insertion of floors, a framed central chimney between a narrow parlour, and a bigger kitchen with two small rooms partitioned beyond this.

LLANGURIG

9070

ST CURIG. The site of a *clas* (or Celtic monastery) founded by Curig, who died on 17 February 550, and from *c.* 1180 controlled by the Cistercian Abbey of Strata Florida, Cardiganshire. In a circular raised churchyard on the N bank of the headwater of the Wye, at *c.* 900 ft. W tower, nave and chancel, N aisle and chancel. The broad tower, with its NE stair-turret, has diagonal buttresses, a wide voussoired W doorway, and a Perp W window, all C15 features, like the dripcourse and the low battered base. The upper parts – window tracery, battlements, and embattled turret – are restoration by *Sir George Gilbert Scott* and *Arthur Baker*, 1877/8. The nave and the rest are slightly off axis with the tower; the explanation may be that the tower is basically C12, like Guilsfield's, but refaced in the Perp

* Cadfan was founder of the church at Tywyn, Merioneth, and first abbot of the monastery on Bardsey Island *c.* 604.

period, and that the nave is late medieval. The three arches to the N aisle and the chancel arch are totally undecorated but probably of the C15. But, excepting the SE angle of the chancel, the Perp E window, the late C15 tracery reset in the vestry, and a nave window, the fabric appears to have been thoroughly remade by the restorers. The N aisle is now under a single pitch of roof with the nave and lit by semi-dormers; the N chancel arcade is in a C15 style; and the roofs – hammerbeams with queer winged angels – are barrel-ceiled in the nave and arch-braced in the chancel. J. Y. W. Lloyd of Clochfaen gave £11,000 towards the work and added a spire. – The SCREEN was made in 1878 from drawings done in 1828 by John Parker of the beautiful late C15 screen which was dismantled in 1834. It has ten bays of foliate and traceried heads and the typical geometrical doorhead. As a conscious attempt at reconstruction it can be compared with fragments of the original at Glansevern, Berriew, and a piece of foliage trail set in the cornice here. – FONT. Perp, octagonal, with two paired trefoil panels a side. – Chancel fittings in the Bodley style, presumably by *Baker*. – STAINED GLASS. Ten faded windows by *Burlison & Grylls*, 1878. The subjects include the life of St Curig, and Lloyd family heraldry. – LYCHGATE with depressed ogee beams, dated 1740.

The exposed village has no other old buildings to show, but it does have a distant breath of Arts and Crafts in the charming lettering on the fountain, 1898, in the tile-hung pub, and in the stone former police station of 1907.

CLOCHFAEN, ¾ m. s. Rebuilt with half-timbering in 1915, by *William G. Drew*. (Turned woodwork in a former hall looks a bit like Comper.)

(TY MAWR, 2 m. w, is cruck-framed; the central truss is arch-braced.)

(RHYD-YR-ONEN, 2 m. NE. A motte and ditches on a site defended by two streams, like Tafolwern, Llanbrynmair. A mid-C12 Welsh castle.)

LLANGYNOG

The working of lead and slate gave rise to this small village at the head of the Tanat valley, but a long time ago. The lead mines on Craig Rhiwarth were discovered in 1692, and in the early C18 a 90 yd vein of almost pure galena yielded great riches to the owners of Powis Castle. The workings were mostly discontinued after forty years, but traces remain on the r., 1 m. up Cwm Rhiwarth. Slate-quarrying flourished *c.* 1775. Thereafter the road over the Berwyns to the Dee Valley was improved. Llangynog was the terminus of the Tanat valley railway from Oswestry which ran from 1904 to 1960.

ST CYNOG. In a small raised circular churchyard. Single-chamber, apparently rebuilt in 1791–2 (blocked N window), and greatly renovated in 1894. The long quoins in the walls may have been re-used from the medieval church. The roof pitch and all the fittings are C19. – MONUMENT. Elizabeth Griffiths, erected 1815. Slate relief with ogee arch and scrolled pediment. – In the vestry, a slab with the Lord's Prayer and an angel, painted in oil; early C19.

NEW INN. Dated 1751.

TAN Y GRAIG, ½ m. E, is the ruin of a stone-built type B house with a tall central chimney and a kitchen added behind it, formed from a cruck-framed, arch-braced C15 hall-house.

(LLWYN ONN, 1¼ m. E. A five-bay cruck hall with an arch-braced central truss. It still has its cruck-framed two-door dais partition, and a one-door passage partition. C17 and C19 alterations.)

PENNANT MALANGELL and PENYBONTFAWR. See pp. 180, 184.

CRAIG RHIWARTH HILLFORT (SJ 055 271). A spectacular hilltop site overlooking the Tanat valley and the peneplain of the Berwyn moorland. Easiest access is from the B4391, passing the remains of early mines on the way up to a narrow original entrance on the NW. Inside the stone rampart there is evidence for upwards of 150 small round huts, mostly sited on the sunny S terraces. They may be recognized either as low walls or as levelled platforms. On the very top is an unusually broad ring which may be an earlier, Bronze Age monument. Medieval *hafodau* can be seen in the E half of the site. The stone huts at Craig Rhiwarth (which have been said to be natural features) are unique in this part of Wales, where wood was normally used. However, excavation is showing that other high-altitude forts were also occupied on a presumably permanent basis and were not simply refuges in times of war.

LLANGYNYW

2 m. NE of Llanfair Caereinion

ST CYNYW. A white-painted single-chamber church, secluded

on a beautiful south-facing hillside, in a partly raised church-yard. Wide, low C15 nave, welcomely intact, and a roof still ceiled. Perp s doorway and a splendid C15 timber porch: corner posts and post-and-panel walls support the arch-braced roof with its cusped wind-braces; oak seats and a cobbled floor. Several Perp windows, the E of three lights with tracery, the chancel s and nave w of two lights. C19 GALLERY, pews, and bellcote. Old pews used as a wainscot. – FONT. Octagonal, Perp, with a Tudor rose. – The SCREEN survives nearly complete, but not so the loft. John Parker drew it unmutilated in 1839. Crossley dated the tracery to the third quarter of the C15, but the pomegranate pattern on the E side of the head-beam to 1500. The beam and central arch remain, and ten narrower tracery heads with the muntins cut off just below. They are of five patterns, two of Herefordshire type (one is of C19 iron, cast at Mathraval forge). The central tracery has a triangular motif and drop-cresting similar to work at Llanwnnog and at Llandefalle (B). The tracery head now between the gallery piers belonged to the w doorway of the screen under the loft; it has a crossed-diagonal motif. – MONUMENT. Canon David Evans † 1787, by *John Nelson* of Shrewsbury. Upright oval and fronds beneath a pediment.

TY MAWR. At the end of a courtyard of timber farm buildings. Square-framed externally, with internal box-frame construction. Signs of the dais canopy remain. Later chimney with two moulded stone stacks. A beam carved with a horse beyond the fireplace. Corbel-posts in the former hall support deep-chamfered beams for an upper floor, which is lit by three dormers with patterned timberwork. Perhaps a C15 house altered to type C *c.* 1600.

LLANIDLOES

9080

In 1280 Llanidloes, which previously had no more than an old-established church, received a market charter from the King (granted to Owain de la Pole) and the benefit of Edwardian town planning and earthwork defences. The present-day street plan follows the C13 grid unashamedly. The defences were earth banks from the confluence of the Clywedog and along Brook Street on the N, beyond High Street on the E, and along Mount Street on the S; and then the river on the W. Its greatest prosperity since the C13 came *c.* 1800–50 from weaving. The population rose to 4,000. The railway to Newtown was opened in 1859 and closed in 1962. About 1860–80 there was a boom at the lead-mines at Van. Llanidloes can boast of the highest dam in Britain (237 ft) holding back the Clywedog reservoir (3 m. NW), which regulates the flow of the Severn. It lost borough status only in 1974. It remains one of the nicest towns in Wales.*

ST IDLOES. W tower, nave and N aisle, S porch. The beautiful early C13 arcade from Cwmhir Abbey in Radnorshire, and the fine roofs erected at its reconstruction in 1542, make this church unusually interesting. Of building before that date there is only the rugged tower and the S nave wall. The late C14 tower has walls of large stones 7 ft thick, a batter at the base, a NE stair-turret, an Early Perp W doorway, and two string-courses. Inside at belfry level a rare rib-vault with random slate infill; in its centre is the opening for raising (C14?) bells. A tall and broad voussoir arch opens to the nave. At the top, a two-tier pyramidal timber bell-stage. Priest's doorway in the S wall, ingeniously blocked. The wall was much rebuilt in 1816. The E.E. S doorway, of c. 1225 or earlier and also brought from Cwmhir, has two roll-mouldings which continue on the oddly flat arch (was it restyled to look Perp?). Splay with widely spaced filleted shafts and knobbly stiff-leaf capitals. The E wall of this single-chamber church was somewhat short of the present one; its uncusped, Late Perp window is now in the E wall of the N aisle.

The ARCADE was set up from the E, where the (then un-buttressed) respond has leaned out. The line is slightly wide of the earlier N wall, and the fifth arch had to be rebuilt narrower than the others, to fit with the tower. One wonders why the spacing was not measured first. The base heights of the piers are uneven; the last two to the E are higher than the rest, which indicates the position of the former raised sanctuary. This splendidly solemn arcade is part of the fourteen-bay aisled nave of the Cistercian church at Abbey Cwmhir (R) some 10 m. SW across the hills. There is no doubt that the material was carted away after the Dissolution, and re-erected in slightly jumbled order at Llanidloes. The Grinshill stone piers are formed of eight groups of three shafts each, the middle one filleted – twenty-four in all – applied on square piers set diagonally (cf. Strata Marcella). The responds have one triplet only and four larger shafts like those of the S doorway. Arches with roll-

* Mr C. E. V. Owen generously gave me much help and information on Llanidloes and its neighbouring houses.

mouldings to the nave, but chamfers only to the aisle, where the outer step is defective all along. The system is that one filleted and one plain roll rise from each cluster of pier shafts, except on the longitudinal angles, where three rolls rise, all filleted.

The stiff-leaf carvings of the round CAPITALS – one to each [19] triplet of shafts – are instructive examples of the development of this quintessential E.E. decoration. The masons for the reconstruction clearly did not distinguish between the six or more patterns at their disposal. Besides the benefits of classification, there is in addition the inferential information the capitals can give concerning the progress of the nave at Cwmhir Abbey. Of the earliest type (c. 1190?) seem to be the two, almost variants of the water-leaf form, on the third pier from the E (N side). On the same pier three capitals show the genesis of stiff-leaf: bunches of four shapes, basically the C12 trumpets, are at the very point of metamorphosis when from the l. a hesitant spray of leaflets pops out. If this type is of c. 1200, then so perhaps are the two sorts of fleur-de-lys designs. These are of flowers, one to a shaft, either beneath a band with a wavy line, or with their tops extended like a crenellation. Examples occur muddled together on all the piers. On the third pier from the E again (SE side) is another indecisive kind, two capitals with wavy patterns meshed behind stalks. That leaves the true stiff-leaf, richly curled on the E respond, in two rows on the first pier, with more on the fourth pier and on the W respond, where the heads droop and are most deeply undercut. The evolution from Transitional to the fully achieved style probably implies nearly a generation in time; Cwmhir's nave would therefore appear to be building by c. 1190 and still in progress c. 1215.

The magnificent ROOF is the most elaborate in the county. [48] Hammerbeams on carved spandrel-pieces support curved ribs and principals, forming a sort of airy tunnel-vault. The framing is all delicately moulded. This type of roof often dates from the C15 (e.g. in East Anglia); but there is no real reason to doubt the date 1542 (on the ninth shield from the NE) and prefer the account that it is originally Abbey Cwmhir's and replaced a stone vault there after a fire. The corbels are odd masonry bits including stiff-leaf from Cwmhir. The base of each bracket is carved, with an archer, grotesque heads, etc. Winged angels holding shields of many shapes are fixed to each hammerbeam; those over the former chancel are charged with the Instruments of the Passion. It is a pity they cannot be seen more easily. Who,

one wonders, proposed this double embellishment? The three
E bays of the roof, together with the chancel, which acts as buttress to the arcade and has a good E window reproduced from
the original Perp, were added to designs by *G. E. Street* in the
restoration of 1880–2, when the other windows were renewed. –
The flamboyant REREDOS panelling was made in 1900 to designs by Street's son, *A. E. Street*. – LADY CHAPEL SCREEN
designed by *Bernard Miller*, 1956. – FONT. Perp, octagonal,
with circled quatrefoil sides and panelled underfaces. –
FUNERAL HELM, perhaps of a Lloyd of Berthllwyd. –
STAINED GLASS. E by *Clayton & Bell*, 1882; S, the True Vine,
1933, to the original designs by *Clayton & Bell*; two N aisle
windows by *Burlison & Grylls*, and two by *Geoffrey Webb*. –
Outside the porch the C18 pedestal of a churchyard SUNDIAL,
once frequent locally.

97 SION UNITED REFORMED CHURCH. 1878 by *John Humphreys* of Swansea; a notable chapel, based on his Tabernacle
Chapel in Swansea of 1872. It occupies one burgage plot of
the C13 town plan, and is dramatically placed at its far end.
Three-bay façade with semicircular upper windows. Portico of
four unfluted Composite columns on bases. The capitals lie
below their heads but carry an arcade over them. Above this a
powerful pediment, sadly lacking its cimatium. The fine,
varnished pine interior contains segmental raked seating. The
gallery, continuous round all four sides, has a parapet with an
openwork band and holds the splendid organ above the pulpit.
It cost only £1,550.

BAPTIST CHAPEL. 1876. Two-storey front with giant pilasters.
Inside there is a U-gallery, and an arch flanked by pilasters
behind the pulpit.

CALVINISTIC METHODIST CHAPEL. Large and with a florid
façade of contrasting stonework. Slate-hung on two sides.
Single-storey portico on the front. Interior with a U-gallery and
the pulpit and organ designed together, and with panelled plasterwork on the ceiling.

55 MARKET HALL. Built *c.* 1600 at the main cross-roads of the C13
town plan. The only timber-framed market hall surviving in
Wales, and not indicative of superflous wealth. Low, open, two-
by-five-bay ground storey with a cobbled floor. Post-and-pan
upper chamber, originally used for the assizes and now the local
museum, supported on segmental arches. No ornament. The
S wall has been replaced in stone, and the N in brick dated
1765. Weathervane on the octagonal lantern dated 1738. The

block of stone at the NW corner served John Wesley as a pulpit. A Historic Buildings Council restoration.

NEW MARKET HALL. *See* below.

TOWN HALL. By *Shayler & Ridge*, 1908. Cefn stone. Of five bays and, like the Market Hall, with a lantern. Open-arcaded ground floor, one bay deep, screened by wrought-iron gates. Ashlar-faced, with mullioned and transomed windows, and a charming Art Nouveau ironwork central balcony. The building is an important, though decently unobtrusive, element of the townscape.

HIGH SCHOOL and JUNIOR SCHOOL. *See* p. 144.

PERAMBULATION. Starting at the three-arched LONG BRIDGE of 1826 over the Severn, in VICTORIA AVENUE are weavers' terraces of brick and a mill of the same period. The houses are double-fronted, i.e. the front doors of separate but addorsed houses open to the street and to a back alley. LONG BRIDGE STREET leads up into the C13 town. Modest C19 terraces, with timber-framing still in use till *c.* 1840, give the town most of its character. This shopping street sports a lion on the Red Lion Hotel and shop-fronts of the 1890s at the end by the Market Hall. In SHORT BRIDGE STREET on the r. CASTLE HOUSE, 1789, has a five-bay front and a C19 Doric porch. Short Bridge was built *c.* 1850. GREAT OAK STREET on the l. from the cross-roads is the main street. In it, the TREWYTHEN ARMS HOTEL, a five-bay, three-storey house of *c.* 1770. Fine portal with four fluted Doric columns and an entablature, an addition of *c.* 1900? Elegant original stair and plaster ceiling in the hall. Next to it is the NEW MARKET HALL of 1838, originally of five bays on a rusticated stucco base. Characteristic neat C19 terraces at the top and in HIGH STREET; but Nos. 43–44 is a C17 regional house. Straight ahead above CAMBRIAN PLACE is a handsome red brick building of eleven bays and two storeys with quoins and round-headed first-floor windows, built in 1864 as the STATION and HEAD OFFICE for three railway companies, including the over-ambitious Manchester & Milford line. Two wings on the entrance side, and a central bow to the platform. Turning r. at the end of High Street the untidily planned MOUNT STREET leads past two weaving mills of *c.* 1840* and the COMMUNITY CENTRE (1962 by *Herbert Carr*) and HEALTH CENTRE (1974 by *Merfyn H. Roberts*, County Architect). These two are built on the levelled bailey of the C12 CASTLE. Llanidloes Mount, which stood

* One recently demolished.

behind the Mount Inn, seems (like Newtown Hall Moat) to
have had a large low motte, 100 ft across the top but only
10 ft high, apparently built much later than the others, to
defend the newly founded borough. Passing between the
Mount Inn and PERLLANDY (a good C17 survival), one meets
China Street coming from the Market Hall, and following l. one
enters SMITHFIELD STREET, broad again and avenued, but
added to the town only in 1826. Terraces and a stone
NATIONAL SCHOOL of 1845. The modern town has spread
further along the Llangurig road, where there is the GARDEN
SUBURB, neat pre-World-War-I houses by *T. Alwyn Lloyd*,
and opposite, the spreading layout of the HIGH SCHOOL and
JUNIOR SCHOOL, 1953–5 and both on the same campus, again
by *Herbert Carr*, the former County Architect. The odd detail
is less utilitarian than at his other schools. Conceptually it
belongs to the modern movement (areas of glass mostly exceed
areas of brick); yet in some ways it looks back to classical elevations, and that individuality is perhaps the shortcoming even
in this, his most expensive project.

DOL-LLYS (Old People's Home), ¾ m. NE. An irregularly
planned two-storey stucco Regency house of *c.* 1810. Tall windows with four-centred heads. The rooms in the two main
curved projections have more elaborate windows. The plan
goes with the Picturesque Villa type, as does the mixture of
Gothic in the quatrefoil piers of the veranda and a vaulted
plaster ceiling, with the simple classical plasterwork in the
drawing room.

(MOUNT SEVERN, ¾ m. SW. A straightforward front of 1827
with a central semi-octagonal two-storey bow and one bay
either side.)

GLYN CLYWEDOG, 2 m. NW, apparently a C17 gatehouse made
into a dwelling-house, is unique among Montgomeryshire
timber buildings. The lower part is of stone, the upper parts
of timber; second quarter of the C17? Single-storeyed, with
originally three large dormers and chimneys at the ends. The
bay and dormer on the l. were added *c.* 1900. A round stone
arch leads to the brick-paved gate passage, with its close-stud
walls and timber arch at the end – itself blocked with timber-
framing. But there is no sign of the manor house beyond. An
C18 stair with turned balusters has been added to the rear
beside a panelled parlour; C17 wainscoting upstairs shows that
this l. side was already the dwelling part of the house.

LLYN CLYWEDOG DAM, 3¼ m. NW. Begun in 1964 by *Sir William Halcrow & Partners*. The dam is 237 ft high, the tallest mass of concrete in Britain. The scheme was primarily to regulate flooding and drought on the Severn for the benefit of many large towns near its lower reaches, but it incidentally provides water locally and is used for recreation. It consists of eleven hollow buttresses, curving downstream at the crest, with stepped spillways between. The hollow buttresses create an astounding spectacle inside, as their vaults soar higher than any cathedral's.

BRYN TAIL LEAD MINE, at the foot of the dam, is in DOE guardianship. The late C19 works include tanks and ovens for processing barytes.

PEN Y GAER (SN 908 869) above the Clywedog reservoir is one of only three stone-walled forts in Montgomeryshire. A single wall at least 12 ft thick encircles the top of the hill, with an entrance on the s, where one end of the wall turns inwards and the other out to create a narrow, oblique passage. Recent damage and clearance have revealed the wall face in several places.

Across the valley is another small hillfort, PEN Y CLUN (SN 926 875), with an earthen rampart around its three weaker sides. The entrance is on the w, where there is a deep ditch and the defences are strongest. The entrance is quite complex: the N arm of the rampart is split to provide cover for a crooked entry passage, which is set askew to the overlapped entrance through a much weaker outer bank which seems only to have existed on the w. The E side of the hill has been damaged by miners prospecting for lead.

DINAS (SN 906 891), an unusual, perhaps unfinished, hillfort above the Clywedog reservoir, is set on the sloping N side of the hill. The E side is steep, and there is little need for extra defence; on the w the scarp and ditch are discontinuous and do not join the only well defined defensive line, a curving rampart clasping the N end of the hill. Outside this N line there may have been a further bank and ditch, since this is the weakest side of the hill. It has been suggested that this unfinished fortification represents the last stand of the British chieftain, Caratacus, against the Romans. Tacitus' account makes it clear that this hurriedly constructed defence was somewhere in Mid Wales, but some have preferred more prestigious sites such as the Breiddin or Cefn Carnedd.

LLANLLUGAN

3 m. NW of Tregynon

A small Cistercian nunnery existed in this remote village from before 1188 until the Dissolution. Its founder was Maredudd ap Rhotpert, and it was supervised by Strata Florida. Even its site is now uncertain, but there is a suitable meadow by the River Rhiw.

ST MARY. An undivided rectangle, with a S porch, in a roundish churchyard. Much is in its C15 state, though the boulder walls could be older than that. The appearance of the masonry is spoiled by over-pointing. S doorway with flat and hollow chamfers continuous to the apex; blocked S priest's doorway with an elliptical head cut from a single stone. The fenestration is Perp – a three-light E window with panel tracery and two-light S windows. Small cusped N window within a blocked doorway with a pointed arch of tumbled voussoirs. Roof of C14/15 type – arched principals with cusped apex braces, and two tiers of cusped wind-braces; also tie-beams in alternate bays, the easternmost one having apparently been cut to admit the E window. Was the church longer once, then? Restoration in 1873. – FONT. Of c. 1200, deep and circular, cut to an octagon at the base. Slender eagle for a stoup. – STAINED GLASS. E, assembled in 1891: three lights with a Crucifixion, a king, and an abbess, of c. 1500 – part was once dated 1453.

GWERNFYDA, 1 m. SW. A long, possibly C15, box-framed hall-house. The hall has ceiling beams of c. 1600, an oaken partition opposite the fire (with space for a seat?), and a big beam over the fireplace carved with a Crucifixion and a hound chasing a stag, a dove, and a dragon. This is thought to have come from the nunnery.

ADFA. *See* p. 75.

LLANLLWCHAIARN

Essentially a rural parish, but its S boundary is the Severn, so it takes in part of 'greater Newtown', including Penygloddfa and the (filled-in) canal basin. Here the Shrewsbury stained-glass-maker David Evans was born in 1793.

ST LLWCHAIARN. Rebuilt on the old site in brick in 1815 (for £1,200).* Brick-quoined nave and pinnacled W tower. Dec chancel by *R. J. Withers*, 1865. The Regency nave, gothicized

* The previous church had chancel, nave, and W bell-turret.

in 1869, has C18 wainscoting from Welshpool church. – REREDOS with Gothic tracery from Welshpool church. – GLASS. Nave S by *Morris & Co.*, *c.* 1870. Full-length figures of St Stephen and St Peter; and predella panels of the Stoning of Stephen and Peter's Escape from Prison, two lucid and well-coloured lights. The latter follows a cartoon by *Ford Madox Brown*. – N by *C. A. Gibbs*, 1874. – Chancel N by *O'Connor*, 1868. – E also 1868. – MONUMENTS. Sarah Baxter † 1774. A hanging cloth against a pinkish marble cartouche, in the manner of Nelson of Shrewsbury. – John Jones † 1808 by *J. Carline*.

ALL SAINTS, 1 m. WSW. By *Aston Webb*, 1888–90. E.E. stepped lancets. Of Llanymynech limestone with Grinshill dressings. S aisle roofed in one with the nave, its pitch punctuated by the gables of two S windows and of the porch. Also on the S of the chancel is the tower, square at the base but turning octagonal at the belfry stage and crowned by a short spire. The interior is less sympathetic. Built for Sir Pryce Pryce-Jones.

In CANAL ROAD is a terrace of DOUBLE-DECKER HOUSES of *c.* 1840, built against a steep fall to the former canal bank. Two-storey cottages face the canal; on top of them another layer of two-storey cottages opening on to the road. Parallels for such extreme economy in housing industrial workers were to be found at Blaenavon and Nant-y-glo in Gwent. Below these a polychrome brick terrace and the SEVERN VALLEY MILLS (1875).

PLAS-Y-BRYN, ½ m. NNE of Newtown. 1881; in the conservative Italianate style favoured by Newtown industrialists.

UPPER BRYN, ½ m. WNW. A square-framed C17 timber house with a date 1660 and the Mortimer motto ('Not we from kings but kings from us') in large renewed letters on the front. This and the porch are jettied. Two doorways with decorated heads.

RED HOUSE, 1¾ m. N. Close studs. A single-storey section with two gabled and storeyed blocks added, and with an early C18 stair.

THE ROCK, 200 yds SW of the parish church. Red brick. The central three bays are Late Georgian, with one projecting bay which has a pediment over the door and vases and balls on its pedimental gable. Matching outer bays added in the C19.

LITTLE ABERBECHAN, 1 m. ENE. With herringbone framing.

(ABERBECHAN, long demolished, was a large late medieval and C17 timber-framed mansion).

NEWTOWN. *See* p. 172.

PENYGLODDFA. *See* Newtown, pp. 172, 174, 177.

1090

LLANMEREWIG

St Llwchaiarn. Founded *c.* 575 by this Celtic saint, who by tradition is buried here: a little upland single-chamber church with s porch and w tower, in a banked oval churchyard with stone stiles. The walls represent a c13 church, but practically all is c19 except the roofs – close-set collars with braces making four-centred arches – which are c15. *John Parker* (1798–1860) was rector in 1827–44. A Gothic-lover and a meticulous draughtsman (his watercolour drawings of Welsh screens are an important record), he erected a fantastic Tower-of-Babel-like pulpit from pieces of the c15 screen.* He also installed galleries (1833) and furniture partly of oak and partly of cast iron, and had the roof ceiled with panelling and bosses and an e window made by *David Evans* (1837). All this went in 1892. Of Parker's time the slender tower with gabled roof on corbels, dated 1838–9; the s porch, round-arched with chevron mouldings but with a trefoiled opening and a hood with lilies, dated 1840; and the s semi-dormer with its almond-shaped light and a lily-finial, dated 1843. Between these two in the s nave wall was an open fireplace, whose octagonal shafted chimney is partly re-erected on the vestry. All this odd, lively work was superintended by *T. G. Newenham. Aston Webb,* who shared Sir Stephen Glynne's view that this personal style was 'generally out of character with the simplicity of a remote village church', prepared plans (executed in 1892 by *W. H. Spaull*) for the familiar heavy windows and furnishings. An unconventional interior by Parker survives at Llanyblodwel, Shropshire, his subsequent living. – Fragment of the c15 SCREEN in the present 1892 one. – GLASS. e signed *Ballantine & Gardiner,* Edinburgh, 1892.

The Old Rectory. Small late c16 timber-framed house of type C but only two-roomed. Central chimney, and an old dormer.

Cilgwrgan, ½ m. wnw. Timber-framed; the l. wing is of *c.* 1600 and square-framed, the two sections to the r. are c17 close studding.

Penarth, 1½ m. sw. The middle portion is a c15 hall, with its floors and the two wings built *c.* 1600. One tall pair of base-crucks survives, arching to a collar and to apex struts. Elizabethan additions are a large chimney and the parlour wing on the l., with dragon-beams supporting the overhangs and fine

---

*Destroyed; known from his drawing in the National Library of Wales.

rafters with double-ogee mouldings on the ceiling. The porch is at this side, not against the r. (kitchen) wing. Hall ceiling with counterchanging joists. The walls are all of close studs including the dais partition, and three of the gables have herringbone framing. The gables are jettied out twice in the normal way.

GLANHAFREN, 2 m. SW. A good mid C17 Severn valley regional Renaissance house, on an old site, with a deep rock-cut well. It has the characteristic two-storey, three-bay front of upright timbers and a large projecting central porch with a shaped door-head. The room above overhangs on plain bressumers. The parlour on the r. is wainscoted and has the cellar beneath.

At GOITRE, 1¼ m. SE, is one of Montgomeryshire's brickworks.

LLANRHAEADR-YM-MOCHNANT 1020

The main part of the village (including the *clas* church of St Dogfan) is in Denbighshire, across the bridge of *c.* 1770 over the Rhaeadr. On the Montgomeryshire side is a huddle of chapels and cottages. SEION METHODIST CHURCH, by *Shayler & Ridge*, 1904, in a massive Arts and Crafts Gothic, has two stumpy towers and bold buttressing down the sides.

RHOS Y BEDDAU CIRCLE (SJ 059 302). A group of Bronze Age ritual monuments on a bleak and atmospheric moorland above Pistyll Rhaeadr (4 m. NE). The steep and narrow path up the cliff beside the waterfall can be a difficult climb, but the walk beside the river is easy from then on. The site stands on a level platform at the confluence of two streams, and a large quartzite boulder directs you to it (perhaps intentionally). The monuments consist of a circle of low stones, and an avenue running SE from the circle towards a very small cairn edged with large boulders (a Kerb Cairn). Just below the plateau is an early estate boundary stone.

LLANSANTFFRAID-YM-MECHAIN 2020

ST BRIDE. A fabric of complicated history, yet consisting of the familiar nave and chancel in one; with N aisle and transept, S porch, W shingled spire. In a circular raised churchyard. The small Norman window in the N wall suggests that the W part of the nave is C12; so perhaps the medieval single-chamber church was extended E from the break in the N roof and the straight join in the S wall. Here the particularly attractive stonework includes courses of dressed red sandstone. The whole building is made of odds and ends of repair. A former pointed s doorway is blocked; the former early C14 E window, three lights with intersecting tracery, is set in the W end. Other medieval fragments are half the PISCINA arch below the ogee s chancel window and the s doorway with its C15 door. Plastered barrel ceiling over the nave. Perhaps in the C17 the porch was built, with fretwork balusters in the sides; also two s windows, three- and four-light, of Jacobean type (dated, with a Latin inscription, 1619); and the dormer above it, dated 1669. Other s windows are dated 1703 and 1706. The Georgian stone-quoined transept, with semicircular-headed window and N door, was added in 1727. Parts of the spire (in origin C17) should probably be attributed to *John Oldrid Scott*, who restored the church in 1891–3. The ponderous two-bay tran-septal arcade is his – the piers are very short – and the renova-tion of the chancel with its carved ceiling, black and white marble floor, and the SCREEN with varied tracery lights and English fan-ribbed canopy. – Georgian ALTAR RAILS. – Carved and dated C17 PEW DOORS re-used as a dado in the chancel. – FONT. C13?; deep bowl with plain rim. – PULPIT. C17, with tester. – GLASS. Chancel s, with a medallion of the Raising of Lazarus, by *David Evans*, *c.* 1847. – CANDELABRUM. Brass, 1808. – MONUMENTS. Hannah Worthington † 1800, by *John Nelson*. – Rev. Griffith Lloyd † 1696, engraved brass. – John Bill † 1796 and Ann Bill † 1797, very refined tablets by *John Nelson* of Shrewsbury. – Wooden plaque to Captain R. K. † 1729.

The village is in three parts. The church group consists of the school and vicarage, the LION HOTEL with Tuscan porch and two-storey bays, and brick and timber-framed cottages. Then comes some new housing round the flour mill together with some brick terraces of the 1830s with X-paned windows. The group round the late C18 BRIDGE, which crosses the River Vyrnwy by two lofty arches and a rounded cutwater, is com-posed of neat little houses of the 1830s and 40s with simple classical details. VYRNWY HOUSE was substantially remo-delled in the 1860s, with towny rounded upper windows and deep eaves.

BRONHYDDON, ½ m. N, is Regency with tripartite windows with fan-fluted tops. Porch with paired Doric columns and an enta-blature.

TY NEWYDD. In two sections at r. angles: one with moulded

bressumer and moulded beams, the other with the date of the whole – 1639. The fine double stone chimney serves both. The kitchen is placed in an outlying position behind the hall, instead of at its end (the traditional service arrangement).

WYDDIGOED is a box-framed house similar to Ty Newydd and again with a tall moulded stone chimney.

DEYTHEUR. *See* p. 99.

LLANWDDYN

0010

ST JOHN. The old church dedicated to St John the Baptist, which was submerged beneath Lake Vyrnwy, had belonged to the Knights Hospitaller. On the N wall were paintings 29 ft long by 6 ft high, depicting nine episodes in Christ's Passion. The substitute building, by *F. V. Holme*, erected in 1887 at the expense of the Liverpool Corporation, has that curious Victorian property of seeming a bulgy excrescence from the ground, in contrast to the look of 'belonging' of the low medieval churches. It has nave, S aisle, and a chancel with transepts and pentagonal apse. E.E. with red brick facing inside. The chancel is quite elaborately equipped with a zigzag-carved PISCINA, trefoiled DOUBLE SEDILIA, and black marble shafts between the lancets. – Georgian CANDELABRUM. – STAINED GLASS by *Curtis, Ward & Hughes*. – The W window of 1909 is to the memory of G. F. Deacon, engineer of the dam.

The village of Llanwddyn had been attached to the consistory of the Knights of St John at Halston; remains of a small HOSPITIUM lie on the hillside W of the lake. Besides the church, the ruins of two chapels, forty houses, and a school are under the water. The upper part of the present village was made soon after the dam, to replace the old. The lower part, Abertridwr ($\frac{3}{4}$ m. to the E), is more recent and has a SCHOOL/COMMUNITY CENTRE by *Herbert Carr* (1948).

LAKE VYRNWY. *See* p. 116.

LLANWNNOG

0090

ST GWYNNOG. In a circular raised churchyard extended to the S, this daughter church of Llandinam is a good example of a Welsh single-chamber church, much restored in 1863. All four walls incorporate medieval stonework, including squared red sandstone robbed from the Roman fort at Caersws. The E

window is still the three-light Perp original. *R. K. Penson*
renewed the roofs, with a canopy and re-used Perp bosses
over the chancel, and built a slated W spirelet on internal
timber supports. – The SCREEN and ROOD LOFT, datable to
c. 1500, are one of Montgomeryshire's treasures, and the best
remaining of some thirty known to have existed. Ten lights
above a low panelled dado, but tracery only in the five to the
N. Low triangular tracery in the doorhead (cf. Llangynyw
etc.). Small motifs are repeated without much overall design.
A full-width cornice of running ornament issues partly from a
wyvern's mouth. The loft, supported by four beams at
bresummer and parapet level, is reached by solid oak steps in
the N nave wall. Formerly there was a pair of posts E and W
of the doorway, each with tracery heads between (cf. St
Margaret's, Herefordshire). The E coving is rib-and-boss surmounted by oak-twig trails and fleur-de-lys cresting. Parapet
of Perp traceries and more running ornament. The W side is
much richer – rib-and-boss coving filled with panels of interlace and circle motifs (cf. Newtown and Llananno, R). The
bressumer has vine-trails again issuing from a wyvern's mouth,
and there are bits of cresting and drop-cresting at the N end.
The parapet might have consisted of niches and statues as at
Llananno, but the existing work is restoration by *David
Walker*, 1873. – STAINED GLASS. E, decorative with three
small scenes, signed *Evans Broth*: (sic), Shrewsbury; *c.* 1863.
– Nave N, a jumble of fragments, including a bishop, from
the E window. Of *c.* 1500. – MONUMENTS. Matthew Pryce
† 1699. Black columns, open segmental pediment, and symbols
of mortality. – David James † 1864. Gothic, with ringed
columns and crocketed canopy. – The grave of the poet John
Ceiriog Hughes is in the churchyard.

PERTHEIRIN, $\frac{3}{4}$ m. w. A beam with the date 1654 over the door –
presumably referring to the building of the lofty close-studded
section behind. The front is faced in brick, and in the C18
originally had two storeys and five bays with pilaster strips at
the angles and on the central bay, and a string-course. C19
alterations.

PARK (PEN PRYS). A house of the Herbert family, in close-
studding of *c.* 1700, but modernized out of recognition.

CLATTER. *See* p. 94.

CAERSWS. *See* p. 85.

GWYNFYNYDD (SO 039 936) is a small enclosed settlement of
about one acre, close to the Roman road from Caersws. Although

it has an impressive clay bank (still high in spite of ploughing) with an outer ditch (recognizable only on the NE), it is not in a defensible position and is best interpreted as a farmstead, perhaps of Romano-British date, since it is so close to the road.

LLANWRIN   7000

ST GWRIN. In a raised circular churchyard with the village close around. Single-chamber with a S porch, of the later C15; old stone-work in all four walls. But the slating on the high-pitched roof-timbers, the W bellcote, and all the windows were renewed in the C19. The restoration – by *Benjamin Ferrey*, 1864 – was not too thorough, and the result inside is really quite good. Trefoiled-ogee PISCINA. Restored Perp E window, with five lights and transom. The roof is of the common Welsh border type, arch-braced, with collars and wind-braces. – FONT. Of local stone, octagonal, Perp. – Low Perp SCREEN dividing off the chancel. An inauthentic doorhead by Ferrey rests on ringed shafts. Fourteen bays of cinquefoiled-ogee traceried lights beside. – STAINED GLASS. In the upper part of the E window, glass datable by Edward IV's badge, the *rose ensoleilée*, to 1461–83; cf. glass at Old Radnor. In the panel tracery are the Virgin and Child enthroned and two acolytes; in the five lights above the transom, Christ crucified, between four saints. – MONUMENTS. William and Margaret Pughe of Mathafarn, erected 1742. Luxuriantly carved Georgian marble monument with a good inscription, surmounted by an urn garlanded with flowers set in an open pediment.

PLAS WRIN. Rebuilt in the late C18 and well proportioned: three by two bays with deep-eaved hipped roof. Formerly the Rectory, and the home of Sylfan Evans, rector in 1876–1903, first professor of Welsh at Aberystwyth, and compiler of the Welsh Dictionary. Below its garden a pretty early C19 SCHOOL with three round-headed windows.

ABERFFRYDLAN, ½ m. SW. The W wing of the older, L-shaped part contains the parlour, whose N wall may be of the C15. The parlour ceiling is exceptionally fine. Its deep beams intersect to form twelve compartments whose joists, datable by the mouldings to c. 1600, are arranged in counterchanging directions. The doorway with carved spandrels looks contemporary. Chimneys abut to the N and W. The S wing was rebuilt in brick in the C18, and the dining room has an C18 fireplace and pilastered doorway. Nearby a brick BARN with freestone quoins, dated 1762.

MATHAFARN, 1¼ m. ENE. This home of the Pugh family was burned down by Cromwellians on 29 November 1644. Just a datestone for 1628 survives, reset, at the back, and only a pair of gate-posts with elegant ball-finials tells of the later C17 rebuilding. The present house is a typical three-bay, three-storey block of c. 1800. Outbuildings include a ruined BREW-HOUSE, perhaps C17, and two interesting BARNS, one of c. 1700, with queen-post roof-framing, and a S side of thin stones with a cart entrance with a flat arch of voussoirs, and at r. angles another with tie-beams, c. 1800? Dafydd Llwyd the poet was squire of Mathafarn c. 1440–90; the future King Henry VII stayed with him on his way to fight at Bosworth.

(BRYNMELIN, 1¾ m. NE. A hall with crucks; the central pair is arch-braced, with cusped struts in the apex.)

BRIDGE, 2 m. W, with two semicircular arches on cutwaters; early C18.

LLANWYDDELAN

1½ m. NNW of Tregynon

ST GWYDDELAN. Rebuilt in lancet style in 1865; the N and E walls perhaps on the old foundations. Single-chamber with W timber belfry, in a small raised churchyard now extended. Perhaps by *J. W. Poundley & D. Walker*. – FONT. C15; octagonal.

LLANYMYNECH

The E half of the village street is in Shropshire (*see The Buildings of England*) and part of the hill. The Montgomeryshire Canal here enters the county from Welsh Frankton. It was open from 1796 to 1936, carrying limestone and coal, and may be returned to working order, anyway as far as Welshpool.

LLANYMYNECH BRIDGE, ¼ m. S. Three shallow smooth stone arches over the Vyrnwy. Rounded cutwaters with niches above. The bridge was designed by *Thomas Penson* (the County Surveyor) in 1826, with advice on the foundations from *Telford*. He also made a design in iron. The cost was £14,000. Penson was also the architect of the village church.

LLIDIART-Y-WAUN

2 m. SE of Llanidloes

CAPEL BANHADLOG was built in 1826 as a chapel of ease to
Llandinam. It has a bellcote and Gothic-leaded windows. –
FONT on a fluted column. – Banhadlog was once a grange of
Wigmore Abbey in Herefordshire.

MACHYNLLETH

Machynlleth lies just S of the River Dovey, where the road from
Newtown to this seaward tip of Montgomeryshire meets the coastal
route from Barmouth to Aberystwyth. The town plan is therefore
T-shaped, and has been so since the time of Edward I. It is West
Welsh, independent, and had a printing-press from the 1790s,
some sort of coach link from Shrewsbury from 1798, and a railway
link from 1864. Apart from a few buildings the appearance of
the town is Victorian.

ST PETER. Inside the W tower, with its C15 walls with deep-
splayed windows, the baptistery was formed in 1894. Quoins
and C18 windows in the upper parts. Battlements and pinnacles
were added in the early C19. The rest of the church was rebuilt
by *Edward Haycock Senior* in 1827. He replaced a (C13?) cruciform plan by a broad nave with galleries. The exterior is an
awkward combination of little neo-Jacobean semi-dormers and
heavily buttressed walls of long blocks of slatey stone. *J. W.
Poundley & D. Walker* made plans for a new chancel in 1864;
it seems that the chancel arch and E window date from a modified
scheme of 1866, and that the galleries were then removed. The
stencilled ceiling is later date. – FONT. C15, octagonal, with
traceried and patterned panels. – STAINED GLASS. E by *Clayton & Bell*, dated 1879. – Several other windows of this period,
including two signed by *Ward & Hughes*, 1886. – N nave wall,
second from W, 1908. – MONUMENT. Sir John Edwards
† 1850, ogee canopy and pinnacles. By *Samuel Manning*.
OUR LADY HELP OF CHRISTIANS (R.C.). By *Sir Percy
Thomas & Son*, 1965. A post-Vatican-II building, full of light.
Bare brick and square, with the altar brought to the centre by
the internal vestry. Ground-to-ceiling windows. Flat roof of
precast concrete members.
PRESBYTERIAN CHURCH. 1867. Dec, with a wheel-window.
(BETHESDA BAPTIST CHAPEL. 1897 by *T. E. Morgan*.)

PLAS MACHYNLLETH (formerly Greenfield) was presented to the town by the Londonderry family in 1947 as corporation offices etc.; before the Londonderrys it belonged to the Edwards family. It looks C19, but within the N wing with regency Gothic multi-paned windows there might be an older house. In front of this a four-bay, four-storey brick block with a hipped roof of *c.* 1770 with contemporary stair and some Late Georgian plasterwork – an oval garland on the hall ceiling – and honeysuckle friezes and fireplaces. Single-storey wings were added at the sides in the C19. A drawing room in one of these has fine gilded wall and ceiling decoration in a French neo-classical manner. In the other, the Council Chamber, two mural paintings of Owain Glyndŵr by *Jack Crabtree*, 1971. This block was given its plaster façade, now lacking some details, with an Ionic colonade, by Sir John Owen *c.* 1846. The date 1653 in the pediment is misleading. The interior of the N wing was remodelled with quatrefoil-panelled doors and cross-vaulted ceilings *c.* 1870. Victorian LODGES, and grounds now municipalized. Next to the former, in Pentre'rhedyn Street, a terracotta doorway in the shape of a horseshoe (*c.* 1900) advertises the former SMITHY. Opposite is an early C19 TOLLHOUSE, and one of the recent brick SCHOOLS by *Herbert Carr*, County Architect. BODLONDEB is C18 and little changed inside. At the cross-roads, the exuberantly carved CLOCK TOWER was put up in 1873 for the coming-of-age of Lord Londonderry's heir, Lord Castlereagh; it is a striking example of the later C19 European mania for semi-political monuments. In a plastic, super-Gothic style possibly influenced by Seddon, by *Henry Kennedy* (architect also of the demolished Christ Church, 1881), and newly cleaned. Behind and in Heol Pen'rallt, severe C18 stone fronts and C19 stucco ones with the usual gables and bows and an iron porch at No. 12. The Doll Street ALMSHOUSES are dated 1868.

MAENGWYN STREET is the main street, wide enough for a market or an avenue, and busy. Various C19 styles, especially a neo-Tudor characterized by lozenge-paned windows. Nos. 32–36 survive of a mutilated late C18 pedimented stone terrace, the only one of its kind in the county. Further down on the N is OWAIN GLYNDŴR'S PARLIAMENT HOUSE. Owain Glyndŵr may have held a parliament at Pennal, N of the Dovey, in 1402 and 1404, but tradition has connected this building with its meetings. It is in fact later than this event – but the event has preserved a rare town house all the same. It is sited along the street. The walls are of small split stones and on the garden side have voussoired arches to a doorway and a window, and an exterior stair to a canted upper-floor entry. The roof spanned an open hall, and its arched collar-trusses are of C15 type, which is the nearest date for the building. The old building was restored (it retains a pitched floor) and the adjoining slate-hung OWAIN GLYNDŴR INSTITUTE built in 1911, at the behest of Lord Davies of Llandinam. Murals in the Parliament House are by *Murray Urquhart* (his Glyndŵr has the face of Lord Davies). PENDRE has a three-bay front and doorway with a big chamfered fanlight of *c*. 1800, and No. 80 also has a front of *c*. 1800 with its Tuscan porch set up to the l. and inside two flights of unexpectedly well-made Georgian stairs. MAENGWYN is C19 with a Doric porch. The cottages opposite, dated 1628 but much renewed, are rare examples of timber-framing on the western seaboard. The HIGH SCHOOL, partly by *Herbert Carr* (County Architect), contains C17 panelling from Parc Pen Prys, Llanwnnog. The CHEST HOSPITAL, thirteen bays and two storeys, the central bay rusticated, was the Poor Law Union, of 1834.

On the E edge of the town, in 1913, *Thomas Alwyn Lloyd* built for Lord Davies the GARDEN VILLAGE; its thirteen gabled terraced houses round a square of trees have a civilized air by comparison with its neighbours. At BRYN-Y-GOG ESTATE (1974–6 by *E. Francis Jones & Partners*), which has just enveloped it, these lessons have not been applied.

LLYNLLOED, ½ m. SE. An C18 two-storey front of seven bays, of dressed stone with a voussoired doorway. The roofs were repaired after a fire in which a crow-stepped gable (C17?) on the r. was destroyed. The rooms however interconnect without passages and have C17 timbering upstairs. C18 wood pilasters in hall and dining room; broad contemporary stairs (added?) at the rear, with dog-gates and pilasters again; and upstairs cupboards uncommonly intact. The plan relates to two houses in South Merioneth, Llwyn, Dolgellau, and Llanfendigaid.

MAESMAWR HALL *see* MEIFOD

MANAFON

1000

ST MICHAEL. Single-chamber with a W timber bell-turret, S porch, and N vestry. Perhaps originally C14, but thoroughly restored twice in the C19. Besides the main walls there survives

the three-light Perp E window and two small windows now in
the vestry; the rest were removed in 1859. The roof is the C15
arch-braced principal one, restored. Stoup beside the s door.
The architect in 1898 was *John Douglas* of Chester, and the
woodwork is characteristic of him. – SCREEN. One narrow and
two wide bays either side of the broad central opening, with
ogee tracery and cresting, but rather un-Welsh in its lack of
varying patterns. – CHOIR STALLS and PEWS. In a modern
Jacobean. – Nice PULPIT. – REREDOS and ALTAR RAILS
also by *Douglas*. – Stripping the walls to bare stone is another
Douglas idea; cf. Llanfechain church. – GLASS. In the vestry
windows two angel heads, c. 1500. – E by *Arthur O'Connor*
c. 1859.

RECTORY. Early C19, three-bay, three-storey whitened front
with ironwork porch. Gwallter Mechain (Walter Davies, 1761–
1849), a writer on Welsh agriculture, was rector here; and so
was the poet R. S. Thomas, from 1943 to 1954.

MANAFON MOAT. A motte scarped from a natural tump.

HENLLYS HALL, ½m. NE. Rebuilt in 1898 for Mrs Perrins-
Williams, who was the patron for the church's restoration –
and for the building of St David, Barmouth (Gwynedd). So
this house is probably by *John Douglas* too. Certainly the hall
woodwork is like that in the church. The neo-Elizabethan s
side has two storeys with four gables. Buttressed porch with
small ogee windows above. In the l. bay a corbelled and castellated upper window. All the windows are of red sandstone,
mullioned and transomed, and have hoods. On the E beside
the chimney a triangular bay with the stonework dying into the
corbelled oriel above. Of gloomy dark stone.

MATHAFARN *see* LLANWRIN

MATHRAFAL

2 m. SW of Meifod

Mathrafal is said, on medieval literary evidence, to have been a
castle and regional capital of the princes of Powys, even from
the Dark Ages. It is mentioned with Aberffraw and Dinefwr
as one of the three ancient royal seats of Wales. The stronger
Powis Castle eventually succeeded under Gwenwynwyn, son
of Owain Cyfeiliog. But Mathrafal remained in use as the head
of a commote till the C15. The evidence of the site – a motte
20 ft high in the NE corner of an earlier 330 ft square enclo-

sure with banks and ditches on the River Banwy – is of C12
occupation of a possibly C11 Welsh site. In 1212 the castle
was garrisoned for King John by Robert de Vieuxpont. It was
seized by Llewelyn the Great but relieved, and its timber buildings were subsequently burned.

MATHRAFAL FARM, ½ m. NW, is a late C19 red brick house. The
nearly open BARN has four round stone piers on one side and
two on the other – a local peculiarity.

MEIFOD   *1010*

STS TYSILIO AND MARY. Nave, W tower, N and S aisles.
Three dedications are recorded within this 9-acre churchyard:
a chapel to St Gwyddfarch, W of St Tysilio; a church of St
Tysilio; and a church of St Mary (bits of its floor were found
on the site of the Congregational Chapel of 1881–3). Pennant
says there was a cell here which was 'as old as Christianity in
these islands'. The site was the burial place of the princes of
Powys (of Mathrafal); a *clas* or Celtic monastic church from
which the churches at Llanfair Caereinion, Guilsfield, Welshpool, and Alberbury (Salop) were founded; and subsequently
belonged to Strata Marcella Abbey. St Mary's church is stated
in the Brut y Tywysogion to have been consecrated in 1156
(cf. Kerry). If, as is consistent with the stonework at the W,
it is the present church that is meant, there must also have been
a change of dedication from Tysilio to Mary.

Of a Romanesque church, anyway, and probably one of
cruciform plan, one and a half arches and one cylindrical pier
are immured in the W outer face of the S nave wall; a free-standing N nave arcade of one and a half bays corresponds to these.
As at Kerry, it is the W end of the C12 aisled church that survives. The piers have capitals of two plain chamfers; the plain
base of the W one is exposed a foot below the level of the present
floor. The arches are two-order but unmoulded. The tower
was built into the last nave bay, and big half-column stones
(from the responds of the crossing arches?) have been re-used
for the piers. Their dressed capitals are Dec like the arch and
vault of the tower, so probably before the C14 the aisles (and
central tower) had fallen into disuse and been demolished. All
the external detail of the tower suggests a C15 date: the battered
base, the stair-turret projecting from the SW angle, the belfry
windows, the gargoyles above, and the battlements.

To return to the nave: a church of quite different plan was

developed from the old one, without a N aisle, but with a s aisle alongside the chancel. Their E walls are aligned. The s arcade is composed of three low two-centred arches, perhaps broken through an earlier wall – see the rood-loft doorway. One octagonal column and moulded capital; no capitals to the responds. The nave E window is Perp; the E window of the s aisle three-light Dec with reticulated tracery. C14 s doorway. Tall s window with cusped Y-tracery. The N aisle, existing as a lean-to in 1795, and noted as having a wooden arcade in 1837, was rebuilt by *Benjamin Ferrey* in 1871-2 with its own gable and a steep and deeply moulded four-bay arcade on cylindrical columns. The rather graceless two-light windows are his too. It was during this work that the C12 arches were found in the s wall. The C14/15 roofs of the nave and s aisle, arch-braced with raking struts and two tiers of trefoiled wind-braces, were raised in the restoration. – FONT with eight panels with initials; Perp or later? – REREDOS. Oak frieze carved with vines, according to Crossley from the wall-plate of the medieval roof; also fragments of arcading from a screen of Dee valley type. – Some C17 PEW work. – Twisted-baluster, late C17 ALTAR RAILS. – Octagonal Jacobean PULPIT at the W end. – More pew work divides off the vestry. – Pretty C19 Gothic ORGAN CASE. – STAINED GLASS. E by *H. Hughes*. – s aisle E by *David Evans*,
88 Salop, *c.* 1856, a monumental, unfussy design in typical strong colours. – Six panels of heraldic glass hanging in the aisles were made in 1838, also by *David Evans*, with arms of Welsh border families. – Other C19 windows by *Ward & Hughes*. –
9 In the s aisle a tapering CROSS SLAB which Dr Nash-Williams compared to some C8 Merovingian sculptured grave-lids in the Poitiers district. Elements of diverse origin are not assimilated into a coherent design. At the top is Christ crucified and a Maltese cross in a circle. Below is a Latin cross encircled with knot-work. Unfamiliar motifs like the circled chi-rho and foliate border have been translated here into a crucifix ring-cross of Irish type, and the Celtic plaits and Viking knots and animals of the local Celto-Norse tradition. To Dr Nash-Williams the introduction of Viking features suggested a C9–10 date; Dr C. A. Ralegh Radford, however, conjectures that it was in fact the tombstone of one of the Princes of Powys, perhaps Madoc ap Maredudd † 1160. – MONUMENTS. Jenkin Parry † 1787, with tapering balusters supporting an obelisk and urns. – Meriel Williams † 1685. Convex slab between black marble columns with white responds; scrolly volutes and an urn above. –

Charles Williams Wynn † 1914 (at Ypres), with a big symbolic relief.

Most building in the village is later than 1825, and there are good examples of the familiar early C19 three-bay, three-storey house, such as TY MAWR and the KING'S HEAD HOTEL with varied fenestration on the centre bay. VYRNWY HOUSE has a fluted Doric porch, and WATERLOO COTTAGE an ogee window. Beside the latter a lane crosses the iron BRONIARTH BRIDGE (by *J. W. Poundley*, County Surveyor), a bit of unattractive functionalism of 1862. A number of older houses face the pastoral scenery along the celebrated Vale of Meifod.

PENYLAN, ½ m. SE. Seven bays with recessed centre: paired Tuscan columns as a porch, with two single columns *in antis* behind them. A picturesque Regency façade when seen from a distance, but quirky close to, since it is contrived with three tiers of windows, but on the l. the upper floor of the house drops below the tops of the first-floor windows, while it is absent altogether on the r. Two Ionic columns screen a delicate Regency staircase from the paved hall. The STABLES are H-plan, with a lantern dated 1812 – the probable date of the façade, too.

GLASCOED, 1 m. SW. A two-storeyed close-studded house, perhaps of *c.* 1600, the timbers massive and close-set throughout. Some alterations.

DYFFRYN, ½ m. SW. Square hipped-roofed farm with a stone porch. Its fine BARNS form two sides of a courtyard (now filled with a huge asbestos shed). They are timber-framed and nogged with red brick with ventilation holes. Late C18?

PENTRE'R GOF, ¼ m. NW. A Severn valley house with a central moulded chimney and unusual ring-patterns in the close-stud framing. Late C17 hipped roof, windows, and some panelling inside.

GOETRE HALL, ½ m. NW. A Severn valley regional house with C19 and C20 additions, but it is the C17 features that are the puzzle. The porch supports the normal upper room, and on its strapwork-carved bressumer is the date 1627. Much of the other woodwork looks built in later, including a James I overmantel: Ionic pilasters and arches over three marquetry panels.

VICARAGE FARM, ¼ m. NW, is a symmetrically planned former vicarage of *c.* 1720 with a spacious two-storey stairwell (and good balusters) beyond the hall. Front of five bays with C19 pediment and dormers.

MAESMAWR HALL, 3 m. SE. Formerly a home of the Lloyd family of Trawscoed, Guilsfield. One, a Royalist, spent the

Commonwealth and Restoration years in Holland and returned to Wales with a Dutch taste for tall brick houses, of which Maesmawr was intended to be a re-creation. It dates from 63 *c.* 1689–92. The front is of seven bays and two main storeys above a basement. Hipped roof with two tiers of dormers with scrolly sides. Cambered windows and brick strings; no quoins. It is quite plain and modest, but the roof has the fashionable sprocketed eaves. The plan is three rooms by two, with the staircase round a big well beyond the hall. The stair has heavy reel-turned balusters up two floors, and plaster garlands on the half-landing ceilings. There are two internal chimneys. In the dining room some good contemporary bolection panelling with geometrical door surrounds; also an early C18 plaster ceiling with three allegorical scenes of Cupid and other figures, and garlands. One of the curious features is the use of timber-framing in an otherwise innovating house. The old techniques were relied on for internal walls: long beams inter-cross on the ceilings, and the joint between wall and hipped roof is managed with small crucks.* Additions were made at the back in 1858, perhaps by *W. H. Hill,* for the same owner as at Brookland Hall, Guilsfield. A lake was formed in the early C19, and a garden was planned by *Edward Kemp,* also in 1858.‡

CEUNANT, ½ m. NE. An open barn with cylindrical and square stone piers by the road. (Another at CWM.)

BRON-Y-MAIN, 1 m. NE. The rebuilding of *c.* 1800 is more architecturally conscious than is common. S front of three bays with a set-back quadrant either side, and two storeys and a blank. Stone pediment over the door.

COED-Y-MAIN, ¾ m. NE. By *Evan Powell* of Welshpool, *c.* 1865.

YSTUM COLWYN. *See* p. 212.

MELLINGTON *see* CHURCHSTOKE

3010   MIDDLETOWN

ALL SAINTS. 1871 by *E. M. Goodwin* of Caernarfon. Nave, bellcote, S porch, chancel, with lancets. Only the C17 SOUTH DOOR is noteworthy; it is studded and panelled with dentils and a depressed arch at the top, and comes from Alberbury, Salop, of which parish Middletown was a township. Wood-carvings tell the strange story of the Ugg of Hell.

---

* Cf. Llangattwg Court, Llangattock (B).
‡ Mr and Mrs Ion Trant gave me much useful information on Maesmawr.

BULTHY FARM, 1¼ m. NE. Brick, three-bay, three-storey, of
c. 1710, with raised gable ends.

MOCHDRE   *0080*

ALL SAINTS. Single-chamber, with w belfry and s porch,
almost totally renewed in 1867 by *E. Haycock Junior*. What does
remain is an unusually ornate Perp roof of seven bays. The customary arch-braced principals with cusped apex braces rest on
somewhat superfluous hammerbeams. On the ends of these are
tubby flying angels. Each bay has three tiers of wind-braces
arranged as quatrefoils, between heavily moulded ribs. The
intersections over the chancel are enriched with bosses. The
roof probably dates from the first half of the C16. Some C17
stalls are set up on the E wall. – Two short wooden medieval
ROOD FIGURES, Christ and the Virgin, found hidden on the   41
wall-plate at the rebuilding, are now in the National Museum
of Wales, Cardiff. Survivals like these are exceptionally few.
The Christ is the more striking, contorted, realistic; the smaller
Mary is a more conventional C15 Gothic figure. Only fragments
of two other such figures, both of Christ, are known. – FONT.
Octagonal, with Tudor roses in quatrefoils on the sides. –
STAINED GLASS. E by *Clayton & Bell*, 1865. – w by *Wailes*. –
MONUMENTS. Richard Ruffe † 1812, tablet with an urn but
also Gothic lettering.

NEUADD GOCH, 1¾ m. SSE. A sturdy close-studded house on a
stone platform. ½ m. below, between two streams, are traces
of a motte and bailey CASTLE.

ESGAIRGEILIOG, 1 m. S. A medieval cruck hall with two
remaining pairs; the middle one is arch-braced and has multi-
foiled struts. Floors have been made in the hall, and a timber-
and-wattle chimney added. Two C17 gabled wings, the w one
with quadrant timbering. Other features of interest are the well
in the cellar, solid oak steps remaining at the bottom of the stair,
and an ogee doorhead.

CWMYRHIWDRE, 2¼ m. S. An ancient farmstead now superseded. A four-cruck-couple structure on a platform site survives as a barn, and some C17 framed buildings.

MONTGOMERY/TREFALDWYN   *2090*

Montgomery stands on sloping ground above the Severn valley,
overlooking the approach to central Wales. It was a strategic site

to command in Iron Age, Roman, and early medieval times. The
county and town name comes from Roger de Montgomery, first
Earl of Shrewsbury, by whom a significant motte and bailey castle
(Hen Domen) was built c. 1070 to guard the Rhydwhiman ford.
Trefaldwyn (the town of Baldwin, after the Norman owner of
Hendomen under Henry I) is the Welsh name of the town and
of the pre-1974 county. The new stone fortress, two miles away
on the rocky ridge above, was constructed in 1223 and after by
Henry III to dominate the invasion route from Shrewsbury. It
was slighted in 1649. Montgomery became a free borough and
ecclesiastical parish in 1227, was the polling place for the
borough's parliamentary seat from 1536 to 1870, and remained
a prospering market town till the industrial age. Then the canal
and later the railway came to serve the lower-lying Welshpool and
Newtown, and anyway stimulated not Welsh manufacture but
markets for English goods. So the town is left – the best planned
and best preserved in Mid Wales – with its medieval church, a
good proportion of Georgian street frontages, and the castle ruins
which from 1964 were excavated by the Department of the Environment. In origin a border stronghold (it is 1 m. from Offa's
Dyke and England), the town and castle were both protected by
an irregular rectangle of walls and ditches begun c. 1227 under
the charter, with four gates – Arthur's to the N, Chirbury to the
E, Ceri to the S, and Cedewain on the castle hill to the W; they
are still partly traceable, since they were rebuilt in stone in 1279–
80 while Bogo de Knovil was Constable of the Castle (cf. Aberystwyth; also Caernarfon etc. in North Wales). But while Leland
saw 'great ruins of the waulle' and 'broken towerets', we cannot.
Practically all the buildings within them are of English, not Welsh
types. With its hilly site and views over Shropshire to Corndon
Hill Montgomery is a delightful place, and as quiet as could be.*

ST NICHOLAS. In a raised churchyard. Single-chamber, divided
by a screen. N and S transepts with two-bay arcades, S porch,
tower at the N of the N transept. The church is first mentioned
in 1227 and the start of the nave was presumably coeval with
the castle, c. 1223. Of rubble stone with C13 red sandstone
dressings, it is long and lofty and has very narrow lancets in
deep reveals – two in the N wall and one in the S. Blocked N
doorway with quarter-round jambs. Also C13, though added
c. 1260 or later, are the S (Lymore) and N (Brockton) transepts,

---

* I am deeply indebted to Dr J. D. K. Lloyd for much information on the
whole town.

the first with broad E and W lancets (with tracery till the C19) and two unequal ones in the S wall (one from the nave). In the W wall a trefoil-headed low-side window. Graceful S arcade with a circular pier; the capitals of the responds and pier, though unalike, have filleted mouldings. The Brockton transept was built *c.* 1275 by Chirbury Abbey, Salop, and has larger single-light windows with tumbled stone heads. The segmental-pointed rere-arch and the jambs of the W window were enriched with a filleted shaft; the E window is similar, but with two nice stiff-leaf capitals and a hoodmould with head-stops. Blocked W doorway with roll-moulding. Both transepts had altars – see the PISCINA in the Brockton transept. The elaborate S doorway is late C13 also, with an inner order of filleted attached shafts continued to the apex within a pair of engaged shafts, with ring-moulded capitals between rolls. A head inserted above. The chancel was extended in the late C13 and now has a large and complex seven-light Perp window – the best in the county. A transom across the main lights and the traceries grouped two, three, and two with six panels – for figures?

The roofs are the structural glory, but their analysis is a puzzle. That over the W half of the nave is a fine one, perhaps of the late C15 or early C16 – slight hammerbeams with arched principals rising to collars with cusped braces. Arcading along the wall-plate decorated with ogee-traceried panels, and four tiers of wind-braces making quatrefoils. The E part of the nave is ceiled with a C16 barrel-vault of rib-and-boss type. Apparently the earlier roof does not continue above this. Perhaps it was meant to extend over the chancel too, or to give emphasis to the rood? Anyhow the existing chancel roof is of 1863 by *George Beadnell* and rather feeble; in 1970 it was ceiled in keeping with the others. The S porch is also by *Beadnell*, 1868, replacing the two-storey stone porch. Modern restoration began in 1816 with the replacement of the low battlemented N tower by the present flimsily detailed, tall buttressed one, at a cost of £1,700 borne by Lord Clive. *G. E. Street* made a report on the church in 1875, in which he recommended that the N arcade be recreated and the chancel roofed according to whatever was found to have been the medieval intention. The work was actually done by *Edward Haycock the Younger* in 1877–8, when the N arcade was added, galleries removed, the W window renewed, and nothing done about the roofs.

FURNISHINGS. FONT. C13; a squat hour-glass-shaped

cylinder, with a band at its waist. – PULPIT designed by *Street* and carved with figures in niches. – REREDOS of Caen stone and alabaster, designed by *R. C. Carpenter* as a frame for the bottom of the E window; the four alabaster figures are by *T. Earp* and the mosaic figures of Evangelists and Prophets by *Clayton & Bell*. – The SCREEN consists of two screens put together. The one facing W, Welsh and made for this parish church, has five openings with large cinquefoiled heads either side of the central doorway with arched and ogee tracery. The rood loft above would have been reached by the stair in the S chancel wall. The existing loft, however, belongs to the other screen, which faces E; and all this and the stalls and misericords in the choir and the canopies above are English, brought from the Augustinian priory of Chirbury at the Dissolution. Crossley compares it to Ludlow and Leintwardine. This Perp monastic screen is also of five bays a side, originally closed by panels. Posts decorated with buttresses and pinnacles. The rood front is pierced by ogee tracery and foliate finials, as are the fine returning stall canopies on the N. The parapet of the rood is backed by planks perforated with little window openings. All this is late C15. There are nine MISERICORDS: an eagle, a priest, a duel, a lost soul taken to hell, and other narrative scenes. The space between the screens formed two pews, and Jacobean gates with little balusters were placed in the way through to the choir. – ROYAL ARMS. 1726. Sumptuously painted in oil on board. – HATCHMENT with the Herbert arms; probably of 1801. – STAINED GLASS. E, 1861 by *Thomas Baillie*. – S, c. 1850. – W, 1902, with St Tyssil, bottom r., holding a model of old Llandyssil church. Designed by *C. Hean* and executed by *G. L. Maerchant*. – MONUMENTS. In the Lymore transept. Two alabaster recumbent effigies of men in armour, much renewed in sandstone c. 1830. The earlier, with a jupon over his armour, is probably Sir Edmund Mortimer † 1408. The later is documented by Lord Herbert of Chirbury as Sir Richard Herbert † 1534, but on stylistic grounds and because of his shoes and Yorkist collar it must have been made c. 1500;
52 from vanished table tombs. – Richard Herbert † 1596. In a magnificent Elizabethan canopied tomb dated 1600; probably designed by *Walter Hancock* († 1599), the master mason/architect of his father-in-law's house, High Ercall, Salop. Herbert lies beside his wife* with his cadaver in alabaster beneath.

---

* Magdalen, subsequently married to Sir John Danvers, died in 1627 and was buried in London.

Their eight children are represented, paired in arcades, behind; they include Lord Herbert of Chirbury and George Herbert. The tomb has a ribbed cross-vault on semicircular arches, with figures of Vanity and Time painted in the spandrels of the big front arch. An entablature above with a painted heraldic frieze breaks forward over four slim Composite columns set diagonally away from the corners, and at these corners supports squat finials. Superstructure of superb strapwork and scrolls and a luxuriant central achievement with the Herbert arms.

PRESBYTERIAN CHURCH. 1885. With a raked floor.

WESLEYAN METHODIST CHAPEL. By *Spaull*.

TOWN HALL. Since the demolition of Llanfyllin's (and of four others in the C19), this is the county's only Georgian town hall. Built by *William Baker*, 1748, for the Herberts, for whom he was then working at Powis Castle. Pale red brick. An early C19 drawing by the Rev. John Pridden shows it, as now, with five-bay arcades. Open till *c.* 1900, they are linked at impost level by simple stone strings and keyed to another string at their crowns. The central slight projection contains a larger arch, attached only to the lower string; then there was originally a thermal lunette, and above eaves level a clock with the Herbert arms breaking into a pediment. Baker's upper floor, lit only from the s otherwise, was replaced by *Thomas Penson* in 1828, at the expense of Lord Clive, with top-heavy though better-lit accommodation for the Quarter Sessions. Large sash-windows, and a pedimental gable termination that set a pattern for respectable farmhouses around. Of 1828 also the rear wing. The clock tower was added in 1921. The predecessor of this building, the Booth Hall, was a half-timbered structure.

COUNTY GAOL. By *Thomas Penson*, *c.* 1830–2. Brick faced with stone. Partly ruined. The governor's house, with the chapel above it, was at the centre of four radiating three- and two-storey wings. One of the yards so formed was fitted with a tread-mill. The gatehouse, built into the wall in 1866 by *J. W. Poundley*, is an ashlar triumphal arch, with four giant semi-rusticated pilasters.

CASTLE. *See* p. 168.

PERAMBULATION. BROAD STREET forms the town's axis. On the w, woodlands rise dramatically behind the town hall up to the castle's rocky bluff; on the e another slope culminates in the church. Seen from above, the C13 town grid is as regular as could be wished for, and Broad Street acts as its central square. The street dips charmingly, and its elevations of Georgian and early C19 red brick houses do not have to compete much with cars or modern street furniture. Cobbles still pave some spaces in front of the houses. At the top, CHINA HOUSE has a mid C18 modillion cornice. On the S, the premises of a bank, with brick quoins, keystones on the windows, and a classical doorcase of the same period, and next to it the late C18 BRONWYLFA, with octagon-fronted bows on three storeys, are the two best (if modest) houses. Three multi-paned Regency shop-fronts can be mentioned, and various fanlights. It needs only a few such domestic buildings to create a sense of order and decorum. In the SQUARE behind the town hall is ROCK HOUSE, basically early C18, three full storeys and dormers in a steep hipped roof. To the r. in ARTHUR STREET a pretty medley of periods begins with the C18 COLOMENDY and a house opposite. As everywhere, the humdrum details are undisturbed. Then the C17 timber-framed OLD BELL, remade in brick, but with the beam of its porch jetty showing beneath a Venetian window, and leaf-carved brackets to the gable. The older PLUME OF FEATHERS, also on the l., of square-framed timbers on a stone base, has Regency Gothic casements.

Across the main road and up SCHOOL BANK to the PRIMARY SCHOOL, a many-gabled stone late-C19-Gothic one and nicely detailed with buttresses and ridge-tiles etc. The new brick hall is by *Herbert Carr* (the former County Architect). The E side of the C13 defences of the town is visible below the school. Going r. from the top, up past the PRESBYTERIAN SCHOOLROOM with its curly Dutch roof and Arts-and-Crafts belfry, and the C18 GLEBE HOUSE with its Gothic casements, we come to the church. Beyond, in LION'S BANK, CLAWDD-Y-DRE has the date 1726 in the old-fashioned way over its door; although built of brick with cambered windows, it has a porch wing as though the date were in the C17. On the N a tiny late C17(?) wing with a shaped gable. The chimneys of the tall double-pile RECTORY, dated 1775, are placed against the gable ends. C19 stucco front. Above a small C18 terrace in BISHOP'S CASTLE STREET, in BACK LANE, stands PLAS TREFALDWYN, a three-gabled brick house of *c.* 1830 whose chimneys are oddly poised over the front gable. Porch of paired Tuscan columns. KERRY STREET leads r., past a doorway with a Gibbs surround, back to Broad Street.

23 CASTLE, ¼ m. NW. The building of the royal castle on its ridge of igneous greenstone was sanctioned by the young Henry III

in October 1223. Twenty miners were sent for from the Forest of Dean on 9 October; by November timber buildings already existed. The site was subsequently developed as a row of wards lying N and S, with the town wall serving as an outer defence to the W, where substantial banks remain. The approach from the S passes a small late C17 brick farmhouse, strangely with dissimilar Dutch gables on either end. This occupies the site of the filled-in outermost ditch, which has an outwork beside it. Two main baileys lie beyond this first one, with possibly a fourth at the N end of the ridge. The importance of their buildings, so thoroughly levelled by order of Parliament in 1649, has only become evident after the recent excavations.

The MIDDLE WARD is defended by a rock-cut ditch which may have been begun before 1229. Its gateway, beyond a bridge, with two D-shaped towers, was the first section of its quadrilateral parallelogram of defences to be replaced in stone in 1251. By 1253 the present walls had been made, with their solid half-round turrets at the SE angle and flanking the E postern into the great ditch which protects the inner ward. The subsidiary tower to the S of these was added c. 1359. They were to support brattices. On the N also the curtain crosses the ditch to the gatehouse. It has a C14 doorway there, but no turrets at all. By the C14 the layout was not dissimilar to that of Powis, but the history of its occupation differs in several conclusive respects. Despite the formation in 1534–43 of the level platform inside the middle ward, to allow extensive timber-framed lodgings to be built (by Bishop Rowland Lee, President of the Council of the Marches), Edward Herbert, into whose family the castle had passed, abandoned it as a dwelling-place c. 1580 and built a 'long, low house' at Blackhall.

Herbert's grandson, Sir Edward (later Lord Herbert of Chirbury), reversed the decision, but sited his NEW BUILDINGS of 1622–5 in this ward rather than in the C13 ward. This house must have been a splendid Renaissance one, in 1680 recalled as 'an elegant and noble pile, beautiful without and richly furnished within'. It occupied the W, S, and E sides of the court and had its principal rooms on the *piano nobile*. The walls were of brick and timber (their bases, in English bond, are now exposed on the W). The builders were two Hertfordshire carpenters, *John* and *Samuel Scampion* of Great Hormead.* Of the Jacobean plaster ceiling made by 'one *Faulkener*', fragments of

* A fine carved Jacobean staircase inserted awkwardly into Lymore (*see* p. 171) was very probably part of the Scampions' work.

geometrical moulded ribbing, diamond bosses, etc., have been found. Lord Herbert surrendered the New Buildings to Sir Hugh Myddelton and Bolingbroke's army in 1644, on condition that the house (and its library etc.) be spared; in 1649, after his death, it and the castle were destroyed.

The INNER WARD has the distinction, shared with Pevensey Castle, Sussex, of possessing one of the earlier twin-towered gatehouses in Britain. 1224 is when heavy expenditure on Montgomery (i.e. on stonework) began; over the next two years £2,000 was spent; in 1233 a tower was being roofed with lead. In 1228 Hubert de Burgh, who may have chosen the site, was granted the castle; though incomplete, it withstood attacks by Llywelyn ap Iorwerth in 1229 and 1231. The innovation of very tall curtain walls protected by circular towers at the entrance is due to Richard I of England's Château-Gaillard. The system was to reach its point of perfection, aesthetically, with James of St George, but some essentials are already present at Montgomery. The solid towers astride the gate passage are combined with the chief dwelling accommodation; the curtain of the polygonal ward, however, while it has two D-shaped towers, does not shew any regularity of plan.

The ditch exposed on the s of the curtain, 20 ft deep and 45 ft across, was bridged. The gatehouse itself consists of the three-quarter-round solid towers, that on the l. with a prison behind which was given a doorway in Bogo de Knovil's remodelling in 1283–8, that on the r. with a guardroom behind, entered by a doorway with segmental-pointed arch. The passage details in red sandstone ashlar include a portcullis groove, jambs of two gateways, and mural cupboards. The three storeys above, consisting of a Knight's Chamber and two private apartments with garderobes, have virtually disappeared. At first-floor level, the chapel, of timber, was built projecting outwards above the passage; the stairs were to its w. The tallest tower, the Well Tower, though of c. 1224 at the base (one lancet), was much rebuilt c. 1359. It stands astride the curtain like a mural keep (cf. Grosmont, Gwent, etc.). The well itself rises from a rock-cut cistern over 200 ft deep. The footings of the N tower alone survive. Among buildings against the walls, the C13 kitchen on the w has its oven under-floor; and the brewhouse on the N, entered by semicircular steps, retains foundations of tanks. Outside to the E a pointed postern door through which the tanks emptied.

LYMORE, ½ m. ESE, demolished c. 1930, was a large and late half-timbered house remodelled by Edward, third Lord Herbert, *c.* 1675 (date on a gable finial) to replace the castle and Black Hall. Its close-studded front had an open three-bay loggia on the ground floor, six gables, and, rising from the centre, a pyramid-roofed look-out tower (cf. the stair-turrets at Plas Mawr, Conwy). A fine carved staircase with diamond-rusticated newels, probably originally made *c.* 1623 for the castle's New Buildings, was moved from Lymore to Aldborough Hall, Ripon, Yorkshire. C18 improvements included a lake.

CWM BROMLEY, 1¾ m. S. A tall, close-studded house with the date 1633 in the ornate bracketed head of the old main doorway. A fine, broad dog-leg stair rises to the attics, with moulded and pierced flat balusters and tapering newel posts. An arch under the second flight.

PEN-Y-BRYN HALL, 1½ m. SE. Built *c.* 1800. Centre of three bays and three storeys, of brick with a stone cornice. Short two-storey wings, on the l. with a Doric porch, on the r. with a blank arch. Lower wings outside these.

PEN-Y-BRYN cottages have attractive Regency iron verandas.

FFRIDD FALDWYN HILLFORT (SO 217 969). One of the great Severn valley forts excavated before the war (see *Archaeologia Cambrensis*, 1942). The earliest fortification on the summit, a palisade enclosing about three acres, was later covered by a rampart, and the area was more than doubled by the construction of a second rampart lower down the slope. Entrances at either end were elaborately defended. The whole fort was refurbished just before the Roman advance. The summit can be reached easily from the road just to the S of it.

CAERHOWEL. *See* p. 85.

HEN DOMEN. *See* p. 111.

NANTCRIBBA *see* FORDEN

NANT MEICHIAID

1010

1¾ m. S of Llanfyllin

PLAS NANT MEICHIAID. A type C timber house with a parlour cross-wing, recently restored. The main range, with the characteristic deep chimney, had a C17 porch at the entry. The cross-wing is well made, with a lateral chimney and with wainscoting inside.

GWAELOD, ½ m. SE. A well preserved small Severn valley regional house with stairs beside the chimney.

NEWTOWN

Newtown has been renewed three times over, which explains its currently untidy appearance. For the already existing medieval village of Llanfair-yng-Nghedewain, Edward I granted a market charter to Roger de Montgomery in 1279. Newtown thus acquired a grid plan, of which Broad Street, and High Street at r. angles to it, leading to the motte and bailey, are obvious survivors despite the town's vicissitudes. One of these was the propensity of the Severn to flood, and only since 1973 have embankments made the low-lying centre of this splendid valley site wholly suitable.

Secondly, the Montgomeryshire Canal reached Newtown in 1819 and seemed to solve the problem of isolation. The population quadrupled between 1801 and 1831, then stood still. With 1200 hand-looms in the town, Newtown rapidly became 'the busy Leeds of Wales'. The magnates of the time were William Pugh, the fourth Lord Sudeley, and Sir Pryce Pryce-Jones. This was also the era of Robert Owen, although it was his less idealistic fellow-townsmen who had the greater influence on their own industries. A uniform type of Late Georgian terraced house, of red brick with pedimented doorcases and one or two floors of big weaving rooms above, was built all round the old town by the hundred; a large number have been demolished since the War, including now some later C19 mills E of Broad Street. One quarter, Penygloddfa, beyond the river, is scheduled for conservation. The later C19 brought bolder brick developments – an ecclesiastical and warehouse quarter – on the New Road.

A third rebirth has been in process since 1965 by which, as one of the Mid Wales Development Corporation's designated towns, Newtown draws on the experience of Cwmbran in Gwent; sectors for factories and for private and public housing arrive with their attendant benefits (and drawbacks) for the very rural locality.

CHURCHES

St Mary. The parish church, by the river, abandoned in the 1840s because of flooding. A broad and low W tower, perhaps C13 in origin, restored in 1939, has C15 windows and a timber bell-stage. The rest is ruined. There was a nave with S aisle of equal length originally divided by a wooden arcade. The standing S wall looks C14, with a priest's doorway under a hoodmould, a PISCINA, and gaping window openings. Within the church a small mausoleum for the Price family of Newtown Hall. – MONUMENT, outside the aisle, to Robert Owen (1771–1858), the humanitarian manufacturer, who was born, and died, at Newtown. By *Alfred Toft*, 1902. A portrait relief, and a relief of labourers receiving justice at his hands. The grave is railed with marvellous Art Nouveau ironwork.

ST DAVID. A large, light, and powerfully vertical church in buff brick by *Thomas Penson*, 1843–7. It cost £4,600. Gothic of the pre-archaeological kind, on the scale of his Christ Church, Welshpool, and on a similar plan – nave with clerestory, N and S aisles, chancel, N porch, W tower – but detailed in an individual C13 fashion with buttresses, bulky pyramidal brick spirelets at the angles, and tall paired lancets with outer and inner hoods. The tower with its saddleback roof and four pinnacles is not quite as gross as Welshpool's, but, like the whole exterior, it suggests some Romanesque abbey. Inside are lofty arcades on piers of flattened octagonal section like the C16 ones in St Mary, Welshpool. Cramped-looking king-post and tie-beam roofs. Bare aisles, originally filled by the N, W, and S galleries removed in the remodelling by *David Walker* of 1874. The yellow brick chancel of 1875 by Walker replaces Penson's short apse – 'more correct but less entertaining', commented Goodhart-Rendel. Big Dec E window. The painting of the internal stonework (1961–4) was an inspiration – a deep lavender blue on the piers; the curious Romanesque-ish enrichment of the arches (in terracotta?) picked out in blue and pink, olive and mauve, etc.; the lancet and clerestory hoodmoulds in grey and yellow. – SCREEN. St Mary, the old church, had an exceptionally fine and long screen of *c.* 1500, the highest in quality of any of the so-called Newtown School except perhaps Llananno (R). Much of it was re-erected here in 1856, but removed in 1875 (surely not by David Walker, who had a sensitive regard for such things?). In 1909 parts were used to line the sanctuary: panels of knotwork, interlacing vine-trails, and geometrical designs, all from the W coving or parapet of the rood loft. *H. L. North* had the rest re-erected in 1938 as a PARCLOSE SCREEN in the N aisle. A delicate length of carving with ribs, bosses, and the most inventive tracery and vine friezes acts as canopy to the altar. There are ten lights in the screen itself, and a triangular-headed doorway. Some parts, particularly the length of vine, leeks, pomegranates, etc., are still coloured gold, red, and green. – PAINTING. The Last Supper, after Poussin; ascribed to *John Dyer*, the poet, *c.* 1730.

– LECTERN. A handsome piece with four lions and a splendid eagle: designed by *Walker*? – Also of the 1875 restoration a good oak PULPIT with a trefoiled arcade. – FONTS. Three in the s aisle: one Perp and octagonal; one of 1847(?); and that of 1874 in use. – STAINED GLASS. E, tracery 1873, main lights 1902, showing Queen Victoria offering her crown to Christ enthroned. – MONUMENTS. Dame Elizabeth † 1731 and Dame Mary † 1739, wives to Sir John Pryce of Newtown Hall. An elaborate wall-monument with a pair of columns supporting an arch with his arms, and two flying putti. – Anna Elizabeth Pryce † 1736. A flying cherub holding a sheet of tasselled material, in marble. – Mrs Morley † 1858, by *Joseph Edwards*.

GOD THE HOLY GHOST (R.C.), Penygloddfa. Formed in 1947 from a C19 brick woollen factory. – PAINTINGS by *Eve Kirk*.

WELSH CONGREGATIONAL CHURCH, Milford Road. 1865. E.E.

ENGLISH CALVINISTIC METHODIST CHURCH, The Crescent. 1879. Dec, with a little spire.

ENGLISH CONGREGATIONAL CHURCH, Park Street. 1876. Dec, with floral glass in the w window. Raked seating.

ZION BAPTIST TABERNACLE, New Road. 1881, by *George Morgan*. An ambitious and handsome chapel in Beaux-Arts Baroque. Front of five bays in bright red (Ruabon?) brick on an ashlar base. Façade with a giant order of Corinthian pilasters, then a cornice with balusters, and above that a shaped brick and stone gable; in front of this projects a full tetrastyle portico and pediment. The order is continued along the flank. The interior also is lavish, with serpentine iron gallery fronts, iron columns beneath, and arcades above. The organ is in a *serliana* recess with marble columns. Schoolroom beneath. The cost was £10,000.

WELSH CALVINISTIC METHODIST CHURCH, New Road. 1875–6. Dec, with raked seating.

WESLEYAN CHAPEL. *See* p. 175.

PUBLIC BUILDINGS

TOWN HALL. By *Colwyn Foulkes & Partners*, 1965–8. Red brick with a hipped pantile roof. Of only two storeys, but nineteen bays long, with regular (but not Georgian) fenestration, an insubstantial stone portico, stone quoins, a cupola – i.e. a hint of a capitol. The effect is low-key and un-urban, which is appropriate, since it stands on the site of Newtown Hall. Beside it is the

DAVIES MEMORIAL GALLERY. 1967, by *Alex Gordon*. Four units, in unobtrusive brown brick, with flat roofs.

MARKET, High Street. With plain iron roofs by *T. Penson*, c. 1850, and a front by the *Development Corporation*, 1976(?). The yellow-brick rear elevation by *David Walker*, c. 1870.

FREE LIBRARY, Broad Street. By far the best building in Newtown. By *Frank Hearn Shayler* of Shrewsbury, 1902. In the Norman Shaw idiom, with a lower storey of François Premier brick and stone, and striking Art-Nouveau-ish timber-framing above – immensely long uprights, a little wooden bow, and a charming balcony on the corner. It is essentially a building on a corner, and the fact that its two clients, having quarrelled, insisted on each side looking different can only have contributed to this highly successful solution. Period interiors.

COUNTY LIBRARY, Ladywell Street. By *Herbert Carr*, County Architect, 1963. The reading room is lit by glass set in its concrete-ribbed tunnel-vault.

COUNTY INFIRMARY, Bryn Road. 1932 by Messrs *Hastwell Grayson* and Messrs *Shepheard & Bower*. Neo-Georgian, round an open courtyard.

FLANNEL EXCHANGE. *See* below.

PERAMBULATION

Standing on the Long Bridge, at the N end of Broad Street, the visitor looks into the C13 town. BROAD STREET was the site of the Tuesday market, of a market hall built c. 1570, and of a successor of 1769 pulled down in 1852. It is to be pedestrianized. In the distance, the grid plan is confused round Market Street and the short Bridge Street. The cinema on the r. occupies the FLANNEL EXCHANGE, built in 1830–2 at the instigation of William Pugh of Kerry (who brought the canal to Newtown). It has paired Doric pilasters on a plinth, with a screen of later columns. In SEVERN PLACE, beside it, public buildings include the former POLICE COURT (*David Walker*, c. 1870) and, at the end on the l., the WESLEYAN CHAPEL, c. 1835 and classical, with a portico of 1878. Back in Broad Street, an uninteresting streetscape of plain terraces of c. 1800 being poorly replaced. The best house, of 1665, was recently demolished to make way for a bank. On the l., behind an early C19 hotel, is old St Mary's, with a former low brick Rectory with iron windows, by the churchyard. This space E of Broad Street, once a place of early C19 mills and terraces, is at the time of writing half-derelict apart from the red-brick TAN-NERY and its characteristic chimney. Further up the street, a Regency shop-front on the l., a large late C19 display of false timbering on the BEAR HOTEL on the r.

More interesting buildings at the cross-roads: the FREE LIBRARY (*see* above) and the confident TOWN CLOCK, cele-brating Victoria's Jubilee, on BARCLAYS BANK, a tomato-coloured, profusely ornamented terracotta office block by *Wood & Kendrick* of Birmingham, 1898. Between them, Severn Street leads to SEVERN SQUARE, the one pre-industrial pocket in the town, with small red brick houses of various C18 dates. To the r. and beyond, a few C17 timber houses. The Wrenian bank, back at the High Street cross-roads, occupies the site of Robert Owen's birthplace (the upper floor contains a small Owen museum). His statue, by *Gilbert Bayes* and *W. C. H. King*, 1953, is straight on over the rise. HIGH STREET is typical for its C19 shop-fronts; the BUCK INN on the r. however is a well-preserved type C timber house of the C17 with a classical brick chimney. High Street leads to the grounds of Newtown Hall, which contain THE MOAT, a large flat earth castle which was probably the town's C13 defence; in 1642 the Parliamen-tarian Sir John Pryce refortified it. Beyond the gardens, the JUNIOR SCHOOL (1953) the COUNTY LIBRARY (1962), and the new POLICE STATION on a rise are all works of *Herbert Carr*, the former County Architect. S of the gardens the Ladywell office block, with vertical brickwork on raking glass as cladding, a piece of forward planning by *J. L. Russell* (Chief Architect to the Development Corporation). Between this and the New Road more weavers' houses survive; yet more on the Welshpool Road. Up the KERRY ROAD is the tallest building by a good margin, the ROYAL WELSH WAREHOUSE, really an early department store, with a red brick Quattrocento eleva-tion, iron supports inside, and a good staircase, by *David Walker* (of Liverpool), 1872. Its builder, Sir Pryce Pryce-Jones, pioneered shopping by post from 1861, and Queen Victoria was a client. 'Industry', says the pediment over the door. Further on, to the l., the Regency rectory of 1813. NEW ROAD, formed *c.* 1821, displays the C19 Newtown, including the poly-chrome brick BOARD SCHOOL by *Benjamin Lay* of Welshpool.

Back to the LONG BRIDGE, an early work (1826) by Mont-gomeryshire's County Surveyor, *Thomas Penson*. Three stone arches of ashlar with rustication on the keystones. The interesting iron-arched footways were added by *Penson* in 1857, after an accident. The bridge leads to PENYGLODDFA (in Llanllwchaiarn parish), the area which most clearly demonstrates the boom which took Newtown's population from 1,700 to 7,000 in a few decades. Housing, at least admirably regularly laid out, began here *c.* 1790. Weavers mostly lived beneath their looms. When power-weaving was introduced *c.* 1850, factories were built near the canal basin. After a period of prosperity, it was Bradford, as everyone knows, that cornered the industry. Penygloddfa retains the evocative presence of the spinning factory cheek by jowl with the houses. CRESCENT STREET leads consistently up the hill, to be crossed by UNION STREET, in which Nos. 1–5, on the l., are a complete row; each three-storey cottage has two cambered windows for its rooms, and two bigger upper windows for the looms. BRYN STREET returns down the hill to COMMERCIAL STREET. Weavers' houses and warehouses again; the poorest (e.g. in Frankwell Street) were flimsily timber-framed even in the early C19. The best examples, Nos. 5–7 Commercial Street, were opened as the most informative NEWTOWN TEXTILE MUSEUM in 1967. Built *c.* 1830, they are in fact six tiny houses, back to back, with iron-railed steps to the doors, and a single room on the storey above reached by a spiral stair. Their top two floors are open from end to end, and the looms stood between the casement windows.

w of Penygloddfa MILFORD ROAD leads past three houses of interest.

CWRT PLAS-Y-DRE (Quaker Meeting House). A small C15 aisled hall moved from the centre of Dolgellau, Merioneth, in 1885. The exterior, as reconstructed, is of stone, with only the gables and the front wall of timber-framing. The latter has square panels on the lower storey, herringbone on the upper. An external stone stair gives access to a gallery along the front. The hall itself is of three bays with collar-beam trusses. The spere-truss stands between the internal cross-passage and the hall proper, and the posts are morticed into the principals (rather than into the tie) of the first roof-truss. The central opening has braces shaped to make a semicircular arch. C17 alterations include the gallery, with turned balusters, carried on an embattled beam round three sides of the hall. Some panelling: and much restoration after the move, which was the work of *A. B. Phipson*. Sir Pryce Pryce-Jones, wrongly, thought this building to have been used for a parliament called by Owain Glyndŵr to Dolgellau in 1404. The house is known to history as the home of Lewis Owen, Baron of the Exchequer, who was murdered on the Welshpool–Dolgellau road by the Gwylliaid Cochion Mawddwy in 1555.

DOLERW (St Mary and St Benedict's School). Built for Sir Pryce Pryce-Jones in 1867. Plain stucco Italianate front with stone dressings, brackets, etc., and a four-column Doric porch. With a tower.

MILFORD HALL, ¾ m. SW of Penygloddfa. A small Early Victorian façade, composed of a pediment and classical detailing to bows and windows.

GRO TUMP, 1 m. NE of Newtown. A deeply-ditched motte and bailey on a bend in the Severn. The motte is c. 35 ft high. A small raised platform to the N is another bailey or hornwork. Probably of late CII date, and perhaps made by Roger de Montgomery.

The MID WALES DEVELOPMENT CORPORATION was established in 1966 with the aim of halting rural depopulation by building factories and houses in six Mid Wales towns. That approaches the philosophy of the New Towns, always remembering that the scale of expansion – from a population of c. 5,500 at Newtown to 13,000 by 1981 or after – and the existing social and economic infrastructure do not call for such extensive planning. The corporation therefore employs the technical resources of Cwmbran Development Corporation; so the Chief Architect (J. L. Russell) is the same for both. An earlier scheme, promoted in 1964, for the Caersws linear town consisted of 'villages' of c. 5,000 people widely scattered along the Severn between Newtown and Llanidloes; its rejection has anyway reprieved this outstanding valley.

Decisions have still to be made on proposals for Newtown's centre; some new buildings have already been noted above. The expansion is zoned for the S side of the river – a number of concrete-clad factories already exist to the E and W at Dyffryn, Vastre, and Mochdre; housing to the W and the S.

GARTH OWEN and MAESYRHANDIR estates were the Urban District Council's, the latter by *Anthony Clarke & Partners*, begun in 1965. Their uniform terraces and squares give no privacy. The addition to Maesyrhandir (1974 by *J. L. Russell*) and particularly TREHAFREN are altogether a different matter. Phase I (c. 1970) is by *Gordon Redfern*, Phases II and III (1972–5) are by *J. L. Russell* (each successively was Chief Architect

and Planner at Cwmbran). The intention was to use a lower
density (thirteen or fifteen houses to the acre) and to disperse
the houses along a pedestrians-only street. That had no need
of width or straightness on its way to the centre, and the result
has plenty of visual variety, plenty to stimulate curiosity. The
attractiveness of the valley situation helps. Materials are chiefly
red brick, with white and black weatherboarding, and slatehanging. The houses are from one to three storeys high,
grouped so as to create spatial interest as well as intimacy. The
other hub of the plan is a meeting hall, shops, etc., on a small
square. Phase III (*J. L. Russell*) comprises more houses com-
pacted into terraces, some with monopitch roofs echoing the
slopes as at Cwmbran, but also much planting and imaginative
landscaping. On the hillside to the S TREOWEN (*Brian Lingard
and Partners*, 1974–) provides a range of intimate to open
spaces, and makes much of contrasting materials and textures.
The groupings are still more varied and informal than Trehafren, and include double-monopitch blocks of flats. The site
is more exposed and the colours are cold grey and yellow
(North Wales colours). In the heart of the town, old people's
FLATS by *J. L. Berbiers* should also be mentioned. Further to
the W, the MAESYDAIL estate (1975–) includes a circular
inward-looking terrace in brick. Nearer the river is the
MONTGOMERYSHIRE COLLEGE OF FURTHER EDUCA-
TION, by *Abbey & Hanson*, 1976–7.
LLANLLWCHAIARN. *See* p. 146.

OFFA'S DYKE

The dyke passes through the E margin of the county. In the Severn
valley and the hills to the S it is thought to be a linking of older
(Bronze Age?) earthworks. Impressive stretches can be seen
near Llandrinio and near Montgomery. See also the Introduction, p. 31.

PENARTH *see* LLANMEREWIG

PENEGOES   7000

ST CADFARCH. The medieval church was replaced by *John
Prichard c.* 1877 with a nave, a sort of crossing, and a chancel
all under a single roof. Externally of grey sawn slate blocks with
sandstone dressings, and rather harsh; the Pembroke slate roof

is a less severe colour. Interior of yellow brick with red and black diapering, and relieving arches. Trefoiled and lancet windows, and a w wheel-window. Wagon ceiling. Richard Wilson's father was Rector of Penegoes (see the tablet on the churchyard wall). – STAINED GLASS. E by *Heaton, Butler & Bayne*, *c*. 1880. – A charming Grecian ORGAN of *c*. 1800.

RECTORY. Regency, dressed stone with a hipped roof; so the birthplace of the painter Richard Wilson (1714–82) is gone.

DOLGUOG, ½ m. NW. In the centre of the N side is a small gabled and dormered house of *c*. 1600 with thick stone walls. To the W a wing with date-stone 1672 and the initials of Francis and Abigail Herbert. E wing *c*. 1750; another W wing *c*. 1800; and a s wing *c*. 1900.

0020

PENNANT MELANGELL

ST MELANGELL. The remote church of Pennant Melangell lies on the side of a beautiful cwm below the Berwyn hills, where Monacella founded a nunnery in the later C8. The legend of her protecting a hare hunted by Brochwel, Prince of Powys, is represented in the frieze from the C15 screen. For her remains an exceptional Romanesque shrine was made (reconstructed in 1958/9). It is of enormous interest both for the architectural type and for the carving. Melangell's festival was held on 27 May. Nearly every century since the twelfth has seen some contribution to this well-loved little building. The church and shrine were perhaps rebuilt by Rhirid Flaidd, who died in 1189, on the Early Christian site.

Nave and chancel are now in one, but only as a result of alterations to the mid C12 church. This consisted of a nave, a long chancel to serve as the feretory, and an apse. Its stonework survives at the SE corner of its nave (between the porch and the narrower chancel), in the opposite wall W of the C19 N window, and in the foundations of the apse in the Cell-y-Bedd, which is abutted against the present E wall. The s doorway, also mid C12, and constructed with chamfered abaci, voussoirs, and a simple chamfered hood, is reset in C17 walling, like the contemporary small rounded N lancet. A reconstruction took place in the C15: the N and E chancel walls were rebuilt on the customary rectangular plan, and so the apse was cut off. The shrine originally stood in the chancel, and the grave is in the former apse (now the Cell-y-Bedd). The plan contrasts with Partrishow (B), where the Cell-y-Bedd is W of the church. It seems that in the C15 a recumbent effigy of Monacella (as a princess) was substituted for the shrine as an object of reverence. Architectural evidence suggests that a S chancel aisle was added then to house the new effigy, and that this aisle and the shrine were dismantled in the C18. The trefoiled S chancel window is C15, renewed. Nave roof of the same period, arch-braced, with cusped apex struts. The rest of the walls are replacements of the earlier work. Everything W of the S door is C17 (stone in the N wall dated 1635); the E remainder of the S wall is C18 and the porch is dated 1737. A W tower was built in the C17, with a timber bell-stage built up from the ground, and reconstructed during the 1877 restoration with a pyramidal roof. – FONT. A plain tapering tub with flat moulded bands at top and base and a filleted roll-moulding round the centre. Second half of the C12. – SCREEN. Late C15. Now 10 ft E of the original position, and mutilated. In the dado a row of six arches pierced with cinquefoils; segmental central arch with rough tracery and drop-cresting, and the eight side openings ogee-headed and richly foliated. Those on the N are dissimilar, those on the S all ogees. Screens of this type are found mostly in the Dee valley. Parts of the parapet of the loft have been re-used on the C18 vestry partition, including a FRIEZE from the W side carved with pretty Newtown-type foliage trails, and – quite exceptionally – with figures representing Brochwel, the huntsman blowing his horn (it stuck to his lips), Melangell with a crozier, the hare and some hounds. It is sad so little is left. – PULPIT. C18. – ROYAL ARMS and BENEFACTION BOARD, also C18. – Corona CANDELABRUM in turned wood, dated 1733. – Painted REREDOS with the Ten Commandments, dated 1886. – Regency ALTAR RAILS. – MONUMENTS. Two recumbent effigies in the nave. First Madog ab Iorwerth, c. 1315: a young man dressed in a surcoat, his sword partly drawn, with the inscription '(HIC IA)CET MADDOC...' round the shield. – Second, St Melangell(?), late C14: she wears the square head-dress of that period and a folded gown, round the waist of which two hares appear to be peeping. That suggested the identification. Both effigies have suffered from ill-use and exposure to the weather. – Tablet to Henry Thomas † 1748, in three colours of marble with a broken pediment.

The CELL-Y-BEDD covers the Romanesque apse foundations and the grave, and contains the shrine. It is structurally C17 but may have had a medieval predecessor dating from after the church's reconstruction in the C15. The beautiful SHRINE

15   is the rarest of survivals, and easily the most delicate piece of
Romanesque architectural design and sculpture in Powys. It
has been dated as early as 1160–70. The material was a reddish
sandstone. A relic chest the size of a coffin is raised on arches
supported by four little columns and two half-columns with
responds, and roofed with steeply pitched gables. Its w end is
structurally joined to an altar of dressed stones, and the whole
stands on a low plinth with a roll-moulding. Enough fragments
were found immured in the church and lychgate walls for a
reconstruction by *R. B. Heaton*; but one wonders whether, in
the absence of original stones, the sarcophagus is quite right;
and whether, had the gables been rebuilt to their full height, it
would not have been altogether too tall. There is nothing of the
kind left in Britain. There were however similar C12 shrines in
England and France. Perhaps the nearest parallel is to be found
on a C12 capital in the crypt of Saint-Denis, which shows an
altar whose E part consists of a gabled shrine supported on
four columns. The bases of the columns and of the capitals are
ringed, and the latters' tops are cable-moulded. The cushion
capitals are shallowly carved on the s with volutes, some
interlacing, and one with fleurs-de-lys between. The s pilaster
and the one old capital on the N have broad sinuous leaf forms.
The twisted foliage is more exuberant again on the spandrels
of the arches, where it is arranged freely, and on the gables
from which it projects as curious little leafed crockets. The face
of the E gable is enriched with lyre-shapes ending in spirals,
arranged in rows. These motifs appear to be very ancient,
perhaps deriving from metalwork decoration. The w gable has
a chevron pattern. The roof itself is of ashlar. Fanciful stonework of this kind exists in a fragment of a shrine at Llanrhaeadr
ym Mochnant, and in other fragments at Llangollen, both in
Denbighshire. This suggests the existence of a local team of
stonemasons.*

The large near-circular churchyard is entered by a LYCH-
GATE dated 1632. Pleasing stonework and arches, and stone
seats within.

LLECHWEDD Y GARTH, ½ m. ESE. In the E wing C17 woodwork
details such as ogee doorheads and carved newel posts on the
stair. Externally the fenestration is C18. Additions and restoration in timber and stone by *Sir Clough Williams-Ellis*, 1907.

* I am grateful to Mrs N. Coldstream for advice on the shrine. The basic
account is of course that of Dr C. A. Ralegh Radford.

LLANGYNOG. *See* p. 137.
PENYBONTFAWR. *See* p. 184.

PENRHOS

2010

HOLY TRINITY. Nave, chancel, S porch, octagonal NW belfry and spire. Pale ochre brick. Lancet windows with ringed terracotta shafts and hoodmoulds on head-stops in the chancel and at the W, all rather self-consciously applied. By *Sidney Smirke*, and dated 1845. – Bath stone PULPIT 1878, replacing a three-decker from the C17 chapel. – MONUMENTS. Margaret Owen † 1816, by *J. Carline*, Salop. Tapering Greek stele with a recessed urn carved with two snakes. – John Owen † 1823, by *R. Milnes*; Neo-Grecian to match. – The chapelry was founded in 1625. The first building was of rubble with a shingled roof.

PENRHOS HALL was a big early C17 timber-framed house which was demolished *c.* 1874.

LLWYN, ½ m. ENE. A cruck-framed central portion of a hall-house standing clear of the slope on a platform. It is unusual locally to see crucks exposed on an end wall. Some C17 additions at the parlour end.

PENSTROWED

0090

ST GWRHAI. Very small single-chamber church entirely rebuilt in 1863. – STAINED GLASS. W by *Powell's*, 1864: Christ appearing to the three Marys. – MONUMENT. Rev. John Herbert † 1876.

GLANHAFREN HALL, 1 m. SE. Brick three-bay, three-storey front of *c.* 1810. The block, one room deep, contains a two-flight stair with honeysuckle ironwork balusters in a segmental recess, and two rooms with classical plaster cornices. A good example of improving a C17 house.

GLANDULAIS, 1½ m. SE. A small Late Georgian house of two storeys and three bays – the outer windows tripartite and with cambered heads. Staircase with fluted balusters. In the drawing room a ceiling with hunting motifs in an oval of leaves, and a frieze of garlands.

PENTRE

2090

1½ m. SSE of Churchstoke

PENTRE HALL. Two timber-framed blocks, one dated 1689 and

with a contemporary staircase. Two-storeyed late C18 stone wing across their ends, the four side windows with triple keystones; good C18 staircase and pilasters on the landing.

ASTON HALL, 1 m. E. Large square-framed C17 farmhouse with an end as well as a central chimney, and a criss-cross l. gable. The added porch, dated 1691, has the usual structure with ropes carried below the corbels.

BISHOP'S MOAT. A motte and bailey on the Sarn Ridgeway at 1,100 ft. The mound is at the opposite end to the entrance. The land was the Bishop of Hereford's.

CAER DIN (SO 274 898) is a small enclosure on flat land close to Offa's Dyke. It was suggested by Sir Cyril Fox that it might be a Dark Age Mercian stronghold connected in some way with this great earthwork, but it may equally be an enclosed farmstead of earlier date.

2010   PENTREHEYLIN

1 m. NW of Fourcrosses

PENTREHEYLIN HALL. A large, very plain neo-Jacobean house of c. 1840 by *Thomas Penson*; ruined.

PENTREHEYLIN NEW BRIDGE. A well proportioned structure erected before 1773. Four arches with triangular cutwaters over the Vyrnwy, and five conduit arches for flood water on the N.

CARREGHOFA AQUEDUCT. Of c. 1796. Designed by *John Dadford*, engineer of the Montgomeryshire Canal as far as Berriew, and *Thomas Dadford*. The contractors were *John Simpson* and *William Hazeldine* of Shrewsbury. It carries the canal over the river on five arches and three dry arches – still. In 1828 distortion of the stonework was checked by the use of iron braces. Yet it can never have looked anything but clumsy; it represents the stage when new problems have not been matched with new techniques.

0020   PENYBONTFAWR

ST THOMAS. In 1855 the lower part of Pennant parish erected its own church, to the design of *R. K. Penson*. Long, dark E.E. nave and chancel with a s tower against the nave near the centre. With its shingled broach-spire and buttressed stair-turret it forms a picturesque grouping. – STAINED GLASS. E by *Hardman*, 1855.

The village proper, as is normal in upland Wales, is a C19 fabric:

that is to say school, terraced houses and their porches, bridge, vicarage, and church are all close in date: it is the scattered farms that are older.

(PENYBONT FARM is a well preserved small stone house of *c.* 1600 with a newel stair beside the chimney. DOE)

GLANHAFON FAWR, 1 m. NW. An L-shaped house of the shrieval Lloyd family, with a C19 front wing. The older part, of *c.* 1600, has a spiral stair beside the chimney and some C17 panelling.

(CILEOS ISAF, ¾ m. NE, is a derelict small mid C16 farmhouse of cruck and post-and-truss construction. Its central hall had an arch-braced collar between the crucks and originally a long seat recessed in the top partition. The lower end was apparently a byre.)

At PARC BACH FARM, ½ m. E, an abandoned house and barn, both cruck-framed.

GARTHGELYNEN FAWR, ¾ m. ENE. The rear, with three stone gables, is perhaps earlier than the front, which is C19 and has a hood over the door with fine acanthus brackets.

LLANGYNOG. *See* p. 137.

PENNANT MELANGELL. *See* p. 180.

PENYGARNEDD

1½ m. ESE of Penybontfawr

1020

BRYNABER HALL. A villa of *c.* 1840. Three single-bay blocks with hipped roofs, the side ones of two storeys, the central one rising to three beneath a depressed arch; lantern on top. The four-column Tuscan porch has been dismantled.

TALWRN. H-fronted farmhouse, part timber- and part stone-built, whose C17 parlour has unusually richly moulded beams.

PENYGLODDFA *see* NEWTOWN, pp. 174, 177

PLASAU DUON *see* CLATTER

PLAS DINAM *see* LLANDINAM

PLAS NEWYDD *see* CARNO

PONT LLOGEL

3 m. NNE of Llangadfan

0010

ST MARY. 1854 by *Benjamin Ferrey*, and paid for by Sir Watkin Williams-Wynn, for whom he reconstructed Wynnstay. A

steep, gabled, strictly E.E. single-chamber church on a hilloc
Spacious and light interior – three big E lancets with pattern(
glass, the central one very tall, and steep scissors truss roof
springing from low corbels. Period fitments.

LLWYDIARTH HALL, 2 m. ENE. This historic house of the
Vaughan and Williams-Wynn families has been replaced by a
dull C19 farm. The only remains of an earlier house are an C18
brick-vaulted cellar behind, and stone stables, whose walls have
a batter, on the road. A Llwydiarth built c. 1420 was frequently
celebrated by the poets of the nobility from the mid C15 to the
end of the C16. Thomas Dinely in his account of the Duke of
Beaufort's Progress in Wales in 1684 sketched an interesting
gabled manor house of c. 1600 with later C17 hipped-roof wings
forming a COURT and fronted by a walled courtyard with a
gatehouse. This was of the North Wales pattern (Trefalun;
Corsygedol): a gabled gate tower flanked by lower gabled
bays.

Two CAIRNS survive in the bottom of the Vyrnwy valley (SJ 039
148 and 015 163), but earlier records mention finds of cists and
other burials from this valley, and from Garthbeibio, which
show that the prehistoric occupation of the area was more
extensive than is suggested by the present remains.

BEDDAU CEWRI – Giants' Graves – is a grandiose name for
what are undoubtedly artificial rabbit warrens (pillow mounds)
of late medieval or early modern date on the hillside at SJ 025
165. These low elongated mounds frequently confuse the
archaeological records, since they can easily be mistaken for
prehistoric graves – at Llanelwedd (R) one happened to overlie
evidence for Neolithic occupation! The commercial production
of 'conies' was quite a widespread industry in the C16–18.

1010   PONTROBERT

ST JOHN EVANGELIST. 1853 by R. K. Penson. Well proportioned gable ends; the slates meet the walls without a coping. Simplest E.E. with a W bellcote, and an equally sensible
interior without structural division. The substantial roof, not
unlike the medieval vernacular, has arched braces resting on
low imposts. Lit at the E by a sanctuary window and three E
lancets.

DOLOBRAN QUAKER MEETING HOUSE, 1 m. ESE. A tiny isolated chapel, dated 1700 over the door, and a cottage under the
same roof; red-brick with drip courses over cambered windows,

and copings on the gables. All the furnishings of the galleried interior have been taken to Pennsylvania and elsewhere. One of the vanished features of this purpose-built meeting house was the openable partition between it and the house. A similar arrangement survives at the Pales, Llandegley (R). Among the members of the meeting were the Lloyd family of Dolobran. The Society of Friends was persecuted in the later C17 – whence the seclusion of the meeting houses – and died out in the area for a century from c. 1850.

DOLOBRAN, ¾ m. ESE. A sad fragment of the home from 1486 to 1780 of one of the most famous Montgomeryshire families, the Lloyds, whose Birmingham branch pioneered the iron industry and banking, represented by the firm of Stewart and Lloyd (now B.S.C.) and Lloyd's Bank. The Lloyds of Dolobran became Quakers in the C17, were concerned with the Mathrafal charcoal forge and built Dolobran forge, and were also concerned in setting up the coke furnace at Bersham, Wrexham, in 1719. It was because of this that they went bankrupt in 1728. The house retains a small wing with William and Mary panelling downstairs, and a sizeable external brick chimney with shaped late C17 supports, joined by a block of c. 1830.

(DOLOBRAN FORGE, ¾ m. SE. The site of this charcoal forge, built in 1719, is beside the Vyrnwy. It was converted into a woollen factory in 1780.)

POOL QUAY

3 m. NE of Welshpool

2010

ST JOHN EVANGELIST. Nave and chancel without division and N aisle in Sweeney Mountain stone; porch and W bell-chamber both in white-painted timber. 1863 by *S. Pountney Smith* of Shrewsbury. The bell-stage is crowned by a little spire. E window of three lancets and a wheel. Goodhart-Rendel said of it: 'A most peculiar church – ambitious, odd and very badly detailed although with a certain competence. It is vaulted in wood internally, the chancel having transverse gables to allow of square (or nearly so) quadripartite divisions. A most elaborate and hideously fantastic carpentry belfry... Proportions bad everywhere but a lot of money spent.'

Before the canal was built Pool Quay was the limit of navigation on the Severn and the port for Welshpool for goods such as iron. Lead from Llangynog was brought down and smelted here. The brick building now called MANOR HOUSE and

SEVERN VIEW may have been used as a warehouse in the C18 but was extensively rebuilt in 1866.

CROWTHER'S CAMP. *See* Guilsfield.

2000   POWIS CASTLE

¾ m. SW of Welshpool

A low MOTTE on the Ladies' Mount, a ridge SW of the castle, is one possible site of a fort of the Welsh princes of Powys, adopted by Cadwgan ap Bleddyn *c.* 1109.

The present red sandstone castle, rightly called Y Castell Coch (the Red Castle), occupies the rock outcrop from which it is built above the Trallwng pool. Its origins are confused. Situated 2 m. W of Offa's Dyke and 5 m. from Shropshire, it is a border castle. It was perhaps the stronghold of Owain Cyfeiliog, master of this province by *c.* 1170 and on friendly terms with England. If so, the rectangular TOWER embedded in the SE angle of the castle could have been built by his son Gwenwynwyn *c.* 1200. This type is not uncommon in South Wales keeps of the Normans (Usk: Whitecastle: Hay), but is rarer in the Welsh castles (but see Dolwyddelan in Snowdonia). This thick-walled tower has dressed sandstone quoins for two storeys but the third is of rubble. On the N of the inner court was the HALL, another thick-walled space approximately reconstituted in Bodley's dining room; this might also belong to the ownership of Gwenwynwyn, in the early C13.

Gwenwynwyn's grandson Owain, who adopted the Norman style 'de la Pole', rebuilt in stone after a sack, particularly of timber buildings, from *c.* 1275 on. The process continued in the early C14 under his daughter, the last of the princely house of Powys, who in 1309 married John de Charleton, and this period produced the bulk of what we see now. This is a CASTLE on the late C13 pattern, consisting of earth outworks, no doubt appreciable before the gardens were formed, of a stone-curtained outer W bailey, etc., and of an inner ward protected by a twin-towered gate (cf. Montgomery) and by tall curtains against which dwelling quarters were built. Taking these in order, the WEST GATE is a replacement in brick, dated 1668, on the plan of the gate blown up by Vavasour Powell's insurrectionists in 1643. The late C13 CURTAIN on the N is externally intact, with an angle stair-turret and a projecting drum tower. That on the S of the W bastion, if it existed, is gone. The l. side of the building facing the court may be contemporary.

The KEEP retains its medieval quality, subsequent help
and hindrance notwithstanding. Two plain half-cylindrical W
towers control the long, narrow, and impressively defended
gate passage. They have small spurs, largely buried. The early
C14 entrance itself lies under a pointed arch with four quarter-
round stepped mouldings, a lintel, then four more pointed
arches. The vaulted, canted passage has two portcullis slots and
arrow loops. The irregular S curtain of squared rubble is mostly
authentic; the second large gate (superseding the postern?), to
the E, has a late medieval character; and the N side too is much
altered, as is the courtyard. As a border castle Powis is particularly strong and up-to-date, but it lacks the finesse of the cen-
tralizing plans of the late C13 royal castles.

The subsequent history concerns its gradual transformation
into a country house, under dynasties of earls instead of chieftains. Sir Edward Herbert, a son of the first Earl of Pembroke,
who bought the castle in 1587, added the *sine qua non* long gallery before his death in 1594. The Herberts were Catholics, and
followed the fate of the Stuart monarchs. Sir Edward's grandson, the second Baron Powis, began to restore the interior after
the Civil Wars, and thus initiated over sixty years of significant
embellishment which continued regardless, apparently, of who
happened to be the occupant at the time. William, third Baron
and first Marquess, lived in exile, and between his death in 1696
and 1722 King William I I I's nephew, William van Zuylesteyn,
created Earl of Rochford, was proprietor. The State Bedroom,
Great Stair, and the start of the terraced gardens belong to the
Restoration, but their European and Dutch-influenced style
did not conflict with the Rochford gardens and wall paintings.
The Powis line resumed with the return of the second Marquess. His great-niece married her distant cousin (a descendant
of Lord Herbert of Chirbury), who was created a new first Earl
of Powis. More internal remodelling; and again more (by *Sir
Robert Smirke*, 1815–18) when the first Earl's great-niece married
the second Lord Clive (for whom the Powis Earldom was
recreated a third time). The windows and skyline of this period
have not changed much. The resulting succession of design is
of great interest and places Powis in a high national category.
It has been in the care of the National Trust since 1965.

We start with the detached N RANGE in the old outer bailey.
It has a few of the tall, thin, cylindrical, Elizabethan chimneys
which occur in clusters on the castle. This building must be
the first of what Leland described as 'two Lord Marchers castels

Powis Castle, plan

1	Inner Court	8	Outer Gateway
2	Dining Room	9	Long Gallery
3	Walcot Room	10	State Bedchamber
4	Tower Rooms	11	Blue Drawing Room
5	East Gate	12	Library
6	Loggia	13	Oak Drawing Room
7	Great Staircase	14	Ballroom

first floor

c. 1200
c. 1300
later

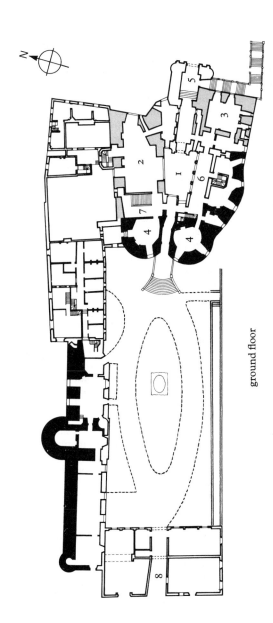

ground floor

within one wall ... the Lord Duddeley's part is almost fallen down. The Lord Powis's part is metely good.' The gabled upper floors, already comprising a long gallery, were converted by *Thomas Farnolls Pritchard*, in 1775–7, into a ballroom and picture gallery. Minimal plaster decoration by *Joseph Bromfield*; vaulted alcoves to C16 windows. The positions of the two faintly 'Gothic' fireplaces show that the room is shortened. Gallery over the entrance on emaciated wood columns with neo-classical motifs in the frieze. Stone windows by *Bodley*?

At the entrance to the gate passage of the INNER WARD the late C17 added a classical doorway (now fronting the orangery). In the l. tower a room with cruciform panels in its Charles II wainscot; in the r. some Chinese paper from Walcot. The inner courtyard gave the space for the long gallery (*c.* 1590). Herbert's work beneath, at ground-floor level, is a Renaissance loggia, four measured bays of simple Doric columns carrying semicircular arches keyed to a string. One of *Smirke*'s improvements was to glaze these openings, put in a neo-Elizabethan ceiling, and to replace the kitchens that occupied this side with bedrooms. In a Smirke bedroom in the C12 tower is another Clive paper from Walcot. Refenestration of *c.* 1818 on this side too. In the centre of this court was the very deep well. On the far side a much less pure C17 classicism appears in a gateway: a diamond-rusticated arch between Doric three-quarter columns which carry a full entablature. This NE GATE TOWER probably dates from the ownership of the Grey family, descendants of the Charletons in the C15. It had three storeys on a rectangular plan till *Smirke* raised it to four to make, highly successfully, a romantic skyline. A beautiful lierne-vault spans the entrance. A fine late C17 rusticated doorway, with an iron gate by *Bodley*, opens to the s. Facing towards the town, its main entrance has a little one-storey Jacobean frontispiece of ashlar with four engaged Doric columns, and two niches with restored statues of the Saxon kings Offa and Edgar.

The N side of the court has two rooms. In the irregular dining room, *c.* 1904, *Bodley* provided an Edwardian atmosphere with heraldic fireplaces, and a neo-Elizabethan ceiling instructively more pompous than the one C16 scrap surviving in a window niche of the old Common Parlour.

61   The GREAT STAIRCASE constitutes the start of the most magnificent interiors in Powys. A product of the Low Countries, spatially and stylistically, and of Italy for pictorial decoration, its twilit grandeur is of a pre-Baroque kind, more restricted and

more rigid. Its counterparts in more fashionable parts of the country were Burghley, Hampton Court, etc., and, more locally, Longnor Hall, Shropshire, *c.* 1670. Powis's may date from *c.* 1668. It is of dog-leg type, with a heavy rail rising at the newels, on balusters enriched with acanthus and small capitals. Bay-leaf garland on the gallery front. The fronts of the treads are inlaid with holly. At the bottom the doorcases are restrained; and the painting on plaster – figures in niches, fruits – is in grisaille. On top comes the contrast of height and colour; and of lavish door frames with pulvinated friezes decorated with acanthus and bay leaves, which support massive double-scroll pediments. The architect seems to be *William Winde*, the Dutch-trained designer of the Powises' Newcastle House in London. His one recorded visit here was in 1698. The ceiling and wall paintings were done for William, Lord Rochford, *c.* 1705. The former is attributed to *Antonio Verrio*. The subject is an allegory adapted from Veronese's 'Apotheosis of Venice' in the Doge's Palace. The scheme of the whole is of columns supporting an entablature, open to the sky as well as to scenes on either side (cf. Burghley, etc.). The walls are signed by Verrio's Dutch pupil *Gerard Lanscroon*. Over the staircase are a 'Triumph of Neptune and Amphitrite' and 'Vulcan forging the arms of Achilles'. Also by Lanscroon the vases of flowers in the pediments and a 'Triumph of Silenus' on the soffit of the landing.

The main rooms are on the first floor. The LIBRARY, remodelled by *Smirke*, has early C18 ceilings by *Lanscroon* there and in an alcove. The OAK DRAWING ROOM, as re-formed by *Bodley* in 1902, lies behind a large canted window facing E. Bodley's are the linenfold panelling, and the lofty and ornate neo-Jacobean ceiling encrusted with pendants. Pennant describes the C16 predecessor of this ceiling as 'stuccoed with most ridiculous paintings of the Zodiac'. Dineley noted busts of Seneca and Aristotle on colums in the chimneypiece. A single window embrasure of this decoration is left, next to a blocked window to the court. The bedroom over the E gateway has nice panelling and fittings designed by Bodley. The third storey of this tower, till 1722 the chapel, has a Jacobean chimneypiece and wainscot.

The superb LONG GALLERY provides for circulation in the 49 s of the house, principally between the Oak Drawing Room and the staircase. It is in fact T-shaped. On the C16 wainscoting, grey and light red overpaint to resemble raised faceted panels, but on the Jacobean doorcase at the end the pilasters and cornice are not *trompe l'œil* but really are in relief. The interesting plaster frieze, dated 1592, consists of stumpy colonnettes dividing painted shields with their white supporters. Some lively man-monsters and mythical beasts in the Elizabethan spirit. The fireplace, dated 1593, includes plaster reliefs of the Temptation and the Expulsion, incongruously beside Sir Edward Herbert's arms. The beautiful contemporary ceiling is patterned, not figural: the ribs, forming in effect a double guilloche design by means of arcs and double-curves, overlap at the intersections. The fields are filled with an interlace of acorns, thistles, etc. In the spur to the l. the infill is more delicate.

62 Beside the long gallery and within the c12 keep the STATE BEDCHAMBER was made. Responsibility for this extraordinary and extravagant casket of a room is probably also *Winde*'s (see the same baluster pattern for the railings, and for the stairs). It is of *c.* 1668. Charles II never used it, but it was slept in by the Duke of Beaufort, the account of whose Progress through Wales in 1684 by Thomas Dineley tells so much. It is unique in Britain in having an alcove for the bed, in emulation of French royal bedrooms, the bed being separated from the room proper by a sort of proscenium, flanked by pilasters and with the monarch's monogram above on a cartouche between festoons, and separated also by a set of rails. The profuseness of the carved and gilded wooden cornice suggests the world of Le Brun. The colours are dull gold on blue. Bolection panelling of geometrical shapes, again with *trompe l'œil* paintwork. Paintings of religious subjects, of vastly lower quality, are set in a frame in the ceiling, and as an overmantel and overdoor.

At the head of the stairs another lofty room, the BLUE DRAWING ROOM, has early c18 panelling arranged in various sizes and painted a light blue: the three tapestries by *Marcus de Vos* are part of the original decor. The ceiling is painted with allegories in harsh colours within fictive frames. As in the library, the figures include portraits of the Powis family, curiously, not the Zuylesteyns.

Between the two medieval portions there is a large (kitchen?) wing, partly of stone and basically Elizabethan, partly c19. One room has part of a late c16 frieze. Over the l. gate tower a room with an intricate ceiling dated 1594. In the N section the construction is of the c17 vernacular timber-framing. This and other parts of Powis received damage from fires in the c18 which may explain *William Baker*'s recorded work (1748–54) and some of the work following *Pritchard*'s survey in 1772. Nothing of theirs appears to have survived the Smirke and Bodley phases, except perhaps the C18 brickwork on the N. Pritchard's chief concerns, other than the offices, were to make more bedrooms (actually done by *Smirke*) and to improve the ground floor (done by *Bodley*).

The famous GARDENS have a strong architectural character. Unlike any others in Britain, they occupy the side of the 100 ft high ridge on which the castle stands by means of four formal terraces each some 200 yds long. Though executed by late C17 Low Countries designers, their ultimate inspiration is surely the civilized extension of Italian villas into their surroundings in the Renaissance. Even the Villa Aldobrandini could not have been more visually dramatic. The most decorative elements are concentrated beneath the castle, and are linked by steps at the sides. The style of each level succeeds the one above. Between ramparts to l. and r. a series of five late C17 red brick niches with alternating triangular and segmental stone pediments seem to date from c. 1675, i.e. the *William Winde* period. On this layer a gardener of genius planted yews, small in the early C18, now bold in colour and shape. Below, a row of arched brick recesses, supporting lead vases. The front of this terrace has a balustrade interrupted by more vases and by four very fine Baroque dancing figures, of shepherds and shepherdesses; they could be by *Van Nost.** This parapet forms the top of the brick orangery on the third terrace. Its centre is set back as an exedra, and the space in front projects forward as well. The name of the engineer who blasted out the rock is given by Pennant as *Adrian Duvall*. The patrons of this substantial section must have been the Rochfords. The rusticated stone doorway of c. 1670, with its flanking Doric columns, was attached to the Orangery by *Bodley*, who had it removed from the w gate towers. On the gentler slopes beneath, after 1722, the Powis family began a water garden, which is shown in Buck's engraving; but it is doubtful how much was achieved. However, Pennant wrote, 'The gardens were filled with waterworks, the whole in imitation of the wretched taste of St Germains en Laye, which the late family had a most unfortunate opportunity of copying.' The terraces retain their original form (though Capability

* Mr Merlin Waterson points out that Van Nost supplied lead figures for Winde's Buckingham House, and could well have made the Powis statuary during Winde's period at the castle.

Brown is said to have urged that they should be reconverted to crags and grass). Following 1772 planting was done and pools were made in the park by *William Emes*. In particular he must have landscaped the ridge opposite the terraces, which to the C18 eye as to our own gave a walk with memorable views.

The fine centrepiece of the outer court is a Baroque statue of Fame, a winged trumpeting female poised on a spirited horse, one of a group originally in the water gardens. The lead of which it is made may be from the vein discovered at Graig-y-Mwyn mine, Llangynog, in 1692.

At the foot of the five flights of steps leading, with the drama of the Baroque, to the E gate tower are William van Zuylesteyn's

68   handsome wrought-iron GATES between rusticated piers. Their maker was *John Warren*, *c.* 1710.* Of the normal elaboration, with an overthrow into which the first Marquess had his own monogram inserted in place of the Dutchman's after 1722; distinguished by large unbroken scallops at the sides.‡

RHYDYCARW *see* TREFEGLWYS

2090   SARN

HOLY TRINITY. Nave, chancel, s tower, by *T. M. Penson*, 1859. Porch under the tower, which has a spire. Scissors truss roofs. The C15 FONT from the vanished chapel of St Michael, Gwernygoe, lies beside the present one. – STAINED GLASS. E by *Mayer*, Munich, *c.* 1876.

(OLD HALL CAMP, 1 m. S. An abortive English castle built in 1228 in the form of a ringwork, intended as a strategic outpost of Montgomery Castle. Probably begun by Hubert de Burgh, and hence identified as 'Hubert's Folly'. De Burgh, who was granted Montgomery Castle in 1228, tried to establish English domination in the Kerry woods. The building work was abandoned after only a few weeks.)

GOETRE, 1½ m. NW. Date-stone of 1749. Goetre was the house of Vavasor Powell, who was in part responsible for the 1647 Welsh Bible.

BETHANY CHAPEL, HODLEY, 2¼ m. WNW. Dated 1840; whitened brick with two Gothic windows.

SNOWFIELDS, 2¼ m. WSW. H-plan, stucco, with odd Gothic

---

* Mr A. Knight very kindly told me the name.
‡ I am most grateful to the Earl of Powis for his help with the account of Powis Castle and with photography there.

details throughout; built *c.* 1860(?) for a tea-planter. Windows
with tracery heads. Screens form porches between the wings.
Two vaulted ceilings with wooden ribs inside; small Gothic
staircase and gallery.

UPPER TREFFIN, 1¾ m. WSW. A Severn valley house with an
overhang all round. Close studding, with the English herringbone timbers on the upper floor. Porch dated 1718, with fret-
cut balusters.

SNEAD   3090

ST MARY THE VIRGIN. Short single-chamber church, almost
completely renewed in 1870; in a square churchyard raised
above the fields. The lower parts of the walls and the voussoired
N and S doorways are perhaps medieval. Nave walls unplastered. Raised tiled chancel. – FONT. C12, circular, four-
lobed, with two handle-like projections. – SCREEN. C19; seven
lights with large ogee traceries.
The Augustinian Priory of Chirbury, Salop, was first established
at Snead.

STRATA MARCELLA ABBEY   2010
2½ m. NE of Welshpool

The Cistercian abbey of Strata Marcella (Ystrad Marchell) was
founded in 1170 by Owain Cyfeiliog, with monks from Whitland, Carmarthenshire. From it, in 1201, Valle Crucis was
established in Denbighshire. A poor abbey, despite endowment
by the C13 princes, it was placed under the control of Buildwas
in the C14. A memorial stone was set up on the Welshpool/
Oswestry road in 1970. The site is now ploughland beside the
Severn, but the church was dug for by Stephen Williams in
1890. With an overall length of 273 ft, it had an aisled nave
201 ft long, transepts only 96 ft long, a short rectangular
chancel, and a 30 ft square tower at the crossing. The long
period of building was from *c.* 1190 till the early C14. There
were buttresses, including clasping buttresses at the W end. The
red sandstone columns of the ten-bay nave had the E.E. pattern
of shafts clustered on piers. Transitional and stiff-leaf capitals
of great beauty reflect the sculptural developments between
c. 1190 and *c.* 1210. Much of this space was occupied by two
monks' choirs. It seems that the elaborate doorway to one of

these may have been the original w doorway. Pier stones with
C14 wavy mouldings were found on the site of the tower. The
cloister on the s has not been excavated. Some actual finds –
C13 tiles and stone fragments – are in the Powysland Museum,
Welshpool. Two local churches possess bits which may origi-
nate here: Buttington's fine stiff-leaf capital, now its font, perhaps from a column in the aisled chapter house; and, at a guess,
Llanfair Caereinion's pinkish s doorway, also datable to just
after 1200. Trewern House has a fireplace.

TRAWSCOED see GUILSFIELD

9090   TREFEGLWYS

St Michael. Nave, chancel, and n porch, substantially rebuilt
on old foundations by *Poundley & Walker*, 1864–5. A lancet
at the w and the Perp e window are re-used from the medieval
church. The w belfry is new, but its stout oaken supports inside
the nave are perhaps C17. Typical *Poundley* Dec windows; the
curious ones in the chancel have nook-shafts, stilted arches, and
dormer heads. Well designed and dull, except for the corbels
and capitals holding the shallow chancel arch, which were
carved with oak and chestnut leaves, ears of corn, and two
doves, by *Griffiths* of Chester.

The village is mostly C19 and C20, except for the Red Lion,
which had a floor of small stones pitched in earth, and the
C18 tithe barn. The slopes of the Trannon valley round
Trefeglwys are however very rich in timber-framed houses,
including nine structures with crucks. Their distribution would
support the theory that the Celts chose to live on ledges above
the valleys, leaving the then undrained bottoms to new settlers.

See
p.
48 Talgarth, ½ m. sw. A large close-studded house, dated to the
1660s. It is of the Severn valley regional type C, but exceptional
in having an oriel window in the jettied end wall of the parlour,
and upper windows under the gable. The central chimney has
been pierced by a staircase. At the time of writing in sad
disrepair.

Ty Mawr, 1 m. sw. A small cruck-framed hall-house built
across the contour. Its timbers have been dendrochronologized
to c. 1500–20. The centre of the three couples has chamfered
arched braces and three foiled struts in the apex. The ends of
the house held separate rooms, the upper ones formed as a result
of the normal C17 conversion – the central chimney creating an

entry lobby. Original panelling opposite the fireplace. There was a canopy above the dais seat. Service rooms up two steps behind. The hall floor is cobbled with a pattern of smooth pebbles set in earth, a circular motif surrounded by squares of stones pointing in opposite directions, and then by a border.

BIRCHEN HOUSE, ½ m. W. A cruck-framed barn opposite; four complete trusses.

RHYDYCARW, 1 m. W. A well preserved Severn valley regional house with the central chimney replaced by stairs and the service rooms removed from the r. end to the back. A big stone chimney in their place. Close-studded, with diamond framing on the first floor. Though built cross-contour, it has a handsome porch. There was a pitched floor in the C17. OLD RHYDYCARW, now a barn, was built, possibly in the early C16, with three cruck trusses, on a stone platform. A well curved couple in the middle have nail-head decoration on the underside and would have had some apex ornament. The dais end pair have a beam between them with a slot for a post-and-panel partition. The parlour lay beyond this, the service room below the (lost) entry screen.

BRYN-DDERWEN, 1 m. N. Four pairs of crucks between square-framed walls. Later stone chimney. The living room has an in-and-out partition and the beam above is cut for the bench.

FFINNANT, 1 m. NE. The C17 door and cross-section stone chimney seem to indicate the conversion of an earlier regional house built against the slope. In fact the framing within includes four box frames. The timber walls have been replaced in brick and stone. In the room on the l. a pitched floor beneath boards. To the rear a close-studded kitchen wing with the date 1677 inside.

PEN Y DDOL. An abandoned house with three cruck couples; of type C since the C17 – or perhaps the half-timbered fireplace is contemporary with the C16 hall.

YSTRADFAELOG, 1½ m. NE. A box-framed C16 house, extended to the r. and converted to the lobby-entry, storeyed type in 1662. In the space of the original open hall there is now a room with a high ceiling of heavily-stopped beams and counterchanged joists in the nine compartments, and a pitched floor under the boards. Pair of square stone chimneys set diagonally.

PEN Y CASTELL, 1½ m. SE. A motte with a rampart round the circumference, at 900 ft.

PWLL GLAS, ½ m. S. An abandoned C17 type C house which had

a pitched floor and a timber-framed, wattle-panelled chimney. As frequently, the structure of the house rests on the fireplace.

TREFNANT HALL *see* CASTLE CAEREINION

0090   TREGYNON

ST CYNON. In a raised round churchyard. Single-chamber, with a good Montgomeryshire w timber bell-turret springing from within the walls; this now has wooden ogee windows and a sundial below the pyramidal roof. The walls were substantially rebuilt in 1787 and again in 1892 by *William Scott Owen*, then Lord Sudeley's agent at Gregynog. He restored the s porch and door and designed the neo-Perp windows. The roof is the usual type of the C15 on: collars and arched braces with cusped wind-braces, much renewed. It is in two sections. The old timber-work supporting the belfry (now enclosed in the vestry) is impressive – huge cross-braced oaken uprights clearly built through the already existing roof. In the C17? Or as late as *c.* 1790? It is interesting to compare the interior reached by Scott Owen with his drawing of it before restoration, when it had a ceiled barrel roof, w gallery, and box pews, and the pulpit was recessed in the N wall. The existing fitments are mostly his doing, like the pews with their quatrefoil openwork. – REREDOS. 1902. Statuettes of white alabaster under canopies of pink. Stencilling on the E wall. – STAINED GLASS. E, a well-designed window by *Clayton & Bell*, made for Street's church of 1875 at Helperthorpe, East Riding, and brought here by Lord Sudeley in the 1880s. – Chancel s. St Dorothea, St Benedict, and an angel, swirling Expressionist figures each with its own colour theme, and strongly leaded; by *Leonard Walker*, *c.* 1921. This lively window is a memorial to William Scott Owen. – MONUMENTS. Large wooden tablet to members of the Blayney family of Gregynog, *c.* 1700. Oval inscription between marbled pilasters, and entablature with urns. –
76   Arthur Blayney † 1795, signed *J. Bacon R.A.* An exquisite neo-classical relief. Tomb decorated with scrolls, cornucopias, and a seated mourning lady, in profile, with on her lap a little nest containing a pelican in her piety. Above this an urn. All carved in cool basso rilievo. The inscription below reads:

Sacred to the Memory of
ARTHUR BLAYNEY, Eſq.ʳᵉ
who, during a long Life paſſed at *Gregynog*,

devoted his Time, his Fortune & his Talents
to the Good of Mankind,
and this Neighbourhood in particular
by ſpiritedly & generouſly promoting Works of great Publick
Utility,
by the conſtant Exerciſe of liberal Hoſpitality,
by a fatherly Attention to his Tenantry & Dependants,
by patiently & ſkilfully reconciling Differences,
by largely encouraging Induſtry & Merit,
and by relieving moſt bountifully the Poor & Diſtressed.

The village is a scattered one, but has a little street by the church
and some black-and-white houses. Some decorated in this
fashion are of brick. There was a brickworks in the parish. A
curiosity is to be found in the neo-Tudor SCHOOL (1872) and
SCHOOLHOUSE by the church, and in the steep and narrow
CONCRETE COTTAGES at the far end: they are indeed entirely
of concrete, roofs and all, yet made to look traditional in construction; in fact at c. 1870–80 they are among the first buildings
erected of that fateful material. The fourth Lord Sudeley, when
owner of the Gregynog estate, pioneered this development. Its
most useful application was for farmhouses, which could be
substantially built at half the price of brick. GWAENTRE-
BEDDAU (1 m. E), FIR HOUSE (1¾ m. SW), DOLYMELINAU
(½ m. NW), and one near Bettws Cedewain (see p. 82) are constructed of it. The material is a pebbly aggregate laid in wet
courses between shuttering directly on the wall (as for cob
walls). The windows, mullioned with semicircular heads, are
also of concrete. For roofs, the technique of pouring the
material on to inclined boards of course produced the now-
fashionable print of the grain in the set concrete. The roofs were
finished with slates, the walls rendered.

In MOAT MEADOW (below the Gregynog drive) a rectangular
ditch or moat looks like the site of an early medieval manor
house or parsonage.

Lewis Dwnn, the C16 genealogist and poet, lived at Ty Mawr,
on the r. above the Bettws road.

GREGYNOG, 1 m. SW. Gregynog and its estate are now used by
the University of Wales as a residential conference and study
centre. Its evolution to quasi-collegiate status should be briefly
described. The earliest known reference to the house is in the
second half of the C12; from the C15 it was the seat of the
Blayney family, and it was celebrated in contemporary poetry

particularly for its hospitality. On the death of the kindly Arthur Blayney in 1795, the property passed to the Hanbury Tracy family. The house was replaced in the life-time of Charles, later first Lord Sudeley, the amateur architect of Toddington, Glos, and Hampton Court, Herefs. His grandson's interests included land improvement here and at Toddington, the use of concrete as a building material, and the woollen industry. He was forced to sell in 1894, partly as a result of prolonged support for the declining Cambrian flannel and tweed mills in Newtown. Lord Joicey was the buyer.

After the First World War Gregynog was bought by Miss Gwendoline and Miss Margaret Davies from their brother the first Lord Davies, the supporter of the League of Nations. They were grandchildren of David Davies of Llandinam. Over the years from 1920 the sisters carried out their intention of making it an artistic centre for Wales. One of the activities was the Gregynog Press, which between 1923 and 1940 produced forty-two books in limited editions. This very distinguished private press, under its controllers starting with R. A. Maynard, continued in the Arts and Crafts tradition and at first printed, *inter alia*, concert programmes, a Life of St David, and the Autobiography of Lord Herbert of Chirbury. Excellence was later achieved also in the wood engravings of Blair Hughes-Stanton and the bindings of George Fisher. The University of Wales restarted the Press (as Gwasg Gregynog) in 1975. Another of the sisters' interests was painting, of which they formed a remarkable collection, particularly of French Impressionists and Post-Impressionists, which was left to the National Museum of Wales. Another was music; a music room was built where festivals and special services of some fame were held. The house and its traditions were a bequest to the University in 1960. As if all this were not surprising enough, the actual fabric of Gregynog should be looked at.*

The first glimpse through oak trees hints at a tall, rickety, Jacobean timber house. One is then startled to find that it is rectilinear and cased in concrete, moulded so that strips stand slightly proud of the surface, in imitation of the local timber-framing and its plaster infill. It is painted intensely black-and-white. The decoration is arranged in bands, broad layers of 'close-studding', chevrons, and diagonals alternating with thinner ones of quatrefoils and more wilful figures. This is certainly inventiveness of a kind, almost kinetic architecture, but who

* I am most grateful to Dr G. T. Hughes for facts and discussions.

was responsible and when – perhaps within the period 1860–70 – is not known. Maybe Henry Hanbury Tracy did it himself, to demonstrate the potentialities of his 'new' material. The result does not quite escape absurdity or even plain awfulness, yet it is masculine and in a way logical.

Anyway the Gregynog of c. 1575 has gone. Moses Griffith's painting shows a two-storey mid C17 brick house of nine bays in all with a slate roof, quite plain but for pedimented doorways. The two-bay wings are cruciform in plan. The nearest parallel is Vaynor Park, Berriew. An inventory of 1795 lists five best rooms, six bedrooms, and thirty service rooms. When this was wholly rebuilt c. 1837 the old arrangement was followed closely: main entrance again to the E, but stable court and outbuildings to the NE. From the Blayneys' house the remarkable panelling in the Blayney Room survives, dated June 22 1636 and tradi- 58 tionally ascribed to Dutch carvers. It decorated a carved dining parlour, sumptuous in effect and specifically displaying the arms of the family (with the Hereford motto 'Virtutis comes invidia') and of their Welsh princely forebears. The arms over the fireplace are those of John Blayney, the probable C17 builder, and his wife.* Most of the fire-surround and the shapely shields of arms, within arcading resting on pairs of tapering pilasters, is the original fanciful work of European post-Mannerist fashion, with C19 additions to fit the larger room. The cellars seem to belong to the rebuilding of 1837, but the rest of the house and the tall Elizabethanizing E-front in particular look much later (Nicholson's Annals shows it as existing in 1872). In 1877 *W. E. Nesfield* published designs (which were not executed) for a more sophisticated façade.‡ The music room, on the NE, partly of the mid 1890s (by *W. Scott Owen?*) and partly by *E. S. Hall c.* 1925, has impeccable architectural manners; the large semi-dormer windows give it bulk, and the black-and-white is real timber post-and-pan. By contrast the brick refectory- and service-wing added behind by *Alex Gordon* in 1967 is straightforward modern with a flat roof.

A plan of the demesne lands was made for Arthur Blayney in 1774 by *William Emes*. His scheme of alterations, including strings of narrow lakes, clumps of trees, and a serpentine path

* The Blayneys bore the three boars' heads erased of Brochwel Ysgythrog; the Lloyds of Berthlwyd the lion rampant erminois. Dr Prys Morgan has skilfully identified the heraldry.

‡ Mr Stephen Levrant has found that *H. R. Ricardo* made alterations (an E bow, central gables) for Lord Joicey *c.* 1895.

linking the beauties of an already well-timbered estate (to use
some of the terminology of the time), was, it seems, largely un-
realized. The broad undivided valley between wooded hillsides
s w of the house is the one area with identifiable c18 planting
and a picturesque landscape vista. The existing layout, like the
house, has a strong Victorian sense of formality, with its
railway-age drives, two concrete BRIDGES (one dated 1880),
and masses of evergreens. As a result the house stands on a
treeless flat terrace of lawns between hollows – still bereft of
Emes's curving pools of water. Landscaping for the University
is being carried on after a plan by *Sylvia Crowe*. A LODGE in
the park and a smaller one on the Bwlch-y-Ffridd drive, both
attractive and half-timbered, are by *Halsey Ricardo*, *c.* 1880.

TRELYDAN HALL *see* GUILSFIELD

2000
TRELYSTAN
1½ m. SE of Leighton

ALL SAINTS. A wonderfully remote church, 900 ft up at the s
end of the Long Mountain. Unique in Montgomeryshire in that
it is timber-built. Single-chamber, with s porch and w belfry;
early c15. Not too happy a restoration in 1856: brick and timber
casing outside and pitched pine inside. None of the windows
is original. c15 roof of principals and arched braces with two
tiers of trefoiled wind-braces – quite typical except that every
other truss was strengthened with a tie-beam, now sawn off and
replaced with iron ties. – SCREEN. Five lights s of the main
opening survive, without their cresting, but with five different
ogee tracery heads robustly carved in oak. Crossley observed
that the semicircular heads and boarding at the base are
characteristic of the Dee valley and resemble the screen at Pennant Melangell. – ALTAR RAILS. Turned, Jacobean. – The
BARREL ORGAN, made by S. Parsons of London, has a Gothic
case. 1827. – STAINED GLASS. E, a pious window, the Agony
in the Garden, perhaps by *David Evans*; in wooden tracery.
BEACON RING (SJ 265 058). A large, simple enclosure of five
acres or more on Long Mountain. It has a single massive
rampart and ditch, in places over 20 ft from top to bottom, but
the effect of the monument has been marred by afforestation
of the interior – particularly unfortunate since it is in the
interior of such sites that one may expect useful results from
excavation. The original entrance was at the s end, where there
is a simple gap, with the rampart ends not exactly aligned.

TREWERN

At the foot of Moel-y-Golfa

COUNTY PRIMARY SCHOOL and COMMUNITY AND YOUTH
CENTRE, 2 m. NE. By *Herbert Carr* (County Architect),
1954(?). Perhaps the most sensitively laid out of the county's
schools, centred round the usual taller hipped-roofed hall/
gymnasium/theatre. The main rooms are grouped by areas so
that they overlook open courts but are not themselves over-
looked. The single-storey brick classrooms have a long side
almost entirely of metal-framed glass, well shaded, and another
light-source opposite. The style has a flavour of neo-Georgian,
yet at the same time is firmly modern (especially in the
detailing).

TREWERN HOUSE. The lower part was an open hall of *c*. 1500,
now reduced in length and with a C17 chimney and floors. The
taller part at r. angles has a jettied gable and woodwork details
– beams on corbel posts, an ogee doorhead – *c*. 1630. The real
interest of the house, however, is the large stone chimney
between the two. Four fireplaces open to it, each with chamfered piers of red sandstone and chamfered lintels. The
ground-floor fireplace to the old hall has two carved heads –
late C13 remnants of Strata Marcella Abbey, it has been
suggested.

MAES FRON. An irregular Late Georgian house with key-fret
ironwork veranda and recessed porch with fluted half-columns
in antis. In the garden a small shell-lined grotto.

POST OFFICE. A good group of estate buildings erected *c*. 1860
for Maes Fron. The seven-bay range has a central gable and
twisted and zigzag brick chimneys. To the l. a STABLE with a
spirelet and lattice windows.

TREWERN HALL, 1 m. W. One of the most handsome timber-
framed houses surviving in the area, formerly the home of the
Kynaston family. It has the date 1610 over the r. porch. Of
earlier date, perhaps the first half of the C16, is the low box-
framed r. wing, with deeply chamfered ceiling beams. The front
is nearly symmetrical: two gables with a hall and other rooms
between, and two-storeyed porches, the l. one built against the
l. wing. The C17 work is post-and-pan with two upper courses
of quadrants, and herringbone in the large gable. It is also
jettied on three sides on corbels, carved with figures and heads
on the front, and of scrolly design on the possibly later rear
wing. A long wood mullioned and transomed window survives

on the front and some stone tiles on the roof at the back. As it is close to the Severn, the house was originally ringed with flood ditches.

BUTTINGTON. *See* p. 83.

TY MAWR *see* CASTLE CAEREINION

9080   VAN
                  2 m. NNW of Llanidloes

The Plynlimon area has been worked for lead, copper, and silver since Roman times at least. Mines were let to Sir Hugh Myddelton in the first half of the C17, and interest in them revived in the late C18. The Van mines, yielding lead and silver, were at their most productive between 1869 and 1881; 550 men were employed after 1865. Some evidence of the workings, two out of eight brick chimneys, housings for the processing machinery of the 1860s on, and a few terraces of houses remain to be seen. The BRYN TAIL mine is in DOE guardianship. The DYLIFE mines were worked from *c.* 1770 to 1896. Bright and Cobden had an interest in them.

VAYNOR PARK *see* BERRIEW

VYRNWY *see* LAKE VYRNWY

2000   WELSHPOOL/Y TRALLWNG

A bustling market town of nearly 7,000 people, the largest in the county – till the expanding Newtown overtakes it – and a gateway to Wales (it is only 4 m. from the Shropshire border). As a centre, and architecturally, it is a much smaller version of Shrewsbury. The English name, originally Pola, distinguishes it from Poole in Dorset. In Welsh it is Y Trallwng, after a lake near the castle; or Trallum Llywelyn, after a Celtic saint, father of Gwyddfarch of Meifod, the site of whose chapel was near the later Domen Castell by the station. This minor castle is mentioned in 1196. But the town grew up under the protection of the lords of Powis' Red Castle. Its charters were given in 1263 by Gruffydd ap Gwenwynwyn, Prince of Powys, and in 1406 by Edward de Charleton. Welshpool's old axis stretches from the dividing of the Llanfyllin and Llanfair Caereinion roads at the W (at a roundabout on which the Gothic lodge to Llanerchydol stands) down past the park of Powis Castle into Mount Street and High Street (which contains

the older buildings) and on to the crossing with the main Shrewsbury to Newtown road. Most of the C19 and C20 building lies
along the latter either way. The fourth road leads from the centre
to the canal, public buildings, and the railway station, and beyond
this to the light industry area on the Severn flats. The Montgomeryshire branch of the Shropshire Union Canal was authorized
in 1794 and the Cambrian railway reached here in 1862. The
borough's prosperity then derived from flannel-working, malting,
and tanning; it was, besides, a port and an agricultural centre.
Its Smithfield, or livestock market, is now the largest in Wales.
Lewis's *Topographical Dictionary* said of it *c.* 1840, 'The whole
town has a cheerful and prepossessing appearance, having more
the character of an English than a Welsh town.' The judgement
holds good.

ST MARY or CYNFELYN. Directly overlooking the town from
a large hilly churchyard. Adam of Usk was its priest in 1411, and
William Morgan (translator of the Bible into Welsh) was vicar
in 1575–8. Probably the church is the Ecclesia de Pola
mentioned in the St Asaph valuation of 1253. A building of
involved evolution, it now has a W tower, nave, chancel, N and
s aisles, and s porch. The church was refounded *c.* 1250 by
Gruffydd of Powys (*see* above); of the C13 are the massive W
tower (to two-thirds of its height) and arch to the nave, and
a three-lancet window, with two little circles as tracery between
the points, set in the N wall of the organ chamber but probably
the E window of the first church. This may have been a double-
naved church whose E wall lay about where the chancel arch
and nave E window are. The chancel was added *c.* 1350 to the
N nave. Three windows with reticulated tracery survive, one
on the N and two on the s. The two-storey porch – like Guilsfield's, to the s nave – is contemporary. The non-alignment of
tower and nave with chancel and other irregularities are per-
plexing, but might result partly from the sack and burning of
Welshpool during the Owain Glyndŵr troubles in 1401. The
present large airy arcades are C16, of pink sandstone, with un- 46
usual Tudor arches and slim piers with flat mouldings and embattled capitals. They then rose to a clerestory and a shallow
roof slightly higher than the present one, with battlements
throughout. Was this done before, or – more interestingly –
after, the Reformation, by the Herberts, one wonders. The
chancel roof, with its Perp beams and coloured bosses, could
be of this period or earlier. The N and s aisles were again rebuilt
in 1773–7 and the tower raised (and its short timber spire

removed). There were two C19 restorers. The first, *John Billing*, in 1856–7 rebuilt the chancel E wall, with its window of five lights of flowing tracery of Shropshire type, a version of the C14 stonework, and erected another of those chancel arches on corbelled shafts. Then in 1870–1 *G. E. Street* put in six handsome flamboyant Middle Pointed windows to light the early C19 galleries in the aisles, and also the nave E window. He had the two SW nave piers built in replica to include the S porch in the aisle area, and added the grand and gloomy open roof, each of whose embattled tie-beams supports a king-post and queen-posts treated as an arcade, with cusped strutting: an extraordinary over-medievalization. Most of the fitments are of this period too, if not all by Street. – FONT, renewed in Mansfield Woodhouse stone. – Elaborate PULPIT (1877) and low CANCELLI (all of stone). – Alabaster, Caen stone, and marble REREDOS, executed by *T. Earp*. – Fine brass ALTAR RAILS and LECTERN. – STAINED GLASS. E by *William Wailes*, 1862. – Much in the aisle windows of *c.* 1875. – TRIPTYCH. Flemish, *c.* 1510. – Fine CHANDELIERS given in 1776.

MONUMENTS. N chancel wall, Sir Edward Herbert † 1594. Painted stone wall-monument with a pair of shallow arches formerly containing figures of his wife and himself kneeling and facing each other. Two detached columns, scrolls above them, and gadrooning and strapwork below the inscription. Dated 1597. – Edward Herbert, second Earl of Powis, † 1848, opponent of the union of the sees of St Asaph and Bangor (in the interest of endowing a new diocese of Manchester with the St Asaph revenues) and patron of building at Montgomery and Powis. Recumbent effigy by *Edward Richardson*, 1852, of alabaster from Chellaston, Derby. The figure, in Garter robes, two angels at the head and an elephant at the feet, lies on a carved chest with brasses by *Waller*. In a recess with Caen stone arch carved by *J. B. Philip*. The whole design was *Sir G. G. Scott*'s. – Third Earl of Powis † 1891. Alabaster recumbent effigy modelled on the above. – Morris Powell † 1729. Small marble as a piece of fabric. – Brass plates to the Rev. S. Davies † 1693, to the Rev. W. Wynne † 1696, and to T. Evans † 1766, in a small Rococo frame. – On the W wall a splendid Stuart ROYAL ARMS. – PLATE. Chalice, 1662, of Guinea gold, presented by Thomas Davies, the Governor of Guinea.*

CHRIST CHURCH. Above Mount Street, on the edge of the park of Powis Castle. A large Anglo-Norman church by *Thomas Pen-*

* The Ven. O. Thomas gave me valuable help with the church.

son, 1839–44, and just earlier than his St Agatha, Llanymynech (Salop). Nave, N and S aisles, apse, S porch, N W tower. Exterior of Welshpool granite, very roughly detailed, with huge conical turrets and massive buttressing. Interior of a grand Romanesque kind, with columns with scalloped capitals, a clerestory, [81] and a flat ceiling. The arches and their ornament are in terracotta, and so is the apsidal rib-vaulting and E arch, but the shafted windows, triforium, and wall arcade are of stone. Giant-size pews. All done for the coming-of-age of Viscount Clive. – FONT of terracotta. – GLASS. Three apse windows probably by *David Evans*, 1844. – PLATE. A C15 alms-dish, probably German, embossed with the Temptation of Eve and Adam (cf. Llanuwchllyn, Merioneth).

ST WINEFRIDE (R.C.). A dizzily steep cruck-framed hall (the timbers are laminated) – an effect avoided by medieval users of the technique. Not a comfortable pitch of gable outside, and an unintimate interior with bare brick walls. The baptistery – movingly – has a glass wall facing the street. By *Weightman & Bullen*, 1963. – GLASS. Designed at Buckfast Abbey.

CHAPELS and PUBLIC BUILDINGS. *See* Perambulation.

PERAMBULATION. At the top end of the town low stone cottages lead to the open curve of MOUNT STREET, and the view beyond to the Long Mountain shows that the tallest buildings are still the parish church and the town hall. On either side, modest C17 timber-framed and C18 brick houses with some C19 replacement. Only slightly townish doorways distinguish them from their country neighbours; e.g. the TOP HAT. HIGH STREET begins with the larger early C18 PLAS GOCH houses, brick with cambered windows and tall roofs. THE MERMAID on the l. is C16, restored. No. 14 on the r. with a fanlight is an example of the late C18 switch from dormers to a full attic storey. Then the METHODIST CHURCH, 1863 by *George Bidlake*, stone with a little Dec spire, and the PRENTICE TRADERS of *c.* 1600 with quadrant woodwork like No. 9 and still with cobbles outside. PARK LANE HOUSE, five bays with an Ionic porch, is a C19 front on an C18 house; beside it a lane runs to the gate of Powis park, where there is a neo-Jacobean LODGE of 1932. Beyond is ANDERSONS, a large C17 brick and timber house containing a fine stair of *c.* 1660 with a gate to the cellars and four complete flights round a well to the attics. Tall newels and pendants, and square balusters with the mouldings slanted on the flights. Opposite, on the bend, Nos. 41–43, good Georgian houses with wooden cornices and classical doorways, but spoiled by improvements. The TOWN HALL is by *Benjamin Lay*, 1873–4, a vaguely French Renaissance stone composition, with pilasters and pediments above a basement, though the facade was changed soon after building – in 1881. Its best feature is the central clock tower with a château roof. It is certainly more prestigious than the late C18 brick town hall, enlarged *c.* 1820, whose arches protruded into the street. Part of this survives down HALL STREET on the l. opposite some C19 shop-fronts. BROAD STREET is the commercial centre, with LLOYDS BANK in a stuccoed Regency house of 1816 with a rusticated ground floor, and next to it a bowed Regency shopfront. Thereafter plain brick three-storey fronts with dates from 1721 to 1803. The NATIONAL WESTMINSTER BANK of 1972, at least in brick, is a clumsy match except for the pitch of the roof. Down a lane on the r. the ENGLISH CONGREGATIONAL CHURCH, a yellow terracotta façade with three pairs of lancets in deep reveals with lots of shafts and dog-tooth. In CHURCH STREET, l. at the cross-roads, there is a good C19 commercial building on the r. (perhaps converted from the old stables of the Royal Oak) – ten pilastered arcaded bays, including the doorways. Opposite St Mary is CHURCH HOUSE, 1892 by *T. E. Price*, of green Criggion stone with a sprocketed roof. Built into the w wall two fine curly open-pedimented sandstone window frames of *c.* 1700. Do they come from Powis Castle? Facing this is the small High Victorian POWYSLAND MUSEUM, in yellow Ruabon brick, by *David Walker*, 1874. It is top-lit with blank pointed windows and Gothic detailing. Here are the archaeological finds of the region, fragments of C13 tiles etc. excavated at Strata Marcella Abbey in 1891, and other objects such as a big bronze group (designed in 1856 by *J. E. Thomas* and modelled by his brother *W. Meredith Thomas*) of the Death of Tewdric Mawr, a subject chosen by Lady Llanover to commemorate Morris Charles Jones, the founder of the Powysland Club which built the museum and which still publishes the most valuable source of county history, the Montgomeryshire Collections. SALOP ROAD starts with pleasant warm red brick early C19 terraces with white detailing, and BRYNTIRION, a Victorian house with oval dormers. Some way further on on the l. WELSHPOOL HIGH SCHOOL, a large complex partly by *Herbert Carr* in his usual pale brown brick. Now r. at the cross-roads down BERRIEW STREET – past the florid MIDLAND BANK of 1876 – where there are still characterful shop-fronts. On the l. is the former NATIONAL SCHOOL of 1821, two simple stone pedimented wings making a little yard. Opposite, a good red brick Victorian SCHOOL with traceried Perp windows. At the end of the town on the r. is OLDFORD CLOSE, the council estate. Conventional at its start c. 1950, it expanded w in the late 1960s with a scatter of prefab-concrete and weather-boarded terraces that raise acutely the problems of an urban vernacular suitable for Wales. This effort is sadly unrelated to its corner of Powis parkland and the Severn valley patchwork beyond. Unbroken flat roofs seldom look well on a hill. Surely housing need not be ugly or slick to be convenient?

Starting again from the cross-roads, SEVERN STREET is consistent with Broad Street with its houses of 1800 and after. The ROYAL OAK HOTEL represents the Late Georgian tradition, with its carefully proportioned red brick, three storeys, tripartite windows, and a good iron sign-bracket. On the r. the MANSION HOUSE, Regency, with a paired-column Doric porch and entablature. Nos. 19–22 are a mid C19 brick terrace with deep eaves. No. 18 on the r., a solicitor's office dated 1863, has a chunky porch with all the detail misapplied, weird-shaped semi-dormers, and feathery ironwork finials. More houses with Georgian details on the l. before the bridge. The CANAL here was thoroughly restored in 1973 as part of the programme to re-open it section by section for leisure use. On the other side boxy government offices face four characteristic detached houses of c. 1800; the last is Clive House. All the other PUBLIC BUILDINGS here are in hipped-roofed neo-Georgian. The COUNTY OFFICES, begun in 1931, were extended in 1941–64 by Herbert Carr (the County Architect) with rather wayward neo-Georgian details. The PRIMARY SCHOOL of 1952 is also Carr's, and so are the sober ALMSHOUSES of 1938. The POLICE STATION (1954) too is in this fail-safe style. The RAILWAY STATION, by Benjamin Piercy (?), c. 1866, is the most disciplined building here. Brick and stone façade of six gables, flanked by two mansard-roofed pavilion bays, with unexpected bits of Gothic detailing and an elegant ironwork platform canopy (made by the S. Morris foundry, Welshpool). DOMEN CASTELL, a motte and bailey castle of the late C12, was cut at the SE for the railway.

GUNGROG HALL, 1 m. E. Mid C19 brick and still Georgianizing, containing some panelling removed from Sir Edward Waldo's house, No. 117 Cheapside, London. The carved room has now returned to Barclay's Bank on that site, but a panelled room of *c.* 1700 with pilasters by the fireplace remains, with more in the hall.

80 LLANERCHYDOL, 1 m. w, was a commote. The present house probably occupies an ancient site. Some part of the core may be brick of 1776, but most consists of Regency Tudor extensions to the s and E of brick and stucco, with ochre sandstone facing on the main range. This remodelling was done after a fire, for David Pugh, whose initials and the date 1820 are on the projecting r. gateway. w wing of *c.* 1870. The exterior is completely irregular and romantic, a turreted wing and a clock tower accenting its ends. Though basically L-planned, the main sides can scarcely be seen together, even from the E, because of the lie of the land. The three-storey juxtaposed ranges in the centre have two slim octagonal turrets, ground to skyline, and are corbelled out at roof-level; the gate arch springs from two similar turrets. Surfaces are massive and unarticulated, except by square window labels. Though shifting in plane and height, they are linked by a parapet of battlements which is continued along a curtain wall to the clock. The house is very much in the picturesque tradition, and the remodelling is perhaps by the *Reptons.** Perp arch on corbels in the hall. Staircase with Perp ironwork balusters climbing round a big well. Drawing room with flat ribbed ceiling and oak-leaf cornice. The dining room has paper imitating tooled leather, perhaps by *Mortons* of Liverpool, who made the Pugh heraldic paper for the stairs at the end of the C19. A Tudor LODGE outside Welshpool stands above four rising sections of Gothic cast-iron railings.

POWIS CASTLE. *See* p. 188.

1010   YSTUM COLWYN
                    ¾ m. SE of Bwlch-y-Cibau

YSTUM COLWYN FARM has a group of minor buildings witnessing to a long continuity of occupation. The farmhouse is C17, made irregular and much repaired in 1825. A BARN nearby has a beam reset as a lintel with the date 1650(?) and the initials of John Williams of Cochwillan, Caernarvonshire, the probable builder. Next to this another BARN with three cruck trusses and also tie-beam trusses. Beside the farmhouse a dignified farm building (cum bothy?), dated 1719, of brick, gable-ended,

---

* Unpublished thesis on the Castle Style by Alistair Rowan, Cambridge University 1965. The informal arrangement is comparable with *Humphry Repton's* proposals for a Tudor 'farm' at Stanage (R).

eight bays and two storeys, with stone quoins and an external chimney. Alongside that a hipped-roof STABLE block dated 1721. This is also of brick, seven bays, with a brick string-course lifted over the arch and good cornices.

YSTUM COLWYN HALL. A featureless stone house of 1866 for a Liverpool cotton magnate.

(PONTYSGAWRHYD, a notable large timber-framed house demolished in 1955, was the home of the Mytton family. Of various builds from the cruck stage on, it contained a wains-coted parlour dated 1593.)

PONTYSGAWRHYD CORN MILL was installed by the Myttons in the early C19. The waterwheel and grinding mechanism are still there.

MEIFOD. *See* p. 159.

RADNORSHIRE
MAESYFED

★

ABBEY CWMHIR

St Mary. Nave, chancel with an apse, and an intriguing s w 91 tower over the porch, in which a ring of colonnettes interrupts a Normandy tower between the broaches and its octagonal spirelet. By *Poundley & Walker*, 1866. Rough-textured stone. Over the porch doorway a relief of the Ascension copied from the tympanum from the abbey. Bell-turret and E windows break the roof-line (a favourite device); the latter are of Poundley's usual lancet-and-circle pattern. The chancel arch, PULPIT, and FONT are ornately carved. – MONUMENTS. Sir Hans Fowler † 1771. – COFFIN LID of *c.* 1200, lettered with the name of Mabli, an abbot of Cwmhir. – STAINED GLASS. Excellent chancel windows by *Heaton, Butler & Bayne*, 1866. Ascension and Crucifixion together in the E, in the deep colours for which they were noted; Christ's Baptism and Agony in the 93 s, the latter an outstanding design by the gifted *R. J. Bayne*, with a sensibility well ahead of its time. – w by *Clayton & Bell*. – St Mary is a foundation of 1680.

Beside the church are a red brick SCHOOL of 1857 and the HAPPY UNION INN, a pleasant little Regency building with iron Gothic windows.

CWMHIR ABBEY. Ruins ¼ m. SE of the church. The Cistercian abbey in the Long Valley was founded (according to the Chronicle of Chester Abbey) in 1143, by Maredudd son of Madoc ap Idwerth; it was refounded in 1176 with monks from Whitland in Carmarthenshire by his brothers Cadwallon and Einion Clud. From Cwmhir, Cymmer Abbey in Merioneth was founded in 1199. The great church originally intended for sixty monks and erected in the early C13 possessed the longest nave in Wales (242 ft). Its fourteen-bay E.E. colonnades are comparable with Canterbury for length; even Wells has only ten bays. That splendour is utterly gone now; the state of the ruins, at the time of writing, is melancholy. If some action cannot soon be taken to secure what remains, the last bits of carved stone will be pilfered, and a short time only will see the remaining walls broken down. The monastic plan and that of the late C12 abbey (of which one corbel head has been found) has yet to be fully established by excavation.

Even the plan of the church is uncertain, for the chancel was never built, and much may have become ruinous both in the C13 and after the Glyndŵr troubles. Foundations of N and S transepts (never completed?), spanning 154 ft, are visible, and so is the collapsed temporary wall in the W crossing arch. The N and S walls of the nave, 63 ft wide, stand in places, but no doorways or windows are intact, and only the bases remain of one crossing pier and of three nave piers. A few triple-shafted responds survive on the walls. Grinshill stone was used. Clearance was wreaked by Thomas Wilson, the owner in 1822–37; but the process evidently began from the day of Dissolution, in view of the re-erection of five bays of the nave arcades at Llanidloes (M) (see p. 140). Those pillars are perhaps over-low; their stiff-leaf capitals suggest a building period from c. 1200 till c. 1230. In 1282, Llewelyn the Last was buried in the church; in such princely connections, as well as perhaps in style, Cwmhir Abbey parallels Strata Marcella (M). Its great size and its first-rate E.E. style may reflect the patronage of Llewelyn Fawr. A carved tympanum now in the farmhouse garden may not have come from the abbey. The subject of the much-weathered relief is the Assumption.

As for the cloister S of the church, nothing is above ground, and the only indication of building is a mound S W of the church, which may be the collapsed chapter house. In the clearance of c. 1825 the abbot's lodging, the refectory, and the dormitories were identified as having been on the E, S, and W sides respectively of the cloister, but this needs confirmation.*

ABBEY CWMHIR HALL. By *Poundley & Walker*, 1867. An interesting pair with the church, in ashlar but again gaily detailed – bands of coloured slates on the steep gables, red and white stone relieving arches. The main characteristic of the mansion is its bargeboards arching across the asymmetrical gables.‡

DEVANNOR, 1 m. E. Massively built, c. 1670, for Richard Fowler

* A detailed paper by Dr C. A. R. Radford on the history and plan of the abbey is to appear in *Archaeologia Cambrensis*.

‡ It was perhaps the preceding house on the site, of 1656(?), which is referred to in the popular jingle, a version of which is:

of Abbey Cwmhir. Of three storeys with gaunt stone walls, battered end chimneys, and diagonal stacks. The plan is symmetrical. The central NE entrance is to a robust four-flight dogleg stair with pierced balusters and elaborate geometrical newels, all tapering from top to bottom. A plain flight also leads down to the kitchen floor, infrequent before this date; one room there has served as a Methodist chapel since 1818.

ABEREDW

0040

St Cewydd. A lovely church beside the River Edw. Nave, chancel, N porch, W tower. The nave might be C14. One Dec window and a steep-pointed Perp doorway. The chancel is in fact no narrower than the nave, and they are probably coeval, but their stone-tiled roofs are not continuous. No E window; in its place tablets with the Decalogue. C16 two- and three-light windows in deep splays. Blocked S priest's doorway. Nave roof of arch-braced collars and curved braces below set on moulded wooden brackets; the chancel has a coved plaster ceiling with wooden ribs. Large porch with a characteristic double bench either side, and in the gable a big oaken foiled truss. Plain two-stage tower with a pyramidal roof; its door to the nave is Tudor and it was probably rebuilt at that period, and repaired again in 1888 by S. W. Williams, who added the clumsy S door and belfry windows. – SCREEN. The demarcation of the chancel is made by a Perp screen of Radnorshire type of fourteen bays with ogee traceries; between that and the wall-plate is a C17 addition of two rows of wavy cut-out rails with a big beam on top. – The ALTAR RAILS are C19 Gothic, of cast iron marked *Hodges & Wright*. – MONUMENTS. James Baskerville † 1792, signed *S. Thomas*, Brecon. – Joan Jones † 1793, signed *R. Millward*, Hay. – (In the porch, a slab inscribed 1.4.1604.)
School (now a house). By *J. L. Pearson*, 1869–70, in an early C14 style.
Aberedw Castle, ¼ m. W. The remains of a C13 stone castle, overgrown by trees. The plan was a square, apparently with towers at the corners, but only the circular one at the SE survives at all clearly. On three sides it has a deep ditch; the W side was

'There's neither a palace, nor park, or deer
Nor either a man in Radnorshire
That's worth five hundred pounds a year,
Except Sir William Fowler of Abbey Cwmhir.'

cut by the Cambrian Railway. Aberedw Castle was the last
refuge of Llywelyn the Last. He died in a skirmish nearby in
1282. The stone fortification almost certainly dates from
c. 1284; Edmund Mortimer's tenant Walter Hakelutel had received licence to crenellate by 1285.

(HEN CASTELL, nearby, is a ditched motte formerly crowned
by a D-plan tower.)

BEGUILDY

ST MICHAEL. Single-chamber and larger than is usual in a
Radnorshire valley; in a circular raised churchyard. Late C15
plan and walls. The chancel was restored in 1885, the nave in
1896. The architect in 1896 was *W. H. Bryden*, who replaced
the fallen W tower with a triple bellcote. E window of three
cinquefoiled lights of Dec or early C15 type; N and S chancel
windows similar, but two-light. Restored S priest's doorway. A
good quantity of old woodwork survives inside. The late C15
arch-braced roofs with alternate tie-beams remain, and three
rows of wind-braces. – SCREEN. A regular and fine Perp screen
with the W posts supporting the loft still *in situ*, forming a W
doorway. Plain dado; seven uniform (English type) tracery
lights either side of a broad shallow-arched central doorhead;
all carved on the W only. The screen bays have panel tracery
above ogees; the triangular doorhead is cusped and subcusped
and the spandrels are filled with circled quatrefoils. The loft
is restoration on the W side, but the coving on the E is original,
with carved bosses and Tudor roses painted in monochrome
on the panels (cf. Tal y Llyn, Merioneth). – STOUP. Inside
the S door. – FONT. Octagonal, C15? – Some rough PEWS. –
Dug-out CHEST. – A DESK END in the choir was used as a
model for the stalls and pew ends. – C18 COMMUNION RAILS.
– PULPIT of the C17, altered. – C16 panels from the old
vicarage and C18 rails have been re-used to form a vestry. –
GLASS. N and S windows in the nave from the workshops of
James Powell, 1945–60.

(LAWN FARM. A C17 central-chimneyed house with wooden
four-light transomed windows under hoodmoulds. One
dormer-gable has quadrant timberwork and an upper jetty on
carved brackets. RCAM)

(PANTYCAREGL, ¼ m. SE. Within a medieval moated site. The
rebuilt house contains medieval carved heads.)

BRYNDRAENOG, 1 m. SE. A timber hall-house on an H-plan,

one of the most complete in the Principality, fortunately repaired twenty years ago as a farmhouse. Bryndraenog was described in the c16 by Sion Dafydd Rhys as the seat of the heirs of Hywel ap Madog of Maelienydd; in the c15 the house had been lauded by Ieuan ap Hywel Swrdwal ('a proud maiden of lime and wood'...'a countess of summer is this court'). Its builder was Llywelyn Fychan. From the c16 to the c18 it was

Beguildy, Bryndraenog, hall (Royal Commission on Ancient and Historical Monuments in Wales)

the home of Morgan Maredudd of Pantycaregl and his descendants. The impressive, (still) open hall is framed as three bays
by huge cruck trusses, each roof bay subdivided by a secondary
arch-braced collar-beam (cf. Amberley Court, Herefordshire).
It is 35 ft long by 19 ft wide. The base-crucks have soaring
arched braces. The modern ceiling hides arcades of trefoiled
ogee tracery between the two collars of the middle trusses, and
three tiers of wind-braces with pierced cusping, very rounded
and full. Also of *c.* 1480 are the porch at the S E corner of the hall,
which led to the screens passage, with a room over; the S wing
containing a pair of service rooms with a pair of blocked arched
doorways to the S of the passage; and above them a solar now
divided in two but with a fine ceiled-in roof with three tiers
of wind-braces. To the W of these, a second (formerly open)
hall, perhaps for the retainers (cf. Tretower). Its roof was formerly decorated with foiled braces and brackets to the tie-
beams, which supported posts and again a second collar. The
corresponding wing N of the hall has been replaced in stone
with C17 window dripmoulds. The original details actually
visible in the hall are the chamfered blades of the immense
crucks; an embattled beam probably to support a gallery above
the S passage; and the high transomed wooden window in the
E wall, with its four ogee lights and blank spandrels, originally
central to the room. A first-floor gallery dated 1636 runs round
three sides, and has contemporary painted panelling at either
end. The exterior was probably square-framed, like the internal
partitions. Alas, the roughcast outside view conceals the house's
beauty. Dendrochronology gives a date *c.* 1560, however.
(CWM-YR-INGEL, 1¼ m. SW, is constructed with five cruck
couples, forming a complete house on the long-house plan.
Now a barn. RCAM)
In the bottom of the Teme Valley, S of Beguildy and close to the
river, is a group of Bronze Age monuments: a squat STANDING
STONE (SO 200 791), a large BARROW (SO 210 783), and a
small BARROW (SO 223 770).
BEACON HILL (SO 177 768) is the highest summit in this area
of moorland; on it are four large, heather-covered BARROWS,
almost 70 ft across and 6 ft high. The southernmost mound
appears to be intentionally flat-topped, as are several barrows
in this area. Other moorland summits in this district also have
prominent barrows. The hill is not easy to reach, and the monuments are perhaps best appreciated from a distance. The
Beacon Hill ones can be well seen from the Kerry Ridge.

PANTY HILL ENCLOSURE (SO 142 833) is a good example of
a small settlement surrounded by quite a substantial bank (no
ditch is visible) but sited on a sloping hillside and obviously
not a defensive work in any true sense. Another may be found
about ¾ m. away at SO 154 835. The date of these sites, which
were probably farmsteads, is not known, but rather similar enclosures were built elsewhere in the Romano-British period.
Such settlements may be more common in Mid Wales than has
previously been thought, for several of the so-called 'forts' are
in very weak positions and are not truly defensive.

BETTWS CLYRO   2040

In fields 2¼ m. NNE of Clyro

HOLY TRINITY (till 1878). A simple rectangle almost completely rebuilt in 1878–9. The roof however is C14, perhaps.
It has two scissor trusses combined with king-post pendants
alternating with three arch-braced collar trusses, and two
carved figures, holding shields, as corbels over the chancel. –
SCREEN. Inserted below the E scissor beam. Two moulded
uprights with capitals and spandrel pieces supporting the rood
beam survive. There are no signs that there was any tracery.
On top has been set the gallery front of twelve simply pierced
bays. Dated by Crossley as late C14 or early C15. – FONT. C13;
circular and tapering.

BETTWS DISSERTH   1050

2 m. N of Hundred House

ST MARY. Rebuilt in 1883 by *J. B. Fowler* of Brecon as a single
chamber with lancets. Plain but well-proportioned. – The
FONT is Perp.
(GLAN YR AFON, ½ m. NNW. C17 timber-framing includes two
pairs of crucks. RCAM)
GWERN HWSMON, ½ m. SW, has an ornate C17 stair. RCAM)

BLEDDFA   2060

ST MARY MAGDALENE. In a round churchyard. Nave and
chancel in one; S porch and W clapboarded bell-turret of
c. 1711. Of a low W tower, newly dug out of its own collapse,
a mural stair is still visible, descending to a doorway, with a

monolithic arched head, level with the floor of the church. The archway to the nave, triangular and of thin stones set almost horizontally, dates it to the early C14. The W part of the nave looks the older (early C13?), with its renewed S doorway and small S lancet. It remains partitioned E of the S door, a relic of its days as a schoolroom. The late C13 E addition is taller and broader but still with lancets (apart from replacements of 1907 by *E. V. Collier*). Roof with alternate tie-beams, king-posts and raking struts, and arch-braced collars, and two tiers of quatrefoil wind-braces in the C15 way. – FONT. Octagonal with a tapering stem; C14? – PULPIT. Partly with rows of Jacobean arcading. – IRON CHEST marked *Coalbrookdale*. – COMMUNION RAILS. Late C17. The balusters are cut out to the silhouette of a spiral. – All the fittings are being made movable (1977) to a scheme of *G. G. Pace* to allow the space to be freely used for liturgical experiment, dramatic or choral performances, etc. A unique development for Powys and one worth watching.

MOTTE, ¼ m. SE. Taken from the Mortimers by Llywellyn ap Gruffydd in 1262. On it, remains of a square tower of 1195.

MONAUGHTY. *See* 258.

1030   BOUGHROOD

ST CYNOG. In a circular churchyard. A small church in a determined Geometrical style, by *C. H. Howell*, 1854. Steeply roofed nave with a N aisle, tall NW tower with a masonry broach-spire, S porch, chancel. Traceried windows. Red-and-blue-tiled roofs. The interior has been entirely whitened, including the lively foliage bands on the arcade capitals and the corbels of the roof trusses, which is a pity. Angel-corbels in the chancel. – Contemporary FONT with elaborate Dec panelling.

The hamlet of Boughrood consists of barely ten houses, but three of them are cruck-framed with C17 alterations: BOUGHROOD COURT, FORGE COTTAGE, and VILLAGE FARM. They lie in their medieval grouping round the churchyard.

BOUGHROOD COURT has three pairs of crucks. The r. end of this old hall-house was interestingly enlarged in the C17. Of this date are the stone overhung porch with a fine studded inner door, the three first-floor windows with hoodmoulds, and a rear stair wing with elaborate pierced balusters and open-work newels.

BOUGHROOD CASTLE, ½ m. E. Begun in 1817 for *Francis Fowke*, probably to his own designs. The s façade is of five bays with a string-course. The design appears to have been changed by Fowke's son in 1820, when the rooms were extended into two-storey bowed bays facing roughly w and e. The elevations were made grander by the addition of a stone pediment on the s, crude colossal piers on ashlar bases beside the end bows, and deep and unhappily thin eaves to the pediment gable and the gables set over the bows. The exterior stucco was stripped off in 1929, when too the s porch and e doorway were altered. The plan consists of an axial hall, divisible by a folding partition, with the main rooms opening off it. Discreet plaster friezes, and fluted pilasters in the hall and on the staircase. At the rear, two wings with the roofs of paired staircases in the angles. Facing this up the hill is the COACH HOUSE with a broad central pediment.

The C12 BOUGHROOD CASTLE belonged to the Gamages family. It is now a ditched tump beside Castle Farm. In 1205 it had a stone tower.

BOUGHROOD BRIDGE, ½ m. s. A level roadway is here carried over the Wye on four main and two flood arches, work of the 1830s for the de Wintons of Maesllwch Castle. The little two-storey Italian-windowed TOLL-HOUSE on the Radnorshire bank was added, perhaps in the 1840s, to a design by *Wyatt & Brandon*.

BOULTIBROOK *see* PRESTEIGNE

BRYNDRAENOG *see* BEGUILDY

BRYNGWYN   *1040*

ST MICHAEL. In a circular churchyard. Nave, chancel, w belfry, s porch; somewhat rebuilt in 1874–7. The nave is a double square, late C13 perhaps – see the paired lancets there and in the chancel. s doorway with Perp mouldings. Large s window with ogee heads in a rectangular frame and a hood with headstops. Small cinquefoiled N window. In the chancel a fine arch-braced roof with two tiers of wind-braces arranged as quatrefoils, and a half-row above, of *c.* 1500. Of the C19 the chancel arch and the nave's tie-beam roof. – In the chancel a COLUMNAR PILLAR STONE with a deeply incised cross. At the ends of its arms and in the centre are ring and dot devices; four crosslets in the angles. Dated by Dr Nash-Williams to the C7–9. – In the porch a COFFIN LID incised with a cross, a chalice, and a missal. – Immured in the SE outer angle of the chancel a stone roughly carved with a female figure set length-wise on either face. – BELL, maybe as old as *c.* 1200.

BURFA *see* WALTON

CAEBACH *see* LLANDRINDOD WELLS

2060

CASCOB

ST MICHAEL. Nave, chancel, s porch, w tower, in a large circular churchyard. The rectangular tower, with a s stairway and a timber-framed bell-stage, is built into a large mound like Bleddfa's, and could be basically of the early C14. There is little indication as to the (probably early) date of the double-square nave except a small splayed C13(?) N window and the paired lancets of the chancel. Big s window of *c.* 1500 but reduced. Restored C15 roofs with three tiers of wind-braces. – SCREEN. Early C16? Five deep round-headed lights on a low dado either side of the doorway, which has a flat quatrefoil-pierced tracery head. The panelled parapet of the rood loft is still in situ. – FONT. Octagonal. C14. – MONUMENT to William Jenkins Rees † 1855, a noted Celtic scholar. – REREDOS with elaborate C19 Dec oak panelling; dating from the restoration of 1895?

CASTELL COLLEN *see* LLANDRINDOD WELLS

CASTELL DINBOETH *see* LLANANNO

CEFNDYRYS *see* LLANELWEDD

0060

CEFNLLYS

Only the church remains of the medieval borough on the bank of the Ithon below the castle. The population declined till the early 1800s, and is now centred on Llandrindod, 1½ m. W. The earliest mention is in a market charter of 1297.

ST MICHAEL. Situated in a meadow humpy with its buried township. Single-chamber, with W tower and slated squat broach-spire. Medieval walls at least not drastically changed, with C16 paired lights in the E and N. Chamfered round-arched s doorway and C16 stone porch with a four-centred arch. The tower is rebuilt. This church and Llandrindod old church were deliberately unroofed in 1893. Restoration in 1895 gave it a lofty hammerbeam and curved-brace roof – probably by *Nicholson & Sons*, since it is so like their work on Llandrindod Old Parish Church of the year before. – SCREEN. C15, with six lights either side of the doorway, a post-and-panel dado, and moulded muntins. The traceries are poor replacements. – PULPIT incorporating carved pew bits dated 1661. – FONT. Perp, octagonal, with curved underside. – MONUMENTS. Rev. Thomas Jones † 1806, by *Davies* of Builth. – John Whittall † 1825 by *Edward Stephens*. – John Whittal † 1832.

A MOTTE 1 m. NNE of the church was the first castle of Cefnllys. It was probably made for Ralph Mortimer between 1086 and 1104.

CASTELL CEFNLLYS occupies a position of outstanding natural strength and beauty, protected by a drop on the NE and by the deep Ithon valley on the other three sides. It consists of the total ruins of two fortresses, the mounds of fallen masonry covering the whole crown of the ridge, within a curtain wall. The site appears to have been used as a prehistoric, presumably Iron Age, fort. The first stone refortification, most likely begun *c.* 1242 for Ralph Mortimer, fell in 1262 to Llewelyn's supporters in Maelienydd. Its entrance gateway must have been at the NW. Beyond that was a 'park'. The bailey in the middle shows traces of a large number of buildings. It had a keep on a mound at its NE. A large rock-cut ditch defends the second keep at the SW, built by the Mortimers on their retaking the site *c.* 1273 under the terms of the treaty of Montgomery. The plan somewhat resembles that of the works at Montgomery Castle. Cefnllys was garrisoned for Edward I in 1282 and taken and burned by Owain Glyndŵr rebels in 1406. A HOUSE was built on the site by Ieuan ap Philip, a constable appointed to the castle by the Duke of York between 1432 and 1459. His bard Lewis Glyn Cothi describes the C15 keep as having an octagonal tower. Ieuan's new hall, of three sections, was decorated with carved oak; the poem names the architect or master carpenter (*pensaer*) who contracted to make it as *Rosier ab Ywain*. Camden records the castle as ruined in 1558.

CILIAU *see* LLANDEILO GRABAN

CLAS-AR-WY, Y, *see* GLASBURY

CLYRO

ST MICHAEL. Rebuilt in 1853 by *T. Nicholson*. Nave, chancel, N aisle, W tower. Only the tower is old – unbuttressed Late Perp to the clock stage, and raised in 1894. Nicholson's work is Dec, and dull. – MONUMENTS. Herbert Beavan † 1778 and others. Sarcophagus with pilasters on lions' feet. – Elizabeth Williams † 1830. Mourning lady kneeling by an urn; palmettes beside the tablet. – This was the church that Francis Kilvert the diarist knew as curate.

In the village, E and S of the church, a number of picturesque low cottages of the C16 and C17. ASHBROOK HOUSE, Kilvert's home during part of his curacy of 1864–76, has a big Regency staircase window. On the S of a housing estate is a large (and late?) motte and bailey CASTLE with a mound with a top diameter of 70 ft. Remains of stone buildings on it. At the other end of the village, CAE-MAWR is Regency with a veranda. At CLYRO COURT FARM uncommon buildings remain from a Cistercian grange of Cwmhir Abbey. Big C14 chamfered archway on the road.* The barn to the r., now obscured by a modern cattle shed, has partly original stone walls and two plain chamfered doorways. One cruck couple remains inside. CLYRO COURT, ½ m. SW, is a florid and grandly proportioned pile in the neo-Jacobean fashion of the 1840s, built for Thomas Mynors Baskerville in a gaudy orange stone. Three large shaped gables over the front. Grand cantilevered staircase, with a gallery. Conan Doyle stayed here to write *The Hound of the Baskervilles*.

(CASTLE KINSEY MOTTE, ½ m. N. Behind the house is the mound. The bailey is occupied by farm buildings. RCAM)

CABALFA HOUSE, 2¼ m. NE. Plain neo-classical additions to the C17 and earlier timber house include the hall with its saucer dome beside the staircase, a neatly detailed drawing room, and a library with two Corinthian columns screening a recess.

CABALFA FARM, 1¾ m. NE. The Late Georgian front block has an ashlar elevation of tripartite windows on three storeys. Beside the spacious and shallow stair are doorcases with fluted entablatures.

COLVA

2¼ m. SW of Gladestry

ST DAVID. Single-chamber, and probably C13 – see the blocked

---

* Recently damaged by a lorry, but one hopes to be repaired.

N lancet. W pyramidal timber bell-turret. The W end is partitioned off; this leaves a well-proportioned space with a roof with alternating tie-beams and arched braces. The walls have been much rebuilt and the windows in their deep embrasures are replacements, bar one. The S doorway has continuous Perp mouldings. The timber porch, also late C15, has stone seats. Few furnishings of interest besides the C18 memorials on the E wall. – FONT. Round, with a two-step moulding to a columnar base; *c.* 1200. – ROYAL ARMS signed *Cartwright de Abaredow*, 1733. – The church is on the 1250 ft contour – one of the highest old sites in Wales.

COLWYN CASTLE *see* HUNDRED HOUSE

CREGRINA   *1050*

ST DAVID. Nave and chancel of separate builds: in a circular churchyard. The nave, which may be C13, was much restored in 1903, and not very well. The wider chancel has the better of the C15 arch-braced roofs, with tie-beams and plain windbraces, and restored details of 1903. It was added at an angle to the nave: the join is marked by plaster infill above the tie-beam, and a little Radnorshire SCREEN of three bays with tracery heads, carved only on the W, either side of the doorway, which has small pinnacles on the jambs. It lacks the floor-to-roof wall-posts at the ends. – FONT. Norman. Plain circular bowl tapering at the base. – Repairs including roughcasting the outside were carried out with help from the Pilgrim Trust in 1958, to plans by *G. Pace*.

PENARTH MOUNT, ¼ m. N. Motte only. In the C15 the home of Bedo Chwith, patron of Lewys Glyn Cothi.

CRUG-Y-BYDDAR   *1080*
3 m. NW of Beguildy

ST PETER. Small; nave and narrow chancel by *H. Lote*, 1856–8. Dec for the E window, Perp for the nave. The Rev. Abraham Thomas may have had a hand in the design. Much renovated by *G. G. Pace* in 1967, when clear glass was put in the windows.

CWMBACH LLECHRHYD   *0050*
2 m. NW of Builth Wells

ST JOHN THE DIVINE. By *J. B. Fowler* of Brecon, 1886–7. Nave and chancel with a rather forbidding exterior. Stone spirelet and triple bellcote over the chancel arch. s porch with inner iron-trellis gates. Inside, the proportions are more agreeable. Pinkish stone. Groups of lancets in the chancel, with marble shafts and hoodmoulds, and a coloured marble reredos. As David Verey says, Fowler's E.E. style is better than S. W. Williams's. – The E GLASS is by *Burlison & Grylls*.

Opposite, an attractive late C19 polychrome brick SCHOOL.

CWMDEUDDWR/
LLANSANTFFRAED-CWMDEUDDWR

9060

ST BRIDE. Totally rebuilt by *F. R. Kempson* in 1866. Nave, chancel, s aisle, and a w tower of Normandy type with a broach-spire. Inside, a low wrought-iron SCREEN. Nothing survived a rebuilding in 1778 except a STOUP in the s porch which is crudely incised with three heads; perhaps Early Norman. – STAINED GLASS. s aisle w, with figures by *Morris & Co.* and by *Stokes*. – Three s windows by *O'Connor*, 1871.

DDERW. Of c. 1870. The brick house designed by *J. W. Hiort* in 1799 has disappeared.

NANNERTH GANOL, $2\frac{1}{2}$ m. NW. A cruck-framed house of early type. Stone walls; windows with close-set diamond mullions. Three pairs of crucks remain, and a post-and-panel partition. The fireplace and winding stair beside the chimney look later – i.e. C17. The ruined end below the cross-passage was possibly occupied by the byre.

RHAYADER. *See* p. 272.

MAEN SERTH (SN 943 698), a tall stone beside an ancient track-way at 1,500 ft, may be prehistoric in origin, but, perhaps in the C7–9, a simple cross was incised on its E face. (There is an early OS bench mark on the w face.) It is the reputed site of the murder of Einion Clud in the C12.

Just above the same trackway at SN 936 699 is CLAP YR ARIAN, a Bronze Age barrow in which an axe-hammer of Preseli (Pembrokeshire) stone was found in the C19. Part of a good stone kerb survives on the w side, and the remains of a possibly medieval *hafod* can be made out on the lower side of the cairn.

Further along the track at SN 926 706 is MAENGWYNGWEDDW, a large block of quartz.

A continuation of the old road system here leads over Esgair-perfedd past a ROMAN MARCHING CAMP at SN 927 699, a site recognized from the air and not easy to see on the ground.

CWMHIR *see* ABBEY CWMHIR

DEVANNOR *see* ABBEY CWMHIR

DISCOED

2060

ST MICHAEL. In a raised (extended) circular churchyard. Rebuilt in 1869. Yet the double-square nave and the chancel are not on axis; old foundations? Goodhart-Rendel particularly admired the restraint of the detail on this little church – the well-proportioned w gable and the handling of the lancets and quatrefoil window above; the slate-shingled bell-turret just E of this with its box-like base, capped with a pyramid from which rises the steep conical spire, he called 'a poem in its way'. Inside he noted the treatment of the join of the chancel and nave roofs, where a decorated tie-beam and low arch supporting the gable end enable a chancel arch to be dispensed with. – GLASS. E by *O'Connor*, London, 1869.

(UPPER HOUSE. An altered C17 timber house. A room downstairs has a ceiling with counterchanged rafters. RCAM)

(MAES TREYLOW, ½ m. NW. Timber-framed, with jetties on slender colonnettes; much repaired. On the upper floor of the cross-wing is a quadrant-moulded gable. One of the open-roofed upper rooms had a central scissor truss. On the site of a Roman fort. RCAM)

CASTLE MOUND. N of the church.

A scenic section of the OFFA'S DYKE path runs S from OS 272 650 – to Burfa, near Walton.

DISSERTH

0050

1¼ m. E of Newbridge-on-Wye

ST CEWYDD. The church stands in a really lovely position beside the Ithon, but the idyll is disturbed by caravans. In a nearly circular churchyard. Broad W tower with a batter at the base, battlements, and a spiral stair in the NE angle. The stair doorways have chamfered jambs; the bottom one has a shouldered head and straight lintel. There is no W door, but an unornamented pointed arch (now blocked) to the church and two buttresses beside it inside the nave. All the windows have voussoir heads and seats in the embrasures; the tracery is Perp renewal. A belfry window retains a re-used piece of Dec tracery with deep mouldings. E first-storey window blocked and cut by the nave roof. The tower basically dates perhaps to *c.* 1400, with some change, and the unitary nave and chancel seem a larger replacement of the mid C15.

The church stands very much as a Victorian architect, called in for advice, might have found many of the Radnorshire churches. At Disserth, however, there was no restoration and the fabric takes one straight into the parish life of *c.* 1700. The walls are whitewashed outside (except the tower) and most of the windows are wood-framed rectangles. The s chancel window, however, is of stone, three lights with trefoiled heads of equal height under a hoodmould. Four-light E window of the same C16/17 pattern, but of oak. Stone s porch with benches, cobbles, and a pointed C14 doorway with monolithic jambs – part of the preceding church? No division between nave and chancel. The fine roofs are C15 – arch-braced collars above tie-beams, and at the second bay from the W a cusped scissors truss, with two tiers of deep foiled wind-braces and some panelling along the wall-plate. All was exposed by *F. E. Howard*, who removed the ceiling of 1839, except over the sanctuary. Stone slab floor without steps. – Of the C15 SCREEN, only the rood beam remains, with one doorpost, and part of the head-beam set against the wall. – The furnishing of the church is simple C17–18 almost to a detail. – BOX PEWS, dated between 1666 and 1722, painted with the names of their later proprietors (e.g. James Watt, who came to live in the area in 1805). – Three-decker PULPIT dated 1687. – C18 COMMUNION RAILS, and an extraordinary arrangement in the sanctuary: BOX PEWS either side of the altar, a recess in the wall behind it, and a blank window to the r. – FONT. Octagonal, on a circular base. – Fragments of PAINTING on the E wall (text and foliage) under plaster, the N wall (supporters and the royal arms), and the s wall (with raised plaster surround). – MONUMENTS. John Davies † 1796, by *Price*, Builth. – Tablet to Ezekiel Williams † 1752 by *W. Watkins.* – One of the BELLS dates from *c.* 1300. Morgan Elfael, † 1563, poet and genealogist, probably came from this locality.

DOLDOWLOD HOUSE *see* RHAYADER

9060   ELAN VALLEY

The Enabling Act permitting the construction of a series of RESERVOIRS in the remote and elevated (yet far from uncivilized) Elan Valley was obtained by Birmingham Corporation in

1892. A smooth masonry dam 122 ft high holds back Caban Coch reservoir. A road bridge with a marine-looking copper-domed valve tower nearby separates the Caban Coch from Garreg Ddu reservoir. It gives the illusion of crossing a shallow lake; in fact it rises well above a submerged dam. Two dams block upper reaches that will be flooded by a new and gigantic Craig Goch dam, to feed the Wye and the Severn. The original scheme was completed by 1904; the engineers were *Ernest Lawson* and *Walter Leahy*.

The Claerwen dam, a separate project, is a mass concrete 100 dam 184 ft high, faced with gritstone from South Wales and Derbyshire. The water flows to Birmingham through a 73 m. aqueduct. Built in 1946–52; the consulting engineers were *Sir William Halcrow & Partners*.

NANTGWYLLT CHURCH. By the bridge. Built in 1903, to a design by *S. W. Williams*, to replace the flooded chapel of ease. Nave and apsidal chancel, with a bellcote over the chancel arch. Lancets etc. – TABLET to Thomas Lloyd † 1782.

(NANT GWYLLT, ¾ m. SE of the church. Drowned. The home of the Lloyd family. A low stone house of eight bays with a pedimental gable and a hipped roof, probably enlarged by Thomas Lloyd c. 1770. Its staircase was 'of massive oak'. Shelley rented it in 1812, and called it 'silent, solitary, old'.)

(CWM ELAN, ½ m. N of the church. Destroyed. A tall mansion of three storeys and three bays with tall thin wings, built after 1792 by Thomas Grove Jun. Shelley, his first cousin, stayed there in 1811 and found 'an appearance of enchantment' in the celebrated landscaping.)

CILEWENT, 1½ m. SW. A stone-walled, cruck-framed long-house in sufficiently complete preservation to have justified its removal to the Welsh Folk Museum at St Fagans. Probably C15, altered in 1734.

RHOS Y GELYNEN. On this moor at SN 902 629 is a good example of a Bronze Age stone alignment – five stones in a straight line, two of them unusually large and impressive. These monuments are mysterious since, though they are often found close to burial monuments, they do not themselves mark burials – in fact quite extensive excavation has provided no hint of their purpose.

ELAN VILLAGE (B) *See* p. 318.

EVENJOBB

ST PETER. 1866–70 by *T. H. Wyatt*. Nave, chancel, low S aisle, and s tower with broach-spire and porch beneath. Solid and ugly. With a wrought-iron chancel screen. Goodhart-Rendel prefaces his criticisms by saying, 'It is the last word in insensitive conventionality, but shews a dreadful knowledge of what generous church builders (the Mynors family) expected at its date.' – GLASS. E by *Clayton & Bell*, 1869.

EVANCOYD. Externally of *c.* 1835 and H-fronted.

NEWCASTLE COURT, 1 m. N. Seven bays and two storeys in local Late Georgian, with a Gothic doorway and bargeboarded gables added *c.* 1880.

(MOTTE. ¼m. SE of the church.)

(CASTLE RING. ½m. NNE of the church.)

FAR HALL *see* LLANFIHANGEL RHYDITHON

2050   GLADESTRY

ST MARY. A handsome church of nave, N aisle, chancel with a sanctus bellcote, s porch, and w tower with a shingled broach-spire. A tall C13 nave, of which the s wall with its single and paired lancets survives, seems to have been enlarged in the late C14. Of the C14 are the lofty double-chamfered chancel arch with the inner order dying into wide responds; the s doorway; and also, set out wide of the earlier wall, the N arcade of three bays with responds and thin moulded capitals on octagonal piers, and two little C14 windows in the lean-to aisle. s porch perhaps C15. C15 nave roof of tie-beams bracketed on corbels (two with carved heads), with king-posts and close-set collars and braces. The tower doorway must have been made before the aisle, and therefore the tower itself, though it looks C16 above the first stage. In the fine chancel, rebuilt as wide as the nave in the C14, four tall C16 Perp windows with rectangular frames. Its C16 roof is a good specimen of arch-braced collar construction, with two and a half rows of complete-quatrefoil wind-bracing and oak studs carved on the underside of the trusses. Restoration in 1910, including the E traceries. – FONT. A circular, plain C13 bowl. – PISCINA. A transitional Norman/ E.E. capital for a four-shafted pier, hollowed as a bowl. The decoration is interlacing foliage with fleshy leaves. Another piscina or stoup in the N aisle. – LECTERN supported by an angel carved in wood. – MONUMENT. Rev. David Jones † 1809.

GLADESTRY COURT is C19 in appearance but has a date-stone

for 1689. Good mid C18 staircase with two turned balusters to a tread and clusters of four for the newels.

The little village is composed of several older stone houses by the church. CORNER HOUSE is box- and cruck-framed. A curious, apparently C18, house next to the Post Office (dated on the chimney) has ogee freestone dripmoulds above two doorways and the upper window, dating presumably from its use as a Baptist Chapel c. 1840.

THE COURT OF GLADESTRY, 1 m. NW, was the home of Sir Gelli Meyrick, fellow-insurgent of the Earl of Essex and patron of the Builth poet Dafydd Goch. The site is partly enclosed by a rectangular bank, but the existing timber-framed farmhouse is late C17.

STONE HOUSE, 1 m. SW. A good later C18 front range: two storeys and a hipped roof with dormers and seven bays with keystones over the windows. The stairs have three turned balusters a tread and fluted newels. (1760?)

(HENGOED, $1\frac{1}{4}$ m. SSW. Farmhouse and barn are both cruck-framed, and perhaps of the late C16. RCAM)

LOWER RABBER, $1\frac{1}{2}$ m. SE. A timber-framed cruck hall of c. 1500; four couples, one with cusped decoration in the apex.

GLASBURY/Y CLAS-AR-WY
1030

Some C18 and earlier houses, and a green, make Glasbury a real village – that rarity in Wales, dependent on long and prosperous settlement. Its origins are ecclesiastical, for, as the Welsh and English names indicate, there was here a *clas* or monastery of the Celtic church. The probable site of the C5 dedication to St Cynidr was c. $1\frac{1}{2}$ m. NNW on Ffynnon Gynydd common. The medieval church, refounded c. 1090, belonged to St Peter, Gloucester. Its site on the flood-plain began N of the Wye; the fallen stonework now lies on the S bank. Floods and a change of course around 1660 brought about its abandonment.

ALL SAINTS. 1881–2 by *Haddon Bros.* on a new site NW of the village. Nave and chancel. W wheel-window. – PAINTING. The Prodigal Son, attributed to *Ribera*.

Round the central triangle of streets are three similar late C18 and early C19 houses with lunette windows in pediments. GLASBURY HOUSE (London Borough of Redbridge Outdoor Education Centre) is of a still more English type, five bays and Late Georgian, with porches either side, and a coach house.

Nearer the river one exceptional house, the OLD VICARAGE, indeed one of the earliest still lived in in Powys, built *c.* 1400 or after. Originally with fairly low rooms open to its complex and beautiful roof structure, it had a hall of four bays above a cross-passage, and a two-bay parlour below. The six trusses survive almost intact, supported on curved wall-braces. The first, over the parlour, is a scissor truss with a king-post. The second and third are closed trusses each with a king-post, and studding. The three hall trusses are arch-braced collars with king-posts (the central one may perhaps be an early example of a hammerbeam). The joints of wall-posts with roof members were decorated with carvings, all cut away but three: a grotesque head, a bishop, and a lady whose headdress gives the nearest date of building. Each roof bay is ornamented as well with three tiers of cinquefoiled wind-braces now hidden by a ceiling. The inscription 1611 on a chimney may indicate the date of the principal modifications to the medieval house: a stone stair-turret, an upper floor, and chimneys of course. Directly next to the vicarage is its TITHE BARN, itself of historic interest, since it preserves one complete cruck couple and another cut away.

THE WOODLANDS (Oxfordshire County Council), ½ m. NW, is a plain, tall Late Regency house of stone. The lowest of its three storeys has a pair of fan-fluted Venetian windows. Coach house with a pediment.

MAESLLWCH CASTLE, ¾ m. NNW. The castellated country house built in 1829–50 for the de Winton family by *Robert Lugar* was mostly demolished *c.* 1951. The first recorded house on the site was the hall house of William Vaughan, who died in 1582. In 1729 it was replaced by a larger house of seven by five bays, with a belvedere parapet on its hipped roof, built for Sir Humphry Howarth. Walter Wilkins, a former Indian merchant, bought the C18 Maesllwch. Lugar planned its replacement a bit further forward – so as to give it the best possible view s across the Wye to the Black Mountains; and to show this to the visitor as a surprise, for he was screened from it while reaching the porch and had to cross the axis of the house to meet the vista. In plan it was symmetrical round a glass-roofed atrium hall. The tall and romantic elevations cast off such classical restraints, the main block having six dissimilar towers, albeit set on the angles and centrally, with bows between. The style was C14 to Perp, with mullioned and transomed windows; the masonry was rusticated. Mr Ffransis Payne rightly men-

tions its undisciplined prodigality. The interiors were completed *c.* 1840, to more eclectic tastes – Norman, Late Georgian,
Gothic. Of this, only the N wall and the two E towers still
stand. To their E, Lugar's service wing of three bays in the
same style. E again, a billiard room, a tower of bedrooms, and
stables, added in 1879 by *E. H. Burnell* and *H. S. Legg*, miss
Lugar's giant playfulness by being too earnest. A LODGE to
the E was perhaps designed by *Lugar.**

MAESYRONNEN. *See* p. 256.
GLASBURY (B). *See* p. 320.

GLASCWM

1050

ST DAVID is thought to be a Dewi foundation. It was also a *clas*
church. Large roundish churchard. Nave and chancel roofed
in one, with a S porch and a W shingled belfry rising through
the roof. Architecturally a finer and larger church than its
neighbours. C13/14 nave on a three-square plan with original
W and S doorways and a wonderful tangled roof of C15 arch-
braced collars with alternating ties and two tiers of trefoiled
wind-braces. The chancel, a C15 addition, entered through an
arch with fluted chamfers almost as wide as the nave, is itself
the same width as the nave and on the same level. There are
still three fine Perp windows with ogee and panel tracery. The
E window and those of the nave were restored in Perp in 1891.
Outside, diagonal and wall buttresses, a low string-course, and
a priest's doorway with a Tudor head. Tie-beams and kingposts
in the porch. The rib-and-panel wagon ceiling of the chancel,
on a battlemented wall-plate, continues over one bay of the nave
to honour the rood. Two lancets for the stair remain in the N
wall. – FONT. C15(?), shaped like a capital. – TABLETS. A
number by local or Black Mountains masons survive, e.g. to
Hugh Evans † 1834 and others, by *S. Morris* of Hay. – Henry
Jones † 1739 with two birds. – Mary Price † 1787, of the local
Rococo type, by *William Jones* of Llanstephan. – Evan
Jones † 1815, small but ornate, by *W. Lloyd.* – The Rev. John
Jones † 1836, with a big urn. – Mary Price † 1816, with a
trumpeting angel, by *T. Jones* of Cusop.

GLASCWM COURT. C17, with mullioned and transomed
windows; with its barns, a picturesque group.

HARPTON COURT *see* NEW RADNOR

* Major G. de Winton kindly supplied much useful information.

HEYOP

1 m. ENE of Knucklas

St David. Rebuilt by *J. L. Pearson* in 1880–2 on the old foundations, the windows and roof very much as in the preceding C15 single-chamber church, and admirably simple. W tower (the W wall is the old stonework) with a new and ungainly shingled broach-spire. – The partly renewed SCREEN is late C15 with five Perp lights either side of the triangular doorhead. The latter had spandrels filled with circled trefoils and with circles containing three circled trefoils. – FONT. Octagonal.

Heyop House opposite was *Pearson's* vicarage; gabled, stone with brick dressings. Dolfelin, 1m.W, is of C17 date. Upper Hall has a quoined early C19 front.

HOWEY

St David. 1904 by *R. Wellings Thomas*, a very small single-chamber church in unpleasantly contrasting dark rubble and red freestone.

Howey Hall. Pedimented stucco front of three bays and two storeys and bay-ended l. wing; c. 1810.

Bryn-y-Groes, 1 m. SE. Apparently C17, with moulded chimney-stacks at the ends, but given a five-bay front and mullion-and-transom windows in the C18, together with interior woodwork and stairs.

HUNDRED HOUSE

Colwyn Castle, ½ m. SW. Perhaps the caput of the commote of Colwyn; subsequently a Marcher stronghold, William de Breos had it rebuilt in 1191. According to the Brut y Tywysogion, a stone castle was erected here for the de Tony family in 1240. The visible remains are a large motte surrounded by a characteristically deep ditch, partly under the farmyard, and no footings of stone at all. A property of the Earls of Warwick from the late C13, it fell into disuse. A document of 1629 records the house, Fforest Farm, as having recently been built by one Davies. As it is built on the motte, it may incorporate the castle stonework, and certainly it has two fireplaces – one lateral – with chamfered stone jambs, one of which has carved stops. The site occupies one end of a very large rectangular embanked enclosure, serving as a bailey, but perhaps originally the defences of a Roman fort.

IRON BRIDGE over the Edw. 1887. Of slight interest for its inscriptions: designed by *S. W. Williams*, County Surveyor, and made by the Horsehay Company, Shropshire.

BRYNLLWYD MOUNT, ¼ m. SE. A motte cut from a moraine beside the Edw, and a banked bailey *c.* 100 yds in diameter. MOTTE. 1 m. SW.

HUNDRED HOUSE BARROW (Bryn Llwyd) (SO 113 543), excavated in the last century, still survives as a large grass-grown mound beside the river. The trench which yielded several cremation burials and urns is still visible. It forms part of a valley bottom cemetery (on either side of the road) and its siting contrasts with the more typical hilltop position of the cairn on Gelli Hill which is visible from the main road on the skyline just E of Hundred House.

KINNERTON   2060

ST MARY. In a raised churchyard. Rebuilt in 1884–5; by *Stephen Williams*? Nave and chancel with shafted triple lancets. Scissor truss roof with a high wooden chancel arch, resting on C13-type imposts. – Well carved PULPIT. – PAINTING. Holy Family with St John, late C17 French?

KINNERTON COURT. Built *c.* 1700 of dressed local stone with external stacks at the ends. The front was remade in the early C19: three bays with a lunette in the pediment. Inside, a curious Georgian staircase, the balusters cut to a sort of Chippendale openwork pattern on the first flight and a lattice balustrade on the second – as it were the Jacobean fashion reappearing. Behind the house is the small ditched MOTTE of a C12 castle.

(EDNOL CHURCH. Foundations only, 1¼ m. NW. It was abandoned *c.* 1830, the fate of many of Radnorshire's remote churches; but having stood till *c.* 1910 it is the most recent to have gone.)

KNIGHTON/TREF-Y-CLAWDD   2070

ST EDWARD. C14 W tower, much restored, but with a three-step chamfered arch to the nave and a trefoiled window. With its reconstructed pyramidal bell-stage, it looks effective against the rising evergreen woodland to the N. The body of the church, rebuilt in 1752 and again in 1875–7 by *S. Pountney Smith*, consists of a nave with a clerestory and a fussy hammerbeam roof, and two aisles. Smooth cylindrical yellow piers and exposed grey masonry. The chancel, rebuilt by *J. L. Pearson* in 1896–7, is much more rewarding; austerely buttressed, and with lancets placed high in the walls. Inside, below the wall-shafts the walls are decorated with red and green stencil-work, and Quattrocento angels with texts from the Gloria. – STAINED GLASS. E by *Ward & Hughes*, 1897. – Chancel lancets and S aisle windows by *Curtis, Ward & Hughes*, c. 1900. – N aisle E, 1860.

METHODIST CHURCH, High Street. Dec with ballflower on the hoods; by *Henry Lote*, 1860.

BAPTIST CHURCH, Norton Street. 1865; with large intersected and Perp traceries. Galleries etc. of 1922.

The borough of Knighton lies just on the 'English' side of Offa's Dyke. The lower part of the town has a level grid of streets that bring to mind an Edwardian plantation. A big Early Norman motte of c. 1100, BRYN CASTELL, lies E of this, and the church too relates to the grid. Beside the latter, the GREEN-PRICE ALMSHOUSES in a c. 1900 vernacular. The HORSE AND JOCKEY, in WYLCWM STREET, is basically a medieval stone house whose hall or solar had an open roof with a truss with apex cusping. In BRIDGE STREET, THE GREAT HOUSE has good C17 and C18 woodwork. Beside it, a late C19 hotel, the gabled NORTON ARMS, has a fine twice-galleried staircase.

The upper part of Knighton consists of narrow streets huddled round a small late C12 MOTTE AND BAILEY, to the S, and on the top – a fortification which fell to Llewelyn ap Gruffydd in 1262. The steep BROAD STREET links the two, and passes the GEORGE AND DRAGON (1637) on the l. Jumbled Late Victorian centre in HIGH STREET, with CLOCK TOWER (*Haddon Bros.*, 1872), banks, slate gables, and bright brick. OLD HOUSE, also on the l., is cruck-built. In its C15 hall roof are raking struts with unusually elaborate cusping. The façade built across the latter has C17 quadrant and arcaded timberwork. In short, the evidence is there for occupation, even prosperity, at both ends of Knighton in the C13, C15, C17, and C19; only the last period dominates the scene and not wholly for its good.

(CWMGILLA, 1½ m. WSW. Four cruck couples. RCAM)

(FARRINGTON, 1¼ m. SE. Stone with dressed details; a demolished cross-wing had the date 1666. RCAM)

KNUCKLAS

The parish was the birthplace of Vavasour Powell, who became the ecclesiastical governor of the border regions under the Long Parliament.

CASTLE. A total ruin of a stone fortress *c.* 30 yds square. One can still pick out the base of a wall and one of the round corner towers. Built by Hugh Mortimer II *c.* 1220–5; destroyed by Llywelyn ap Gruffydd in 1262.

VIADUCT. Built, perhaps in 1883, for the London and North Western Railway. Thirteen masonry arches. The battlemented parapet has a pair of half-round corbelled turrets at either end, in sympathy with the former castle above. The architect was *H. Lote.*

LLANANDRAS see PRESTEIGNE

LLANANNO

ST ANNO. The old church beside the Ithon was completely rebuilt in 1876–7 by *David Walker* of Liverpool. His little single-chamber replacement has distinctive large neo-Perp windows of clear glass and carefully designed bench pews. Above all, his restoration preserved the glorious SCREEN. Appropriately renewed in 1880 (and again in 1960), it is now the best example left reasonably intact of the work of the imaginative Newtown school of screen-carvers. It dates from the turn of the C15 and C16. Ten tracery lights of six different designs, some 'Newtown arabesques', some Herefordshire Perp. The triangular central doorhead has five circles (three with whorl motifs) in each spandrel. Lavish, partly restored running ornament above: serrated leaf-fronds with intertwined stalks on the W and astonishingly delicate water-plant interlace on the E. The LOFT has the coving characteristic of Wales, with slightly curved longitudinal ribs, and bosses (one a duociput, others knots or flowers) underneath. On the W these are fitted with tracery panels, mostly geometrical and repetitive; many are copies. The inventiveness of these seventeen formal designs is very enjoyable, and is well matched by the execution. What can have inspired it all? Only Newtown, Llanegryn (Merioneth), and Daresbury (Cheshire) possess such variety. The lower and upper bressumers of the parapet are carved with bands of running ornament, first of pomegranates and leaves and then of beautifully stylized crinkly vine-trails coming from the mouths of two wyverns. The top beam has the exuberant water-plant interlace again, tellingly contrasted with large, smooth, heart-shaped leaves. Each of these patterns is not carved in the solid, but undercut, so that the oak forms, once coloured, stand like a filigree against the shadowed ground. The parapet has its original triangular canopies with pinnacles above and buttresses between, but the twenty-five figures are replacements carved *c.* 1880 by *Boulton* of Cheltenham. Christ in the centre; on the l. Patriarchs, Kings, and Prophets, and on the r. the twelve Apostles. (Such rich and varied work was to be found in many Mid Wales churches till destruction started in the C18.) – BOX PEW with woodwork dated 1681. – C15 octagonal FONT.

CASTELL DINBOETH or DINBAUD, ¾ m. NNW. Named after Maud, widow of Roger Mortimer. One of three Mortimer castles in Radnorshire (with Cefnllys and New Radnor) garrisoned in the war of 1282–3. At 1332 ft. The characteristically deep late C13 rock-cut ditch is further protected by earth outworks to the N and S. Inside this moat was a polygonal stone keep whose walls have quite gone, except for a fragment of a NE gate tower. It served no later purpose. Just NE of the castle are a pair of PLATFORM SITES of pre-Norman? farmhouses. Stone footings of one measure *c.* 45 ft by 17 ft.

(MAES-YR-HELM, 1¼ m. NNW. Cruck-built, with a single-bay open hall, and two rooms above the dais partition; now a barn.)

(CRYCHELL, 1 m. W, is partly late C15. The central cruck truss of an open hall, with trefoiled cusping in the apex, and an upper truss containing the wooden partition and doorways remain *in situ*. Probably the walls were always of stone, and not square-framed, as was the common case. C17 adaptations include the timbered dormer. RCAM)

0060

LLANBADARN FAWR

1½ m. E of Penybont

ST PADARN (or Paternus). Internally a successful rebuilding of 1878 by *S. W. Williams*; but not pleasing outside. Nave, and chancel scarcely narrower, with a low S tower, and porch beneath. The detail is simple: pale warm stone inside and, rightly, no stained glass. The windows are in deep reveals, especially in the E wall, which reproduces the C12 effect. Double-chamfered chancel arch and a traditional nave roof of arch-braced principals and wind-braces. The inner side of the S

doorway has a roll-moulding, in sympathy with the SOUTH
DOORWAY, which contains one of only two Romanesque
carved tympana in Wales. The reset oblong stone in the
TYMPANUM is carved, not with the Christ-figure of the second [13]
half of the C12, but with two leaping lion-like animals with
trefoiled tails in profile, facing a tree (of life) which grows from
the frontally placed head of an animal. Beneath the smaller
creature on the l. is a sun-disc. Tau-pattern on the lintel,
which rests on two imposts, the W carved with a head, the E
similar but defaced. These motifs are old ones, suggesting a
date c. 1100–1150. The doorway has a pair of engaged columns,
the W on a moulded base with the cushion capital decorated
with fantastic creatures, the E on a fluted base with a capital
decorated with two figures (Adam and Eve?) and between them
a head not unlike the tympanum's. On these are two abaci, the
W ornamented with lozenges, the E with serpents. They support
the hoodmoulded arch, of two orders, the outer with incised
zigzags, the inner with out-turned zigzags, which confirms an
early C12 date for this outlying work of the Herefordshire
carvers.* – FONT. The C17 font stands beside the new;
octagonal, with a recess in one side. Font cover dated 1678. –
STONE inscribed VALFLAVINI, in the s porch wall; perhaps
brought from the Roman fort at Castell Collen (2 m. SW). –
MONUMENTS. Rev. James Jones † 1733, inscribed in a roundel
in a large armorial tablet. By *Davies*, Builth. – John Price
† 1798. Tabernacle-type on an ogee bracket; the pediment
curves to a point. Signed *T.B.*, Newbridge. – Evan Davies
† 1834. – Evan W. Davies † 1838, with a broken column under
a weeping willow. – David Williams † 1793.
(MOTTE. 1 m. SSE.)

LLANBADARN FYNYDD   0070

St PADARN. Single-chamber with a W bellcote; considerably
restored by *S. W. Williams* in 1894. Only one old window, flamboyant Dec, in the N wall, but the roof of c. 1500 remains intact.
Arched braces resting on corbels, two in the chancel carved
with roses; one tie-beam; cusped strutting in the apexes. – The
head beam of the ROOD SCREEN is still there, with some vine
and waterleaf running ornament like Llananno's. It was drawn
by John Parker in 1830. – Laudian-type ALTAR RAILS with

* Professor Zarnecki very kindly helped me with this description.

turned balusters dated 1716. – PULPIT with C17 panels. – FONT. A round bowl chamfered to an octagonal base; probably early C14.

(GWERNLAS, 2 m. NE. Cruck-framed, with a timber partition and one doorway in the dais truss, and a single-bay (18 ft) hall. RCHM)

(Near CASTELL-Y-BLAIDD, a ringwork 2 m. NE, are the PLATFORM SITES of four houses grouped together near a junction of ridgeways SW of Castell-y-Blaidd, at over 1300 ft. They represent two pre-Norman(?) farms. All have the characteristic scarped 'hoods'. None was large – one house, of wood, was c. 24 by 14 ft. Another had a circular structure beside it. All have banked enclosures beside them.)

RHIW PORTHNANT (SO 112 823). A group of three Bronze Age BARROWS on the N end of a small moorland ridge. Two are typical rounded barrows; the third is of a rather more unusual kind – a flat-topped mound, a profile which appears to be original and not the result of modern disturbance. This mound, over 60 ft across and about 4 ft high, is known as 'Dicky's Stool'. The group is easily reached from the cross-roads on the mountain road to Llanbadarn Fynydd.

LLANBADARN-Y-GARREG

1040

ST PADARN. A little rectangular church with a bellcote, painted white, beside a pretty stream. Perhaps C13 or C14, but there is no obvious way of telling – there is a pointed unmoulded S door, a shallow sixteen-sided FONT on a cylindrical base, and the walls themselves. The single-framed scissor truss and collar roof, of twenty-eight close-set trusses, might be C14 or C15. A plain rood beam bears the (obliterated) Royal Arms. Everything else is later: ALTAR RAILS and PULPIT are C17, the wooden windows C18. The church was restored in 1960.

LLANBEDR PAINSCASTLE

1040

1½ m. W of Painscastle

ST PETER. Nave and W bellcote, chancel, S porch. Nave perhaps C14, with a rough E arch through to the added C15 chancel. S priest's doorway with an elliptical arch. The fenestration is crude but untampered with: in the nave a large trefoiled window and two-light cusped windows; debased Perp tracery in the w and also in the n and s chancel walls; cusped mullions for the panel lights. Only a small window high up in the E wall of the chancel, and a wagon roof. Stoup in the porch. The nave roof is c19 and the church was new-pewed in 1879 by *J. Evins* of Hereford. – FONT. c12. Bowl tapering to the cylindrical stem. – TABLET. Among others of the local type, Elizabeth Tuck † 1797, by *I. Millward*, Hay. – Circular plinth of the CHURCHYARD CROSS.

OLD LLANBACH HOWEY, ½ m. sw. Early c17. End walls of stone, the front refaced, the rear wall of close-stud timber-work. The gable ends support tall pairs of chimneys set diagonally; in the l. end also a two-storey spiral staircase.

MOTTE, 1½ m. sw. Ditched.

(LLEWETROG, 1 m. wnw. On an early long-house plan, altered in the c17. RCAM)

LLANBISTER *1070*

ST CYNLLO. In a rounded churchyard on hilly ground. Nave and chancel in one, picturesquely built up at the w to compensate for the falling ground and with a tower abutted at the E end, the only available place. Broad nave perhaps of *c.* 1300, with small lancets in the n and s walls, but much repaired. The s doorway with a double chamfer and the s priest's doorway are c14. One s window dated 1732. To the restorers of 1908, *W. D. Caröe* and *H. Passmore*, is owed much, both for exploiting the unusually steep site and for keeping the woodwork which gives the church its character. The roof is largely new work, tie-beams (formerly with crown-posts and raking struts) alternating with every two collared trusses for the nave, and just arched braces over the chancel. Four tiers of wind-braces throughout (the model dates from the c15). The s porch contains steps which the restorers continued up into the nave; beside these, a baptistery for total immersion. Immediately above is the GALLERY, dated 1716, with a stair and parapet with turned balusters. At the n beneath the gallery a little schoolroom was partitioned with contemporary carpentry. These parts were given windows on both storeys by the restorers. – c16 TOWER, greatly reduced in height, with diagonal buttresses, an elliptical s doorway under a triangular relieving arch, and a nw stair-turret, entered by a rounded door in the chancel. Two-tier pyramidal bell-stage dated 1732. – FONT. c14, octagonal (with a base chamfered to a square). – PEWS,

reduced from box pews. A bench at the rear dated 1688. – C18
PULPIT and TESTER, moved from the S. – SCREEN. On a
stone step. Sixteen lights with wooden tracery heads apparently
copied from Llananno. The doorway has moulded shafts
applied to the jambs and a head copied from screens. Deep
head-beam with restored brattishing. – CHOIR STALLS, by
Caröe (?) – ALTAR RAILS dated 1828. – REREDOS. A Christ in
Majesty, emphatically of *c.* 1950. The choir windows beneath
flattish relieving arches. – Remains of C17 WALL PAINTING. –
MONUMENTS. Classical marble and slate tablets to Edward
Meredith † 1833; the Rev. David Lloyd † 1838 by *Davies* of
Clun; Evan Williams † 1790; Elizabeth and Richard Bywater
† 1830 and 1867 by *B. Davies* of Clun. – Re-used fragments of
E.E. CARVING, probably from Abbey Cwmhir, notably the
stoup by the S door and a hollowed capital beside the font. –
Some C18 and C19 GRAVESTONES in the churchyard were
brought from Llananno.

(BRONDRE FAWR. A C17 stone house with a three-storey porch,
all altered. RCAM)

(UPPER CROES CYNON and LOWER CROES CYNON, 1 m. E.
Both are cruck-framed, with two doorways in their dais partitions. RCAM)

1040   LLANDDEWI FACH

In fields 1½ m. WSW of Painscastle

ST DAVID. Small nave and chancel with a W belfry, entirely
rebuilt by *Prichard* and *Seddon* in 1860, on an older site. Communion rails dated 1712. Fireplace on the N.

CWM FARM was the vicarage. It is a late C17 house with
mullioned and transomed windows and chimneys at the ends.

1060   LLANDDEWI YSTRADENNI

ST DAVID. In a circular churchyard. Entirely rebuilt in 1890 by
S. W. Williams. Nave and chancel in one and a W bellcote. In
the S wall a low Romanesque priest's door, of reassembled bits.
Two-step jambs; shafts in the angle with foliage capitals; round
arch with the roll-moulding behind two square ones. One of
the r. jamb-stones has a fragment of a C13 inscription. – FONT.
Octagonal; early C14. – MONUMENT. Andrew Phillips † 1701.
Wall-memorial with two columns, putti standing beside them,

figures on the pediment, and other once-gilded plaster decoration.

LLANDDEWI HALL. Part of the C16 house of the Phillips family. What survives is on a T-plan. Thick and tall stone walls and square-framed internal partitions. The round-headed chamfered stone front doorway has been removed from a demolished w wing. This house and Far Hall (2 m. E) share a traditional connection with Cwmhir Abbey; and also some Elizabethan panelling with a fantasy frieze. But other features of the woodwork suggest a mid C16 date: two Tudor doorheads with carved spandrels and heads carved in the apexes and a small cupboard with a door with a quincunx of circles. Fine hall ceiling of deep-chamfered beams with counterchanged joists. C17 stair.

TOMEN BEDD-UGRE, ¾ m. NW. A small motte sited on the circumference of a round bailey.

(DOLYDRE, ½ m. SSW. A fine five-bay C17 cruck-framed barn, with a central threshing bay. The end bay was framed off as a byre. RCAM)

CWM CEFN Y GAER. There are two hill-top enclosures on this ridge. The w one (SO 114 698) is a small but quite elaborate hillfort with widely spaced multivallate defences; the E hill-top (SO 121 699) is surrounded by only a single stone rampart with a sharply inturned entrance at the E end. The area enclosed is nearly 10 acres.

LLANDEGLEY   1060

ST TECLA. In a circular raised churchyard. What seem to be the N and S walls remain of a late medieval single-chamber church. Dec S priest's doorway with a graceful septifoil head, supposed to be spoil from Abbey Cwmhir. A thorough rebuilding was undertaken in 1876 by S. W. Williams, who re-roofed the whole church, adding a slightly narrower chancel with no arch but a tie-beam with partitioning in the old Radnor fashion at the division. Unfortunate Perp windows. An attractive w tower with a short broach-spire was built in 1953, with stones from Llwynbarried Hall, Nantmel. – SCREEN. Perp, with four-centred doorhead and six tracery lights on either side, of two different patterns. – FONT. Rounded bowl on cylindrical stem; c. 1200. – C19 classical ledger-stones are fixed to the S exterior walls.

THE PALES QUAKER MEETING HOUSE, 1 m. N. A simple,

isolated C18 building where many features are uniquely preserved from the C19 and before. The site was used for unmarked
burials from 1683 and the first chapel built in 1716. The existing
stone and thatch building is rather later, but has C18 benches
and on the dais two benches facing the meeting. On the SE,
towards a wonderful view, is a porch inside which two doors
dated 1828 open r. into the half for meetings and l. into a schoolroom with a fireplace. Between the rooms are three large windows with removable shutters – an arrangement perhaps dating
from the opening of the school in 1867.

FFALDAU. The main part is cruck-framed (two pairs) and perhaps of *c.* 1500. Exterior of rubble stone. Mullioned and
transomed windows in the N wall and hoodmoulds over the
windows in the late C17 cross-wing.

0040   LLANDEILO GRABAN

ST TEILO. At the N of a banked circular churchyard high above
the Wye. Nave, chancel, S porch, W tower. A double-square
nave plan, perhaps of the C14. The pointed E opening was
apparently broken through when the chancel was made. Two-
light trefoiled windows throughout; the Perp E window has big
mullions, with tall panel tracery. Wooden barrel roof with
carved bosses in the nave; wall-plates with brattishing in the
choir. S priest's doorway. The porch has a simple chamfered
doorway like the nave's, a truss with foiled struts above, and
an octagonal stoup. Quite a bit of replacement was carried out
by *E. V. Collier* in 1897, particularly on the low tower, which
has a pyramidal roof, and on the walls. – FONT. C14; on an
octagonal stone base. – ALTAR RAILS. C17.

PENISARPLWYF, 1½ m. ESE. A small L-plan C17 house with
many old features – windows, beams, stairs, and a post-and-
panel partition with two camber-headed doorways, one with
the date 1641.

CILIAU, 1½ m. SE. An unusually interesting small late medieval
stone farmhouse, perhaps of the second half of the C15. The
core is a hall (once open) with two arch-braced collar trusses.
Reminders of the three-unit cross-passage plan are the doorways in C15 post-and-panel partitions on opposite sides. The
W leads directly to the parlour; to the E two doorways with elaborately shaped wooden heads communicate with the service
rooms. The tall lateral chimney indicates gentry status. One
cambered stone cyclopean doorway, and C17 windows. The

original wings either end of the hall made an H-plan; their upper storeys were timber-framed and jettied. An arabesque panel gives the date 1701 – is this the date of the corbel-posts and the upper floor in the hall, and also of the nice William and Mary stair with its newels, drop pendants, and shapely turned balusters? (RCAM)

LLANDRINDOD WELLS

0060

HOLY TRINITY (the old parish church of Llandrindod) is on the hill above the lake ½ m. SE of the town. It was originally a C13/14 single chamber, with a S porch now nearer the E end, and W spirelet. After a strange episode in the course of which the Archdeacon had Llandrindod and Cefnllys churches unroofed, to force people to attend the town church, it was rebuilt in 1894 by *Nicholson & Sons*, and extended to the W in 1911. Tie-beam roof trusses (a localism copied from the old work) over the nave, and over the chancel hammerbeams carrying braces steeply arched to a point, with curved brackets and quatrefoils below. – MONUMENTS. John Hope † 1761. Bronze, with engraved coat of arms. – Tablet to Eliza Dale and child † 1806. – David Jones † 1817, a stone with traces of colour. – Morgan Davies † 1835, by *Price*, Builth. – Thomas Whittall † 1826, by *Stevens*. Ornate sandstone tablet carved with spiral-fluted colonnettes, a frieze of flowers and urns, and a larger urn above; painted grey and white. – GLASS. E *c.* 1951. – A sheela-na-gig in relief, with one side of the stone later marked with a cross-crosslet, was found in 1894 buried beneath the floor.

HOLY TRINITY, Llandrindod Wells. S nave and chancel, S aisle; N nave and chancel, N aisle – a complicated plan; but the building is no older than 1871. It was erected by *T. Nicholson* of Hereford as an aisled church, with round columns with carved capitals, and bands of dark stone throughout. Apparently a tower was intended to rise from the S aisle. The lighter N nave and aisle were added in 1905 by *R. Wellings Thomas* of Llandrindod. Everything E of the chancel arches is his design too – windows with nook-shafts and flowing Dec tracery. He also enlarged the S chancel in 1910, but kept the window tracery of 1871. This chancel arcade has clusters of grey marble columns with detached shafts. Double order round the E windows. Roof of double hammerbeam construction with lots of tracery carving and winged angels. It could all be fifty years earlier. – Elaborate SCREEN to the N chancel and pulpit – an ingenious device which keeps the S chancel dominant. – STAINED GLASS. N aisle, the Good Samaritan, 1923; N nave W, 1969; N aisle W, 1973.

ST DAVID (R.C.). 1971 by *Weightman & Bullen*. A broad tribune with a summer nave that can be shut off. Externally a bit uncoordinated, but culminating in a glazed gable and a Celtic cross. Internally of buff fair-faced brickwork and gabled boarded ceilings.

PRESBYTERIAN CHURCH OF WALES. 1905 in Perp or Tudor, by *Ewen Harper Bros.* of Birmingham. It cost £6,000 including the stone tower and spire.

CHRISTIAN CONFERENCE CENTRE. Also neo-Perp. By *W. Beddre Rees*, 1907.

CONGREGATIONAL CHURCH. By *J. M. Smith*. In strongly red brick with a red brick spire.

TABERNACLE BAPTIST CHAPEL. By *E. Peters Morris*, 1907, in mixed styles.*

The origins of the spa town go back even to the late C17; saline and sulphur springs were discovered in the 1730s. 'In 1756', says Jonathan Williams, 'a Dr Wessel Linden published a book on the medicinal value of the springs, which had the effect of giving them considerable publicity.' In 1748 the *Gentleman's Magazine* chortled, 'Let England boast Bath's crowded springs/Llandrindod happier Cambria sings.' About 1749 a Mr Grosvenor of Shrewsbury converted LLANDRINDOD HALL, a house immediately below the old church, into what Lewis's *Topographical Dictionary* described as 'a spacious hotel, capable of accommodating numerous families'. The alterations and additions he made for this purpose included a suite of rooms for balls, concerts, and billiards, and shops for supplying various articles of use or luxury. It appears that this establishment, with its 100 beds, really was what we would think of as a hotel today – its manager-successors aim at similar facilities – and it is an early example of a building type which developed in spas. It closed in 1787; there is nothing else of C18 Llandrindod remaining.

A second wave of hotels, the Pump House and the Rock House, located round the springs near the river Ithon, began *c.* 1805 and a third *c.* 1870; use of the spa itself finally ended in 1971. People have opted for the coasts both times. The lake by the

* I am grateful to Mr Vernon Hughes for information on chapels in Llandrindod.

Pump House was created in the 1870s by *W. N. Swettenham*,
the hotel was rebuilt in 1888. The baths, pump room, and
market hall at the ROCK HOUSE were designed by *S. W.
Williams c.* 1872. *T. Nicholson* made a development plan for
Mr Middleton Evans in 1868.

Present-day Llandrindod reflects this past in little more than
name. The Powys County Council occupies the former PUMP
HOUSE HOTEL of *c.* 1886 (there is no County Hall). There the
pump room is intact, and beside it the prettily arcaded former
bath-house and the twin pepper-pots of the boiler house.
£30,000 in all was spent. The town is an oasis of red brick in
the greenest of landscapes; of secure Edwardian streets in an
area of farms. Its urban environment, built perhaps in just two
decades, *c.* 1890–1910, is coherent and above all ordered. It
possesses qualities of the residential resorts on the North Wales
coast, but has more trees. Ruabon is the likely source of the
cheerful and raucous bricks in its plush terraces of predominantly
red or predominantly yellow houses, and these colours often
contrast with ornate white cast-iron arcading just like the Late
Victorian developments in the North. Like them it relied on its
railway station. The best groups are near the post office. Only
one or two buildings can be singled out – the copper-turreted
HOTEL METROPOLE of *c.* 1899 as the essence of the town,
with an attractive Art Nouveau veranda; COOMBS' in
Middleton Street for a commercial front almost entirely in glass;
the red-brick GLEN USK HOTEL for its very profuse iron
balconies. In ROCK PARK the nostalgic shapes of pavilions and
spa architecture survive in thick woods. They are in the polychrome style of *c.* 1890. The local(?) designers were improving
when growth stopped abruptly.

CAEBACH CHAPEL, ¾ m. N. A small independent place of worship founded by the Rev. Thomas Jones in 1715. A complete
C18 interior, though with later ogee windows. Side entrance;
box pews, raked at the rear; a gallery at the rear as well; coved
plaster ceiling. Semi-octagonal pulpit. The lighting still (at the
time of writing) by candles and lamps. – A large TABLET of
1810 to the Jones family of Trefonnen combines two marbles,
grey for the flanking pilasters and white for the urn.

½ m. SE of Caebach Chapel is TREFONNEN, the ruined C17 and
C18 house of the Jones family.

NEUADD, ¾ m. ESE of the chapel, is a cruck-framed house with
two early windows. In the centre a bulky C17 chimney with
four separate diagonal stacks.

CASTELL COLLEN ROMAN FORT (SO 055 628) is a large fort with a chequered history of abandonment and refurbishment; it has also suffered a good deal from excavators. The diagonal trenching carried out in 1913 has not been filled in; though this is very shocking, it does make the site rather more interesting to visit than many Roman forts. The first fort on this site, perhaps founded in A.D. 75–8, was a large one, about five acres in extent, initially surrounded by a ditch and a turf rampart, later revetted in stone. Under the Severan reorganization of Britain (c. A.D. 210) the garrison here was reduced and a large part of the NW side abandoned. A new line of defence was built defining a square fort only $3\frac{1}{2}$ acres in extent. Remains of the stone headquarters building and the commandant's house can still be recognized as well as a single large stone granary; the barrack buildings must have been wooden throughout the history of the fort, which seems to have been in use up to the C4. To the S there was a large bath building, excavated more recently and now covered up. Finds from the excavations are exhibited in Llandrindod Wells Museum.

S of the town on LLANDRINDOD COMMON is a group of small PRACTICE CAMPS; there were originally eighteen of them, the largest group in the Roman Empire. Fourteen can still be recognized from the air, but they are very difficult to see on the ground. They lie just to the W of the main road and railway from SO 050 590 to 058 608 alongside the original Roman road which ran to the W. These camps would be dug by the troops as exercises; they had to build similar marching camps each night when they were on campaign.

LLANELWEDD

0050

ST MATTHEW. In a raised churchyard overlooking the Wye. Nave, chancel, N aisle, S porch, W tower, substantially dating from 1877; but by all accounts *John Norton*, the restorer, did what he could to preserve or copy the old work. Simple chamfered priest's door, porch doorway, and round S doorway. Three-bay N arcade of double-chamfered piers of C15 type. Plain C14 Brecon-type tower with machicolations added in place of a pyramidal roof. – FONTS. One is octagonal, on two circular steps. – Another found buried in the churchyard is now outside the chancel. – Five old PEWS at the back. – The CHANCEL SCREEN is dado-height only, and on it stand eight winged angels. This, the PULPIT, the CHOIR SEATS, and the

ALTAR FRONT were carved by Miss *Amy Thomas* and a Miss *Faltin*. – STAINED GLASS. E by *Clayton & Bell*; nave windows by *Burlison & Grylls*.

SCHOOL. Built *c.* 1892. Stone. Ogee windows. 'Designed as a labour of love' by *Commander Algernon Thomas*.

LLANELWEDD HALL (Royal Welsh Agricultural Society). The fine Queen Anne plaster ceiling of the dining room has been destroyed by fire.

GELLI CADWGAN. Cruck-framed on a stone base. Stone walls. A long-house plan. Converted to a storeyed house with a central chimney in the C17.

TYNCOED, 2 m. N. Mid C18; five bays with a hipped roof and a good contemporary stair.

PENCERRIG, 1¼ m. NNW, was the family home of Thomas Jones (1743–1803), the landscape and portrait painter who in his early twenties was a pupil of Richard Wilson of Penegoes (M). In 1831 his house – a five-bay hipped-roofed building whose late C18 staircase is still there – was engulfed by additions. The C19 work includes elaborate Gothick doorways, 'in the style of King Henry the 7th', in the words of *William Whittington* the surveyor. The late C18 STABLES still stand, with their seven-bay brick front with a pediment above three bays, and an octagonal lantern. The lake below was made *c.* 1825 for Jones's daughter. But these are small changes compared with the endurance of the countryside he painted.

CEFNDYRYS, 1 m. NW. Built in 1787–90 for David Thomas on a picturesque see-and-be-seen site. Five-window façade with a central accent: a gable pediment with a lunette, two niches flanking the first-floor window, and a porch with slender paired Tuscan columns. Cross-axial plan. Hall with a depressed arch on columns; bow-ended dining-room. Additions to the r. of *c.* 1840. Gothic-fenestrated STABLES of three bays, with a pediment and lantern.

On the broken rocky summit of the CARNEDDAU ridge are three hillforts, cairns, and, beneath the relatively modern pillow mounds in the vicinity of the quarry, evidence for Neolithic occupation, although no monuments of that date survive. The hillforts differ in design, but all make good use of the natural defensive properties of the terrain; they cannot be accurately dated but may be assumed to belong to the last centuries B.C. or first centuries A.D. CWMBERWYN CAMP (SO 073 548) has only a single rampart for most of its circuit, but a formidable ditch; CAER EINION (SO 063 531) has two stone ramparts but also incorporates several lengths of natural cliff; GAER FAWR (SO 058 531) is the largest and most impressive, with multiple ramparts and a complex entrance.

For the BRIDGE over the river Wye, ½ m. SW, *see* Builth Wells (B).

0050

LLANFAREDD

1½ m. ESE of Llanelwedd

ST MARY. A small single-chamber church in a round church-yard. The walls are clearly ancient, but much renewal was done by *E. V. Collier* in 1891. Roof with arch-braced trusses, and tie-beams at the W, but all very much renewed too. The S door and its wooden frame are C17. Of the same century are the ALTAR RAILS. − FONT. Perp, on a slender octagonal shaft. − TABLETS. William James † 1765, and others, by *Games* of Talgarth. − In the W spirelet a BELL of *c.* 1280.

0060

LLANFIHANGEL HELYGEN

1¼ m. SE of Nantmel

ST MICHAEL. A little church on the simplest rectangular plan, in a near-round churchyard. W end partitioned off as the vestry, with a W bellcote over. Arch-braced collars with raking struts and two tiers of cusped wind-braces in the roof. − BOX PEWS neatly arranged, and a TWO-DECKER PULPIT. − Stone-flagged floors. − FONT. Circular, on a slim cylindrical base; C13? Formerly a stoup? − Diamond-shaped TABLET to Thomas Joseph † 1805, and others. − The church was happily restored in 1956 by the Pilgrim Trust. The walls were mostly rebuilt *c.* 1812, and an E window was put in after an appeal by the curate, Thomas Price (Carnhuanawc). Part of his training in drawing and antiquities was given by Theophilus Jones of Brecon (*see* Cwmdu (B)).

GREAT HOUSE, ½ m. NW. C17 or earlier, with a central moulded stone chimney, and stopped and chamfered beams. Sited across the contour.

1050

LLANFIHANGEL NANT MELAN

2½ m. SW of New Radnor

ST MICHAEL. In an extended churchyard: the close ring of large yews marks an early or pre-Christian site. Norman Revival.

Small nave and semicircular apse, by *Thomas Nicholson* of Hereford, 1846; said to have been consciously modelled on Kilpeck church – the nave and apse do have lesenes, roll-moulded windows, and a corbel-table, but this is merely trim and ceases altogether on the N. s porch door and w window with shafts and zigzag. Engaged columns and a roll for the chancel arch, and engaged columns with vaulting ribs in the apse. The nave has a shallow pent roof. – PULPIT and DESK also neo-Norman. – FONT. Perp, octagonal. – MONUMENT. T. Butts † 1793, by *Davies*, Builth. – The church belonged to William de Breos and was given in the later C12 to the Knights of St John. As at Llandegley, memorials are fixed to the outside of the s wall. John Lewis of Llynwene, the historian, † 1616, was a native of this parish.

CASTELL CRUGERYDD, 1½ m. NW. A raised circular bailey *c.* 50 yds in diameter with a small independently ditched motte at the w. It is mentioned by Giraldus Cambrensis on his journey with Archbishop Baldwin through New Radnor to preach the First Crusade in 1188. Llewelyn Crug Eryr the herald-bard lived here *c.* 1300. (His descendants were patrons of Lewis Glyn Cothi.)

GREAT HOUSE, opposite the church, is clearly a long-house. Dwelling-house and byre under the same roof; the door between them is blocked, but its wooden frame can be seen in the byre.

MOTTE. 1½ m. WSW.

TOLLGATE, 1 m. W, next to the Forest Inn. Early C19, one-storey with a bay.

TOMEN CASTLE, 1½ m. NW. A ditched motte.

MAESMELAN. A C17 central-chimneyed house with a good C18 stone-tiled corn-barn with byre beneath, built at r. angles to the house.

LLANFIHANGEL RHYDITHON   *1060*

ST MICHAEL AND ALL ANGELS. In a rounded raised church-yard, now enlarged. Nave, short chancel, w tower; entirely rebuilt by *B. Wishlade* in 1838; the chancel by *S. W. Williams*, 1891. – FONT. Small, C14, octagonal. – GLASS. E by *J. Stephenson* of Bath. – MONUMENTS. Benjamin Bore † 1834, chunky classical, by *Davies*, Clun.

Below the church an octagonal tollgate of *c.* 1800, converted into a SCHOOL in 1848.

FAR HALL, 1 m. N. A plain C17 T-plan house with a stone clustered chimneystack. The internal details – parlour beams and
a central chimney – are typical of the period, but the upper
floor is unusual in having wainscoting in most rooms. Interesting overmantel carved with five figures in Elizabethan dress,
with vines in the arches between them and wavy tendril and
leaf decoration on the frieze. A second overmantel is partially
re-erected in a small room panelled with pilasters with strapwork figuring and a frieze of fantastic animals.

CASTELL CYMARON, 2 m. N. A motte and bailey built for Hugh
Mortimer, and rebuilt in 1195. Retaken by Llywelyn ab Iorwerth in 1202. It continued as the Mortimers' manorial court
till the end of the C13.

MOTTE AND BAILEY, 3¼ m. N. At c. 1150 ft.

₂₀₇₀   LLANGYNLLO

ST CYNLLO. Nave and chancel under one roof but divided by
a chancel arch and N transept, rebuilt on the old foundations
by *John Middleton*, 1878. W battlemented tower (1894) and S
porch (1896) rebuilt by *F. R. Kempson*. Lancet windows
throughout. Large SEDILIA. The roof also is wholly new but
of C15 type. The only old bits are the four-centred doorway
re-used at the W, and a tiny N lancet. – MONUMENTS. James
Meyrick † 1739, with an open pediment. – Mary Evans † 1834,
by *B. Davies*, Clun.

        LLANSANTFFRAED-CWMDEUDDWR *see*
                  CWMDEUDDWR

₀₀₅₀   LLANSANTFFRAED-IN-ELVEL

ST BRIDGET. In a circular churchyard, and within a smaller
near-complete ring of old yews. Rebuilt by *F. R. Kempson*,
1895; a long single chamber with old timbers in the S porch
roof, and two bells hung in the window recesses in the W wall.
Bits of window tracery, the altar rails, and oak for the pews
were re-used. The stone-flagged floor and arch-braced roof
with tie-beams make the interior much more likeable than the
exterior. – FONT. Perp.

At Llansantffraed a Cistercian nunnery was founded before 1176
by an early abbot of Strata Marcella. The village consists of
a handful of houses only. LLANDRE is cruck-built; the former
VICARAGE has a Regency veranda.

(LLWYNMADOC, ¾ m. WNW. Formerly the home of the Vaughan family.)

CASTLE BANK (SO 087 561). The stone rampart of this Iron Age hillfort can be well seen from the road from Crossway to Hundred House. The elongated hill has, in fact, two stone enclosures and a cairn on it. The S hillfort, the earlier defence, was used as an outer enclosure when the second fort was built on the N end of the ridge. The original entrance is at the S end.

LLANSTEPHAN   *1040*

1¼ m. NNW of Boughrood

ST STEPHEN or YSTYFFAN. At the N of a large circular church-yard, on a hillside with distant views. C18 (?) LYCHGATE with gates for people and carts and an added stable for the parson's horse. Nave, chancel, S porch, W tower. The C13 nave plan, a double square of the same size as Llandeilo Graban's, is also broken through for the C14 chancel. S doorway and round-arched W doorway from the C14(?) tower. Some C15 windows in the S wall and a Perp E window with panel tracery like Llandeilo's. C17 unceiled wagon roof over the chancel. A new nave roof, chancel arch, etc. by *Thomas Nicholson*, 1867–8. The low tower rises two and a half stages like Aberedw's, and was probably rebuilt in the C16; it has oak to reinforce the weak stonework and a pyramidal roof. – FONT. Octagonal on a modern base.

DOLWEN, ¼ m. SE. A cruck hall on the usual down-the-hill site. Two trusses survive, one arch-braced and decorated with quatrefoil and trefoil cusping in the apex, the other plain and blocked at the bottom by a wood partition with a Tudor doorway.

LLANSTEPHAN HOUSE was demolished in 1972; the replacement is by *N. Johnston*, 1974–6.

(CELYN, 1 m. NE of the church. A ruined cruck-framed house (three pairs remain) comprising the byre and living-room of the early long-house plan. After the usual enlargement in the C17, when stairs etc. were added, it has become a barn.)

SUSPENSION BRIDGE. Built by *David Rowell & Co.*, 1922. Across the Wye.

LLANYRE   *0060*

ST LLŶR. In a small raised churchyard now enlarged. The

medieval church had an unusually ornate roof. The C19 dedication was to All Saints. Entirely rebuilt by *S. W. Williams*, 1885–
7. Nave, chancel, three-sided apse. Pale bare stone interior with
knowledgeable E.E. decoration; the w window is a group of
five stepped lancets with detached shafts. – FONT. An oblong
octagon; Late Norman? – MONUMENT. Thomas Williams
† 1845. Grecian. – GLASS. E by *A. L. Moore.*

LLOWES

1040

ST MEILIG. In a circular churchyard. St Meilig came from
Clydeside *c*. 650 and founded a *clas* here. Nave and chancel
entirely rebuilt in 1853–5 by *W. J. Worthington*; the upper
(Perp) part of the w tower was added later, to stonework
existing at the first stage. – FONT. Circular, with a raised band
round the middle and octagonal undercutting. Early C13.
Broken. – CROSS. C11. A tall tapering slab decorated front and
back with a large cross in high relief. On the front a Latin
wheel-cross of Celtic type, its arms and upper stem filled with
lozenge patterning. The cross on the reverse is similar but has
no wheel or ornament. Moved into the church in 1956.

LLOWES COURT. A stone house three storeys tall was built
c. 1570 by Thomas Fychan. This, with its spiral stair, seems
to be embedded in an early C18 remodelling. Front of five bays,
reduced to three windows. Stair of the same date added at the
rear, with a panelled room at its head.

MOTTE. 1 m. S.

MAESLLWCH CASTLE *see* GLASBURY

MAESYRONNEN

1040

1 m. N of Glasbury

INDEPENDENT CHAPEL. Formed in 1696–7, and thus amongst
almost the earliest in use in Wales. Structurally, however, the
building is older than that: a cruck truss in the wall between
chapel and caretaker's cottage reveals that this was a C16(?) farm
and barn, the former rebuilt by the C17 and the latter (not un-
typically) later converted into a meeting house. The chapel roof
was replaced in the C18, on leaning walls, with tie-beams. s front
with mullioned and transomed windows under gablets, and end
doorways. The remarkable interior preserves to a detail the
FURNITURE of the C18 and C19: a pew and table dated 1727;

1 *Landscape:* Breconshire and the Brecon Beacons

2 *Landscape:* The Vale of Meifod, Montgomeryshire

3 *Town Scenery:* Llanidloes (M)

4 *Village Scenery:* Tretower (B)

5 Glyntawe (B), Cerrig Duon, Bronze Age

6 Caersws (M), Cefn Carnedd hillfort, Iron Age

7 Aberyscir (B), Brecon Gaer, south gateway of Roman fort, *c.* A.D. 140

8 The Llywel (B) Stone (now in the British Museum),
eighth century or later

9 (left) Meifod (M), Sts Tysilio and Mary, cross slab, perhaps ninth or
tenth century
10 (right) Neuadd Siarman Cross (now in Brecknock Museum, B), tenth century

11 Partrishow (B), St Ishow or Issai, font, *c.* 1055

12 Brecon (B) Cathedral, font, *c.* 1130–50

13 Llanbadarn Fawr (R), St Padarn, tympanum, first half of the twelfth century

14 Kerry (M), St Michael, arcade, 1176 (?) and early fourteenth century

15 Pennant Melangell(M), St Melangell, shrine of St Monacella, *c.* 1160–70 (reconstructed in 1958/9)

16 Tretower (B) Castle, keep, mid twelfth century

17 Hay-on-Wye (B) Castle, keep, *c.* 1200, the gateway 1233

18 and 19 Llanidloes (M), St Idloes, arcade from Cwmhir Abbey (R),
c. 1200–1230, re-erected c. 1542, with detail of capitals

20 Brecon (B) Cathedral, chancel, 1201–8; vault by Sir George Gilbert Scott, 1861–2

21 Brecon (B), Christ College, chapel, *c.* 1240 and early fourteenth century

22 Llanddew (B), Holy Trinity, largely late thirteenth century

23 Montgomery (M) Castle, begun 1223

24 Bronllys (B) Castle, early or mid thirteenth century

25 Powis Castle (M), keep, *c.* 1300

26 Presteigne (R), St Andrew, nave, first half of the fourteenth century

27 Brecon (B) Cathedral, monument to Walter and Christina
Awbrey, 1312

28 and 29 Brecon (B) Cathedral, north arcade of the nave,
Decorated, and canopy in the Corvizors' Chapel, *c.* 1340

30 Kerry (M), St Michael, tower, largely early fourteenth century

31 Llanelieu (B), St Ellyw, screen, fourteenth century and later

32 Guilsfield (M), St Aelhaiarn, nave, late fourteenth or early fifteenth century; ceiling *c.* 1500

33 Llanfair Caereinion (M), St Mary, effigy of Dafydd ap Gruffydd Fychan, *c.* 1400

34 Brecon (B), Christ College, Small Hall, fourteenth century

35 Presteigne (R), St Andrew, south aisle and tower, later fifteenth century

36 Montgomery (M), St Nicholas, east window, Perpendicular

37 Llandefalle (B), St Matthew or Maelog, second half of the fifteenth century

38 Tretower (B) Court, great hall, *c.* 1470

39 Tretower (B) Court, gatehouse and curtain wall, *c.* 1480

40 Old Radnor (R), St Stephen, early fifteenth century

41 Mochdre (M),
rood figures (now
in the National
Museum of Wales),
fifteenth century

42 Old Radnor (R), St Stephen, stained glass figure of
St Catherine, late fifteenth century

43 Llananno (R), St Anno, screen, perhaps *c.* 1500, with figures of *c.* 1880

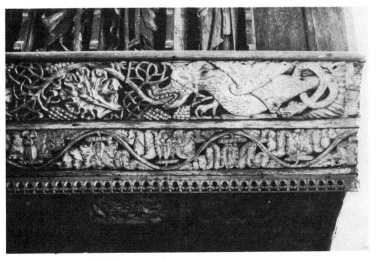

44 Llananno (R), St Anno, screen, detail

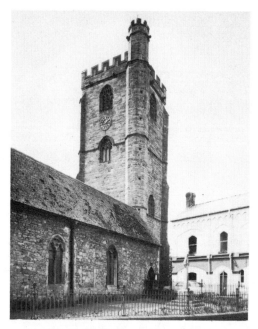

45 Brecon (B), St Mary, tower, *c.* 1510–20

46 Welshpool (M), St Mary, nave, early or mid sixteenth century

47 Old Radnor (R), St Stephen, organ case, early sixteenth century

48 Llanidloes (M), St Idloes, roof, 1542

49 Powis Castle (M), long gallery, *c.* 1592 (*Copyright Country Life*)

50 Llanfaes (B), Newton, 1582

51 Monaughty (R), *c.* 1575 (?) and later

52 Montgomery (M), St Nicholas, monument to Richard and
Magdalen Herbert by Walter Hancock, 1600

53 Felindre (B), Old Gwernyfed, probably before 1613

54 Brecon (B) Cathedral, monument to Sir David Williams † 1613 and wife

55 Llanidloes (M), Market Hall, c. 1600

56 Llanfihangel Rhydithon (R), Far Hall, overmantel, Elizabethan

57 Hay-on-Wye (B) Castle, seventeenth-century house before the fire
(*Copyright Country Life*)

58 Tregynon (M), Gregynog, overmantel in the Blayney Room,
1636 and nineteenth century

59 Clatter (M), Plasau Duon, mid seventeenth century

60 Aberhafesp (M), Aberhafesp Hall, staircase, *c.* 1675

61 Powis Castle (M), staircase, probably by William Winde, c. 1668, the walls painted by Gerard Lanscroon, c. 1705

62 Powis Castle (M), State Bedchamber, probably by William Winde, *c.* 1668

63 Meifod (M), Maesmawr Hall, c. 1689–92

64 Trefecca (B), Trefecca Fawr, ceiling in the parlour, c. 1680–90

65 Maesyronnen (R), Independent Chapel, converted *c.* 1696

66 Brecon (B), Christ College, chapel, monument to Bishop Lucy † 1677

67 Brecon (B), Christ College, chapel, monument to the Rev. Richard Lucy † 1690,
his wife and his son Gam † 1697, by William Stanton

68 Powis Castle (M), gates by John Warren, *c.* 1710

69 Llanfyllin (M), St Myllin, early eighteenth century

70 Montgomery (M), Town Hall, by William Baker, 1748, and
Thomas Penson, 1828

71 Trefecca (B), College, perhaps by Howell Harris, 1751–73

72 Llanbedr Ystrad Yw (B), Moor Park, *c.* 1760

73 Llangattock (B), St Catwg, tablet to William Morgan † 1746
and his wife Alice † 1750

74 Llandrinio (M), bridge, 1775

75 Guilsfield (M), St Aelhaiarn, monument to the Rev. James Egerton † 1772,
by John Nelson

76 Tregynon (M), St Cynon, monument to Arthur Blayney
† 1795, by John Bacon

77 Berriew (M), Glansevern, by Joseph Bromfield, *c.* 1801–7

78 Stanage Park (R), by Humphry Repton, J. A. Repton, and
Edward Haycock, c. 1807–45

79 Guilsfield (M), Garth, by John C. Loudon, begun 1809 (demolished 1946)

80 Welshpool (M), Llanerchydol, perhaps by the Reptons, 1820

81 Welshpool (M), Christ Church, by Thomas Penson, 1839–44

82 Llandinam (M), bridge, by Thomas Penson, 1846

83 Brecon (B), Brecknock Museum (formerly Shire Hall), by T. H. Wyatt and D. Brandon, 1839–43

84 Battle (B), Penoyre, by Anthony Salvin, 1846–8

85 Llangasty Tal-y-Llyn (B), St Gastayn, by J. L. Pearson, 1848–56, chancel

86 Leighton (M), Leighton Hall, library, ceiling decoration
by J. G. Crace to designs by A. W. N. Pugin, *c.* 1855

87 Brecon (B) Cathedral, monument to Sophia Watkins
† 1851, by John Evan Thomas

88 Meifod (M), Sts Tysilio and Mary, window by David Evans, *c.* 1856

89 Brecon (B), Christ College, collegiate buildings, by John Prichard and J. P. Seddon, *c.* 1861

90 New Radnor (R), monument to Sir George Cornewall Lewis, by John Gibbs, 1864

91 Abbey Cwmhir (R), St Mary, by J. W. Poundley and D. Walker, 1866

92 Llandysilio (M), St Tysilio, by G. E. Street, 1867–8

93 Abbey Cwmhir (R), St Mary, window by Heaton, Butler & Bayne, 1866

94 Abermule (M), Cefn Bryntalch, by G. F. Bodley and Philip Webb, 1869

95 Llandinam (M), Plas Dinam, by W. E. Nesfield, 1873–4

96 Llandinam (M), Presbyterian Church, by Szlumper & Aldwinkle, 1872–3

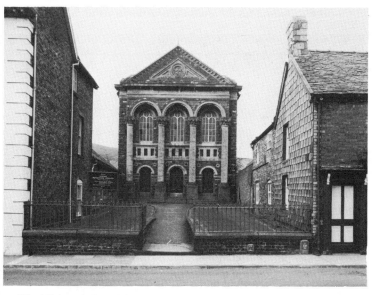

97 Llanidloes (M), Sion United Reformed Church, by John Humphreys, 1878

98 Llyswen (B), Llangoed, by Sir Clough Williams-Ellis, 1913–19

99 Llangammarch Wells (B), St Cadmarch, by W. D. Caroe, 1913–16

100 Elan Valley (R), Claerwen Dam, by Sir William Halcrow & Partners,
1946–52

101 Newtown (M), housing at Trehafren, by J. L. Russell, 1972–5

three BOX PEWS; the PULPIT in the centre of the long N wall, among C19 memorial TABLETS. No vernacular building speaks plainer than this quintessence of Radnorshire.

MICHAELCHURCH-ON-ARROW   2050

ST MICHAEL. Nave, chancel, and low W tower with a saddleback roof. The tower dates from the C13 (one lancet), the nave and chancel perhaps from the C13 or C14 too. Much restoration in 1869 by *Thomas Nicholson* (diocesan architect of Hereford). The chancel is divided from the nave by a Late Perp SCREEN, of Welsh construction. The dado is pierced by circled quatre-foils. It has a continuous band of tall traceries wholly English (of the Herefordshire school) in their fluent lines, particularly so the bold subsidiary ogee doorhead with its big leaf crockets, and the pinnacles. C19 wood cusped chancel arch with boarding above in the traditional Radnorshire manner, which is pierced with a distinctive arcade placed on the arch. The sanctuary has the remnants of a pre-Reformation CIBORIUM (cf. Brilley, 1 m. into Herefordshire). Two moulded wall-posts with fleurons supported a bracket and arch screen of some sort, and an EASTER SEPULCHRE on the N wall. Against the now window-less E wall two more posts with little finials and an embattled beam form the frame for a reredos. Crossley thought all these members originally formed a rood screen and loft like Llan-elieu's (B), which was replaced by the present screen less than a century later. The coved ceiling over the reredos is restored, but the ribs and bosses in the centre are original: a bishop (of Hereford), Henry IV, and Joan of Navarre are the identifica-tions of the heads, which points to a date c. 1410. Outer arch with a cresting of inverted cusping and sub-cusping. – FONT. Octagonal on a circular base, but recut. – GLASS. S chancel by *Mayer & Co.*, Munich and London, 1873.

CHURCH HOUSE FARM, box-framed, has a C17 parlour with a compartmented ceiling.

BAYNHAM HALL, 1 m. WNW. A house of c. 1700 added to an earlier wing. Of good simple William and Mary proportions, with a tall hipped roof, pedimental gable containing a Venetian window, and tall external chimneystacks at the ends. Stone; five bays. Staircase with elegant contemporary turned balusters. To the r. a fine large C18 stone BARN, L-shaped, with a stone-slate roof. It combines a corn-barn with byres.

2060

MONAUGHTY

2 m. E of Bleddfa

51 A large Late Elizabethan house – the largest in the county – built for the Price family (several of whom were High Sheriff and M.P. between 1552 and 1622) and little altered. H-plan, but not symmetrical. Gaunt walls of random brownish stone with freestone flush quoins on the wings. All the windows have stone transoms and mullions; some have dripmoulds. The central, storeyed section contains the hall and could date from *c.* 1575. This is entered through two stone Tudor doorways on opposite sides with armorial carved spandrels. It originally had a porch and an oriel on the E, both of two storeys. Two coats of arms in a single panel on the E, one in a subcusped quatrefoil. On the S the low wooden screen, unusual in its bold early mouldings, preserves its two triangular doorheads; both are decorated with fronds and one also has the Price arms. Below the passage the full-height partition is of plain stout framing, and below that were pantry and buttery. Deeply chamfered ceiling beams over the hall form fifteen compartments in which the joists were originally set in counterchanging directions. Lateral Tudorarched fireplace, with formerly a half-spiral stair beside leading to the Great Chamber. This contains fragments of a geometrically ribbed plaster ceiling. Of the gabled wings, which both have two external chimneys with tall ashlared stacks, the N (solar end) originally had its own stair and has plain wainscotting in an upper room. The S has its own crudely carved doorway to the kitchen; the original broad elliptical fireplace arch remains there. On the upper floor a ruined tower garderobe. Timber-framed partitions throughout. A timber stairturret was inserted in the angle between wing and hall in 1638; sturdy balusters up the two steep circuits of the well.*

1 m. NW, by the Lugg, is a rectangular ENCLOSURE, the remnant of a grange of Cwmhir Abbey, from which Monaughty (or Mynachdy) takes its name.

NANTGWYLLT *see* ELAN VALLEY

0060

NANTMEL

ST CYNLLO. In a circular churchyard with an C18(?) LYCH-GATE with two openings. The angle-buttressed base of the W

---

* Mr D. Blain gave me most useful information on Monaughty.

tower is C17 or earlier; its embattled upper half, and the unaisled nave, were rebuilt in 1792. However the nave windows and doors are redone in a poor neo-Norman style.

ST MARK, YSFA, 3 m. SW. Single-chamber with an apse; built in 1871. – FONT. C14, octagonal, with crenellation along the bottom of the bowl. – GLASS. E by *O'Connor*, 1871.

LLWYNBARRIED HALL, 1 m. WSW. A parlour ceiling with deep-chamfered beams and Tudor rose bosses at their intersections suggests this was a C16 house of good standing. Much alteration of the 1870s, including a neat neo-Jacobean staircase, by *S. W. Williams*. A BARN built as late as 1772 has crucks combined with box-framing. Stone from embattled garden towers of *c.* 1820 is re-used at Llandegley church.

(DOLAU, 1 m. W. A small C17 cruck-framed house and similar barn. RCAM)

(CEFN CEIDO HALL. An C18 three-window front and a doorway with a scalloped fanlight. A late C15 timber-framed hall-house nearby, now a BARN, has a unique arching cruck couple with a king-post above the collar in its two-bay hall. On the upper side a passage with a room above; in square-framed walls. Below, a parlour with two crucks, one with a post and panel partition. A stone BARN has a semicircular-headed doorway. RCAM)

(GWERNCYNYDD, 1 m. SW. An early C17 three-cruck house. RCAM)

(CHURCH COTTAGE – near the church – is a small cruck building of *c.* 1700. RCAM)

NEWBRIDGE-ON-WYE 0050

ALL SAINTS. A competent if rather bland, multicoloured church. Nave, chancel, five-sided sanctuary, and N tower; by *S. W. Williams*, 1883, and about his best. Largely sponsored by the Venables family. Plain Dec exterior. Tall tower with a broach-spire. The nave has smooth masonry walls and the roof rises clear of the windows on wall-shafts. Well-proportioned sanctuary with five windows with contemporary glass and relieving arches on red marble shafts. Wooden vault also on slender shafts. Some additions of 1894, and an intarsia pavement of 1909.

Newbridge grew up as a small spa town in the C19. The timber BRIDGE, one of the few old routes connecting Radnorshire with

Brecon, was rebuilt in ferro-concrete in 1910. Who were the engineers?

PONT A'R ITHON, $\frac{1}{2}$ m. s. Two segmental arches with circular flood openings at the sides. C19.

LLYSDINAM (B). *See* p. 357.

See p. 357.

2050

NEWCHURCH

ST MARY. Rebuilt in 1856–7 with nave and unarticulated chancel arch, short chancel, w tower with a broach-spire. In a large raised churchyard. – The FONT is a slightly tapering cylindrical monolith. It could be C10 or C11, and so of the Celtic church.

GREAT HOUSE. This complex of structures is representative of the main periods of building in Mid Wales. A two-bay cruck hall is built down the contour, the middle set of its couples having quatrefoil and trefoil bracing in the apex above arch-braces. It is of *c.* 1490, and the widest span existing in Wales (28 ft). Beyond a partition was a fourth cruck-framed bay for a parlour. Conversion to a storeyed house – with a fine door in the porch, rebuilt diagonal chimneys, oversailing dormer – took place perhaps in 1661 (date on a doorway). A wing was added to the N in 1790. The house forms one side of a characteristic farmyard.

(TYN Y CWM, 1 m. SW. A fine timber-framed barn dated 1713. RCHM)

DOLBEDWIN. A small Late Elizabethan stone house with lateral chimneys. Inside, interesting woodwork such as post-and-panel partitions with elaborate mouldings and simple door-heads, and crude tapering newel posts on the stair.

$\frac{1}{4}$ m. w is a CASTLE MOUND.

2060

NEW RADNOR

ST MARY. w tower with the porch beneath and stair to the w gallery, nave with diminutive transepts, and a five-sided quasi-chancel. Planned by *Adams* and erected in 1843–5 by *Thomas Dashwood*. An extreme case of unsuitable rebuilding. The late medieval parish church was completely removed and its substitute is Gothic in name only – just buttresses and lancets on a Late Georgian plan. The useless little apse has been superseded by bringing the altar forward on polygonal steps, to designs by *George Pace* (1964). – ALTAR RAILS, made with traceries from the Perp screen. Of an unusual scissors pattern, combined with panels and cusping. – Two eroded medieval recumbent EFFIGIES in the porch, one a man with a round shield, the other a woman, have not been securely identified. – The church was probably founded in the C12 or C13 under the castle's protection.

The CASTLE directly overlooks the town. The visible remains now are earthworks – entrenchments round a bailey *c.* 90 yds by 180 yds, and NE of that a large ditched mound *c.* 55 yds across. Owain Glyndŵr sacked the castle in the early C15 and Leland saw only ruins. It was probably established by Philip de Breos, one of the Marcher barons, in 1096. A rebuilding in stone took place in the C13, as at Cefnllys and Castell Dinboeth, perhaps for Edward Mortimer, who garrisoned it for Edward I in 1282–3. Thomas Rees in 1815 records the keep as nearly square, with square towers (for the gate?) on the SE side. Seven pointed arches were dug out in 1773, and more in 1864.

New Radnor has a grid plan and is still protected on the N, W, and S by earth ramparts and ditches.* Three main streets intersect five transverse streets in an area of twenty-six acres. Such regular towns are frequent adjuncts to important C13 castles (e.g. Montgomery); they were not infrequently economic non-starters, though seldom so obviously as this one. Its original plots are not all occupied yet, nor are there buildings of a dignity to match its status as a borough from 1562 to 1833. No. 10 HIGH STREET, part timber and part stone, alone has a C16 origin. Running parallel to the S of High Street are BROAD STREET and WATER STREET with its stream. The former's Town Hall and Market Cross have gone. The Regency, stone-built LAURELS stands out amongst the C19 cottages. One hopes that future infilling will respect the village's historic plan and modest scale. The 77 ft high MONUMENT to Sir George Cornewall Lewis (of Harpton), a mid-Victorian Chancellor of the Exchequer, stresses its dedicatee's eminence in an alien culture; by *John Gibbs* of Oxford, 1864, with figures by *W. Forsyth*, its Gothic belongs to the florid, Ruskinian style.

DOWNTON HOUSE, 1 m. E. A plain mid-Georgian house of brick under stucco; five bays and two storeys, with two more bays to the l. added *c.* 1840–50. Hall with a small arch on colonnettes without capitals; plaster friezes of triglyphs and rosettes. Drawing-room ceiling in the Adam style.

HARPTON COURT, 1½ m. ESE. A broad avenue stretches from the mid-C19 Italianate LODGE on the road to the site of the

* Murage grants were made in 1251–90, however.

mansion of the Lewis family, which was demolished in 1956. It had two façades. The N front, of nine bays and two storeys, on a basement, of stucco on brick, with even-length quoins at the angles was erected by Thomas Lewis in 1750. The s façade, also of nine bays, was of bare ashlar except for full-height Doric pilasters supporting a pediment. This seems to have been by *John Nash*, who between 1805 and 1812 built a first-floor suite of entrance hall, staircase, library, and dining room, for Thomas Frankland Lewis. Attached to that were the parts still standing: a neo-C17 wing, and a STABLE COURTYARD, apparently of *c.* 1870 – though Nash was paid for a design in 1805.*

₃₀₆₀ NORTON

ST ANDREW. Substantially rebuilt by *Sir George Gilbert Scott* in 1868. Nave and chancel in one, with small N and S transepts added by Scott. C17 W timber bell-turret in two stages with a shingled spire supported on timbers in the nave. The W end of the roof is hipped, so that the tower seems to rise through triple pyramid roofs. Scott reproduced the old work only approximately, e.g. the polygonal ribbed ceiling over the choir. Some old woodwork was kept in the low SCREEN, which has four flat quatrefoil-headed lights to either side of a wide cambered archway. Scott used a cusped wooden arch at the break in the roof above. – FONT. C15. – Oak REREDOS and PULPIT, 1905 and 1916. – GLASS. E by *Clayton & Bell.* – MONUMENTS. Mistress Elizabeth Flower † 1637. – SUNDIAL on the tower, to Mildred Drage, 1947.

MOTTE. Taken from the Mortimers by Llewelyn ap Gruffydd in 1262.

NORTON MANOR, ½ m. W. A large neo-Jacobean house of 1858 on the site of an earlier house. With a colossal top-lit stairwell.

OLD IMPTON, ¾ m. W. An L-shaped stone house of the C16 and C17. The C16 range has beams and two big stone chimneys. About 1625 a Somerset family named Flower added an over-hung wing. Its timber porch is uniquely decorated: richly moulded beams, the jetty on brackets carved *inter alia* with a set of carpenter's tools, and an inner doorhead decorated with arabesques; geometrical figures interlaced. Parlour with elaborate counterchanged-joist ceiling. Panelling.

UPPER DOLLEY, 1½ m. SW, has a twice-jettied gabled solar wing, added perhaps by Hugh Lewis (High Sheriff in 1609), soon after

* I must thank Sir Andrew Duff-Gordon for his help.

1600, to an earlier stone house. Small quadrant timberwork on the upper floor. Both rooms have fireplaces with quarter-round mouldings; that on the first floor is panelled.

OFFA'S DYKE

The earthwork crosses the Teme valley at Knighton, giving it its Welsh name Tref-y-Clawdd, 'the town on the dyke'. From here to Discoed there are fine stretches. It then goes down the Radnor border to Hay; but in Archenfield, once in the jurisdiction of the bishops of Hereford, there is a break. See also the Introduction, p. 31.

OLD RADNOR/PENCRAIG

2050

St Stephen (or the c6 St Ystyffan). Old Radnor church is English in type (the parish, unlike most of Radnorshire, stayed in the diocese of Hereford after 1920), and good for an English county, so still better for a Welsh one. It stands proudly, in a large round churchyard, on a hill overlooking the Radnor basin. Nave and chancel, N aisle and chapel, S aisle and chapel, S porch, W tower. The four-bay double-chamfered nave arcade 40 is of one build, with tall early c15 octagonal piers with moulded capitals on square bases. No chancel arch, but the S aisle has one to the Lady Chapel. The N aisle is a narrow lean-to; the broader S aisle has its own gable. This irregularity, which probably followed a Glyndŵr burning of the church in 1401, means that the N roof slopes low, in harmony with the falling ground. All that remains of the c12 church is a scalloped capital (placed behind the organ). N aisle roof with Perp beams and rough bosses. The other roofs are Tudor, almost flat, with carved foliage or emblem bosses at the rib intersections. Late Perp windows in the N aisle and Lady Chapel. c16 camber-headed cinquefoil windows in the S aisle; most of the traceries and headstops are renewed. The E end was taken down and rebuilt by *F. Preedy* of Worcester in 1882. The two-bay chancel arcades remain, with four-centred arches, and a trefoiled PISCINA with a head either side, but the E window was new and the roof beams were set on corbels, with an arched truss to mark the chancel. Pointed c15 S doorway. Porch with a Perp arch with multiple mouldings. Three niches above with restored sculpture. Broad three-stage Perp tower with diagonal buttress, battlements with arrowslits, and a crowning NE stair-turret. (Later S doorway.)

FONT. An impressively large doleritic erratic boulder, roughly rounded and flat-topped; the bowl is in the broad cylindrical section above four stumpy legs. C8(?). – SCREEN across nave and aisles. A splendid example of the Gloucestershire type (cf. Cirencester). Late C15; its gilding and paintings of saints were removed in the C19. The posts, with shafts attached, run through the rails to the floor (Welsh screens do the opposite). In each bay there is blank arcading at the bottom of the dado, with an openwork quatrefoil band above this. In the heads, elaborate trefoil tracery with roses which rise to the profile of the vaults. In the nave and S aisle the central doorways have two bays of this tracery over lower cusped doorheads. W side with tierceron-vaulting all along, a frieze of drop-cresting, running vine ornament carved in the solid, and cresting. The E canopy is a plain coving with a frieze, and the tracery heads have carved spandrels disguising this inconsistency, except in the Lady Chapel, where there is vaulting again. Some restoration in 1872. – PARCLOSE SCREENS N and S of the chancel, with the narrow lights, and the muntins dying into the rails, on the Welsh pattern. With restored traceries. – STALLS with traceried fronts, and simple poppyheads, against the main and the parclose screens. C15. – ORGAN CASE. Early C16: the earliest in the British Isles. Linenfold panels below, with some reset on their sides in 1872, when the present organ, by Messrs *J. W. Walker*, was inserted. The large pipes are grouped in three angular towers, freely carved with foliated ogee heads, the short ones in two flat sections between. The style of their foliage, though still Gothic, is impure. On top is a beautiful cresting with pinnacles between semicircles, and also with beasts (ferrets?) and dragon ornament etc. The forms, fantastic yet not unrestrained, of the decorative elements are in the spirit of the early Renaissance, especially of Venice. The exceptional quality of the woodwork suggests a metropolitan provenance. – EASTER SEPULCHRE in the N vestry. – Foliated CALVARY CROSS in the nave floor. – TILES. By *Godwin*. – Some medieval glazed tiles in the W bay of the N aisle and in the Lady Chapel doorway. – PAINTINGS. Moses and Aaron; Italian, C18. – Three HATCHMENTS on the W wall. – GLASS. N aisle E window, St Catherine, late C15, on a background of *Roses Ensoleillées*. Very engaging, for all its crudeness. – E by *Hardman*, 1882. – MONUMENTS. John Lewis † 1797, by *Flaxman*. A flat sarcophagus on corbels. – Thomas Lewis † 1777, by *W. Tyler*, a large pyramidal tomb which blocks the Lady Chapel E window. Woman sitting diagonally with her arm round an urn; portrait medallion above. – Ann Lewis † 1785. Less rhetorical than her husband's; mourning lady on a pyramidal slab with putti beside, on a tapering base with lions' feet. – Thomas Lewis † 1724. Shaped orange marble tablet of 1778 with white detailing. – Stephen Harris † 1740 and Arabella Harris † 1792. – The churchyard is sited amongst prehistoric earthworks.

HARP INN. C17, stone; restored by the Landmark Trust in 1971.

PAINSCASTLE   *1040*

Painscastle was the head of the commote of Lower Elfael till the Conquest.

CASTLE. Of Norman origin, and named after the Marcher family of Fitzpayn. To strengthen his control of the border country, Henry III began its reconstruction in stone in 1231. Carpenters were impressed at Reading in 1233 for work on this temporarily important royal holding. The site comprises an outer entrenchment enclosing c. 12 acres, and an inner bank c. 120 yds by 50 yds, with a big, independently ditched, early C12(?) motte at its S. There may have been a round keep on this. The outer ward appears to have been protected by a stone curtain with angle towers and an E gateway, but this has gone, together with any timber buildings. The Earl of Warwick maintained a garrison of thirty-six here as late as 1401.

The village of Painscastle has the interesting peculiarity that its farms are nucleated, so that the lands radiate from farmhouses built in the shelter of the castle. This practical piece of Norman(?) planning accounts for the group of worthwhile buildings. UPPER HOUSE has embedded in its walls and roof the timbers of an aisled hall of early type, perhaps even of c. 1400 and connected with the castle, against the bailey of which it stands. Two aisle trusses, one either side of the arch-braced one spanning the hall. The hefty roof is held in place by ingenious wind-bracing. In the lower tier the outer end of each pair rests vertically on the speres, while the inner end lies with the slope of the roof; in the upper, faintly ogee-pointed tier, they go conventionally. The house retains a C17 post-and-panel partition and staircase and has a lower cross-wing and porch.★
CASTLE FARM, directly below the mound, possesses a hand-

★ Upper House was found by Mr H. Brooksby; I am indebted to him for telling me about this important discovery.

some five-bay Georgian front. On the crossroads is a corn-
barn, and beyond that a small white BAPTIST CHAPEL of
1848. PENDRE, on the N of the village, has C17 doorways and
a porch. Opposite these is a small cruck house. Painscastle's
later fame was as a gathering point for cattle drovers; the cows
were shod here for the journey to Hereford. A market house
survived till the C19.

(GLYN, 1 m. E. Cruck-framed (one truss), but rebuilt with C17
dormers and doorways. RCAM)

(WERN-NEWYDD, 1 m. SE, has a storeyed porch complete with
its studded door and an ornate staircase. RCHM)

PENCERRIG see LLANELWEDD

PENCRAIG see OLD RADNOR

0080

PEN-ITHON HALL

2½ m. NNW of Llanbadarn Fynydd

Built by *George Augustus Haig c.* 1855; he seems to have been his
own architect. The plan is the Irish solution of a central hall
from which all the main rooms open. Round the first floor is
a complete gallery for the bedrooms, and a third, upper court
was made around the skylight. Front with a rough and ready
portico and projecting end bays. Two wings at the rear. A late
case of Regency design.

1060

PENYBONT

Next to the common are BRYNITHON, a Regency-windowed cottage, and a C19 travellers' inn, the SEVERN ARMS HOTEL.
The latter, a twin-gabled three-bay block with a lower six-bay
wing on the l., has ornate iron windows with small panes of
Regency (here probably *c.* 1850) pattern, and straight heads
under hoodmoulds. The interior is a period piece.

PENYBONT HALL, across the Ithon, began in 1755 as a small
house. About 1800 a simply detailed Late Georgian dining
room and staircase were added. The house was greatly enlarged
and remodelled in a nondescript gabled style in 1877 by *H.
Sheffield*, but the additions, with the exception of a tower, have
recently been pulled down.

(NANT-DDU, 1½ m. S. A barn containing three cruck trusses.
RCAM)

PILLETH

2060

ST MARY. In a quite beautiful position overlooking the Lugg valley and approached through fields and then up formal steps. Broad, much buttressed C13 or C14 W tower with a later saddle-back roof and a SW stair-turret. A holy well beside it. A fragment of larger C15 tracery in its W window. Extended down the contour from this is a single-cell nave, whose roof burned in 1894. Restoration in 1911 by *W. J. Tapper*, with a lower-pitched roof. In the chancel are two reticulated two-light windows with cusping. Flat-ogee-headed PISCINA. Restored E window. C14 S doorway. – FONT. Deep bowl with rough scalloping on the underside. A lobed stoup of *c.* 1200 nearby.

Pilleth is one of very few places in South Wales to be noted in Domesday Book. A decisive battle against Sir Edmund Mortimer was won by Owain Glyndŵr in 1402, beside the Lugg.

PILLETH COURT. The centre and N wing survive of an H-plan house, possibly built by the Prices of Monaughty. Brick with flush stone quoins, materials remaining at the base of the C19 S wing also. Large windows with dripmoulds on the E bay. Stout C17 newel stair inside. But external chimneys on the N and W, together with chamfered stone fireplaces, are the best evidence for a date of *c.* 1600 for the core of the house.

CASTELL FOEL-ALLT, ½ m. S. A motte and large bailey, on the Lugg.

NANT-Y-GROES, ½ m. ESE, was the home of Dr John Dee, the Elizabethan mathematician.

PRESTEIGNE/LLANANDRAS

3060

Presteigne is a lucky town, lying low (for Radnorshire) in the gentle valley of the Lugg (a Herefordshire river), on an isthmus of land which links it with the wealthier and mellower east. 'For beautious building it is the best in the shire, a towne of Commerce', wrote Saxton in 1575. Its townscape still offers more diversity than any in the county, hasn't yet suffered intrusions, and wears the fashionable air of its coaching and railway days.

ST ANDREW. Presteigne's church, architecturally much the best in Radnorshire, drew its wealth from the Herefordshire part of the parish, and is still in the diocese of Hereford. From the C13 to the Reformation the Augustinian Canons of Wigmore Abbey held the rectory of Presteigne. The church consists of a rather austere basilical nave of the early C14, with the choir

S aisle and Lady Chapel enlarged and the chancel rebuilt in the mid C15, which gives it a tremendous increase in light and spaciousness.

Evidence of C10 or C11 Saxon origins is visible externally in the lower part of the E end of the N aisle wall, and internally in the stones of half a tall semicircular arch at the E. The conjectured Saxon plan is a nave extending W to the middle pier of the present arcade, and a narrower chancel. This work came to light in the restoration of 1889–91. In the W wall the S half of an immured arch represents the end of an Early Norman lengthening of the nave. Two blocked splayed windows in coursed stonework again in the N wall are Norman too. About 1200 rebuilding was begun, then halted – see the two W piers of the N arcade, which are circular with a ring-moulding at the bottom of their capitals and octagonal tops. The old nave however does not seem to have become the aisle of the new till the early C14, when the continuation of the N arcade would have involved its destruction. The NW respond is similar to the rest of the six-bay arcades of octagonal columns, and all the arches are pointed and double-chamfered. Clerestory of small ogee trefoiled lancets and a roof of close-set trusses forming a two-centred arch. This roof is single-framed, and has braces rising to a collar-purlin, on which the collars are placed. All the members are closely spaced (except for some tie-beams). Is this the C14 roof? Contemporary S doorway. The Perp additions to the S are the first stage of the tower, which doubles as the S porch and has a broad doorway and ribbed cross-vault with a hole for raising the bells; and the ashlar-faced S aisle with the Mortimer arms on a buttress, the early C14 aisle having been rebuilt c. 1460 probably as three chantry chapels, each having a large triangular-headed window with unusual tracery. This aisle is independently roofed with arch-braced collars alternating with tie-beams joined by upright struts to the collars. The late C14 N respond of its E arch has a squint to the chancel. The arch itself has been rebuilt round and dies into the S wall. In the wider Lady Chapel, a flattish shouldered ogee S doorway with a three-light cinquefoiled window (see two others in the N aisle) re-used above, and a small PISCINA, are also in the Dec style. The stonework of the early C14 chancel arch dies into the piers. Jonathan Williams records it as painted with figures of Moses and Aaron on the W and Death and Time on the E. The last N nave arch is carried to the wall instead of falling to a respond; in place of the respond there is a fragment of the big C14 E arch. Beside it are the lower and upper entrances to a rood-loft stair in a Perp turret. The entire chancel is fully developed Perp – buttresses in Downton stone, a double S arcade with wavy mouldings, and a Tudor panelled roof with moulded beams supported on brackets. It was erected by the Canons of Wigmore. All the windows have Perp tracery, the E with an embattled transom; also the nave W window and doorway and more windows in the Lady Chapel. Perp too the top of the tower and the diagonal buttresses. Three restorations in the last century have secured the fabric. The first was undertaken c. 1855; in 1889–91 *J. L. Pearson* repaired the nave, the aisle W windows, and the roofs generally, and also designed the ornate chancel and S aisle teak SCREENS; and in 1927 the walls were stripped. No pews. – FONT. Plain C14 octagonal. A small bulbous bowl of c. 1200, found near Stapleton Castle, lies near it. – PULPIT. Stone; designed by *Pearson*. LECTERN of brass on a tripod base. – WARDENS' TABLE dated 1666. – SCULPTURE. St Andrew; small Romanesque(?) relief high over the W window outside, seated full-face with his r. hand raised in blessing (cf. St Peter at Bromyard, Herefs.). – TAPESTRY. Christ's Entry to Jerusalem. Woven in Flanders in the early C16. From one of the same cartoons as a set made for Canterbury Cathedral, which are now in La Chaise Dieu, Aix-en-Provence. – PAINTINGS. The Holy Family with the infant St John and another child; executed in the style of *Rosso Fiorentino*. – Presteigne Church, a late C17 perspective in oil with figures in another hand. – There are fragments of wall paintings at the NW of the nave. – GLASS. In the Tudor gallery window in the Lady Chapel, a jumble of early C15 pieces (reconstructible?) remaining from famous windows already spoiled in the C17. – E by *Powell's*, 1855; also two panels at the W. – In the tower a CARILLON made in 1728. – Beautiful Georgian three-tier CANDELABRUM. – MONUMENTS. In a low semicircular arched recess in the N aisle, a tapered coffin lid with a large foliate cross in relief; c. 1240. The cross is circled and has curled leaf enrichment; the shaft has fleurs-de-lys branching from it and rests on semicircular arcading. – In the chancel: Rev. James Bull † 1799. – Rev. James Beebee † 1841 by *Gardner*, Cheltenham. – Francis Owen † 1686. – An illegible tablet with Baroque surround above, c. 1690. – Evan(us) Davies † 1686. Curly columns, putti on the pediment, and gilded stone foliage. – Elizabeth Owen † 1705. Straight columns and the inscription in an oval garland; again gilded stone with putti on the pediment. – Thomas Owen † 1732, by *Richard Kingsland*. Tabernacle with composite pilasters. – Edward Parsons † 1812 by *Gardner*. – Richard Owen † 1748. Open pediment with marble pilasters.

SHIRE HALL. 1829. Stone, with a stucco façade. Nine bays in all, of which three stand forward beneath a tetrastyle Tuscan portico on a basement storey.

MARKET HALL. By *Thomas Nicholson*, 1869. Red brick with black brick and white stone trim. Open three-bay arcades on the ground floor, round-headed windows on the first. At one side is a clock tower, as though this was a little Italian town hall-cum-market. It cost £1,300.

The streets s w of the church, Broad Street, High Street, and St David's Street, suggest a C13 rectilinear layout. There is no evidence of walls, however. The town held a Wednesday market by the early C13 – in Broad Street? – and was given a charter in 1482. The central area was twice burned, by Owain Glyndŵr and in 1681, possibly with confusion to the early streets.

PERAMBULATION. Leaving the churchyard by THE SCALLIONS, the border river down to the l. is crossed by a short C17(?) packhorse BRIDGE. BROAD STREET, on the r., starts with the OLD RECTORY behind the church, brick, of the second quarter of the C18. Its tithe BARN has a reused late C15 curved-brace roof. Next on the r. are the first of many timber-framed houses of *c.* 1590–1680, here with gables to the street. WELL HOUSE, built across CANON'S LANE, is the most picturesque. In HAFOD, an upper room has an open roof with a truss with apex cusping, and wind-braces. The imposing neoclassical Shire Hall stands opposite (*see* above). Presteigne was the assize town from the C16 till the C20. On the same side of the street, RED HOUSE, with an altered C18 front and brick quoins, and the DUKE'S ARMS, which had a C17 galleried wing. On the r., where the road broadens, some substantial C18 houses; WHITE HOUSE has pilasters at the angles, OSSINGTON HOUSE quoins and heavy window frames. The cheerful Market Hall (*see* above) manages its corner site by rounding the wall, sprouting an ogee niche, and supporting the end of the gable on a frog as corbel. HEREFORD STREET, on the l., has at Nos. 43–45 a square-framed gabled house. Further on on the r. is JOHN BEDDOES SCHOOL, founded by a cloth-merchant as a grammar school in 1565, but newly rebuilt in unimaginative semi-high-rise. GREEN END, opposite the Market Hall, starts with a C17 house and a curious Tudor-pargetted front of the 1890s.

HIGH STREET, running r., displays modest C19 applied details – pediments, dormers, oriel windows, and so on – a feature of the town. But the façade of Messrs BENNETT'S (Mansion House) conceals one of the very few medieval town houses in Powys; Presteigne's were of timber, and one or two survived fires and fortune, though greatly changed about. This one was a large C15 open hall, and has tracery-carved spandrels and fragments of roll-moulded beams. Still on the W of the street is the RADNORSHIRE ARMS HOTEL, a fine close-studded house dated 1616 on the porch. Diagonal stone chimneystacks. It has its original studded door, and a panelled room with ceiling compartments with moulded joists. A lane on the l. leads to Presteigne's own park, WARDEN. A platform of earth at the top, about 45 by 30 yds, is the remnant of a Norman motte and bailey levelled by Llewelyn the Last in 1262.

ST DAVID'S STREET turns NE from High Street. ST DAVID'S HOUSE, behind its Late Georgian front, seems to embody a box-framed hall of c. 1500. Enlargements of the C17 brought some wainscoting in the inserted upper floor. A stair added in the courtyard has open-fret balusters and ornamental newels. The OLD MANOR HOUSE, also on the l., served as the judge's lodgings. Two-storey plastered stone front of c. 1840 with two pedimental gables projecting slightly from a three-bay centre. In the central hall, however, late C16 beams detailed similarly to Old Impton, Norton, and an early C17 overmantel brought from Stapleton Castle (Herefs.). The houses in CHURCH STREET, which connects behind the church with BROAD STREET, range from timber-framing to plaster of c. 1800.

CARMELITE CONVENT, ½ m. SE. With a chapel of 1954.

WEGNALL, 1 m. SE. An interesting square-framed farmhouse, datable to c. 1600, with close-studding and a jetty on the front. Two first-floor oriels still. Cluster of four diagonal chimneys at the r. end. The porch has been removed. At the back a close-studded solar wing, as common near Presteigne: this too is jettied at the end, and has its oriels on both floors. The fireplace in the lower room has mitre stops; in the upper room the fireplace arch is cambered, and there is part of a moulded plaster ceiling.

BROAD HEATH, 1¼ m. ESE. A small Georgian house with an ogee window in the pediment. Simple additions of c. 1925 by *Sir Clough Williams-Ellis*.

BOULTIBROOK, ¾ m. NW. An older centre – a tall three-bay block with two windows in blank arches – incorporated between low, plain, five-bay wings, all plastered, whose lower windows are also set in blank arcading. This enlargement probably all belongs to the Regency, but the extension at the r. was made in 1872. Sir Harford Jones Brydges, the Persian scholar and diplomat, employed *Robert Smirke* in 1812–15 to add a library. This projects to the rear and is entered through a domed anteroom. Of red brick. A very elongated octagon on plan, it has no windows (though one Smirke bookcase still) but is top lit. Plaster cornice with egg-and-dart and a foliage frieze. The central dome is coffered; the others have fleur-de-lys designs. A small pedimented COACH HOUSE with lantern beyond.

At FOLD FARM, a brick hay-barn with the date 1740 is the earliest dated use of brick in the county.

RHAYADER/RHAEADR GWY

ST CLEMENT (formerly St Cynllo). Nave and chancel, N aisle, W tower. By *S. W. Williams* of Rhayader, 1887 (date on the W tower) to 1897; E.E. The arrangement of the chancel is an intelligent compromise between the local single-chamber plan and Victorian convention. The choir keeps the width and height of the nave but has special treatment in the S window (with its clustered wall arcade) and in the N parclose screen; only the sanctuary narrows with an arch. Pure C13 E triple lancet. The only old remnant, even from the church of c. 1772, is the C11/12 FONT, circular and with four projecting heads (like St Harmon's).

GAUFRON CHURCH, 1¾ m. E. Built c. 1894.

TABERNACLE CONGREGATIONAL CHAPEL, Bridge Street. 1836 by *T. Hope*. Pedimental gable to the street.

Rhayader is something of a lonely town, but nonetheless with its four main streets beside the Wye bridge not destitute of architectural interest. Across NORTH STREET from the church is the former VICARAGE, by *F. R. Kempson*, in red brick. On the l. turn beyond is the COMMUNITY CENTRE (1974 by *G. Williams*, then Rhayader R.D.C.'s Chief Planning Officer), whose laminated-cruck-supported roof spans 40 ft. EAST STREET, l. from the crossroads, has a little CLOCK TOWER (by *B. Lloyd*, 1924) on the site of the timber-framed Town Hall of 1762. On the corner between South Street and Bridge Street a lowly timber-framed house of 1683, THE OLD SWAN. In SOUTH STREET, on the r., PENRALLY HOUSE has the only Regency brick front, of five bays. BRIDGE STREET was the street of early times. The CWMDEUDDWR ARMS, on the r., is the town's oldest building, of the C17 regional type. Nearer the bridge were the motte-and-bailey castle recorded in 1178, and a contemporary cell of Dominicans; neither has left any trace. The BRIDGE itself replaced the first stone arch here (1780) in 1929.

The TOLLGATES outside the town were erected in 1792.

An C18 TANNERY has been re-erected at the Welsh Folk Museum, St Fagans.

CEFNFAES, ¾ m. N. Built in 1803 but much altered c. 1911. Tuscan porch.

(At MIDDLE NANTSERTH, 1¼ m. N, are two cruck-framed buildings, an early C17 house and a contemporary barn, enlarged in 1828. RCAM)

PENLANOLE, 3½ m. SSE. A tea-planter's retirement villa of c. 1840, for Daniel Reid. Two storeys and seven bays, the middle three of which, beneath a pedimental gable, were originally protected from the weather by a colonial double-decker iron veranda. 'If the Wye ... could by any stretch of imagination be converted into the Ganges, the illusion would be complete', said Burke.

(SUSPENSION FOOTBRIDGES, ranging in date from the early C20 to recent carpentry ones by Mr Hope, link the Breconshire farms with the roads E of this reach of the Wye.)

DOLDOWLOD HOUSE, 5 m. SSE. To the r. of a small farmhouse bought by James Watt, the inventor, his son James (with professional help from R. W. Mylne) added a fine S range based on his own Elizabethan house, Aston Hall, near Birmingham. This competent four-bay block of c. 1827 is an early example of the style's renaissance. The effect was subtly altered in 1878 when S. W. Williams replaced the old farmhouse with an extension, still in the Elizabethan style but with a Victorian feeling for irregular grouping and an acentral tower. In the first build the elaborate staircase and the earlier and nice ceiling designs.

Two Bronze Age BARROWS stand on a low ridge (SN 985 684 and SN 990 687) just N of the A44, from which they are clearly visible. The W one is over 6 ft high and covered with trees; the E one is equally fine, and parts of the stone kerb which retained the earthen mound can be seen around the base.

CWMDEUDDWR. See p. 228.

1040 RHOSGOCH

CHAPEL. Small. Two doors in the side, and two early C19 multi-paned windows.

RHOSGOCH MILL is still in working order, and has been grinding corn for 450 years. The building is largely C19.

GREAT HOUSE. A C16 range has thick stone walls and the remains of huge crucks. The C17 part contains a small but fashionable Jacobean stair with ornate newels. In the yard a fine box-framed CORN BARN.

HONDON. A small C16 cruck hall, with its internal partition etc., Jacobean fireplace beam, a C17 staircase wing, and more additions. Disused.

1050 RHULEN

1½ m. SE of Cregrina

ST DAVID. The most unassuming of all the Radnorshire rural churches. White-painted, and shaped like a hull – the walls lean out every which way. In a circular churchyard. Nave and chancel in one and probably of *c.* 1300. The W part is shut off with a wall, its own W door, and carries a wooden pyramidal belfry; the E part is extended, but still with the S door well to the E. Barrel-ceiled roof. S porch. S doorway with a steeply shouldered top, in a reveal similar in shape, with a C17 door. Lighting the sanctuary are the only windows, a trefoiled N one and a three-light wooden S one dated 1723. No E window; instead a recess, again shouldered, behind the altar. – FONT. Octagonal; *c.* 1400.

(CWM-FILLO, ½ m. NW, incorporates three possibly medieval trusses of a cruck house in later walls. RCAM)

9070 ST HARMON

ST GARMON. The site of a Celtic mother church and of a *clas*. In a raised circular churchyard. Nave, S porch, and chancel – in fact the hall-church of 1821 by *W. Evans*, with a chancel added and the W gallery taken out. The pleasant Regency Gothic windows, pyramidal W bellcote, ball-finials, etc., have been replaced by more churchy fixtures of 1908. Tie-beam trusses exposed after being hidden by a plaster ceiling. – FONT. Circular, with four human heads projecting; C11–12. –

(CANDELABRUM. Dated 1771.) – MEMORIAL. Rev. John
Davies † 1818, by *Edward Stevens*, Llandegley. – Francis Kilvert the diarist was vicar of St Harmon in 1876–7.

DYRYSGOL, 2 m. WNW. Two platforms were the sites of houses
in the Dark Ages or early Middle Ages. They are *c.* 25 ft wide
by *c.* 120 ft and *c.* 106 ft long, and built with the tops dug into
the hill and the ends terraced out.

BEILI BEDW. A number of platform sites occupied in the C14
and C15.

(BABYLON. A cottage with a floor pitched in squares. Dated
1768. In the same range are byre and barn.)

(CWM Y RYCHAN, 2¾ m. NW. A medieval house, now restored.
One of two cruck couples surviving has a tall cusped post
between the collar and tie-beam; there were partitions either
side of a central opening below the tie.)

GRUGYN TUMULUS (SN 983 723). A very fine Bronze Age barrow clearly visible from the road. A bronze spearhead is said
to have been found in it – a weapon which is rather rarely found
with burials.

BANCGELLI BARROW (SN 980 708) is another fine, large barrow
visible from the road.

The group of three BARROWS N of St Harmon (SN 990 740) cannot be easily recognized now. One was excavated and produced
evidence of cremated burials and burnt planks.

THE MOUNT (SO 012 755) is a large grass-grown Bronze Age
burial mound set at the confluence of two streams. It is a large
example, measuring about 80 ft in diameter and standing over
6 ft high.

In the head of the Afon Dulas there is a small group of Bronze
Age monuments. A tall STANDING STONE, with the stump
of what may have been another nearby, lies in the centre of
the field at SN 964 776. The BARROW in the next field is less
easy to see. Further up the valley at SN 951 769 is another tall
STANDING STONE. A flat stone beside it may also have been
standing at some time, for it does not seem to be a natural
boulder.

RHYDDHYWEL, *c.* 5 m. NE. Five large Bronze Age barrows are
visible along the W edge of this high moorland ridge. They
dominate the skyline and their siting is very typical of this kind
of monument, designed to make a striking impact in the landscape.

STANAGE PARK
                   2¾ m. E of Knighton

'The wild and shaggy Genius of Stanedge' was how *Humphry
Repton*, not being given to understatement, conceived the picturesque house and landscape he proposed to Charles Rogers
in 1803. Stanage is within eight miles of Downton Castle and
Croft Castle, Herefordshire, and in the late C18 it belonged to
the Johnes family of Croft, who took down the C16 and C17
house on the site. Repton's suggestions for replacing it and its
formal gardens were set out in one of his Red Books. 'The most
judicious mode of combating the difficulty which prudence
opposes to magnificence, will be to follow the example set at
Downton, where the *inside* was first consulted, and the *outside*
afterwards made to conform to *that*, under the idea of a *picturesque outline*. . . . I will endeavour to restore that sort of importance, which formerly belonged to the old Manor house. . . .'

78   The existing informal grouping, begun in 1807 and mostly
continued in the initial spirit, is only partly attributable to Repton himself. His cut-out drawings seem to relate to the lower
'Elizabethan' S portions. One of the gateways between their
flanking turrets has a date 1807. Embattled and step-gabled
outbuildings stretch round these. More spacious rooms were
added to the N, it seems, by *John Adey Repton* in 1822 – in a
stucco-faced Tudor style with asymmetrical towers and battlements. Rear elements in this idiom include a delightful dairy
or game larder, with pinnacles and a pyramid roof. The fabric
was further remodelled in 1845 by *Edward Haycock*, who added
incidental bows, a porch, turrets, and a dining room with windows of a more ecclesiastical sort. Of interiors, the big cantilevered staircase, with dense neo-classical coffering round the
lantern above, and the dining room with a stained-glass window
are Haycock's, the library is J. A. Repton's.

In the park, Repton formed a large new pond at the head
of the stream. A long scenic drive leads along this up to the
house, from his LODGE on the Knighton road, which has a loggia
of four Tudor arches. A two-storey park-keeper's cottage has
gone. Between 1807 and 1809 65,000 trees (oak, larch, Spanish
and horse chestnut, ash) were planted, by a William Hope.

Thomas Johnes evidently thought of settling at Stanage
before he began Hafod, for *Robert Adam* made designs in 1780
for a neat neo-Palladian villa here with a giant Doric portico.
Adam also made drawings for an octagonal parish church with

a projecting atrium, but whether this idea, also unexecuted, was for Stanage or Hafod it is impossible to tell.*

TREF-Y-CLAWDD *see* KNIGHTON

WALTON

2050

WALTON COURT. Part of a cruck hall, of which a truss and part of the central cusped apex remain, stands beside two C17 square-framed wings. Thomas Herrick, *c.* 1700, rebuilt in stone with a coursed front and a Dutch-gabled dormer over the door. The staircase has arched openings and vertically symmetrical balusters.

HINDWELL FARM, ½ m. N. A C17 house, with a late C18 front facing the Pool. The Wordsworths stayed here in 1810–12 (his brother-in-law, Thomas Hutchinson, was the farmer).

At WOMASTON, ¾ m. NE, is a moated MOTTE (at the site of a castle of Edward the Confessor). The house, remodelled in 1927, has a Regency lodge.

BURFA, 1½ m. NE, is a restored late medieval timber-framed house. It has the gable trusses, the partition, and the cross-passage truss of a C15 cruck long-house. A close-studded solar block of two storeys was added to its upper end in the later C16; its woodwork is partly painted internally with Jacobean decorative patterning. Subsequently the main hall in the upper end of the cruck house was replaced by a C17 storeyed cross-wing.

¼ m. SW of the house is a MOTTE. Burfa stands just above OFFA'S DYKE, and a rewarding stretch for walkers runs N to Discoed. BURFA CAMP (SO 284 610), crowning the hill to the E, is an important multivallate hillfort, but it has been badly damaged by forestry. Though the complex barbican entrance on the S side has now been partially cleared, it is still difficult to trace the defences in detail.

BARLAND, 2 m. NE. The home in the C18 of a Moravian community. A MOTTE lies ¼ m. to the S.

Walton is an area with several BRONZE AGE MONUMENTS – standing stones and barrows – and the local fields were the source of a large number of flint implements, suggesting extensive settlement at this time. The barrows at Knapp Farm can be clearly recognized from the road (as can the large motte), but those near Hindwell Farm are more difficult to pick out.

*I am grateful to Mrs G. Coltman Rogers for her assistance.

The FOUR STONES (SO 246 608) are the only Welsh example of an unusual ritual/burial monument – a Four-Poster – more often found in Scotland and akin to the more common Stone Circles of the period. On the SE stone there are 'cup marks' – small artificial hollows – feature which is common on this type of site, but whose purpose is unexplained.

WEGNALL see PRESTEIGNE

2060

WHITTON

St DAVID. In a circular churchyard. A small rebuilding, the nave in 1867 and the chancel without division in 1910. Low shingled W spire. The E wall has a reredos of E.E. blank arcading in two tiers with black marble shafts. – Tall SCREEN with only three arches. – FONT. C14. – STOUP. C12? In the chancel. –PULPIT with carved panels, late C17, brought from Pilleth church. – MONUMENT. John Price † 1597, brought from Pilleth church and much restored in 1908. Two female figures beside the tablet, one holding a skull, the other a bird.

BRECONSHIRE
BRYCHEINIOG

★

ABERBRÂN

1 m. ENE of Penpont

(PONT AR FRÂN, over Nant Bran. Rebuilt in 1823 by *Benjamin James*.)

ABERBRÂN BRIDGE. Three elegant arches across the Usk. A plaque records the builder as *James Parry* (architect also of the Wye bridge at Builth); 1791, repaired in 1854.

ABERBRÂN FAWR was built by the Games family before Newton, nearer Brecon. The main hall of the Tudor manor house has almost gone. On its E is the large moulded fireplace, and there are two C16 doorheads, one of them the (blocked) entry to the extant farmhouse, which was the retainers' and service wing at r. angles to the hall (cf. Great Porthaml, Talgarth). With its big external side chimneys it is a picturesque structure. It was mostly rebuilt *c.* 1746.

ABERCAMLAIS *see* PENPONT

ABERCRAF

ST DAVID. Nave, chancel, S W porch and tower, by *J. Cook-Rees*, 1911. The bell-stage of the tower is ashlar, with paired lancets under shallow continuous hoodmoulds. Simple but good roof. – GLASS. E, 1912 etc.

The coal in this part of the Upper Swansea Valley was first worked at Taren Gwyddon in 1758; at Gwaunclawdd in 1770. (A FURNACE for smelting iron had come by 1826; the base remains, 1¼ m. W, by the basin of the Swansea Canal.) Several collieries were active in the C19.

(YARD BRIDGE, 1 m. WSW. A fine stone bridge that carried a colliery tramroad over the river Tawe, built for Mr Harper in 1805.)

CAPEL TY'N-Y-COED, ½ m. NE. 1829 (date-stone). A good

Independent chapel of the George IV period. SW and SE sides stucco with stucco quoins. Tall round-headed windows with intersected tracery and quoined surrounds. Hipped roof with deep eaves and consoles. An attractive interior too, with a gallery with an ornamented parapet supported on fluted iron columns, and a *set-fawr* with twin curved steps.

CAPEL COELBREN, 1½ m. ESE. Nave and chancel, rebuilt in 1799 and 1900.

WAUN-LWYD. The circular cattle house (1¼ m. W) seems to be unique in the United Kingdom, though several were built on a similar plan in the early C19 in the eastern United States. The design is a central cylinder of stone with a conical roof with good timberwork, divided by a cross-passage. From the segmental rooms so formed, four openings give into two crescentic cattle sheds which surround the centre either side of the doorways. At the time of writing it is falling down.

(HEN-NEUADD. C16. The oldest part is four-storeyed, including the cellar and the attic which has one upper cruck.)

ABERCYNRIG *see* LLANFRYNACH

ABERHONDDU *see* BRECON

9020　　　　　　　　ABERYSCIR

ST MARY AND ST CYNIDR. In a circular churchyard. Nave and chancel in one under a steep roof, and a tall W bell-turret. Largely by *C. Buckeridge*, 1860 – till then it was primitive enough to have an earth floor. Vestry added in 1884. C15 N doorway. – STOUP. – MONUMENT. A large tapering slab incised with a foliate cross and inscribed round the border; *c.* 1500?

ABERYSCIR CASTLE. At the confluence of the River Yscir with the Usk. Motte only.

ABERYSCIR COURT, nearby, is a plain stucco house of five bays; 1837.

PONT-AR-YSCIR, ½ m. N. Two-arch bridge with cutwaters and refuges; C18.

BRECON GAER ROMAN FORT (SO 002 297). This site may be rather difficult to find (though sign-posted) down a number of small lanes, but it is worth a visit because of the quantity of Roman masonry exposed – a very fine length of wall fronting the earth and clay rampart stands over 6 ft, and both the S and W gates and guardrooms have been cleared, as well as one of the corner towers. Excavation revealed that the bath-house was inside the fort and that there had been a civil settlement outside the N gate. This large fort was designed for a garrison of 500 cavalry. The original timber buildings of *c.* A.D. 75 were replaced by stone ones about 140. The fort was excavated in 1925–6 by Sir Mortimer Wheeler (*The Roman Fort Near Brecon*). A tombstone found nearby suggests that the garrison in the early C2 came originally from Spain.

ALLTMAWR   *0040*

ST MAURITIUS. Tiny – only about 35 ft long, and one of the smallest churches in Wales. Single-chamber, with a three-sided apse added at the end of the C19. The plan is probably of the same date as the circular, round-bowled FONT with octagonal stem: i.e. the C13. The font was brought from Aberedw (R). Tie-beam roof. C18 wooden windows, pulpit, and box pews at the back of the church. – MONUMENT. Lord Trevethin † 1936 and his wife. Their relief portraits, depicted at the time of their marriage, face each other. By *Ernest Gillick.*

(ALLTMAWR ISAF, ¾ m. NW. A C17 cruciform plan, like Pool Hall, Crickadarn, with early C18 additions. A plaster cartouche in an outbuilding tells us that it was built by Richard Price in 1716.)

BATTLE   *0030*

ST CYNOG. Single-chamber, rebuilt by *J. Bacon Fowler* of Brecon in 1880. Surprisingly, he kept the ribbed and plastered barrel ceiling of *c.* 1500. – STOUP.

PENOYRE, ½ m. E. Built by *Anthony Salvin*, 1846–8, for Col. 84 Lloyd Vaughan Watkins, to replace a house of 1799 built for his father, the Rev. Thomas Watkins. Very precise. Ashlar. Externally, a combination of informal Regency-villa grouping and Barry's Italian Renaissance style. The W side incorporates a bow. The main elevation is correctly detailed from early C16 palazzi and urban in type. It is Roman in scale too – though of only five bays and three storeys with triangular pediments for the *piano nobile* windows. Smooth surfaces with bands of Vitruvian scroll and guilloche. It faces a stunning view of the Brecon Beacons. The upper storey of Salvin's colossal entrance tower, asymmetrically placed on the E side, is an open loggia articulated with pilasters – a reference to the Cubitts' Osborne of 1846–9? Strip rustication round the doorway and keystone masks. The main block has an arcade of Tuscan columns supporting an entablature and balustrade, and broken by rusticated aedicules at the angles. To balance this, a strong cornice with lion-masks. The conservatory to the W had a glass dome, demolished in 1899.

The lavish interiors are partly preserved. An octagonal anteroom with niches (formerly containing statues) alternating with doors, leads to the dining room on the r., with a decorated ceiling; to a library on the l. with a screen of scagliola columns; and ahead to the staircase hall. Though the balusters of the divided stairs are clumsy, the composite scagliola piers of the upper gallery, the low segmental arches painted with arabesques, and the two stucco-ceilinged domes are what one would have expected half a generation earlier – from the Grecian fashion rather than the Italianate of the 1840s and 50s. Beyond the stairs are two small drawing rooms, one with the bow facing W. The cost was £33,000, not including large gardens, particularly balustraded terraces, which have only partially survived.

A rectangular stony MOUND here (SO 006 306) has a very tall (13 ft) stone at one end. The date and purpose of the monument are unknown.

PEN Y CRUG. A multivallate hillfort at SO 029 303. The ramparts run round the top of an isolated hill, the inner one surviving to a height of over 3 ft, the outer ones very slight. On the steep SW side the fourth rampart was never built. Oblique entrance on the S side, with an annexe which might have been part of an earlier fort, of which there is another hint in the curving bank within the interior.

9050   BEULAH

EGLWYS OEN DUW (Church of the Lamb of God), ¾ m. NW of Beulah. Nave and chancel with a Germanic flèche over the chancel arch. By *John Norton*, 1867. His E.E. is very strict, but the interior compensates with coloured bands of brick and tile on the floor and red brick walls. At the E a gold mosaic REREDOS and a three-lancet window with marble shafts. E glass by *Clayton & Bell*, and good. The well-designed Victorian fitments include a little ironwork PULPIT; carved CHOIR STALLS and DESK; a brass CORONA CANDELABRUM; and a pair of two-tier altar CANDELABRA. Two brass CANDLE-SCONCES in the form of water lily leaves with frogs. More glass by *Clayton &*

Bell in the big five-lancet W window, 1868; two sanctuary windows by *Burlison & Grylls*, c. 1877. In all a thoughtful and lavish Victorian interior. – At the W are the FONTS from Llanfihangel Abergwesyn church (demolished 1964), plain and circular and perhaps of the C13; and from Llanddewi Abergwesyn church, perhaps C12, small, square in section, and tapering. Norton's new font is a big low pillar with four columns supporting a carved square top.

LLWYN MADOC, 1½ m. NW. Built for Evan Thomas in 1747. Nine bays, two storeys, and a tall pedimental gable. C20 alterations by *Philip Tilden* include a mansard roof.

(TWDIN, ½ m. S. A small oblong ringwork.)

(CAERAU, ½ m. S. A farm sited on a Roman fort with a medieval motte.)

BRECON/ABERHONDDU   ₀₀₂₀

CATHEDRAL CHURCH OF
ST JOHN THE EVANGELIST

HISTORY. The Benedictine priory church became a cathedral in 1923 on the formation of the diocese of Swansea and Brecon. This was architecturally appropriate, since it is pre-eminently the most splendid and dignified church in Mid Wales. And it was a happy result for the most comprehensive group of conventual buildings remaining habitable in Wales: beside the C13 and C14 church there are the prior's lodging, guest house (?), a tower (now the canonry), almonry, and tithe barn, though these are all later than the church. The building continued in use as the parish church from 1537 till 1923, so the monuments are here rather than in the town church. There were two periods of restoration, in 1861–2 and in 1872, under *Sir George Gilbert Scott*, the restorer also of Hereford Cathedral. The chancel vaulting and other roof work are his designs.*

The site is a ridge above the River Honddu a few hundred yards NE of the castle. Bernard de Neufmarché established the important Norman castle at Brecon in 1093 and gave a church, named in the grant as 'the church of St John the Evangelist without the walls', to his confessor Roger, a monk of the Benedictine Abbey at Battle in Sussex. Roger and another monk,

---

* There is a most informative new (1973) guide, by the Very Rev. W. U. Jacob. I am grateful to Dr Jacob for his help, and for correcting proofs. I am also much indebted to the Chapter Clerk, Lt.-Col. R. M. Pryce, for his suggestions.

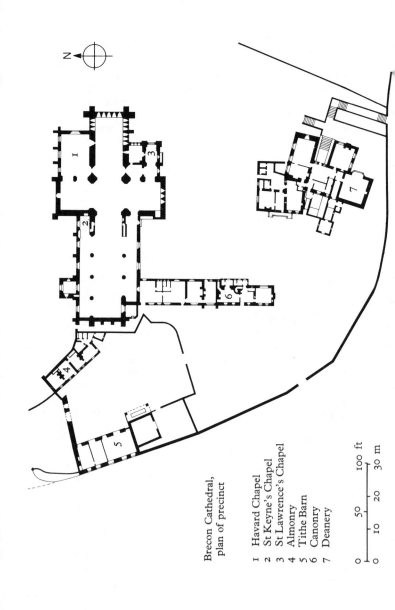

Brecon Cathedral,
plan of precinct

1 Havard Chapel
2 St Keyne's Chapel
3 St Lawrence's Chapel
4 Almonry
5 Tithe Barn
6 Canonry
7 Deanery

0   50   100 ft
0   10   20   30 m

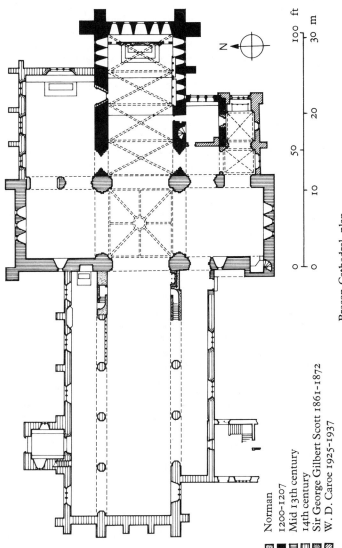

Brecon Cathedral, plan

Norman
1200–1207
Mid 13th century
14th century
Sir George Gilbert Scott 1861–1872
W. D. Caroe 1925–1937

N

100 ft
30 m

50

20

10

0
0

Walter, founded a community which became a priory of Battle
Abbey, later consisting of prior and about eight monks. Their
new church probably followed the Romanesque monastic
cruciform plan like Bury St Edmunds Abbey (begun in 1081).
It may have reached its full size in the mid C12.

The existing fabric is a replacement of the Norman church.
The E parts date from the time of William de Breos, and the
nave arcades, the tower, and the N transeptal chapel probably
from the time of Humphrey de Bohun, who held the Lordship
of Brecknock from 1298 to 1321. During the C15, the period
when the Staffords, Dukes of Buckingham, held the Lordship,
the nave was furnished with a three- or four-storey screen, the
Golden Rood, the aisles were occupied by guild chapels, the
only survivor of which is the Corvizors' on the N, and the tower
was again heightened.

The monastery buildings as existing were constructed in the
C14 and C15, and enclosed within a battlemented curtain. The
complete plan is uncertain. The chapter house has disappeared
(see Gwernyfed, Felindre), and the cloister finally decayed in
the C18. They were granted, together with the priory
endowments, to Sir John Price, one of the visitors of the Welsh
monasteries charged with their dissolution. He made his own
residence in the prior's house; the W side of the cloister became
his stables. In the C19 these were properties of Marquess
Camden, who underwrote much of the repairs. They were
repurchased in 1925, and appropriated to something nearer
their former uses – the Priory House became the deanery, a
chapter house, etc., and the former hospitium, etc., choir
vestries and the canonry. *W. D. Caröe* carried out this work,
and also strengthened the central tower, rebuilt St Lawrence's
Chapel (1930), and designed the high altar reredos (1937).

EXTERIOR. At only 205 ft long, the church of Brecon Priory was
a relatively small one. It is stark and massive. Even the chancel
shows practically no enrichment. Angle buttresses, at the N and
S with pinnacle clusters added by Scott. Corbel-table and parapet, continued on the nave by Scott but not on the transepts.
The lancet mouldings are flush with the wall, this sturdy plainness contrasting tellingly with the elegance inside. The Havard
Chapel extends along three N bays of the chancel; the windows
Scott had to recreate, and he was guided by the early C14 N
aisle. On the transepts the lancets have a drip-course moulded
over them as a hood. The nave itself had embattled walls. Lean-
to N aisle, the windows with two full-height mullions, the outer

two lights with lancet heads (cf. St Mary, Abergavenny). St
Keyne's Chapel is lit by a reticulated dormer window, whose
tracery is not upright but slightly tilted. Three niches for statuary over the door of the N porch, and upper paired lancets.
N clerestory with two-light windows of alternating basic Dec
cusped patterns. The W front has no façade or doorway. Its
corbelled parapet predates Scott. Angle buttresses again. Large
geometrical window of five lights grouped two, one, and two,
beneath a circle filled with four quatrefoils. This replaced one
like the S W nave window, which has circles between intersecting
tracery, all the elements cusped. The S aisle W window is
meagrely reticulated. Its other windows were copied by Scott.
The S clerestory windows are a little earlier in style than the
N ones, if not much different in date: three-light intersecting
traceries. E of the S transept *Caröe*'s rebuilding of St Lawrence's
Chapel. He carefully reproduced the mid C13 detail.

INTERIOR. As it stands, the priory church follows to a certain
extent the Norman plan. The early C12 structure had an aisleless parochial nave, of which the foundations of the W front
lie beneath the later work. This continuing function accounts
for the existence of the font, as well as for the erection of
memorials before (and after) the Reformation. Beyond a screen
were the crossing, transepts, and chancel, which formed the
monastic church. The short stretches of blank walling W of the
crossing belonged to the C12 nave. Rebuilding began in 1201
at the E. The patron was William de Breos, Lord of Brycheiniog
till 1207/8. The arrangement (a fresh start) was a straight-ended
CHANCEL of four bays, flanked by rectangular-ended chapels 20
en échelon of two and one bays respectively. The plan is common
to other Benedictine priories. Completion was forestalled by
William de Breos's disgrace.* The stone vaulting of the choir
was never made, but preparatory springers exist, as also in the
crossing and chapels. The chapels are rebuilt except for the first
to the S; the rest is intact C13 work. The architecture of the
chancel is a very beautiful specimen of the first phase of pure
Early English. Five lancets fill the E wall, and three groups of
three the N and S walls. At the E, the central three are slightly
stepped, and the outer pair are short; their widths also decrease
from the middle outwards. The lateral groups are similar, and

* And Dr Ralegh Radford suggests that William's son Philip, who was
Bishop of Hereford, moved the team of masons to that cathedral (then rebuild-
ing), and that this accounts for the close relationship of the more elaborate
Lady Chapel there with the choir at Brecon.

much narrower. Each light is in a deep embrasure, and the clusters of slender shafts of pinkish-grey stone on the sharp inner edges between – they alone represent the wall surface – give a sense of graciousness and structural strength. The whole design stresses the height of the chancel, though it is actually quite broad. The E clusters between lancets are quintuplets, and carry filleted rolls and hoods. The N and S clusters are triplets, with one shaft detached; the inner arch mouldings are chamfers, then rolls and again hoods. Some capitals with dogtooth bands. The shaft-rings, capitals, and bases on the continuous sill provide a consistent horizontal accent all round. But, though of the same composition as those dividing the lancets, the vaulting-shaft clusters are more widely spaced and their capitals are set lower than the others, so that the vault reinforces the sense of verticality. Here is a consequence of a scheme which omits a triforium. The vaulting, as indicated above, dates from 1861–2 and resulted from Scott's conviction that the choir begged to be finished in this way in order to mask its flat Perp wooden ceiling. His quadripartite rib-vault has transverse arches alternating with the bays over the windows, and no ridge-rib; the model is the quadripartite system of the Hereford Lady Chapel. There can be little doubt that in deciding that a restorer should practise 'conservation' (his word) he was right in this case. One might only wish that the stone in the panels had been the local purple-grey instead of the yellow he used. All the same, the effect is impressive. On the S the triple PISCINA and triple SEDILIA, with detached shafts and trefoil arches, were much reconstructed by Scott. One damaged stiff-leaf capital.

Against the fourth bay of the choir the original CHAPELS had upper storeys, so there are no windows. Two fine archways lead N and S to these chapels, however, each with quintuplet clusters of plain and filleted shafts, and three engaged shafts in the obtuse splays on either side. The arches they support have various alternate chamfered and filleted mouldings, and hoods with head-stops. The SACRISTY, directly S of the chancel, has three E lancets with shafts, and a DOUBLE PISCINA on the S, all a bit simpler. This is as far as the best work goes. While still fine, the CROSSING AND TRANSEPTS date from around the second quarter of the C13 and are aesthetically less stimulating. Each face of the crossing piers has twin shafts in front and single ones on its canted sides, all of just more than semicircular projection only. Ring-moulded capitals. Two-order chamfered arches and a lesser outer moulding with a concave chamfer. The twin shafts of the E and W crossing arches terminate in foliage bosses clear of the height of the stalls of the monastic choir which shut off the transepts. In the latter at the N and S are triple stepped lancets with single unringed shafts. Wall-passages pass in front of these and the N windows, which are lancets and small but with larger chamfered rere-arches with hoods. Entry to the night stair at the S W. The original roof-lines were restored by Scott. Arches to the inner chapels on a similar pattern to the crossing. Also the arch leading to the S aisle and door to the cloister. Interruption of the work at this point may have been caused by the Welsh re-conquest of Brycheiniog in 1262. Resumption took place towards the end of the century, and again the designs are less elaborate, reflecting presumably another drop in wealth. The HAVARD CHAPEL replaced the two N transeptal chapels (see their gable-lines on its W wall). Its N W arch is of c. 1300. In 1923 *Sir Charles Nicholson* adapted it for use as the REGIMENTAL CHAPEL OF THE SOUTH WALES BORDERERS. At the S E corner a fine doorway with a trefoiled inner profile. The two-step mouldings include a row of ballflower, and a quadrant with smaller ballflower. Foliage-crested hood and flanking pinnacles. Contemporary arch to the E chapel off the S transept, with a late C13 niche at the base of the r. jamb. ST LAWRENCE'S CHAPEL to its E has low stone quadripartite vaults, as for the initial project. C13 PISCINA. Also by c. 1300 the second stage of the tower with the paired inner windows. These have chamfered arches on engaged shafts within continuous outer chamfers.

The NAVE developed in accordance with other liturgies. The oblation of the Rood was introduced in the C13; the great W screen and its Golden Rood were formed in the C15. The sections of blank wall at the E of the nave with their stair openings and corbels to support the woodwork give an idea of its importance. A S niche is by Scott. These lengths of wall antedate the responds of the arcades. The aisles are of slightly different dates: first the plainer three-bay S arcade of octagonal piers and double-chamfered arches, a S aisle largely renewed by Scott, and the clerestory windows over the piers; then the four-bay N arcade with three bands of concave mouldings in the arch 28 chamfers. This enlargement to an aisled nave is explicable by the prosperity of the borough of Brecon and its clergy after c. 1300 and the formation of additional chapels. The N aisle became the GUILD CHAPEL OF THE CORVIZORS. The

29   dedication is now to St Keyne. In its N wall an ogee sepulchral
recess of c. 1340 with multiple mouldings, two rows of ballflower, and a septifoil inner profile. C14 S PORCH with a muni-
ment room above; the inner doorway replaced in E.E.
(wrongly) by Scott. Scott restored the nave in 1872; scraped
the walls; and added arch-braces and arcading to the roof
trusses. The latest pre-Dissolution structural addition to the
priory church was the massive early C16 upper stage of the
tower – massive in style more than structure, however, since
it needed drastic internal strengthening in 1913.

FURNISHINGS. CHANCEL: REREDOS. By *W. D. Caröe*, 1937;
the end of the wholehearted Gothic Revival which starts with
Essex's reredos at Lincoln in 1792. Of stone, with small panels,
and in the intricately decorated manner of c. 1500. Figures
under canopies, and reliefs. Four diagonal buttresses, rather
like the woodwork of Llanfilo screen, continue the verticals of
the windows. – RELIEF OF THE ROOD. Tall, worn C15 panel
of stone with two figures kneeling below. – PAINTING. The
Mocking of Christ, ascribed to *Honthorst*. – GLASS. Three S
lancets by *Clayton & Bell*, 1864.

HAVARD CHAPEL: PAINTING. The Baptism of Christ by
Albani. – PEWS by *W. D.* and *A. D. R. Caröe*. – GLASS. The
Adoration and the Entombment, by *Horace Wilkinson*, 1929. –

27   MONUMENT. Walter and Christina Awbrey of Abercynrig,
formerly dated 1312. A single slab carved with the two recumbent effigies; his hair is curled, her head is covered by a cap
and wimple. He is holding a carved crucifix against his chest,
and the pillow between them is filled with a Rood with Mary
and St John either side. Angels swinging censers in the pedimental canopy of the slab. Inscribed: 'Waler le Fiz Water
Aubrey git ici Iesus de sa alme eit merci', etc.

NORTH TRANSEPT: MONUMENTS. Henry Williams
† 1736; with a relief of children's heads. – Mary Ann
Clifton † 1809. A garland of white marble branches on black. –
Sir John Meredith † 1780. Figure of a woman prostrated over
two coffins, beneath a vault. By *John Bacon the Elder*
(Gunnis). – Susanna Watkins † 1847, perhaps copied from the
preceding. – Rev. Thomas Watkins † 1829. The relief rhe-
torically shows two angels appearing at his deathbed. By *J.
Thomas & Sons*. – Mary Watkins † 1762 and John Lloyd
† 1812. High relief of the donor mourning beside two urns. –
George Price Watkins † 1843. The lifesize group of mourners
includes a woman and two children. – Sophia Watkins † 1851.

By *I. E. Thomas*. Definitely Early Victorian taste. A large relief 87 of her rising in the arm of an angel. – Eliza Watkins † 1855. Full-face portrait bust in a roundel.

CROSSING: CHOIR STALLS by *Scott*, 1872.

SOUTH TRANSEPT: CUPBOARD. C17, with sacred reliefs including the Baptism and Deposition, panels of *c.* 1500 said to have come from Neath Abbey. – ORGAN by *H. Bevington & Sons*, late C18 in a Victorian case. – MONUMENTS. William Morgan James † 1798 and the Rev. Thomas James † 1812. Two relief figures, one holding a tall cross and one mourning; by *Flaxman*. – Thomas Maybery † 1829, by *John Evan Thomas*. Gothic, with two figures beneath the pinnacles. – Walter Jeffreys † 1748, by *Tho. Paty*, Bristol. Handsome Doric pediment and pilasters. – Frederick Jones † 1834, by *J. Thomas & Son*. Trophy. – John Powell † 1809, by *J. E. Thomas*. – Samuel Pryce † 1813. – John Price † 1719, by *Tho. Paty*. With a broken pediment. – Bishop Edward Williamson † 1953. With a full-face relief by *Ayres*. – Bishop Edward Bevan † 1934. Bronze recumbent effigy by *W. Goscombe John*.

NAVE: FONT. Large circular bowl with an only partly 12 decipherable Latin inscription on the rim. Carved in shallow relief with a series of grotesque masks alternating with roundels containing fantastic birds and beasts (cf. Eardisley, Herefs.). Band of interlace above. The short circular pedestal has Romanesque intersected arcading. Of *c.* 1130–50. – CHANDELIER. Brass. Given by Elizabeth Lucy in 1722. Three tiers of seven branches. – CRESSET STONE. With thirty sockets for lights, the largest known. C12. – CHEST in the S aisle. A magnificent piece of North European Mannerist carving with figures and projecting heads; *c.* 1550. – PULPIT incorporating carved bits from the C15 screen. – Two fragments of WALL PAINTINGS in the W crossing arch. – GLASS. W, 1898. – MONUMENTS. At the W: D. Price † 167–? With a fragile open pediment broken forward on colonnettes. – Margaret Powell † 1774 and Charles Powell † 1796, a pair of *c.* 1800, by *H. Wood* of Bristol. – David Price † 1835 (signed illegibly). Grecian, draped. – Four pretty slabs on the floor beneath these, with inscriptions on the margins; perhaps C16. – In the S aisle: A simpler slab with a circled cross, on the wall. – Esther Davies † 1813. – Sir David Williams † 1613 and wife, of Gwernyfed, 54 Felindre. Two alabaster recumbent figures. Very stiff. The finery they wear is interesting, however. – Joann Hughes † 1741. With a bust above the tablet. – The Games Monument. A wooden recumbent figure of the wife of one of three men of the Games family once commemorated by an all-wood three-tier tomb. Of c. 1555, which is late for a figure of wood; some mutilation; very fashionably dressed. – John Maund † 1850. A pair of half-pillars with urns, curiously placed in a double Perp niche. – The tomb of Hugh Price, the founder in 1571 of Jesus College, Oxford, has not been found.

ST KEYNE'S CHAPEL. PARCLOSE SCREEN. Buttressed uprights and an embattled rail, panelled dado and paired lights with traceries, all of early C16 type and English in design. Bosses from the Late Perp choir ceiling are fixed to it. – GLASS. Two windows by *Powell's*, 1910 and 1911. – MONUMENT. The effigy in the recess is supposed to be the founder of the chapel; he is a civilian in tunic and coat and a plain example of the mid C14.

The CONVENTUAL BUILDINGS of the C13 do not survive. There is no direct evidence of the cloister S of the church; but Dineley wrote, 'Its windows are of good artifice in stonework, arch'd with timber in square panes, but the want of repair hath much decayed it.' The chapter house and slype etc. have not been dug for. However, within the C15 embattled wall of the precinct there are buildings deserving mention as palimpsests. The partly C19 DEANERY at the SE of the group has some early C17 windows with wood architraves and diagonal chimneys; its E part is a C17 H-plan. Structurally it is also partly medieval, with a blocked (C14?) arch in the S wall, a doorway with a similar chamfered pointed arch in a corridor (both of these next to the present chapter house), and a lancet in the clergy house wing. Along the W side of the space where a cloister should be, that is to say running S at r. angles from the W end of the S aisle, is a two-storey range which has been greatly remodelled – most recently by *Caröe* in 1926–7. At the N end the lower floor has early C17 stable woodwork and fireplaces. In the upper floor small cusped C15 lights facing E, five widely spaced and three together. Was this a guest house? A library? One can only conjecture. Then the four-storey tower of the CANONRY, with one straight-headed E window of three ogee lights, and inside a spiral stone stair and two fireplaces with corbelled lintels and one chamfered and elliptical, perhaps all of the early C16. The S end is entirely of c. 1700. The precinct wall forms an enclosure W of this range. It has two gateways, to the W (with an elliptical-headed postern beside it); and to the N, a cambered head with two niches above. Flanking the inner side of the N gate the small ALMONRY, whose blocked cambered doorway and tiny lancet are set in the wall itself, and the TITHE BARN, early C17 as far as the timber-work – ovolo-mullioned windows and queen-post roofs – is concerned. It has gargoyles on the W.

CHRIST COLLEGE (originally the DOMINICAN FRIARY OF ST NICHOLAS). Neither the date of foundation, nor the founder's name (or indeed where the friars came from) has been found for this friary outside the former walls of Brecon on the road to Cardiff and Neath. The earliest architecture in the chapel is datable to c. 1240; Milo Fitzwalter gave land to Malvern Priory about this time. The Awbrey family of Abercynrig are thought to have been the benefactors in the C14. The first mention is in the western visitation of the Dominicans in England, of 1269. The choir of the friary church, its roofless nave, the C14 refectory and an adjoining building survive, and that so much has done so is due to their having been granted after the Dissolution to William Barlow, Bishop of St Davids. He transferred the College of Abergwili to the site in 1541; the College of Christ Church trained clergy here till the opening of St David's College at Lampeter attracted men there. The college became a public school in 1853. More important perhaps even than *J. P. Seddon*'s excellent restoration of the chapel in 1859–72 are the Gothic Revival school buildings of 1861–4 and after by *John Prichard* and *Seddon*, the architects to Llandaff diocese.

The CHAPEL is the choir and screen passage of the friary 21 church. It is 66 ft long, the nave 88 ft. The plan has no transepts, in common with the friaries of Chichester and Winchelsea. Externally, the E end is wholly occupied by a window of five stepped lancets enclosed in one overall frame, an example of the C14 style creating a large, unified design, if not yet quite in terms of tracery. Angle buttresses. N wall of four good lancets for the sanctuary and seven deeper ones for the choir, which looks soundly mid C13; but let Seddon have his say: 'In restoring ... the beautiful chancel, which alone existed of the former church, I laid its tottering N wall stone by stone on the turf and set it up again and might defy anyone to tell it had been touched.' After four corresponding lancets on the S the wall is blank; the vestry was abutted in the middle of it (see the squint to the altar), and a two-storey range ran S of its W part with on its upper floor the dormitory (see the blocked C15 doorway of the night stair). This was on the E of the cloister, to which we shall return. A blocked arch stands between the screen passage and the E cloister.

The C13 NAVE shows the base of its large W window. Tomb
recess on the S. In perhaps the first quarter of the C14 a N aisle
was built, the arcade of which is quite gone except for the responds. Large N doorway with two orders of shallow quadrant
mouldings continuous over a semicircular arch. A chapel
remains in use at its E. The ANTECHAPEL is rebuilt on the
plan of the two C13 masonry screens. The central doorway to
the choir has a chamfer and a sunk chamfer, perhaps con-
temporaneous with the AWBREY CHAPEL on the N. The early
C14 triple trefoiled lancet E window there is restored. Plain
three-lancet N window. DOUBLE PISCINA with a detached
shaft and trefoil arches. The CHAPEL proper has an organ case
by *Seddon* in a loft by *Caröe*, and a panelled wagon ceiling which
is decorative though a bit flat. Also some nice sea-things on the
tiles. Attached shafts framing the lancets on the N and S. In
the N sanctuary wall an early C14 sepulchral recess, the arch
with two rolls with fillets, and a hoodmould. On the E wall two
of the nook-shafts belonging to the original lancets were left
in the jambs of the C14 window. The quadruple (which is unusual) SEDILIA on the S and the DOUBLE PISCINA have trefoiled arches and hoods with foliate stops. Even at this end the
Dominican building was not lavish; its E.E. is abstemious in
its non-decoration of surfaces. Further restoration in 1926 by
J. L. Phillips and *W. D. Caröe*.

FURNISHINGS. CHAPEL. E GLASS, the Calvary, designed
by *Seddon c.* 1864. The leading used as definition; otherwise
in the palest 'Cathedral' colours, like the lancets. Made by *Clayton & Bell*, 1865. An effective design. – REREDOS. Panelling,
probably by *Caröe*, covers the original tile reredos. – STALLS,
to designs by *Seddon*, 1863. – MONUMENTS. The Rev. Charles
Pryse † 1696. Aedicule with twisted columns abundantly
decked with symbols of mortality. A putto in the open pediment. Latin inscription. – Thomas Lloyd † 1755. With a relief
of a weeping amorino lying in front of ruined buildings, inserted
in a broken pediment, and above this an urn and pyramid
(added in 1792?). – Thomas Bullock Lloyd † 1796. With an
oval relief of a tall lady with an urn. By *Wood* of Bristol. –
The Rev. George Bull † 1709, by *John Rickets*, Gloucester.
With a severe classical surround.

ANTECHAPEL. Six remaining STALLS, ordered to be completed (together with other repairs) by Bishop Lucy in 1664,
but basically of c. 1400. Their MISERICORDS include a horse,
an angel, two lions, and a skeleton. – The big cinquefoiled

DOUBLE PISCINA came from the nave. – Magnificent eighteen-branch C17 CANDELABRUM. – MONUMENTS. Martha Lucy † 1676. Cartouche with strapwork framing and flowers. – William Lucy, Bishop of St Davids, † 1677. A half-length portrait bust – the only one of the kind in Breconshire. Vigorous head; in episcopal robes. The enjoyable surround consists of a pediment with two putti, active and contemplative, beside the figure, and an inscription placed in a splendid wreath of putto heads, leaves, and drapes circled by two snakes. – The Rev. Richard Lucy † 1690, by *William Stanton* (1697), and his wife Florence Games † 1709. Lifesize alabaster figures on a tomb-chest, he recumbent, his bewigged head on a pillow, she leaning on her l. arm looking out. Play is being made of the (nick-) name Gam, meaning one-eyed. – Gam Lucy † 1697, their eldest son, is represented standing on the step of the chest; again lifesize, his fashionable dress speaks for the family's position, as do the columns and open pediment of this uncommon conversation piece. – Martha Lucy † 1674. With upturned volutes and an open pediment.

AWBREY CHAPEL. John Awbrey † 1596. Incised slab depicting a man in armour and his wife. – Another with a foliate Greek cross.

COLLEGIATE BUILDINGS. A competition to reconstruct the school came in 1859. The cloister lay S of the nave, from the E screens to the width of the W range away from the W wall. It was finally destroyed in 1660. *Pritchard*'s LIBRARY of 1861 is built down the centre of its site at r. angles to the nave, creating the W enclosure of a new quadrangle. It is in the E.E. style and augustly institutional; paired blank arcading with trefoiled windows subdivided by buttresses on the first storey, then triple lancets based on the chapel's on the second. At the S end a tall oriel holds the stair. Here the style shifts to the C14 'Venetian'. SCHOOL HOUSE, S of the quadrangle, is quite a different building, domestic, smooth-surfaced, of multicoloured stone, by *Prichard & Seddon*, c. 1861. Smaller two- and three-light windows with relieving arches in red and white stone lower down; the largest windows are in the semi-dormers. Seddon's original drawing shows a tall central tower. It seems that Ruskin's museum at Oxford was the model. An octagonal room (looking like a monks' kitchen, and a kitchen is what it was at first) with plate tracery and the characteristic steep-pitched roof serves as a link with the other early residential building. This is tall again, of the local deep red sandstone, with a charming variety of freestone windows, a different type on each floor; once more the series becomes more expansive the higher one looks. As a group, and individually, these buildings are convincing in their free use of correct medieval forms, and what has been done since doesn't compare.

With Alway House we have turned into a small open court, facing s. Though far from the cloister, the other Dominican buildings are here: they are surprising survivals. E–W is the long LARGE HALL, originally the C13 infirmary(?) and much restored by *Prichard & Sedden*. With its three-sided apsidal end with buttresses and the fireplace in its N wall it is clearly medieval, but extensively renewed. Low C14(?) roof of five bays of arch-braced collar-trusses, with simple curved wind-braces. A wing at r. angles looks like an early kitchen with its external chimney; one notices two paired shouldered windows on the E. It abuts the notable C14 SMALL HALL, possibly originally the guest hall. Here, too, much is 1860s work – the entire W wall with plate tracery in the windows (were the architects careful to copy the old evidence?), the hooded fireplace on its simple corbels. The fine roof, four bays of trusses braced with big trefoil arches and with wind-braces of the same ample trefoil shape, looks like the original. A complex little window in the N gable unites a triquetra and a trefoil in a spherical triangle, a conceit close to the spirit of the Dec style. Schoolrooms opposite the N door were added by *J. B. Fowler* in 1880–2. A boarding house (1889) and recent additions continue an expansion to the w.*

OTHER CHURCHES

ST MARY's position in Bulwark and its splendid C16 tower make it scenically the most prominent building in Brecon (rather than the secluded cathedral); yet its role as the parish church began only in 1923, and it has still to weather the results of a series of devitalizing restorations. It began as a chapel of ease to the Benedictine priory; the circular pier in the N arcade, which has a broad scalloped capital supporting a square abacus, alone remains of the short aisled church of the mid C12. The arches E and W of this pier are low, pointed, chamfered, and of rubble; between them is a niche. Extension of this arcade to the E and the W and the building of the s arcade – now with only one original circular pier, opposite the C12 one but taller and slenderer than that, so that the whole looks post-1200 – continued till the early C14. Of this date the s w octagonal pillar, the stops

* I am grateful to Mr E. Parry for corrections to this account of Christ College.

of which return it to a square base. The plan is thus of a nave with no division between it and the chancel; a s aisle of the same length, the PISCINA indicating that it had its own altar; and a shorter N aisle. The s windows have Y-tracery, two with and two without cusping; the E and one of the aisle windows are three-lancet groups and cusped and uncusped respectively, but all of the early C14. The N aisle was rebuilt a little later and has one Dec window unrestored. Added to this plan are the small s porch, roofed with arched braces and trefoil-cut principals and with a quatrefoiled ceiling, late C15; and the extension of the choir together with a five-light transomed Perp E window. Lastly, c. 1510–20, Edward Stafford, Duke of Buckingham, had the w tower constructed at a cost of £2,000. Large w arch with Tudor mouldings and a large w window with renewed Late Perp tracery. There are springers for a vault, now dismantled. The tower illustrates the importance of the Somerset Perp style as far up the Usk as this, given a grander-than-local patron. About 90 ft high, it has an octagonal NW stair-turret, diagonal buttresses, and big traceried windows, on a scale which makes it the finest in Powys and causes its red battlements and carved waterspouts to be visible all over the town. The fabric was repaired in 1831; in 1856, when the renewal of the arcades in yellow railway stone was probably done by *T. H. Wyatt* (and also perhaps the open-truss wagon roof was constructed, with its flattened section); and in 1928 by *W. D. Caröe* – the reredos, stalls, organ case, and finally the screen (1949). – STOUP. The base is a cluster of shafts and the bowl a half-octagon decorated with ogival arches and pinnacles carried on four corbel-figures. Early C15? – ALTAR. On the w pilaster of the s arcade. A shallow slab with two blank trefoiled panels as a reredos. Late C14? – The FONT and PULPIT look like *Wyatt*'s, particularly the latter, which stands on eight colonnettes of coloured marble and shows that expense is no substitute for careful design. – GLASS. E, 1856 by *Charles Gibbs*; bright and mainly decorative. – MONUMENTS. A coffin lid with a raised foliate cross; foliage too on the shaft, all very stylized; and six arrows. C14? C15? – A slab in the porch incised with a cross. C14?

ST MICHAEL (R.C.), Wheat Street, p. 300.
DR COKE MEMORIAL CHAPEL, Lion Street, p. 299.
BAPTIST CHAPEL, Watergate, p. 301.
PRESBYTERIAN CHURCH, Watton, p. 301.
(PLOUGH CHAPEL. Rebuilt in 1841 and enlarged in 1897.)

PUBLIC BUILDINGS

CASTLE. Above the confluence of the Usk and Honddu and now
divided by CASTLE SQUARE. Bernard de Neufmarché's military headquarters and caput of the lordship of Brecon was a
motte and bailey on a naturally defended (and prehistoric) site.
It was established by 1093 in succession to castles at Abergavenny and Crickhowell, after the defeat of Rhys ap Tewdur,
ruler of South Wales. The holder of the lordship in the late
C12, William de Breos, was the probable builder of the small
Ely Tower on top of the motte (in the garden of the bishop's
residence); the remains are a polygonal turret and part of the
shell keep. The bailey ran s towards the Usk. The C13 added
a stone curtain, towers, and gatehouse, which have all gone.
Of the buildings within the walls, the chapel too is gone, but
part of the great hall of Humphrey de Bohun is attached to
the hotel. It had an aisled undercroft of octagonal piers with
vaults. The s wall of the ruined hall, of c. 1280, has large trefoiled lancets in big splays, and a corbelled embattled parapet.
To the SE a contemporary round stair-turret, with loops, and
a semi-octagonal latrine tower of c. 1300. The hall was magnifi-
cently re-roofed c. 1550 but already dismantled under James I.

83 BRECKNOCK MUSEUM (formerly the SHIRE HALL), Glamorgan Street. By *T. H. Wyatt & David Brandon*, 1839–43. In
Greek Revival, still (cf. Smirke's at Hereford), and turned into
a museum without architectural incongruity. Of Bath stone.
Tetrastyle fluted Doric portico in Combe Down stone, of heavy
proportions like e.g. the temples at Paestum. Inner porch of
two columns of the same order *in antis*. Triglyph frieze all
round, with anthemium cresting at the sides. The Court Room
had an Ionic-columned exedra, filled now with its old fittings;
altered in 1889. Some architectural fragments are displayed
inside; also some of the Early Christian monuments of Brecon-
10 shire, including the C10 PILLAR CROSS from Neuadd Siarman,
Maesmynys. This is c. 6 ft high and unquestionably the finest
and most complete in Powys, of a type found also in southern
England. The cross is wheel-headed. Its arms spread to a
circular profile and have deeply scooped pits between. Both
faces and the sides are carved in relief with panels of various
types of elaborate knotwork and interlace. Its peculiar feature
is the treatment of the angles, which have moulded shafts with
intermittent reel ornaments.

GUILDHALL, High Street Inferior, p. 299.

COUNCIL CHAMBER, Glamorgan Street, p. 300.
COUNTY LIBRARY, Ship Street, p. 300.
CEMETERY, Cradoc Road, p. 301.
MARKET HALL, High Street Superior, p. 301.
GAOL, Postern, p. 301.
BARRACKS, Watton, p. 301.
COUNTY GAOL, see Llanfaes.

PERAMBULATION

The natural meeting-place is the bronze STATUE OF WELL-
INGTON, E of St Mary, given to the town by its sculptor, *John
Evan Thomas* of Brecon (1810–73), a pupil of Chantrey. Made
in 1852, it has reliefs of Peninsular War and Waterloo incidents.
It stands at the head of THE BULWARK, more or less in the
middle of the almond shape of the lost C13 ten-towered walls
that enclosed the borough between here and the castle. The
layout dates from the second half of that century, the town having been burned by Llewelyn ap Iorwerth in 1233. The walls
on Speed's map have five gates. They were demolished *c.* 1640–
50, except for one tower behind Buckingham Place, in Captain's
Walk. On the r. down HIGH STREET INFERIOR are Early
Georgian houses and an Edwardian bank. The GUILDHALL,
on the site of its timber predecessor of 1624 by *John Abel* (a
three-gabled court room on three bays of columns, above a market), is a disappointment – three bays by seven of blank sandstone arcades; stucco above with a pedimental gable. It is partly
of 1770 but mostly of 1888. The end of the street is an agreeable
market-town mixture of plain C18 and C19 houses, including
the birthplace of Sarah Siddons (1755), a Corinthian-columned
C19 shop-front, and LLOYDS BANK on the site of Brecon Old
Bank, founded in 1778. On the corner of HIGH STREET
SUPERIOR another pretty C19 shop-front: three glazed bows
with barley-sugar columns. Sharp r. is LION STREET. An alley
on the l. leads to the DR COKE MEMORIAL CHURCH, with
a low-relief Italianate stucco façade on a rusticated base. (Inside, the monuments to Dr Coke's family are by *J. E. Thomas*.)
No. 12 was the birthplace and home of Theophilus Jones (1759–
1812), Breconshire's historian. Next to it, CHURCH HOUSE,
with a four-bay early C18 façade with quoins, an egg-and-dart
cornice, and carved consoles; it is otherwise largely C17 and
built beside a rear courtyard. Further down, No. 6 is an C18
double-pile, and No. 5 has the low hipped and sprocketed roof

and the chimney clusters characteristic of *c.* 1700, and plaster ceilings inside. No. 4 is a handsome house, possibly by *John Crunden, c.* 1740, and most exceptional in this region in being of red brick. Three storeys and five bays, of which the centre three break forward. Keystones on all the windows. Doorway with Gibbs surround, broken pediment, and fanlight. Nice ironwork in the gateway and railings. (Inside, a good Georgian chimneypiece with pediment.) We emerge at the foot of Bulwark at WATTON MOUNT, a C19 house with Doric columns above a basement door.

THE BULWARK itself widens greatly towards St Mary. On its s, big C18 buildings with C19 fronts. No. 12 has an early C18 door surround fronting a Jacobean house with a fine staircase; No. 11 two orders of pilasters on a rusticated base, and a pediment. The C18 WELLINGTON HOTEL has a C19 portico over the pavement with a little pediment on each side. The bank's house next on the r. retains its late C18 quoins and fluted frieze. The four-storey front with a Doric portico is the last of these mostly C19 stucco façades. Retracing our steps to the Museum, GLA-MORGAN STREET is sharp on the r. Immediately on the l. a funereal COUNCIL CHAMBER (1962) of doubtful parentage. The former English Independent Chapel opposite of *c.* 1835 has a pleasant classical stucco front and Regency intersecting windows. The URSULINE CONVENT SCHOOL occupies an C18 house with a tall C19 plaster front behind good railings and gates, and the early C17 HAVARD HOUSE. Beyond these buildings and Captains Walk the meadows, undeveloped, still reach to the heart of the medieval town. On the corner of WHEAT STREET is BUCKINGHAM PLACE, rare in being left stone-fronted and not stuccoed, and rare too in being Tudor in origin (see the main four-centred moulded doorhead). In the C16 apparently with hall and detached solar, in its C17 state the hall was storeyed (see the relieving arches). A fireplace had the Awbrey arms. ST MICHAEL'S R.C. CHURCH is on the l., a plain Gothic nave and chancel by *C. Hansom,* 1851. SHIP STREET turns downhill between the only building with exposed timber-framing in the town (C16), and a N side now opened out by the construction of the COUNTY LIBRARY (1969, by *J. A. McRobbie,* County Architect). In as tight-fitting an environment as Brecon, the danger is for even modest innovation to be too powerful; this one acknowledges the fact. (No. 13 Bridge Street has the yard of an C18 coaching inn.) At the bottom the seven-arch BRIDGE across the Usk, while

not medieval, originates from 1563. Of seven segmental arches.
Enlargements certainly in 1794 by *Thomas Edwards*; in 1801
by *John Maund*; and recently. Christ College is on the far bank.
Just upstream the Honddu is crossed by WATERGATE. The
bridge is modern. Beside this a BAPTIST CHAPEL of *c*. 1880,
and a Penfold hexagonal pillar box (1866–79). In the early C19
riverside walks existed.

Up CRADOC ROAD is the CEMETERY by *H. J. Powell* of Cardiff,
1858. Quite a good pair of chapels in the usual Second Pointed,
banded stone, with a lodge – and a wonderful view of the Beacons. Brecon has wisely expanded in the C20, particularly in
this NW sector.

The N turn from the junction of SHIP STREET and HIGH
STREET INFERIOR leads past the entrance gateway of the
MARKET HALL, a single big stone arch with Tuscan pilasters
and entablature, by *T. H. Wyatt*, 1857. CASTLE STREET on
the l. approaches the castle, and across the Honddu on the r.
is POSTERN, in which stands a small building with blank arches
inscribed 'BRECON GAOL 1842'. STRUET, which keeps to the
near side of the river and is closely lined with small houses with
nice Late Georgian details, leads N towards the cathedral.

WATTON is the axis of the contemporary growth to the SE, but
is by contrast with Struet also a planned approach to Bulwark
and the old centre. It leaves the town with orderly terraces and
an avenue. The Gothic PRESBYTERIAN CHURCH (by *W. F.
Poulton*, 1872) has a good steeple. On its N are the BARRACKS
of the South Wales Borderers. Designs for the brick arsenal
(now a museum) were made *c*. 1805 by *John Maund*. The big
keep that succeeded it, with concrete and iron floors, dates from
1876–9. The stone barrack buildings round the parade ground
were mostly designed by Colonel *Ord*, R.E., 1842–4. The
terminal range, nineteen bays and two storeys with a central
clock tower, was cavalry and infantry barracks. In CAMDEN
ROAD, behind, CAMDEN COURT, in boring Elizabethan but
massed round a central tower, was erected as the Congrega-
tionalist Memorial College by the Rev. *Thomas Thomas*. Dated
1869.

s of Watton in flat ground is the terminal basin of the BRECON
AND MONMOUTHSHIRE CANAL, begun in 1792, opened in
1801, and connected with the Monmouth Canal in 1812 for the
iron trade. The engineer was *Dadford*. So this was the 'industrial area' of a town which mostly earned its prosperity from
the cloth industry and agriculture – and is still an important

agricultural centre. On the subject of communications, Brecon was a centre of early tramroads and of a railway network now closed. The first tramline here, to Glangrwyne Forge (1794), just preceded the canal. Apart from the Hay Railway (1812), for which one bridge survives, lines went to Eardisley, Brynmawr, Ystradgynlais, and Neath. The BRECON AND MERTHYR RAILWAY, involving a climb of 1,000 ft in six miles, was built by *David Davies* and *Thomas Savin* (contractors) and *Henry Conybeare* (engineer) between 1860 and 1863. Connections followed with Hay, Hereford, and the Great Western (1864), Builth and the Cambrian Railway (1864), and Neath and the Great Western (1867). Stations for these were again near Watton.

MOTTE, 1½ m. ENE.

LLANFAES. *See* p. 335.

BRECON GAER *see* ABERYSCIR

1030

BRONLLYS

ST MARY. Nave and chancel, drastically and uninterestingly rebuilt in 1887 by *Nicholson & Sons* but apparently on the C12 or C13 plan; so a narrow chancel arch remains, a C14 N priest's door, and a rood-loft stair. The odd bulbous FONT with four projections could be C12 or C13. A big C16 Tudor SCREEN with buttressed posts and three bays of foliage-carved spandrels (one spandrel has a 'green man' – a human head sprouting leaves from the mouth) now stands at the W. This and other changes at the E are by *G. G. Pace*. C16 timber N porch, with an arched entrance and wind-braces in its roof. – PULPIT. Of *c.* 1700. Brought from Llandefailog Tre'r Graig. – The (medieval?) detached tower stands NE of the chancel; though described in *Archaeologia Cambrensis* as 'the erection of a nineteenth century humourist', there are other detached towers. LYCH-GATE at the churchyard entrance.

24 BRONLLYS CASTLE. A steep motte formed against an outcrop; on it, a C13 round tower. The castle was first fortified by Richard Fitz Pons of Clifford (Herefs.) soon after the Norman Conquest of Brycheiniog in 1091–3, and the tower was probably built by his descendant Walter de Clifford II between 1221 and 1263 (DOE). The keep is entered above the battering base by a pointed doorway which leads into a hall with two lancets. Vaulted cellar below. The second storey, a C14 domestic addi-

tion, has a fireplace and two ogee cinquefoil windows. The third storey has a hooded chimney. By 1521 it was beyond repair. This keep and Tretower's are similar in type, and of French origin, introduced by the Marcher Lords. Stretching down beside the Llynfi is a large, formerly stone-walled, inner bailey, at the far end of which a house was picturesquely placed in the 1790s. A fragment of the great hall was incorporated into the stables. There are signs of an extensive outer bailey which before the Conquest may have constituted a llys. Bronllys became the capital of the cantref of Selyf under Richard Fitz Pons.

BRONLLYS HOSPITAL, ½ m. W. Formerly a tuberculosis sanatorium, built on a widely spaced pavilion-system plan in 1913–20 by *Edwin T. Hall* and *Stanley Hall*. The CHAPEL, dedicated in 1920, is a Latin cross with the sanctuary beyond a semi-circular arch. The external detailing is of high quality. W herringbone stone tympanum. Deep eaves and buttresses with triplet windows, but only the E and transept ones have arched voussoirs. Low-eaved roof, the scissor trusses amazingly economical. The SE campanile has an exaggerated perspective. The sanatorium lies in the park of PONT-Y-WAL, a late C19 house replacing one built by Howel Harris in 1759.

TREPHILLIP, 1 m. W. A farmhouse of the end of the C17 and the early C18. Two bays, a two-storey porch projection, and another bay. Hipped roof. Good stair with twisted balusters, in the traditional place behind the chimney and not in the back wing.

BRYNMAWR *

Brynmawr grew up in the C19 with the iron and coal industries of north Monmouthshire. The streets have the orderliness of Regency planning, though in fact most of the layout dates from *c.* 1840–60. That it differs so strikingly from the towns down in the valleys is the responsibility of John Thomas, who was actually a public health inspector. Those streets which do not form part of a grid follow the track of the old tramroads. Thus there are streets of modest but well-proportioned and well-integrated buildings. Since in the C20 the local ore proved unsuitable for steelmaking and the collieries were run down, this town of terraced houses, improbably situated at 1,200 ft amongst bare hills, has lived by means of light industry.

* Transferred to Gwent in 1974.

St Mary. Rebuilt by *Nicholson & Hawtree*, 1900. Nave, n and s aisles, chancel. Inside, a big ornate PULPIT, and a REREDOS by *Scott* of the 1860s from St Mary, Richmond, Yorks. Beside the tower a C12 STOUP, perhaps from Llanelly church. – (Next to the church the VICARAGE, *c.* 1881, possibly after a design by *J. D. Sedding*. Of stone, the gables and first floor slate-hung.) Many chapels of different classical styles were built in Brynmawr in the C19, since Nonconformity established itself early here. BETHESDA CHAPEL, Alma Street, of 1850 has a prominent front with three tall Regency Gothic (intersecting) windows. The pyramid-roofed ZION CHAPEL, built in 1844 in Clarence Street to the l., has a segment-pedimented portal. R. into Beaufort Street and r. again into Davies Street for the two-storey TABOR BAPTIST CHAPEL of 1835, gaily classical, with round-headed upper windows and ice-cream-pink colourwash. St Mary is at the top of DUMFRIES PLACE, a street of very small mid C19 houses NE of Beaufort Street. Parallel to this, a few streets w, is Queen Street, where the CONGREGATIONAL CHURCH'S façade seems to be based on the paired segment-headed windows of Monmouth Shire Hall. CONTROL DATA LTD at the e of the town is a volumetrically compact complex of *c.* 1970.

0050 BUILTH WELLS/LLANFAIR YM MUALLT

St Mary. The dedication to St Mary is Norman, but the tower of *c.* 1300 is the earliest part now. Slightly splayed base, small lancets, battlements. The explanation for its curious position s of the chancel is that the nave of 1793, which had replaced the medieval one (the two roof-lines are visible on the e side of the tower, above its filled-in arch), was left standing while its Victorian successor was being constructed. Nave, chancel, and s aisle are by *John Norton*, 1875. Two-storey s porch. Round tower with a conical roof beside it. Trefoil-arch-braced nave roof and Dec windows. – STAINED GLASS. e, four lights and tracery, by *Kempe*, 1877. – w, two lights in pairs, with circles and a wheel above, 1945. – s by *Heaton, Butler & Bayne*. – FONT. C14, with raised stops on the base. – MONUMENT. A worn recumbent effigy in the porch: John Lloyd † 1585, 'Ysquer to the bodye' to Queen Elizabeth, in military dress, his head on a helmet.

CASTLE. Earthworks only now. A motte-and-bailey was begun just before 1100 for Philip de Breos, head of the lordship, to protect the important crossing of the Wye. The defences were razed by Llewelyn ap Gruffydd in 1260. Much of what can now be seen was probably in existence by then. A motte sloping 60 ft in all down to the N has two crescentic hornworks attached on higher ground to the W, S, and E. A wet ditch and bank surrounds them. Between 1277 and 1283 Edward I had the castle refortified. *John fitz Adam of Radnor* was paid for overseeing temporary timber buildings in 1277. In the same year stone replacements were started; the work from 1278 may have been under the control of *James of St George*. (Two master masons and two master carpenters are named in the accounts from then on.) The fortifications consisted of a great tower (probably a shell keep), a stone curtain with six towers, a drawbridge flanked by two more towers, and a stone wall and ditch to the inner bailey; the outer bailey was also to have had a stone wall. Payments ceased *c.* 1283 with the work still unfinished and with North Wales the centre of conflict. The stone was probably removed in Elizabeth I's reign; some foundations have been found and excavation would be illuminating. The great interest of Builth Castle is its concentric plan, the precursor of Edward's North Wales castles begun by Master James during the campaign of 1282.

PERAMBULATION. The small town of Builth, one of Breconshire's three markets, consisting of about eighty houses, was entirely destroyed by fire on 20 December 1691. The surveyor for rebuilding was *Edward Price*. There is nothing of this date left apart from Nos. 13–15 High Street, brick and of five bays. The town has little planning – it lived from the tourist trade in the C19, and lives from its market today. A walk anticlockwise round the town and churchyard from near the BRIDGE leads through a variety of C19 narrow streets. The small STRAND HOUSE near the river has stone quoins and the date 1756 in the pediment. Chapels stand all round the large churchyard. The first is ALPHA PRESBYTERIAN CHAPEL, 1903 by *Habershon, Fawkner & Groves*, but originally built in 1747 under Howell Harris's direction. Opposite, LLANFAIR, a small villa of 1820 with a Tuscan porch. Next is HOREB CONGREGATIONAL CHAPEL, 1869 by *R. Moffatt Smith*, with a spire, and then the BAPTIST CHAPEL of 1899 by *George Morgan & Son*. Then the low C18 OLD HALL, and the early C19 HAFOD with a Venetian window and PETERWELL with tiny two-storey Regency bows. Turning l. down High Street and Broad Street to the early C19 LION HOTEL, there is the town's best building – the MARKET HOUSE by *Haddon Brothers*, 1875.* It is of stone, with an arcade of seven varied openings below, some with traceries, then terracotta portrait roundels, terracotta machicolations, and a big red-tiled hipped roof. The prototype, roughly, is Italian C13/14 town halls, carried out here in colourful materials. It stands beside the six-arched BRIDGE, first built by *James Parry* of Hay in 1779 but widened on the downstream side in 1925.

ABERDUHONW, 1¼ m. E. Behind the C19 front is a mid C17 staircase. BARN with attractive arched openings, such classicism being a feature of mid C19 Breconshire builders. (DAIRY(?) with upper-cruck roof.)

BWLCH

CASTELL BLAENLLYNFI, ½ m. NW. The strategic castle controlling the small lordship of Blaenllynfi has an obscure and confused history. It was held by many prominent Marcher families in the C13 and C14. When it received its wet moat and stone curtain is not known exactly. The later, well cemented square buttresses are now more intact than the walls themselves. The plan of the defences and interior buildings has been partly revealed by recent excavation.

CROSFIELD HOUSE (British Legion). The home of the Games family from the C16 and of the Gwynne-Holford family in the C19, when it was called BUCKLAND. Rebuilt by *S. W. Williams* after a fire in 1895 in Elizabethan style. In the large main room, which looks W, a great dividing stair with an arcaded gallery above. An Elizabethanizing 86 ft long gallery passes this. The house built for Roderick Gwynne of Glanbran, Carmarthenshire, *c.* 1775 had a three-storey NE front with a colonnade and pediment, and wings beside. The NW façade had Ionic pilasters on a basement supporting a balustrade, and pediments on the wings. The grounds included a lily-garden designed by *Avray Tipping*.

PEN Y GAER (SO 169 219), a small Roman fort belonging to the earlier half of the occupation of Wales, lies on the road from Abergavenny to Brecon Gaer. The large rampart has been heightened and strengthened with a stone wall on two occasions, and it is this defence which is all that can be recognized today. The N side is clear, but the others have been somewhat confused by later banks and buildings.

* Now converted into the Wyeside Arts Centre, without excessive loss of character.

CAER BERIS *see* CILMERI

CANTREF   0020

1¼ m. WSW of Llanfrynach

ST MARY. W tower; nave and chancel in one. The tower, of
c. 1600, is broad and quite plain, with rectangular chamfered
windows, the belfry window mullioned. Pyramidal roof. Low
pointed E doorway. Nave rebuilt in 1829, and altered in 1867
by *C. Buckeridge*. The claustral look of thickly plastered walls
is typical of him. Trefoiled lancets. The demarcation of the
chancel is gracefully managed, for once – E.E. shafts from floor
level with foliate capitals supporting a septifoil wooden truss. –
FONT. Circular and tapering, on a cylindrical base; C12 but
recut, probably.

CAPEL Y FFIN   2030

CHURCH. Just a rudimentary rectangular hall, only *c.* 25 by
13 ft inside, in an enclosure of ancient yews. The date is perhaps
1762. Rectangular windows. Pyramidal W bellcote, stone-tiled
like the roof. S porch of 1817. Steps in the SW corner lead to
the GALLERY which occupies the W wall and then runs right
to the E wall. – Other contemporary furnishings are the octagonal PULPIT, 1780, the ALTAR RAILS, and the SETTLES (one
dated 1783). – The FONT looks medieval; an octagon, tapering
below a vertical rim. The base is also old. – CHURCHYARD
CROSS. Moulded rectangular shaft, and base.
MONASTERY. Father Ignatius (the Rev. Joseph Lyne) established an Anglican Benedictine monastery at 1,150 ft in the
Honddu valley in 1869, calling it Llanthony Tertia. After his
death in 1908 it became dependent on the Caldey Island priory,
and in 1924 passed into the possession of Eric Gill. The cloister
was begun in 1870, the church in 1872, by *Charles Buckeridge*
(† 1873) and continued by *J. L. Pearson*, who took over his
practice.
    CHURCH. The three-bay chancel, the one part of an ambi-
tious plan to reproduce Llanthony to be realized on such an
awkward site, was to have four lateral chapels. Building continued till 1882; the vaults fell *c.* 1920. Its noble style was based
on the transitional Romanesque/E.E. of its model; so the wall-
shafts are very slender but have scalloped capitals. SEDILIA
etc. in late C13 E.E. Some restoration, e.g. to Father Ignatius'

grave, *c.* 1970. The flamboyant German reredos is at St Julius and St Aaron, near Newport, Gwent.

The separate CLOISTER, up the slope on the SW, and far smaller than the full monastic establishment of the first conception, is to a design of pristine simplicity by Buckeridge. Paired lancets under hoods, between buttresses, below: lancets by ones above. The N side of the quadrangle was closed by the erection of a CHAPEL (Our Lady and St David) among the roof members in the late 1920s. Some inscriptions on the beams by *Eric Gill*; also an early gravestone (1907). On the S side a double doorway opens to the refectory, which has ceiling beams on corbels. On the wall a notable Crucifixion painted by *David Jones c.* 1930 in a moving Byzantinizing style; also a humorous mural by *D. Tegetmeier*, 1934.

1030

CASTELL DINAS
2¾ m. SSE of Talgarth

The Dinas Brân of South Wales, dominating the W flank of the Black Mountains. At 1,476 ft this is the highest castle site in Wales or England. Inside an extensive Iron Age hillfort with multiple ramparts are the traces of a C12 castle with two wards and a hornwork. Apart from fragments of the medieval walls (e.g. near the N postern and main W gates) at the surface, it is difficult to distinguish the elements of the defences. The oblique entrance to the earlier fort may be recognized at the N from air photographs. The upper (N) ward, completely walled, with five or six square towers (one still has a two-centred arch), was divided from the middle ward by a ditch. At its centre the collapsed late C12 rectangular stone keep, *c.* 65 ft by 40 ft, within a chemise wall. The deep rock-cut dry moat round both wards is medieval. Owain Glyndŵr seems to have held Castell Dinas as his operational base *c.* 1401.

In the hills around are a number of Long Cairns.

See
p.
20 TY ISAF LONG CAIRN (SO 182 291). The classic Breconshire 'Severn Cotswold' neolithic tomb, excavated by Professor Grimes (*Proceedings of the Prehistoric Society* IV, 1939). However, though the cairn 100 ft long and 50 ft broad remains, the complex chambers have been filled in and are scarcely visible.

CWM FFOREST (SO 182 292). Another long cairn of the same type, also showing evidence of a chamber and dry-stone walling.

MYNYDD TROED (SO 161 284). Another 'Severn Cotswold'

long cairn with some evidence of stone chambers in the centre. Excavation revealed dry-stone walling along the sides, a very characteristic feature of these cairns.

CASTLE MADOC *see* LOWER CHAPEL

CATHEDINE   *1020*

ST MICHAEL. Chancel with a Dec window and N tower with a steep pyramidal roof by *E. H. Martineau*, 1868; nave with lancets rebuilt by *S. W. Williams* in 1894. – FONT. C13; plain, circular. – GLASS. E, mostly patterned, *c.* 1868. – S sanctuary by *Mayer & Co.*, Munich.

TREHOLFORD. Stucco. With a segmental two-storey bow at the r. end of each of three sides. Partly late C18 and partly built in 1837 for the Gwynne Holford family, and more Victorian than Regency in plan but not in elevation.

CATHEDINE FAWR, $\frac{3}{4}$ m. N. The sandstone emblem over the door has the date 1699. Five bays and two storeys with the dripcourse rising above the mullioned and transomed ground-floor windows. Pedimental gable. Hipped roof and end chimneys.

CEFNCOEDYCYMMER*   *0000*

ST JOHN. 1874 by *Robinson* of Cardiff. Nave, and chancel with an individualistic buttressed S steeple.

ST TUDOR. 1888.

Cefncoedycymmer belongs geographically with Merthyr Tydfil in the area N of the confluence of the Taf Fawr and the Taf Fechan, and embraces an incongruous whorl of postwar houses at Trefechan. The drama of its position is in its rivers and their bridges. The earliest, taking a road over the Taf Fawr, PONT-Y-CEFN, has a single elliptical arch of *c.* 1804 (or earlier).

CEFN COED RAILWAY VIADUCT. By *Savin & Ward* (contractors) and *Henry Conybeare* and *Alexander Sutherland* (their engineers), 1865–6. A gigantic, confident bridge curving round high over the houses and 122 ft above the river. There are fifteen arches in all. The cost was £25,000. Abandoned by the Brecon–Merthyr railway line, it now serves as the best point from which to see Cyfarthfa Castle and Merthyr Tydfil downstream, and from which to view the concrete ROAD VIADUCT, by *Rendel, Palmer & Tritton*, for the Heads of the Valleys route

* Transferred to Mid Glamorgan in 1974.

just upstream (1964), whose slender deck and supports make a telling contrast with the sturdy masonry tradition of the Victorian engineers.

(ST MARY, NANTDDU, 5 m. NNW. A nave-and-chancel chapel rebuilt by *C. Buckeridge* in 1863.)

CERRIG DUON see GLYNTAWE

CHRIST COLLEGE see BRECON, p. 293

0050

CILMERI
Llanganten parish

ST CANNEN. Only a few yards from the River Chwefru. Small nave and chancel, rebuilt in 1882 by *Lewis Powell* of Hereford. – FONT. C12. Circular, with four angular projections. – MONUMENTS. Posthuma Price † 1712 and Rees Price † 1712; a local, armorial pair.

CEFN-Y-BEDD, ¼ m. W. On a grassed mound protected by a hedge, a jagged, 15 ft high monolith of Caernarvonshire granite was erected in 1956 to mark the place where Llywelyn, the last native Prince of Wales, was killed in a skirmish on 11 December 1282.

CAER BERIS, 1¼ m. ESE. A tall C12 MOTTE on a stony ridge in a loop of the River Irfon. On the bailey a large neo-Jacobean timber-framed house built between 1896 and 1911 by Harcourt Wood has a replica of a courtyard of an English border counties manor house. Its S wing is built out on elm baulks over sharply falling ground. In the dining room a C16 stone fireplace and panelling perhaps from Emral Hall, Flintshire.

2010

CLYDACH*

The iron industry controlled by the Hanbury family in the Clydach gorge was in existence by the last decade of the C16. Forge Row works had the date 1603 over a door. Part of a C17 charcoal FURNACE remains (*see* Llanelly). Clydach works was set up at the end of the C18 (when the Brecon and Monmouthshire Canal was also being built). W. H. Cooke and E. Frere bought out the Hanburys and in 1790 started tinplate-making. Remains of coke-fired BLAST FURNACES built into the hillside. The

* Transferred to Gwent in 1974.

industry closed down in 1884, and the tenement housing was recently demolished. A small IRON BRIDGE survives, dated 1824; its shallow arch is formed of four girders with Gothic strutting.

CLYDACH HOUSE. Five bays and three storeys. Original William and Mary windows at the rear. Over the door are the arms of Francis Lewis, who came here as manager of the Llanelly Furnace, and the date, 1693, when the house was built. The centrally placed staircase, rising in two storeys round a well, has twisted balusters and other carved details.

CRAI/LLANILID   *8020*

ST ILID. By *J. B. Fowler*, 1882. Single-chamber with three-sided apse.

(TANYFEDW, 1 m. NNW. A shed with a trefoiled ogee window (late C15) in its wall might have been an ecclesiastical building.)

(TIRCAPEL, 2 m. NNW. Partly built from stones from the Celtic chapel of St Ilud, where the Llywel stone (now in the British 8 Museum) was found. Date-stone 1831. DOE).

LLYWEL. *See* p. 359.

CRAIG-Y-NOS *see* GLYNTAWE

CRICKADARN   *0040*

ST MARY. In a circular raised churchyard. Nave and chancel in one, perhaps C14, with a sightly C16 three-stage embattled tower and a NW stair-turret with a Tudor arch to the nave. The two-centred S doorway and S priest's doorway and the single and paired lancets in the N wall are the earliest details. Perp the E window (cf. Llandefalle) and the two ogee S windows. The nave roof is ceiled, but a large tie-beam and braces over the site of the former screen are visible. Very good C15 S porch of the Wye valley type (cf. Aberedw, Radnorshire). Two trusses, both with quatrefoil and trefoil cusping and the outer one also arch-braced, and a trefoil arched truss between them, together with two tiers of foiled wind-braces, were used in its elaborate little roof. A rough stoup on the l. Restorations in 1867 and 1895, and again *c.* 1910, when *Sir Clough Williams-Ellis* buttressed the leaning walls and provided at the W an oval vestry window, a balcony, and the fireplace. – FONT. C14/15, plain, octagonal. – MONUMENT. William ap David Lloyd † 1607.

Large slab with a fleur-de-lys cross, a coat of arms, and lettering round the margins; the widespread C17 local format.

POOL HALL, ½ m. w. On a cruciform Restoration plan. The original door within the open arched porch has the initials. of the builder (later High Sheriff) Howel Powel, and the date 1670. The typically massive character of the period is exemplified in the carved doorheads, and more strongly in the timber stair with its traditional Jacobean diamond-finialled newel-posts and sturdy, but turned, balusters.

(Two medieval EARTHWORKS, ¼ m. SW, and 1¾ m. WSW.)

CRICKHOWELL/CRUCYWEL

2010

ST EDMUND. Large but plain, on a C14 cruciform plan with a central crossing tower and N and S aisles. All but the chancel much altered. The land was given by Lady Sibyl Pauncefoot in 1303, when the church was built. Much of interest in the chancel. The intersecting three-light E window is restored, but the N and S ones are narrow trefoiled lancets. PISCINA and a trefoil-headed SEDILE. N and S priest's doorways. Vestry added beyond. On the N three sepulchral recesses with, from W to E, early C14 keeled mouldings and a hood; a double order of late C14 wavy mouldings, the inner resting on colonnettes; and again two keeled rolls, with foliate stops to the hood. On the S only two recesses, both with quarter-round mouldings. Double-chamfered crossing arches. Tall two-lancet transept windows with Geometrical tracery. The transepts were known as Rumsey Chapel and Gwernvale Chapel. The nave arcades are not of the first build and not identically set out; their E arches are now wide (but not of the same width) and lack responds – for the sake of a screen perhaps? Restored W window with C14 trefoiled tracery. In the S aisle a Perp cinquefoiled niche with pinnacles. The aisle walls were pulled down in 1765 and replaced in 1826 and 1835. Restoration in the early 1860s included work on the tall post-medieval(?) broach-spire on the tower; for this the architect was *J. L. Pearson*. At a further restoration in 1897 the roofs were all renewed. – FONT. A serpentine-section bowl dated 1668 with C19 additions. – Lady Chapel (S transept) REREDOS, a fine Crucifixion designed by *W. D. Caröe*, c. 1934. – Main REREDOS, c. 1893, with the Last Supper beneath ornate canopies in stone. – GLASS. E of the 1890s (?); W of c. 1870 and excellent in colour; S transept by *C. A. Gibbs*, London. – MONUMENTS. In one S chancel

recess, Sir Grimbald Pauncefoot († 1287), first quarter of the
c14. Cross-legged recumbent effigy with the legs and r. arm
mutilated, in a chain mail helmet. His shield charged with
three lionels. – In the N recess opposite, Lady Sybil
Pauncefoot † 1326, a recumbent effigy lacking the hands, in a
long folded robe. The head is naturalistic and fairly well preserved. – Sir John and Lady Joan Herbert, 1690. Alabaster
figures, she lying in front on a cushion, he in armour, con-
fidently leaning on his l. arm, looking out. His achievement
of arms above. On the r. of the tomb small kneeling figures
of Elizabeth and William LeHunt † 1694 and 1703.*

CASTLE. Scattered ruins of uncertain history. Abandoned in the
c15, the castle was mostly pulled down by the c19. The earliest
part is a large motte, perhaps of the c11; on top are the fallen
remains of a shell keep c. 25 yds in diameter. E of that are two
abutted towers, one circular and one rectangular, both of the
same date. G. T. Clark suggested that the circular one was the
gate tower. It has three storeys, the second and third octagonal,
but placed so that the walls of the lower support the angles of
the upper; these two floors have early c14 windows and the
remains of fireplaces. The rectangular tower had four floors.
Just W of the mound is the ruin of another circular tower, this
one of the early 1300s. These buildings were made for Sir
Grimbald Pauncefoot. The ground between is a raised bailey.
On the river side there appears to have been an eight-acre enclosure, which Buck's engraving (1741) shows defended with
a curtain wall and angle drum-towers. In TOWER STREET a
pair of small battlemented drum-towers (one almost destroyed)
with c15 windows, supposed to be the gateway to the town.
The town received a murage grant in 1281; no sign of walls
exists today.

CRICKHOWELL BRIDGE. Gently curving upstream on a series
of substantial piers, this and Llangynidr Bridge are the loveliest
bridges surviving across the Usk. A comparatively broad roadway is carried over the river on eight arches, and on another
five dry arches on the w bank. It is of c16/17 type with segmental arches and cutwaters with refuges. Widened in 1810 and
often repaired. A bridge here is mentioned in 1558.

PERAMBULATION. Richard Fenton in 1804 called Crickhowell
'the most cheerful looking town I ever saw'. It certainly has
a worthwhile diversity of buildings and a neat prosperity deriv-

* The Rev. Cyril James kindly corrected me on several points concerning
the church.

ing from the C19. The borough charter was granted in 1283. The market hall stood at the junction of Beaufort Street with High Street, where the Lucas Memorial is. Starting from there, HIGH STREET leads SW between early C19 stucco-fronted houses. On the l. JUBILEE HOUSE, which has a Grecian front with two pediments on Ionic and Tuscan pilasters, was the new Market and Town Hall built in 1833–4 by *T. H. Wyatt*. The BRITANNIA INN is C17 with a C19 front. On the corner of TOWER STREET the YOUTH HOSTEL, a five-bay house of 1719, with flat keystone heads over the windows, and Ionic pilasters and a pediment round the door. Gabled roof with modillion cornice, and a pediment with a lunette – early C18 details rare in Wales. (Opposite a terrace of small stucco fronts with a pediment.) Next on the l. is an C18 house, the DRAGON, with a Venetian window with triglyph frieze pushing up the cornice on the first floor, and on the r. opposite LATHAM HOUSE, also C18, with an open doorway pediment. At the top of BRIDGE STREET on the r. is HERBERT HALL, a C17 house with an Early Victorian stucco front of five bays with an eaves gable. At the bottom, by the bridge, BETHABARA BAPTIST CHAPEL, which was rebuilt in 1840 with a two-storey front, round-headed windows on the first floor, and a Tuscan porch.

Back in CASTLE ROAD, DAN-Y-CASTELL has a classical door-case of c. 1790. L. again round the castle and l. into the main road (BEAUFORT STREET) for the CLARENCE HALL, 1891. Up STANDARD STREET is THE MALT HOUSE, the former house of the Rumsey family, a large altered C16 and C17 house, H-fronted, with a small two-storey GAZEBO with Gothic upper windows, of c. 1800, behind. Some stone-hooded windows in the E wing. A hundred yards beyond the BEAR, a former coaching inn standing by a cobbled pavement at the top of the SQUARE, is a long embattled wall. The gateway in it, PORTH MAWR, has Tudor arches, C19 vaulting, an upper chamber lit by two hooded windows, and a stair-turret and battlemented parapet. It is coeval with Great Porthaml's but deeper. It was built by the Monmouthshire Herbert family for their house, Cwrt-y-Carw, which has gone, but was probably quite small. PORTHMAWR HOUSE on the old site has a stucco W façade of five bays and a low sprocketed roof. Fashionable details include a dainty triglyph frieze below the eaves, and fan-ironwork in the spandrels of the veranda.

On PEN-Y-DRE FARM below is a small C19 gazebo.

GLAN-NANT, ½ m. NW. A square Regency Tudor-windowed house of *c.* 1800 with a semi-octagonal corner wing.

GWERN-VALE (HOTEL), ¾ m. N. The central block with a segmental bow was built by *John Newby*, *c.* 1795. The porch at the side, of six Tuscan columns (with Ionic responds), the central four supporting an entablature and pediment, and a drawing room with a screen of slender Corinthian columns are nearly intact. The house was the home of Sir George Everest, after whom the mountain was named.

GWERNVALE BURIAL CHAMBER (SO 201 192) has been recently excavated because of roadworks. Formerly only the central chamber was visible, but the base of an exceptionally long trapezoid cairn, a 'dummy portal' and forecourt, and two lateral chambers at the W end have now been exposed. All these features are highly characteristic of the Severn-Cotswold group of Neolithic tombs.

MOTTE, 1 m. NW. The earlier castle of Crickhowell. Possibly built by Sir Humphrey Burghill of Brecon Castle, and a few years later in the possession of the Turberville family, according to Theophilus Jones. They are mentioned in 1121.

MAESCELYÑ, 1¼ m. NW. 1873. Rather pedestrian; possibly by *Pearson.* Clusters of round chimneys, and an oriel over the porch. Half-timbered LODGE of 1887.

CRUG HYWEL (SO 225 206). A small hillfort on a spur of the Black Mountains above Crickhowell. The pear-shaped area is defended by a rampart and deep ditch with a smaller (counterscarp) bank on the outside. Inturned entrance on the W side.

CRUCYWEL *see* CRICKHOWELL

CWMDU   *1020*

ST MICHAEL. In part of good Perp architecture. The W tower with battlements, turret, and W doorway may encase the only masonry remaining from the church whose consecration by Herwald in the C11 is recorded in the Liber Landavensis, together with that of Partrishow and Llanbedr churches. Contemporary with the tower are the components of a fine church of the 1430s, consisting of nave, N and S aisles, and choir, which was extensively rebuilt in 1831–3 at a cost of £2,000 for the incumbent, Thomas Price (known also by his bardic name Carnhuanawc; the antiquary, and Celtic and Welsh historian);

hence the very short chancel of contemporary orthodoxy – but hence also the retention of any of the old work at all. The plans were drawn by Mr *Pratt* of Crickhowell. The church was rebuilt again by *Caröe* with *Hunt & Baldwin* in 1907, when the N aisle was removed. Windows of extreme length remain, a big E window with panel tracery and a five-light straight-headed S window particularly. Fine W arch; the others much renewed. C15 S porch, the doorway earlier than the windows, with a barrel ceiling. Priest's porch too, with a pointed but similar ceiling, and two niches of the 1830 work. In it are two fragments of stone crosses of the C11–12. In the S buttress a late C6–early C7 PILLAR STONE incised with a Latin inscription, CATACUS HIC IACIT/FILIUS TEGERNACUS, and Ogams. – ROYAL ARMS. In stone, early C19, by *J. Jones*, Crickhowell. – SCREEN. The dado, muntins, traceries, and head-beam with running ornament (late C15) are placed round the sanctuary. – CHURCHYARD CROSS. Steps, base, and part of the shaft only. – (In the churchyard a PILLAR STONE with a Latin cross incised in the C7–9, and a later burial inscription.)

A VICARAGE was made for Thomas Price *c.* 1840 from a barn; he had a cromlech and a menhir built in the garden.

Llanfihangel Cwmdu was the old Welsh settlement, Tretower (*see* p. 379) the Norman one.

(FELINDRE FARMHOUSE, ½ m. SSW. C17, with a Tudor-headed rear doorway, and panelled bedrooms with arched doorways. DOE)

MIDDLE GAER, 1½ m. SSW. Built in the third quarter of the C16 with separate Tudor doorways to the cross-passage and lower room. An early instance of the plan-type B with the fireplace abutting the passage. It was entirely of two storeys from the start, as the corbelled chimney to the first-floor room at the lower end shows.

A narrow BRIDGE at Felindre crosses over the Rhiangoll by two arches, with cutwaters and refuges. Built perhaps *c.* 1700. Most of the tributaries flowing into the Usk from the N are crossed by old bridges, but few on the S.

DDERW *see* LLYSWEN

9020   DEFYNNOG

St CYNOG. Nave and chancel in one, N aisle, S porch, W tower. The font, stoup, and an incised stone are exceptional evidence of Christianity in this wild upland area before the Norman Conquest. Part of the N nave wall, with a squarish blocked window formed of two jambs and a lintel slightly cut into for the head and far overlapping the jambs, seems to survive from the Celtic church. Tall tower with three storeys of round- and camberheaded small windows, a SE stair-turret, and details of the late C15 – a deep splayed base, gargoyles, and battlements. Big coursed Tudor stonework. The body of the church appears to date from *c.* 1500. Broad nave with a barrel-ceiled roof, the moulded ribs set close together. N chantry chapel, similarly roofed, built with its E end aligned with the chancel's and divided by a three-bay Perp arcade. The N respond looks earlier. Fenestration throughout with two odd Perp types. In the N and S walls an almost round-headed frame with two mullions, the outer pair of lights with a single cusp at impost level, the inner with a trefoil head but otherwise plain. The two E windows are four-light, then eight tall lights of panel tracery; no transom. The W end of the nave was partitioned off to make a schoolroom. Some restoration in 1888. S porch with outer and inner C15 doorways. – STOUP. Pre-Norman? Square, with raised panels on three sides. – FONT. Early C11? The base is square, rising to a flanged circle from which four fleurs-de-lys run back into its corners (cf. Partrishow font for this leaf-form). Two round stones with a ring-moulding between them form the shaft. The bowl is deeply undercut and decorated on the sides with a band of billets and a band of crosses and spaces. On the rim the only example of Runic writing in Wales, an indication of Viking settlement here despite the distance from the sea. A further inscription in Lombardic letters, repeating the Runic, reads: SIWURD + GWLMER. – PULPIT. C18. – REREDOS. Carved oak; 1907. – PILLAR STONE. Immured at the S W corner of the base of the tower. Inscribed RUGNIATIO [FI] LI VENDONI, and with Ogams. At the top a Celtic circled cross and a St Andrew's cross design. The inscription must be C5 or C6, the crosses C7–9. – MONUMENTS. Evan David † 1761; with a simple Last Judgement. – GLASS. Chancel S by *Mayer & Co.*, Munich. – The two E windows appear to be by the same maker. – The church is fitted with delightful oil STANDARD LAMPS. – LYCHGATE (transoms and tracery across the arches), 1903.

VICARAGE. Built for the Rev. Moses Williams, the Welsh scholar and bibliographer, and dated 1721 in the roof. Three bays, two storeys, and the usual sprocketed hipped roof; i.e. the familiar type of vicarage on a modest scale. Four rooms and central stairs, with contemporary details.

CHURCH ROW. C19 estate cottages with Tudor chimneys and window hoods and pointed doors. The line is broken by three projecting gables.

(TREPHILIP is an early C19 white stucco-fronted house with long Regency windows and a portico.)

ELAN VILLAGE

9060

Elan Village was built in 1906–9 on the Breconshire side of the Elan valley reservoir complex, to provide for the maintenance staff. A suspension bridge crosses the river to it. The pairs of cottages – C20 stone traditionalism – are widely spaced along the naturally garden-city riverside site. The school has pride of place on a rise behind. The architects were *Buckland, Haywood & Farmer* of Birmingham.

LLANNERCH-Y-CAWR, 3 m. SW. A cruck-built long-house – a good example of the medieval house-type. Probably early C16. Two trusses survive in the hall. The wide doorway on the long (SE) side leads l. to the upper, dwelling section, and r. to the byre. C17 details in the hall include the chimney, stone spiral stair, upper floor, and post-and-panel partitions. At and after the same period, the original timber walls were replaced with stone. It is 77 ft long.

ELAN VALLEY (R). *See* p. 230.

FELINDRE

1030

1½ m. S of Glasbury

53 OLD GWERNYFED. A large stone Jacobean manor house built, probably, by Sir David Williams, M.P. for Brecon, between his purchase of the estate in 1600 and his death in 1613. The Williams family also built Llangoed, Llyswen, and made that their home from *c.* 1730 instead. The front is symmetrical, the plan an E. The main rooms and stair were in the SW wing – a shell since a fire *c.* 1780. Fortunately it is intact enough not to mar one of Breconshire's best set-pieces. The middle section is of five bays, and in the full-height porch projection one is curious to see a C13 doorway employed as the outer arch. This has a two-centred arch and two orders, the inner a continuous quarter-round moulding, the outer ringed jamb-shafts with scalloped capitals and a roll-moulding. Llanthony was tradi-

tionally taken as its provenance.* The inner door has a wicket.
On the r. a secondary doorway with rustication of *c.* 1700 and
a Tudor head. The r. wing, the service wing, is set about with
big external chimneys, one of which serves a (later?) fireplace
with a 12 ft arch. Inside the main door a cross-passage screened
from the hall on the l. by fluted wooden columns with egg-and-
dart as capitals, and panelling – all confused evidence now.
They carry a gallery (above the passage) with spiral balusters.
Big fireplace with a deep flush lintel. The ceiling of this tallest
room retains part of its early C17 geometrical plaster ceiling of
interlaced ribs and separate leaf ornament; the wainscoting was
moved from upstairs. On the first floor fragments of contemporary ceilings and of wall painting. A date on a fireplace (1680)
tells of alterations.

SE of the house a pair of circular DOVECOTES with conical
roofs and Tudor doorways belongs to the original forecourt layout. The pair of rusticated GATEPIERS between them was
moved *c.* 1930 from the NW. They and a second pair *in situ* –
both late C17 and with ball-finials like ones at Hay Castle –
seem to correspond with the old drive. Another set, on the road,
carved with lions and oak branches, was moved from *Nesfield*'s
Gwernyfed Park.

TREGOYD (Fellowship House), 1 m. NE. Rebuilt after a fire in
1900. Red brick with a segmental portico. Neo-Georgian wing
and alterations of 1914. Its predecessor was the C17 gabled
house of Lord Hereford.

(PEN TWYN, *c.* 1 m. E. A cruck-trussed barn, C16 (?).)

(BRIDGE. C17(?); with two segmental arches on cutwaters.)

GARTHBRENGY   *0030*

1 m. NE of Llandefaelog Fach

ST DAVID. C17 W tower. Nave and chancel in one, with a low
Perp N arcade of three bays, walled in; the three two-light cinquefoiled windows are those of the N aisle demolished in the
mid C19. Restorations in 1834 by *William Jones*; also in 1874
and in 1901. – FONT. Octagonal, C15? – STOUP. C12; four-
lobed. – Low SCREEN dated 1912. – MONUMENT. John
Jones † 1835 and others, by *S. M. Sarne.* This type with

* Dr Ralegh Radford has suggested that this was the doorway to the chapter
house in the vanished claustral buildings of Brecon Priory, with a date in the
second quarter of the C13.

several memorials worked into one design is not uncommon. –
Others in the *Brute* style.

(PANTYCORED. Long, early C17 house with a staircase wing; the
front with early C18 windows. The elaborately moulded parlour
doorway has vase stops.)

GELLI, Y, *see* HAY-ON-WYE

2010

GLANGRWYNE

HALL FARM, ½ m. N. A small Tudor farmhouse with the original
door and stone door frame; other details obscured.

LLANGRWYNE COURT (formerly Sunny Bank). A three-
storeyed stuccoed front with semicircular bows and the look
of the 1850s, though the plan would be a common one for
c. 1830.

GLANGRWYNE BRIDGE, over the Grwyne, was built in 1773
by *Andrew Maund* of Brecon. Three arches, the central one the
highest. Still with the traditional large cutwaters and refuges.

THE FORGE HOUSE. A sophisticated front range for the Welsh
borders: three-sided central bay of one storey only, flush plaster
quoins, and pedimental doorcase with detail of *c*. 1800.

Below on the Grwyne is the site of Walter Watkins's iron forge,
which worked till 1842; it is reputed to have been started in
1720. Watkins and his son-in-law, Charles Cracroft, built the
Pen-y-cae furnace at Ebbw Vale in 1790.

IRON BRIDGE of *c*. 1856 over the Usk. A very long span, with
flat girders on iron columns, but of no visual interest.

GLANUSK PARK *see* PENMYARTH

1030

GLASBURY

The old village is in Radnorshire (*see* p. 233), but the Wye was
crossed here from 1777 by a bridge built by *William Edwards*
of Pontypridd. It was carried away in 1795. After the river
changed its course *c*. 1660 the old church was abandoned and a
new one built on the Breconshire bank.

ST PETER. By *Lewis Vulliamy*, 1837–8. Goodhart-Rendel described it as 'a large meeting house thing, at present ungalleried,
with a w tower, in pseudo-Romanesque'. Strip pilasters,
corbel-tables, and windows beneath relieving arches, details
weakly copied by the later chancel (1881). The tower has stark

corner spirelets with pyramidal points, and a shafted W doorway. Big aisleless interior, with a roundel above the chancel arch and an elaborate trussed roof. – The iron SCREEN was part of the alterations of 1881. – Terracotta and mosaic REREDOS by *Powell*'s of Blackfriars, 1894. – FONT dated 1635, octagonal still, and with crude raised and incised ornament. From the chapel at Aberllynfi. – MONUMENT. Walter de Winton † 1840, Gothic, by *J. E. Thomas* of Brecon. – GLASS. W, the Woman of Samaria, monogrammed E.F., 1890. – N, Christ and St Peter walking on the water, *c.* 1933. By *Comper*?

Only mounds mark the collapse of the OLD CHURCH on the Wye flats ¼ m. N of St Peter.

TREBLE HILL BAPTIST CHAPEL. 1866. Red brick with a front of four stone pilasters and a pediment.

BROOMFIELD. An 1830ish Italianate villa, the centre of three storeys and a basement, projecting from lower wings. On the r. a porch with fluted Doric columns.

MOTTE AND BAILEY, ½ m. SW.

ABERLLYNFI HOUSE. Mid Georgian, with a careful front: both roof and dormers are hipped, and the central accent is a Venetian window with a bull's eye over.

LLWYNAU BACH, ½ m. NE. A large barn built in the early C19 for a horse-threshing engine. At r. angles a stable, also hipped-roofed and with a round window. Possibly associated with the Hay and Brecon Tramway of 1812, which ran just above.

GLYNTAWE   *8010*

ST CALLWEN. Rebuilt in 1893 by *S. W. Williams*. Single-chamber.

CRAIG-Y-NOS (ADELINA PATTI HOSPITAL), 1½ m. SW. The designs for the original house (called Bryn Melin) for Rhys Davies Powell, built in 1841–3, were by *T. H. Wyatt* (and shown at the Royal Academy as *Wyatt & Brandon*). The landscape appears to have called for a baronial response, and as much as was built forms the central section. A sort of tower-house bristles with Scottish quirks – an embattled porch, a recessed panel above (at first with queer machicolations), a pair of pyramidal roofs with a gablet between, a tourelle at the side. Step-gable in the r. wing. Tasteless extensions of 1891 to N and S in bright pink Crai stone, including a clock tower, for Dame Adelina Patti. Her winter garden, moved to Swansea, is known as the Patti Pavilion. Her THEATRE here is the mecca for her devotees. Its pilastered façade abuts the clock tower at the bay next its frontispiece. The architects were *Bucknall & Jennings* of Swansea, 1890; decoration by *Jackson & Sons* of London. The plan is a miniature version of Bayreuth's (it holds 150) with a segmental back wall. An order of free fluted Corinthian columns runs all round, including (in the form of pilasters) the back wall. Proscenium flanked by paired columns. Continuous frieze inscribed with the names of composers of opera – Rossini's in pride of place. Coved ceiling. The colours are gold, pastel green, and peach. Ingenuity contrived a floor which can be level through to the back of the stage; or which after the removal of boards and the lowering of jacks can provide an orchestra pit and a raked auditorium. On the stage remain a set of garden scenery painted in oils by *Steinhardt* and a curtain drop by *Hawes Craven* depicting Madame Patti as Semiramide.

DAN YR OGOF CAVE. A less well known part of this cave system, OGOF YR ESGYRN (SN 839 160), revealed evidence for occupation in the Middle Bronze Age (pottery and metalwork) and in the Romano–British period. Caves were quite often inhabited in the later period, but it is rare to find Bronze Age occupation sites of any kind.

5 CERRIG DUON AND MAEN MAWR (SN 852 206). On a small flat-topped promontory just on the W side of the river is an important group of Bronze Age ritual monuments: a large circle of low stones approached at a tangent by an 'avenue' of even smaller stones (often rather difficult to find – they are on the NE side of the circle but do not lead into it). Just outside the circle to the N is a very large stone (Maen Mawr) which makes the monument easy to spot from the road. Behind it are two more low stones set in line. Seen from behind Maen Mawr the circle is outlined against the dramatic view of the valley to the s, a careful siting no doubt important to its builders in the mid second millennium B.C., though some claim that there may have been additional astronomical significance in the alignment of these monuments. This group, with circle, avenue, outlier, and cairns to the s, is characteristic of several Welsh sites of this period; it is also one of the finest, and easy to reach. Another large prehistoric stone may be seen further N on the E side of the valley. Several Breconshire valleys have these large stones at the head (cf. Maen Llia).

GREAT PORTHAML *see* TALGARTH

GWENDDWR
0040

1¾ m. WNW of Crickadarn

ST DUBRICIUS. A simple single-chamber church extensively repaired in 1886. Of the old work the C14 S and blocked priest's doorways; two chancel N lancets and a Perp sanctuary window; and the small octagonal FONT. The C15 S porch roof resembles Crickadarn's, with its two quatrefoil and trefoil trusses and an arched one between and pairs of foiled wind-braces. W tower much rebuilt. – MONUMENT. A floreated cross to a member of the Gunter family † 1580(?). – The Cistercian Abbey Dore, Herefordshire, had a priory at Gwenddwr.

GWERNYFED see FELINDRE

HAY-ON-WYE/Y GELLI
2040

ST MARY. A church appropriated to Brecon Priory and dedicated between 1115 and 1135 collapsed c. 1700, leaving only the embattled C15 W tower. The present sub-Georgian nave and short chancel are by *Edward Haycock Senior*, 1834; big lancets alternating with buttresses, and inside, a gallery added round the W and N sides. Some additions to the chancel of 1866, by *Nicholson*(?): a semicircular apse, the base steeply battered, then three small lancets under dogtooth hoodmoulds and a corbel-table and steep roof. Also an intrusive three-bay chancel screen of banded stone with spreading transitional C12 leaf capitals. – Alabaster PULPIT of 1879, with half-length figures of Christ and the four Evangelists in quatrefoils, standing on eight colonnettes in the manner of Giovanni Pisano's mid C13 pulpits at Siena and Pistoia. – MONUMENTS. A recumbent effigy, perhaps of the C14, lies defaced and broken by the S door. – Elizabeth Gwynn † 1702.

E of the church beyond the stream is a MOTTE. The castle is first mentioned in 1121, and in view of the frequent Norman juxtaposition of castle and church, this was certainly its site.

CHAPEL OF ST JOHN, Lion Street. Possibly formed in 1254. Long known as Eglwys Ifan, and the Guild church of Hay in the Middle Ages. Restored in stone in 1930, when the E end was reconverted into a chapel, with a C17 oak reredos at the S.

CASTLE. A large ringwork crowns the hill above the town. On its N a roughly square keep was built c. 1200 by Matilda de Breos. Norman are the S windows to the two floors, the upper one with two round-headed lights and a mullion. After vicissitudes in the early C13 Henry III had the castle rebuilt in 1233, when the keep gained its first-storey E entry, though the major addition was to reface the main gateway. Opening directly from the town, this now stands impressively on a battered footing. The C13 arches are shallow, segmental, and double-chamfered; in between is a portcullis slot, and the C14 inner opening has a three-step arch with one capital. It still possesses medieval wooden doors. The town was burned by Llywelyn ap Iorwerth in 1231, and the town walls went up c. 1236; a section along the N of the ringwork was common to town and castle. The castle was reduced by Simon de Montfort in 1265. Damage in 1460, when it was the property of the Dukes of Buckingham, may have been the cause of repairs to the tower – see the pairs of Early Tudor windows on the N.

The MANSION adjacent to the keep, begun for James Boyle of Hereford c. 1660, is tall and stone-built, of two storeys, with tall moulded brick chimneys. On the N seven shaped dormer gablets of the third quarter of the C17, on the S five with sunk quatrefoil panels, all finialled on the apex and kneelers. On these two sides the windows are early C19 sashes, but the stone mullions and transoms under labels have not been replaced on the W and E. S porch with a four-centred doorhead and a parapet of finials the same as on the gablets. Modish late C17 rusticated gatepiers and balls (cf. Gwernyfed). Much original decoration, including an elaborate Early Jacobean staircase and hall and a room with strapwork carving on the cornice and a plaster overmantel, perished in a fire in the E half of the house in 1939. Restoration c. 1910 by *Caröe*. The W half, gutted in a second fire in 1977, is to be rebuilt. Stabling of the early C19. The C13 walled town of Hay was more or less contained by the walls till their destruction between the late C18 and mid C19. So the parish church and the castle were outliers on the S and W until the early C19. The three gates went early; fragments of the walls, though, remain at the back of the Cattle Market and near the former Water Gate off Newport Street. Two distinct elements of Hay are the pleasing mesh of streets and alleys on the slopes of its fortress precinct, and its modest provincial early C19 classicism in warm grey stone, at the SW particularly. HIGH TOWN combines both characteristics – the jumble of C17 timber-built houses with C19 fronts below the castle, and at the start of MARKET STREET a view of the Cheese Market and the Butter Market. The lower floor of the two-storey CHEESE MARKET is open at either side, where there is a single column

in antis. The deep-eaved pediment faces up the street. The site
is probably that of the C17 market house; the present structure
was made in 1835 for Joseph Bailey, who in 1844 bought the
castle. The BUTTER MARKET, just beyond, is two years its
senior. It is quaintly ambitious, for all its diminutive size – an
uncouth Doric temple three bays by nine, and till recently open
along seven of those. The little columns all have a pronounced
entasis. Follow the street to the BULL RING, a small square
on the far side of which is PEMBERTON HOUSE, early C19 and
well detailed. In LION STREET on the l. the attractive tiled
shop-front of Messrs. WILLIAMS (1886). At the bottom the
TOWN CLOCK (1881), that indispensable if now unfashionable
focus of the Mid Wales towns. This is in off-the-peg Gothic,
with a high plinth and a two-stage spire. The Pavement and
Broad Street converge here. Some variety in BROAD STREET,
for instance the row opposite the clock – a Regency front, a
lower early C18 house with a stone-tiled roof, and the plain late
C19 CROWN HOTEL. The next stretch, going N, is mostly
stucco fronts of the earlier 1800s, with a good five-bay three-
storey example on the r. Either side of the BRIDGE STREET
turning, on the l. farther up, are two timber-framed buildings,
the CAFÉ ROYAL, dated 1623, with a jettied upper floor, and
the THREE TUNS, a small C16 cruck hall with an early C17
conversion to storeys and a large central chimney. The BRIDGE
itself is skeletally constructed with prestressed concrete piers
and beams; engineers *G. Maunsell & Partners*, opened 1958. It
replaces the Hereford, Brecon and Hay railway bridge, built
in 1865 by *Thomas Savin*, which in turn succeeded a road bridge
of 1795 which carried the tram-road too after 1815. Bridge
Street becomes NEWPORT STREET past the Regency-fronted
UNITED REFORMED CHURCH on the r., at the former limit
of the town walls.

sw of the castle swells the broad curve of the early C19 CHURCH
STREET. The VICARAGE on its E, built apparently as late as
c. 1840 as the George Inn, has a pedimented doorcase in its five-
bay front and on the r. its own stable and archway. Nearby,
the TRINITY METHODIST CHAPEL with a nice Italianate
tower. In OXFORD ROAD is the small red-brick Gothic BETH-
ESDA EVANGELICAL CHURCH, on its front the legend
'Primitive Methodist Chapel 1865' in intricately undercut
stone letters. Back on the corner of Church Street the largish
SWAN HOTEL, rebuilt *c.* 1812 in ashlar. Quite bare façade
of seven wide bays with a pedimental gable over the middle

three. A little further on, still on the r., are two sets of HARLEY
ALMSHOUSES, the first a row of six with Tudor windows and
a pediment, dated 1822, the second just beyond dated 1826.
The way to St Mary's is beside the Swan Hotel, and beyond
the church on the l. is HAY POOR LAW UNION, dated 1837,
a low classical building with an eight-bay front. The cruciform
central block behind is of the normal three storeys; from it
radiate two-storey wings.

LOWER SHEEPHOUSE, 1 m. SW. Late Georgian, of five bays and
two storeys, with a lunette in the pedimental gable. Double-
pile plan.

UPPER SHEEPHOUSE. A renovated C17 house containing a staircase from Penyrwrlodd, Llanigon.

(LLANGWATHEN, 2 m. SE. A hall-house – two pairs of crucks
remain – rebuilt as a type B house with, perhaps, a byre below
the passage.)

LLANAFAN FAWR

9050

ST AFAN. Single-chamber nave and chancel, rebuilt on a smaller
scale by *S. W. Williams* in 1887. Well-proportioned. Arch-
braced roofs with a double arch as a division. Plain battlemented
W tower, and a stone reading, 'This steeple was erected ... by
Thos. Thomas Undertaker ... 1765.' – Besides the new carved
FONT there is a small C13 one; also incised (early medieval?)
fragments in the porch. – In the sanctuary a PILLAR STONE
with a circled cross; C7–9.

RED LION INN. A cruck-framed former hall-house opposite the
church.

RING MOTTE, 200 yds W. A low mound with an outer ditch and
bank, in all *c.* 45 yds across.

CRIBARTH, 2 m. SW. Double-pile plan of *c.* 1690. Five bays, with
a sprocketed hipped roof, coved eaves, and end chimneys. The
central staircase occupies a spacious well; yet the balusters are
of a repetitive turned Jacobean kind. A good number of solid
and sensible houses of this simple William and Mary appearance were built at prosperous Breconshire farms around 1700.

LLANAFAN FECHAN
2 m. WSW of Cilmeri

9050

ST AFAN. In a raised roundish churchyard. Small single-
chamber; rebuilt in 1866 by *C. Buckeridge*. – FONT. C14, octagonal, with raised stops on the base.

LLANBEDR YSTRAD YW   2020

Llanbedr is in the old commote of Ystrad Yw. Artistically it is of note as the home in the C18 and C19 of the Brute family, who may actually have invented the style of memorial tablet in which the fine and varied calligraphy which slate permits was combined with simple classical raised ornament, and with foliage borders coloured with their own still-brilliant dyes.

ST PETER. Nave and chancel, s aisle and chancel in one, w tower and s porch. A consecration of Llanbedr church in 1060 is recorded in the Liber Landavensis. It may be represented by the present nave, which seems however to have been widened to the N by the C16. C14 tower with a ringers' squint into the church. The shape and appearance now are late C15 or early C16. Enlargement by means of a six-bay s arcade (two to the chancel) with formless capitals. The result is an equivocal plan – the N aisle has a chancel arch, rebuilt by *J. L. Pearson* in 1897, and a separate chancel; the s aisle has no division, but it has a PISCINA. Over this aisle is a ribbed plaster barrel ceiling; the nave had a shallow-pitched sloping panelled ceiling but is now open to the collars. There are several varieties of Late Perp windows, including a flattened ogee head with incised figuring at the w of the s aisle, and later C16 E windows. The N nave windows, again by Pearson, have a row of quatrefoils and square tops to match the s windows. Good Perp s porch and doorway. Contemporary s priest's doorway. Earlier restorations in 1868 and in 1883 by *F. R. Wilson* of Alnwick. – FONT. Goblet-shaped and with large stops on the base; *c.* 1500. – PAINTINGS. Diaper fresco with knots, etc., as a background to the rood above the chancel arch, discovered when Pearson stripped the walls. – MONUMENT. Thomas Brute † 1724 – one of the local family of stonemasons. – In the churchyard the stepped base of a CHURCHYARD CROSS, and a LYCHGATE.

MOOR PARK, ½ m. S. Built for John Powell *c.* 1760; a wing of 72 *c.* 1903 by *H. L. Beckwith*. A tiny ideal villa with a curiously mondain Baroque plan. It consists of four round towers partially inset in a taller octagonal core. The four main rooms are arranged to lie diagonally with the main axis, so that each has its window in a bowed end. These are tripartite, and recessed in semicircular-headed niches. Conical roofs round the octagon. Chimneys on top of the straight sides. Spiral stairs mount from the central hall, beginning with a serpentine twist away from the direction of the door. The upper floor has a circular gallery in a near-octagonal landing. Graceful locally wrought iron balustrades.*

PACKHORSE BRIDGE, ¼ m. SW. Below Upper Cwm Bridge, on the Grwyne Fechan.

GUDDER, ¼ m. E. A plain rectangular stone six-bay house. The stair climbs round a well and has turned balusters of just post-1700 type.

HENBANT FACH and HENBANT FAWR, ½ m. NE, are next to each other. Henbant Fach is a C15/16 hall-house with a later chimney. Arch-braces and cusped decoration in the roof. At the SW external corner a pointed stone archway leads into the lower beast-house. The BARN opposite is similarly built across the contour on a battered basement; three pairs of upper crucks support the roof.

PEN-YR-HEOL, 1½ m. NE, with four cruck trusses, was converted early in the first quarter of the C17 by the normal insertion of a central stone chimney and a post-and-panel partition with triangular doorheads.

LLANDDETTY

2 m. WNW of Llangynidr

ST TETTA (or DETIU). In a circular churchyard beside the Usk. Single-chamber with a S porch. W bellcote of 1878. Tudor S doorway and priest's doorway and Late Perp E tracery and other windows, but the plan is C13 or earlier – see the traces of broad W door jambs. The ribbed barrel-vault was well reproduced in 1934. Restorations in the 1870s. – ROYAL ARMS. Painted on the N wall; Hanoverian. – FONT. Octagonal; E.E. cushion stops at the base. – PILLAR STONE. C9, and 4 ft 3 in. high. The inscription reads GUADAN SACERDOS/ FECIT CRUX P(RO) AN(IMA) NI(N) ID ET ANI(MA) GURHI/GUADAN. Incised on each side linear ornament and three crosses (one of which is ringed). – GLASS. E perhaps by *Comper*. – Base of the CHURCHYARD CROSS S of the porch.

LLANDDETTY HALL. Basically early C17, but with alterations, including small metal Gothic windows, probably for George Overton *c*. 1815; he and Dixon built the Bryn-oer tramroad from the Trefil limestone quarries to Talybont on the Breconshire Canal, a drop of 1,000 ft in about eight miles. Later the home of Disraeli's wife, Mrs Lewis.

* I wish to thank Mr S. Hopton for help on Moor Park.

(MAESMAWR. Of the C18 and earlier. Venetian window to the Georgian staircase.)

LLANDDEW 0030

Llanddew was a *clas*, or Celtic Christian community. The Bishop of St Davids established a palace here in the C12.

HOLY TRINITY or ST DAVID. In a roundish churchyard. 22 Cruciform, with a crossing tower. The tower 'newly erected and made in ... 1620', with the result that it now stands a little S of the E–W axis, and has big arches to the chancel and nave but only small openings (pointed and semicircular) to the transepts, all without ornament or mouldings. The importance of Llanddew in the C12, both ecclesiastical and military, suggests that part of the church – perhaps the nave – may also be of that date. The nave is almost entirely rebuilt, however. Two loose pieces of lintel in the S transept, comparable with those of *c.* 1100 at Llanfilo, are carved with bands of lozenges and patterns of triangles, and one has a Maltese cross at one end. They and the broad circular FONT with a rounded chamfer beneath seem to antedate everything E of the nave. The fine chancel, the same width as the nave, has three E.E. lancets a side and an E triplet of lancets, the centre one the taller, with a triple hood. Small C13 PISCINA. The S priest's doorway is Dec, trefoiled, with a hood. The transept walls, with a batter one third of their height, are also C13 – see the narrow E lancet-slit in the N transept (now vestry) which had an altar beneath. Both have squints to the chancel. The pyramidal roof of the tower dates from *c.* 1780. The nave was restored – lancets, a new roof, and the walls stripped – in 1900 and the E parts of the church in 1884. – STONE with a ring-cross; C11? – Two STOUPS, one bulbous, C12/13, the other a late C12 capital for a four-shafted pier. Cable-mouldings etc.

BISHOPS' PALACE. Giraldus Cambrensis as Archdeacon of Brecon came to live here in 1175. The palace is now in ruins. At the S a C14 doorway with a hoodmould resting on corbelled shafts. Along the W a dilapidated early C14 defensive wall with a semicircular revetment, and on the outside near this Bishop Gower's well, made *c.* 1340, under a cambered arch. In the middle of the site are the ruins of a hall, 47 ft by 22 ft, also of the early C14, with big windows in the N and W walls and a lancet in the S. The VICARAGE was built on the site in 1867.

THE PEYTONVIN, $\frac{1}{2}$ m. WNW, a ditched site commanding a crossing of the River Honddu, was given to Sir Richard Peyton by Bernard de Newmarch to protect Brecon Castle during its construction in 1093.

PYTINGWYN, 1 m. WNW. The second of the chain of mottes in the Honddu valley. The farmhouse incorporates fragments of the medieval manor house belonging to the Gam family: lateral fireplaces, and a blocked window of *c.* 1500 with mullion and transom.

PYTINGLAS, 1$\frac{1}{2}$ m. WNW. A third motte in this series of castles.

ALEXANDERSTONE, 1 m. ESE. A small motte with a bailey behind the rebuilt late C16 farm.

0040

LLANDDEWI'R-CWM
1$\frac{1}{2}$ m. S of Builth Wells

ST DAVID. In a circular churchyard. Nave, chancel, W tower with windows only on the N. The church is mentioned in the Taxatio of 1183. E.E. lancets in the chancel and a S priest's doorway. Much repair in 1847, by *Joshua Daniels*, and later, including a wagon roof over the chancel with moulded ribs over the altar. – FONT. Square, with chamfered edges, on a round base. C12–13.

(MAES-Y-CWM, $\frac{3}{4}$ m. NE. An early C16 cruck-framed barn.)

0030

LLANDEFAELOG FACH

ST MAELOG. Beside the River Honddu. C16 W tower with blocked S doorway and pyramidal roof. Nave and chancel rebuilt in 1831 by *Maund* of Brecon and again in 1856 by *W. G. & E. Habershon*. The late C19 fitments are unusually good. – Alabaster REREDOS carved with the Deposition, Entombment, and Resurrection. – Marble arcading and a PISCINA. – Mosaic chancel floor. – Carved CHOIR STALLS. – Pretty ironwork SCREEN. – PULPIT, also with an alabaster figure. – Brass LECTERN. The bookrest is a pelican in her piety; on a twisted column. – FONT. Circular, C13. – STOUP. Incised with lines; one face missing. – GLASS. E by *Ward*. – CROSS SLAB. About 8 ft high, tapering downwards. At the top a Latin cross with four knotted ends. Below, a section with a relief of a large frontal figure holding a club (?) and a dagger, surrounded by knotwork. Then an inscription '+ BRIAMAIL FLOU' in a cable-moulded panel. At the base, a compartment

of plaitwork. Late C10. – MONUMENTS. Under the tower, C16
and C17 slabs with crosses. – William Prytherch † 1776;
erected 1793. – Pennoyre Watkins † 1792 and Sarah Watkins † 1818. With a Gothic surround. – LYCHGATE by *F. R.
Kempson*, 1897.

(A PARSONAGE designed in 1857 by *C. Buckeridge* for the Rev.
Gilbert Harries, who introduced him to the Breconshire
churches, does not seem to have been built.)

LLANDEFAELOG HOUSE. Ashlar. S front of three bays. E front
of *c.* 1790, with two very shallow two-storey bows. Date-stone
for 1630 with the worn arms of the Prytherch family on the
older range behind. The house is sited directly by a Norman
MOTTE.

LLANDEFAILOG TRE'R-GRAIG   *1020*

ST MAELOG. Single-chamber, in a circular churchyard with
yews. Probably C13 – see the N lancet, and perhaps the two
heads in the porch – but reconstructed in 1710 by the rector.
One S window of *c.* 1540; C18 N and S windows. Roof of 1901.
Perp S porch doorway. – FONT. Norman; circular and tapering. – There is an interesting group of C17 and C18 MONU-
MENTS. Johan ? † 1617, Blanch Parry † 1630, Anne Parry
† 1645, William Howell † 1633; all slabs with ornate quatrefoiled crosses and heraldry. – John Gould † 1780 and Thomas
Jones † 1790, both signed by local masons. – Rev. Gregory
Parry, erected 1774. A putto with the circled serpent for
eternity and an urn and marble pyramid; all on a sarcophagus. –
Rev. Gregory Parry † 1785. A plaster oval of a lady garlanding
an urn, between Rococo and neo-classical. – Early C14 COFFIN
LID fragment with a foliate quatrefoiled cross.

FARMHOUSE. Formerly the home of the Parry family, who held
offices at Elizabeth I's court; Blanch Parry was High Sheriff
of Breconshire in 1619. Squarson descendants rebuilt the
church. The houses here are an example of the unit system,
that is distinct dwellings constructed adjacent to each other.
The building on the l. has a blocked Tudor doorway, but the
rest of the details are C17 – dripmoulds, diagonal chimneys,
and a solid oak stair. The hall, now divided, has a late C17 plaster
ceiling of garlands and rakes, alluding to successful harvests.
The separate C18 house on the r. (perhaps replacing one contemporary with the house on the l.), of two storeys and five
bays, is now connected to the first. Opposite is a long range

of whitewashed FARM BUILDINGS, including a stable of
c. 1600, which makes this an outstanding vernacular group.

LLANDEFALLE

ST MATTHEW or MAELOG. A big Perp church in a round
churchyard, all on its own except for the early C18 rectory
below. One wonders what the explanation is. From its predecessor of *c.* 1300 remain the re-erected S doorway, which has
two roll-mouldings in plane with each other in the intrados;
a N window with Y-tracery; and the W nave wall. W tower (the
upper two stages probably rebuilt *c.* 1661), nave and S aisle
divided by the usual double-chamfered arcade and roofed in
one, and chancel. The nave roof has tie-beams and is barrel-
ceiled, and so is the chancel roof. Chancel arch with its original
SCREEN of *c.* 1500; five tracery lights either side of the
(restored) central doorway, all of the same pattern – crossed
diagonals with circled quatrefoils; cf. Llangynyw (M) and Partrishow (B). Above is a vine-trail extended between two fantastic beasts. The loft is gone but the N stair-turret remains.
Almost all the windows are Perp, the E and S aisle E of a rectilinear type and the N and S of a curvilinear type. Two three-
light windows of local design of *c.* 1700 in the S chancel wall.
PISCINA in the S aisle. Perp S porch with an arch-braced roof
and a C16(?) door. A stoup beside this. – FONT. C13; round
and squat. – ALTAR RAILS with the gates higher than the rest
but all with spiral balusters; *c.* 1660. – GLASS. A few C15
fragments in the aisle E window. – MONUMENTS. Thomas
Williams † 1730 and Benjamin Williams † 1742, both with
fanciful lettering by *T. Brute.* – Thomas Williams † 1779 and
Roderick Gwynne † 1780, both by *Powel,* Talgarth. – In the
churchyard a stone LYCHGATE.

BRECHFA INDEPENDENT CHAPEL, beside Brechfa Pool, 1½ m.
NNE of the church. Built in 1803 and small. The W gallery and
fittings look later.

LLAN FARMHOUSE, ¼ m. E. 1824, with an arcaded cart-house
in the same range.

TREBARRIED, ¾ m. SSE. The former home of the Vaughan family,
at the time of writing abandoned. The plan is the usual rectangle, with a porch and with the stair and service rooms in a
rear wing. This feature and the good Jacobean staircase place
it near the end of the occurrence of this type – perhaps *c.* 1650.
Three-light Tudor window re-used above the porch. Inside,

some carving and panelling. At the back unusual OUTBUILD-
INGS of the early C18, with hipped sprocketed roofs, form a
courtyard of three even two-storey ranges. Local tradition connects Trebarried with Shakespeare and the Midsummer
Night's Dream.

FELIN-NEWYDD, ¾ m. ENE. C18, but enlarged in the C19 and
also gothicized; that is, alternate gables and pinnacles were
added to the upper storey.

LLANDEILO'R FAN
8030

4 m. NNW of Sennybridge

ST TEILO. Single-chamber, much restored in 1873. Blocked
priest's doorway. The roof however is a fine C16 one; collars
and braces, and king-posts with trefoil heads in the openings
between the struts. – SCREEN. Plain dado, posts, and head-
beam only. – STOUP. – FONT. C14, octagonal. – GLASS. E
1914. – MONUMENTS. Rev. Richard David † 1614. – Edward
Jones † 1820, by *Henry Westmacott*. – David Lloyd † 1865,
Gothic, by *Williams*, Brecon.

ABERLLECH, 2 m. SE. Built c. 1780. Small. Two Venetian windows on the ground floor, and classical pilaster and staircase
details. Long range of barns with rows of columbaria on the
l.; detached bakehouse etc. on the r.

LLANELIEU
1030

1¾ m. E of Talgarth

ST ELLYW. A peaceful C13 single-chamber church on the N
of a big round ancient churchyard. The plan is almost three
squares. The C13 evidence is the S priest's doorway, which
simply has a continuous quarter-round chamfer and a two-
centred head. (Possibly also C13 the round-headed splay of the
NE lancet.) Continual small changes and improvements. The
S wooden doorway is later than the ribbed door, which, though
remade, is of c. 1600 and appears to belong to the blocked doorway just to the E. Two-light W window also Late Perp. Tie-
beam roof with one tier of cinquefoiled wind-braces. Gentle
C19 repairs, roof, bellcote, porch, etc., by *Baldwin* of Brecon,
1905. – Parts of an elaborate C14 SCREEN are still *in situ*. A 31
so-called 'veranda' of posts with sunk quadrant mouldings and
solid spandrels, the central opening narrower than the lateral

ones, supports the joists for a loft. (Originally there was wainscoting between the posts and the screen wainscot, to enclose the side altars.) Over the loft the roof trusses are arch-braced, apparently to form a ciborium; behind is the rood beam, and boarding, pierced by squints, from the floor of the loft up to the former ceiling. This tympanum and the front of the screen are painted purplish-red with white roses; the partition with a white cross also. – In the sanctuary a small PISCINA and turned Laudian ALTAR RAILS. – FONT. A slender goblet-shape; perhaps C16 or C17. – MONUMENTS. Three slabs with sunk raised lettering: Richard Aubrey † 1610; Thomas Aubrey † 1669; William Aubrey † 1716 (outside, on the E wall). – William Davies † 1786, with colouring, by *Hughes*, Llanvillo. – On the N wall a fragment of the (C18?) painted ROYAL ARMS. – Against the porch a small PILLAR STONE incised with a cross in a circle and four small rings in the angles; a second PILLAR STONE has a cross ringed with three circles. Both are C7–9. – Near this a SUNDIAL dated 1686.

LLANELIEU COURT. A problematic building. A pointed archway leads to a passage from which another pointed but chamfered doorway opens – i.e. a type B house? It is said to be a relic of a C14 monastic cell connected with Llanthony Priory. At the angle of the house are dismantled stones from a Tudor-arched gateway dated 1676. Also three contemporary Latin inscriptions.* The house was the home of the Aubrey family.

FFOSTILL LONG CAIRNS (SO 179 349). Two Neolithic tombs of Severn Cotswold type. Such pairing is relatively common in this group. The N one is the larger and more complex, with the remains of three chambers visible within the cairn. The E chamber is the main one and has the characteristic closed portal which in some monuments becomes simply a 'blind entrance'. The S cairn is shorter and contains only one visible chamber, a rectangular structure which has been badly damaged. The sites were excavated without notable result in the 1920s.

2010 LLANELLY‡

ST ELLI or ELLYW or ALMEDA. An ancient circle of yews surrounds the church. There are wide views N and E over the Usk

---

* Mr Peter Howell has identified two, from Virgil's Eclogues and from Ovid's Heroides.

‡ Transferred to Gwent in 1974.

valley. As at Llanbedr and Llangenny churches, there are two
naves. The s part is probably a Norman or C13 nave with an
(added?) chancel – see the blocked priest's doorway. C15 s
porch. The w tower, perhaps of the C13, very broad and not
high, has a sw stair-turret. The later N aisle has a five-bay
arcade without capitals, three arches in the nave and two in the
chancel. The latter are the earlier, and they, the C15 or earlier
PISCINA by the N altar, and the E and two N aisle windows,
which have Late Perp tracery, suggest that the date 1626 refers
not to the building of the aisle but possibly to the slender ribbed
barrel ceiling. The nave and chancel have barrel ceilings too,
but they look modern. Restorations in 1867 (rebuilding of the
nave arcade) and 1896 (the broach-spire placed on the tower). –
FONT. A deep boulder; C11 or C12. – ALTAR TABLE. Elizabethan, with bulbous gadrooned legs. – GLASS. All C20. Nave
E, The Good Shepherd, with a fresh-coloured landscape,
c. 1901. – N aisle E, St Elli, with scenes of coal-mining and iron-
making; c. 1966. – N aisle N, St Elli and the church, c. 1913;
and an intense World War I window, with the risen Christ and
soldiers in the trenches. By whom? – MONUMENTS. John
Maund † 1850, Gothic, by *W. Meredith Thomas*. – Elizabeth
and Edward Lewis † 1711 and 1713. A bronze plate fixed to
a slab carved with two dragons' heads, thistles, etc. – s of the
church the stepped base (and shaft?) of the CHURCHYARD
CROSS.

DANYGRAIG, ½ m. NNE. The front is Regency, c. 1810, a cheerful
design of the two-storey bows under deep unbroken eaves, with
round heads to the upper windows.

(IRONWORKS, ½ m. SSE. The Llanelly furnace existed by the end
of the C17. The ruined stone blast-furnace is built as usual at
the bottom of a slope, to permit charging from the higher
ground. Behind this, another stone building may have been the
charcoal store.)

CLYDACH. *See* p. 310.

LLANFAES

Expansion along the main road w of the Usk bridge has made
Llanfaes seem part of its large neighbour, Brecon. Otherwise it
is a typical rural parish.

ST DAVID. Next to the site of the medieval church. Nave, N and
s aisles, chancel, w tower and spire. By *J. Clayton*, 1859, but

almost entirely conventionally rebuilt in 1923–5. The tower and spire and the aisle windows, which belonged to the nave before enlargement, are C19, and so is the N aisle W window, formerly at the E, three lights with Dec tracery and filled with *Clayton & Bell* glass of *c.* 1859. – STAINED GLASS in the N aisle E window by *Morris & Co.*, *c.* 1935. – ROOD. 1940. – FONTS. One medieval and recut; one of 1945 carved with an ark, symbols of the Evangelists, etc.

CHRIST COLLEGE. *See* Brecon.

CWRT TARELL. Remodelled from the three-block GAOL of 1858, by *Colwyn Ffoulkes & Partners*, 1975, as flats.

BRIDGE over the Tarell, ⅛ m. W. A single arch with circular openings in the haunches. By *Job Thomas*, 1829.

FFRWDGRECH, 1 m. SW. A Grecian villa of 1828. The E and W sides have two gable pediments as deep as the deep wooden eaves, and one bay between. Stone porch with paired unfluted Ionic columns, and stone bracketed architraves over the windows. Anthemion detailing in the ceiling medallions; egg and dart cornices. Addition to the N in 1892.

CILWHYBERT, 2 m. SW. A good medium-sized motte surrounded by a ditch and bank, next to the farm.

HEOLFANOG, 2½ m. SSW, belonged to the Havard family in the C16. It is a total ruin.

CWMGWDI, 2 m. SSW. An outstandingly well preserved farmhouse of *c.* 1600. The main part runs E and W of a central chimney with four diagonal stacks. On the l. are the cellar, parlour, bedrooms, and attic; on the r. the kitchen and a stone well stair, then bedrooms and attic. Many shaped doorheads and the original studded doors. Late Tudor stone doorway to the cellar stair. The entrance is to a N projecting wing. Stone corbels to the parlour beams; others project from the S walls, for the former pentice.

50 NEWTON, ½ m. NW, was built by John Games, High Sheriff of Breconshire, descendant of Sir David Gam who was knighted at Agincourt. (An earlier house was called Trenewydd.) On the great hall fireplace is the date 1582. The double-pile plan (surviving trusses show that originally the two roof-lines were constructed E and W) is thought to be the earliest example in Wales, and is contemporary with the earliest in England – Whitehall, Shrewsbury. Its large compact mass is four floors high, and an early C18 pyramidal roof now accentuates this extreme height (cf. Treowen, near Monmouth). Only part of the building is still habitable. At the S a porch wing with some blocked (?)

Elizabethan stone windows, and a door with a wicket. The still medievally-conceived two-storey hall at the s w corner has over its Tudor fireplace a slab which traces in raised letters the family descent; in the centre is their coat of arms. At the w end, the dais. The screen between the hall and the entry passage at the E is partly obscured. The visible parts are two fluted columns with cornice mouldings as capitals (cf. Old Gwernyfed), the intervals filled with wainscoting. Though this is c17, the framed partition of the second storey looks c16. It has turned rails (from a gallery?). Pedimented central doorway of c. 1700. This seems to be the date of the staircase also, which climbs a well in the N w corner of the house and has gracefully designed half-balusters. In the formerly important chamber above the hall fragments of an overall Elizabethan plasterwork decoration – fleur-de-lys and rosettes in the window embrasures, the surround of a coat of arms over the fireplace, and two corbels with just the springing of plaster ceiling ribs. Also a fireplace with foliage in the Tudor spandrels. Among stonework details that are as expected, the re-use of two c15 traceried windows (from an earlier house or from the church?) on the third floor at the N is not. Further alterations of c. 1700 include the six great chimneys capping the pyramid of the roofs. In the drawing room a little c18 carving and bolection panelling.

BRECON. *See* p. 283.

LLANFAIR YM MUALLT *see* BUILTH WELLS

LLANFIGAN 0020
½ m. s w of Pencelli

ST MEUGAN. Ralph de Mortimer of Pencelli Castle built a church on the old site *c*. 1272. The existing nave etc. is rebuilt, but the N arcade and aisle seem datable to the c14 by style, an addition to the E.E. church, with some details re-used in the N wall. This rustic work could alternatively date from after the Glyndŵr troubles. The arcade is four bays of low rubble arches chamfered once. The two capitals of the three E bays are rudimentary – five diminishing squares of stone. Their short columns are ashlar and octagonal but the top and bottom stones are dressed to a square. The E respond has a similar capital and continuous chamfers; the w is a rubble pier with a thin responding capital. The fourth (w) bay has a continuous chamfer and dressed stone jambs, without capitals. Three two-light windows: N lancets which are unaltered; one with inserted cusped Y-tracery; the E with later trefoil heads. Blocked C13 N doorway. No division between nave and chancel. The nave roof is the habitual ribbed cradle-vault of the late C15 on. Two pairs of big three-light cinquefoiled s windows with straight heads; also a small window with Y-tracery. s priest's door with Tudor head. Nave s doorway two-centred. The windows etc. were repaired by *S. W. Williams* in 1891; the obtrusive repointing of the unplastered stone is more recent. A small arch joins to the w tower, which is contemporary with the nave and has a stepped base, water-spouts, and battlements. – FONT. Late C13; octagonal, on a circular base. – AUMBRY(?) inside the s door. – STALLS. Of *c.* 1700; the small benches possibly C17. – PULPIT and ALTAR RAILS incorporating C17 work. – A section of the SCREEN in the N aisle comprises a two-centred doorway, buttresses, and a painted moulded head-beam; attributed to the C14. – MONUMENTS. Lewis Gunter † 1683, with curly serpents at the sides. – Rev. Walter Williams † 1866, Gothic. – Some ornate slabs of *c.* 1700 in the chancel. – CHURCHYARD CROSS, base and shaft only.

PANTLLEFRITH. A classic small farmhouse of just after 1600. Regional plan type A. In the projecting two-storey porch an inner post-Tudor doorway and door, fitted with a small wicket and a draw-bar, leading to a cross-passage at the end of which is a stair down to a cellar dairy. Beside the chimney of the bigger room on the l. a fine little late C17 stair with turned balusters, and a service room. A smaller room and end chimney to the r.

PENCELLI. *See* p. 364.

8050

LLANFIHANGEL ABERGWESYN

4 m. NNW of Llanwrtyd Wells

ST MICHAEL. This ancient foundation is now represented only by the ruins of the medieval church, and the floor of *R. J. Withers*'s church, demolished in 1964.

LLWYN-DDERW (HOTEL), ½ m. SW. The elegant front range was added for David Jones in 1796. He possessed more than 10,000 sheep, according to Theophilus Jones. Carefully dressed small stones, three storeys and five bays, with a modillion cornice and a Tuscan porch. Good Georgian details inside too, including pilasters supporting arches in the stairwell, and door and fireplace details. In the N wing a big fireplace with stone voussoirs, perhaps of the C17.

LLANFIHANGEL BRYN PABUAN

4 m. WNW of Builth Wells

ST MICHAEL. In a circular churchyard. Single-chamber with
a S porch. C13? Much old stonework in the walls, and early C16
arch-braced roofs both in the porch and in the church. Plain
struts and panelled wall-plate in the latter. One small trefoiled
light near ground level on the S; a 'low-side' window? The
windows and other repair are by *C. Buckeridge*, 1868. – STOUP.
Circular; with a corbel carved with a head set above it. – FONT.
Circular, perhaps C13, but recut.

(NEUADD RHOSFERIG. Small late C16 house with hall and
parlour only but a chimney and stair in either gable. Elaborate
hall beams.)

LLANFIHANGEL FECHAN *see* LOWER CHAPEL

LLANFIHANGEL NANT BRÂN

3½ m. NNE of Sennybridge

ST MICHAEL. C16 or C17 W tower with SE stair-turret and pyramidal roof. Single-chamber nave and chancel by *J. L. Pearson*,
1882. Wooden chancel arch and a little tracery below a tie-beam
to mark off the chancel. – GLASS. E, 1914.

LLANFIHANGEL TAL-Y-LLYN

ST MICHAEL AND ALL ANGELS. In a partly round churchyard.
Perp W tower with battlements. S porch of *c.* 1500 with a round-
arched doorway and an arch-braced roof with cusping. In it
a pagan columnar PILLAR STONE with a socket in the top.
Short C15 (or Norman?) nave, with a chancel, all thoroughly
and characterlessly restored in the 1870s. – FONT. Norman.
Circular, carved as a bowl with a cable-moulding near the rim,
then a widening stem with rings of flat and roll-mouldings.

NEUADD has a five-bay front block and contemporary staircase
of *c.* 1720.

HEMLEY HALL is C16, built down the contour, with a detached
kitchen beside – a layout common in Breconshire till the C18.

The Hay Railway, to the SW, passed through one of the earliest
RAILWAY TUNNELS, 674 yds long, built in 1812–16.

LLANFILO

St Bilo (or St Milburg, abbess of Wenlock in the c7. The church is in many ways a delight, and the interior with its early c16 screen is in a good state after being attentively restored by W. D. Caröe and others between 1913 and 1951. The walls of the E half of the nave are Norman, and two diapered lintels of c.1100 remain, one over the blocked N doorway, the other unmoved in the S porch. The former is carved with two rows of, as it were, flat dogtooth with a border of diamonds, the latter with a chequer of diamonds and a dot and bar motif. To this the medieval chancel and an extension of the nave were added. In the S porch a c15 timber roof whose arched brace and transverse ribs have a pleasing architectural quality. Plain chamfered S doorway and door, with outer boards of 1767. W tower, with slated broach-spire and an unfortunate E arch, rebuilt in 1851. In the nave a c15 ribbed barrel ceiling. Later windows: the two-light S window perhaps c17, a similar four-light N window restored on the model of the Jacobean/Early Georgian S chancel window, and a tall insertion of c.1680 to light the pulpit. Beneath this outside is the head of an E.E. lancet. The stone floor slopes all the way from W to E. The chancel, beyond the plaster partition of the rood, and a step lower, has an intimate character – it was partly rebuilt c.1710 with a stone flagged floor and a coved plaster ceiling. Red sandstone window of c.1913 at the E. – Two stone MENSAE or altar-slabs were found in the floor, one of which, of c.1200, is the altar under the loft, and the other at the E. – The ROOD LOFT, reached by its N mural stair, and the SCREEN are the focus of the little nave. Their ochre to silver colouring matches the re-used pew work and the six PEWS of 1630 in the nave, the unvarnished PULPIT of 1680, and the memorials left in place along the walls. The screen, of six lights and a doorway, has ogees and two quatrefoils (the Hereford-shire pattern) in the tracery. The head-beam is carved with vine-trails coming from the dragon's mouth at the N. Cresting above. Then the flat-ribbed coving of the Welsh screens, deeper on the W side and with vine and rose bosses. The W parapet has new drop-cresting, two bands of running ornament, and at the top, trefoils and a trail of pomegranates. Between is a panelled front divided now by six triangular pilasters (four renewed), with Perp carving and foliate capitals and bases, which may have supported the rood figures above the parapet. The relief figures between them are, from the N, St Peter, St

James the Great, the Virgin and Child, St Luke, and St Paul. They and the central canopy were carved by *Nathaniel Hitch*, between 1926 and 1930. The ROOD on the E nave wall above is also his work. It was dedicated in 1925, together with the enlarged ALTAR TABLE. – Early C15 Angelus BELL in the chancel. – ALTAR RAILS of *c.* 1630. – FONT. Probably Norman. A boulder with a two-ring moulding at the rim. – MONUMENTS. Coffin lid carved with a cross and fleur-de-lys border; late C13. – Characteristic memorials from the C17 to the C19 include two signed by *T. Brute*. – In the circular churchyard to the S the base of the medieval preaching CROSS, and to the E a LYCHGATE built *c.* 1700.

(TREDOMEN, I m. S. A hamlet of four small farmhouses, of which TREDOMEN COURT has the earliest structure (C16). The buildings are mostly C17 to C19; the early C17 MIDDLE HOUSE, consisting of hall, parlour, dairy wing, and byre, is the best preserved.)

LLANFRYNACH

ST BRYNACH. In a very large roundish churchyard, from which many of the gravestones have regrettably been cleared. C14 W tower; the nave and chancel were replaced by a local builder, *William Jones*. The date is 1855, so the chancel arch is narrow and steep. In 1864 the tower wall was simply broken through to create a W window and a set of pews for the de Winton family. – FONT. C14, octagonal, but looks recut. – A tall SLAB, dated by Dr Nash-Williams to the C10–11. A figure with arms raised (a Crucifixion?) above, then knot interlace, and at the very top and near the bottom Maltese crosses (cf. Llanhamlach). – GLASS. E by *Hardman's* of Birmingham, *c.* 1859. An emotive and strongly coloured Crucifixion. – W, stylistically similar, *c.* 1864. – Two S sanctuary windows by *Warrington & Sons*, 1863. – MONUMENTS. Charlotte de Winton † 1826. An obelisk draped in a shroud, in which a putto hides his face and on which is the inscription. By *I. E. Thomas*, London. – Richard de Winton † 1841, by *I. E. Thomas*. With a portrait medallion and military symbolism. – The CHURCHYARD CROSS was copied from one at Merthyr Mawr, Glamorgan, in 1910.

TY MAWR, beside the church, seems to have originated as a fortified manor house. Sections of wall remain E of the present house, including a blocked arch perhaps of the C15, and the main corridor of the house passes through a substantial masonry gateway 8 ft wide. Besides Tretower comparable houses might be Great Porthaml, Talgarth, and Porth Mawr, Crickhowell. The rector in the early C19, Charles Clifton, is said to have been a friend of Nash. About 1820 he set about converting what he found into an irregular, Strawberry Hill kind of Gothic house: it has big ogee windows and doorways and pinnacles on the s, but has been rather subdued by additions of c. 1860–80. Nonetheless plenty of plasterwork remains downstairs, including a big niche with crockets and ribbed vaulting in the corridor. The staircase ornamentation is partly wood carvings by *Thomas Price* (Carnhuanawc), rector of Cwmdu (B).

TY-FRY is a C17 porched farmhouse. The r. wing has an outside stair leading to what was the schoolroom for the village in the C19.

MAESDERWEN, ½ m. W. A plain Doric stucco villa dating from the early C19, two bays and three storeys, with short bowed wings.

ABERCYNRIG, 1 m. NNW. Externally a fine, well preserved William and Mary manor house, mostly built by the Jeffreys family. The front typically has two short (though unequal) wings, all once with mullion and transom windows, and stone-tiled steep hipped and sprocketed roofs. The owners from the C13 were the Awbreys. But there are traces of a substantial C16 house in a Tudor doorway on the l. of the front and a Henry VIII fireplace – a deep chamfered stone lintel set on moulded corbels – in a NW room. The beams in this room have ribbed chamfers of C16 type, too. A hypothetical central hall was filled in c. 1690 with two panelled rooms with ornate bolection-moulded fireplaces; these are now joined. In the overmantels two C17 panel paintings of the Diana and Actaeon story. They resemble French Mannerist narrative work in that the wooded parks of fine classical buildings are the dominant subject, not the mythologies. In the N and S wings are two late C17 staircases; the one round a well, though similar to the other, is of a later type, since that is of the dog-leg pattern. Other contemporary woodwork of the same Mannerist kind.

(ROMAN BATH HOUSE, ½ m. W. Part of a mosaic pavement found in 1775 is in the National Museum of Wales.)

LLANGAMMARCH WELLS

9040

ST CADMARCH. By *W. D. Caröe*, 1913–16. W tower,* low nave 99 and chancel; squinches but no chancel arch. Although not altogether satisfactory as a whole, the church represents an interesting phase of style. The basis is an intelligent use of the traditional plan-type. The historical references are to the local Perp, but the treatment is Arts-and-Crafts. The structural framework is rough (though carefully pointed) masonry, which results in some lack of intensity and sense of finish – deliberate, presumably, in the arcade for the unbuilt N aisle. As always with Caröe, the detail of the fitments is of high quality. – REREDOS of oak, with statues of St Cadmarch and St David. – LECTERN with openwork tracery. – A new FONT with the C15 one beside it. – Simply designed PEWS. – Above the S porch doorway a C7–9 PILLAR STONE carved with a circled cross, part of a figure, and a spiral ornament. – MONUMENTS. Theophilus Jones † 1812, 'Author of the History of Breconshire'. – Joseph Richards † 1841. Local Gothic. – Theophilus Evans, one of the greatest of Welsh prose writers (a history of Wales etc.), was vicar from 1738 to 1763.

PARC FARM, 1 m. SE. The central dwelling-portion is of *c.* 1600. The spiral stairs have been replaced by C19 ones in the cross-passage. On the far (lower) side of a wooden partition in this passage is the beast-house; above the house a barn completes the total length of 144 ft, one of the longest in Wales.

(CWMFYNNON, 2½ m. SW. Remnant of a late medieval timber house, now a byre. It has jointed crucks.)

(CEFN BRITH, 2 m. SW. C17, with a camber-headed porch and seats. The birthplace of John Penry, one of the founders of Independency in the reign of Elizabeth I.)

LLANGANTEN *see* CILMERI

LLANGASTY TAL-Y-LLYN

1020

ST GASTAYN. Rebuilt by *J. L. Pearson*, with a new chancel. Begun in 1848; furnishing was still in progress in 1856. Small E.E. nave and chancel and a plain, massive W tower. The patron was Robert Raikes of Treberfydd, who had come into contact with the Tractarians at Oxford in the 1830s, and whose building programme included the neighbouring school (and the rectory). Mark Girouard has stressed the unpretentiousness of these

* Added in 1927.

buildings. Raikes's impressive and austere church is a remarkably intact survivor of the Oxford Movement's ideas on liturgical arrangements (e.g. the STOUP in the porch). The chancel is evocative of their appeal to medieval piety and richness together, with its triple E lancet and wall-shafts, and its ironwork parclose screen. All the more so with the decoration newly repainted; this includes stencilling on the walls and a frieze of texts. The low chancel SCREEN is made from pieces of the C16 one, carved in the solid, with exotic canopied panels. – GLASS. E probably by *Wailes*, dated 1849. – W of similar date.

SCHOOL AND MASTER'S HOUSE. By *Pearson*, 1848–50. Single-storey with trefoiled lancets; built beside the churchyard lych-gate. Altogether an attractive, serious-minded group.

TREBERFYDD, ½ m. s. Robert Raikes came to Llangasty Tal-y llyn in 1848 to start a centre of Tractarian worship for the area. He bought a square late C18 house, Treberfedd Villa, and over the years 1848–52, particularly the last two, had it progressively replaced by an Elizabethan Gothic family house. Eastlake calls it 'manorial' Gothic. *J. L. Pearson*, who had built three churches near the Raikes family's home near Hull, was the chosen architect for the house as well as for the church and school. He had to rebuild on the old room-plan, and so the design evolved piecemeal, the garden tower for instance being added after the earlier drawings. The scale is domestic throughout, and local stone was used; for this reason it is also a harmonious feature in the panorama of the lake. Bath stone dressings. The entry front has a tower with carved animal bosses. The rest is two storeys of square-headed Elizabethan windows, with one oriel and one bow, beneath irregular gables. Though quiet, the elevations are not without intensity, particularly at the roof-lines' prettily tiled gables and Elizabethan chimneys. The conservatory, stone with a wood and glass roof, looks a contemporary addition. Inside, the tiles in the hall are probably by *Minton* and the stair banister etc. is pitch-pine. Hooded fireplace. Gothic Revival of the period of the Great Exhibition is the style of much of the furnishings. The drawing room has two Puginesque fireplaces, but decoration of *c.* 1900 has replaced a Pugin wallpaper. The library is unchanged. The interestingly detailed L-shaped STABLES, with a gate tower beside the house (cf. Great Porthaml, Talgarth), incorporated a forge and a dovecote. The style seems quite natural to their functions. Their weathervane is dated 1852. The complete gardens – three geometrical parterres, planting, drives, and a walled garden –

designed in 1850 by *W. A. Nesfield* are somewhat altered. A small COTTAGE (ORNÉ) by *Pearson* in the garden was built in 1857.

TY MAWR, 1 m. w. The old manor house of Llangasty dates from the C17 but has been greatly changed. Round it are grouped an C18 corn-barn and two tall hipped-roofed C18 granaries, one with blank arcading.

MOTTE, ½ m. SW. Small and partly eroded.

BRYN-LLICI, 1½ m. w. A solid house of *c.* 1705. Central stairway with slender turned balusters. Tall end chimneys and hipped sprocketed roof. The long front has six bays of mullioned and transomed windows.

TREBINSHWN, 1¼ m. S. The Regency stuccoed façade was made *c.* 1805 for Admiral Sir Edward Hamilton, two half-octagon wings and a three-bay centre, the angles with rusticated quoins. The house has two low storeys dictated by the stone house behind, of *c.* 1630. This had a half-H plan. In the middle is a paved hall, with a fashionable Regency staircase. Other rooms now with pilasters, friezes, and simple ceiling mouldings. In the NW wing features earlier than 1630: an arched fireplace and segmental stone doorways, probably datable in South Wales to the later C16. Christopher Fry lived here after World War II.

LLANGATTOCK

2010

ST CATWG. In a near-circular churchyard with a LYCHGATE. Large W tower, replacing one built in Stephen's reign and not aligned with the nave. Two almost identical chambers, of which the S is the nave, each with its own chancel. A continuous C14 arcade divides them, and the pair of chancel arches springs from the second pier from the E. The fenestration is Late Perp (one S window), Tudor (W tower window), and Elizabethan (chancel windows). Ribbed ceilings with a Tudor arch over nave and N aisle, which were roofed together in a single pitch in 1785. In the frequent C19 restorations the chancel roof and some windows were replaced. There is a fine Tudor S doorway, a porch, and a second S porch for the priest. The tower, also of Tudor date, with three stages, battlements, and an octagonal NE stair-turret, has a great arch with moulded responds to the nave. – STAINED GLASS. Nave E and N aisle, early windows by *Clayton & Bell, c.* 1866 and 1860. – Chancel windows of 1886 and 1888.

MONUMENTS. Richard Harcourt † 1723. Early Georgian. –

Anna Williams † 1772. – On the tower walls a fine group of later C18 Rococo stones with coloured raised ornament, made by local masons. – On the s, William and Alice Morgan † 1746 and 1750, with coloured 'tulip' border. – Mary Moses † 1777 by *A. Brute*, a particularly pretty one. – Thomas Williams † 1780 by *T. Jones*. – Mary Herbert † 1782, with cherubs. – Henry Watkins † 1800, by *J. Brute*. – Margaret Saunders † 1785, by *A. Brute*. – William Lewis † 1782, with elegantly curled fronds, by *T. Jones*. – Jennet Cunvin † 1775, by *A. Brute*. – On the N a tablet to Anne Lewis † 1773; 'Being a Midwife, she was an Instrument in the Hand of providence to bring to this World 716 Children'. By *J. Brute*. – Village stocks and whipping-post in the N aisle. – Outside the priest's porch is the base and shaft of the CHURCHYARD CROSS.

73

GARN GOCH (SO 212 177) is a large Bronze Age barrow in the centre of the village, now covered in trees.

Llangattock is a pleasantly varied village, like Crickhowell on the opposite side of this favoured length of the Usk. A narrow street of C18 and C19 houses leads to the church, and there are some larger houses of a certain standing before the industrial age.

THE OLD RECTORY, built in 1852, is Tudor, with a porte cochère.

LLANGATTOCK CWRT. Two houses, one a small C17 farm-house perhaps, at an angle to another of *c.* 1695–1705 and joined to it by a passageway with a Late Jacobean doorway. This second house has a symmetrical exterior, five windows wide by two storeys high, and a deep-eaved cornice; the same moulding occurs on the modillions and the window entablatures, a shallow alternation of rectangular and semicircular dentils. Over the doorway a bracketed hood of William and Mary design with a hemispherical undersurface. Hipped roof constructed with substantial upper crucks, the early Welsh way of dealing with this new-fashioned feature. The roof is stone-tiled, with three similar hip-roofed dormers. The plan is a considerable puzzle – it appears that a passage ran round the back of the house, outside the main (and so older?) walls and chimneys, but within the roof span. It leads to a small late C17 stair, but not to any service areas. Drawing room panelled in chestnut, *c.* 1700, with a mid C18 fireplace. Traditionally the home of the Williams, or Conway, family.

PLAS LLANGATTWG was the home of the Morgan family. The pleasant façade grew over the whole of the C18. (Remnants of the Late Tudor house behind were altered by *T. Alwyn Lloyd* in 1937.) The main block is of the tall plain type of *c.* 1700, three storeys and a hipped roof, three bays wide only; but two-storey wings were added in the middle of the century and the composition improved with quoining on the three sections, and a cornice and pediment with a bull's eye. The fanlight porch and pilasters are faintly neo-classical of *c.* 1790. Lastly a revision of *c.* 1800, when the windows of the lower two storeys were lowered and the centre was given a veranda of pretty Regency ironwork and a tent-shaped canopy above the middle window. In the garden a GLASSHOUSE or orangery of *c.* 1850, whose profile from base to wall is curved.

LLANGATTOCK PARK HOUSE, ½ m. SSW. By *T. H. Wyatt* for the Duke of Beaufort *c.* 1838. A smallish stone neo-Tudor house with one-storey projecting bays. One on the E side has round masonry columns with windows between, a pierced balustrade, and lions with shields.

GLANWYSC, ½ m. NNW. A villa built by *John Nash* for Admiral Gell in the 1790s, not large, with a portico, and cruciform in plan, so much remodelled in the pleasant stucco Italianate manner of the 1850s that it is not recognizable now – unless it contains the earlier plasterwork etc.

HÊN GASTELL, 1 m. SSE. A square motte within a wet ditch. On the platform was a square stone curtain. Its date might be *c.* 1300.

DAN-Y-PARK, 1¼ m. SE. Demolished; built by Edward Kendal in the late C18.

LLANGENNY

ST CENAU. A short medieval nave and its added chancel have become the N aisle of a single-chamber Late Perp nave with a S porch. The plan development seems to correspond with the sequence at Llanbedr Ystrad Yw. Arcade of octagonal piers (one a monolith), three bays in the nave and two in the chancel. Nave and porch have ribbed barrel ceilings, and the porch arch is roughly semicircular too, but not the S nave doorway and the priest's doorway, which are four-centred. The old nave has a pair of squints beside the chancel arch, at the sites of the medieval altars. At the enlargement and refenestration of the church in the late C15 or early C16, or during the restoration in 1863 by *C. Buckeridge*, the S aisle was made the nave; it has the taller E window and a PISCINA. Flat C16 ceiling in the N aisle; low-pitched Tudor ceiling in the N chancel. Evidence for a screen is the small blocked S window and the removal of the E nave respond. – FONT. Circular, with a rope moulding beneath. C12. – MONUMENT. Lewis Morgan † 1688. With an open pediment. – STOUP in the porch. – The LYCHGATE is dated 1639.

SCHOOL beside the church in a simple Tudor; dated 1886.

LLANGENNY BRIDGE has a single arch with the abutments lightened with circular holes. Probably late C18.

(PEN-LAN, 1¼ m. NE. Well preserved small farmhouse of post-Tudor type; with a date-stone (on a stair-turret) for 1686, the probable date also for the plaster ceiling in the small parlour.)

PENDARREN. Rebuilt in 1876 for Andrew Doyle, builder also of the school.

CWRT-Y-GOLLEN, ½ m. SSW. The family home of the Morgans, a late C17 house remodelled c. 1800 by the Rev. Richard Davies, burned down in 1909. It had then a three-storey centre and wings. A. M. Gear & Associates designed the existing buildings for the Welsh Brigade Depot.

The STANDING STONE at Cwrt-y-Gollen (SO 232 168), close to the main road, is the most impressive of several on the valley bottom to the N.

LLANGOED see LLYSWEN

LLANGORSE

ST PAULINUS. Nave, chancel, W tower, and S aisle. Restoration by T. Nicholson in 1874 has left no old nave and chancel detail except two C15 N windows. He built (or rebuilt?) the chancel arch and all the chancel but kept the roof. S arcade of conventional C15 design: three bays to the nave and one to the chancel. Early Tudor S doorway, S windows, and S priest's doorway. The tracery of the S aisle, E and sanctuary windows is also of c. 1840. The good and complete barrel roof of the aisle, of moulded ribs without plaster infill, like the chancel's, is presumably again part of the late C15 enlargement. Perp W tower of three stages with a slightly stepped base. – There are three fragments of EARLY CHRISTIAN STONES in the church: at the E of the S aisle one incised with a Latin ring-cross, C7–9, and inscribed † GURCI BLEDRUS; one incised with a foliate cross(?), C10 or early C11; and at the W an C11/12 one with a Latin burial inscription, HIC IACET (S)I(U)LERD (F)ILIUS/VULMER (Dr Nash-Williams). – FONT. Octagonal, with a carved underside; c. 1300?

GILFACH, 1 m. SE. A farmhouse of *c.* 1600. Below the cross-passage the woodwork is C17. A stone doorway leads to the older part above, where there is evidence of one cruck, stud and panel partitioning, and, on the rear wall, a later stone stair-turret.

(CARN Y CASTELL, 2 m. NE. A motte.)

(TREWALTER, 1½ m. NNW. A much ruined type B house, built in 1653. The chimney and stair backing into one side of the cross-passage served the main room, beyond which oak screens divided off two smaller rooms; on the other, beyond a screen, was a large parlour with its own chimney.) *See* p. 47

LLANGYNIDR 1010

ST KENNETH. In a roundish churchyard. Nave, chancel, W porch; by *Clifton West*, 1873. After a fire in 1928, only a broken FONT, perhaps of the early C13, a STOUP in the S wall, and S of the church the square base of a CROSS remain of the old church.

LLANGYNIDR BRIDGE, ½ m. NW. Second only to Crickhowell Bridge, perhaps, of all the bridges across the Usk, and certainly one of the oldest – *c.* 1600. Like its sister at Crickhowell it arcs against the current, but though only six arches (80 yds) long, its greater height lends its sheer cutwaters a little grandeur.

OLD PEN-Y-BRYN, 1¼ m. E. A small C17 farmhouse, of great interest because the high seat in the hall is still in position against the moulded stud-and-panel partition facing the hearth. The seat is a unique detail (but see Cwm-gu Fach, Tretower). It has one tall shaped end. Beside the fireplace is a two-storey spiral stair; shaped doorways to it on the first floor. The gable end of the attached byre has a wood-mullioned window. The house originally had pentises either side.

LLANHAMLACH 0020

ST PETER AND ST ILLTYD. Perp W tower with battlements and W doorway. C15 N porch. Nave and chancel under one roof, rebuilt in unsympathetic Dec by *S. W. Williams* in 1887. The walls are plastered, unlike Llansantffraed. – FONT. Octagonal. Perp. – MONUMENTS. Jane, wife of Sir Humphrey Stanley. A recumbent stone effigy wearing a cloth bound under her chin; datable to *c.* 1325. The lettering on the slab and pillar was cut in the C17. – THE MORIDIC STONE. A C10–11 pillar stone which has lost several inches at least at the top. Inscribed on the r. side (I)OHANNIS,/MORIDIC SUR(R)EXIT. HUNC LAPIDEM, in letters and language of the period before the Norman invasion. The other side decorated with knots. The face is carved with a Latin cross with forked ends. Beneath the arms on the l. a small male figure, on the r. a larger female figure, both with raised hands. These are, naturally, identified as St John and the Virgin Mary. The rest of the surface is filled in with various knot patterns. The treatment is linear and childlike.

PETERSTONE COURT was the home of the Walbeoffe family after the Conquest. The present house, built in 1741 for John Powell, is a straightforward, handsome Georgian design of a higher standard than the Breconshire norm and a type most uncommon throughout Mid Wales. Front of five bays, the middle three slightly breaking forward. The third storey was added in the C19 below the pediment and cornice. Door with Gibbs surround. Addition of 1901 on the r. Good staircase and landing details. On the l. a small panelled room containing a pine overmantel with excellent *rocaille* decoration. Another room is said to have a contemporary plaster ceiling.

The name comes from a C6 cylindrical PILLAR STONE next to the A40 in front of the house. The stone is inscribed N(EMNI)I FILIUS VICTORINI.

At CEFN BRYNICH, I m. NW, are two substantial BRIDGES. One, perhaps built in the C18, carries a road over the Usk on four massive arches and has cutwaters; the other just downstream conveys the Monmouthshire and Brecon Canal, again on four arches, and probably dates from 1800. The engineer for the canal was *Thomas Dadford Jun*. This conservative stone structure, though the largest work in the system, called for no more invention than the road bridge.

TY ILLTYD LONG CAIRN (SO 097 263). A Severn Cotswold tomb of Neolithic date. A rectangular chamber towards the N end retains its capstone and is fronted by an open rectangular area which may have been an open forecourt. Carvings on stones in the 'forecourt' and the chamber are probably medieval.

2040 LLANIGON

ST EIGEN. In an old near-round churchyard with a LYCHGATE at the SW. Nave and chancel. C14 S porch, with an outer arch with unusual chamfered and half-round mouldings on plain capitals, supporting a bell-stage added in 1670. Nave with renewed paired lancets, perhaps of c. 1300, with its three-lancet E window now in the W wall. Ceiled roof. The chancel arch and E window are restoration of 1857. In the sanctuary a S window with Y-tracery and cusping. – ALTAR RAILS. C18. – TILES on the sanctuary floor. – The old FONT (in the porch) is C13, circular, with three lines incised at the rim. – GLASS. E by *J. Bell*, 1856.

TY-MAWR, just below the E end of the church, is timber-framed, which is rare in Breconshire. On the r. of the cross-passage are the hall and then another room; in both the floor of the upper storey seems, from the placing of the carved corbels, to be an insertion.

½ m. NW is a small MOTTE.

TYNLLYNE, 1 m. SW. A T-plan farmhouse of *c.* 1600. A central-chimneyed wing was added about 30 years later, making an H-front. Gabled E porch, also C17. The doorway has a Tudor head. The plan of the older part is an interesting one: the main chimney stands between a cross-passage and the hall/kitchen with its nine-compartment deep-beamed ceiling. In the W wing the parlour with a fireplace stair at the gable end and service rooms more ingeniously arranged than usual, though less advanced than Dderw, Llyswen.

MIDDLE MAESTORGLWYDD BARN, 1½ m. S, is particularly informative for studying a late medieval cruck hall. It has five cruck trusses. The end bays have been partitioned for rooms at the upper end and perhaps for a byre at the lower. The central pair of bays was the hall. The central couple is sunk-chamfered, arch-braced, and has trefoil cusping in the apex struts; the couple above the dais has a big trefoiled arched brace, and a head-beam cut away for the dais canopy. Wind-braces. The timber-framed walls seem to have been replaced with stone in the C16 – see the pointed-arched door at the NE of the hall (which has a round head inside), both of rubble voussoirs. The hall escaped conversion to a storeyed house in the C17.

(WENALLT ISAF, ¾ m. SSE. Part of a cruck hall (three couples survive), with a chimney inserted behind the pointed arch-braces of the hall truss.)

(WENALLT UCHAF, 1½ m. SE, is built with the fireplace backing onto the passage.)

PENYRWRLODD, ½ m. SSW. The E range, of stone with window

hoodmoulds, has a doorway with the date 1650, a studded door, and pendants from the gable above. It was built for William Watkins, a Parliamentary soldier. Within is a moulded stud-and-panel partition. In 1707 a tall stone cross-wing with a five-bay front and sprocketed roof was added; its dentil cornice forms a pediment over the central bay. Some mullioned and transomed windows with stone architraves. Contemporary panelling inside, and a good low-relief plaster ceiling. c18 BARNS and STABLES, one, of five bays, and dated 1707, built to provide a Dissenting Chapel on its upper floor. Until recently it had an ornate plaster eaves cornice. The mid-c17 staircase has been moved to Upper Sheephouse, near Hay.

PEN Y WYRLOD (I) LONG CAIRN (SO 225 398). One of the Neolithic tombs of Severn Cotswold type. A simple rectangular chamber is exposed at the E end of a pear-shaped mound which also contains the remains of a smaller chamber at the W end. Excavations in the 1920s were inconclusive, but it has been suggested that this W tail might be an addition to an essentially circular mound containing the larger chamber; however, stones to the N of this chamber suggest the possibility of a passage of Pipton type.

TWYN Y BEDDAU (SO 242 386). A large burial mound beside a mountain road. Excavation in the last century (three trenches can still be seen) produced evidence for five cremation burials covered by a layered mound of stone and hard and soft earth.

LLANILID see CRAI

LLANILLTYD

4½ m. WSW of Brecon

ST ILLTYD. A bare circular churchyard at 1,100 ft containing, according to Theophilus Jones, the saint's burial-place (A.D. 480). The dull mid-c19 church (by *William Jones*, 1858) is abandoned.

BLAENCAMLAIS CASTLE, 1 m. W. On a lonely site at 1,050 ft. The tall mound, though lacking a bailey, is capped by the collapsed stonework of a substantial circular tower, 42 ft in diameter (cf. Bronllys and Tretower). It was almost certainly built by Llywelyn ap Gruffydd c. 1262. By 1265 it had been destroyed by the future King Edward I.

MOUNTAIN CENTRE, ½ m. E. An innovatory information and picnic facility for visitors by car to the Brecon Beacons National

Park. The idea came from the Carnegie U.K. Trust in 1965. The executant architects were *S. Colwyn Foulkes & Co.*, and the site chosen was a remote common on Mynydd Illtyd from which the views of the Beacons are glorious. It sensibly combines covered ways and loggias for wet weather with two floors of terraces for fine; through the use of local building materials and local planting species, it strikes a compromise between visual modernism and the real vernacular.

St John, Libanus, 1½ m. ese. Small nave and chancel in one, by *F. R. Kempson* and *J. B. Fowler*, 1891.

Bedd Illtyd (sn 974 264). An annular cairn about 45 ft across, with a hollow centre in which lies a large stone. It may be a Bronze Age ring cairn, but the siting is not characteristic. Ring cairns are not necessarily burial monuments and may have something in common with stone circles. However it may be later, as the name suggests.

Twyn y Gaer (sn 990 280) is a small univallate hillfort with an inturned entrance on the ne. On the slopes below are a ditched round mound, ten pillow mounds (artificial rabbit warrens), and a medieval platform house (the terraced site of a stone building). The Roman road from Brecon Gaer to Neath is also visible in this area.

LLANLLEONFEL

1½ m. n of Llangammarch Wells

Church (dedication unknown). On an ancient hilltop site in a circular enclosure. Single-chamber. Gone to ruin when Kilvert visited it; restored by *R. J. Withers* in 1874. He put in lancet windows in deep splays, a chancel arch with responds, etc. Double w bellcote. The sloping floor still gives an old feel, though. – glass. e, three lancets, 1889. – pillar stone. Inscribed with a metrical epitaph: i(n) (s)in(d)one muti ioruert ruallaunq sepulcris + iudicii adv(e)ntum specta(n)t i(n) pace trem(en)dum. c7–c9 ? – Four matching c18 tablets to the Gwynne family of Garth.

Maesllech, ½ m. sw. A barn at the farm has four pairs of rudely dressed late crucks; c17?

Garth House, ¼ m. se. The former home of the artistic Gwynne family, c17 at the ne but much rebuilt in the c18 and c19. Above garden terraces.

LLANSANTFFRAED

ST BRIDE. Nave, chancel with N (Buckland) chapel, and slender
octagonal S spire. Totally renewed by *Stephen Williams* of
Rhayader in 1884–5. Interior of reddish ashlar with white
corbels, and white E.E. foliage capitals on the chancel arches
(cf. Llanyre, R). The late C13 FONT, octagonal with curved
undersurfaces and cushion stops at the base, and porch stoup
were retained. Also some unusually dignified MONUMENTS.
Games Jones † 1681, with a segmental pediment and an epitaph attributed to Henry Vaughan. – Edmund Jones † 1683.
Inscribed on a convex slab, in an open-pedimented aedicule. –
Margaret Jones † 1695. On a fictive cloth with putti and garlands and formal frame. – Thomas Jones † 1713. In a surround of flowers, fruit, and putti (no architecture). – Thynne
Howe Gwynne † 1826. The inscription is apparently inserted
in an early C18 Corinthian tabernacle. – Henry Vaughan,
whose brother was rector here, was buried in the churchyard
in 1695. The large Grecian sarcophagus is not to him, however,
but to Col. Gwynne Holford, and was erected in 1847.
NEWTON FARMHOUSE, ¾ m. NW, or rather its predecessor,
was the birthplace of Henry Vaughan, the Silurist, in 1620.

LLANSPYDDID

ST CADOG. C14 nave and chancel in one. Cusped Y-tracery in
one N and three S windows. S porch with a C16 carved barge-
board. *C. Buckeridge* re-roofed the church in 1870, and gave it
a regular and boring interior and a W bellcote. – STOUP or
PISCINA. Late Norman, with dogtooth round the square rim.
– FONT. C13; recut. – The SOUNDING BOARD over the
pulpit is made from vine-trails and part of the coving from the
late C15 screen. – STAINED GLASS. W by *Charles Gibbs*,
c. 1856. – PILLAR STONE. In the churchyard to the N. Incised
with two circled crosses, one with four small circles placed
round it. C7–9. Said to mark the grave of Aulach, father of
Brychan. – Also in the churchyard a marble sarcophagus to
John Pearce † 1856, by *John Evan Thomas*. Carved with arms,
torches, etc.
BOLGOED, 1 m. SW. An early C19 three-storey house with a
veranda. Also a summer-house privy, square on plan, with a
pyramidal roof from which rises a narrower octagonal tower
with ogee windows.

LLANWRTHWL   9060
2¾ m. s of Rhayader

St Gwrthwl. Nave and chancel, by *J. G. Finch Noyes*, 1875.
The site is perhaps pre-Christian – see the raised churchyard
and the standing stone by the s porch. – FONT. Circular, with
four projecting heads. CII–12. – GLASS. E of 1874. – W by
Leonard Walker, 1936. St Paul. Almost abstract.

(TALWRNMAENOG. A small early C17 farmhouse with its original doorway, a panelled partition with carved doorheads, etc.
DOE)

(TALWRN, 2 m. W, was a cruck hall, partly rebuilt in 1668 and
1864.)

There are several stone BURIAL CAIRNS on the moorlands of
Gamriw and Cefn y Ffordd which may be visited on foot if
the weather is not too wet.

On GAMRIW are seven hill-top cairns, large simple piles of stone
on the top of the ridge, commanding fine views but uncharacteristically hidden from below. The largest one (SN 944
612) has a small shepherd's house built into it. The second cairn
from the N (SN 957 620) has a smaller cairn abutting one side,
a peculiarity of design which seems to be popular in this area,
since it also appears at Cefn y Ffordd.

CARNAU CEFN Y FFORDD comprise a cemetery group on the
col SE of the old trackway. Such siting is very characteristic
of a number of these monument groups. This cemetery contains
both large and small cairns, a low standing stone, and a block
with what appear to be artificial 'cup marks'. The two large
cairns, which can be easily seen across the valley, overlook the
smaller ones, but are not mutually intervisible. Both are large,
about 60–70 ft across, but can never have been high. The N
one may even have been a Platform Cairn. It has a good kerb
and a reasonably flat profile.

SAITH MAEN (SN 949 603) is a short alignment of seven small
stones. Only two of them are at all conspicuous, and the whole
group is rather difficult to find. It is on the SW side of the col,
below a boggy area. The purpose of alignments is unknown,
but they are an occasional component of these Bronze Age
monument groups.

Other cairns may be found on Drum-ddu and the surrounding
moorland, which is smooth, open, and relatively dry. The landscape and the monuments are highly characteristic of Bronze
Age environment and design and their aesthetic impact can be

well appreciated here. Similar groups may be found on other moorland areas in Mid Wales, but some of these moors are inaccessible and even dangerous. This one can be reached fairly easily from Llanwrthwl.

LLANWRTYD

1¼ m. NW of Llanwrtyd Wells

ST DAVID. In a circular churchyard. Probably an ancient foundation, but a seemingly C14–15 church. Nave with two Tudor windows. Short, non-aligned chancel with an unmoulded, off-centre arch. S porch with a chamfered round-headed doorway. S rood-stair turret; W bellcote. Restoration by *C. Buckeridge*, 1862; one of his emergency, low-cost ones. – PILLAR STONE. A stone incised with a circled cross divided horizontally; C7–9; brought from Llawdre farm. – FONT. C14–15, recut. William Williams Pantycelyn was curate here in 1740–2.

LLYN BRIANNE, 4 m. WNW. The reservoir for Swansea in the Upper Tywi Valley is partly in Powys, but the 300 ft high dam (1968–72) is just in Dyfed.

LLANWRTYD WELLS

ST JAMES. By *David Jenkins*, 1896.

Llanwrtyd Wells became a local watering-place in the late C18, and has small hotels and chapels of late last century. Edwardian CONGREGATIONAL CHAPEL. The BAPTIST CHAPEL of 1910 is in violent red and yellow terracotta. Of this period the spa buildings also.

A WOOLLEN FACTORY from Esgairmoel, 1 m. SE, built c. 1760, has been translated, with its looms, etc., to the Welsh Folk Museum, St Fagans.

LLANYNYS

2½ m. W of Builth Wells

ST LLYR. Remotely sited in fields beside the River Irfon. Nave, chancel, S porch, W bellcote. Repaired or rebuilt in 1687, c. 1778, 1894. The exterior is whitened. – FONT. C14. – ALTAR RAILS. C17. – GLASS. S, c. 1867.

(BERLLANBER, 1 m. ESE. Rebuilt in the C17 and after on the plan of a late medieval long-house.)

LLANYWERN

¾m. WNW of Llanfihangel Tal-y-llyn

St Mary. W porch; C14 nave and short chancel. Very small and scarcely touched in the C19, except for the windows. It is lit, at the time of writing, by oil lamps. Flagged floors. The nave has a scissor-truss roof, the chancel a ribbed canopy of *c*. 1500. The beams over the site of the rood are painted madder (cf. Llanelieu). – FONT. Circular and rounded; C13. – STOUP. – MONUMENTS. Thomas Powell † 1794, by *Hughes*. – Thomas Williams † 1828, also by *Hughes*. – Some worn C17 slabs. – The churchyard was, and is, a bog (hence the name).

Llanywern is an undisturbed and appealing hamlet of four adjoining farms and farmhouses of the C17–19. Ty Mawr is partly of *c*. 1600, with a late C17 addition with a porch.

LLYN BRIANNE *see* LLANWRTYD

LLYSDINAM

½ m. W of Newbridge-on-Wye

The home of the Venables-Llewelyn family, rebuilt since 1934 by *Guy Elwes*, and latterly by *Claude Phillimore*. Stucco, with an art-deco porch bow. A bedroom with decoration of *c*. 1820 was transported intact from Penllergaer, Glamorgan. In its C19 state partly by *S. W. Williams*. (½ m. W is a neat ringwork.)

NEWBRIDGE-ON-WYE (R). *See p. 259.*

LLYSWEN

St Gwendoline. According to Theophilus Jones, the site (in Llangoed Park) was given to the See of Llandaff *c*. 560. The present building, in a small circular churchyard, was largely renewed by *Charles Buckeridge* in 1863. Nave, chancel, timber S porch, and W tower. The retention of the Norman plan accounts for the slight axial discrepancies. The interior is almost unornamented, and the austerity of white walls and a dark wagon roof is particularly effective in the deep narrow chancel. Lancets there, and paired lancets and quatrefoils in the nave. – FONT. Norman, and round, on a masonry base. – GLASS. Four sensitive and beautifully executed small windows in the chancel. By *Carl Edwards*, *c*. 1946 to 1973.

400 yds SW of the village is a small MOTTE.

DDERW, ½ m. SE, was the home of the Morgan family, who were
later connected by marriage to the Morgans of Tredegar, near
Newport. Four gables, the r. one (the kitchen) a C17 addition
to the C16 three-gable house; but this front with its central
Venetian window is altered. The plan of c. 1590 was a half-H,
with the hall and cross-passage in the centre, a parlour and
buttery on the l., and the service wing on the r. The parlour
has a decorated fireplace. In the William and Mary period a
fine dog-leg staircase was added at the back; the C16 stair is in
the service wing. Near the house is an imposing group of C17
BARNS. The largest, a corn-barn with two porches, has a
plaque reading 'Erected 1681, Rebuilt 1854'.

PENTRE SOLLARS, 1 m. SE. The N wing preserves one cruck
truss, with braces making a pointed arch, from a C15 hall-house.
The S wing has a big plain fireplace of c. 1600 and heavy
mullioned and transomed windows.

LLANGOED, 1½ m. NW. A house was built on this large estate
in 1633 by Sir Henry Williams.* His father Sir David Williams
built Gwernyfed (B), which remained the family home till
c. 1730, when they moved to Llangoed. The C17 house is the
present S wing, five bays but not with the original windows,
and remodelled inside in the C18. Two-storey porch,
approached now by semicircular steps and with lateral arches
as well as the front cambered one. Over the latter is a heraldic
date-stone charged with the Williams' three cocks.‡

98   The greater part of Llangoed is by *Sir Clough Williams-Ellis*.
This commission, from Mr Archibald Christy in 1913, was his
first major work. As with Lutyens's contemporary houses, the
style is an attempt to recreate the country house tradition in
modern terms. The building period was between 1913 to 1914,
the date over the entrance, and 1919, the date on the forecourt
gatepiers. The main SW front is a broad E with hipped-roofed
blocks in the angles; the one on the r. contains the staircase.
Gable-ended wings with a sense of Cotswold Jacobean mass-
ing. A plain parapet above the first floor divides the elevation
roughly into two, for the central hipped roof is very tall. In
complete contrast with all these 'vernacular' features, the entry
tower, of clean Gwespyr stone, is sophisticated, classical,
French. Doorway arch keyed directly to the top of the short
rusticated basement of an attenuated Doric *piano nobile*. On
the first storey a C17 type window and a balcony. The free

* There seems no reason for it to be called a castle.
‡ Mr G. Chichester kindly helped me on Llangoed.

Doric entablature has triglyphs only on the single pilasters, the date-inscription running between them as a frieze. Hipped roof with a cartouche and swags perched on the eaves over the window. The broad garden front, with three bows in a comfortable Edwardian regularity of mullioned and transomed windows set against local dressed stone, is without distinctive features except for a Venetian window in a surprising white dormer. The preceding house and estate buildings were grouped round the courtyard, and there was a hipped roof (this being a consistent motif of the new house also). Dining room with vigorous fluted Doric pilasters and again an intermittent frieze. The polished wood staircase, grandly conceived with mural paintings of gorgeous birds by *F. Hodge*, emerges at a gallery of unfluted Ionic columns. The work at Llangoed, in addition to formal gardens, included a laundry and a light-hearted STABLE COURT, with a turreted cottage on the l. It has a splendid pedimented cupola. On account of its delicacy and use of bright colour, this group is in fact a truer portent of its architect's exuberant mature style than the more monumental house.

NEW LLANGOED, 2 m. NW. By *Nicholas Johnston*, 1977–8. A large prehistoric STANDING STONE can be seen in the middle of a field below the road (SO 123 395). It is a fine stone, now leaning, but almost 11 ft tall.

BOUGHROOD BRIDGE, ½ m. NW. *See* Boughrood (R).

LLYWEL   *8030*

1 m. NW of Trecastle

LLYWEL CHURCH or ST DAVID. The church, founded by Llywel, a disciple of Teilo, in the C5, was granted to the Chapter of St David's in the C13. Now there is a good Perp building of about the 1480s which has kept most of its details. The early Tudor years were a period when very many Breconshire churches were reconstructed – here the nave, S porch, and chancel. The W tower has a W doorway (exceptional in this area) with a stoup beside it. Its two-centred arch has a continuous hollow chamfer and is recessed into the tall and widely splayed base of the tower; three corbels carry the drip-course over it. Three tiers of small windows; gargoyles and battlements. SE embattled stair-turret. No other mouldings or buttresses. This plainness and the obstructed upper window to the nave suggest a C14 date and alteration in the C15. No E arch either, but in the

entrance are placed three bays of the SCREEN, removed in 1869. Tall round-headed openings with vines etc. carved in the spandrels. The arches descend onto crocketed pinnacles, characteristically C16 in their detail and subordinate position. The nave windows have the common Late Perp tracery, three ogee lights and then two heart-shapes, each divided by a mullion. Small two-light Tudor windows at the W. Lower and upper doorways to the N rood stairs. Low chancel arch and now a screen of 1925 made by *Harry Hems*. S priest's doorway. Similar windows again in the chancel; the E window is four lights grouped two and two by the tracery arches. At the N a shallow tomb recess with a Tudor arch. Nave and chancel both have barrel-vaults with a chequer of moulded ribs and no plaster infill, and so does the porch. Its outer doorway is two-centred; the inner is four-centred and has the original door. *Scott* was in charge of repairs in 1869. – PILLAR STONE. About 5 ft 7 in. tall; marked with Ogams with the name TARI-
CORO. C5. – The LLYWEL STONE. Plaster replica of a find at Capel Ilud in the neighbouring parish, now in the British Museum; *c*. 6 ft high, tapering downwards. Incised on one side in the C8 or later with pictographs or linear symbols in four panels, including a saltire, two figures, and bishop with a staff. The decoration most resembles pre-Christian art in Brittany. The introduction of figures does not, according to Canon J. Jones-Davies, suggest a Celtic origin. On the other side is a burial inscription, probably primary, of *c*. A.D. 500: (M)ACCU-
TRENI † SALICIDUNI. The cross between the words may have been added in the C7. The name is repeated in Ogams. –
– FONT. C11/12 (pre-Norman); disused. – STOCKS. Made in 1798. Under the tower. – LECTERN. Brass; 1917. – GLASS. E by *Cox & Sons*, *c*. 1872. – MONUMENTS. Sibil Morgan † 1600. Slab with lettering only. – Lewis Powell † 1867. With pretty Gothic decoration.

CRAI. *See* p. 311.

0030 LOWER CHAPEL/LLANFIHANGEL FECHAN

ST MICHAEL. Founded *c*. 1790 and rebuilt in 1863–4 by *Thomas Nicholson*. Nave, E bellcote, and small semicircular sanctuary, for once a happy treatment of an E end. Fitments of *c*. 1880. – GLASS. S, 1906. – MONUMENTS. Charles Powell † 1796, by *H. Wood*, Bristol. – Roger Watkins † 1858.

CASTLE MADOC, ¾ m. NNW. The date-stone on the W reads

'... Ty Newydd. T(homas) P(owell). 1588'. By the late C17 the house had a s front of three storeys and six bays, and on the w gable end a characteristic two-storey porch with an arched doorway. This w front seems to have been enlarged c. 1825 and given a hipped roof. On the r. of the s side the Italianate stucco porch was added c. 1850, two storeys (with rustication on the lower) and a pediment. Further extensions at this end include a three-bay E entrance front of c. 1880. To the N a STABLE BLOCK of c. 1800 which has a tall pedimental gable with a bull's eye window. N again a pyramidal-roofed DOVECOTE of the same period. The early history of the site begins with the Powell family, who in the C11 or C12 built a ringwork on higher ground NE of the house. This seems to have been abandoned two centuries later for a stone bailey, on to the walls of which the present house was constructed; the MOTTE of this second castle is directly behind the house.

GAER FAWR and GAER FACH. Twin hillforts on either side of the Honddu valley. Gaer Fawr on the NE side (SO 020 380) is a long oval enclosure with two ramparts around most of its circuit except on the naturally steep s side. Inturned entrance at the SE end. Gaer Fach (SO 009 366) is a smaller fort with only one main rampart. On the SW and NE corners, however, this is doubled, and on the steep s side it never existed. The defences are best preserved on the w.

MAEN MAWR see GLYNTAWE

MAESMYNYS   0040
2½ m. SW of Builth Wells

ST DAVID. Nave and chancel, rebuilt in 1878. Bulky lychgate of 1903. The sanctuary was brightly refurbished in 1963 by *George Pace* and *Ronald Sims*. Its E window (Christ in a vesica of cherubs' wings) and the five painted REREDOS panels (Crucifixion, Annunciation, and Nativity), by *Henry Harvey*, were designed as a correlating group.

ABERCNEIDDON, ½ m. NW. Built by *Edward Price*, the surveyor of Builth after the fire of 1691, as his home. The material is brick (English bond), which was very rarely used in Breconshire before c. 1850. The pattern, the local late C17 one – hipped sprocketed roof, and a five-bay front – is particularly well-proportioned here. Flattened segmental heads to the lower windows, including the two narrow ones beside the door; the first-floor windows are similarly spaced, but with blank bays above the narrow windows. Fine central staircase with William and Mary woodwork.

MERTHYR CYNOG

St Cynog. In a large circular churchyard, by tradition the burial-place of Cynog. The existing church however is post-Conquest. The broad and low (Norman?) w tower has thick walls, a square NE stair-turret to two thirds of its height, and corbel-table and battlements. Single-chamber nave and chancel of unusual length, with a junction in the build just w of the screen. The tower and w half are perhaps C12 and C13; the E half has two trefoiled N lancets of the C14. C14 S doorway. Tudor details in the tower. C16 arch-braced roof, much renewed. This is another restoration by *C. Buckeridge* – 1860–1. – PISCINA. – SCREEN. C14, which is a considerable rarity. Massive plain timbers. A two-centred, buttressed central archway and broad openings either side. – STOUP. C12(?); round. – FONT. Circular and goblet-shaped. C12/13(?).

YSCIRFECHAN, 1¼ m. w. Largely of *c.* 1670 – see the two-storey porch with moulded outer and inner doorways – but developed from a medieval hall, formerly owned by a branch of the Vaughan family.

BAILYBRITH, 2 m. NE. Early C17, built round remains of a hall-house of *c.* 1500. Part of an arch-braced collar-beam points to the hall. Large two-storey gabled range with a porch with a voussoir-arched doorway, the original front door, stairs beside, etc. Large hall with stone arched entrance. Diagonal chimneys.

MOOR PARK *see* LLANBEDR YSTRAD YW

NEUADD SIARMAN

1½ m. sw of Maesmynys church

At Neuadd Siarman Farm stood the C10 PILLAR CROSS now in the Brecknock Museum at Brecon (*see* p. 298).

NEWTON *see* LLANFAES

OLD GWERNYFED *see* FELINDRE

PARTRISHOW/PATRISIO

4½ m. NE of Crickhowell

St Ishow or Issui. Little and lonely, in a remote site with far views, Partrishow church demonstrates the liturgical arrangements of several periods, and one is scarcely surprised to find that the conservation of this exceptional building is c20 work. It was entrusted to *W. D. Caröe* and done in 1908–9 (date on the LYCHGATE). The church consists of nave and chancel, and of an EGLWYS Y BEDD abutted at the W but with its own entrance and altar. This chapel has a c14 arch-braced roof, s doorway and trefoil window, and a c13 W lancet. The altar is placed acentrally on the r., over the grave of Issai. Though the site is that of the original shrine, what it is abutted to must be an older fabric, and an opening with a grille was made to join the two. Beside the grille a cinquefoiled niche. The Norman nave has no N windows, and only Tudor s windows and door. c15 porch with a stoup. Outside, along the s side of nave and chancel is a stone seat facing the base and shaft of the CHURCHYARD CROSS, perhaps of *c.* 1300, except for the lantern by *Caröe* dated 1918. The chancel was rebuilt in Elizabethan Perp – at least it has the paired lights with ribbed panelling above and a label with square stops of the local variety in its E window. Late c15 chancel arch. In front of it the famous SCREEN and ROOD LOFT, surviving with little impairment and datable to *c.* 1500. The central door has a shallow triangular head. On either side are four narrow openings with cusped lancet tracery, and at the ends two wider bays (above the altars) with intersected-diagonal traceries. The underside of the loft is a restored rib-and-boss flat coving. On the lower bressumer three bands of running ornament, including one of water-leaf and one of vines with splendid dragons either end; on the upper, bands of a geometrical motif and cresting. The parapet itself is of muntins with panels of Late Perp tracery patterning which strengthens the screen's shimmery character. On the N the rood stair-turret. Beneath the loft are two stone altars, older than the screen (and not destroyed in 1550 at the order of Edward VI). The barrel-ceiled nave roof has moulded ribs and wallplate, all late c15; the chancel roof, however, also ceiled and with battlemented tie-beams, was put in by *Caröe*. Many JACOBEAN FITMENTS. – The ALTAR RAILS with fret-cut balusters are of *c.* 1640 (Archbishop Laud's requirement). – PULPIT. Also mid c17. – Painted on the walls (W) a DOOM FIGURE, (N) the perished ROYAL ARMS, and several panels of texts. – FONT. This alone remains of the church dedicated by Herewald before the Norman invasion. It dates from *c.* 1055. The design is aesthetically a good solution; a simple cylinder, the broad rim carved with two rolls terminating in leaves, and inside this the inscription MENHIR ME FECIT I(N) TE (M) PORE GENILLIN in Hiberno-Saxon minuscules. Cynhillin was Lord of Ystrad Yw. The leaf is of the Winchester manuscript type, a form which appears in carving in other counties.* −MONUMENTS. Fourteen memorials dated between 1757 and 1804, their raised ornament, usually with floral borders, strongly coloured and gilded. They are attractive work of the *Brute* family and their followers, though only a few are signed. − William Sanders † 1757, by *T. Brute*. − Anne Griffiths † 1804, by *J. Brute*. − John Powell † 1788 and William Powell † 1766 by *A. Brute*. − To round off such a compendium of antiquities, the parson's horse had a STABLE by the lychgate.

NEUADD, 1½ m. SE. A small, low C15 hall-house of a type common in England but rarer in Wales: that is a one-storey hall with an arch-braced and wind-braced roof between short storeyed end sections. The stud-and-plank partitions between these parts remain. They had triangular doorheads. A two-centred E archway opened to the original cross-passage. The hall itself was fitted about the end of the C16 with a chimney with monolithic jambs, a Tudor stone doorway to a wide cross-passage behind it, and an upper floor.

TYN-Y-LLWYN, ¼ m. SE, below the church, is a striking C15 and C16 farmhouse converted to a cruciform plan in 1649. Its particular interest is in the number of minor but unchanged domestic features. The S end, on falling ground, slopes sharply back and has C17 diagonally-placed chimneys. The fireplace beneath has a bressumer carved (in 1678?) with the arms of the Herbert family − two dragons and two fleurs-de-lys, with an arching moulding. The plan consists of a cross-passage between two broad original doors, outside which the wings were added; and a large loft above which has a big fireplace and a post-and-panel partition, of the C16, with doorways to two upper rooms. A spiral stair leads to a room still lit by unglazed wood-mullioned windows with shutters.

(TYN-Y-PANT, ½ m. SE. Ruined cruck long-house.)

(Y COED, ½ m. NNE. A rebuilt cruck long-house with one truss remaining.)

(GRWYNE FAWR masonry dam was built high in the Black Mountains in 1930 by the Abertillery Water Board.)

---

* Professor Zarnecki pointed this out to me.

PENCELLI

0020

1½ m. SE of Llanfrynach

PENCELLI CASTLE belonged to Ralph de Mortimer. It overlooks the Usk halfway between Blaenllynfi and Brecon castles, but on the S bank. There may have been a motte, but the remains now are the bases only of a large bailey wall and of a roughly rectangular tower, and a section of wall SE of the house. Buck's print of 1741 shows a late C13 gatehouse with two possibly semi-circular towers. In the C16 Pencelli was the property of the Herberts of Montgomery. Is it possible that the FARMHOUSE, much altered as it is, was their house? It is a double-pile, two storeys plus attics and fairly lofty. Main S doorway with a good Tudor arch with carved spandrels. On the door the date 1583. Comparison would have to be made with Newton. Another feature in common is the re-use of old material – lancets, from the castle presumably – for the stairwell at the N. However that may be, the front with sash-windows seems C18, and has a nice castellated parapet. Porch with sharply-pointed arch.

PENCELLI COURT. Dated 1691 on a chimney. Five bays long, with lattice windows.

LLANFIGAN. *See* p. 337.

PENDERYN*

9000

ST CYNOG. Very small W tower, on a battered base and crowned with a corbel-table and battlements, of C15 type. The nave and chancel, much rebuilt but agreeable, are mostly late C19. – STOUP. In the large S porch. Octagonal, with a snowflake pattern cut on three sides. – STAINED GLASS. E, the Adoration, three lights, 1886, in a *cinquecento* manner. – Chancel S, the Presentation of Christ to Simeon, also 1886, and by the same artist. – Nave S, 1882. – N, by *Morris & Co.*, *c.* 1919. – LYCHGATE.

(BODWIGIAD, ¾ m. E. A five-bay house of 1815, with a gabled porch and Gothic window. DOE)

CAIRNS in Cwm Cadlan (SN 986 110). A group of three Bronze Age monuments runs down the valley to the S of the road. The E one is badly ruined; the middle one is a fine large cairn about 60 ft in diameter; the W one is a very good example of a large Ring Cairn with a boulder at the centre. Other cairns may be found on the ridge to the N of the road but the walk is a long one. (Beware of swallow holes in this area.)

* Transferred to Mid Glamorgan in 1974.

PENMYARTH
2 m. WNW of Crickhowell

CHURCH (in the park at Penmyarth). Small nave and chancel,
a Norman to E.E. design of 1852 with plain shafts at the wide
chancel arch and beside the three E lancets. A far from conventional w tower of three short stages with a low pyramidal
stone spire of overlapping stones, above a corbel-table with
grotesque heads. The w arch has shafts again and is open to the
porch. Diagonal buttresses complete its eclectic but picturesquely agreeable oddness. – The STAINED GLASS is quite
fine. E, 1852. – N and S sanctuary lancets. – Nave: the first on
the N, 1858 (the three Marys at the Tomb) and the first on the
S, 1860 ('Suffer Little Children . . .'), are a pair. – The second
on the N and S, both of 1861 (The Good Shepherd, etc.) and
perhaps by *Clayton & Bell*, are a pair and very richly coloured.
– MONUMENT. Sir Joseph Bailey M.P. † 1858. His portrait in
relief, and a woman kneeling praying by it; by *J. E. Thomas*.
The only non-Gothic design here – to the builder of the church.
GLANUSK PARK, on the S side of the Usk. The house of 1825–
30 by *Robert Lugar* was demolished in 1954. It was built for
Sir Joseph Bailey (1783–1858), nephew of Richard Crawshay
of Cyfarthfa Castle – the second of Lugar's big houses in South
Wales. Sir Joseph made his fortune by reviving the Nant-y-
Glo ironworks, and from the Beaufort ironworks in Gwent.
At the three park entrances are LODGES of the same date; the
drive crosses a bridge over the Usk and passes beneath a rock-
faced gatehouse, both a little self-important and apparently of
the same date by another hand. The STABLE COURTYARD is
of this kind too, except for the delightful GATE TOWER, which
must surely be *Lugar*'s. Four slim corner turrets with fanciful
arrow-loops rise on squinches to octagonal ogee domes, a play-
ful piece of Gothic-cum-Elizabethan, and reminiscent of the
style of the house. Glanusk was earlier and more elegant than
Maesllwch (R); it was, however, similarly foursquare with
fronts on opposite sides, and had a two-storey hall colonnaded
like an atrium. The SE front, a three-storey range, had an eye-
catching skyline of lofty octagonal ogee turrets and pinnacles,
towering against the wooded Myarth hill behind. The new
house on the site is by *Louis Hurley*, 1978.
Two estate COTTAGES at Pont-y-bryn-hurt look as if they are
by *J. L. Pearson*.
GLIFFAES, I m. w. Built for the Rev. W. West in 1881; by

whom? Now a hotel. The site is terraced to overlook the Usk, but the whole arrangement is informal. The house is Italianate – though that is a bad description of a simple stone villa adorned only with Lombard brick campanili at either end. (Lugar designed a house here in 1841, but surely it is not the present one.) The LODGE is a delight. Of appealing materials inventively used, it compresses a number of charming details – a spiralling stair tower, a campanile, another turret – into one miniature group round the porch.

TRETOWER. See p. 378.

PENOYRE see BATTLE

PENPONT   9020

BETTWS PENPONT CHURCH. Rebuilt in 1864 by *Sir George Gilbert Scott*; however the design is not up to the quality of e.g. Bwlch-y-Cibau (M). The previous building was an C18 chapel of ease of Llanspyddid, and both were erected by the Williams family of Penpont. Small, short nave with a scissor-beam roof, and a round apsidal chancel with a hemicyclical wood-ribbed vault (cf. Bwlch-y-Cibau). Circular w tower with conical roof. This forms a narrow w apse inside and serves as the baptistery. Some features of the old building were kept, which possibly accounts for the repeated use of curved forms and certainly for those of the tower. – STAINED GLASS. Five E lancets by *Hardman*. – Nave S by *Burlison & Grylls*. – W, 1892. – ORGAN by *Flight & Robson*, 1804. – Two HATCHMENTS.

PENPONT. The façade to the E is austerely, and rather ineptly, neo-classical. Ashlar. Three storeys. The first-floor windows have entablatures and the centre of these alone has brackets. This upper part is five bays wide; the portico beneath extends to seven to mask the lengthening of the main rooms. Colonnade of the Tuscan order, rather bleak, with no fluting or frieze. Its centre bay breaks forward further than the end bays, carrying the panelled parapet with it. At the angles the columns are coupled. These alterations, of *c.* 1810 and probably for Penry Williams (Sheriff 1804, Lord Lieutenant 1836), are the work of an unknown architect. Might it be *Hopper* (cf. Erddig, Clwyd) or *Smirke*? Penpont was originally built *c.* 1666 by Daniel Williams (in whose family it remains). His double-pile house survives at the end of a hall corridor with slight Gothic plaster vaulting. Its stairs, occupying a generous two-storey well, have unusual balusters – two twists at the bottom, then vase shapes with slanted top mouldings – and newels with arch and keystone panels and ball-finials. Upstairs a room with flat late C17 panelling and tapestries of the Queen of Sheba. Dining room and drawing room are remodelled alike: twin Ionic columns form screens in place of the old walls, of brown and yellow scagliola respectively. Panelled plaster ceilings of late C17 type, respectively with laurel and garland decoration. In the drawing room, an early C19 fireplace with relief figures by *J. E. Thomas*, but panelling and an open-pedimented doorway again on late C17 patterns. Beside the house a mid C19 conservatory.

The complement of late C17 to early C18 buildings of different types around the house is worth noting. The LODGE (or dower house) near the church, apparently of 1686 and later, is two-storeyed with semicircular end walls. Its pediment is filled with a Baroque limewood carving with the Boleyn arms and swags of fruits. On the W of the house the STABLES, of seven bays with a pedimental gable, the end bays treated as two-storey pavilions. On the N, thus forming a courtyard, the three-bay COACH HOUSE, also pedimented and with a lantern. Windows with stilted depressed arches on both. Square DOVECOTE to the W, built on piers, with timber-framed brick-nogged walls and a lantern on its pyramidal roof. The LAUNDRY on the river bank has ogee windows to the N. The handsome BRIDGE over the Usk was built at the same time as the house (*c.* 1666); quite broad, of four arches with cutwaters, it makes its contribution to the valley landscape here.

ABERCAMLAIS, ½ m. W. Since *c.* 1571 the home of the Williams family, a cadet branch of which later in the C17 built Penpont (originally Abercamlais Isaf). Such a pair of large houses so close is exceptional in the county in view of their outbuildings and bridges; moreover they share affinities of date and plan-type, both having three main floors and grand staircases centrally placed in the back half of the house. The S front here is of *c.* 1710, seven bays of dressed local stone, its only enrichment a wooden cornice of foliage consoles and an egg-and-dart frieze which breaks over each one. On the E side possible evidence of the early C17 house. Attic dormers added in 1910 by *Caröe*. The interior, also mostly early C18, has contemporary panelled rooms and Early Georgian fireplaces. In the entrance hall a ceiling with a central whorl, but a frame in another style. In the drawing room the fireplace (said to have come from Fonthill) is carved with two fine neo-classical relief figures with flowing draperies. The plaster ceiling – essentially a Late Baroque cartouche – like the hall ceiling seems to have come from elsewhere. As at Penpont, ingenious staircase design has produced some attractive work, including turned boxwood balusters and a gently widening lower flight. The smaller E stair has a variety of baluster forms.

A Tudor LODGE shows the excessive rustication of the mid Victorian fashion. Vastly more interesting as a rural type is the early C18 PIGEON HOUSE, a tall stone octagon supporting a cupola. Its square lower part is built to bridge the stream, and so made a latrine – simplicity itself, with useful and ornamental qualities into the bargain. Abercamlais has its own BRIDGE as well, across to the N bank of the Usk, of four arches and originally very early – c. 1600. Its roadway was widened c. 1680 over the cutwaters on the upstream side. A spindly mid-C19 SUSPENSION BRIDGE spans the river 200 yds downstream.*

PETERSTONE COURT see LLANHAMLACH

PONT-AR-HYDFER
1½ m. SW of Trecastle

8020

ST MARY, TRAEANGLAS. By *J. B. Fowler*, 1890. The reredos is tiled.

ABERHYDFER BRIDGE. 1855 by *William Williams*, County Surveyor.

PONT GWENLLIAN, ¾ m. NW. Rebuilt in 1833, single arch; *W. Watkins*, Surveyor.

MEITY ISAF, 1 m. SSW. A small cottage, yet with chamfered pointed stone doorways in the N and W walls, and remains of Tudor Perp windows.

NANT TARW CIRCLES (SN 819 258). A pair of Bronze Age stone circles and a ruined cairn stand on a col between two moorland streams – a setting very characteristic of these groups of religious monuments. Both circles are roughly the same diameter, but the stones of the W circle are on the whole slighter and less evenly spaced, perhaps due to destruction. About 400 ft to the SW is a large fallen monolith with two smaller stones behind it, and on the E side of the W circle another, an arrangement very reminiscent of that at Cerrig Duon, where the outliers are the most conspicuous features of the complex from a distance,

---

* I am grateful for information on Abercamlais to Captain N. Garnons-Williams.

which would be the case here were they standing. The nearby cairn, which undoubtedly belongs to the group, is now badly ruined, but earlier records speak of a large kerb.

SCETHROG

1½ m. NW of Llansantffraed

HEN BERSONDY. Probably of *c.* 1600, to go by remains of a wood-mullioned window and a corbelled chimney. In plan, a single row of rooms, all very much modernized. In the angle between it and the tithe barn is a deep well.

SCETHROG HOUSE. Date-stone for 1691, the period of its enlargement in the prosperous William-and-Mary fashion (cf. Abercynrig). So there are hipped sprocketed roofs and clustered square chimneys, and inside some good woodwork – panelling, bolection-moulded fireplaces, and particularly two large staircases, both very close in date, at either end of the house. An older wing at the rear.

SCETHROG TOWER, ¼ m. SW, built by a branch of the Picard family, is one of the two tower-houses in Breconshire (the other is at Talgarth). It stands on a knoll in flat ground beside the Usk. The lower part of the walls has a batter (inside which was a cellar) and other stonework suggesting an early C14 date, particularly the pointed doorway to the mural stair and two fireplace corbels on the first floor. The doorway, windows, internal features, and roof are Tudor or later.

LLANSANTFFRAED. *See* p. 353.

SENNYBRIDGE

CASTELL DU or RHYD-Y-BRIW. A tower and walled court were built in the reign of Edward III near the confluence of the Senni and the Usk. Earthworks only remain, apart from a fragmentary round tower on the S. In 1271 the castle was the seat of Einion Sais.

GLAN-USK. Early Victorian stucco villa with a Doric porch.

LLWYNCYNTEFIN. Two-storey porch with a chamfered, rounded doorway and above it a stone with the coat of arms of the builder, Hugh Penry, and the date 1634. Wooden ovolo-moulded windows on this and on the bay to the l. A trefoiled stone window in its gable. Original inner door with a wicket. The hall with through-passage behind this has plain late C17 plasterwork between the beams. L. wing rebuilt in local early C18 style. Much Victorian alteration.

PONT LLWYNCYNTEFIN. A fine span of two arches with a cutwater over the Usk; dated 1750.

TALACHDDŪ

ST MARY. In a raised circular churchyard. Small nave and chancel perhaps as early as the C14, much restored in 1864 by *Thomas Nicholson*, who inserted the chancel arch and substituted the W wooden belfry for a W tower. Both nave and chancel have C15 ribbed barrel ceilings. The S porch doorway and neat arch-braced roof (cf. Llanfilo) are also Perp; the Tudor-headed S doorway and a N and a S window are nearer to *c*. 1600. – FONT. A triple-clustered column with a shallow bowl; last quarter of the C13.

GLYN CELYN, ¼ m. SE. A Late Regency house of pink ashlared stone; the three-window front with its two pedimental gables steps back for the central bay. Canted bows on the r. Built by the Rev. Charles Griffith *c*. 1833. Two-storey LODGE in the same style.

TALGARTH

ST GWENDOLINE. St Gwendoline, according to tradition, was buried at Talgarth. This is a large church for the area, now with a nave and chancel in one, N vestry, W tower, S aisle, and S porch. The vestry with its random stone segmental S arch and broad squint to the chancel seems to be the N transept of a cruciform church of the C13. Such plans are commonly associated with *clas* foundations. The nave (with the new aisle) was apparently rebuilt *c*. 1400 with a four-bay nave arcade and a single-bay chancel arcade. That almost makes two naves. They share details of the Y-tracery of *c*. 1300 with later insertions like the Perp S aisle E window. No chancel arches, but a timber arch and a new E window were inserted in the nave in the extensive restoration of 1873 by *Thomas Nicholson*. Perp additions are the tall and gaunt three-stage tower and the S porch, which has an earlier stoup inside. Blocked late C16 doorway in the N nave wall. At the W a fragment of vine-trail from the SCREEN. – MONUMENTS. Late C13 cross slab, the cross with carved foliage in a quatrefoil round it, and fronds also branching from the stem, all in high relief. – Howell Harris (the religious reformer) † 1773, a lettered memorial, by *Games*. – Joseph Harris † 1761. A fine oval design, the inscription fitting the lower half of the slab, an urn the upper. – William Vaughan † 1774; on a shaped armorial bracket. By *A. Brute*. – William Vaughan † 1631. A slab lettered round the margins in the medieval fashion.

The village is largely C19 growth on the main road and tramway routes between the Wye and Usk valleys. The plain classical TOWN HALL dates from 1877. Groupings near the church are older. A distinct and pretty hamlet exists below on either bank of the River Enig. Beside the bridge is a TOWER HOUSE, one of two in Breconshire (the other is at Scethrog on the Usk). It is three storeys high and has a C17 pyramidal roof. A straight mural stair in the E wall has been destroyed. The remaining details – machicolation on the N and a small two-centred window, and a similar window and a garderobe shaft on the W – look C14. A little below on the same bank is GREAT HOUSE FARM, which is partly C17. It faces an C18 brick barn with pigeon-holes in the gable.

GREAT PORTHAML, 1 m. NNE, was the home of Sir William Vaughan, who became the first High Sheriff of Brecknockshire in 1539. Henry VII stayed here on his way to Bosworth, and essentially the house is the one existing then. Hall with three open scissor trusses; though one of the best medieval roofs in Wales, it is now invisible above a ceiling. Two of the trusses incorporate pierced spandrel-boards and king-pendants (cf. Old Court, Bredwardine, Herefordshire). Below the screens passage, cut off by a framed partition, are three plainer bays, originally roofing the first-floor great chamber with their arch-braced collar trusses. Lateral fireplace. An original wing of great interest extended behind, before the regrettable recent rebuilding. The house is mentioned by Leland. The vaulted porch (to the cross-passage), with its doorway with a four-centred head beneath a segmental hood with square stops, and the gate tower alone remain to be seen from a Tudor forecourt more grandiose than the house. This tower is also an unusual survival, though a feature of C16 Border houses, architecturally competent and English in type. It has a cross-vault, then a chamber above with a fireplace and Tudor windows. The main archways and the windows have hoodmoulds again with diagonal square stops. Stair in the N wall to the embattled look-out. At the time of writing it is in poor repair. Only two Tudor doorways re-used in a later barn survive from the rest of the C16 work: the large timber-framed barn is C17.

MID WALES HOSPITAL, ½ m. SE. 1900 by *Giles, Gough & Trollope*. Separate CHAPEL with plain lancets.

TREGUNTER, I m. W, the fine mid Georgian house built by Thomas Harris, was demolished *c.* 1924. Thomas, an elder brother of Howell Harris of Trevecca (and father-in-law of Perdita Robinson), spent his London-made fortune on the Tregunter estate between 1765 and 1775. The house was of brick, five bays and three storeys flanked by three-bay wings of two storeys. Much good carved panelling from the interior was dispersed in 1914. Lakes seem to have been made in the grounds. Tregunter was later the home of Joseph Harris's granddaughter, following the death of her husband W. A. Madocks (*see* Tremadoc, Gwynedd).

At TREGUNTER FARM a two-storey granary of *c.* 1766–7 still stands. Five cart-openings beneath – a simple Italianate composition much imitated in the following century in the vicinity.

TREFECCA. *See* p. 376.

PENDRE CAMP (SO 155 326), 4 acres in extent, is defended by two circuits of ramparts surviving in places to a height of 10 ft. It is on a naturally defended site above a bend in the river.

THREE COCKS 1030

GWERNYFED PARK (SECONDARY SCHOOL). By *W. E. Nesfield*, 1877–80, for Col. Thomas Wood. In stone, and in a rather commonplace Jacobean, the porch gate no more prominent than the rest of the front. Some familiar detail – a sundial and pediment on a chimneystack, and of course East Anglian brick chimneys and his 'pies' and rosettes on the lead parapets. But this is not the top of Nesfield's form; and modern classrooms have been added on the r. The STABLE RANGE on the l. is the better proportioned part and the more historicist, and no doubt alludes to the C17 house (Old Gwernyfed, Felindre) that Col. Wood also owned. Some tile-hanging and half-timbering. The pale-coloured LODGE has wooden bows and a porch projecting from a conventional stone centre.

Nesfield (or his father in old age?) laid out gardens also.

ABERLLYNFI CASTLE, ¼ m. NW. Motte, formerly with a bailey, refortified in 1233. Nearby, the total ruin of Aberllynfi church (?).

TREVITHEL, 1¼ m. SW. The façade, of just after 1700, shows a determination, not comparable with other local houses, to make an organized design in terms of the Queen Anne style. The front is of dressed stone, five bays, the ends articulated with battered rusticated pilasters, and with a richly moulded string with consoles above it, surviving (after C19 change) on the l. On the ground floor of the one-bay, slightly projecting porch are a pair of crude tapering pilasters worked with zigzag and lozenges, then an abacus, and 'capitals' carved with the Prince of Wales's feathers. The rest of the façade, below the tall hipped roof, is missing. The house is L-shaped and lofty, and mostly mid C17. Fine central staircase round a well with two turned balusters a tread, fluted newels, and with scrolly sides to the treads. The first flight is walnut and the second oak.

LITTLE LODGE LONG CAIRN (SO 182 380). One of the lesser known Neolithic burial chambers of Severn Cotswold type, but one of the more interesting to visit since the cruciform chamber can be well seen at the S end, under a tree. Stones to the W suggest the existence of an entrance passage from that side, and there may have been additional chambers in the N half of the cairn. The site was excavated without much result.*

The ROUND CAIRN at Pipton, ½ m. W, a Bronze Age burial monument about 55 ft across, can be seen from the road on flat land beside the river. It is grass-grown, but there is evidence of stone within. It has been disturbed in the centre. The earlier LONG CAIRN, a Neolithic burial monument of very complex plan, is not accessible to visitors, and in any case the stone chambers are not visible. A model may be seen in the National Museum of Wales and the excavation is reported in *Archaeologia Cambrensis*, CV (1956).

8040

TIRABAD

Llandulas parish

3 m. S of Llanwrtyd Wells

CHURCH. Rebuilt on a new site in 1716, and altered in 1871. – MONUMENT to Sackville Gwynne of Glanbran † 1734, who built it.

9020

TRALLONG

¾ m. NW of Penpont

ST DAVID. Single-chamber nave and chancel of two builds. Blocked priest's doorway with a C16 rounded arch in the E

* *Man* (Feb. 1929), 34–6.

section; also a Dec trefoiled N window. A C16 S triplet. The new
roof, W bellcote, windows, etc., and timber N porch are by *C.
Buckeridge*. This job was done in 1861 at the instigation of the
Rev. Gilbert Harries and saved the building from demolition.
During the operations, an Early Christian PILLAR STONE was
found serving as a lintel in a window. It is 5 ft 3 in. tall and
the broad end was originally bedded *c.* 16 in. into the ground.
The Latin inscription reads CUNOCENNI FILIU(S) CUN-
OCENI HIC IACIT; the Ogams on the side of the stone give
a similar meaning. Dr Nash-Williams dated these inscriptions
to the C5–early C6. The Latin ring-cross, however, was cut
on the previously buried end in the C7–9. – FONT. C13 but
recut.

ABERCILIENI BRIDGE, 1¼ m. W. 1826; a single arch.

TWYN Y GAER (SN 969 306). A small oval univallate enclosure
on the high ground at the entrance to the Nant Bran.

TREBARRIED *see* LLANDEFALLE

TREBERFYDD *see* LLANGASTY TAL-Y-LLYN

TRECASTLE   8020

MOTTE AND BAILEY. An outpost of Brecon Castle, taken (from
Llanlleonfel) in 1160, and a good specimen of C12 fortification.
The motte is *c.* 30 yds broad on top, steep and ditched all
round; the bailey is raised, *c.* 200 ft long, and protected by a
counterscarp bank.

The castle belonged to the Gwyn family, who lived at Camden
House. A few buildings such as Castle House have details
dating from the expansion of the village in the 1830s; as a
trading centre it declined with the railway age.

PANTYSGALLOG BRIDGE, 1½ m. E. A graceful single arch across
the upper Usk. Second half of the C18. (Still with solid
haunches.)

TRECASTELL MOUNTAIN (SN 833 310). A group of Bronze Age
circles and two superimposed Roman marching camps may be
found at the end of the military road (originally a Roman road
from Brecon Gaer to Llandovery). The STONE CIRCLES are
of different diameters, but both are built of relatively small
stones. Several stones have been removed, but the holes are still
visible. A short alignment of low stones leads SW from the
smaller circle in the direction of a small burial mound, S of the
ceremonial circles.

Y Pigwn. A very characteristic pair of overnight marching camps both probably built during the early Roman campaigns in Wales (i.e. before A.D. 75). The camps are 38 and 25 acres in extent, enclosed by a bank and ditch with four typical protected entrances (*claviculae*). The best preserved of these curving banks is at the NE entrance, the one nearest the Bronze Age circles. The two camps are superimposed, with a very slightly different alignment; the overlap can best be seen on the W. The S side has been badly damaged by mining in the C18.

Llywel. *See* p. 359.

1030   TREFECCA

1¼ m. SW of Talgarth

71 Trefecca College (Coleg Trefeca). Howell Harris (1714–73) had spent the years before 1752 in founding Methodist societies in Wales and England. In that year he assembled about one hundred of his Welsh supporters in a 'Family' at Trevecka Fach, his own home, and began his astonishing Strawberry Hill Gothic accommodation for them. William Williams Pantycelyn called it 'the castellated monastery'. The style was as progressive as the concept. Howell Harris was open to a variety of influences: the inspiration for his community came from the Moravians' settlement at Fulneck in Yorkshire; its architectural appearance must have been absorbed from fashionable style at first hand. 'Madam' Sidney Griffith of Cefnamwlch, Caernarvonshire, had by 1752 given him £900 for building. Who the architect was is unknown: Harris himself, perhaps. N façade of three blocks thrown out from the older nucleus, of one, two, and one bays. All had small, narrow ogee windows and circular corner turrets. The outer wings were two-storeyed and gabled, the inner three-storeyed with a flat parapet. A larger semicircular turret projected in the middle. It was completed by 1772. It is undeniable that the design was not of the quality, say, of the next nearest example of the Gothick taste in the 1750s, Shobdon church in Herefordshire. What is interesting is that this is a very early use of the style, and that it is used for the premises of an idealistic commune.

Inside there is no contemporary detail. The S side of the college contains the Home at the W end. (It may date from 1706.) Two low storeys, an L-plan; at the corners Venetian windows, after which the cornice oddly droops for the space between. Interiors of *c.* 1730 surviving here are the little parlour which has a ceiling with two egg-and-dart cornices and an IHS in a sunburst; and Harris's friend Lady Huntingdon's dining room, whose ceiling pattern is a modillion cornice, then an octagon with, originally, an eye in a triangle in the centre. Also cupboards with ogee doors, panelling round the fireplace, and a loose open pediment with scrolls for sides above it. The clock-tower and angel weathervane were added in 1754; by 1758 there were a chapel, infirmary, bath house, and dovecote too.

The Family arrived at self-sufficiency, not only in the building trades, but in agriculture (Howell instigated the founding of the Brecknockshire Agricultural Society in 1755, and his scientist brother Joseph promoted new farming methods), and through the manufacture of clothing. Their private printing-press published more than a hundred religious books between 1758 and 1806, including a Life of Harris in 1791. For John Wesley Trefecca was 'a little paradise'. During the early C19, however, the group died away. Their charming building has lost its l. wing to the very Chapel-Gothic HOWELL HARRIS MEMORIAL CHAPEL (by *R. G. Thomas*, 1872),* dating from its period as a Calvinistic Methodist Theological College (1842–1906); opposite, the new block for the Residential Centre for Mission Work (1973) has further sapped its spirit. Facing the Home is a six-house TERRACE of twenty-four lodgings for students, of 1867.‡

COLLEGE FARM, ¼ m. N. A C16 farmhouse which in 1768 became an academy for Methodist preachers, founded by the Countess of Huntingdon. The farm is interesting in its own right. Twin E gables of red sandstone, one a porch with Perp outer and inner arches and a broad door with original ironwork. Then a cross-passage between the hall and other rooms on the r. Another, blocked, Tudor doorway entered from the w. Date inscription of 1576 over the front door, scratched on an emblem stone with four angels in a circled cross. The badly preserved College occupied the hall as an assembly room or chapel, and a new wing beyond. Its Gothic stucco E front had three bays and two storeys, all of broad delicate ogee-traceried windows grouped round the door. Of this period (1772) the hall (now a store) retains a large w window with three ogee heads proportioned as in a Venetian window. Also the iron rails and platform. The

*This houses an excellent exhibition, together with relics of the Harris circle.

‡ In connection with Trefecca College, I wish to thank Mrs O. Davies, the curator of the museum.

style is directly connected with Lady Huntingdon's Chapel (now Trinity Presbyterian Church) at Bath, of 1765. She had an acquaintance with Horace Walpole, possibly employed the same architect for both works, and thus introduced a purer Gothic to Wales than that of Harris's college. The academy moved to Cheshunt in 1791.

TREFECCA FAWR, ½ m. s. Apart from the harmonious H-front, with its armorial relief over the arched doorway and some wood ovolo-moulded mullioned and transomed windows, little is revealed outside. The house faces medieval (and perhaps religious) foundations in a moat, and is probably built of stone from there. About 1660 Rebecca Prosser, after whom the hamlet is named, began a farmhouse comprising the hall and kitchen to its l. beyond a central chimney. The hall now has geometric panelling with Ionic pilasters and a modillion cornice, all of *c.* 1700. Its ceiling mouldings are a circle inside a square inside a circle, with harvesting motifs freely arranged. The r. side of the forecourt is a wing of *c.* 1680–90. Parlour with deep bolection panelling and an 'artisan mannerist' elaboration of this for
64 the fireplace. The plaster ceiling is the most remarkable in Powys. Beams make nine compartments of it. The sides are enriched with foliage and the undersides with a profusion of cider apples and so on. Strongly moulded elliptical garlands fill the fields between. It worthily celebrates the fruitfulness of the land. In the wing also a substantial dog-leg stair with turned balusters up four flights. The l. wing is C18. Thomas Harris of Tregunter, the owner later in the C18, rented Trefecca Fawr as a farm to his brother Howell (*see* above).*

(On a ridge ¾ m. SE is a small badly preserved RINGWORK. The entrance was at the E.)

MOTTES. Two C12 forts face each other across the River Llynfi. The one at Tredustan Hall, small and partly cut away, revealing its construction, is better than the damaged one on the Trefecca bank.

TREDUSTAN COURT, ½ m. NW. A late C17 L-plan. Front with five bays and some tall mullioned and transomed windows; the similar side elevation also with five bays. In plan it is conservative.

PENTWYN nearby contains a pair of crucks.

TREDUSTAN HALL, ¼ m. WNW. A symmetrical seven-bay design of *c.* 1700 with new windows under stone entablatures. Hipped and sprocketed roof.

---

* I must thank Major Lewis for his kind cooperation with photography at Trefecca Fawr.

TALGARTH. *See* p. 371.

TALGARTH. *See* p. 371.

PEN Y WYRLOD (II) LONG CAIRN (SO 150 315), a recently discovered Severn Cotswold tomb, has been partially excavated but public access is not yet available. The N half of the tomb had been damaged by quarrying, which revealed the presence of at least three lateral chambers and a 'blind entrance' at the E end. A larger chamber may open from the S side, or it may have balancing lateral chambers. The cairn was edged with very fine dry-stone walling, a characteristic of this style of tomb-building. The bodies were unburnt and were placed in the chambers as piles of bones; no datable objects were found with them, but a radiocarbon date obtained from the bones suggested that the tomb had been built before 3,000 B.C., a date rather earlier than might have been expected for this group.

TREGUNTER *see* TALGARTH

TRETOWER   *1020*

ST JOHN THE EVANGELIST. Rebuilt in 1876–7 by *J. L. Pearson* for the Baileys of Glanusk. The old dedication was to St Michael, and the building was probably a chapel attached to Tretower Castle. Of local red stone with yellow dressings, it has nave, chancel, S porch, and a double bellcote over the chancel arch. Lancet-style, and typically serious-minded. – GLASS. Three E lancets dated 1906. The church has an important scenic role to fulfil and it does it well – the right weight when seen from the gateway of Tretower Court, and sufficiently formal when its plain E.E. details are the foreground to the view of the castle.

CHURCH HALL. Just N of the church and alike in style but with a lower roof-line. Also by *Pearson*, 1887–8. A semicircular bow, with a conical roof and paired lancets, answers the vestry wing of the church.

In the village are some attractive minor buildings; but there is nothing small-scale about the grand views of the Usk and Rhiangoll valleys.   4

TRETOWER COURT INN. Two separate houses built adjoining – i.e. unit houses. The larger is the older, perhaps late C16, has a corbelled first-floor chimney. S range early C17 with a broad cross-passage; four-centred doorheads.

TRETOWER HOUSE. Neat early C18 house with a five-bay front and a hipped sprocketed roof.

(LLANDDEGMAN-FAWR, ½ m. ESE, like Tretower Court Inn, consists of two C17 houses in one yard. The main range is a former long-house; the other touches it only at the corner but now connects.)

CWM-GU, 1 m. ESE. Two small C17 houses: first CWM-GU COTTAGE, with representative vernacular details outside – a diagonal chimney and a shaped doorhead; also a pentice or sheltering roof along the entrance wall – sensible enough in the rainy vicinity of the Black Mountains. Dated 1633. CWM-GU FACH, altered in the C19, still has its post-and-panel partition and C17 high seat.

TRETOWER COURT AND CASTLE, 200 yds S of the church. Picard, one of the Norman lords who participated in Bernard de Neufmarché's occupation of the Usk valley at the end of the C11, received from him part of the Ystrad Yw district. He built his castle mound and bailey with its timber defences in marshy ground at the bottom of the Rhiangoll valley. In the middle of the C12 his son Roger had a stone curtain erected round it, and inside a first-floor hall and solar (and kitchen below), the ruins of which are among the best Romanesque domestic work left in Wales. These structures were partly removed by his great-grandson Roger Picard, to make space for a tall circular keep (cf. Bronllys Castle) and a stone-walled bailey. Evidence in documents of 1230-40 suggests that they were put up then. The Castle continued in use as a garrison during the C14 and was held for the King by Sir James Berkeley against Owain Glyndŵr, then at Castell Dinas.

The Court, some 200 yds SE of the Castle, had however quite likely succeeded the Castle as the dwelling around 1300. A survey of the possessions of John, Roger's son, who died in 1305, mentions the Castle and adds that it was worth nothing. This dating is corroborated by the discovery of detail of c. 1300 reused in the later medieval buildings of the Court. The heiress of the Picards, Amicia, brought Tretower to her husband, Ralph Bluet of Raglan, Monmouthshire, in the early C14. The N range of the present courtyard belongs to that period, though much altered in the C15. At the end of the C14 the heiress of the Bluets married James de Berkeley; about 1420 their son sold Tretower and Raglan to Sir William ap Thomas. Sir William's wife Gwladys, the daughter of Sir David Gam of Brecon, had two sons – Sir Roger Vaughan the younger (by her first marriage to Sir Roger Vaughan), and William Herbert, later created Earl of Pembroke. Herbert gave Tretower to his elder half-brother, who, between 1457 and his death in 1470, rebuilt all but the lower (service) storey of the N range, adding the noteworthy timber gallery along the upper floor. This floor has a hall with on its W a solar and bedchamber and on its E a two-room guest chamber. Being a man of wealth and standing, Sir Roger then doubled its size by adding the interesting W range, whose ground floor includes the hall, screens passage plus buttery plus pantry, and beyond these the retainers' hall. This would seem to mean that there were two households living separately. Sir Thomas his son completed the courtyard plan c. 1480 by building the gatehouse on the E and the curtain wall walks, and embellished the solar in the W range with an oriel. Charles Vaughan (the uncle of the C17 poet Henry Vaughan of Scethrog), who inherited Tretower in 1613 and died c. 1636, remodelled part of the courtyard in a mid C17 style, interrupting the wooden gallery which had circled it to make a symmetrical two-storey E façade of mullioned and transomed casements with a central (C20 reconstruction) doorway into the hall. The S end of this late C15 W range was adapted as living quarters, reached from the gatehouse by a new covered passage along the S wall. It has two gables to the W surmounted by twin diagonal chimneys and more C17 windows. Tretower was finally sold out of the Vaughan family in 1783; it became a farm.

Since 1930, when the Brecknock Society, having bought it, transferred it to the predecessors of the DOE, the modern and many of the C17 accretions have been stripped away, and we now see the bare but durable bones of the medieval structure.* It is a curious experience. The Court in its previous state must have been as unrecognizable as the bailey of the Castle is today, chock-a-block with farm buildings. All the features of the N range and the arrangement of the W were discoveries. Decayed or destroyed woodwork is being meticulously restored in oak; so too is the stone, but less successfully. One consequence of the pursuit of historical authenticity is the lack of a sense of the habitable anywhere. Of course the painstaking recovery e.g. of the unusual domestic plan of the W range more than justifies a period of emptiness. One wonders what the next step will be, logically or imaginatively. To furnish from the resources of a public collection? Or to let the renewed fabric speak for itself?

The lane which leads by the Court is as innocent of the twen-

* Mr C. A. R. Radford is the author of the admirable official DOE guidebook, on which this entry chiefly depends.

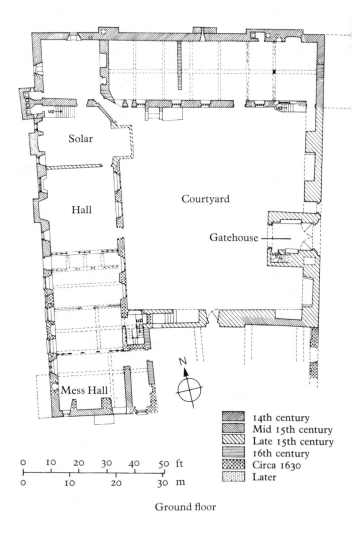

Ground floor

Tretower Court, plan (D. of E.)

tieth century as could be.* On one side is the BARN, built partly
of materials from the Court, stone from the tower, C17 wood-
mullioned windows, and so on. Its N end is older and was
storeyed once – and so domestic. ½ m. S is HEOLDRAW, a C19
house whose C17 porch was a lodge to the tower. It is two-
storeyed with a round stone archway and a hoodmould. Corbelled, overhanging upper floor.

The COURT has ordinary rubble walls. The parapet along 39
the walls, slightly corbelled out, has lost some of its merlons
and arrow-loops. Two corbels on the gabled end of the N range
supported a wooden porch over a door (now blocked) between
the road and the courtroom. Long seven-light Elizabethan
window on the living floor. In the gate tower a low arch with
continuous Perp mouldings; the inner arch has a hood. On the
r. a similar postern doorway, its upper floor also corbelled out
(notice the pistol-holes) but still barely flush with the curtain.
It rests on a flat rib-vault. The inner window tells us that there
were trefoiled ogees with blank spandrels. Steps ascend to the
vanished third storey.

On the r. on entering the courtyard is the range begun in
the early C14. Its two-centred doorway is original. The E room
downstairs, the courtroom (for Tretower was the caput of a
lordship), had its own S door, and still has a C15 fireplace, a
lancet window, and grooves in the beams for a boarded ceiling.
Apart from a steward's room, the rest of the space was for
storage: the cider cellar was built in the C16. By recent steps
the square-framed gallery is reached, roofed in one with the
upper rooms, which, together with the reconstruction in stone
and timber, is mid C15 work. The domestic quarters are up
here. Only the S wall is square-framed; in it are characteristic
doors and windows into the rooms. Along the N wall C15 fireplaces with smooth deep lintels, windows with stone seats, and
two garderobe shafts projecting on the exterior. The E end, a
two-bay hall heated by its C14 fireplace with a projecting hood,
and a one-bay chamber, is not yet partitioned off. The chamber
contained the original stair. The central hall is of three bays,
demarcated by tie-beam trusses painted red, with leaves
painted on their white plaster infill. Two open arch-braced
trusses with cusping above the collars: no wind-braces. It is
fine; but first-floor halls in Herefordshire, for example, are
finer. Next the solar, and, the other side of the stone
partition, a large heated bedchamber, with a further garderobe

* Since this was written, several houses have been built opposite the church.

facing W; this was Sir Roger Vaughan's, and is mostly C14. The site of the medieval kitchen is lost.

By contrast the main rooms of the later C15 W range are on the ground floor; though more complex, they still body forth the medieval household of a Welsh aristocratic family. The solar has some single lights, all ogee, and an oriel of *c.* 1480 (replaced in reconstituted stone). The adjoining hall is again of three bays, but vastly more spacious, rising through the building to a fine roof also of arch-braced principals with cusped strutting, and with three tiers of foiled wind-braces as well. The system continues over the chamber above the solar. Between the two is a post-and-panel partition with a moulded and embattled head-beam; the space between this and the collar is filled by four trefoil-headed panels between the uprights. Big transomed ogee windows and a lateral fireplace in its outer wall. The S side of the hall is closed by a similar partition with two Tudor-headed doorways leading to the screens passage, and beyond to four one-storeyed service rooms, two for the masters, two for the men, divided by further screens. Finally at the S the mess hall: like the hall, it was open to the roof, and has three doorways, devised to keep the retainers separate from the household. Here too there is a two-light transomed window, its upper lights ogee-headed. As already mentioned, the C17 dwelling occupied this end, and now that floors, stairs, and all are dispensed with, only the windows either side with their embattled architraves tell of this. The W external wall has tall lateral chimneys.

The CASTLE passed through four phases as a stronghold controlling roads in the Usk and Rhiangoll valleys which skirt the Black Mountains. The low mound and bailey of *c.* 1100 is exceptional only in that the mound was revetted in stone. It had a wet moat. Civilized life in the fortress reached its peak *c.* 1150 with the construction of a polygonal SHELL KEEP outside the mound. Of its rectangular E gate tower there are just foundations and a pit. The dwelling, in stone, was built inside the curtain but with windows looking out. Its kitchen, the main room of the lower storey, occupied the S projection. It was lit by three small loops in deep splays, and its semicircular fireplace is intact except for the hood. Immediately to the r. of the kitchen is the stair up to the hall, of which there is little enough to see. The room was about 25 ft long. One S window has two-step dressings to the outside; as on the doorway (of which a jamb survives) in the stone partition between the hall and the solar, there are traces of chevron patterns. Evidence here was lost with the collapse of the s w angle in 1947. The solar, nearly 30 ft in length, was at r. angles along the w wall and again above a basement, in which there were two small windows. Blocked fireplace with a cambered arch of voussoirs. One small window survives in its gable wall, beside the hall window. The inner mouldings (of its l. side) are similar on the jamb and elliptical arch: one plain order either side of a quarter-column with a base, twisted shaft, and (eroded) capital. Another to the w has a plain elliptical rere-arch. Access to the solar was either by the hall stair, or by a spiral stair in the s w corner which rose from ground level via the solar to the wall walk, which could also be reached by the gatehouse stair. Apart from the demolition of their inner walls, the C12 rooms are further confused by the considerable heightening of the masonry above the string-course and the blocking of openings undertaken in process of making the taller and more massive curtain required in the C13. The oven and the straight stair on the w belong to C14 or C15 use of the site.

The circular TOWER stood defended not only by the rein-forced curtain but also by the massive walls of the large bailey, of which parts including a round NE tower have been spared. The tower itself rises from a battered base, within which was the dungeon. Entry was to a second-storey hall. Fireplace with a hood on moulded imposts. Lancets, with stone seats in the wide splays. There were two mural spiral stairs leading up. In the third storey (now inaccessible), which was also heated, is the doorway which gave on to a covered bridge across to the wall walk. The fourth floor has three big cusped windows but no fireplace. On top were battlements. The large triangular bailey retains stone curtains and round corner towers.

CWMDU. *See* p. 315.

PENMYARTH. *See* p. 366.

TREVITHEL *see* THREE COCKS

TYN-Y-LLWYN *see* PARTRISHOW

VAYNOR*

0010

ST GWENFREWI. Nave, chancel, and s w tower. Built for Robert Thompson Crawshay of Cyfarthfa (whose extraordinary tomb is in the churchyard) by *Robinson* of Cardiff in 1870; his

* Transferred to Mid Glamorgan in 1974.

idiosyncratic stonework and his enthusiastic tower distinguish his work from that of his more correct colleagues. The tower has regrettably lost its lucarne windows and its spire; the replacement saddleback roof is by *G. G. Pace.* – GLASS. E by *Clayton & Bell*, 1872. – w, 1908. – MONUMENTS. William Williams, by *J. Edwards*, 1874. A figure ascending; dangerously near High Victorian mawkishness. – William Harris † 1956. Full-length relief of a man in a friar's habit; illustrative and formal qualities admirably balanced. By *Ayres.* – Richard Crawshay † 1903. A casket encrusted with Renaissance motifs placed against a gold mosaic lunette; typically Edwardian in taste.

The ruined MEDIEVAL CHURCH stands 100 yds w of the modern one. A small C16 tower is built within the w end of the nave.

R. T. Crawshay's grave (1879) is covered by a pink granite slab weighing 12 tons, with the legend 'God Forgive Me'.

MOTTE, 100 yds w of the church. With a bailey.

HY-BRASAIL. A ponderous Italian folly applied to a cottage. Ashlar; dated 1912. Three-storey tower, the upper floor an open loggia. On its r. a gallery over an open arcade and a shorter tower at the end. The explanation of this warm-climate recreation is said to be the builder's love of an Italian *contessa.*

PONTSARN VIADUCT, ½ m. sw. Seven masonry arches carried the Brecon and Merthyr railway 90 ft above the Taf Fechan. 1866, by *Savin & Ward* and their engineers *Henry Conybeare* and *Alexander Sutherland.*

YSTRADFELLTE

ST MARY. The lack of details earlier than *c.* 1500 suggests that all was rebuilt in the C16. The broad nave and short chancel are linked, however, by a simple and irregular chancel arch that might well have been broken through an earlier E wall. Entrances to the rood stairs survive in the N wall. Fine moulded-rib barrel-vaults, with the timberwork left open, in both nave and chancel. Two blocked doorways. In the chancel are the only old windows: a Late Perp two-light cusped s one, and a N single-light window. The gaunt w tower on a battered plinth has a w door which leads through to the nave (cf. Llywel). It tapers to a corbel-table and then battlements. – FONT. Octagonal, with bands cut round each face and round the rim. C16? – REREDOS. Carved oak surround to the E window. –

GLASS. E, 1891. – MONUMENT. Edward Walters † 1824.
Shaped slab with colouring. – LYCHGATE. C19.

CASTELL COCH, ¾ m. NNE. A classic castle site on a spur above
the confluence of the Rivers Llia and Dringarth. The outer bailey is protected only by a ditch to the S and a rampart and ditch
on the ridge to the N. The small size may mean a Welsh castle.
Just behind the collapsed round tower at the S angle (C13), and
enclosed in its attached stone curtain, is the foundation of a
rectangular stone hall, c. 35 by 55 ft, which appears to be of
C12 date.

MAEN MADOC, 1½ m. NNW. A C5 or C6 pillar stone, probably
marking a Christian burial beside the Roman Sarn Helen,
which runs between Brecon Gaer and a fort near Coelbren on
the way to Neath. (The Roman road is E of the stone.) The
Latin inscription reads DERVAC(IVS) FILIVS IVST(VS)
(H)IC IACIT.

HEPSTE FAWR, 1½ m. SE, is one of the last authentic Welsh long-
houses still inhabited both by farmers and their cattle. From
a lobby formed in the byre passage, doors open r. into the
dwelling, l. into the beast-house. This vital element of internal
communication between the two has in almost all cases been
severed. Stone. The timber detail looks C17.

(NANT-Y-MOCH is a platform site occupied by a long-house in
the C16.)

MAEN LLIA (SN 927 189). A fine example of a standing stone, set
in the head of the pass. It is a sandstone conglomerate, 13 ft
high and 8 ft wide. Nearby are a ringwork with double bank
and a cairn which may be part of the same complex of monuments. Across the valley a later settlement can be seen on the
E slopes when the light is right.

YSTRADGYNLAIS   7010

ST CYNOG. Nave, N and S aisles, chancel. 1861. By *Benjamin
Ferrey* (GR); but so odd that it might have been largely by the
Rev. *Thomas Walters*, the vicar. Stone arcades set on spindly
paired iron colonnettes with carved capitals. Clerestory of
paired circular trefoiled windows. Scissor truss roofs with big
cusped bracing. The interior is large, bright, and ungainly. –
In the SE wall of the chancel above some steps parts of two
Early Christian PILLAR STONES inscribed HIC IACIT (C6)
and ADIVNE (C5 or C6). – GLASS. Aisle windows, c. 1920–60,
with makers' monograms and rebuses. – MONUMENTS.

Morgan Aowbry † 1648. – A nameless early C18 tablet with columns and a scrolly open pediment. – The previous small Norman church stood on raised ground just to the N.

YNYS-CEDWYN HOUSE (R.D.C. OFFICES), ½ m. SW. Late C18. Five bays and three storeys. The stair has a Venetian window. Formerly the home of the Gough-Aubrey family.

YNYS-CEDWYN IRONWORKS, ½ m. SSW. The two roofless and wall-less yellow brick arcades of an unfinished works and a tall chimney (1872) are visible from the road, and also a massive stone curtain on the site of the six mid C19 furnaces beyond. They were fuelled with anthracite coal, a discovery of George Crane and David Thomas. Ruins also of a tinplate works of 1889. The long industrial history of the Ynys-Cedwyn Company goes back at least to 1612, a date found on a pig of iron. In the C19 Claypon's Tramroad was built and several coal mines were sunk. (TWO BRIDGES on the tramroad, designed in 1832 by *John Brunton*, ½ m. NE and ¾ m. NNE of the ironworks.)

GLOSSARY

ABACUS: flat slab on the top of a capital

ABUTMENT: solid masonry placed to resist the lateral pressure of an arch or vault.

ACANTHUS: fleshy, serrated leaves used as part of the decoration of a Corinthian capital and in some types of leaf carving.

ACHIEVEMENT OF ARMS: in heraldry, a complete display of armorial bearings.

ACROTERION: pedestal on the ends or top of a classical pediment, sometimes with a statue.

ADDORSED: two human figures, animals, or birds, placed symmetrically back to back.

AEDICULE: framing of a window, door, or monument by columns and a pediment.

AFFRONTED: two human figures, animals, or birds, placed symmetrically face to face.

AISLE: wing or lateral part of a church separated from the nave by a row of columns.

AISLE TRUSS: roof truss supported mainly on aisle-posts within the walls of a building.

ALABASTER: soft, slightly translucent limestone used for sculpture.

ALCOVE: recess, usually semicircular, in a wall.

ALIGNMENT: Bronze Age (?) ritual monument with several upright stones set in a row.

ALTAR: table in Christian churches for the celebration of the Holy Eucharist. A *Mensa* is the stone slab on its top.

ALTAR TOMB: monument resembling an altar.

AMBULATORY: semicircular or polygonal aisle enclosing an apse.

ANNULET: shaft-ring.

ANTA: classical order of oblong section used at the ends of a colonnade or portico, which is then *in antis*.

ANTEFIXES: upright ornaments placed in rows on a classical cornice.

ANTEPENDIUM: altar frontal in metalwork or textiles.

ANTHEMION: classical ornament like a honeysuckle flower (*see* Fig. 1).

A   P   A   P   A

Fig. 1. Anthemion and Palmette Frieze

APRON: raised, shaped panel below a window sill.

APSE: semicircular or polygonal end of a chancel, chapel, or room.

ARABESQUE: light and fanciful surface decoration using flowing lines, tendrils, etc., interspersed with vases, animals, etc.

ARCADE: range of arches supported on piers or columns. BLIND ARCADE: the same attached to a wall.

ARCH: structure of wedge-shaped stones (voussoirs) or bricks spanning a void, and supported at the sides (*see* Fig. 2). *Semi-*

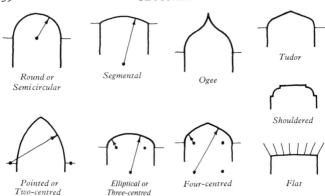

Round or   Segmental   Tudor
Semicircular   Ogee

                                                    Shouldered

Pointed or   Elliptical or   Four-centred   Flat
Two-centred   Three-centred

Fig. 2. Arch

circular arch: a semicircle drawn from a centre on the springing line. *Pointed arch:* formed of two intersecting arcs of the same radius. *Segmental arch:* drawn from a centre below the springing line. *Elliptical* or *three-centred arch:* a half ellipse drawn from the springing line.

centred arch: pointed arch with the two lower arcs drawn from centres on the springing line and the two upper arcs drawn from centres below it. *Tudor arch:* like a four-centred arch but with straight lines in place of the two upper arcs. *Ogee arch:* a pointed arch formed of two S-shaped curves. *Shouldered arch:* with stones projecting inwards from the imposts. *Flat arch:* with a straight horizontal profile. *Relieving arch:* incorporated in a wall to carry weight away from an opening some way beneath. *Rere-arch:* at the inner face of an embrasure, window recess, etc. *Transverse arch:* across the main axis of an interior space, especially between bays in a vault. *Dia-* *phragm arch:* transverse arch with solid spandrels. *Strainer arch:* inserted in order to buttress walls internally. *Skew arch:* where the axis is not at right angles to the face. *Intrados* or *Archivolt:* undersurface of an arch.

ARCH-BRACE: curved timber fixed in the angle between the horizontal and the inclined or vertical members of a truss.

ARCHITRAVE: lowest of the three main parts of the entablature of an order.

ARCHIVOLT: *see* Arch.

ARRIS: sharp edge at the meeting of two surfaces.

ASHLAR: masonry of large blocks wrought to even faces and square edges.

ASTRAGAL: colloquially, a glazing bar; in classical architecture, a convex moulding.

ASTYLAR: of an elevation: without columns or other vertical members.

ATLANTES: male counterparts of caryatids.

ATRIUM: inner court of a Roman

house; also open court in front of a church.

ATTACHED: *see* Engaged.

ATTIC: storey above the main entablature, hence the top storey beneath the roof.

AUMBRY: recess or cupboard to hold sacred vessels for Mass.

AXE HAMMER: shafted stone tool of Bronze Age date with blade at one end and hammer at the other.

BAILEY: open yard or court of a castle; *see also* Motte-and-Bailey.

BALDACCHINO: tent-like roof supported on columns.

BALLFLOWER: globular flower of three petals enclosing a small ball. A decoration used in the first quarter of the C14.

BALUSTER: small pillar or column of fanciful outline.

BALUSTRADE: series of balusters supporting a handrail or coping.

BARBICAN: outwork defending the entrance to a castle.

BARGEBOARDS: fret-cut or carved boards fixed to the eaves of a gable.

BARROW: round barrow, a circular mound of earth covering a burial, normally of Early Bronze Age date. Circular arrangements of stakes or stones may also be found beneath them (stake circles, cairn rings, etc.).

BARTIZAN: *see* Tourelle.

BASE: the projecting foot of a column, used in all the Orders except the Greek Doric.

BASEMENT: a storey or high plinth below the main storey or order, but not (as in modern use) below ground.

BASILICA: a Roman public build-

ing; in medieval architecture, an aisled church with a clerestory.

BASTION: projection at the angle of a fortification.

BATTER: inclined face of a wall.

BATTLEMENT: parapet with a series of indentations or embrasures with raised portions or merlons between. Also called Crenellation.

BAYS: divisions of the length of a building, externally by fenestration or an order, internally by an order on the walls or by compartments in the ceiling or roof.

BAY-WINDOW: angular or curved projection of an elevation with ample fenestration. If curved, also called Bow-window. If corbelled out from the wall, also called Oriel window.

BEAKER PEOPLE: group distinguished by the use of a pottery appearing at the end of the Neolithic period (*c.* 2000 B.C.) and originating in the Netherlands. They seem to have been the catalyst in many social and technological changes, notably the introduction of metallurgy.

BEAKHEAD: Norman ornamental motif consisting of a row of bird or beast heads with beaks biting usually into a roll moulding.

BELFRY: structure to hang bells in. A BELLCOTE stands on a gable; a BELL-STAGE is a room on top of a tower; a BELL TURRET is built on a roof.

BERM: level area separating ditch from bank on a hillfort or barrow.

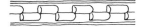

Fig. 3. Billet Frieze

BILLET FRIEZE: Norman ornamental motif made up of short blocks placed at regular intervals (*see* Fig. 3).

BIVALLATE: of a hillfort: defended by two concentric banks and ditches.

BLOCKED COLUMN: column interrupted by regular projecting blocks, e.g. on a 'Gibbs surround'.

BLOCKING COURSE: low continuation of the wall above the cornice.

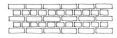

English Bond

Flemish Bond

Fig. 4. Bond

BOND: *see* Fig. 4. *English Bond*: method of laying bricks so that alternate courses or layers on the face of the wall are composed of headers or stretchers only. *Flemish Bond:* method of laying bricks so that alternate headers and stretchers appear in each course on the face of the wall.

BOSS: knob or projection usually placed to cover the intersection of ribs in a vault, roof, or ceiling.

BOW-WINDOW: *see* Bay-window.

BOX: convenient term to describe a compact minor dwelling, e.g. a small country house.

BOX-FRAME: truss composed of two storey-posts and a tie-beam, usually braced at the angles; used in hall houses, barns, etc.

BOX PEW: pew with high wooden sides and doors.

BRACKET: small supporting piece of stone or wood, to carry a projecting horizontal member.

BRESSUMER: long beam, usually jettied outwards, supporting the upper part of a timber house or rood loft.

BRICKWORK: a *Header* is a brick laid so that the end appears on the face of the wall; a *Stretcher* is one laid so that the side appears on the face of the wall.

BROACH: half-pyramidal reinforcement to the base of a castle tower. *See also* Spire.

BRONZE AGE: the period when bronze tools were dominant; in Britain *c.* 1800 to 600 B.C. It is broadly divided into Early, Middle, and Late Bronze Age at 1400 and 900 B.C., and may be further subdivided into phases according to the type of tools made, usually called after a typical hoard, as Penard Phase, Wilburton Complex, etc.

BUCRANIUM: ox skull.

BULLSEYE WINDOW: small circular window.

BUTTRESS: vertical masonry member projecting from a wall to resist the thrust of an arch or vault, or built against it to stabilize it (*see* Fig. 5). *Flying buttress:* with an arch or half-arch to transmit thrust from the upper part of a wall to a detached buttress. At the corners of a building there are four types. *Diagonal buttress:* one placed at 135° to each of the two walls. *Angle buttress:* two, meeting at 90° at the angle itself. *Set-back buttress:* two, set slightly back from the corner. *Clasping buttress:* wholly enclosing the corner.

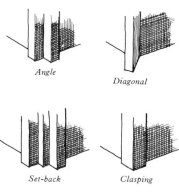

Angle

Diagonal

Set-back

Clasping

Fig. 5. Buttress

CABLE MOULDING: Norman moulding imitating a twisted cord. *Rope mouldings* are also used on timber houses.

CAIRN: heap of stones, in prehistory normally covering a burial. *Long Cairns* cover Neolithic burial chambers; *Round Cairns* (like Barrows, *q.v.*) cover Early Bronze Age burials. There are several variations of design among round cairns, e.g. *Kerb Cairns*, *Platform Cairns*, and *Ring Cairns*. Some of these variant monuments are for ceremonial rather than burial and may be akin to to Stone Circles (*q.v.*).

CAMBER: slight rise or upward curve of an otherwise horizontal feature.

CAMP: Roman military site. *Auxiliary:* camp for the auxilia (non-legionary troops); *Marching:* earthworks dug each night by the army on campaign; *Practice:* earthworks dug during training.

CAMPANILE: free-standing bell-tower.

CANOPY: projection or hood over an altar, pulpit, niche, statue, stall, etc.

CANTED: of a bow or end of a wing: half-hexagonal or half-octagonal on plan.

CAPITAL: head or top part of a column, pilaster, or shaft (*see* Fig. 6). The Romanesque types include: *Cushion capital:* a cube with its lower angles rounded off. *Scalloped capital:* like a cushion capital but with several convex ridges converging on the neck. *Waterleaf capital:* carved with broad flat leaves. The Gothic types include: *Crocket capital:* with rows of upstanding leaves. *Stiff-leaf capital:* with stylized foliage consisting of upright branching and curling leaves. *Bell capital:* an inverted cone with horizontal mouldings. For classical types, *see* Orders.

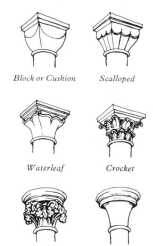

Block or Cushion   *Scalloped*

Waterleaf   *Crocket*

Stiff-leaf   *Bell*

Fig. 6 Capitals

CARTOUCHE: tablet with an ornate frame, usually enclosing an inscription or coat of arms.

CARYATID: whole female figure supporting an entablature or other similar member. Cf. Atlantes.

CASEMENT: window hinged at the side. *See also* Mouldings.

CASTELLATED: decorated with battlements.

CELURE: panelled and adorned part of a wagon roof above the rood or the altar.

CENOTAPH: funerary monument which is not a burying place.

CHAMFER: surface made by cutting off a square angle, usually at an angle of 45°. *Sunk chamfer:* where this face is recessed. *Hollow chamfer:* where the surface is concave.

CHANCEL: that part of the E end of a church in which the altar is placed, usually applied to the whole continuation of the nave E of the chancel arch or screen.

CHANCEL ARCH: arch separating the chancel from the nave or crossing.

CHANTRY CHAPEL: chapel attached to, or inside, a church, endowed for the saying of Masses for the soul of the founder or some other individual.

CHEMISE WALL: small wall surrounding a keep.

CHEVET: French term for the E end of a church (chancel, ambulatory, and radiating chapels).

CHEVRON: Norman zigzag ornament.

CHOIR: the part of a church where services are sung; in monastic churches this can occupy the crossing and/or the E bays of the nave, but in cathedral churches it is usually in the E arm.

CIBORIUM: canopied shrine for the reserved sacrament.

CINQUEFOIL: five-leaf form in the head of a window, etc., produced by cusping.

CIST: stone-lined or slab-built grave. *Short Cists* are normally Early Bronze Age in date; *Long Cists* belong to the Early Christian period.

CLAPPER BRIDGE: bridge made of large slabs of stone, some built up to make rough piers and other longer ones laid on top to make the roadway.

CLAS (Welsh): early quasi-monastic system in Wales and also in Cornwall and Ireland, existing from the dark ages to *c.* 1200. *Clasau* comprised a number of secular canons, and their later churches had more elaborate plans than a simple chancel and nave.

CLASSIC: term for the moment of highest achievement of a style.

CLASSICAL: term for Greek and Roman architecture and any subsequent styles inspired by it.

CLERESTORY: upper storey of the nave walls of a church, pierced by windows.

CLOSE STUD: method of constructing a wall by using closely spaced upright timbers.

COADE STONE: artificial (cast) stone made in the late C18 and the early C19 by Coade and Sealy in London.

COB: walling material made of clay, straw, and sand, etc.

COFFERING: sunk square or polygonal panels used to ornament a ceiling, vault, or arch.

COLLAR: *see* Roof.

COLONNADE: range of columns.

COLONNETTE: small column.

COLUMN: in classical architecture, an upright structural member of round section with a shaft, a capital, and usually a base. *See* Orders.

COMPOSITE: *see* Orders.

CONSOLE: carved bracket with a compound curved outline (*see* Fig. 7).

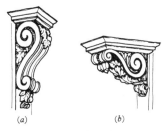

(a)   (b)

Fig. 7. Console

COPING: capping or covering to a wall.

CORBEL: block of stone projecting from a wall, supporting some feature on its horizontal top surface. *Corbel table:* series of corbels below the roof of a Norman church or to carry a parapet.

CORINTHIAN: *see* Orders.

CORNICE: in classical architecture the top section of the entablature, whether on an order or doorcase, etc. Also a decorative feature in the angle between wall and ceiling.

CORONA: lit. 'crown'; used of spires and chandeliers.

COUNTERCHANGING: of joists in a ceiling divided by beams into several compartments, when they are placed in opposite directions in alternate squares.

COUNTERSCARP BANK: small bank on the down-hill or outer side of a hillfort ditch.

COURSE: continuous layer of stones etc. in a wall.

COVE, COVING: concave undersurface, like a hollow moulding but on a larger scale, often linking wall to ceiling or an outside wall to the eaves.

CRADLE ROOF: *see* Roof.

CREDENCE: table or shelf near an altar to hold the sacramental elements.

CRENELLATION: *see* Battlement.

CREST, CRESTING: ornamental finish along the top of a screen, etc. Where it hangs below the bottom of a rood loft it is called *drop-cresting*.

CROCKET, CROCKETING: leaf decoration placed on the sloping sides of spires, pinnacles, gables, etc., in Gothic architecture.

CROCKET CAPITAL: *see* Capital.

CROG-LOFFT (Welsh): low cottage with a loft under the roof.

CROMLECH: word of Celtic origin used of single free-standing stone chambers of Neolithic date.

CROSS DYKE: bank and ditch cutting off a promontory or dividing a ridge.

CROSSING: space at the intersection of nave, chancel, and transepts.

CROSS-PASSAGE: space between opposed doorways at the end of medieval halls and later storeyed houses.

CROSS-VAULT: *see* Vault.

CROSS-WINDOW: window with one mullion and one transom.

CRUCK: cruck construction is a method of timber-framing in which the ridge beam is supported by pairs of curved or inclined timbers extending from floor to apex. *Base cruck:* one terminating at the collar. *Scarfed cruck:* of two pieces mortised together. *Upper cruck:* one springing from the wall-plate.

CRYPT: underground room, usually below the E end of a church.

CUP MARK: small artificial hollow cut in stone, Early Bronze Age in date and of unknown, but assumed religious, purpose.

CUPOLA: small polygonal or circular domed turret crowning a roof.

CURTAIN WALL: outer connecting wall between the towers of a castle. In C20 architecture, a non-load-bearing wall applied round a framed structure.

CUSHION CAPITAL: *see* Capital.

CUSP: projecting point between the foils (*q.v.*) in a foiled Gothic arch.

CUTWATER: the pointed form of a bridge's piers; if built up to road level, the triangular platform forms a *Refuge.*

CYCLOPEAN: masonry executed in exceptionally large stones.

DADO: decorative covering of the lower part of a wall.

DAGGER: tracery motif of the Dec style, of lancet shape but rounded or pointed at the head, pointed at the foot, and cusped inside (*see* Fig. 20).

DAIS: raised platform at one end of a room, occupied by the head of the household and his family.

DEC ('DECORATED'): historical division of English Gothic architecture covering the period from *c.* 1290 to *c.* 1350.

DEMI-COLUMN: column half sunk into a wall.

DENTIL: part of a classical cornice, composed of a series of regular blocks.

DIAPER WORK: surface decoration composed of square or lozenge shapes.

DIAPHRAGM ARCH: *see* Arch.

DOGTOOTH: typical E.E. ornament consisting of a series of four-pointed stars in relief like a pyramid and set diagonally (*see* Fig. 8).

Fig. 8. Dogtooth

DORIC: *see* Orders.

DORMER (WINDOWS): windows placed vertically in the sloping plane of a roof.

DOUBLE PILE: *see* Pile.

DRAGON-BEAM: a diagonal beam to support the corner of a jettied floor.

DRESSINGS: parts of an elevation in worked stone, e.g. quoins, which contrast with walling of another texture or colour.

DRIPSTONE: *see* Hoodmould.

DROP-CRESTING: *see* Cresting.

DRUM: circular or polygonal vertical wall of a dome. Also one of the stones of a column.

DRYSTONE: stone construction without mortar.

E.E. ('EARLY ENGLISH'): historical division of English Gothic architecture roughly covering the C13.

EASTER SEPULCHRE: recess, usually in the N wall of a chancel, to receive an effigy of Christ for Easter celebrations.

EAVES: overhanging edge of a roof.

EAVES CORNICE: cornice below the eaves of a roof.

ECHINUS: convex moulding supporting the abacus of a Greek Doric capital, sometimes bearing an egg and dart pattern.

EGG AND DART: architrave decoration from the Ionic order.

ELEVATION: one side of a building; an elevation drawing represents a single wall.

EMBATTLED: furnished with battlements.

EMBRASURE: small splayed opening in the wall or parapet of a fortified building.

ENCAUSTIC TILES: glazed and decorated earthenware tiles used for paving.

ENGAGED COLUMNS: columns attached to, or partly sunk into, a wall.

ENTABLATURE: in classical architecture, the whole of the horizontal members (architrave, frieze, and cornice) above a column. See Orders.

ENTASIS: very slight convex deviation from a straight line; used on Greek columns and sometimes on spires to prevent an optical illusion of concavity.

ESCUTCHEON: shield for armorial bearings.

EXEDRA: apsidal end of a room. See Apse.

FAÇADE: main front of a building.

FANLIGHT: window in the tympanum of a doorway, originally with fan-like glazing bars.

FAN-VAULT: see Vault.

FERETORY: place behind the high altar where the chief shrine of a church is kept.

FESTOON: carved garland of flowers or fruit suspended at both ends. See also Swag.

FILLET: narrow flat band running down a shaft or along a roll moulding.

FINIAL: top ornament on a canopy, gable, or pinnacle.

FLAMBOYANT: properly, the latest phase of French Gothic architecture where the window tracery takes on undulating lines.

FLÈCHE: slender wooden spire on the centre of a roof. Also called Spirelet.

FLEURON: small decorative carved flower or leaf.

FLUTING: vertical or spiral channelling in the shaft of a column.

FOIL: concave arc formed by the cusping (q.v.) of a circle or an arch. Trefoil (three), quatrefoil (four), cinquefoil (five), multifoil, express the number of leaf shapes to be seen.

FOLIATED: carved with leaf shapes.

FOLLY: amusing or fantastic structure, so named since presumed more costly than useful.

FOSSE: ditch.

FRATER: refectory or dining hall of a monastery.

FRESCO: wall painting applied to wet plaster.

FRET, KEY FRET: Greek running ornament with lines at right angles; cf. Vitruvian scroll.

FRIEZE: horizontal band of ornament, esp. middle division of a classical entablature (see Orders). A *Pulvinated Frieze* has a bold convex profile.

FRONTAL: covering for the front of an altar.

FRONTISPIECE: tiered decoration

at the entrance of an Elizabethan building.

GABLE: wall at the end of a double-pitch roof, between the eaves and the apex. If the gable wall rises higher than the roof, it may be coped or stepped. *Dutch gable:* with multi-curved sides crowned by a pediment. *Shaped gable:* with multi-curved sides meeting at a point (*see* Fig. 9).

Dutch Gable

Shaped Gable
Fig. 9. Gable

GADROONING: short-ribbed enrichment on sloping and vertical surfaces.

GALILEE: chapel or vestibule usually at the W end of a church enclosing the porch. Also called Narthex (*q.v.*).

GALLERY: in church architecture, the upper storey above an aisle, opened in arches to the nave, often erroneously called Triforium (*q.v.*). In domestic architecture, a covered passage, whence the long Elizabethan upper room; by extension a room for the display of works of art.

GARDEROBE: lavatory or privy in a medieval building.

GARGOYLE: water spout projecting from the parapet of a wall or tower, carved into a grotesque human or animal shape.

GAZEBO: lookout tower or raised summer house overlooking a garden.

'GEOMETRICAL': *see* Tracery.

'GIBBS SURROUND': C18 treatment of a doorway or window consisting of a surround with intermittent large blocks of stone in the jamb mouldings and a flat arch with multiple keystones (*see* Fig. 10).

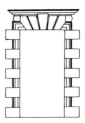

Fig. 10. 'Gibbs surround'

GROIN: sharp edge at the meeting of two cells of a cross-vault; *see* Vault.

GROTESQUE: fanciful classical wall decoration, usually incorporating human figures. See *also* Arabesque.

GUILLOCHE: flowing classical ornament composed of two bands interweaving to form circles (*see* Fig. 11).

Fig. 11. Guilloche

GUTTAE: small downwards-projecting discs on a Doric cornice.

HAFOD (Hafodau): simple houses used during the summer by those minding the herds on upland grazing lands. Normally dating from the C15 to the C18.

HALF-TIMBERING: *see* Timber-framing.

HALL CHURCH: church in which nave and aisles are of equal height or approximately so.

HALL HOUSE: house in which the main room occupies the full height of the building.

HAMMERBEAM: *see* Roof.

HEADBEAM: bressumer or straight beam above the tracery of a screen, a part of its structural frame.

HEADER: *see* Brickwork.

HERM (lit. the god Hermes): male head or bust on a pedestal.

HERRINGBONE WORK: masonry or brickwork laid in a zigzag pattern.

HEXASTYLE: term describing a portico with six columns.

HILLFORT: late Bronze Age–Iron Age earthwork enclosed by a ditch and bank system; in the later part of the period the defences multiplied in size and complexity. They vary from about an acre to over 30 acres in area, and are usually built with careful regard to natural elevations or promontories.

HIPPED ROOF: *see* Roof.

HOODMOULD: projecting moulding above an arch or a lintel to throw off water. Also called Dripstone or Label.

HORNWORK: raised outwork, usually isolated by ditches, for the defence of the weak approach to a medieval castle.

ICONOGRAPHY: the science of the subject matter of works of the visual arts.

IMPOST: block, usually moulded, from which an arch springs.

INDENT: shape chiselled out in a stone slab to receive a brass.

INGLENOOK: recess for a hearth with provision for seating.

INTERCOLUMNIATION: the interval between columns.

INTRADOS: *see* Arch.

IONIC: *see* Orders.

IRON AGE: the period after the introduction of iron to the coming of the Romans (*c.* 600 B.C. to A.D. 50).

JAMB: straight side of an archway, doorway, or window.

JETTY: overhanging upper floor of a building.

JOIST: one of the smaller timbers in a ceiling, supporting the floorboards.

KEEP: strongest tower of a castle. A *Shell Keep* is polygonal and built on a motte.

KERB CAIRN: *see* Cairn.

KEY PATTERN: continuous fret ornament, like a Vitruvian scroll, but drawn with straight lines at right angles (*see* Fig. 12).

Fig. 12. Key Pattern

KEYSTONE: wedge-shaped stone in the apex of an arch or rib-vault.

KING-PENDANT: member of a roof truss like a king-post but ending in a boss.

KING-POST: *see* Roof.

KNEELER: horizontal decorated projection at the base of a gable.

KNOTWORK: ornament of interlacing bands on Early Christian monuments.

L

LABEL: *see* Hoodmould.

LABEL STOP: ornamental stop at the end of a hoodmould.

LACED WINDOWS: windows linked together visually by strips, which continue vertically the lines of the vertical parts of the window surrounds.

LANCET WINDOW: slender pointed-arched window.

LANTERN: in architecture, a small circular, square, or polygonal turret with windows all round crowning a roof (*see* Cupola) or a dome.

LANTERN CROSS: churchyard cross with lantern-shaped top usually with sculptured representations on the sides of the top.

LEAN-TO: *see* Roof.

LESENE or PILASTER STRIP: pilaster (*q.v.*) without base or capital.

LIERNE: *see* Vault.

LIGHT: in architecture, the part of a window between two mullions.

LINENFOLD: Tudor panelling ornamented with a conventional representation of a piece of linen laid in vertical folds.

LINTEL: horizontal beam or stone bridging an opening.

LOGGIA: covered space behind a colonnade (*q.v.*).

LONG-AND-SHORT WORK: quoins consisting of stones placed with the long sides alternately upright and horizontal.

LONG HOUSE: house and byre in the same range, with internal access between them.

LOUVRE: opening, often with lantern (*q.v.*) over, in the roof of a room to let the smoke from a central hearth escape.

LOZENGE: diamond shape.

LUCARNE: small opening to let light in, especially on Gothic spires.

LUNETTE: semicircular window or surface.

LYCHGATE: gate structure with a roof placed at the entrance to a churchyard to shelter a coffin.

LYNCHET: long terraced strip of soil accumulating on the downward side of prehistoric and medieval fields due to soil creep from continuous ploughing along the contours.

M

MACHICOLATIONS: missile holes opening downwards from a gallery constructed on the outside of castle walls, in the spaces between the corbels supporting it.

MAJOLICA: ornamented glazed earthenware.

MANDORLA: pointed oval frame round a (holy) figure.

MANSARD: *see* Roof.

MAUSOLEUM: monumental tomb, so named after that of Mausolus, king of Caria, at Halicarnassus.

MEDALLION: round or oval decorated plaque.

MEGALITHIC TOMB: burial chamber built of large slabs and originally covered by a cairn, normally long. Built in many parts of Britain and Europe during the Neolithic for the communal burial of the dead. Also known as 'chambered tombs'.

MENSA: *see* Altar.

MERLON: *see* Battlement.

MESOLITHIC: 'Middle Stone Age'; the post-glacial period of hunting and fishing communities dating in Britain from *c.* 8000 B.C. to *c.* 4000 B.C. when farming communities arrived.

METOPE: the space between the triglyphs in a Doric frieze.

MEZZANINE: low storey placed between two higher ones.

MISERICORD: carved shelf on the underside of a hinged choir stall seat which, when turned up, provided the occupant of the seat with a support while standing. Also called *Miserere*.

MITRE: raised moulding like a half-pyramid.

MODILLION: small bracket of which large numbers are placed below some types of cornice.

MOTTE: steep mound forming the main feature of C11 and C12 castles.

MOTTE-AND-BAILEY: Norman and Welsh defence system consisting of an earthen mound (the motte), originally topped with a wooden tower, and sometimes placed within a bailey, with enclosure ditch and palisade.

MOUCHETTE: motif in curvilinear tracery, a curved dagger (*q.v.*), specially popular in the early C14. *See* Tracery (Fig. 20).

MOULDINGS: enrichments of a member of a building, of uniform profile whether concave or convex or both. *Ovolo:* of quarter-round convex section, as in C17 window mullions. *Cavetto:* of quarter-round concave section. *Bolection:* projecting moulding joining two surfaces, as used round doorways and panels *c.* 1700. *Keel:* moulding whose outline is in section like that of a keel of a ship. *Casement:* deep hollow in the outer reveals of Perp window frames. *Roll:* C12 moulding of more than 180° section. *Bowtell:* Gothic moulding similar to, but smaller than, a roll. *See also* Chamfer.

MULLIONS: vertical members dividing a window into 'lights'.

MULTIVALLATE: of a hillfort: defended by three or more concentric banks and ditches.

MUNTIN: post, as a rule moulded, and part of a screen.

NAILHEAD: E.E. ornamental motif, consisting of small pyramids regularly repeated.

NARTHEX: enclosed vestibule or covered porch at the main entrance to a church (*see* Galilee).

NEOLITHIC: 'New Stone Age', dating in Britain from *c.* 4000 B.C. to *c.* 1800 B.C. when metal became prevalent. The period of the first settled farming communities.

NEWEL: central post in a winding staircase; also the principal post when a flight of stairs meets a landing.

NICHE: upright recess in a wall.

NOOK-SHAFT: shaft set in the angle of a pier or respond or wall, or the angle of the jamb of a window or doorway.

OBELISK: lofty pillar of square section tapering to the top and ending pyramidally.

OGAM: British and Irish script of the Dark Ages; its letters are formed of parallel notches read vertically down a line.

OGEE: flowing S-shaped curve.

ORATORY: small private chapel in a house.

ORDERS: in classical architecture, the different styles of column, each with its proper base, shaft, and capital, and its proper entablature, composed of architrave, frieze, and cornice. The rules of proportion and design are very elaborate; *see* Fig. 13 for the three Greek and two of the Roman orders. The *Greek Doric* has a thick fluted shaft, no base, and triglyphs and carved metopes in its frieze. The *Ionic* has a fluted shaft with a base, and characteristic volutes on the capital. The *Corinthian* has the slenderest shaft, a capital carved with acanthus leaves, and a much-moulded entablature. The *Roman Doric* has a base and a fluted shaft; the *Tuscan* has a plain shaft with a base and a plain frieze. The *Composite* com-

bines the features of the Corinthian with the volutes of the Ionic in its foliate capitals.

ORIEL: *see* Bay-window.

OVERDOOR: painting or relief placed above a doorway.

OVERMANTEL: decorative panel above a fireplace.

OVERSAILING COURSES: series of stone or brick courses, each projecting beyond the one below it.

OVERTHROW: decorative upper crest on top of C18 iron gates.

OVOLO: *see* Mouldings.

PALAEOLITHIC: 'Old Stone Age'; the first period of human culture, commencing in the Ice Age and immediately prior to the Mesolithic; the Lower Palaeolithic is the earlier phase, the Upper Palaeolithic the later.

PALLADIAN: architecture follow-

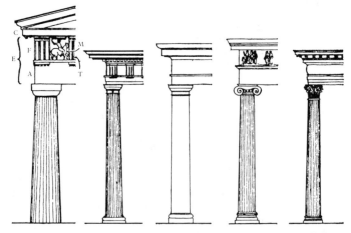

Fig. 13. Orders of columns (Greek Doric, Roman Doric, Tuscan Doric, Ionic, Corinthian) E, Entablature; C, Cornice; F, Frieze; A, Architrave; M, Metope; T, Triglyph

ing the ideas and principles of
Andrea Palladio (1508–80).

PALMETTE: classical ornament
like a symmetrical palm frond;
for illustration *see* Anthemion,
Fig. 1.

PANEL: subdivision of a surface,
e.g. between stone ribs, or the
field between stouter wood- or
stonework. *See also* Tracery.

PANTILE: roof-tile of S-shaped
section.

PARAPET: low safety wall at any
drop, e.g. on a bridge, castle,
housetop, etc.

PARCLOSE SCREEN: *see* Screen.

PARLOUR: the small 'best' room in
vernacular houses.

PATERA: small, round or oval
ornament in shallow relief in
classical architecture; a roundel;
a 'pie'.

PAVILION: secondary balancing
wing of a house; a pleasure
building.

PEDESTAL: in classical architecture, a stand sometimes used
to support the base of an order.

PEDIMENT: low-pitched gable
derived from Greek temples,
used in classical, Renaissance,
and neo-classical architecture
above a portico and above doors,
windows, etc. It may be triangular, or curved like an arc on a
chord. *Broken Pediment:* one
where the horizontal base is
interrupted at the centre. *Open
Pediment:* one where the apex of
the sloping sides is left out (*see*
Fig. 14). *Scrolled Pediment:* an
open pediment where the sloping sides end in volutes.

PENDANT: ornamental feature
projecting down from a vault,
ceiling, roof, or staircase.

PENDENTIVE: concave triangular
spandrel   between   adjacent

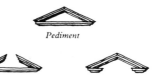

Pediment

Broken   *Open*

Fig. 14. Pediment

arches supporting a drum or
dome, constructed as part of a
hemisphere.

PERISTYLE: in classical architecture, a range of columns all
round a building, e.g. a temple,
or an interior space, e.g. a courtyard.

PERP (PERPENDICULAR): historical division of English
Gothic architecture covering the
period from c. 1335–50 to
c. 1530.

PERRON: *see* Stair.

PERSPECTIVE: the science of
drawing in three dimensions;
hence an architect's drawing so
representing a proposed building.

PIANO NOBILE: principal storey
of a house with the reception
rooms; usually the first floor.

PIAZZA: open space surrounded
by buildings.

PIER: strong, solid support, frequently square in section or
composed of many shafts (compound pier).

PILASTER: classical order treated
as a shallow pier attached to a
wall. *Pilaster Strip: see* Lesene.
Termini Pilasters: pilasters with
sides tapering downwards.

PILE: row of rooms. *Double Pile:*
rows placed so that a house is
two rooms deep.

PILLAR PISCINA: free-standing
piscina (*q.v.*) on a pillar.

PINNACLE: ornamental, usually tapering, form crowning a tower, buttress, etc., especially in Gothic architecture.

PISCINA: basin for washing the Communion or Mass vessels, provided with a drain. Generally set in or against the wall to the s of an altar.

PLATE TRACERY: *see* Tracery.

PLATFORM CAIRN: *see* Cairn.

PLATFORM SITE: house site of medieval date, a rectangular platform at right angles to a slope, formed by excavating at the head to build up at the foot.

PLINTH: projecting base of a wall or column, generally chamfered (*q.v.*) or moulded at the top.

PODIUM: continuous base to a building.

POINTING: mortar joints in stone or brick facing; they have a telling effect on its appearance.

POPPYHEAD: carved leaf ornament used to decorate the tops of bench or stall ends.

PORTCULLIS: openwork gate constructed to rise and fall in vertical grooves; used in gateways of castles.

PORTE COCHÈRE: porch large enough to admit wheeled vehicles.

PORTICO: centrepiece of a house or a church with classical detached or attached columns and a pediment. A portico is called *prostyle* or *in antis* according to whether it projects from or recedes into a building. In a portico *in antis* the columns range with the side walls.

POST-AND-PANEL: method of constructing a wooden partition with boards slotted upright into thicker posts.

POSTERN: small gateway at the back of a castle.

PREDELLA: in an altarpiece, the horizontal strip below the main representation, often used for a number of subsidiary representations in a row.

PRESBYTERY: the part of a church lying E of the choir, where the altar is placed.

PRINCIPAL: *see* Roof.

PRIORY: monastic house whose head is a prior or prioress, not an abbot or abbess.

PROSCENIUM ARCH: visual division or frame in front of a stage, state chamber, etc.

PROSTYLE: with free-standing columns in a row.

PULPITUM: stone screen in a major church provided to shut off the choir from the nave and also as a backing for the return choir stalls.

PURLIN: *see* Roof.

PUTLOG HOLE: putlogs are the short horizontal timbers on which the boards of scaffolding rest during construction. Putlog holes are the holes made in the wall for putlogs, which often are not filled in after construction is complete.

PUTTO: small naked boy.

QUADRANGLE: inner courtyard in a large building.

QUARRY: in stained glass, a small diamond- or square-shaped piece of glass set diagonally.

QUATREFOIL: *see* Foil.

QUEEN-POSTS: *see* Roof.

QUOINS: dressed stones at the angles of a building. The stones are often bonded alternately in either wall.

RADIATING CHAPELS: chapels projecting radially from an ambulatory or an apse.

RADIO CARBON DATING: method of dating organic material, normally charcoal, from archaeological sites by measuring the amount of surviving radioactive carbon 14. This isotope begins to decay at a known rate at the moment of 'death'. However it has been shown recently that these dates are younger than the true date by a factor of some 100–300 years.

RAFTER: *see* Roof.

RAIL: horizontal timber in a screen or panelling.

RAKE: slope or pitch.

RAMPART: stone or earth wall surrounding a castle, fortress, or fortified town. *Rampart Walk:* path along the inner face of a rampart.

REBATE: rectangular recess cut out of an edge.

REEDING: decoration with parallel convex mouldings, the reverse of fluting.

REFECTORY: dining hall of a monastery, etc.; *see* Frater.

RENDERING: plastering of an outer wall.

REPOUSSÉ: decoration of metalwork by relief designs, formed by beating from the back.

REREDOS: sculptured or painted screen behind and above an altar.

RESPOND: half-pier bonded into a wall and carrying one end of an arch.

RETICULATION: *see* Tracery.

REVEAL: that part of a jamb (*q.v.*) which lies between the glass or door and the outer surface of the wall.

RIB-VAULT: *see* Vault.

RINCEAU (lit. little branch) or antique foliage: classical ornament, usually on a frieze, of leafy scrolls branching alternately to left and right.

RING CAIRN: *see* Cairn.

RINGWORK: early earthwork defence in the form of a circle.

ROCK-FACED: term used to describe masonry which is hewn to produce a natural, rugged appearance.

ROCOCO: latest phase of the Baroque style, current in most Continental countries between *c.* 1720 and *c.* 1760.

ROMANESQUE: that style in architecture which was current in the C11 and C12 and preceded the Gothic style (in England often called Norman). (Some scholars extend the use of the term Romanesque back to the C10 or C9.)

ROMANO-BRITISH: term applied to the period and cultural features of Britain affected by the Roman occupation of the C1–5 A.D.

ROOD: cross or crucifix and figures, usually over the w end of a chancel. *Rood Loft:* singing gallery on the top of the rood screen, above which the rood was fixed. *Rood Screen:* screen dividing the chancel from the nave of a church, supporting the rood or a rood loft. *Rood stairs:* stairs to give access to the rood loft.

ROOF: for external forms *see* Fig. 15. *Lean-to:* a single pitch built against a wall. *Double pitch:* two slopes with gables at the ends. *Saddleback:* a double-pitch roof on a tower. *Hipped:* with sloping ends in place of gables. *Half-hipped:* where the ends are gabled but have small slopes

Lean-to   Double-Pitch   Mansard

Hipped   Gabled Hip   Half-Hipped

Fig. 15. Roof Forms

below the ridge. *Gabled Hip:* where the ends are sloped but have small gables below the ridge. *Mansard:* double-pitch roof with two slopes, the lower being steeper than the upper. *See also* Gable.

For structural members *see* Figs. 16–18. *Wall-plate:* timber laid longitudinally on top of a wall. *Tie-beam:* beam connecting the two slopes of a roof at wall-plate level, to prevent the roof from spreading. *Rafter:* timber sloping up from the wall-plate to the ridge. The covering slates, tiles, etc., are fixed (by means of battens etc.) to the rafters. *Principal:* massive rafter in a roof truss, dividing the roof into bays which may or may not correspond with those of the structure below. *Purlin:* longitudinal timber laid parallel with the wall-plate, either on the outer face of the principals (*through purlins*) or tenoned into them (*tenon purlins*). *Collar:* horizontal beam joining the sloping rafters well above the wall-plate. *Braces:* diagonal timbers strengthening a transverse member. *Arched braces:* timbers of arched profile employed to strengthen a collar truss. *Windbraces:* diagonal or shaped timbers placed to strengthen the purlins, and to resist distortion. *Ridge piece:* timber laid longitudinally at the apex of a roof. *King-post:* central upright timber carried on a tie-beam and supporting the ridge beam. *Queen-posts:* two upright timbers carried symmetrically on a tie-beam and supporting the purlins or collar beam. *Wall post:* vertical member placed below the wall-plate to strengthen the wall below a truss. *Strut:* secondary small member used to join the main timbers. *Ashlar pieces:* short upright timbers supporting the rafters on the wall-plate. *Sprockets:* short timbers planted on the bottom of rafters to produce a slight flattening at the

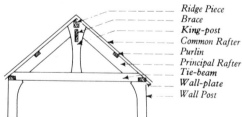

Ridge Piece
Brace
King-post
Common Rafter
Purlin
Principal Rafter
Tie-beam
Wall-plate
Wall Post

Fig. 16. King-post roof

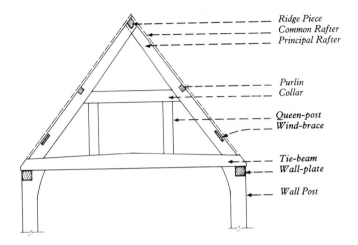

Ridge Piece
Common Rafter
Principal Rafter

Purlin
Collar

Queen-post
Wind-brace

Tie-beam
Wall-plate

Wall Post

Fig. 17. Queen-post roof

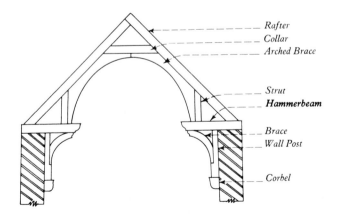

Rafter
Collar
Arched Brace

Strut
Hammerbeam

Brace
Wall Post

Corbel

Fig. 18. Hammerbeam roof

eaves. *Scissor truss:* where the braces of principal or common rafters, rising from the wall-plate, intersect below the ridge. *Wagon* or *cradle roof:* having a curved undersurface, either ceiled or left open, like a canvas tilt over a wagon; this is formed by close-set rafters with arched braces. *Hammerbeam roof:* constructed with beams projecting from the tops of the walls, supported on wall posts, and carrying arched braces or hammer posts on their inner ends. *Single-framed:* if consisting entirely of transverse members (such as rafters with or without braces, collars, tie-beams, etc.) not tied together longitudinally. *Double-framed:* if longitudinal members (such as a ridge beam, purlins, or wind-braces) are employed. As a rule in such cases the rafters are divided into (stronger) principals and (weaker) common rafters, and so into bays.

ROPE MOULDING: *see* Cable Moulding.

ROSE WINDOW (or WHEEL WINDOW): circular window with patterned tracery arranged to radiate from the centre.

ROTUNDA: building circular in plan.

ROUGHCASTING: coating of cement and small stones to protect a wall from the weather.

RUBBLE: building stones, not squared or faced or to size; they may be laid in regular courses (coursed rubble), or laid without conscious pattern (random rubble).

RUNNING ORNAMENT: repetitive undulating foliage carved on Gothic screens, etc.

RUSTICATION: surface treatment of stones for emphasis. *Smooth:* if the ashlar blocks are smooth and separated by V-joints. *Banded:* if the separation by V-joints applies only to the horizontals. *Diamond:* if the blocks are faceted like diamonds. *Rock-faced:* if the surfaces are left rough like rock.

S

SADDLEBACK: *see* Roof.

SALTIRE CROSS: equal-limbed cross placed diagonally.

SANCTUARY: (1) area round the main altar of a church (*see* Presbytery); (2) sacred site consisting of wood or stone uprights enclosed by a circular bank and ditch. Beginning in the Neolithic, they were elaborated in the succeeding Bronze Age. The best known examples are Stonehenge and Avebury.

SARCOPHAGUS: elaborately carved coffin.

SASH: glazed window frame; specifically one hung on cords in vertical tracks.

SCAGLIOLA: material composed of cement and colouring matter to imitate marble.

SCALLOPED CAPITAL: *see* Capital.

SCARP: artificial cutting away of the ground to form a steep slope.

SCREEN: wood, stone, or metal partition, usually at the W end of a chancel. *Parclose screen:* one separating a chapel from the rest of the church. *See also* Rood Screen.

SCREENS PASSAGE: screened passage between the hall of a medieval house and the entrances to kitchen, buttery, etc.

SECTION: representation of the interior of a building on a vertical plane; also profile of a moulding.

SEDILIA: seats for the priests (usually three) on the S side of the chancel of a church.

SERLIANA WINDOW: *see* Venetian Window.

SET-FAWR (Welsh): deacons' pew beneath the pulpit of a Nonconformist chapel.

SET-OFF: *see* Weathering.

SEVERN-COTSWOLD TOMB: Variety of megalithic tomb (*q.v.*) having a very complex ground plan and found in the Cotswolds and to the W of the Severn in Gwent, Glamorgan, and Breconshire.

SEXPARTITE: *see* Vault.

SGRAFFITO: pattern incised into plaster so as to expose a dark surface underneath.

SHAFT: upright member of round section, especially the main part of a classical column.

SHAFT-RING: motif of the C12 and C13 consisting of a ring round a circular pier or a shaft attached to a pier. Also called Annulet.

SHEILA-NA-GIG: fertility figure, usually with legs wide open.

SILL: horizontal member at the bottom of a window or timber-framed wall.

SLATEHANGING: covering of walls with overlapping rows of slates; tilehanging is similar.

SOFFIT: underside of an arch, lintel, etc. Also called Archivolt.

SOLAR: upper living-room of a medieval house, reached from the dais end of the hall.

SOUNDING BOARD: horizontal board or canopy over a pulpit. Also called Tester.

SPAN: the horizontal distance between two supports, e.g. the piers of a bridge, walls, or abutments.

SPANDREL: triangular surface between one side of an arch, the horizontal drawn from its apex, and the vertical drawn from its springer; also the surface between two arches.

SPERE-TRUSS: an aisle truss placed at the division between screens passage and hall. The screen itself, placed between the speres or posts, was originally movable.

SPIRE: tall pyramidal or conical pointed erection often built on top of a tower, turret, etc. *Broach Spire:* a broach is a sloping half-pyramid of masonry or wood introduced at the base of each of the four oblique faces of a tapering octagonal spire with the object of effecting the transition from the square to the octagon.

SPIRELET: *see* Flèche.

SPLAY: chamfer, usually of the reveal of the window.

SPRINGING: level at which an arch or vault rises from its supports. The first stones of an arch or vaulting-rib are called springers.

SPROCKET: *See* Roof.

SPUR: solid angular projection at the base of a tower.

SQUARE-FRAME: system of constructing a wall by the use of vertical and horizontal timbers morticed together.

SQUINCH: arch or system of concentric arches thrown across the angle between two walls to support a superstructure, e.g. a dome.

SQUINT: hole cut in a wall or through a pier to allow a view of the main altar of a church from places whence it could not otherwise be seen. Also called Hagioscope.

STAIR: *Spiral* or *newel:* with steps

radiating from a central support, and in a cylindrical shaft. *Well:* with steps in three flights and a landing on the fourth side of a rectangular well. *Dog-leg:* in two parallel flights with landings at either end. *Cantilevered* or *flying:* with self-supporting steps bonded into the wall on one side only. *Dividing* or *double return:* starting with a single central flight, which branches against an end wall, to return on each side wall. *Perron:* on a double-curved plan, leading to an exterior doorway. *See* Fig. 19.

STAKE CIRCLE: *see* Barrow.

STALL: fixed seat for clergy, choir, etc., often in rows and under canopies.

STANDING STONE: large monolith, traditionally dated to the Bronze Age. They may have been erected for a number of reasons: some may be markers of routes, territories, etc.; others stand near graves.

STAUNCHION: upright structural member, of iron or steel or reinforced concrete.

STEEPLE: the tower of a church complete with its spire or lantern.

STELE: upright gravestone used by the Greeks, carved with figures beneath a gable.

STIFF-LEAF: stylized foliage carved on E.E. capitals, consisting of upright branching and curling leaves.

STONE CIRCLE: ceremonial site of Bronze Age date. Excavation has provided little evidence for the precise use of stone circles and, from their upland siting, it has often been suggested that they played some role in the worship or study of the stars.

STOREY-POSTS: the principal posts of a timber-framed wall.

STOUP: vessel for the reception of holy water, usually placed near a door.

STRAINER ARCH: *see* Arch.

STRAPWORK: C16 and C17 decoration consisting of interlaced bands resembling cut and bent leather.

STRETCHER: *see* Brickwork.

STRING COURSE: intermediate stone band or moulding projecting from the face of a wall.

STUCCO: plaster work; smooth rendering on an external wall.

STUDS: the subsidiary vertical members of a timber-framed wall.

STYLOBATE: the level base of a colonnade.

SWAG: festoon (*q.v.*) formed by a carved piece of cloth suspended from both ends.

TABERNACLE: ornamented niche to contain the reserved sacrament.

Dog-leg

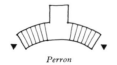

Perron

Double Return

Fig. 19. Stair

TERMINAL FIGURE or TERM: upper part of a human figure growing out of a pier, pilaster, etc., which tapers towards the base.

TERRACOTTA: fired, but usually unglazed, clay, used for ornament.

TESSELLATED PAVEMENT: mosaic flooring, particularly Roman.

TESTER: *see* Sounding Board.

TETRASTYLE: term describing a portico with four columns.

THERMAL WINDOW: semicircular, with two mullions.

THREE-DECKER PULPIT: pulpit with clerk's stall below, and reading desk below the clerk's stall.

TIE-BEAM: *see* Roof.

TIERCERON: *see* Vault.

TILEHANGING: *see* Slatehanging.

TIMBER-FRAMING: method of construction where walls are built of timber framework with the spaces filled in by plaster, brickwork, etc.

TIMBER-LACED BANK: hillfort (*q.v.*) rampart built of earth strengthened by a framework of heavy logs.

TOMB-CHEST: chest-shaped stone coffin, the most usual medieval form of funerary monument.

TOURELLE: turret corbelled out from the wall; also called Bartizan.

TOWER HOUSE: compact fortified house with the main hall above ground and at least one storey above that.

TRACERY: pattern of arches and geometrical figures either in the upper part of a stone-mullioned window, to support the glass, or applied decoratively on screens, walls, and vaults (*see* Fig. 20). *Plate tracery:* early form of tracery where decoratively shaped openings are cut through the solid stone infilling in a window head. *Geometrical tracery:* tracery characteristic of *c.* 1250–1310, consisting chiefly of circles or foiled circles. *Y-tracery:* tracery consisting of a mullion which branches into two, forming a Y shape; typical of *c.* 1300. *Intersecting tracery:* tracery in which each mullion of a window branches into two curved bars, each being drawn with the same

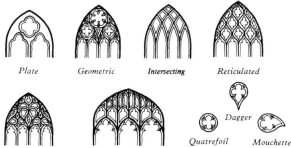

Plate   Geometric   *Intersecting*   Reticulated

Flowing   Perpendicular   Quatrefoil   *Dagger*   Mouchette

Fig. 20. Tracery

radius from a different centre. Every two, three, four, etc., lights together form a pointed arch; also typical of *c.* 1300. *Reticulated tracery:* tracery typical of the early C14, consisting entirely of circles drawn at top and bottom into ogee shapes (or double-ended daggers) so that a net-like appearance results. *Flowing tracery:* complex form of flowing lines, ogees and geometrical shapes woven together. *Panel tracery:* Perp tracery formed of upright straight-sided panels with cusped heads, above the lights of a window.

TRANSEPT: transverse portion of a cross-shaped church.

TRANSOM: horizontal member dividing a window.

TRANSVERSE: *see* Arch and Vault.

TREFOIL: *see* Foil.

TRIBUNE: *see* Gallery.

TRICIPUT: sign of the Trinity expressed by three faces belonging to one head.

TRIFORIUM: arcaded wall passage or blank arcading, facing the nave at the height of the aisle roof and below the clerestory windows.

TRIGLYPHS: blocks with vertical grooves separating the metopes in the Doric frieze. *See* Orders.

TRIUMPHAL ARCH: large arch between two narrower bays, as in the arch of Constantine in Rome.

TROPHY: sculptured group of arms or armour, as a memorial of victory.

TRUMEAU: stone mullion supporting the tympanum of a wide doorway.

TRUSS: main frame in a timber structure, supporting a roof (*q.v.*)

TUDOR FLOWER: diamond-shaped leaf ornament, used in screens of the Tudor period, etc.

TUMBLED: of brickwork, laid at an angle of 45° as reinforcement.

TUMULUS: *see* Barrow.

TURRET: small tower, round or polygonal in plan.

TUSCAN: *see* Order.

TYMPANUM: space enclosed by the lintel of a doorway and the arch or pediment above it.

UNDERCROFT: vaulted room, sometimes underground, below a church or hall.

UNIVALLATE: of a hillfort: defended by a single bank and ditch.

VAULT: an arched ceiling constructed of stones. *Barrel-* or *tunnel-vault:* of semicircular or of segmental pointed section. *Groined* or *cross-vault:* formed by two barrel-vaults meeting at right angles, and named from the diagonal edges at which the planes change. *Rib-vault:* with diagonal ribs projecting along the groins. *Quadripartite vault:* where each bay is divided into four compartments. *Sexpartite vault:* where each quadripartite bay is subdivided into six compartments by a transverse rib. *Domical vault:* square or polygonal dome rising on a bay of the same shape. *Fan-vault:* late medieval vault composed of inverted half cones springing, like the equal ribs, from a single point of support (*see* Fig. 21). The main components of a vault are: the projecting *ribs* (*diagonal ribs*; *wall ribs*; *transverse ribs*;

ridge ribs; *tiercerons*, which rise from a main springer to the ridge rib; *liernes* or *tertiary ribs*, which from the C14 were used to link the main ribs and tiercerons), the *webs* of stone in the compartments between, and the *bosses* at the main intersections (*see* Fig. 22).

VAULTING-SHAFT: vertical member leading to the springer of a vault.

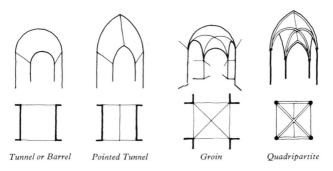

Tunnel or Barrel   Pointed Tunnel   Groin   Quadripartite

Fig. 21. Vaults

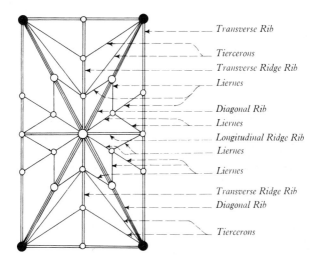

Transverse Rib

Tiercerons

Transverse Ridge Rib

Liernes

Diagonal Rib

Liernes

Longitudinal Ridge Rib

Liernes

Liernes

Transverse Ridge Rib

Diagonal Rib

Tiercerons

Fig. 22. Ribs of a Late Gothic Vault

VENETIAN WINDOW: window with three openings, the central one arched and wider than the outside ones (*see* Fig. 23). Also called Serliana.

Fig. 23. Venetian Window

VERANDA: open gallery against a building with a roof on light, usually metal, supports.

VERNACULAR: local style, employed for smaller houses, utilitarian buildings, etc., and using local materials.

VESICA: oval with pointed head and foot; also called Mandorla (*q.v.*).

VESTIBULE: anteroom or entrance hall.

VILLA: (1) Roman country house-cum-farm; (2) the type built by Palladio in the Veneto, with a portico and wings; its popularity in Britain led to (3), in Gwilt's definition (1842), 'a country house for the residence of opulent persons'; whence it came to mean (4) a slightly pretentious suburban house.

VITRUVIAN OPENING: doorway or window which diminishes towards the top, as advocated by Vitruvius.

VITRUVIAN SCROLL: running ornament of spirals like wavelets, also called Running dog (*see* Fig. 24).

Fig. 24. Vitruvian Scroll

VOLUTE: spiral scroll, the distinctive part of an Ionic capital. The form is more generally used to decorate brackets or buttresses.

VOUSSOIR: wedge-shaped stone used in arch construction.

WAGON ROOF: *see* Roof.

WAINSCOT: timber panelling in framed fields to cover internal walls.

WALL-PLATE: *see* Roof.

WALL POST: *see* Roof.

WATERLEAF: broad leaf shape used in later C12 capitals. *See* Capital.

WEATHERBOARDING: overlapping horizontal boards, covering a timber-framed wall.

WEATHERING: sloping projection to throw water off the wall below.

WEEPERS: small figures placed in niches along the sides of some medieval tombs. Also called Mourners.

WHEEL WINDOW: *see* Rose Window.

WICKET: small door formed in a larger one.

WIND-BRACE: *see* Roof.

LANGUAGE GLOSSARY

(Adapted, with omissions and a few augmentations, with the permission of the Director General of the Ordnance Survey, from the O.S. publication *Place Names on Maps of Scotland and Wales*.)

a = adjective
ad = adverb
f = feminine
n = noun masculine

nf = noun feminine
np = noun plural
pl = plural
pr = preposition

abad, *n* abbot
abaty, *n* abbey
aber, *n & nf* estuary, confluence, stream
adeiladu, *verb* to build
aderyn, *pl* adar, *n* bird
ael, *nf* brow, edge
aelwyd, *nf* hearth
aethnen, *nf* aspen, poplar
afallen, *nf* apple-tree
afon, *nf* river
ailadeiladu, *verb* to rebuild
allt, *pl* elltydd, alltau, *nf* hillside, cliff, wood
Annibynol, *a* Independent
ar, *pr* on, upon, over
ardd, *n* hill, height
argoed, *nf* wood, grove

bach, *a* small, little, lesser
bach, *pl* bachau, *nf* nook, corner
bala, *n* outlet of a lake
banc, *pl* bencydd, *n* bank, slope
bangor, *nf* monastery originally constructed of wattle rods
banhadlog, *nf* broom patch

banw, *n* young pig
bar, *n* top, summit
bechan, *a* *see* bychan
bedd, *pl* beddau, *n* grave
Bedyddwyr, *a* Baptist
beidr, *nf* lane, path
beili, *pl* beiliau, *n* bailey, court before a house bailiff
bellaf, *a* far
bendigaid, *a* blessed
betws, *n* chapel
beudy, *n* cow-house
blaen, *pl* blaenau, *n* end, edge; source of river or stream; highland
bod, *n & nf* abode, dwelling
bôn, *n* stock, stump
braich, *n & nf* ridge, arm
brân, *pl* brain, *nf* crow
bre, *nf* hill
brith, *f* braith, *a* speckled; coarse
bro, *nf* region; vale, lowland
bron, *pl* bronnydd, *nf* hill-breast (breast)
bryn, *pl* bryniau, *n* hill
bugail, *pl* bugelydd, bugeiliaid, *n* shepherd
bwla, *n* bull

bwlch, *pl* bylchau, *n* gap, pass

bwth, bwthyn, *n* cottage, booth

bychan, *f* bechan, *pl* bychain, *a* little, tiny

caban, *n* cottage, cabin

cader, *nf* stronghold

cadlas, *nf* close, court of a house

cae, *pl* caeau, *n* field, enclosure

caer, *pl* caerau, *nf* stronghold, fort

cafn, *n* ferry-boat

canol, *n* middle

cantref, *n* hundred (territorial division)

capel, *n* chapel

carn, *pl* carnau, *nf* heap of stones, tumulus

carnedd, *pl* carneddau, carneddi, *nf* heap of stones, tumulus

carreg, *pl* cerrig, *nf* stone, rock

carrog, *nf* brook

carw, *n* stag

cas (in Casnewydd etc.), *n* castle

castell, *pl* cestyll, *n* castle; small stronghold; fortified residence; imposing natural position

cath, *nf* cat. (In some names it may be the Irish word cath meaning 'battle'.)

cau, *a* hollow; enclosed

cawr, *pl* ceiri, cewri, *n* giant

cefn, *pl* cefnydd, *n* ridge

cegin, *nf* kitchen

ceiliog, *n* cock

ceiri, *np* *see* cawr

celli, *nf* grove

celynnen, *pl* celyn, *nf* holly tree

celynnog, clynnog, *nf* holly grove

cemais, *n from np* shallow bend in river, or coastline

cennin, *np* leeks

cerrig, *np* *see* carreg

cesail, *nf* hollow (arm-pit)

ceunant, *n* ravine, gorge

cewri, *np* *see* cawr

chwilog, *nf* land infested with beetles

cil, *pl* ciliau, *n* retreat, recess, corner

cilfach, *nf* nook

clawdd, *pl* cloddiau, *n* ditch hedge

cloch, *nf* bell

clochydd, *n* sexton, parish clerk

cloddiau, *np* *see* clawdd

clog, *nf* crag, precipice

clogwyn, *n* precipice, steep rock hanging on one side

clwyd, *pl* clwydydd, *nf* hurdle, gate

clynnog, *nf* *see* celynnog

coch, *a* red

coeden, *pl* coed, *nf* tree

collen, *pl* cyll, coll, *nf* hazel

colwyn, *n* whelp

comin, *pl* comins, *n* common

congl, *nf* corner

cornel, *nf* corner

cors, *pl* corsydd, *nf* bog

craf, *n* garlic

craig, *pl* creigiau, *nf* rock

crochan, *n* cauldron

croes, *nf* cross

croesffordd, croesheol, croeslon, *nf* cross-roads

crofft, *pl* crofftau, *nf* croft

crug, *pl* crugiau, *n* heap, tump

cwm, *pl* cymau, cymoedd, *n* valley, dale

cwmwd, *n* commote (territorial division)

cwrt, *n* court, yard

cyffin, *n* boundary, frontier

cyll, *np* *see* collen

cymer, *pl* cymerau, *n* confluence

Cynulleidfaol, *a* Congregational

cywarch, *n* hemp

dan, *pr* under, below

derwen, *pl* derw, *nf* oak

diffwys, *n* precipice, abyss

dinas, *n & nf* hill-fortress (city)

diserth, *n* hermitage

disgwylfa, *nf* place of observation, look-out point

dôl, *pl* dolau, dolydd, *nf* meadow

draw, *ad* yonder

du, *a* black, dark

dwfr, dŵr, *n* water

dyffryn, *n* valley

eglwys, *nf* church

(ei)singrug, *n* heap of bran or corn husks

eisteddfa, *nf* seat, resting place

eithinog, *nf* furze patch

elltyd, *np* *see* allt

ellyll, *n* elf, goblin

eos, *nf* nightingale

erw, *pl* erwau, *nf* acre

esgair, *nf* long ridge (leg)

esgob, *n* bishop

ewig, *nf* hind

-fa, *nf* *see* ma-

fach, *a* *see* bach

faenor, *nf* Vaynor

fawr, *a* *see* mawr

ffald, *pl* ffaldau, *nf* sheep-fold, pound, pen, run

ffawydden, *pl* ffawydd, *nf* beech tree

fferm, *nf* farm

ffin, *nf* boundary

ffordd, *nf* way, road

fforest, *nf* forest, park

ffridd, ffrith, *pl* ffriddoedd, *nf* wood; mountain enclosure, sheep walk

ffrwd, *nf* stream, torrent

ffynnon, *pl* ffynhonnau, *nf* spring, well

fry, *ad* above

gardd, *pl* gerddi, garddau, *nf* garden; enclosure or fold into which calves were turned for first time

garth, *n* promontory, hill enclosure

garw, *a* coarse, rough

gefail, *nf* smithy

(g)eirw, *np* rush of waters

glan, *nf* river-bank, hillock

glas, *a* green

glas, glais (as in dulas, dulais), *n & nf* brook

glo, *n* charcoal, coal

glyn, *n* deep valley, glen

gof, *n* smith

gogof, *pl* gogofau, *nf* cave

gorffwysfa, *nf* resting place

gris, *pl* grisiau, *n* step

grug, *n* heath, heather

gwaelod, *n* foot of hill (bottom)

gwastad, *n* plain

gwaun, *pl* gweunydd, *nf* moor, mountain meadow, moor-land field

gwely, *n* bed, resting-place, family land

gwen, *a* *see* gwyn

gwerdd, *a* *see* gwyrdd

gwernen, *pl* gwern, *nf* alder tree

gwersyll, *n* encampment

gwrych, *n* hedge, quickset hedge

gwryd, *n* fathom

gwyddel, *pl* gwyddyl, gwyddelod, *n* Irishman

gwyddrug, *nf* mound, wooded knoll

gwyn, *f* gwen, *a* white

gwynt, *n* wind

gwyrdd, *f* gwerdd, *a* green

hafn, *nf* gorge, ravine

hafod, *nf* summer dwelling

hafoty, *n* summer dwelling

helygen, *pl* helyg, *nf* willow

hen, *a* old

hendref, *nf* winter dwelling, old home, permanent abode

heol, hewl, *nf* street, road

hir, *a* long

is, *pr* below, under

isaf, *a* lower (lowest)

isel, *a* low

iwrch, *pl* iyrchod, *n* roebuck

lawnd, lawnt, *nf* open space in woodland, glade

llaethdy, *n* milkhouse, dairy

llan, *nf* church, monastery; enclosure

Llanbedr St Peter's church

Llanddewi St David's church

Llanfair St Mary's church

Llanfihangel St Michael's church

llannerch, *nf* clearing, glade

lle, *n* place, position

llech, *pl* llechau, *nf* slab, stone, rock

llechwedd, *nf* hillside

llethr, *nf* slope

llety, *n* small abode, quarters

llidiard, llidiart, *pl* llidiardau, llidiartau, *n* gate

llom, *a* *see* llwm

lluest, *n* shieling, cottage, hut

llumon, *n* stack (chimney)

llwch, *n* dust

llwch, *pl* llychau, *n* lake

llwm, *f* llom, *a* bare, exposed

llwyd, *a* grey, brown

llwyn, *pl* llwyni, llwynau, *n* grove, bush

llyn, *n & nf* lake

llys, *n & nf* court, hall

lôn, *nf* lane, road

ma-, -fa, *nf* plain, place

maen, *pl* meini, main, *n* stone

maenol, maenor, *nf* stone-built residence of chieftain of district, rich low-lying land surrounding same, vale maerdref, *nf* hamlet attached to chieftain's court, lord's demesne (maer, steward + tref, hamlet)

maerdy, *n* steward's house, dairy

maes, *pl* meysydd, *n* open field, plain

march, *pl* meirch, *n* horse, stallion

marchog, *n* knight, horseman

marian, *n* holm, gravel, gravelly ground, rock debris

mawnog, *nf* peat-bog

mawr, *a* great, big

meillionen, *pl* meillion, *nf* clover

meini, *np* *see* maen

meirch, *np* *see* march

melin, *nf* mill

melyn, *f* melen, *a* yellow

menych, *np* *see* mynach

merthyr, *n* burial place, church

Methodistaidd, *a* Methodist

meysydd, *np* *see* maes

mochyn, *pl* moch, *n* pig

moel, *nf* bare hill

moel, *a* bare, bald

môr, *n* sea

morfa, *n* marsh, fen

mur, *pl* muriau, *n* wall

mwyalch, mwyalchen, *nf* blackbird

mynach, *pl* mynych, menych, myneich, *n* monk

mynachdy, *n* monastic grange

mynwent, *nf* churchyard

mynydd, *n* mountain, moorland

nant, *pl* nentydd, naint, nannau, *nf* brook

nant, *pl* nentydd, naint, nannau, *n* dingle, glen, ravine

neuadd, *nf* hall

newydd, *a* new

noddfa, *nf* hospice

nyth, *n & nf* nest, inaccessible position

oen, *pl* ŵyn, *n* lamb

offeiriad, *n* priest

onnen, *pl* onn, ynn, *nf* ash-tree

pandy, *n* fulling-mill

pant, *n* hollow, valley

parc, *pl* parciau, parcau, *n* park, field, enclosure

pen, *pl* pennau, *n* head, top; end, edge

penrhyn, *n* promontory

pensaer, *n* architect

pentref, *n* homestead, appendix to the real 'tref', village

person, *n* parson

pistyll, *n* spout, waterfall

plas, *n* gentleman's seat, hall, mansion

plwyf, *n* parish

poeth, *a* burnt (hot)

pont, *nf* bridge

porth, *n* gate, gateway

porth, *nf* ferry, harbour

pwll, *pl* pyllau, *n* pit, pool

rhaeadr, *nf* waterfall

rhandir, *n* allotment, fixed measure of land

rhiw, *nf & n* hill, slope

rhos, *pl* rhosydd, *nf*   moor,
   promontory
rhyd, *nf & n*   ford

saeth, *pl* saethau, *nf*   arrow
sant, san, *pl* saint, *n*   saint,
   monk
sarn, *pl* sarnau, *nf*   causeway
simnai, simdde, *nf*   chimney
siop, *nf*   shop
sticil, sticill, *nf*   stile
swydd, *nf*   seat, lordship,
   office
sych, *a*   dry

tafarn, *pl* tafarnau, *n &
   nf*   tavern
tai, *np   see* tŷ
tâl, *n*   end (forehead)
talwrn, *pl* talyrni, tylyrni,
   n   bare exposed hill-side,
   open space, threshing floor,
   cockpit
tan, dan, *nf*   under, beneath
teg, *a*   fair
tir, *n*   land, territory
tom, tomen, *nf*   mound
ton, *pl* tonnau, *nf*   wave
ton, tonnen, *pl* tonnau, *n &
   nf*   grassland, lea
torglwyd, *nf*   door-hurdle,
   gate
towyn, *n   see* tywyn
traean, traen, *n*   third part
traeth, *n*   strand, shore
trallwng, trallwm, *n*   wet
   bottom land

traws, *a & n*   cross,
   transverse
tref, *nf*   homestead, hamlet,
   town
tros, *pr*   over
trwyn, *n*   point, cape (nose)
twr, *n*   tower
twyn, *pl* twyni, *n*   hillock,
   knoll
tŷ, *pl* tai, *n*   house
tyddyn, ty'n, *n*   small farm,
   holding
tylyrni, *np   see* talwrn
tywyn, towyn, *n*   sea-shore,
   strand

uchaf, *a*   higher, highest
uchel, *a*   high
uwch, *pr*   above, over

ŵyn, *np   see* oen

y, yr, 'r (definite article)   the
yn, *pr*   in
ynn, *np   see* onnen
ynys, *pl* ynysoedd,
   nf   island; holm, river-
   meadow
ysbyty, *n*   hospital, hospice
ysgol, *pl* ysgolion, *nf*   school
ysgubor, *pl* ysguboriau,
   nf   barn
ystafell, *nf*   chamber, hiding-
   place
ystrad, *n*   valley, holm, river-
   meadow
ystum, *nf & n*   bend shape

INDEX OF PLATES

INDEX OF ARCHITECTS ETC.

INDEX OF PLACES